The Dodecanese

and the east Aegean islands

written and researched by

Marc Dubin

www.roughguides.com

BULGARIA
GREECE
TURKEY
İstanbul
Kavála
Thássos
Alexandhroúpoli
Thessaloníki
Samothráki
Thássos
Bandırma
Límnos
Gökçeada
(Imbros)
Mýrina
Moúdhros
Vólos
Skiáthos
Alónnisos
Áyios
Efstrátios
Sígri
Ayvalık
Mytilíni
Dikili
Lésvos
Skópelos
Skýros
TURKEY
Kými
Halkídha
Évvia
Psará
Híos Town
Híos
Çeşme
İzmir
Rafína
Pireás
Athens
Ándhros
Karlóvassi
Vathý
Kuşadası
Kéa
Tínos
Ikaría
Pythagório
Sámos
Ermoúpolis
Foúrni
Mýkonos
Agathoníssi
Kýthnos
Sýros
Pátmos
Lipsí
Sérifos
Léros
Páros
Náxos
Sífnos
Kálymnos
Kós Town
Marmaris
Datça
Mílos
Síkinos
Íos
Amorgós
Astypálea
Kós
Folégandhros
Níssyros
Sými
Tílos
Anáfi
Thíra
(Santoríni)
Ródhos Town
Kýthira
Hálki
Rhodes
Andikýthira
Dhiafáni
Kárpathos
Haniá
Réthymno
Iráklio
Sitía
Pigádhia
Kássos
Áyios Nikólaos
Crete
(Kríti)
Metres
1500
1000
500
200
100
0
N
0
100 km

◀ Thessaloníki 
Kastellorizo, Cyprus & Israel ▶

Introduction to the

Dodecanese

and the east Aegean islands

The Dodecanese archipelago forms the remotest territory of the modern Greek state, up to 250 nautical miles from Athens. All of it is closer to Turkey than mainland Greece, a fact not lost on either country; indeed these scattered islands have only been part of Greece since 1948, representing the last successful phase of the *Megáli Idhéa*, a century-long campaign to reclaim historically Greek territories. Greek nationalists began referring to the islands as the *Dhodhekánisos* (Twelve Islands) after 1908, though in fact there are fourteen major and four minor inhabited isles in the group, plus nine more, large and small, which make up the more northerly east Aegean islands, part of Greece since 1912. Even now numerous military bases and smaller watch-points counter the threat (real or imagined) of invasion from Turkey. Despite the high-level civilian rapprochements which have taken place between Greece and Turkey in recent years, the Greek armed forces clearly prefer to keep their powder dry.

These stepping stones en route to the Middle East or Anatolia have always been fated for **invasion and occupation**: too rich and strategic to be ignored, but never powerful enough to rule them-

Fact file

● Greece is currently the easternmost member of the EU, with a **surface area** of 131,957 square kilometres (50,949 square miles) divided into 51 provinces. No other country, with the exceptions of Indonesia and the Philippines, has so many islands, though they form only about 10 percent of Greece's total territory. The **population** is overwhelmingly **Greek-speaking** and 96 percent are **Greek Orthodox**; there are noticeable Catholic, Sunni Muslim, Jewish and evangelical Christian minorities, plus (mostly on the mainland) pockets of Turkish-, Romany- and Macedonian-speakers. Around 370,000 people live in the Dodecanese and east Aegean, nearly half of these in towns of over 5,000 people.

● Per "native" total population of roughly 10.4 million, Greece has the highest proportion of immigrants in Europe – estimated at 800,000 to 1.1 million, most of these Albanian.

● Since 1974 Greece has been a **parliamentary republic**, with the president as head of state, and a 300-seat, single-chamber parliament led by a prime minister. At present PASOK, the (approximately) social-democratic ruling party, is enjoying its third consecutive term in office, something hitherto unheard of in the perennially unstable – and historically rightist – Greek political world.

...the Dodecanese and east Aegean conform remarkably well to their tourist-board poster image of purple-shadowed islands and promontories, floating on a cobalt-and-rose horizon

selves. Romans, Byzantines, crusading Knights of St John, Genoese, Venetians, Ottomans and Italians have for varying periods controlled these islands since the time of Alexander the Great. Whatever the rigours of these occupations, their legacy includes a wonderful blend of architectural styles and cultures: frescoed Byzantine churches and fortified monasteries, castles of the Genoese and Knights of St John, Ottoman mosques and grandiose Italian Art Deco buildings. Such **monuments** are often juxtaposed with (or even rest upon) ancient Greek cities and temples that provide the foundation for claims of an enduring Hellenic identity down the centuries; **museums**, particularly on Sámos, Rhodes and Límnos, amply document the archeological evidence.

But it was **medieval** Greek peasants, fishermen and shepherds, working without an indigenous ruling class or formal Renaissance to impose models of taste or patronize the arts, who most tangibly and recently contributed to our idea of **Greekness** with their songs and dances, costumes, weaving and vernacular architecture, some unconsciously drawing on ancient antecedents. Much of this has vanished in recent decades under an avalanche of *bouzoúki*-instrumental cassettes, "genuine museum copies" and bawdy postcards at souvenir stalls, but enough remains in isolated pockets for visitors to marvel at its combination of form and function. Indeed, only on two islands included in this guide – Rhodes and Kós – has local character come to be determined by tourism, and even here pockets of traditional life persist.

Most visitors come primarily for hedonistic rather than cultural pursuits: going lightly dressed even on a scooter, swimming in balmy waters at dusk, talking and drinking under the stars until 3am. Such pleasures amply compensate for certain enduring weaknesses in the Greek **tourism** "**product**": don't expect orthopedic mattresses, state-of-the-art plumbing, Cordon-Bleu cuisine or obsequious service. Except at a limited number of upmarket facilities, rooms can be box-like, and the food at its best is fresh and simply presented.

But what impresses most is how, despite the strenuous efforts of

- **Tourism** is the country's main foreign-currency earner, with over 10 million visitors from overseas in a good year. **Shipping**, which used to occupy second place, is in crisis and has been replaced by **agricultural products**, especially olive oil and olives, citrus, raisins and wine. **Mineral extraction** – in particular chromium and bauxite – were formerly important but are also now in decline, except for marble-quarrying. Locally manufactured clothing and household items are aimed at the domestic market, though exports to central Europe are increasing.
- In November 2000, Greece became the first country to have more mobile phones than fixed phones (roughly 6.5 million of the former).
- 97.6% of all Greek homes now have a colour television.
- Greeks have dropped from first to fourth worldwide in frequency of sex (Americans are now first), though they are still in second place for the number of sexual partners (behind the French).
- The Greeks are the fattest people in Europe, with 22% classed as "overweight" and 15% as "clinically obese".
- Greece is typically in violation of more EU directives than any other EU member state, except Italy.
- Inflation has dropped from 19.8 percent in the early 1980s to 2.7 percent in 2001.

Place names: a warning!

The art of rendering Greek words in Roman letters has for years been in a state of uproar. It's a major source of confusion with place names, for which each local authority, and each map-maker, uses a different system. The word for "saint", for instance, one of the most common prefixes, can be spelt Áyios, Ágios, or Ághios. And, to make matters worse, there are often two forms of a name in Greek – the popularly used *dhimotikí*, and the old "classicizing" *katharévoussa*, with different spelling and accentuation. Thus you will see the island of Inoússes written also as Inoússai; or Póthia, capital of Kálymnos, as Póthea. Throw in the complexities of Greek grammar – with different case-endings for names – and the fact that there exist long-established English versions of Classical place names, which bear little relation to the Greek sounds, and you have a real tangle.

In this book, we've used a modern and largely phonetic system, with Y rather than G for the Greek gamma when preceding I or E; Y also for ypsilon wherever possible; DH rather than D for delta; and H or KH (not CH) for the letter chi, in the spelling of all modern Greek place names. We have, however, retained the accepted "classicizing" or "English" spellings for the ancient sites, and for familiar places like Athens (Athína, in modern Greek). We have also accented (with an acute mark, or sometimes a diaeresis) the stressed letter of each word; getting this right in pronunciation is vital in order to be understood.

developers, arsonists and rubbish-dumpers, the Aegean **environment** has not yet been utterly destroyed. Seen at the right time of day or year, the Dodecanese and east Aegean conform remarkably well to their tourist-board poster image of purple-shadowed islands and promontories, floating on a cobalt-and-rose horizon. Island beaches vary from discreet crescents framed by tree-fringed cliffs to deserted, mile-long gifts deposited by small streams and backed by wild dunes, ideal for enacting Crusoe fantasies. But inland there is always civilization, whether the tiny cubist villages of the remoter outposts, or burgeoning resorts as cosmopolitan – and brash – as any in the Mediterranean.

If you're used to the murky waters of the open Mediterranean in Spain, France or Israel, the **Aegean** will come as a revelation, with forty-foot visibility the norm, and all manner of sea creatures visible, from starfish and octopi on the bottom to vast schools of fish. The sea here is also a **water-sports** paradise: the joys of snorkelling and kayaking are on offer to novices, and some of the best windsurfing areas in the world beckon. Yacht charter, whether bareboat or skippered, is big business, particularly out of Rhodes and Kálymnos; only the Caribbean can rival the Dodecanese for interest. And during the months when the sea is too cold or the weather too blustery, many islands offer superb **hiking** on surviving donkey-trails between hill villages, or up the highest summits.

The islanders

To attempt an understanding of the **islanders**, it's useful to realize how recent and traumatic were the events that created the modern Greek state. The east Aegean and the Dodecanese islands remained in **Ottoman or Italian** hands until the early (or mid-)1900s; meanwhile, many people from these "unredeemed" territories lived in Asia Minor, Egypt, western Europe, mainland Greece or the northern Balkans. The Balkan Wars of 1912–13, Greece's 1917–18 involvement in World War I, the Greco-Turkish war of 1919–22, and the organized **population exchanges** – essentially regulated ethnic cleansing – which followed each of these conflicts had profound effects. Orthodox refugees from Turkey suddenly made up a noticeable proportion of the east Aegean's inhabitants, and with the forced or

Landscapes vary from lush groves of cypress, pine and olive, to volcanic crags, wind-tormented bare ridges, salt marshes or even year-round streams

voluntary departure of their Levantine merchant class, Muslims and (during World War II) Jews, both these islands and the Dodecanese lost their multicultural traits. Even before the last world war, the Italian occupation of the Dodecanese was characterized by progressively stricter suppression of Greek Orthodox identity, though in general the 1940s hereabouts were not quite so dire as on the mainland.

After World War II, benign neglect was about the best most islands could expect until the late 1960s. Given the chance to **emigrate** to Australia, North America or Africa, many islanders did so, continuing a **depopulation** which ironically had begun as soon as the various archipelagos had been united with the "motherland". This trend was only reversed in the 1970s, as worldwide recession and the advent of retirement age for the original migrants started to spur a return home. There are still a dwindling number of islanders who were born Ottoman subjects before 1912, educated in Italian between 1920 and 1926, lived through fierce battles in 1943 and 1944, left for Australia, Africa or Canada after 1948, and who have returned as pensioners to live out their days in a modern Greek state that's part of the unified EU. Get talking to any of them and you'll have a first-hand idea of how the twentieth century affected the Dodecanese and east Aegean.

...frescoed Byzantine churches and fortified monasteries, castles of the Genoese and Knights of St John, Ottoman mosques and grandiose Italian Art Deco buildings

The dawn of **mass tourism** in the 1960s arguably saved some islands from complete desolation, though local attitudes towards this deliverance have been decidedly ambivalent. It galls local pride to have become a class of seasonal service personnel, and the encounter between outsiders and villagers has often been **corrosive** to a deeply conservative, rural society. Though younger Greeks adapt happily as they rake in the proceeds at resort areas, visitors still need to be sensitive in their behaviour towards the older generation. The mind boggles imagining the reaction of black-clad elders to nude bathing, or even scanty apparel, in a country where – despite being increasingly out of step with majority sentiment – the Orthodox church remains an all-but-established religion and self-appointed guardian of national identity. In the presence of Italian coffee bars, internet cafés and street-corner cash machines, it's easy to believe that Greece at one stroke became thoroughly European when it joined the EU – until a flock of sheep is paraded along the main street at high noon, or the 1pm ferry shows up at 3pm, if at all.

Wayside shrines

Throughout Greece you'll see, by the side of the road, small shrines or *ikonostáses* designed to hold a saint's icon, an oil lamp, a few floatable wicks, a box of matches and not much else. Unlike in Latin America, they don't necessarily mark the spot where someone met their end in a motoring accident (though occasionally they do); typically they were erected by one family or even one individual in fulfilment of a vow or *támma* to a particular saint to reciprocate for any favours granted. *Ikonostáses* come in various sizes and designs, from spindly, derrick-like metal constructions to sumptuous, gaily painted models of small cathedrals in marble and plaster which you can practically walk into. Often they indicate the presence of a larger but less convenient (and often locked) church off in the countryside nearby, dedicated to the same saint, and act as a substitute shrine where the devout wayfarer can revere the icon it contains. *Ikonostáses* are usually well maintained with fresh supplies of oil – except for the forlorn, abandoned ones on footpaths which are no longer trodden since a new, parallel road was built.

Where to go

There is no such thing as a "typical" east Aegean or Dodecanese island; each has its distinctive personality, history, architecture, flora – and unique tourist clientele. **Landscapes** vary from lush groves of cypress, pine and olive, to volcanic crags, wind-tormented bare ridges, salt marshes or even year-round streams. Setting aside the scars from a few unfortunate man-made developments, it would be difficult to single out an irredeemably ugly island, and amongst possible destinations there is something for everyone.

The **east Aegean** islands alternate in character: harsh, masculine **Límnos**, **Híos** and **Ikaría**, with their dry climates and stark scenery, bracketing lusher, damper and greener **Sámos** and **Lésvos**, the most important of these islands in antiquity. The latter two are perhaps the best "all-rounders", especially for a two-week holiday, with Sámos offering the best island-hopping connections if you've arrived on a flight-only arrangement. The **Dodecanese** also display equally marked topographic and economic contrasts. The dry limestone outcrops of **Kastellórizo**, **Hálki**, **Sými** and **Kálymnos** have always relied on the sea for their livelihoods, and the wealth generated by this maritime culture – especially in the nineteenth century – fostered the growth of their attractive port towns. The first three in particular appeal to a fairly upmarket

Boatyards

Even in the more touristed islands and mainland coastal resorts, a remarkable number of traditional boatyards (*karnáyia*) still survive. As long as there are commissions for wooden fishing boats and tourist kaïkia, they will probably continue to do so, though much of the order book these days consists of repairs to existing craft. Small craft are built in the time-honoured way, with the keel and framework assembled first from seasoned pine – which abounds in Greek coastal regions – and then overlaid with planking. You can often spot *karnáyia* from some distance by the bright orange *mínio* or red-lead paint applied to the exposed wood – long illegal in most of the EU but still the preservative of choice in Greece. Equipment can be low-tech, with wooden trellising and launching rollers the rule; serious accidents caused by hulls lurching the wrong way at the wrong time are not unheard of.

clientele which values a spirit of place over four-star beaches; Kálymnos' "annexe" islet of **Télendhos** has been discovered of late, a car-free alternative to the west-coast strip of its larger neighbour. The sprawling, relatively fertile giants **Rhodes** (Ródhos) and **Kós** have had their traditional agricultural economies almost totally displaced by a package-tourism industry attracted by good beaches and nightlife, as well as the most exciting ensembles of historical monuments in the Dodecanese – none better than at Ródhos old town. **Kárpathos**, marooned between Rhodes and Crete, has some of the best beaches and walking in the Dodecanese; **Tílos**, despite its relative lack of trees, has ample water and more fine beaches and hiking, though the green volcano-island of **Níssyros** is dry. **Léros** shelters softer contours and more amenable terrain than its jagged map outline would suggest, while **Pátmos**, the atmospheric island of Revelation, and **Astypálea**, at the fringes of the archipelago, boast architecture and landscapes more appropriate to the Cyclades.

When to go

Most islands and their inhabitants are far more agreeable, and resolutely Greek, outside the **busiest period of early July to late August**, when crowds, soaring temperatures and the effects of the infamous *meltémi* wind detract considerably from enjoyment. The **meltémi** is a cool, fair-weather wind which originates in high-pressure systems over the far north Aegean, gathering momentum as it travels southwards and assuming near-gale magnitude between Híos and Sámos; the lee of the latter (and of the Antaolian landmass) provides some shelter for the northern Dodecanese, but generally north-facing coasts (especially at Rhodes) bear the full brunt of its howling, which often results in cancelled sea transport.

You won't miss out on warm weather if you come **between late May and mid-June**, or in **September** when the **sea is warmest** for swimming. During **October** you are likely to hit a week's stormy spell, but for most of that month, *kalokeráki* or "the little summer of Áyios Dhimítrios", the Greek

The Evil Eye

Belief in the Evil Eye is pan-Mediterranean and goes at least as far back as Roman times, but nowhere has it hung on so tenaciously as in Greece (and neighbouring coastal Turkey). In a nutshell, whenever something attractive, valuable or unusual – an infant, a new car, a prized animal – becomes suddenly, inexplicably indisposed, it is assumed to be *matisméno* or "eyed". Blue-eyed individuals are thought most capable of casting this spell, always unintentionally or at least unconsciously (unlike *máyia* or wilful black magic). The diagnosis is confirmed by discreet referral to a "wise woman", who is also versed in the proper counter-spell. But prevention is always better than cure, and this involves two main strategies. When admiring something or someone, the admirer – blue-eyed or otherwise – must mock-spit ("*phtoo, phtoo, phtoo*!") to counteract any stirrings of envy which, according to anthropologists, are the root-cause of the Eye. And the proud owners or parents will protect the object of admiration in advance with a blue amulet, hung about the baby's/animal's neck or the car's rear-view mirror, or even painted directly onto a boat-bow.

equivalent of Indian summer, prevails. While autumn choice in nightlife or food can be limited – Greece still eats by season, and as yet imports little produce – the light is softer, and going out at midday becomes a pleasure rather than an ordeal. The first migratory **fish** from the Dardanelles also arrive in early October, with various species caught until May. As a rule, the further south you go, the longer the tourist season: Lésvos and Sámos, for instance, pretty much shut down by early October, even though their last charters leave at the end of the month, while Rhodes and its closely neighbouring islets see "summer" trade well into **November**, when swimming at noon is not unheard of. If you're a fish enthusiast, you can take advantage of the main netting season while on a winter break in Rhodes.

December to March are the **coldest** and least comfortable months, though glorious **wild flowers** begin to bloom very early: January in the Dodecanese, February in the east Aegean for the same species. The more northerly islands endure the coldest and wettest conditions, with the higher peaks of Sámos, Híos and Lésvos wearing a brief mantle of **snow** around the turn of the year.

As **springtime** proceeds, you simply shift focus further north, remembering that a distance of fifty nautical miles may mean the difference between open or still-shut tourist facilities as well as blossoms gone or in bloom. **April** weather is notoriously unreliable, though the air is crystal-clear, the landscape green and colours brilliant – a photographer's dream. **May** is more settled, with an added bonus of the last winter fish and a cornucopia of **spring vegetables**; the south Dodecanesian sea **warms up** comfortably again by early May, though around the more northerly islands the water is too cool for prolonged dips.

Other factors affecting the timing of a visit have to do with the level of tourism and the related **amenities** provided. Standards, particularly in tavernas, invariably slip under peak-season pressures; the food can be the dreariest representation of Greek cuisine possible – a monotonous sequence of tomato salads, pre-pak Belgian chips and frozen North Sea or California squid, with no fish to speak of. Room rates are at their highest from July to September, and rental cars and bikes booked days ahead. If you can only visit during midsummer, reserve a package well in advance, or plan an oddball itinerary taking in islands with sparse seagoing connections or no airport. Between November and April, you have to contend with pared-back ferry schedules (and almost nonexistent hydrofoil or catamaran departures), plus skeletal facilities when you arrive, except on Rhodes, which has significant "winter sun" tourism. You will, however, find fairly adequate services to the most populated islands, and at least one hotel and taverna open in their main town.

Average temperatures (°C) and rainfall (cm)

	Jan		Mar		May		July		Sept		Nov	
	°C	Rain	°C	Rain	°C	Rain	°C	Rain	°C	Rain	°C	Rain
Rhodes												
	11	14	13	10	20	2	27	0	25	1	16	12
Kós												
	11	17	13	11	19	2	25	0	23	1	16	12
Lésvos												
	9	12	12	8	20	3	26	1	24	1	14	11

things not to miss

It's not possible to see everything that the Dodecanese and east Aegean islands has to offer in one trip – and we don't suggest you try. What follows is a selective taste of the region's highlights: outstanding beaches and ancient sites, natural wonders and unique villages. They're arranged in four colour-coded categories, which you can browse through to find the very best things to see and experience. All highlights have a page reference to take you straight into the guide, where you can find out more.

01 **Pátmos, Ayíou Ioánnou Theológou monastery** Page **288** This monastery in the *hóra* of Pátmos is an architectural showcase, as well as a bulwark of the Orthodox Church; shown is the courtyard arcade.

02 East Aegean islands, distinctive lodging Page **329** • The *Aïdhonokastro* complex in the village of Valeondádhes, Sámos, is typical of high-quality restoration accommodation on these islands.

03 Límnos, Kondiás Page **415** • The third largest settlement on Límnos has the typical basalt-built, tile-roof houses of both this volcanic island and neighbouring Lésvos.

04 Rhodes nightlife Page **116** • Ródhos Town is famous for its nightlife, which is no longer confined to the modern districts of Neohóri but spills over into the Old Town.

05 Lésvos, Skála Eressoú Page **396** The long, outstanding beach and resort village of Skála Eressoú in the southwest of the island, seen from Vígla hill.

07 Ikaría, Armenistís Page **342** • Mesakhtí beach is arguably the best beach on Ikaría, with a strong surf guaranteeing action for those with boards.

06 Astypálea mosaics, Tallarás bath Page **253**
The Byzantine mosaics of these baths at Análipsi are superb; shown here is Time personified.

08 Híos, mastic villages Page **360**
Strings of sun-drying tomatoes are a common sight during autumn in these architecturally unique villages; shown is Pyrgí.

10 *Hokhláki* mosaics Page **173** • The art of *hokhláki* or pebble-mosaic work reaches its zenith in the Dodecanese, particularly in the courtyard of Áyios Nikólaos church, Hálki.

09 Sámos, north-coast foothills Page **328** • Terraced vineyards below Manolátes village present some of the loveliest scenery on the north slope of Sámos.

11 Foúrni Page **347**
The laid-back island of Foúrni is an ideal spot for a reasonably priced and fresh seafood meal, courtesy of this active fleet.

12 Níssyros, the volcanic caldera zone Page **211**
No stay on the island would be complete without a visit to its dormant central volcano; shown is Stéfanos crater.

13 Kastellórizo harbour Page **179** • The intimate port-town of Kastellórizo island, with the coastal mountains of Turkey in the background, basks in its reputation as the location for the film *Mediterraneo*.

14 Rhodes, Lindos Acropolis Page **126** • From the Hellenistic acropolis of Lindos, refortified by the Knights of St John, you look north along the length of Rhodes island.

15 Yachting, the Dodecanese Page **267** • The perfectly protected fjord of Vathýs, on the east coast of Kálymnos, is a popular haven for the many yachts which cruise these islands.

16 Rhodes, Byzantine frescoes Page **138** Along with those of nearby Thárri monastery, the late Byzantine frescoes of Kímisis Theotókou church in Asklipió village are the finest in the entire Dodecanese.

17 Kárpathos, Ólymbos village Page **159** Windswept Ólymbos village in the far north of Kárpathos offers sweeping views along the island's rugged west coast.

18 Ródhos Old Town Page **98** • The well-preserved medieval walls offer an excellent vantage point over Ródhos Old Town, deservedly a UNESCO Heritage Site; in the foreground is the Ottoman Sülemaniye mosque.

19 Níssyros, Mandhráki Page **207** • The atmospheric port village of Mandhráki, seen here from its castle of the Knights, sees relatively few overnight visitors.

20 Kós, Khristós peak Page **237** • A hike up 846-m Khristós peak in Kós' Dhíkeos range rewards you with stunning panoramic views; shown is the summit chapel of Metamórfosis.

21 Knights' castles Page **276** • The castle above the villages of Pandélli and Plátanos on Léros is one of the best preserved of many erected by the Knights of St John between the thirteenth and sixteenth centuries.

22 Léros, Italian Art Deco monuments Page **274** • Built during the late 1920s as an Italian naval base, the port of Lakkí on Léros still retains marvellous Art Deco/ Internationalist monuments of the era.

23 Kárpathos, Kyrá Panayiá beach Page **159** • This is perhaps the best of many sand-and-pebble beaches hidden along the calmer east coast, reachable by boat, jeep or on foot.

24 **Lazy fishing ports** Page **292** • Despite recent development, the port of Lipsí remains a relaxing backwater where fisherman still tend their nets.

25 **Astypálea, Hóra** Page **249** • Lovingly preserved houses in this protected settlement sport both Neoclassical iron balconies and the traditional wooden *poúndia*.

26 **Sými's back country** Page **192** • The frescoed chapel of Áyios Vassílios, overlooking Lápathos bay, is just one of many possible destinations for walkers on forested Sými.

27 Kós, Brós Thermá thermal springs Page **233** • A soak in these shoreline hot springs is a popular outing, especially on moonlit autumn nights.

28 Tilos, Ayíou Pandelímona monastery Page **203** • This fortified oasis-monastery in the far west of Tílos is the island's greatest sight – and start-point of some excellent walks.

29 Kálymnos, Télendhos straits Page **264** • The view across the straits between Massoúri or Myrtiés and the car-free islet of Télendhos is among the most stunning in the Dodecanese.

contents

Using the Rough Guide

We've tried to make this Rough Guide a good read and easy to use. The book is divided into five main sections, and you should be able to find whatever you want in one of them.

front section

The front colour section offers a quick tour of Dodecanese and east Aegean islands. The **introduction** aims to give you a feel for the place, with suggestions on where to go. We also tell you what the weather is like and include a basic country fact file. Next, our author rounds up his favourite aspects of the region in the **things not to miss** section – whether it's great festivals, amazing sights or a special restaurant. Right after this comes the Rough Guide's full **contents** list.

basics

You've decided to go and the basics section covers all the **pre-departure** nitty-gritty to help you plan your trip. This is where to find out which airlines fly to your destination, what paperwork you'll need, what to do about money and insurance, about internet access, food, security, public transport, car rental – in fact just about every piece of **general practical information** you might need.

guide

This is the heart of the Rough Guide, divided into user-friendly chapters, each of which covers a specific region. Every chapter starts with a list of **highlights** and an **introduction** that helps you to decide where to go, depending on your time and budget. Likewise, introductions to the various towns and smaller regions within each chapter should help you plan your itinerary. We start most town accounts with information on arrival and accommodation, followed by a tour of the sights, and finally reviews of places to eat and drink, and details of nightlife. Each chapter concludes with **public transport** details for that region.

contexts

Read Contexts to get a deeper understanding of how the islands tick. We include a brief **history**, an article about the local **music**, a detailed further reading section that reviews dozens of **books** relating to the country, and a **language** section which gives useful guidance for speaking Greek, and a glossary of words and terms that are peculiar to the country.

index + small print

Apart from a **full index**, which includes maps as well as places, this section covers publishing information, credits and acknowledgements, and also has our contact details in case you want to send in updates and corrections to the book – or suggestions as to how we might improve it.

chapter map of **The Dodecanese and east Aegean islands**

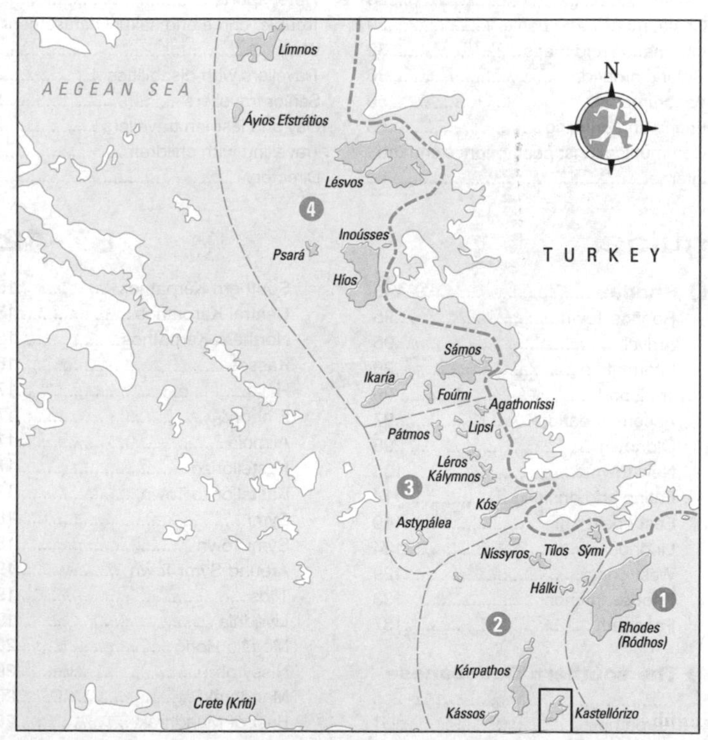

contents

colour section i–xxiv

basics 9–85

guide 87–421

map symbols

symbols

maps are listed in the full index using coloured text

- Paved road
- Dirt road
- Footpath
- Pedestrianized street
- Ferry route
- National border
- Chapter division boundary
- River
- Airport
- Heli-pad
- Bus stop
- Parking
- Campsite
- Mountain peak
- Viewpoint
- Cave
- Spring
- Waterfall
- Castle
- Archeological site
- Lighthouse
- Church (regional maps)
- Monastery
- Mosque
- Synagogue
- Information office
- Post office
- Taxi rank
- Wall
- Building
- Church (town maps)
- Cemetery
- Park
- Marsh
- Beach

basics

basics

Getting there

It's close on 2300 miles from the UK or Ireland to virtually any of the Dodecanese or east Aegean islands, so for most north European visitors flying is the only viable option. There are seasonal direct flights to the largest of the islands from several major British airports; flying time is four to four-and-a-half hours, depending on your start point and island destination.

Only two carriers currently fly direct to Greece from North America, so most North Americans travel to a gateway European city, and pick up an onward connecting flight with an associated airline. You may discover that it's cheaper to arrange the final Greece-bound leg of the journey yourself, in which case your only criterion will be finding a suitable, good-value North America–Europe flight; such onward flights from the UK are detailed below.

It's fairly easy to track down flights from Australia to Athens, less so from New Zealand. But given most people's travel plans, you might be better off with a Round-the-World (RTW) ticket that includes Greece. If London is your first destination in Europe, and you've picked up a reasonably good deal on a flight there, it's probably best to wait until you reach the UK before arranging your onward travel to Greece.

Airfares to Greece from Europe and North America always depend on the **season**, with the highest in effect from June to August (plus Easter week), when the weather is best; fares drop during the "shoulder" seasons – April/May and September/October – and you'll get the best prices during the low season, November to March (excluding Christmas and New Year weeks when prices are hiked up and seats are at a premium). Note also that flying at weekends from North America ordinarily adds $50 or so to the round-trip fare; price ranges quoted below assume midweek travel. Australian and New Zealand fares have their low season from mid-January to the end of February and October/November; high season is mid-May to August, plus December to mid-January; and shoulder season the rest of the year.

You can often cut costs by going through a **specialist flight agent** – either a consolidator, who buys up blocks of tickets from the airlines and sells them at a discount, or a **discount agent**, who in addition to dealing with discounted flights may also offer special student and youth fares and a range of other travel-related services such as travel insurance, rail passes, car rentals, tours and the like. Some UK agents specialize in **charter flights**, which may be cheaper than anything available on a scheduled flight, but again departure dates are fixed and cancellation penalties are high. For Greece, you may even find it more cost-effective (especially from the UK) to pick up a **package deal**, with accommodation included, from one of the tour operators listed on pp.14–15.

Booking flights online

Many airlines and discount travel websites offer you the opportunity to book your tickets online, cutting out the costs of agents and middlemen. Good deals can often be found through discount or auction sites, as well as through the airlines' own websites. Even if you don't end up actually buying your ticket online, the websites are worth a visit to clue you up on what the prevailing published economy fares are; however, these sites often don't have the really inexpensive, transient deals. The cheapest of the airlines' published fares is an APEX (Advance Purchase Excursion) ticket, which has certain restrictions. You may be expected to book – and pay – at least 14–21 days before departure, keep to a minimum/maximum limit on your stay (typically 30 or 60 days), and be liable to penalties (including total loss of ticket value) if you change your schedule. Some airlines also issue "student" tickets to those under 26, often extending the maximum stay to a year. There is also a number of "Senior" or "Golden" fares available for those over 60. When exploring a quoted fare on a website, always click the "Rules" link – all conditions will be spelled out in small print. Any reputable site will have a secure, encrypted facility for making credit-card payments – if it doesn't, you're probably better off not using the site to purchase.

Online booking agents and general travel sites

ⓦwww.etn.nl/discount.htm A hub of consolidator and discount agent web links, maintained by the non-profit European Travel Network.

ⓦwww.princeton.edu/Main/air800.html Has an extensive list of airline toll-free numbers and websites.

ⓦwww.flyaow.com Online air travel info and reservations site.

ⓦwww.smilinjack.com/airlines.htm Lists an up-to-date compilation of airline website addresses.

ⓦhttp://travel.yahoo.com Incorporates a lot of Rough Guide material in its coverage of destination countries and cities across the world, with information about places to eat and sleep etc.

ⓦwww.cheaptickets.com or www.cheaptickets.co.uk Discount flight specialists.

ⓦwww.cheapflights.com Flight deals, travel agents, plus links to other travel sites.

ⓦwww.lastminute.com Offers good last-minute holiday package and flight-only deals.

ⓦwww.deckchair.com Bob Geldof's online venture, drawing on a wide range of airlines.

ⓦwww.expedia.com or www.expedia.co.uk Discount airfares, all-airline search engine and daily deals.

ⓦwww.travelocity.co.uk Destination guides, hot web fares and best deals for car rental, accommodation and lodging as well as fares. Provides access to the travel agent system SABRE, the most comprehensive central reservations system in the US.

ⓦwww.travelselect.com Useful, fairly easy-to-use site without most of the guff and banner adverts of the better-known sites. Linked to walk-in travel agency in the UK (London storefront) and the USA (two premises) if you want to talk to a human.

ⓦwww.hotwire.com Bookings from the US only. Last-minute savings of up to forty percent on regular published fares. Travellers must be at least 18 and there are no refunds, transfers or changes allowed. Log-in required.

ⓦwww.priceline.com or www.priceline.co.uk Bookings from the US/UK only. Name-your-own-price website that has deals at around forty percent off standard fares. You cannot specify flight times (although you do specify dates) and the tickets are non-refundable, non-transferable and non-changeable.

ⓦwww.skyauction.com Bookings from the US only. Auctions tickets and travel packages using a "second bid" scheme. The best strategy is to bid the maximum you're willing to pay, since if you win you'll pay just enough to beat the runner-up regardless of your maximum bid.

ⓦwww.travel.com.au Australian website with a good range of discounted air fares; no-nonsense, easy to use and interpret.

ⓦwww.travelshop.com.au Australian website offering discounted flights, packages, insurance and online bookings.

Flights from the UK and Ireland

Most of the cheaper flights from Britain and Ireland to Greece are **charters**, which are sold either with a package holiday or (less commonly) as a flight-only option. The flights have fixed and unchangeable outward and return dates, and usually a maximum stay of four weeks.

For longer stays or more flexibility, or if you're travelling out of season (when few charters are available), you'll need a **scheduled flight**. As with charters, these vary widely in price, and are again often heavily discounted by agents. Useful advertisements for discounted flights are found in the weekend-supplement travel sections of newspapers like *The Independent*, *The Guardian*, *The Observer* and *The Sunday Times*, as well as weekly listings magazines such as *Time Out*.

You can fly **direct** to the islands of Rhodes, Lésvos, Límnos, Sámos and Kós, though you'll find that the cheapest tickets to Greece tend to be to Athens, or sometimes Thessaloníki. With any Olympic flight to Athens or Thessaloníki, or an Aegean-Cronus flight to Athens, you can get a heavily discounted **domestic connecting flight** on the same airline to any island which they currently serve.

Charter flights

Travel agents throughout Britain sell **charter flights** to Greece, which usually operate from late April or May to late October (Sámos, Kós, Lésvos) or mid-November (Rhodes); late-night departures and early-morning arrivals are common, though you may have a choice of more civilized hours. Even the high-street chains frequently promote "flight-only" deals, or discount all-inclusive holidays, when their parent companies need to off-load their seat allocations. Charter airlines include Air 2000, Flying Colours, Britannia, JMC and Monarch, but you can only book tickets on these through their designated agents (see p.13), and you may find that flight-only deals are rare indeed at peak season.

The greatest variety of **flight destinations** tends to be from London Gatwick and Manchester. In summer, if you book in advance, you should have a choice of most of the international east Aegean and Dodecanesian airports. Flying from elsewhere in Britain (Birmingham, Bristol, Cardiff, East Midlands, Luton, Stansted, Glasgow or Newcastle), or looking for last-minute discounts, you'll find options more limited, most commonly to Athens, Rhodes and Kós.

The **cost** of charter flights can be reasonable; sample summer return fares to Rhodes or Kós, gateways to the Dodecanese, range from £170 to £210 from London Gatwick, but in general you pay dearly for the convenience of a direct flight to the holiday island of your choice, skipping Athens. For less-visited isles like Sámos or Límnos, with only a couple of services a week from Britain on a single airline, you can expect to pay up to £350 in high season, and very rarely less than £300. To these figures, add £10–20 for departures from Manchester and Birmingham, and as much as £40 for take-off from Cardiff, Glasgow and Bristol. In some cases scheduled, semi-direct services on Olympic Airways or Aegean-Cronus are no more expensive and may have an edge in terms of flexibility (see below). Outside of high season (which includes Easter), bargain flights can be snapped up for as little as £120 return. Costs can often be highly competitive if you buy a flight as part of an all-inclusive package: see pp.14–15 for details of holiday operators.

Summer charters operate **from Dublin and Belfast** to Athens and there are additional services to Rhodes. A high-season charter from Dublin to Athens costs upwards of €317 return, while a week's package on Rhodes costs from €635 per person for two weeks.

It's worth noting that **non-EU nationals** who buy charter tickets to Greece must buy a round-trip ticket, to return after no fewer than three days and no more than four weeks, and must accompany it with an accommodation voucher for at least the first few nights of their stay – check that the ticket satisfies these conditions or you could be refused entry. In practice, the "accommodation voucher" has become a formality; it has to name an existing hotel, but you're not expected to use it (and probably won't be able to if you try).

The other important condition regards **travel to Turkey** (or any other neighbouring country). If you travel to Greece on a charter flight, you may visit another country only as a day-trip; if you stay overnight, you will possibly invalidate your ticket. This rule is justified by the Greek authorities because they subsidize charter airline landing fees, and are therefore reluctant to see tourists spending their money outside Greece. Whether you go along with that rationale or not, there is no way around it, since the Turkish authorities clearly stamp all passports, and the Greeks usually check them. We have, however, had reports of charter-flight-only patrons flying to Kós, happily spending a week in Turkish Bodrum, and then returning without incident, but it would be wise to double-check if the rule is still in effect.

Student/youth charters can be sold as one-way flights only. By combining two one-way charters you can, therefore, stay for over a month. Student/youth charter tickets are available to anyone under 26, and to all card-carrying full-time students under 32.

Finally, remember that **reconfirmation** of return charter flights is vital and should be done at least 72 hours before departure. If you've travelled out with a package company, this service will usually be included as part of the rep's duties, but you should not assume that it has been done. Personal visits to the airline's representative office are best, as phone numbers given on ticket wallets are typically engaged.

Scheduled flights

The advantages of **scheduled flights** are that they can be booked well in advance, have longer ticket validities (30, 60, 90 or even 180 days), involve fewer or none of the typical restrictions applicable to charters, and often leave at more sociable hours.

However, many of the cheaper, shorter-duration fares do have advance-purchase and/or minimum-stay requirements, and also severe restrictions on date changes or refunds. As with charters, discount fares on scheduled flights are available from most high-street travel agents, as well as from a number of specialist flight and student/youth agencies – though it's always well worth contacting the airlines direct, using the telephone numbers below. Like charters, they must be reconfirmed within 72 hours of the return leg (in practice, 36 hours is usually enough).

Scheduled airlines

Aer Lingus in Republic of Ireland ⓣ01/705 3333 or 844 4777, ⓦwww.aerlingus.ie.
British Airways ⓣ0845/773 3377, in Republic of Ireland ⓣ0141/222 2345, ⓦwww.britishairways.com.
British Midland ⓣ0870/607 0555, in Northern Ireland ⓣ0845/755 4554, in Republic of Ireland ⓣ01/283 8833, ⓦwww.flybmi.com.
Cronus Airlines ⓣ020/7580 3500, ⓦwww.cronus.gr.
EasyJet ⓣ0870/600 0000, ⓦwww.easyjet.com.
Olympic Airways ⓣ0870/606 0460, in Republic of Ireland ⓣ01/608 0090, ⓦwww.olympic-airways.gr.
Ryanair ⓣ0870/156 9569, in Republic of Ireland ⓣ01/609 7800, ⓦwww.ryanair.com.

The widest choice of scheduled flights from the **UK to Greece** is with the Greek national carrier **Olympic Airways** and with **British Airways**, who both fly from London Heathrow to Athens (twice daily on BA, three times daily on Olympic). Olympic also offers a daily early-evening service from London Gatwick to Thessaloníki, plus three weekly flights to Athens from Manchester. BA also offers one daily morning service from London Gatwick to Athens, but nothing to Thessaloníki, and the Gatwick service may fall victim to proposed route cuts in 2002. Both airlines have a range of special fares and, even in July and August, discount flight agents or websites can come up with deals, valid for sixty days away, for as low as £200 return, including tax; more realistically, you'll pay around £250 return during high season from London, £300 from Manchester. It may be worth avoiding absolutely rock-bottom fares, as Olympic in particular no longer allows changes to your return date on tickets of under ninety days' validity. In the spring or autumn, return fares to Athens run to about £180 including taxes, and in winter dip to about £150. As this route is common-rated between these airlines, you'll also be able to book onward connections simultaneously to domestic Greek airports, though discounts will apply only if using Olympic on all legs of the journey.

Note that flights from British regional airports route through Heathrow or Gatwick in the first instance, with a supplement applicable. Olympic has a code-sharing partnership with British Midland, which should ease the pain (and possibly the cost) of connections from Scotland and the north of England in particular.

Aegean-Cronus Airlines, so far the only privately run Greek airline to challenge Olympic on international routes to Britain, offers daily late-evening services to Athens from London Heathrow, arriving at dawn the next day. Any advertised fares to Thessaloníki all currently go via Athens, with a two-hour layover; direct services have yet to consistently materialize. Fares to either city weigh in at about £170 low season, tax included, or £250 high season. From Athens you may be able to get advantageous domestic add-on fares to Rhodes and Lésvos, the two islands in this guide currently served by Aegean-Cronus.

Potentially the cheapest, no-frills service is provided by **easyJet**, out of London Luton to Athens only; fares vary from £29 to £159 one way, tax included, with the exact amount depending on the season, how far in advance you book and availability for the particular flight – a last-minute booking for three weeks from the end of August will probably result in a combined return fare of £210, but for January–February can be as little as £65, taxes included. Departures vary slightly by season, but typically there are two flights daily, in the early afternoon and quite late in the evening. The cheaper tickets are obviously very restrictive, and there's no on-board meal service. On the plus side, easyJet usually offers special train fares from central London (Blackfriars, King's Cross, West Hampstead) to Luton Parkway (free shuttle bus from there to airport) in co-operation with Thameslink.

Irish travellers will find year-round scheduled services with Aer Lingus and British Airways operating from both **Dublin** and **Belfast via Heathrow** to Athens, or from Dublin via Heathrow on British Midland and

Olympic, but you'll find them pricey compared to charters. Youth and student fares are offered by USIT Now (see box below for address).

Travelling to London and buying a separate ticket there is an alternative if direct flights from Ireland are in short supply, and may sometimes save you a little money, but on the whole it's rarely worth the time and effort. For the record, budget flights to London are offered by British Midland, Aer Lingus and Ryanair.

Flight and travel agents in the UK and Republic of Ireland

Air 2000 ⓣ0870/750 0001, ⓦwww.firstchoice.co.uk. Flight-only division (charters) of First Choice Holidays.
Aran Travel International Galway ⓣ091/562 595, ⓕ564581, ⓦwww.iol.ie/~aran/aranmain.htm. Good-value flights to all parts of the world.
Argo Holidays 100 Wigmore St, London W1H 9DR ⓣ020/7331 7000. Designated consolidator for Olympic, Aegean-Cronus and BA; however service has suffered of late, with unnecessarily expensive 60- or 90-day tickets offered when 30-day is required.
Avro Vantage House, 1 Weir Rd, London SW19 8UX ⓣ020/8715 4440, ⓦwww.avro.co.uk. Seat-only sales of all Monarch charter flights to Athens and Rhodes from a selection amongst Gatwick, Luton, Manchester and Glasgow.
CIE Tours International Dublin ⓣ01/703 1888, ⓦwww.cietours.ie. General flight and tour agent.
Co-op Travel Care Belfast ⓣ028/9047 1717, ⓕ471 339. Flights and holidays around the world.
Cosmos ⓣ0870/908 4299, ⓦwww.cosmos-holidays.co.uk. Offers flight-only arrangements on Monarch from Manchester, Gatwick and Birmingham to a variety of holiday islands.
Greece & Cyprus Travel Centre 44 Birmingham Rd, Sutton Coldfield, West Midlands B72 1QQ ⓣ0121/355 6955, ⓦwww.greece-cyprus.co.uk. Flight consolidator and general Greek packages specialist.
JMC ⓣ0870/758 0194, ⓦwww.jmc.com. Good selection of flights only to Kós, Sámos and Rhodes from a half-dozen UK airports.
Joe Walsh Tours Dublin ⓣ01/872 2555 or 676 3053, Cork ⓣ021/427 7959, ⓦwww.joewalshtours.ie. General budget fares agent.
Lee Travel Cork ⓣ021/427 7111, ⓦwww.leetravel.ie. Flights and holidays worldwide.
Liffey Travel Dublin ⓣ01/878 8322 or 878 8063. Package-tour specialists.
The London Flight Centre ⓣ020/7244 6411, ⓦwww.topdecktravel.co.uk. Long-established agent dealing in discount flights.
Mondial Travel 8 Moscow Rd, London W2 4BT ⓣ020/7792 3333. Good consolidator agent for scheduled flights to Greece; can nearly match easyJet prices on the major airlines.
North South Travel Moulsham Mill Centre, Parkway, Chelmsford, Essex CM2 7PX ⓣ01245/608291, ⓦwww.nstravel.demon.uk. Friendly, competitive flight agency, offering discounted fares worldwide – profits are used to support projects in the developing world, especially the promotion of sustainable tourism.
Rosetta Travel Belfast ⓣ028/9064 4996, ⓦwww.rosettatravel.com. Flight and holiday agent.
STA Travel ⓣ0870/160 6070, ⓦwww.statravel.co.uk. Worldwide specialists in low-cost flights and tours for students and under-26s, though other customers welcome. A dozen branches across England, especially on or near university campuses.
Student & Group Travel Dublin ⓣ01/677 7834. Student and group specialists, mostly to Europe.
Thomson ⓣ0870/550 2555, ⓦwww.thomson-holidays.com. Limited flight-only deals on Britannia to Corfu, Rhodes, Iráklion (Crete), Thessaloníki, Zákynthos, Kós, Sámos, Kefalloniá, Skiáthos and Kavála (for Thássos) on Britannia Airways.
Trailfinders ⓣ020/7628 7628, in Republic of Ireland ⓣ01/677 7888, ⓦwww.trailfinders.com. One of the best-informed and most efficient agents for independent travellers; for scheduled flights only; all branches (there's at least one in all the UK's largest cities, plus Dublin) open daily until 6pm, Thurs until 7pm.
Usit Campus ⓣ0870/240 1010, ⓦwww.usitcampus.co.uk. Student/youth travel specialists, offering discount flights, with town branches in London, Birmingham, Bristol, Cambridge, Edinburgh, Manchester and Oxford, as well as a presence in all YHA shops and many university campuses across Britain.
USIT Now Belfast ⓣ028/9032 7111, Dublin ⓣ01/602 1777 or 677 8117, Cork ⓣ021/427 0900, Derry ⓣ028/7137 1888, ⓦwww.usitnow.ie. Student and youth specialists for flights and trains.

Packages and tours

Virtually every British **tour operator** includes Greece in its programme, though with many of the larger, cheap-and-cheerful outfits you'll find choices limited to the established resorts on Rhodes, Kós, and to a lesser extent Lésvos or Sámos. If you buy one of these at a last-minute discount, especially in spring or autumn, you may find it costs little more than a flight – and you can use the accommodation offered as much or as little as you want.

For a more low-key and genuinely "Greek" resort, however, it's better to book your holiday through one of the **specialist agencies** listed below. Most of these are fairly small-scale operations, offering competitively priced packages with flights (unless otherwise stated) and often more traditional village-based accommodation. They also make an effort to offer islands without overdeveloped tourist resorts. Such agencies tend to divide into **two types**: those which, like the major chains, contract a block of accommodation and flight seats (or even their own plane) for a full season, and an increasing number of bespoke agencies which tailor holidays to your needs, making all transport and accommodation arrangements on the spot, using hotels/apartments which may or may not have vacancies at the time you want. These can work out somewhat more expensive, but the quality of flights and lodging is often correspondingly higher.

The **walking** holiday operators listed opposite either run trekking groups of ten to fifteen people plus an experienced guide, or provide customers with a printed, self-guiding itinerary, and arranged accommodation at the end of each day. Walks tend to be day-long hikes from one or more bases, or point-to-point treks staying in village accommodation en route.

Sailing holidays usually involve small flotillas of four-to-eight-berth yachts, taking in different anchorages each night, or are shore-based, with instruction in small-craft handling. All levels of experience are catered for. Prices start at around £520 per person, flights included, in a group of four on a two-week flotilla. Alternatively, confident sailors can simply arrange to charter a yacht from a broker; the Greek National Tourist Organization has lists of companies.

Specialist package operators

Villa or village accommodation

Argo Holidays 100 Wigmore St, London W1H 9DR ⓣ020/7331 7070, ⓦwww.argo-holidays.com. Packages to luxury hotels and top villas on the larger east Aegean and Dodecanese islands (including a "Winter Sun" programme on Rhodes).

CV Travel 43 Cadogan St, London SW3 2PR ⓣ0870/606 0013, ⓦwww.cvtravel.co.uk. Some quality villas on Hálki and Pátmos.

Direct Greece Granite House, 31–33 Stockwell St, Glasgow G1 4RY ⓣ0141/559 7111; Manchester ⓣ0161/236 2838; London ⓣ020/8785 4000, ⓕ0141/553 1752. Moderately priced villas, apartments and restored houses on Rhodes (Líndhos, Péfkos, Haráki), Hálki, Kálymnos and Lésvos (Sígri).

Elysian Holidays 16 High St, Tenterden, Kent TN30 6AP ⓣ01580/766599, ⓦwww.elysianholidays.co.uk. Began as Volissós (Híos) restored-house specialists, now have a wide programme of quality premises on a dozen islands, including Pátmos.

Greek Islands Club 10–12 Upper Square, Old Isleworth, Middlesex TW7 7BJ ⓣ020/8232 9780, ⓦwww.greekislandsclub.com. Extremely high-quality villa portfolio includes a few on Pátmos.

Greek Sun Holidays 1 Bank St, Sevenoaks, Kent TN13 1UW ⓣ01732/740317, ⓦwww.greeksun.co.uk. Good-value package holidays, including some fly-drive options, on Kárpathos, Kássos, Astypálea, Pátmos, Foúrni, Ikaría, Sámos, Híos and Límnos; also tailor-made island-hopping itineraries.

Hidden Greece 47 Whitcomb St, London WC2H 7DH ⓣ020/7839 2553, ⓕ7839 4327, ⓔhiddengreece@ntours.co.uk. A bespoke agency running for forty-plus years now, arranging accommodation on and transport (on scheduled flights) to thirty less-visited islands, including most Dodecanese (bar Kárpathos & Kássos), Foúrni and Ikaría.

Island Wandering 51a London Rd, Hurst Green, Sussex TN19 7QP ⓣ01580/860733, ⓦwww.islandwandering.com. Tailor-made island-hopping itineraries on and between Pátmos, Lipsí, Léros, Kálymnos, Astypálea, Kós, Níssyros, Kárpathos, Ikaría and Sámos. Deals range from pre-booked accommodation only (this tends to be on the basic side) to mini-tours, with local ferry or air transfers arrranged.

Laskarina Holidays St Marys Gate, Wirksworth, Derbyshire DE4 4DQ ⓣ01629/822203, ⓦwww.loaskarina.co.uk. Top-end villas, quality hotels and restored houses on Hálki, Sy*mi, Tílos, Kálymnos, Télendhos, Léros, Lipsí, Pátmos, Ikaría and Sámos; scores consistently high marks for

customer service.
Simply Travel Kings House, Wood Street, Kingston-upon-Thames, Surrey KT1 1UG, ⓦwww.simply-travel.com. Administers three separate programmes; ring Simply Greece ⓣ020/8541 2277 for high-quality apartments, villas and small hotels for Sámos and Pátmos.
Sunvil Holidays Sunvil House, 7–8 Upper Square, Old Isleworth, Middlesex TW7 7BJ ⓣ020/8568 4499, ⓦwww.sunvil.co.uk/greece. Durable and consistently high-quality outfit specializing in upmarket hotels and villas across Greece; islands covered in this book are Límnos, Sámos, Ikaría and Pátmos.
Travel à la Carte First Floor, 32 High St, Thatcham, Berks RG19 3JD ⓣ01635/863030, ⓦwww.travelalacarte.co.uk. Established Corfu specialist, now branched out to quality waterside villas on Hálki, and hillside ones on Sými – plus luxury Sými hotels.

Walking and wildlife holidays

Limosa ⓣ01263/578143. Springtime birding on Lésvos.
Marengo Guided Walks 17 Bernard Crescent, Hunstanton P36 6ER ⓣ01485/532710, ⓦwww.marengo.supanet.com. Annually changing programme of easy walks guided by ace botanist Lance Chilton; past one-week offerings have included Sámos, Sými, western Kós and northern Lésvos.
Ramblers Holidays Longcroft House, Fretherne Road, Welwyn Garden City, Herts AL8 6PQ ⓣ01707/331133, ⓦwww.ramblersholidays.co.uk. An outfit which has shed its former fusty image and actively courts a younger clientele; its easier outings include trips to Sámos and Pátmos.
Waymark Holidays 44 Windsor Rd, Slough SL1 2EJ ⓣ01753/516477, ⓦwww.waymarkholidays.co. Spring and autumn walking holidays (10–14 days) on Sámos.

Sailing holidays

The Moorings Bradstowe House, Middle Wall, Whitstable, Kent CT5 1BF ⓣ01227/776677, ⓦwww.moorings.com. Operates bareboat charters out of Kós Town.
Nautilus Yachting 4 Church St, Edenbridge, Kent TN8 5BD ⓣ01732/867445, ⓦwww.nautilus-yachting.co.uk Bareboat yacht charter out of Kós and Rhodes.
Seafarer Cruising & Sailing Albatross House, 14 New Hythe Lane, Larkfield, Kent ME20 6AB ⓣ01732/229900, ⓦwww.seafarercruises.com. UK agent for Vernicos Yachts (Greece), with bareboats out of Rhodes, Kós and Sámos.
Sportif ⓣ01273/844919, ⓦwww.sportif-uk.com. Windsurfing packages on Kós, Rhodes and Kárpathos. Instruction clinics in conjunction with nearby accommodation.
Sunsail The Port House, Port Solent, Portsmouth, Hampshire, P06 4TH ⓣ02392/222222, ⓦwww.sunsail.com. Resort-based tuition in dinghy sailing, yachting and windsurfing at five locations in Greece, including Kamári on Kós; one- or two-week flotilla sailings northwards out of Kós Town. Good facilities for non-sailing children.

Flights from North America

The Greek national airline, Olympic Airways, flies out of New York (JFK), Boston, Montréal and Toronto. The airline – and also its domestic competitors Aegean-Cronus – can offer reasonably priced add-on flights to the islands of the Dodecanese and east Aegean. Delta is the only North American carrier currently offering any direct service to Athens, though American Airlines and USAir have code-sharing agreements with Olympic, and in conjunction with Olympic quote through fares to/from Chicago, Dallas/Fort Worth, Denver, LA, Miami, Ottawa, Quebec, SF, Seattle, Tampa, Vancouver, and Washington DC.

Generally, there isn't enough traffic on the North America–Athens routes to allow for very cheap direct fares; you may have better luck flying another national carrier (for example Lufthansa or Alitalia) and arriving at Athens after a stopover at their European hub.

From the USA

The daily (5 weekly in winter) flights **to Athens out of New York (JFK)** (non-stop) **and Boston** (1 stop) on Olympic start at around US$700 round trip in winter, rising to around US$1400 in summer for a maximum thirty-day stay with seven-day advance purchase. Delta has four weekly direct services from New York (JFK) to Athens, but high-season published discount fares are vastly overpriced at close to US$2000; you can save a bit by changing in Paris to another European airline) for the final leg. In general, one-stop flights are less expensive; at the time of writing, Alitalia was offering the cheapest summer fares New York–Athens (via Rome) at just over US$1000, less than half that in winter. Travelling during the May and October "shoulder seasons" will also yield significant savings.

Common-rating (ie price-fixing) and marketing agreements between the various airlines means that fares to **Athens from the Mid-West, Deep South or the West Coast** are little different; from Chicago, Miami, Dallas, Seattle, or Los Angeles you're looking at US$1700–1900 high season, US$500–600 in winter, something in between at shoulder season. These tickets typically involve the use of American Airlines, Air France, Alitalia, Iberia and KLM, via their European gateway cities. With little to distinguish these itineraries price-wise, you might examine the stopover time at their respective European hubs, as these can sometimes be overnight. You may be better off getting a domestic add-on to New York and heading directly to Athens from there.

From Canada

As with the US, air fares **from Canada to Athens** vary depending on where you start your journey, and whether you take a direct service. Olympic flies non-stop out of Montréal and Toronto four times weekly (3 in winter) for a scheduled return fare of about CDN$1400 in winter, climbing to nearly CDN$3000 in summer. Indirect flights on Air Canada and British Airways (both via London Heathrow), or KLM or Air France will cost about CDN$500 less in summer, though in winter their fares are little different from Olympic; frequencies via the European hubs are daily or nearly so. From Calgary or Vancouver, there are no direct flights; expect to pay CDN$2800–3000 during summer, on such combinations as Air Canada/Lufthansa or Air Canada/KLM.

Scheduled airlines in North America

Air Canada ⓣ1-888/247–2262, ⓦwww.aircanada.ca.
Air France ⓣ1-800/237-2747, in Canada ⓣ1-800/667-2747,ⓦwww.airfrance.com.
Alitalia ⓣ1-800/223-5730, in Canada ⓣ1-800/361-8336, ⓦwww.alitalia.com.
American Airlines ⓣ1-800/433-7300, ⓦwww.aa.com.
British Airways ⓣ1-800/247-9297, ⓦwww.british-airways.com.
Continental Airlines domestic ⓣ1-800/523-3273, international ⓣ1-800/231-0856, ⓦwww.continental.com.
Delta Air Lines domestic ⓣ1-800-221-1212, international ⓣ1-800/241-4141, ⓦwww.delta.com.
Iberia ⓣ1-800/772-4642, ⓦwww.iberia.com.
KLM/Northwest US domestic ⓣ1-800/225-2525, international ⓣ1-800/447-4747, in Canada ⓣ514/397-0775, ⓦwww.klm.com.
Lufthansa ⓣ1-800/645-3880, in Canada ⓣ1-800/563-5954, ⓦwww.lufthansa-ca.com.
Olympic Airways ⓣ1-800/223-1226 or 212/735–0200, ⓦwww.olympic-airways.gr.
US Airways domestic ⓣ1-800/428-4322, international ⓣ1-800/622-1015, ⓦwww.usairways.com.
Virgin Atlantic Airways ⓣ1-800/862-8621, ⓦwww.virgin-atlantic.com.

Discount travel agents

Air Brokers International ⓣ1-800/883-3273 or 415/397-1383, ⓦwww.airbrokers.com. Consolidator and specialist in RTW and Circle-Pacific tickets.
Airhitch ⓣ1-800/326-2009 or 212/864-2000, ⓦwww.airhitch.org. Standby seat broker: for a set price, they guarantee to get you on a flight as close to your preferred western European destination as possible, within a week. Costs are currently $165 (plus taxes and a $29 processing fee) from or to the East Coast region; $233 (plus tax & $29 reg. fee) from/to the West Coast or (when available) the Pacific Northwest; $199 (plus tax & $29 reg. fee) from/to the Midwest; and $177 (plus tax & $29 reg. fee) from/to the southeast. (Taxes for all Europe itineraries are $16 eastbound and $46 westbound.)
Airtech ⓣ212/219-7000, ⓦwww.airtech.com. Standby seat broker; also deals in consolidator fares and courier flights.
Educational Travel Center ⓣ1-800/747-5551 or 608/256-5551, ⓦwww.edtrav.com. Student/youth discount agent.
High Adventure Travel ⓣ1-800/350-0612 or 415/912-5600, ⓦwww.airtreks.com. Round-the-world and Circle-Pacific tickets. The website features an interactive database that lets you build and price your own RTW itinerary.
New Frontiers/Nouvelles Frontières ⓣ1-800/677-0720 or 212/986-6006, ⓦwww.NewFrontiers.com. French discount-travel firm. Branches in New York, LA, San Francisco and Québec City.
Skylink US ⓣ1-800/AIR-ONLY or 212/573-8980, Canada ⓣ1-800/SKY-LINK. Consolidator.
STA Travel ⓣ1-800/777-0112 or 1-800/781-

4040, ⓦ www.sta-travel.com. Worldwide specialists in independent travel; also student IDs, travel insurance, car rental, rail passes, etc.
Student Flights ⓣ 1-800/255-8000 or 480/951-1177, ⓦ www.isecard.com. Student/youth fares, student IDs.
TFI Tours International ⓣ 1-800/745-8000 or 212/736-1140. Consolidator.
Travac ⓣ 1-800/872-8800, ⓦ www.thetravelsite.com. Consolidator and charter broker, with another office in Orlando.
Travel Avenue ⓣ 1-800/333-3335, ⓦ www.travelavenue.com. Full-service travel agent that offers discounts in the form of rebates.
Travel Cuts Canada ⓣ 1-800/667 2887, US ⓣ 416/979 2406, ⓦ www.travelcuts.com. Canadian student-travel organization.
Travelers Advantage Cendant Membership Services, Inc ⓣ 1-877/259-2691, ⓦ www.travelersadvantage.com. Discount travel club; annual membership fee required (currently $1 for 3 months trial).
Worldtek Travel ⓣ 1/800-243-1723, ⓦ www.worldtek.com. Discount travel agency for worldwide travel.
Worldwide Discount Travel Club ⓣ 305/534-2642. Discount travel club.

Specialist package operators

Cloud Tours ⓣ 1-800/223-7880, ⓦ www.cloudtours.com. Arranges island-hopping itineraries between the big names (eg Rhodes); uses expensive hotels.
Hellenic Adventures ⓣ 1-800/851-6349, ⓦ www.hellenicadventures.com. Small-group, human-scale tours, led by an enthusiastic Greek–American; the five hiking and sailing itineraries are much better than average, taking in unusual highlights on the mainland, plus Híos and Límnos. The website is fun and easy to use, too.
Meander Adventures (ex-Avenir Travel), ⓣ 1-800/367-3230, ⓦ www.meanderadventures.com. Excellent small-group and tailor-made tours to Greece and Turkey; for the territory of this book, offers top accommodation on Sými; one-week Rhodes plus Sými hiking package (US$825 land only); and a two-week Greek Easter expedition encompassing Rhodes, Sými and Sámos (US$2595 land only). Can also arrange yacht and kaïki cruises around the Dodecanese (excl Rhodes). Established since 1991 with Shirley Smith, part-time Sými resident, at the helm; loyal repeat clientele.
Valef Yachts ⓣ 1-800/223-3845, ⓦ www.valefyachts.com. Offers a choice of fixed, 8-day motor-yacht cruises in the Dodecanese or the Ionian islands; a bit rushed, but affordable at $900–1150 per person. Also very expensive bareboat charter (sailing or motor yacht); pick your craft from the online brochure.

Flights from Australia and New Zealand

With the huge Greek-emigrant community in Australia, Olympic does a fair job of providing direct links to Greece, though they're seldom the cheapest option. The airline offers three weekly flights (two in winter) to Athens from Sydney, and two from Melbourne, via Bangkok, with onward connections to other Greek destinations. There are no direct flights from New Zealand – you'll have to get yourself to Australia, Southeast Asia or a nearby European hub for onward travel.

Tickets purchased direct from the airlines tend to be expensive; travel agents or Australia-based websites offer much better deals on fares and have the latest information on limited specials, Round-the-World fares and stopovers. Some of the best discounts are through Flight Centres, Trailfinders and STA, who can also advise on visa regulations.

If Greece is only one stop on a longer journey, you might want to consider buying a Round-the-World (RTW) fare. Some travel agents can sell you an "off-the-shelf" **RTW ticket** that will have you touching down in about half a dozen cities (Athens is on many itineraries); others will have to assemble one for you, which can be tailored to your needs but is apt to be more expensive. Figure on A$2250/2600 low/high season for a RTW ticket including Greece, on Star Alliance airlines. In the past, Qantas and British Airways have also offered RTW fares, dubbed the "Global Explorer". RTW fares from any point in Australia are usually common-rated, ie the price is the same from whichever Australian airport you commence travel from. From New Zealand, allow over NZ$3500 for the same programmes.

For a **simple return fare**, you may have to buy an add-on internal flight on whatever has replaced the lately defunct Ansett Airlines to reach the international gateways of Sydney or Melbourne. Because of the way Australians travel, most tickets are **valid for one year**; at the time of writing, **high-season** departures could be had for A$1770 (one-stop flight on PIA and Qantas) to A$1900 on Olympic, the latter valid all the way to any domestic airport in Greece. Cheaper multi-stop fares on Egyptair (A$1500), Emirates ($A1720) or Gulf Air (A$1800) tend to be reserved for students or over-60s. Leaving at **low season** means fares of A$1460 (Olympic) to A$1520 (combination of United, Lufthansa and Singapore Airlines); students can try Egyptair (A$1360), while seniors currently have Gulf Air (A$1410). Other airlines which in the past have had advantageous fares to Greece include Aeroflot (via Singapore and Moscow), Alitalia (via Rome or Milan), Royal Jordanian (via Amman), and Thai Airways (via Bangkok).

From New Zealand, the usual routes to Athens are either westbound several times weekly via Bangkok, Sydney or Singapore, on Thai Airways, Singapore Airlines or Air New Zealand, or eastbound almost daily via Los Angeles with Air New Zealand. Published return fares are currently edging up to NZ$3500, and even discount outlet tickets close to NZ$3000, so a RTW fare as described above may be your best option.

Scheduled airlines

Aeroflot Australia ⓣ 02/9262 2233, ⓦ www.aeroflot.com.

Air New Zealand Australia ⓣ 13/2476, New Zealand ⓣ 0800/737000 or 09/357 3000, ⓦ www.airnz.com.
Several flights weekly to Athens via LA or Bangkok from major Australian and New Zealand cities (in partnership with the "Star Alliance" and other code-share arrangements).

Alitalia Australia ⓣ 02/9244 2400, New Zealand ⓣ 09/ 302 1452, ⓦ www.alitalia.it.

British Airways Australia ⓣ 02/8904 8800, New Zealand ⓣ 09/356 8690, ⓦ www.british-airways.com.

Egypt Air Australia ⓣ 02/9267 6979, ⓦ www.egyptair.com.

Gulf Air Australia ⓣ 02/9244 2199, New Zealand ⓣ 09/308 3366, ⓦ www.gulfairco.com.

Lufthansa Australia ⓣ 1300/655727 or 02/9367 3887, New Zealand ⓣ 09/303 1529 or 008/945220, ⓦ www.lufthansa.com.

Olympic Airways Australia ⓣ 1800/221663 or 02/9251 2044, ⓦ www.olympic-airways.com.

Qantas Australia ⓣ 13/1313, New Zealand ⓣ 09/357 8900 or 0800/808767, ⓦ www.qantas.com.au.

Royal Jordanian Airlines Australia ⓣ 02/9244 2701, New Zealand agent: Innovative Travel ⓣ 03/365 3910, ⓦ www.rja.com.jo.

Singapore Airlines Australia ⓣ 13/1011 or 02/9350 0262, New Zealand ⓣ 09/303 2129 or 0800/808909, ⓦ www.singaporeair.com.

Thai Airways Australia ⓣ 1300/651960, New Zealand ⓣ 09/377 3886, ⓦ www.thaiair.com.

Flight and travel agents

Anywhere Travel Australia ⓣ 02/9663 0411 or 018/401014, ⓔ anywhere@ozemail.com.au.

Budget Travel New Zealand ⓣ 09/366 0061 or 0800/808040.

Destinations Unlimited New Zealand ⓣ 09/373 4033.

Flight Centres Australia ⓣ 02/9235 3522 or for nearest branch ⓣ 13/1600, New Zealand ⓣ 09/358 4310, ⓦ www.flightcentre.com.au.

Northern Gateway Australia ⓣ 08/8941 1394, ⓔ oztravel@norgate.com.au.

STA Travel Australia ⓣ 13/1776 or 1300/360 960, New Zealand ⓣ 09/309 0458 or 09/366 6673, ⓦ www.statravel.com.au.

Student Uni Travel Australia ⓣ 02/9232 8444, ⓔ Australia@backpackers.net.

Thomas Cook Australia ⓣ 13/1771 or 1800/801 002, New Zealand ⓣ 09/379 3920, ⓦ www.thomascook.com.au.

Trailfinders Australia ⓣ 02/9247 7666.

Usit Beyond New Zealand ⓣ 09/379 4224 or 0800/788336, ⓦ www.usitbeyond.co.nz.

Specialist package operators

Kompas Holidays Australia ⓣ 07/3222 3333 or 1800/269968, ⓦ www.kompasholidays.com.au.
Scores for its Greek island-hopping programme, covering 11 of the better-known islands; they arrange hotels (3-day minimum stay per island) and all ferry transfers.

Sun Island Tours Australia ⓣ 02/9283 3840, ⓦ www.sunislandtours.com.au. An assortment of island-hopping, fly-drives, cruises and guided land-tour options.

Getting there from mainland Greece

Given the limitations of direct flights to the Dodecanese and the east Aegean, many travellers – of necessity those from North America and Australasia – will touch down first at Athens' Eleftherios Venizelos airport, with a few Brits flying into Thessaloníki or Kavála as well. From Athens or Thessaloníki you have a choice of making your way to the island of your choice by plane or ferry. Rhodes, Kastellórizo, Kárpathos, Kássos, Kós, Astypálea, Léros, Sámos, Híos, Lésvos and Límnos all have airports served by Olympic Airways'/Olympic Aviation's domestic flights; Aegean-Cronus flies to Lésvos and Rhodes; while Axon, which may in fact have bought a controlling interest in Olympic by the time you read this, links Athens with Sámos and Rhodes.

Flights

Flying out as soon as possible will probably be the most attractive option, especially if you've arrived jet-lagged from another continent. Olympic Airways offers a good incentive for using them for the international leg of your trip: a hefty discount on the internal return flight from Athens or Thessaloníki to the selected island. As an example, Athens to Sámos costs the equivalent of about £76 return if purchased within Greece, but as little as £50 if purchased as part of an all-Olympic itinerary originating overseas – the same (or possibly a bit less than) the cost of a round-trip cabin ticket on an overnight ferry. Making your **onward connection** involves nothing more strenuous than taking the escalator up from the ground-floor arrivals level to the departure concourse, with layovers often as short as ninety minutes. Your luggage will be checked through to your final destination – though this seems to be allowed of late even if you change carriers – and moreover you're entitled to the full international 20- to-23-kilo **baggage allowance**, not just the puny 15-kilo Greek domestic one.

Olympic flight frequencies (see "Travel Details" at the end of each island account) from Athens are adequate – three to six daily for the biggest islands – though seats are in heavy demand during peak season. You can have **same-day connections** from the **UK** by using the slightly more expensive 12.20pm flight from Heathrow. This arrives in Athens in time for the final (April–Oct) evening onward service to Límnos, Híos, Lésvos, Kós and Rhodes; getting to Sámos on the same day has become problematic, and you may have to use the morning BA flight out of Gatwick, assuming it still exists, to ensure a connection.

For all the other smaller islands, your best option is to take Olympic or BA's "red-eye" flight out of Heathrow, historically at around 10.30pm, to make a quick connection on the first flight out on the following day – usually sometime between 6am and 9am. If you fly Aegean-Cronus from London, you don't have the option of a same-day connection, as they only offer red-eye service, again at about 10.30pm. EasyJet's early afternoon service arrives just in time (c. 7.30pm) to mesh with the last flights of the night out to Rhodes, Kós, Lésvos and Límnos – see overleaf for the strict Athens airport rules on layover times.

Ferries

For those islands without airports, or Athens-bound travellers who prefer to island-hop, the first order of business will be getting to Pireás (Piraeus), the port of Athens, and onto a ferry bound for the island of your choice (for routes, see pp.40–41). Boats heading for the east Aegean usually depart in the early evening, while those bound for the Dodecanese leave in the afternoon. There are just a few morning sailings to the east Aegean, mostly in high season, so if you arrive on a pre-dawn charter, you could face a wait of up to twelve hours. Travellers arriving in Thessaloníki or Kavála will find ferry connections to the east Aegean pretty sparse – at most two or three weekly, even in summer.

Travelling via Athens and Pireás

If you opt for a cheap flight to **Athens**, you may find yourself with some time on your hands in the Greek capital before the Aegean leg of your journey. This is not necessarily a hardship; the city is, admittedly, no holiday resort, with its concrete architecture and air pollution, but it has modern excitements of its own, as well as some superlative ancient sites. A couple of nights' stopover will allow you to take in the Acropolis, the ancient Agora and some major museums, wander around the old quarter of Pláka and the bazaar area, and sample some of the country's best restaurants and clubs.

Otherwise, a very early morning flight arrival in Athens would allow you just enough time to take a look at the Acropolis and Pláka, before heading down to the port of **Pireás** (Piraeus) to catch one of the afternoon or evening ferries to the east Aegean or the Dodecanese.

What follows is a brief guide to getting in and out of the city, and some pointers on what to do while you're there. For a full account of Athens, see *The Rough Guide to Greece*.

Arriving at – and surviving – Athens airport

Athens' **new Eleftherios Venizelos airport** at Spáta opened on 28 March, 2001, replacing the old, cramped but undeniably convenient one at Ellinikó, south of town. The new terminal has made itself widely unpopular with travellers for its distance east of Athens (27km), indirect public transport connections (thus far) into town, battery-farm architecture and its enormous size (claimed third largest in the world), this last factor making **missed connections** a distinct possibility. Poor signposting makes mad dashes down nightmarishly endless concourses and up escalators (there are a few lifts for luggage trolleys) doubly stressful. To add insult to injury, you have to pay for baggage trolleys in arrivals (about €1 in coins, more if you use a card; keep euro coins handy).

Printed airport rules stipulate a minimum of 55 minutes between your incoming flight's arrival and onward flight's departure, but most airlines – for example Olympic – are insisting on a **minimum connection time of 90 minutes**. Given Olympic's habitual lateness, the presence of security checks even for transfer passengers, and the fact that all aircraft for domestic flights are parked a very long shuttle-coach-ride away on the runway, prudence would dictate observing this rule when buying fares. Some, but not all, ticketing systems won't let you book an itinerary if the layover is too short. If you miss your onward domestic flight owing to non-observance of this rule, ground staff will be rudely dismissive of you, even more so if the two airlines were different.

Now, the good news: the departure concourse **shops are excellent** (you can sometimes even find a few Rough Guides in the bookstore), and eating opportunities are fairly abundant, though seats are in short supply (as they are in all departure lounges). There are ample banking facilities in the arrivals hall, including several cash machines. Best of all – and the only conspicuous advantage of the new unified terminal – you can have your **luggage checked through to your final domestic destination**, even if your international- and domestic-leg airlines are different. Do this at the outset as a precaution, and even if your inbound flight is hideously late, you stand a good chance of getting yourself and your carry-on to the end of your itinerary as planned, even if your baggage only shows up the next day.

Getting from the airport to Athens or Pireás

As yet there are **no light-rail or underground** links the whole way into town; space has been left for tracks in the median strip of the Attikí Odhós or giant ring road around northern Athens, but don't expect project completion until late 2003 at best.

If you're happy to carry your own bags around, there are fairly good **express bus services** to Athens and Pireás. Line E94 (every 16min 6am–8.30pm, half-hourly 8.30pm–midnight) departs from outside the arrivals hall, halts at the current last metro stop, Ethnikí Ámyna, and then continues into the centre. Otherwise there's line E95 all the way to central Sýndagma Square (every 25min 6am–7.50pm; every 35min otherwise), incidentally your only option from midnight to 6am. From Ethnikí Ámyna to the airport, allow 45min to 90min depending on time of day. Finally, line E96 heads for Pireás port (every 20min 5am–7pm, half-hourly 7pm–8.30pm, every 40min 8.30pm–5am), going via the beach suburbs. Journey time varies from 80min to 2hr depending on traffic. All three services cost €3, but for the price you automatically get a "one-day" travelcard valid for 24 hours on all Athenian public transport.

A **taxi** to Athens should cost no more than about €18, to Pireás no more than €24 – at most times of the day your driver will find it quicker to imitate the E96 by heading southwest to Vári and Voúla and then north through the southerly beach suburbs, rather than struggle through traffic in the northern suburbs. This amount should include a

Contact numbers for Greek domestic/international airlines

Aegean-Cronus City centre ⓣ010/33 15 502, Óthonos 10, Platía Syndágmatos, or countrywide ⓣ0801/20 000; airport ⓣ010/35 34 294, ⓣ010/35 30 101; ⓦwww.aegeanair.com or ⓦwww.cronus.gr.

Olympic Airways City Centre ⓣ010/96 66 666, Syngroú 96, or countrywide ⓣ0801/44 444; airport ⓣ010/93 65 529.

Contact numbers for other international airlines

British Airways ⓣ010/89 06 666 (Glyfádha suburb); airport ⓣ010/35 30 452.

Delta ⓣ0800/4412 9506 (Óthonos 4, Platía Syndágmatos); airport ⓣ010/35 31 150.

easyJet ⓣ010/96 70 000 (no in-town walk-in office), ⓦwww.easyJet.com.

General airport information ⓣ010/35 30 000.

€1.20 airport surcharge and €0.15 for each item of luggage, but but make sure the meter is working (fares begin at €0.70, minimum fare €1.50) and visible from the start – double or even quintuple overcharging of newcomers is the norm. When obtaining money from human tellers at the airport exchange booths, secure small-denomination euro notes and coins – presenting a taxi driver with €20 or €50 notes is just inviting a rip-off.

Athens accommodation

Finding **accommodation** in Athens poses few problems except during mid-summer – though it's always best to phone ahead. A small selection of moderately priced places is listed below. The main branch of **EOT** (the Greek National Tourist Organization) at Amerikís 2 can supply you with a decent folding map of the central districts.

It is possible, if not very savoury, to overnight in the port of **Pireás**, but to make the most of your time in Athens the best place for a short stay is **Pláka**, the oldest quarter of the city, which spreads southwest of Sýndagma Square (Platía Syndágmatos); it's within easy walking range of the Acropolis, and has many outdoor restaurants and cafés. All the listings below are in Pláka, except for *Marble House* and *Art Gallery*, which lie just south in Veïkoú/Koukáki district. Prices are for a double room in high season (see box on p.50 for price categories).

Acropolis House Kódrou 6–8 ⓣ010/32 22 344. Mostly en suite, if slightly pricey spot in a converted mansion. ❹

Adonis Kódrou 3 ⓣ010/32 49 737. Modern, all-en-suite building just opposite the *Acropolis House*. ❹

Art Gallery Pension Erekhthíou 5, Veïkoú ⓣ01/92 38 376. Good location near Syngroú/Fíx metro station; middlingly maintained en-suite rooms. ❹

John's Place Patróöu 5, Pláka ⓣ010/32 29 719. Dark single/double/triple rooms with baths in the hall but neat and well kept. In a peaceful backstreet off Mitropóleos. ❷

Marble House Pension In a quiet alley off Anastasíou Zínni 35, Koukáki ⓣ010/92 34 058. Quiet, en suite, friendly, excellent value pension, renovated in 2001; all rooms with fans, most en suite and with balconies. Good location near Olympic Airways head office, and Syngroú/Fíx metro. ❷–❸.

Nefeli Iperídhou 16, Pláka ⓣ010/32 25 800. Modern, bland but salubrious and primely located C-class hotel free of tour groups. ❹

Phaedra Herefóndos 16, Pláka ⓣ010/32 38 641. Enduring non-en-suite 1960s-vintage cheapie, on a usually quiet pedestrian lane. ❷

Student and Travellers' Inn Kydhathinéon 16 ⓣ010/32 44 808. Popular, clean and well-run former hostel has singles, doubles and triples with shared bathrooms. Also offers luggage storage and internet facilities. ❸

Athens eating

Pláka is bursting with touristy **restaurants**, most of them very pleasantly situated but representing poor value. Three with nice sites *and* good food are *Iy Ipiros*, actually on Platía Ayíou Filíppou in the Monastiráki flea market, for *mayireftá*; *O Thanasis*, nearby at Mitropóleos 69, for dynamite *souvláki* and kebabs; and *Kafenio Dhioskouri*, Dhioskoúron, for seafood snacks with an unbeatable view of the ancient agora. *Eden* (Liossíou 12) is one of the city's few vegetarian restaurants. In **Koukáki**, *Ouzeri Evvia* at Yeoryíou Olymbíou 8, and *Iy Gardhenia* at Anastasíou Zínni 29 (lunch only), are both good value and close to the area's accommodation.

Athens: the city

Central Athens is a compact, easily walkable area. Its hub is **Sýndagma square** (Platía Syndágmatos), flanked by the Parliament building, banks, airline offices and the eponymous central metro station. The EOT office on Amerikís is just a short walk north along Stadhíou. Pretty much everything you'll want to see in a fleeting visit – the Acropolis, Pláka, the major museums – lies within twenty to thirty minutes' walk of here. Just east of the square, too, are the **National Gardens** – the nicest spot in town for a siesta, though don't doze off with your valuables strewn about.

Pláka and the bazaar

Walk south from Sýndagma, along Níkis or Filellínon streets, and then briefly west, and you'll find yourself in Pláka, the surviving area of the nineteenth-century, pre-Independence village. Largely pedestrianized, it is a delightful area just to wander around – and it straddles most approaches to the Acropolis.

For a bit of focus to your walk, take in the fourth-century BC **Monument of Lysikrates**, used as a study by Byron, on Shelley Street, and the Roman-era **Tower of the Winds** (Aéridhes), a bit west on Dhioyénous. The latter adjoins the **Roman Forum** and the eminently worthwhile **Museum of Greek Popular Musical Instruments** (Tues & Thurs–Sun 10am–2pm, Wed noon–8pm; free). Climb south from the Tower of the Winds and you reach **Anafiótika**, with its whitewashed Cycladic-style cottages (built by workers from the island of Anáfi) and the eclectic **Kanellopoulos Museum** (Tues–Sun 8.30am–3pm; €2.40).

Head north from the **Roman Forum** (Tues–Sun 8am–3pm; €1.50), along Athinás or Eólou streets, and you come to an equally characterful part of the city – the **bazaar** area, which shows Athens in its most Near Eastern aspect. **Monastiráki Square**, home to another metro station, is flanked by an Ottoman mosque that now serves as a museum of ceramic art (daily except Tues 9.30am–2pm; €1.50). This is an annexe of the **Museum of Greek Folk Art** (Tues–Sun 10am–2pm; €1.50) back on Kydathinéon, which includes some work by Theophilos of Lésvos (see p.385). On Sundays a genuine **flea market** sprawls around Platía Avyssinías, west beyond the lane of tourist shops promoted as the "Athens Flea Market".

The Acropolis and ancient Agora

Even with just a few hours to spare between flight and ferry, you can take in a visit to the **Acropolis** (summer Mon 11am–6.30pm, Tues–Sun 8am–6.30pm; may close 2.30pm in winter; €6). The complex of temples, rebuilt by Pericles in the "Golden Age" of the fifth century BC, is focused on the famed Parthenon. This, and the smaller Athena Nike and Erechtheion temples, are placed in context by a small museum housing some of the original relief art left behind by Lord Elgin.

If you have more time, make your way down to the **Theatre of Dionysos**, on the south slope (Tues–Sun 8.30am–2.30pm; may open longer July–Aug; €1.50), and/or to the Ancient (Classical Greek era) **Agora** (southeastern entrance down the path from the Areopagus; northern entrance on Adhrianoú; Tues–Sun 8.30am–3pm; €3), presided over by the Doric **Thiseion**, or Temple of Hephaestus.

Major museums

Athens' major museum is the **National Archeological Museum** (Patissíon 28; summer Mon 12.30–7pm, Tues–Sun 8am–7pm; winter Mon 10.30am–5pm, Tues–Sun 8.30am–2.45pm; €6). Its highlights include the Mycenaean (*Odyssey*-era) treasures, Classical sculpture and, upstairs, the brilliant Minoan frescoes from Thíra (Santoríni).

Two other superb museums, very close to each other, are the **Benáki** at Koumbári 1, corner of Vassilísis Sofías (Mon, Wed, Fri, Sat 9am–5pm, Thurs 9am–midnight, Sun 9am–3pm; shut Tues; €6), a fascinating, recently overhauled collection of medieval, antiquarian and folk treasures, and the **Goulandris Museum of Cycladic and Ancient Greek Art** at Neofýtou Dhouká 4 (Mon–Fri 10am–4pm, Sat 10am–3pm; €3), with its wonderful display of figurines from the Cycladic island civilization of the third millennium BC.

On to the islands: Pireás

For those who have stopped off in Athens for the day or overnight, it's about 9km from the city centre to the ferry port of **Pireás** (Piraeus). The easiest way to get there is by **taxi**, which should cost around €4.50–6, depending on your starting-point and how many bags you have. You may find that you have fellow passengers in the cab: this is permitted, and each drop-off will pay the full fare. Otherwise, Line 1 of the metro (Kifissiá-Pireás) will get you there easily, passing through Omónia and Monastiráki stations and depositing you, at the port, within moderate walking distance of many boat-berths. The journey takes about 25 minutes – trains run from 6am to midnight – with a flat fare of €0.60 (€0.75 if you've used Line 2 or Line 3 as well).

You can buy **ferry and catamaran tickets** from agencies at the harbour in Pireás, or in central Athens (see the list below); Amalías and Vassiléos Konstandínos are on the west and southwest sides of the National Gardens, respectively. Try to get a ferry that makes a reasonably direct run to your destination. There may be little or no choice to relatively obscure islands such as Astypálea or Foúrni, but ferries to the larger Dodecanese or east Aegean islands can take very different routes – ie "expresses" stopping only at Kós and Rhodes, versus the "milk run" calling at two or three Cyclades plus every intervening Dodecanese before reaching the end of the line.

Other mainland ports

Although Pireás has the widest choice of ferry and catamaran departures, some of the east Aegean islands can be reached more quickly from other ports on the mainland.

Alexandhróupoli

The third northern port (6hr by bus from Thessaloníki, 20min by taxi from its own airport) has one weekly summer sailing on NEL to Límnos, Lésvos, Híos, Sámos, Kós and Rhodes. It's a somewhat unenticing place to stay – you'd really only use it as a jump-off point if coming from Istanbul. If you get stuck, the *Lido* at Paleológou 15 (☎05510/28 808) represents by far the best budget-hotel value.

Useful ticket agency: Kykon Tours, Venizélou 68 (☎05510/25 455), handles NEL.

Kavála

The second port of northern Greece (3hr by bus from Thessaloníki, 45min by taxi from its own airport at Khryssoúpoli, 32km northeast) has regular links to **Límnos** and **Lésvos**, less often to **Híos**. The city has a line of good tavernas in the old quarter below the castle, but pleasant, affordable hotels are in short supply. In ascending order of comfort and price, try the *Akropolis* (☎0510/223 543) at Venizélou 29, the *Panorama* (☎0510/224 205) at Venizélou 32/c or the *Esperia* (☎0510/229 621) at Erythroú Stavroú 42, opposite the archeological museum.

Useful ticket agency: Nikos Miliadhes, Platía Karaolí Dhimitríou (☎0510/226 147 or 223 421) represents NEL; the *Saos II* to Límnos has its own agency a few steps further along the quay (☎0510/835 671).

Ráfina

This small port near Athens (reachable by a taxi ride or infrequent bus from the airport, or by regular bus from the Mavromatéon terminal downtown) has far more regular connections than Pireás – typically three to four weekly – to **Áyios Efstrátios** and **Límnos**.

Information: dial the port police on

Ferry company main outlets

Most of the phone numbers below will be constantly engaged during business hours; you usually have to go in person to the address listed or (more easily) to an authorized agent on the Pireás quay.

DANE Aktí Miaoúli 33, Pireás ☎010/42 93 240.
G&A Ferries Kanthárou 2 corner Aktí Miaoúli, Pireás ☎010/41 99 100 or 45 82 640; also Amalías 32, Athens ☎010/32 10 061.
Hellas Ferries/Hellas Flying Dolphins Etolikoú 2, cnr Aktí Kondhýli, Pireás ☎010/41 99 000; also Vassiléos Konstandínou 2, Athens ☎010/75 12 356.
LANE Aktí Possidhónos 30a, Pireás ☎010/42 74 009.
NEL Astíngou 2, Pireás ☎010/41 15 015.

☎02940/22 100 for sailing times and the current representative of NEL.

Thessaloníki

The northern capital is a fairly busy alternative port; to reach the harbour area from Macedonia Airport, 16km out, take the #78 bus (€0.50) into town, which passes within a few blocks of the harbour passenger terminal. Alternatively, a taxi won't be much more than €6. Between June and September, there is a once-weekly long-haul ferry to **Kós** and **Rhodes** via **Sámos**, and a slightly more frequent stopping service to **Límnos**, **Lésvos** and **Híos**.

If you have a day in hand, it's worth exploring the Byzantine churches, especially the Áyios Yeóryios Rotunda and tiny Ósios David with their fine mosaics, as well as the Archeological Museum. Hotels are plentiful if mostly uninspiring, noisy and often vastly overpriced; worthwhile exceptions include the *Tourist* on Mitropóleos 21 (☎0310/276 335), the *Nea Mitropolis* at Syngroú 22 (☎0310/525 540), the *Bill* at Syngroú 29, corner Amvrosíou (☎0310/537 666) and the *Orestias Kastorias* at Agnóstou Stratiótou 14 (☎0310/276 517).

Useful ticket agencies: Omikron, Salamínos 4 ☎0310/555 995 (DANE, G&A); Karacharisis, Koundourióti 8 ☎0310/524 544 (NEL).

Visas and red tape

UK and all other EU nationals (plus those of Norway and Iceland) need only a valid passport for entry to Greece; you are no longer stamped in on arrival or out upon departure and, in theory at least, enjoy the same civil rights as Greek citizens. US, Australian, New Zealand, Canadian and most non-EU Europeans receive entry and exit stamps in their passports and can stay, as tourists, for ninety days. If you arrive on a flight or boat from another EU state, you may not be stamped in routinely – make sure this is done to avoid unpleasantness upon exit.

Visa extensions

If as a non-EU/EFTA national you wish to remain in Greece for longer than three months, you should officially apply for an **extension**. This can be done in Ródhos Town at the *Ypiresía Allodhapón* (Aliens' Bureau); brace yourself for concerted bureaucracy. In other locations you visit the local police station, where staff are usually more co-operative.

Unless they are of Greek descent, visitors from **non-EU countries** are currently allowed only one six-month extension to a tourist visa, for which a hefty fee is charged – up to €150. In theory, EU nationals are allowed to stay indefinitely but, to be sure of avoiding any problems, it's best to get a resident visa and (if appropriate) a work permit – see "Work", p.77. In either case, the procedure should be set in motion at least four weeks before your time runs out. If you don't already have a work permit, you will be required to present pink, personalized bank **exchange receipts** (see, p.30) totalling at least €1500 for the preceding three months, as proof that you are importing sufficient funds to support yourself without working. Possession of unexpired credit cards, a

Greek embassies abroad

Australia 9 Turrana St, Yarralumla, Canberra, ACT 2600 ☎02/6273 3011.
Britain 1a Holland Park, London W11 3TP ☎020/7221 6467, ⓦwww.greekembassy.org.uk.
Canada 80 Maclaren St, Ottawa, ON K2P 0K6 ☎613/238-6271.
Ireland 1 Upper Pembroke St, Dublin 2 ☎01/676 7254.
New Zealand 5–7 Willeston St, Wellington ☎04/473 7775.
USA 2221 Massachusetts Ave NW, Washington DC 20008 ☎202/939-5800, ⓦwww.greekembassy.org.

Greek **savings account passbook** or travellers' cheques can to some extent substitute for the pink receipts; the pages of the passbook in particular should be photocopied and given to the police.

Certain individuals get around the law by leaving Greece every three months and re-entering a few days later, ideally via a different frontier post, for a new, ninety-day tourist stamp. However, with the recent flood of Albanian and Eastern European refugees into the country, all looking for work, security and immigration personnel don't always look very kindly on this practice.

If you **overstay** your time and then leave under your own power – ie are not deported – you'll be hit with a huge spot fine upon departure, effectively a double-priced retroactive visa extension; no excuses will be entertained except perhaps a doctor's certificate stating you were immobilized in hospital. It cannot be overemphasized just how exigent Greek immigration officials often are on this issue.

Insurance

Even though EU health care privileges apply in Greece (see p.26 for details), you'd do well to take out an insurance policy before travelling to cover against theft, loss, illness or injury. Before paying for a whole new policy, however, it's worth checking whether you are already covered: some all-risks homeowners' or renters' insurance policies *may* cover your possessions when overseas, and many private medical schemes (such as BUPA or PPP in the UK) offer coverage extensions for abroad.

In Canada, provincial health plans usually provide partial cover for medical mishaps overseas, while holders of official student/teacher/youth cards in Canada and the US are entitled to meagre accident coverage and hospital in-patient benefits. **Students** will often find that their student health coverage extends during the vacations and for one term beyond the date of last enrolment. Most **credit-card issuers** also offer some sort of vacation insurance, which is often automatic if you pay for the holiday with their card. However, it's vital to check just what these policies cover – in the UK, frequently only death or dismemberment.

After exhausting the possibilities above, you might want to contact a **specialist travel insurance** company, or consider the travel insurance deal offered by Rough Guides (see box, p.26). A typical travel insurance policy usually provides cover for the **loss** of baggage, tickets and – up to a certain limit – cash, cards or cheques, as well as **cancellation** or curtailment of your journey. Most of them exclude so-called **dangerous sports** unless an extra premium is paid: in the Greek islands this means motorbiking, windsurfing and possibly sailing, with most visitors engaging in one or the other at some point. Many policies can be chopped and changed to eliminate coverage you don't need – for example, sickness and accident benefits can often be excluded or included at will. If you do take medical coverage, ascertain whether benefits will be paid as treatment proceeds or only after return home, whether there is a **24-hour medical emergency number**, and how much the deductible sum is (sometimes negotiable). When securing baggage cover, make sure that the **per-article limit** – typically under £500 in the UK – will cover your most valuable possession. Travel agents and tour operators in the UK are likely to **require travel insurance** when you book a package holiday, though after a change in the UK law in late 1998 they can no longer insist that you buy their own – however you will be required to sign a declaration saying that you have a policy with a particular company.

If you need to make a **medical claim**, you should keep receipts for medicines and treatment, and in the event you have anything stolen or lost you must obtain an **official statement** from the police or the airline

Rough Guide travel insurance

Rough Guides offers its own travel insurance, customized for our readers by a leading UK broker and backed by a Lloyd's underwriter. It's available for anyone, of any nationality, travelling anywhere in the world.

There are two main Rough Guide insurance plans: **Essential**, for basic, no-frills cover; and **Premier** – with more generous and extensive benefits. Alternatively, you can take out **annual multi-trip insurance**, which covers you for any number of trips throughout the year (with a maximum of 60 days for any one trip). Unlike many policies, the Rough Guides schemes are calculated by the day, so if you're travelling for 27 days rather than a month, that's all you pay for. If you intend to be away for the whole year, the Adventurer policy will cover you for 365 days. Each plan can be supplemented with a "Hazardous Activities Premium" if you plan to indulge in sports considered dangerous, such as skiing, scuba-diving or trekking. Rough Guides also does good deals for older travellers, and will insure you up to any age, at prices comparable to SAGA's.

For a policy quote, call the Rough Guide Insurance Line toll-free on ⓣ0800/015 0906 (in the UK); on ⓣ1-866/220-5588 (in the USA); or, if you're calling from elsewhere ⓣ+44 1243/621046. Alternatively, get an online quote at ⓦwww.roughguides.com/insurance

which lost your bags. In the wake of growing numbers of fraudulent claims, most insurers won't even entertain one unless you have a police report. There is usually also a **time limit** for submitting claims after the end of your journey.

Health

British and other EU nationals are officially entitled to free medical care in Greece upon presentation of an E111 form, available from most post offices. "Free", however, means admittance only to the lowest grade of state hospital (known as a *yenikó nosokomío*), and does not include nursing care, special tests or the cost of medication. If you need prolonged medical care, you should make use of private treatment, which is as expensive as anywhere in western Europe – this is where your travel insurance policy (see p.25) comes in handy. The US, Canada, Australia and New Zealand have no formal health-care agreements with Greece (other than allowing for free emergency trauma treatment).

There are no required **inoculations** for Greece, though it's wise to ensure that you are up to date on tetanus and polio. The **water** is safe pretty much everywhere, though you will come across shortages or brackish supplies on some of the drier and more remote islands. Bottled water is widely available if you're feeling cautious.

Specific hazards

The main health problems experienced by visitors have to do with **overexposure to the sun**, and the odd nasty from the sea. To combat the former, don't spend too long in the sun, cover up limbs, wear a hat, and drink plenty of fluids in the hot months to avoid any danger of **sunstroke**; remember that even hazy sun can burn. In terms of sea-gear, goggles or a dive mask for swimming and footwear for walking over wet or rough rocks are useful.

Hazards of the deep

In the sea, you may have the bad luck to meet an armada of **jellyfish** (*tsoúkhtres*), especially in late summer; they come in various colours and sizes ranging from purple "pizzas" to invisible, minute creatures. Various over-the-counter remedies for jellyfish stings are sold in resort pharmacies; baking soda or diluted ammonia also help to lessen the sting. The welts and burning usually subside of their own accord within a few hours; there are no deadly man-of-war species in Greek waters.

Less vicious but more common are black, spiky **sea urchins** (*ahiní*), which infest rocky shorelines year-round; if you step on or graze one, a sewing needle (you can crudely sterilize it by heat from a cigarette lighter) and olive oil are effective for removing spines; if you don't extract them they'll fester. You can take your revenge by eating the roe of the reddish–purple ones, which is served as a delicacy in a few seafood restaurants.

The worst maritime danger – fortunately very rare – is the **weever fish** (*dhrákena*) which buries itself in shallow-water sand with just its poisonous dorsal and gill spines protruding. If you tread on one, the sudden pain is excruciating, and the exceptionally potent venom can cause permanent paralysis of the affected area. Imperative first aid is to immerse your foot in water as hot as you can stand, which degrades the toxin and relieves the swelling of joints and attendant pain, but you should still seek medical attention as soon as possible.

Somewhat more common are **stingrays and skates** (Greek names include *platý*, *seláhi*, *vátos* or *trígona*), which mainly frequent bays with sandy bottoms where they can camouflage themselves. Though shy, they can give you a nasty lash with their tail if trodden on, so shuffle your feet a bit when entering the water.

When snorkelling in deeper water, you may happen upon a brightly coloured **moray eel** (*sméma*) sliding back and forth out of its rocky lair. Keep a respectful distance – their slightly comical air and clown-colours belie an irritable temper and the ability to inflict nasty bites or even sever fingers.

Sandflies, dogs and mosquitoes

If you are sleeping on or near a **beach**, it's wise to use insect repellent, either lotion or wrist/ankle bands, and/or a tent with a screen to guard against **sandflies**. Their bites are potentially dangerous, as these flies spread leishmaniasis, a parasitic infection characterized by chronic fever, listlessness and weight loss. It's difficult to treat, requiring long courses of medication.

In Greece, the main reservoirs for leishmaniasis are **dogs**. Transmission of the disease to humans by fleas has not been proven, but it's wisest not to befriend strays as they also carry echinococcosis, a debilitating liver fluke. In humans these form nodules and cysts which can only be removed surgically.

Mosquitoes (*kounóupia*) in Greece carry nothing worse than a vicious bite, but they can be infuriating. One solution is to burn pyrethrum incense coils (*spíres* or *fidhákia*), which are widely and cheaply available, if pungently malodorous. Better, if you can get them, are the small electrical devices (trade names Vape-Net or Bay-Vap) that vaporize an odourless insecticide tablet; many accommodation proprietors supply them routinely. Insect repellents such as Autan are available from most general stores and kiosks.

Creepy-crawlies

Adders (*ohiés*) and **scorpions** (*skorpií*) are found throughout Greece; both creatures are shy, but take care when climbing over drystone walls where snakes like to sun themselves, and don't put hands or feet in places, like shoes, where you haven't looked first. The wiggly, fast-moving **centipedes** (*skolópendres*) which look like a rubber toy from Hong Kong should also be treated with respect, as they pack a nasty bite.

The number of annual deaths from **snakebite** in Europe is very small. Many snakes will bite if threatened, whether they are venomous or not. If a bite injects venom, then swelling will normally occur within thirty minutes. If this happens, get medical attention; keep the bitten part still; and make sure all body movements are as gentle as possible. If medical attention is not nearby then bind the limb firmly to slow the blood circulation, but not so tightly as to stop the blood flow.

Many reptiles, including snakes, can harbour *Salmonella* bacteria, so should be handled cautiously and preferably not at all. This applies particularly to tortoises.

In addition to munching its way through a fair fraction of Greece's surviving pine forests, the **pine processionary caterpillar** – taking its name from the long, nose-to-tail convoys which individuals form at certain points in their life cycle – sports highly irritating hairs, with a poison worse than a scorpion's. If you touch one, or even a tree-trunk they've been on recently, you'll know all about it for a week, and the welts may require antihistamine to heal.

Pharmacies, drugs and contraception

For **minor complaints** it's enough to go to the local *farmakío*. Greek pharmacists are highly trained and dispense a number of medicines which elsewhere could only be prescribed by a doctor. In the larger towns and resorts there'll usually be one who speaks good English. Pharmacies are usually closed evenings and Saturday mornings, but all should have a monthly schedule (in both English and Greek) on their door showing the complete roster of night and weekend duty pharmacists in town.

Greeks are famously hypochondriac, members of one of Europe's champion medicine-gobbling nations, such that pharmacies are veritable Aladdin's caves of **arcane drug and sundry formulas** – just about everything available in North America and northern Europe is here, and then some. **Homeopathic** and **herbal** remedies are quite widely available, too, and the largest towns have dedicated homeopathic pharmacies, identified by the characteristic green cross.

If you regularly use any form of **prescription drug**, you should bring along a copy of the prescription, together with the generic name of the drug; this will help should you need to replace it, and also avoids possible problems with customs officials. In this regard, it's worth being aware that **codeine is banned** in Greece. If you import any you might find yourself in serious trouble, so check labels carefully; it's the core ingredient of Panadeine, Veganin, Solpadeine, Codis and Empirin-Codeine, to name just a few common compounds.

Hayfever sufferers should be prepared for the early Greek pollen season, at its height from April to June. If you are taken by surprise, you'll be able to get tablets and creams at a pharmacy, but it's cheaper to come prepared. Commercial antihistamines like Triludan are difficult to find in smaller towns, and local brands can be overpriced.

Contraceptive pills are more readily available every year, but don't count on getting these – or spermicidal jelly/foam – outside of a few large island towns, over-the-counter at the larger *farmakía*; Greek women tend not to use any sort of birth control systematically, and have an average of four abortions during their adult life. **Condoms**, however, are inexpensive and ubiquitous – just ask for *profylaktiká* (the slangy terms *plastiká* or slightly vulgar *kapótes* are even better understood) at any pharmacy or corner *períptero* (kiosk).

Women's hygiene supplies are sold in pharmacies or in supermarkets near the toilet paper and nappies. Sanitary towels ("Always" brand) are ubiquitous; tampons, known by the trademark catch-all of "Tampax", can be trickier to find in remoter spots, especially on the smaller islands. Where there is no Tampax as such, "OBs" are similar.

Doctors and hospitals

You'll find English-speaking **doctors** in any of the bigger towns or resorts; the tourist police, hotel staff or even your consulate should be able to come up with some names if you have any difficulty.

For an **ambulance**, phone ⓣ166. In **emergencies** – cuts, broken bones, etc – treatment is given free in **state hospitals**, though you will only get the most basic level of nursing care. Greek families routinely take in food and bedding for relatives, so as a tourist you'll be at a severe disadvantage. Somewhat better are the ordinary state-run **out-patient clinics** (*yiatría*) attached to most public hospitals and also found in rural locales. These operate on a first-come, first-served basis, so go early; usual hours are 8am to noon, though it's sometimes possible to get attended to between 1 and 5pm.

Costs, money and banks

The cost of living in Greece has spiralled during the years of EU membership: the days of renting an island house for a monthly pittance are long gone, and food prices at corner shops now differ little from those of other member countries. However, outside the established resorts, travel between and around the islands remains reasonably priced, with the cost of restaurant meals, short-term accommodation and public transport still cheaper than anywhere in northern or western Europe except Portugal.

Prices depend on where and when you go. The larger tourist resorts and trendier islands (like Rhodes, Kós, Sými and Pátmos) are more expensive, and costs everywhere increase sharply during July and August, or at Christmas, New Year or Easter. **Students** with an International Student Identity Card (ISIC) or under-26s with an International Youth Travel Card can get discounted (sometimes free) admission at many archeological sites and museums; those **over 60** can rely on site-admission discounts of 25 to 30 percent, as well as similar discounts for transport. These, and other occasional discounts, tend to be more readily available to EU nationals.

Some basic costs

On most islands a **daily per-person budget** of £23–27/US$32–38 will get you basic accommodation, breakfast, picnic lunch, a short ferry or bus ride and a simple evening meal, as one of a couple. Camping would cut costs marginally. On £35–38/$49–54 a day you could be living quite well, plus sharing the cost of renting a large motorbike or small car.

Inter-island **ferries**, a main unavoidable expense, are reasonably priced, subsidized by the government in an effort to preserve remote island communities. The cheapest cabin for the overnight journey from Athens to Sámos, an eleven-hour trip, costs about €37, a deck-class ticket for the four-hour trip from Rhodes to Kós costs about €11. For €4–7 you can catch a short-hop ferry to the numerous small islands that lie closer to Rhodes, Kós and Sámos, the most likely touchdown points if you're flying to the Dodecanese or east Aegean on a direct charter.

The simplest double **room** generally costs around €20.50–26.50 a night, depending on the location and the plumbing arrangements. Bona fide single rooms are rare, and cost about seventy percent of double rates. Organized **campsites** are little more than €4 per person, with similar charges per tent and perhaps 25 percent more for a camper van. With discretion you can camp for free in the more remote, rural areas.

A basic taverna **meal** with local wine can be had for around €9–10 a head. Add a better bottle of wine, seafood or more careful cooking, and it could be up to €20 a head; you'll rarely pay more than that. Sharing seafood, Greek salads and dips is a good way to keep costs down in the better restaurants, and even in the most developed of resorts, with inflated "international" menus, you'll often be able to find a more earthy but decent taverna where the locals eat.

Much has been made in some publications of the supposed **duty-free** status of the Dodecanese, making those islands attractive for the purchase of luxury goods and alcohol. Alas, this quirk became a casualty of EU convergence in 1993, its only legacy a slightly lower local rate of VAT than the rest of Greece – which is normally cancelled out by simply raising the basic price of items.

Banks and exchange

Greek **banks** are normally open Monday to Thursday 8.30am–2pm, and Friday 8.30am–1.30pm. Certain branches in major towns or tourist centres are open extra hours in the evenings and on Saturday mornings for exchanging money. Always take your passport with you as proof of identity and be prepared for at least one long line.

Outside these times, the largest hotels and travel agencies can often provide this service, albeit sometimes with hefty commissions. On small islands with no full-service bank, "authorized" bank agents will charge yet another extra fee (1–2 percent) to cover the cost of posting a travellers' cheque to the main branch.

The safest, though most expensive, way to carry money is as **travellers' cheques**. These can be obtained from banks (even if you don't have an account) or from offices of Thomas Cook and American Express; you'll usually pay a commission of between one and two percent, though it pays to be aware of any special commission-free deals from your travel agent or your home bank. You can cash the cheques at most banks, though rarely elsewhere. Each travellers' cheque encashment in Greece will incur a minimum commission charge of €1.20–2.40 depending on the bank for amounts of up to €60 equivalent, so you won't want to make too many small-value transactions. For greater amounts, a set percentage will apply. Make sure you keep the purchase agreement and a record of cheque serial numbers safe and separate from the cheques themselves. In the event that cheques are lost or stolen, the issuing company will expect you to report the loss forthwith; most companies claim to replace lost or stolen cheques within 24 hours.

Small-denomination **foreign bank notes** are also extremely useful, and relatively unlikely to be stolen in Greece (see "Trouble, crime and sexual harassment", p.75). Since the freeing up of all remaining currency controls in 1994, a number of authorized brokers for exchanging foreign cash have emerged in major tourist centres such as Rhodes. When changing small amounts, choose those bureaux that charge a flat percentage commission (usually one percent) rather than a high minimum. There are also a small number of 24-hour automatic **foreign-note-changing machines** in a few resorts, but again a high minimum commission tends to be deducted.

In 1998, the Greek **post office** largely abandoned the business of changing money – a nuisance, as many tiny islands have a post office but no bank. If you have a UK-based Girobank account, you may still be able to use your chequebook to get money at some remote post offices. You may also find that main post offices (in provincial capitals) are the designated receiving points for Western Union Moneygrams (see opposite).

Finally, there is no need to **purchase euros** before arrival unless you're coming in at some ungodly hour to one of the remoter land or sea frontier posts, or on a Sunday. Airport arrival lounges will always have an exchange booth or cash machine for passengers on incoming international flights.

The euro

Greece is one of twelve European Union countries which have changed over to a single currency, the **euro** (€). The transition period, which began on January 1, 1999, was lengthy, however: euro notes and coins were not issued until January 1, 2002, with the Greek drachma (*dhrakhmí*, the oldest currency in Europe) remaining in place for cash transactions, at a fixed rate of 340.75 drachmes to 1 euro, until they were scrapped entirely on February 28, 2002. You will be able to exchange any left-over drachma coins into euros until March 2004, and any old drachma paper notes until March 2012, at branches of the Bank of Greece. For the most up-to-date **exchange rates** of the US dollar or the pound sterling against the euro, consult the very useful currency speculators' website, ⓦwww.oanda.com.

You should not be charged commission for changing euro-denomination **travellers' cheques** in any of the twelve countries within the euro zone (also known as "Euroland").

All **local prices** in this book are given in **euros**. Amounts were derived from the last known drachma price of late 2001, and usually rounded up – as the Greeks will almost certainly do, if the experience of decimalization in the UK is anything to go by. Also judging by past practice, Greek shopkeepers are unlikely to bother much with shortfalls of 10 euro-cents or less, whether in their favour or yours.

Euro notes exist in **denominations** of 5, 10, 20, 50, 100, 200 and 500 euros, and coins in denominations of 1, 2, 5, 10, 20 and 50 cents and 1 and 2 euros. The bills are the same across Euroland, but individual countries can propose specific designs for the coins.

Visa Travel Money (@www.visa.com)

This is a disposable debit card pre-paid with dedicated travel funds which you can access from over 457,000 Visa cash machines in 120 countries with a PIN that you select yourself. When your funds are depleted, you simply throw the card away. Since you can buy up to nine cards to access the same funds – useful for couples/families travelling together – it's recommended that you buy at least one extra as a back up in case your first is lost or stolen. There is a 24-hour Visa global customer assistance services centre which you can call from any of the 120 countries toll-free. The number to call from Greece is 00 800 11 481 0304. In the UK, many Thomas Cook outlets sell the card.

Credit cards and cash dispensers

Major **credit cards** are not usually accepted by cheaper tavernas or hotels, but they're almost essential for renting cars, for buying Olympic Airways tickets and for expensive souvenirs. Major travel agents may also claim to accept them, but for buying ferry (as opposed to air) tickets a **three percent surcharge** is typically passed on to the consumer. Visa and Mastercard are widely accepted, American Express far less so and Diner's hardly at all.

You can easily use the growing network of Greek **cash machines** (ATMs), by learning the PIN numbers for your debit/credit cards. Larger airports (such as Athens, Kós, Rhodes and Thessaloníki) have at least one of these in the arrivals hall, and almost any town or island with a population larger than a few thousand (or substantial tourist traffic) also has them. The most well distributed are those of the National Bank/Ethniki Trapeza, the Trapeza Pireos/Bank of Piraeus, and the Commercial Bank/Emboriki Trapeza, which happily and interchangeably accept Visa, Mastercard, Visa Electron, Plus and Cirrus cards; those of the equally widespread Alfa Trapeza/Alpha Bank and its increasingly rare subsidiary the Ionian Bank/Ioniki Trapeza are somewhat more restrictive, accepting only American Express and Visa-affiliated cards.

Cash machine transactions with **debit cards** linked to a cheque account via the Plus/Cirrus systems attract charges of 2.25 percent on the sterling/dollar transaction value, subject to a minimum of £1.75, making them the **least expensive** way of getting money in Greece as long as you withdraw more than £80 equivalent in euros (about €130). By contrast, using **credit cards** at a cash dispenser is one of the **dearest** ways of obtaining cash: a cash advance per-transaction fee of £1.50 minimum typically applies in the UK – often working out much greater – plus a "foreign transaction" surcharge of up to 2.75 percent on the total, depending on the card issuer.

Wiring money

All told, learning and using the PIN numbers for any debit or credit cards you have is the quickest and least expensive way of securing moderate amounts of funds from abroad. In an emergency, however, you can arrange to have more substantial amounts of **money wired** from your home bank to a bank in Greece. Receiving funds by SWIFT transfer takes a minimum of two working days and can take up to ten working days if your sender picks the "non-express" service. From the UK, a bank charge of 0.03% percent, with a minimum of £17, maximum £35, is typically levied for a two-day service; some building societies charge a £20 flat fee irrespective of the amount. If you go this route, your home bank will need the address and (ideally) the branch number of the bank where you want to pick up the money. It's unwise to transfer more than the equivalent of €10,000 (currently about US$8500 or £6000); above that limit, as part of measures to combat money-laundering, international terrorism and organized crime, the receiving Greek bank will begin asking awkward questions and imposing punitive commissions.

Having money wired from home using one of the **companies** listed below is never convenient – local affiliate offices other than the post office are thin on the ground in Greece – and is even more expensive than using a bank, and should be considered as a last resort. However, unlike with banks, the funds should be available for collection at Amex's, Thomas Cook's or Western Union's local representative office within hours, sometimes minutes, of being sent.

Money-wiring companies

In Australia
American Express Moneygram ⓣ1800/230 100, ⓦwww.moneygram.com.
Western Union ⓣ1800/649565, ⓦwww.westernunion.com.

In New Zealand
American Express Moneygram ⓣ09/379 8243 or 0800/262263, ⓦwww.moneygram.com.
Western Union ⓣ09/270 0050, ⓦwww.westernunion.com.

In North America
American Express Moneygram ⓣ1-800/926-9400, ⓦwww.moneygram.com.
Western Union ⓣ1-800/325-6000, ⓦwww.westernunion.com.
Thomas Cook US ⓣ1-800/287-7362, Canada ⓣ1-888/8234-7328, ⓦwww.us.thomascook.com.

In the UK and Ireland
Western Union Money Transfer ⓣ0800/833 833, ⓦwww.westernunion.com.
Moneygram ⓣ0800/018 0104, ⓦwww.moneygram.com.
Thomas Cook ⓣ01733/318922, Belfast ⓣ028/9055 0030, Dublin ⓣ01/677 1721.

Information and maps

The National Tourist Organization of Greece (Ellinikós Organismós Tourismoú, or EOT; GNTO abroad, ⓦwww.gnto.gr) maintains offices in most European capitals, and major cities in Australia and North America (see box below for addresses). It publishes an impressive array of free, glossy, regional pamphlets that are good for getting an idea of where you want to go, even if the actual text should sometimes be taken with a spoonful of salt. Also available from the EOT are a reasonable fold-out map of the country and a large number of brochures on special interests and festivals.

Greek national tourist offices abroad

Australia
51 Pitt St, Sydney NSW 2000 ⓣ02/9241 1663, ⓔhto@tpg.com.au.
Canada
91 Scollard St, 2nd Floor, Toronto, Ontario M5R 1GR ⓣ416/968-2220, ⓔgrnto.tor@sympatico.ca.
Israel
5 Shalom Aleichem Street, Tel Aviv 61262 ⓣ03/517 0501, ⓔhellenic@netvision.net.il.
Netherlands
Kerkstraat 61, 1017 GC Amsterdam ⓣ20/625 4212, ⓔgnot@planet.nl.
UK
4 Conduit St, London W1R 0DJ ⓣ020/7734 5997, ⓔEOT-greektouristoffice@btinternet.com.
USA
645 Fifth Ave, New York, NY 10022 ⓣ212/421-5777, ⓔgnto@greektourism.com.
The GNTO website lists a dozen more non-English-speaking countries with full tourist offices. If your home country isn't listed there, apply to the embassy. There are no Greek tourist offices in Ireland, South Africa or New Zealand.

Tourist offices

In the Dodecanese and east Aegean there are official **EOT offices** only in Ródhos Town, Vathý (Sámos) and Mytilíni (Lésvos); elsewhere, specifically on Kós, Híos, Kálymnos, Mólyvos and again Ródhos Town, you'll find **municipal tourist offices**. Staff at either breed of office are happy to provide advice and photocopied sheets on ferry and bus departures, the opening hours for museums and sites, plus occasionally assistance with **accommodation** – though there have been scandals in the provinces concerning certain staff taking backhanders to steer potential clients towards particular outfits. In the absence of any of these, you can visit the **Tourist Police**, essentially a division (often just a single delegate) of the local police. They can sometimes provide you with lists of rooms to let, which they regulate, but they're really where you go if you have a **serious complaint** about an accommodation or eating establishment.

Maps

No authoritative, authentic maps . . . . Well, isn't that as it should be? Why does anybody need maps? If an individual wants them he's a spy. If a country needs maps it's moribund. A well-mapped country is a dead country. A complete survey is a burial shroud. A life with maps is a tyranny!

That extract from Alan Sillitoe's unjustly forgotten 1971 satire, *Travels in Nihilon*, pretty much sums up the prevailing attitude towards **maps** in Greece, which are an endless source of confusion and often outright misinformation. Each cartographic company seems to have its own peculiar system of transcribing Greek letters into English – and these, as often as not, do not match the semi-official transliterations on the road signs.

The most reliable **general map** of the Dodecanese and east Aegean islands is the GeoCenter map "Greek Islands/Aegean Sea", which covers all points described in this book at a scale of 1:300,000. It's not perfect, and like all double-sided maps can be cumbersome to use; the single-sided Freytag-Berndt (1:650,000, with index booklet) is a possible alternative, while Michelin #980 (scale 1:700,000) ranks a distant third despite revisions in the mid-1990s. All of these are widely available in Britain and North America, less easily in Greece (see p.34–35). Freytag-Berndt also publishes a series of more detailed **regional island maps**, including *Kos–Samos–Ikaria* (1:150,000), *Rhodos* (1:100,000) and *Hios–Lesvos–Lemnos* (1:150,000); these are best bought overseas from specialist outlets.

Maps of **individual islands** are more easily available on the spot, and while some are wildly inaccurate or obsolete, with strange hieroglyphic symbols, others are reliable and up to date; we've indicated in the guide where particular maps are worth buying or not. Large-scale products always worth keeping an eye out for are those published by Athens-based **Road Editions** (Ⓦwww .road.gr); based on army topographical maps, they're usually quite accurate but as of writing available for only a few islands covered in this book – Rhodes, Kárpathos/Kássos, Kós, Sámos, Híos and Lésvos. In the UK they can be purchased at the Hellenic Book Service, Stanfords and other good map shops (see p.34 and p.502 for addresses). Two domestic competitors to Road, Emvelia (Ⓦwww.emvelia.gr) and Anavasi have recently emerged, but thus far Emvelia has concentrated on the mainland and major cities, whilst Anavasi specializes in mountain hiking maps, plus the islands of the Sporades and Cyclades, though this of course may change. Out in the islands, Road and Anavasi maps can often be found in the bookstore chain Newsstand.

Hiking and topographical maps

Hiking and topographical maps of the east Aegean and Dodecanese islands, including Rhodes, are almost impossible to obtain in Greece. The Greek government's equivalent of Ordnance Survey or USGS topographic maps are unavailable indefinitely for "security reasons" owing to continuing tension with Turkey and other Balkan neighbours. Should the rules change, you can try your luck at the Army Geographical Service (*Yeografikí Ypiresía Stratoú*) in Athens at Evelpídhon 4, north of Aréos Park (Mon, Wed & Fri 8am–noon).

At present, the best available hiking maps are those prepared before and during World War II by foreign powers. For the **east Aegean islands** you want those prepared by the British War Office at a scale of 1:50,000, with twenty- or forty-metre contour intervals; while they don't show paths, they depict roads more accurately than many contemporary Greek tourist maps, and also indicate the magnetic declination from true north. All of this series is quite useable except the one for Ikaría, which was evidently hastily produced (the contour lines don't join up correctly).

For the **Dodecanese**, under Italian occupation from 1913 to 1943, the map set published by the Instituto Geografico Militare in Florence from 1927 onwards is your best choice. Sheets for each island have been published at a 1:25,000 scale, with ten-metre contour intervals. Because of that, and their calligraphic lettering, they have a deceptively antiquarian appearance, but are eminently reliable for natural features and village positions, and often show trails remarkably accurately. Difficulties arise principally from the Italianization of all Greek place names, eg Terrarossa for Kokinohóma, so you have to "decode" between two probably unfamiliar languages.

These two series are not commercially available overseas, let alone in Greece, so you'll have to make do with **photocopies** of originals kept by certain large institutions. In the US or Canada, try the map room of a major university library; most will have at least the Italian set, and charge nothing or a nominal fee for copying. In the UK, the only source of both the British and Italian cartography is the map library of the Royal Geographical Society, Kensington Gore, London SW7 2AR (ⓣ020/7591 3050, Mon–Fri 11am–5pm only; no mail order service but ⓕ020/7591 3001 for enquiries). Before you're allowed to make copies (around £1.50 per large A2 sheet), you first have to petition the Directorate of Geographic Information, Military Survey, Block A, Government Buildings, Hook Rise South, Tolworth, Surbiton, Surrey KT6 7NB by letter or fax for permission to use Crown Copyright material (ⓣ020/8335 5338, ⓕ8335 5387).

Finally, for hiking in particular areas of Sámos, Rhodes, Sými and Lésvos, maps-with-guide booklets published by **Marengo Publications** in England also prove very useful. Stanfords keeps a good stock of these, or order from Marengo direct at 17 Bernard Crescent, Hunstanton PE36 6ER (ⓣ & ⓕ01485/532710, ⓔmarengowalks@aol.com, ⓦwww.marengo.supanet.com). The municipality of Níssyros issues a free, laminated, GPS-compatible topographic map of that island, prepared by two German visitors.

Map outlets

UK and Ireland

Blackwell's Map and Travel Shop 53 Broad St, Oxford OX1 3BQ ⓣ01865/792792, ⓦwww.bookshop.blackwell.co.uk.
Easons Bookshop 40 O'Connell St, Dublin 1 ⓣ01/873 3811, ⓦwww.eason.ie.
Heffers Map and Travel 20 Trinity St, Cambridge CB2 1TJ ⓣ01223/568568, ⓦwww.heffers.co.uk.
Hodges Figgis Bookshop 56–58 Dawson St, Dublin 2 ⓣ01/677 4754, ⓦwww.hodgesfiggis.com.
James Thin Melven's Bookshop 29 Union St, Inverness IV1 1QA ⓣ01463/233500, ⓦwww.jthin.co.uk.
John Smith and Sons 26 Colquhoun Ave, Glasgow G52 4PJ ⓣ0141/552 3377, ⓦwww.johnsmith.co.uk.
The Map Shop 30a Belvoir St, Leicester LE1 6QH ⓣ0116/247 1400.
National Map Centre 22–24 Caxton St, London SW1H 0QU ⓣ020/7222 2466, ⓦwww.mapsnmc.co.uk.
Newcastle Map Centre 55 Grey St, Newcastle upon Tyne NE1 6EF ⓣ0191/261 5622, ⓦwww.traveller.ltd.uk.
Ordnance Survey of Northern Ireland Colby House, Stranmillis Ct, Belfast BT9 5BJ ⓣ028/9066 1244, ⓦwww.osni.gov.uk.
Ordnance Survey Service Phoenix Park, Dublin 8 ⓣ01/820 6100, ⓦwww.irlgov.ie/osi/.
Stanfords 12–14 Long Acre, London WC2E 9LP ⓣ020/7836 1321, ⓦwww.stanfords.co.uk; maps by mail or phone order are available on this number and via ⓔsales@stanfords.co.uk. Other branches are within the British Airways offices at 156 Regent St, London W1R 5TA ⓣ020/7434 4744, and 29 Corn St, Bristol BS1 1HT ⓣ0117/929 9966.
The Travel Bookshop 13–15 Blenheim Crescent, London W11 2EE ⓣ020/7229 5260, ⓦwww.thetravelbookshop.co.uk.

USA and Canada

Adventurous Traveler Bookstore PO Box 64769, Burlington, VT 05406 ⓣ1-800/282-3963, ⓦwww.AdventurousTraveler.com.
Book Passage 51 Tamal Vista Blvd, Corte Madera, CA 94925 ⓣ415/927-0960, ⓦwww.bookpassage.com.
Elliot Bay Book Company 101 S Main St, Seattle, WA 98104 ⓣ206/624-6600 or 1-800/962-5311, ⓦwww.elliotbaybook.com.
Forsyth Travel Library 226 Westchester Ave, White Plains, NY 10604 ⓣ1-800/367-7984, ⓦwww.forsyth.com.
Globe Corner Bookstore 28 Church St, Cambridge, MA 02138 ⓣ1-800/358-6013, ⓦwww.globercorner.com.
GORP Adventure Library Online only ⓣ1-800/754-8229, ⓦwww2.gorp.com.
Map Link Inc 30 S La Patera Lane, Unit 5, Santa Barbara, CA 93117 ⓣ805/692-6777, ⓦwww.maplink.com.
Open Air Books and Maps 25 Toronto St, Toronto, ON M5C 2R1 ⓣ416/363-0719.

Phileas Fogg's Travel Center #87 Stanford Shopping Center, Palo Alto, CA 94304 ⓣ1-800/533-3644, ⓦwww.foggs.com.
Rand McNally 444 N Michigan Ave, Chicago, IL 60611 ⓣ312/321-1751, ⓦwww.randmcnally.com; 150 E 52nd St, New York, NY 10022 ⓣ212/758-7488; 595 Market St, San Francisco, CA 94105 ⓣ415/777-3131; around thirty stores across the US – call ⓣ1-800/333-0136 ext 2111 or check the website for the nearest store.
Travel Books & Language Center 4437 Wisconsin Ave, Washington, DC 20016 ⓣ1-800/220-2665, ⓦwww.bookweb.org/bookstore/travellers.
The Travel Bug Bookstore 2667 West Broadway, Vancouver V6K 2G2 ⓣ604/737-1122, ⓦwww.swifty.com/tbug.
Traveler's Choice Bookstore 22 W 52nd St, New York, NY 10019 ⓣ212/664-0995, ⓔtvlchoice@aol.com.
Ulysses Travel Bookshop 4176 St-Denis, Montréal, PQ H2W 2M5 ⓣ514/843-9447, ⓦwww.ulysses.ca.
World of Maps 118 Holland Ave, Ottawa, Ontario K1Y 0X6 ⓣ613/724-6776, ⓦwww.itmb.com.
World Wide Books and Maps 1247 Granville St, Vancouver V6Z 1G3 ⓣ604/687-3320, ⓦwww.worldofmaps.com.

Australia and New Zealand

The Map Shop 6 Peel St, Adelaide ⓣ08/8231 2033, ⓦwww.mapshop.net.au.
Mapland 372 Little Bourke St, Melbourne ⓣ03/9670 4383, ⓦwww.mapland.com.au.
Mapworld 173 Gloucester St, Christchurch ⓣ03/374 5399, ⓕ03/374 5633, ⓦwww.mapworld.co.nz.
Perth Map Centre 1/884 Hay St, Perth ⓣ08/9322 5733, ⓦwww.perthmap.com.au.
Specialty Maps 46 Albert St, Auckland ⓣ09/307 2217, ⓦwww.ubd-online.co.nz/maps.
Travel Bookshop, Shop 3, 175 Liverpool St, Sydney ⓣ02/9261 8200.
Worldwide Maps & Guides, 187 George St, Brisbane ⓣ07/3221 4330.

Greece on the internet

Greece is strongly represented on the internet, with numerous websites offering information on most conceivable subjects. Some of the better sites, however, are Greek-only, or require Java and/or the downloading of Greek fonts to be completely useable. Almost every island will have its own website, though some of these, in bizarre renditions of "Gringlish", are barely readable or packed with turgid, obscure ancient history. Others – mastered by expatriate residents – are fluent enough but rather vague as to specifics so as to avoid raising local hackles. Moreover, the most visited spots like Rhodes, Kós or Sámos tend to have the worst maintained sites; you generally have better joy with the remoter, less-known islands, which are keener to promote themselves with interesting sites. Country-wide and regional sites recommended below are reasonably useful, balanced and literate.

ⓦwww.greektravel.com
Subjective, North-American-orientated but useful site maintained by North Carolinan Matt Barrett, who's been visiting Greece for over three decades. Lots of recommendations, destination thumbnails, tricks and shortcuts, plus hundreds of links to affiliated sites.

ⓦhttp://forecast.uoa.gr
Excellent one-stop site for the temperature, wind direction and rainfall country-wide, maintained by the University of Athens physics faculty. Pick a specific city or island for an all-parameters report; English option available.

ⓦwww.poseidon.ncmr.gr
Greek oceanographer's site maintained by the National Centre for Marine Reserach that profiles Aegean weather meticulously, including groovy graphics of sea currents and surface winds, based on satellite imaging. Slow-loading but sophisticated, good for yachties, reports one topic (rain, temperature, etc) at a time.

ⓦwww.culture.gr
The Greek Ministry of Culture's website. The best bit is its alphabetical gazetteer to monuments, archeological sites and museums. Not complete, and the opening hours are probably unreliable, but it does have a lot of info about the more obscure sites.

ⓦwww.athensnews.gr
On-line edition of the *Athens News*, Greece's longest-running quality English-language newspaper, with the day's top stories. A bit slow, but easy to find your way around.

ⓦwww.kathimerini.com/news/news.asp
On-line edition of the abridged English translation of *Kathimerini*, one of Greece's most respected dailies. Fully archived for years back, excellent search facility.

Ⓦwww.greekworks.com
US-based e-zine covering Greece- and Greek-related personalities, topics and events. It's $75 a year to register, and little of the content is free, but you get what you pay for in top-flight writing.

Ⓦwww.hellenicbooks.com
Website of the UK's premier Greek bookstore. Full, opinionated reviews of their stock, possibility of buying on-line, and witty descriptions of every island compiled by proprietor Stelios Jackson and his assistant Markos Stefanou.

Ⓦwww.ktel.org/frontpage.shtml
Bilingual website of the KTEL, or national bus syndicate. Fairly reliable schedules, organized by province; the main problem is that most of the Aegean islands are not covered.

Ⓦwww.gtp.gr
Website of Greek Travel Pages, the fat (and expensive) printed manual on every Greek travel agent's desk. Mostly resorted to for its ferry schedules (also kept on a separate site, Ⓦwww.gtpweb.com). Completely revamped in 2001, though still not 100 percent reliable (as with anything to do with Greek shipping).

Ⓦwww.thegreektravel.com
A literate, fairly informative general island-travel site which concentrates on the more obscure destinations: Astypálea, Hálki, Léros, Kárpathos and Níssyros in the Dodecanese, and Híos and Límnos in the east Aegean.

Ⓦwww.lesvos.com
Excellent overview of Lésvos, compiled by Matt Barrett (see previous page). Reliable restaurant recommendations, though these are compiled on the basis of his summer-only residence and can go a year between updates.

Ⓦwww.island-ikaria.com
Literate, interesting and fairly current, covering everything from hot springs to festivals; well organized, with sensible internal links.

Ⓦwww.chiosnet.gr
The municipality's official site; a bit dull, but kept current.

Ⓦwww.symivisitor.com
Current news for aficionados, a range of accommodation, restaurant and beach profiles, presented by the publishers of the monthly island newspaper.

Ⓦwww.kalymnos-isl.gr
Official website, with the English pages edited by expatriated radio journalist and author Faith Warn and thus fluent. However, the news pages can get stale, and tourism specifics are a bit anodyne.

Ⓦwww.leros.org
A bit of Gringlish to contend with, but clearly devised with love, and gives a fun, thorough flavour of the island's landscapes, people and traditional architecture.

Ⓦwww.astypalaia.com
General all-purpose site detailing island sights, eats and accommodations, though links sometimes "stick".

Ⓦwww.kastellorizo.de
Fairly good, if inevitably biased (author Monika is locally married) site giving a fair overview of this tiny islet; slightly ropey English text available.

Getting around

Island-hopping is one of the intrinsic features of a holiday in the Dodecanese or east Aegean, as much a pursuit in itself as a means of transport. The local ferry, catamaran and hydrofoil network is extensive, and few of the 27 inhabited isles featured in this book are difficult to reach. Inter-island plane flights are expensive, costing up to four times as much as a deck-class ferry ticket and twice as much as a first-class cabin, but useful if you need to save time or when boat links are inadequate. Especially in the Dodecanese, planes are being replaced by more competitively priced hydrofoils and catamarans.

Mainline ferry companies: principal routes

DANE (home port: Ródhos Town)
Rhodes–Tílos–Kós–Kálymnos–Léros–Pátmos–Pireás
Rhodes–Kós–Kálymnos–Astypálea–Pireás
Rhodes–Níssyros–Kós–Léros–Pátmos–Pireás
Rhodes–Kós–Sámos–Thessaloníki

G&A Ferries (home port: Pireás)
Vathý–Karlóvassi–Foúrni–Áyios Kírykos–Náxos–Páros–Pireás
Vathý–Áyios Kírykos–Mýkonos–Sýros–Pireás
Kastellórizo–Rhodes–Sými–Tílos–Níssyros–Kós–Kálymnos–Léros–Pátmos–Náxos–Páros–Sýros–Pireás
Rhodes–Kós–Kálymnos–Astypálea–Pireás
Rhodes–Kós–Léros–Pátmos–Foúrni–Áyios Kírykos–Pireás
Rhodes–Kós–Léros–Lipsí–Pátmos–Áyios Kírykos–Pireás

Hellas Ferries (Hellas – ex-Minoan – Flying Dolphins) (home port: Pireás)
Mytilíni–Híos–Pireás
Mytilíni–Híos–Sámos (Vathý)–Sýros–Pireás
Vathý–Karlóvassi–Évdhilos–Mýkonos–Sýros–Pireás

LANE (home port: Áyios Nikólaos, Crete)
Rhodes–Hálki–Kárpathos (both ports)–Kássos–Sitía (Crete)–Áyios Nikólaos (Crete)–Mílos–Pireás

NEL (home port: Mytilíni)
Mytilíni–Híos–Pireás
Mytilíni–Límnos–Kavála or Thessaloníki
Mytilíni–Híos–Mýkonos–Sýros–Pireás
Límnos–Áyios Efstrátios–Sígri–Rafína
Rhodes–Kós–Sámos–Híos–Mytilíni–Límnos–Alexandhroúpoli

Non-Athens-based ferry companies

ANEK (Kalymnian Shipping Co) 852 00 Kálymnos ☎02430/29 612, Ⓕ24 144.
DANE Afstraliás 92, Ródhos Town, 851 00 Rhodes ☎02410/43 150, Ⓦwww.helios.gr/dane.
LANE Sfakianáki 5, Áyios Nikólaos, Lassíthi, Crete ☎08410/26 764.
Miniotis Lines Neoríon 21, Híos Town, 821 00 Híos ☎02710/24 670, Ⓦwww.miniotis.gr.
NEL Pávlou Koundouriótou 47, 811 00 Mytilíni, Lésvos ☎02510/26 299 or 26 251.

NB Reverse itineraries are valid in most cases, but note that these represent ideal itineraries; in many cases islands may be omitted in one or both directions, eg Hálki can be skipped on LANE's Rhodes–Crete run, and Kálymnos may be dropped from Kós–Astypálea runs.

For getting around the islands themselves, there are basic bus services, which most tourists choose to supplement at some stage with motorbike or car rental.

Sea transport

There are four types of craft carrying passengers around the islands: medium-sized to large **conventional car ferries** (which connect the Dodecanese and east Aegean with each other, the mainland, the Cyclades and Crete); small to large, **high-speed catamarans** (which operate both between certain Dodecanese, and between the east Aegean islands and Pireás); **hydrofoils** (confined to relatively sheltered waters between neighbouring islands and the lee of Asia Minor); and local **kaïkia** (small passenger-only boats which in season undertake short hops and excursions). Costs are very reasonable on the longer journeys, though proportionately more expensive for shorter, inter-island connections.

We've indicated **ferry connections** on the maps as well as in the "Travel Details" at the end of each island account. Be warned, however, that schedules are notoriously erratic, and must be verified on the spot; the details given are essentially for departures between mid-June and mid-September inclusive. **Out-of-season** services are severely reduced, with many islands served only once or twice a week. However, in spring or autumn those ferries that do operate are often compelled by the transport ministry to call at extra islands to compensate for other craft still in dry dock, making possible some interesting connections.

The most reliable, up-to-date information is available from the local **port police** (*limenarhío*), who can be found on or near the harbour of every sizeable island; smaller places may only have a *limenikós stathmós* (marine post), often just a single room with a VHF radio. Their officers rarely speak much English, but they keep complete schedules posted – and, meteorological report in hand, are the final arbiters of whether or not a ship will sail in stormy weather.

Apagorevtikó, or obligatory halt of all seaborne traffic, is applied for weather in excess of force 7.5 on the Beaufort scale; hydrofoils tend to be confined to port at force 6 or above, with catamarans falling somewhere in between. There are, however, exceptions to this depending on the direction of the wind (southerlies are considered exceptionally dangerous), and port police maintain elaborate charts collating additional factors such as wave height; catamarans, for example, can sail in windier conditions than hydrofoils, but have a poor tolerance for disrupted sea surface. Since the sinking of the *Express Samina* (see box below), port police have been erring on the side of caution, though a few can seem to be (and sometimes are) unreasonable and arbitrary. Travellers stuck on a remote island with a flight home to miss often ponder the possibility of chartering a fishing boat to get them to the airport island; the fishermen are entitled to risk their lives at will, and often do sail off in dodgy weather, but they're heavily fined if caught risking passengers' lives, so this is usually a non-starter.

Few ferry companies, with the honourable exceptions of the *Dodekanisos Express*, Kyriakoulis Maritime, Miniotis Lines and NEL Lines, produce regular

The wreck of the *Express Samina* – and beyond

September 27, 2000, was a sort of Judgement Day for the Greek domestic ferry industry. Around midnight in gale conditions, the *Express Samina* (née the *Golden Vergina*), bound ultimately for Ikaría, Sámos and Lipsí and the oldest ship in the domestic fleet, slammed full speed into the Pórtes rocks outside Páros harbour in the Cyclades, and sank within minutes. The bridge was unstaffed by senior officers, all of whom were elsewhere watching a football match on television. The British and Greek Navies exercising in the area, plus swarms of fishing boats from Páros, together plucked most of the 500-plus aboard from the water, including numerous foreign tourists, but 82 passengers drowned. It was the worst maritime disaster in Greece since the ferry *Iraklion* went down in December 1966, with 226 casualties.

Skipper Vassilis Yiannakis, and the first mate, were quickly charged with manslaughter and criminal negligence, and as of writing are still on remand, awaiting trial when submarine investigations of the wreck are completed. Once the initial furore died down, the pair – especially the captain, who had been involved in two prior collisions – seemed on reflection to be easy scapegoats. The boat had previously been owned by Agapitos Lines, one of several shipping companies swallowed up by Minoan Flying Dolphins in its several-year drive to acquire eighty-percent dominance of the Greek passenger-ferry industry (among larger companies, only ANEK, NEL and DANE have escaped their grasp) – and a near-monopoly on sailings to the Cyclades and the Dodecanese. In this they had been assisted by a previous merchant-marine minister in the PASOK government, who also became a focus of opprobrium, along with Minoan Flying Dolphins management (one of whom, general manager Pandelis Sfinias, committed suicide on November 30 by jumping from the sixth floor of his Pireás headquarters).

It also emerged that the 34-year-old *Express Samina* was the worst but by no means the only rust-bucket in the Greek domestic fleet well past its scrap-by date. EU regulations normally require ships to be retired after 27 years of service, but Greek shipping interests had wheedled an extension to 35 years from Brussels – in much the same way that Minoan Flying Dolphins had cajoled the Greek government ministry into granting it, rather than any remaining smaller competitors, licences for any route, profitable or otherwise. With an effective monopoly and regulated fares, there was little incentive (as there is on the Greece–Italy lines) to keep boats up to date. Greek newspapers quickly tallied 18 ferries 29 years old, or older. The age of the *Express Samina* was a critical factor in her rapid sinking; newer craft have multiple airtight compartments, so that a single breach in the schedule sheets or booklets, the excuse being that precise routes and frequencies change unpredictably over the course of any given year. For Miniotis and NEL, sheets or booklets are unlikely to appear before July, with a revision in mid-September. The only attempt at an all-inclusive Greek ferry guide is the yearly "Greek Travel Routes, Domestic Sea Schedules", co-produced by the GNTO, and the Greek travel agents' manual, the GTP; be prepared to master an array of bewildering abbreviations for ports and shipping companies. The printed guide is available at GNTO/EOT offices, usually from July onwards, but you'll find a very sporadically updated version at Ⓦwww.gtpnet.com.

Regular ferries

On most **ferry** routes, your only consideration will be getting a boat that leaves on the day, and for the island, that you want. Departures for the more obscure islands, the so-called *agonés grammés* or subsidized lines, are famously user-hostile: there may be no boat for five days, and then suddenly two appear within two hours of each other, at 3am to boot. The Ministry of Transport, which pays the subsidies for this behaviour, seems unwilling or unable to compel more **logical schedules**. However, when sailing from Rhodes or Kós to the other Dodecanese islands, you should have a choice of two – possibly three – sailings, and may want to bear in mind a few of the factors below.

Routes taken and the speed of the boats can vary considerably. The journey from Rhodes to Pátmos, for instance, can take anything from eight to ten and a half hours. Before buying a ticket it's wise to establish how many stops there will be before your island, and the estimated time of arrival. Many agents act only

hull would not be fatal, but the *Express Samina* had just a single compartment, and was effectively doomed the moment the rocks tore a three-metre gash in her side (though the crew having left bulkhead doors open did not help). Most lifesaving equipment, from the ancient, cork-buoyed lifejackets to the snail-slow lifeboats, was inadequate or scarcely used at the critical hour. Only the year before, an inspection engineer had resigned in protest that his verdict on the boat as unseaworthy was being ignored by Minoan.

The government had to be seen to be doing something, and so made a show of granting some minor routes to Minoan's competitors during the weeks following the sinking, and pushed for a thirty-year limit on service time for boats in early 2001. It's in the medium term, however, that the fallout from the disaster has had most effect. The oldest members of the domestic fleet were instantly confined to port, pending safety inspections – which several did not pass, leaving a shortfall. Those ships which could be brought into compliance with EU standards were refitted, but clean bills of health were often issued in an arbitrary and biased manner; a loophole in the law allows substandard craft to continue operating if their destination is a non-EU country. As a result, much of 2001 saw very skeletal connections to certain of the remoter Dodecanese; Kastellórizo and Tílos were particularly hard hit, losing their catamaran schedule mid-season when the boat in question switched to more lucrative ports. In the prevailing climate of protecting profits (and one's legal behind) before service, matters are likely to get worse before they get better. Only a few newly commissioned ferries – such as NEL's high-speed catamarans *Aeolos Express, Aelos Express II* and *Aeolos Kenteris* – have taken to the water since the sinking. Investigation of the wreck is still underway, and Minoan Flying Dolphins remains the target of a vast number of civil suits for wrongful death, and a criminal investigation as well – not, perhaps, unrelated to the directors' July 2001 decision to rechristen the company Hellas Flying Dolphins. Terrified of another public-relations disaster in the run-up to Greece's hosting of the 2004 Olympics, port police have become far stricter about confining boats to port in marginal weather conditions, compounding the effect of already sparse departure frequencies.

Ferry schedules only stabilized (relatively speaking) from July 2001 onward, and the route of the *Express Samina* in particular was not adequately substituted by another craft – for the first time in over half a century, there was no mid-summer connection between Sámos/Ikaría and Páros/Náxos to Sámos.

for one specific boat (they'll blithely tell you that theirs is the only available service), so you may have to ask around to uncover alternatives. Especially in high season, early arrival is critical for getting what may be a very limited stock of accommodation.

Since the *Express Samina* disaster (see box on p.38), a few of the most elderly craft have been consigned to the scrap heap or dumped overseas. Though spanking-new **boats** are still a rarity, you will more often than not be surprised to encounter a former English Channel or Scandinavian fjord ferry, rechristened and enjoying a new lease of life in the Aegean.

Regular ferry **tickets** are, in general, best bought on the day of departure, unless you need to reserve a cabin berth or space for a car. Buying tickets in advance will tie you down to a particular craft at a particular time – and innumerable factors can make you regret that. Most obviously there's bad weather, which, particularly off-season, can play havoc with the schedules, causing some small boats to remain at anchor and others to alter their routes drastically. (The ticket price is refunded if a boat fails to sail.) There are only three periods of the year – March 23–25, the week before and after Easter, and most of August – when all categories of ferry facility (seat, cabin, car space) need to be booked at least a couple of days in advance.

Following cases in 1996 of captains loading ferries to double their rated capacity, **obligatory advance ticketing** was universally introduced in 1998. Staff at the gangway will bar you from embarking if you don't have a ticket, and tickets are absolutely no longer available on board. In many cases there may not even be a last-minute sales booth at the quayside. The only exception to this rule in 2001 was the *Nissos Kalymnos*, which was still selling fares on the gangplank, but the word is that their tickets will be computerized as of 2002, and this anomaly will cease.

Fares for each route are currently set by the transport ministry and should not differ among ships or agencies though, curiously, tickets for journeys towards Athens are marginally more expensive than those in the opposite direction. There is usually a twenty-percent discount on round-trip fares. The cheapest class of ticket, which you'll probably automatically be sold, is **deck class**, variously called *tríti* or *gámma*. This gives

The Nissos Kalymnos

The small, slow but reliable **Nissos Kalymnos** (cars carried) is the most regular lifeline of the smaller Dodecanese (aside from Kárpathos and Kássos) – its "milk run" visits them all twice a week between mid-March and mid-January. This community-owned ship can be poorly publicized on islands other than its home port; if you encounter difficulties obtaining information, you should phone the central agency on Kálymnos (☎02430/29 612). Specimen schedules, observed for some years now, are as follows:

Mid-March to April, and mid-Sept to mid-Jan: Mon and Fri 7am, leaves Kálymnos for Kós, Níssyros, Tílos, Sými, Rhodes; out to Kastellórizo late afternoon, turns around at midnight. Tues and Sat 9am, departs Rhodes for Sými, Tílos, Níssyros, Kós, Kálymnos, with a Tues evening return trip to Astypálea. Wed and Sun departs Kálymnos 7am for Léros, Lipsí, Pátmos, Arkí (Wed only, omitted in 2001), Agathónissi, Pythagório (Sámos), returning from Sámos at 2.30pm bound for Kálymnos via the same islands. Thurs 7am from Kálymnos to Astypálea, returns immediately at 10.30am.

May to mid-June: Mon and Fri 7am, leaves Kálymnos for Kós, Níssyros, Tílos, Sými, Rhodes; out to Kastellórizo late afternoon, turns around at midnight, arrives Rhodes 5am. Tues and Sat 9am, departs Rhodes for Sými, Tílos, Níssyros, Kós, Kálymnos, with an evening return trip both days to Astypálea. Wed and Sun departs Kálymnos 7am for Léros, Lipsí, Pátmos, Arkí (Wed only, omitted 2001), Agathónissi, Pythagório (Sámos), returning from Sámos at 2.30pm bound for Kálymnos via the same islands. Thurs, idle.

Mid-June to mid-Sept: Mon and Thurs 7am, leaves Kálymnos for Kós, Níssyros, Tílos, Sými, Rhodes; out to Kastellórizo late afternoon, turns around at midnight. Tues and Fri 9am, departs Rhodes for Sými, Tílos, Níssyros, Kós, Kálymnos, with an evening return trip both days to Astypálea, arriving Kálymnos 1.30am. Wed and Sun departs Kálymnos 7am for Léros, Lipsí, Pátmos, Arkí (Wed only, omitted 2001), Agathónissi, Pythagório (Sámos), returning from Sámos at 2.30pm bound for Kálymnos via the same islands. Sat, 7am from Kálymnos to Astypálea, returning immediately.

Miniotis Lines services

Híos-based Miniotis Lines operates two small, slow, tugboat-like ferries, the *Kaptetan Stamatis* and the *Hioni*, the latter facing compulsory retirement in 2003. This company specializes in *agonés grammés* or unprofitable lines, collecting huge subsidies from the government to run somewhat unpredictable, complicated schedules at uncivilized hours. Based on late 2001 patterns and prior experience, itineraries in future are likely to resemble the following:

Sun

Craft 1 departs Híos Town 7pm for Karlóvassi/Vathý on Sámos, overnights there.

Craft 2 departs Híos Town 8pm for Psará, overnights there.

Mon

Craft 1 leaves Vathý/Karlóvassi 6am, bound for Foúrni and Ikaría, returns mid-morning to Sámos, out again mid-afternoon to Foúrni/Ikaría, returns to Pythagório (8.30pm).

Craft 2 departs Psará at 7am for Volissós, returns to Psará 2pm.

Tues

Craft 1 departs Pythagório 7am for Agathoníssi, Arkí, Pátmos, Lipsí and Léros (arrival noon), returning via the same islands to Pythagório at 5.30, continuing to Vathý, Karlóvassi and Híos (arrival 12.30am Wed).

Craft 2 leaves Psará 7am for Híos Town, returns to Psará 3pm.

Wed

Craft 1 idle.

Craft 2 departs Psará 7am for Volissós, returns Psará 2pm, continues to Mytilíni (arrives 7pm).

Thurs

Craft 1 departs Híos Town 7am for Psará, returns immediately; 5pm departure for Sámos (Karlóvassi, Vathý, Pythagório), final arrival 2am Fri.

Craft 2 departs Mytilíni at 8pm for Psará, overnights there.

Fri

Craft 1 departs Pythagório 7am for Agathoníssi, Arkí, Lipsí and Pátmos (arrives 11am), returns via same islands to Pythagório (3pm), immediate departure to Foúrni–Áyios Kírikos–Foúrni (5–7pm), back to Vathý, Karlóvassi (11pm) and Híos (final arrival 2am Sat).

Craft 2 leaves Psará 7am for Volissós, returns 2pm to Psará, then sails to Híos Town (arrival 7.30pm).

Sat

Craft 1 idle.

Craft 2 departs Híos Town 7am for Psará, returns 2pm for Híos Town (arrival 5.30pm).

you the run of most of the boat except for the upper-class restaurant and bar. On the shorter, summer journeys the best place to be, in any case, is on deck – space should be staked out as soon as you get on board. However, boats acquired recently seem – with their glaring overhead lights and moulded-plastic bucket seats – expressly designed to frustrate those attempting to sleep on deck. In such cases it's well worth the few extra euros for a cabin bunk, especially if you can share with friends (cabins are usually quadruple, occasionally double or triple). Class consciousness has increased since the early 1990s, so deck-class passengers may find themselves firmly locked out of second-class facilities at night to prevent them from crashing on the plush sofas, and may have to make do with pullman-type seats. **First-class** cabin facilities usually cost scarcely less than a plane flight and are not terrific value – the main difference between first and second being the presence of a bathroom in the cabin, and a better location. Most cabins, incidentally, are overheated or overchilled, and pretty airless; ask for an *exoterikí* (outer) cabin if you want a porthole (though these are always bolted shut).

Since bookings are now computerized, this should preclude **overbookings**, but occasionally you may be sold a cabin berth at an intermediate port only to find that they are "full" when the boat arrives. Pursers will not refund you the difference between a cabin and third class, palming you off by telling you to take the matter up with the issuing agent. Your first- or second-class fare entitles you to a bunk, and this is clearly stated (in Greek) on the verso of your ticket. Make a scene if necessary until you are accommodated – there are often cabins in the bilge, set aside for the crew but generally unused, where you can sleep.

Motorbikes and cars get issued extra tickets, in the latter case four to five times the passenger deck-class fare, depending on size. Subject to quirks too complex to explain (Lésvos–Sýros is less than Lésvos–Sámos, for instance), car fees are roughly proportionate to distance: Sámos–Ikaría is €26–29.50 depending on port and direction, while Sámos–Pireás is about €73.50. Technically, written permission is required to take rental motorbikes and cars on ferries, though in practice few crew will bother to quiz you on this – in any case, it's almost always cheaper to rent another vehicle at your destination.

Some ferries sell a limited range of **food on board**, though it tends to be overpriced and mediocre. Honourable exceptions include the meals served by DANE or NEL on their overnight sailings. On the short, daytime hops between the various islands of the Dodecanese and east Aegean, it's a good idea to stock up beforehand with your own provisions; Miniotis Lines, the *Dodekanisos Express* and the *Nissos Kalymnos* in particular offer nothing other than biscuits, greasy, prefab pizzas, coffee and soft drinks.

Hydrofoils and catamarans

Hydrofoils – commonly known as *dhelfínia* (dolphins) – are roughly twice as fast (and at least twice as expensive) as ordinary ferries. However, they are a useful alternative if you are pushed for time, and their network can also neatly fill gaps in ferry scheduling. Their main drawback (aside from frequent engine breakdowns) is that they were originally designed for cruising on placid Russian or Polish rivers, and are quite literally out of their depth on the open sea; thus they are extremely sensitive to bad weather, and even on a moderate sea are less than ideal for the seasick-prone. Most services don't operate – or are heavily reduced – from October to June, and are prone to arbitrary cancellation in any season if not enough passengers turn up. Following the *Express Samina* sinking, hydrofoils are no longer allowed to carry scooters or bicycles as in the past.

Because of their need to hug sheltering landmasses, hydrofoils sometimes sail well inside **Turkish territorial waters**, hooting at fishing boats flying the star and crescent. Despite poor relations between the two countries, this is specifically allowed, and almost unavoidable anyway on the runs between Rhodes and Kós, Kós and Léros, or Sámos and Híos.

Two **hydrofoil companies**, Kyriakoulis Maritime and Laoumtzis Flying Dolphins, serve the Dodecanese between mid-May and mid-October, operating out of Rhodes, Kálymnos and Sámos (Kyriakoulis only), plus Kós (both companies). We have excluded those companies that only offer charter services to tour agencies, as opposed to scheduled services approved by the Ministry of Transport. Specimen routes are detailed in the box opposite.

Kyriakoulis Maritime has nine craft in theory, inherited from the amalgamation of previously existing companies Samos Hydrofoils and Dodecanese Hydrofoils, but only five or six of these are active at any given time – most likely the "dolphins" provided with more reliable GM Caterpillar engines, replacing the obsolete, temperamental Russian Cometa ones. Routes are complicated but fairly predictable. In peak season, there is a daily link Rhodes–Kós and back, north in the morning and south in the evening; on successive weekend days it may detour via Sými or Níssyros. Another craft leaves Kálymnos between 7 and 11am for Kós and a selection of islands north to Pythagório on Sámos, returning from there between 12.30 and 2pm; while the third craft, based in Pythagório, leaves Sámos between 7.30 and 8.15am, arriving via Pátmos, Lipsí, Léros and Kálymnos at 11.30–11.45pm, and returning between 1 and 2pm to Sámos via the same islands. Twice a week Agathoníssi is served by either the morning or afternoon craft; there are plans to include Arkí in these discretionary itineraries once its new jetty is completed. Several days a week, either a northbound, Kós-based craft or a southbound, Pythagório-based craft includes Ikaría (Áyios Kírykos) and Foúrni in its run, just before or after Pátmos. Still another craft based on Kálymnos leaves at dawn for Rhodes via Kós, returning between 4 and 6pm; once or twice a week it will call at Hálki and Tílos in either direction. There is also a nominal Saturday service from Kálymnos to Astypálea, but owing to weather conditions and lack of passenger demand this tends to run at most three times in any summer. Services north of

Hydrofoils: principal routes

Ports of call in brackets are served once or twice weekly as adjuncts to the daily route shown. Detailed frequencies are given in the "Travel Details" following each island account.

Kyriakoulis Maritime
Rhodes–(Sými)–Kós–(Sými)–Rhodes
Kálymnos–Kós–Rhodes–(Tílos)–(Hálki)–Rhodes–Kós–Kálymnos
Rhodes–Kós–(Níssyros)–Kós–Rhodes
Rhodes–Kós–Kálymnnos–Léros–Pátmos & reverse
(Rhodes)–Kós–Léros–Lipsí–Pátmos–(Agathoníssi)–Pythagório & reverse
Kós–Léros–Pátmos–(Foúrni)–(Ikaría)–Pythagório & reverse
Pythagório–(Agathoníssi)–Pátmos–Lipsí–Léros–Kálymnos–Kós & reverse
Pythagório OR Vathý–Foúrni–Ikaría–Pátmos & reverse
Vathý–(Évdhilos)–Híos–Lésvos

Laoumtzis Flying Dolphins
Kós–Sými–Rhodes & reverse
Kós–Pátmos–Kós
Kós–(Níssyros)–(Tílos)–(Hálki)–Rhodes & reverse

Sámos, from Vathý to Híos and Lésvos (occasionally via Évdhilos, Ikaría) sputter along unreliably in peak season only if at all, highly prone to the same disabilities as the Astypálea service. Some of the unusual runs to the smaller islands can get completely booked by transfers of package tour groups. For current routes and schedules, phone ⓣ02420/25 920 (Kós), ⓣ02410/78 052 (Ródhos Town) or ⓣ02730/80 620 (Sámos).

Laoumtzis Flying Dolphins, based in Kós, has two craft with a fairly set pattern. One craft always leaves Kós at around 8am for Rhodes, returning shortly after 5pm. Twice weekly there are diversions via Sými in each direction, and on Saturday there's the "milk run" via Níssyros, Tílos and Hálki, designed to get package patrons to/from their weekend charters. Twice a week the other craft provides an express run up to Pátmos in the morning, returning in the late afternoon. For exact details ring ⓣ02420/ 26 388.

High-speed **catamarans** have been a prominent feature of Greek maritime life since the late 1990s, attempting to combine the speed of hydrofoils – or even faster, at 40 knots per hour – with the (relative) reliability and vehicle-carrying capacity of larger ferries. The fact that they are new and sleek, purpose-built in France or Scandinavia, has not prevented numerous breakdowns, since they are constantly playing catch-up to fill in weather-cancelled itineraries and thus miss necessary maintenance. **Inside** they are rather soulless: ruthlessly air conditioned, with no deck seating to take the air and the most banal Greek TV blaring at you from numerous airplane-type screens. Indeed the whole experience can been likened to flying, right down to the seat type. Cabins are non-existent and food facilities even more minimal than on conventional ferries – after all, you'll be at your destination within six to seven hours, the longest trajectory at present. Car fares are normal, though passenger **tickets** are at least double a comparable ferry journey, ie similar to hydrofoil rates.

There are two large high-speed catamarans plying the east Aegean: NEL's French-made *Aeolos Express* and *Aeolos Kenteris*, each of which can carry a couple of hundred vehicles as well as passengers in a sealed interior (there is no sun deck). Two smaller ones serve the Dodecanese: the *Dodekanisos Express*, also known as *O Spanos* after the supermarket chain which owns it, and the *Sea Star*. The *Dodekanisos Express*, based on Rhodes, can carry 4–5 cars and a slightly larger number of two-wheelers; it's a sleek new Norwegian-built craft, with a limited amount of deck space (but no deck chairs). The *Sea Star* does not carry vehicles, and is the much less reliable of the two, fitfully serving the line Tílos–Rhodes with occasionally other nearby islands thrown in. 2001 was the *Dodekanisos Express*' second year of operation, and service patterns seem to have settled down, but it has never called at Astypálea, Agathoníssi, Hálki, Kárpathos or Sámos (Pythagório) and is unlikely to in the future. See the box on p.44 for specimen routes.

Catamarans: principal routes

NEL operates three large catamarans, with two active in the east Aegean. Routes of the two craft are as follows:
Aeolos Express: Sámos–Ikaría (either port) –(Kéa)–(Náxos)–(Páros)–Pireás
Aeolos Kenteris: Lésvos–Híos–Pireás
NB The *Aeolos Kenteris* departs both Pireás and Lésvos at 4pm year-round; the *Aeolos Express* departure from Sámos varies seasonally, typically after midnight in summer, having set out from Pireás at 6pm.
Dodekanisos Express:
Rhodes–(Tílos)–(Níssyros)–Kós–Kálymnos–Léros–(Lipsí)–Pátmos
Dodekanisos Express:
Rhodes–Kastellórizo–Rhodes (May only)
NB In all cases *Dodekanisos Express* departs Rhodes daily at 8.30am, returns 6–7pm.

Small ferries, kaïkia and taxi-boats

In season, **kaïkia** (caiques) and **small ferries** of a few hundred tonnes displacement sail between adjacent islands and to a few of the more obscure ones. These small boats can be extremely useful and often very pleasant, but are no cheaper than mainline services. In fact, if they're classified as tourist agency charters, and not passenger lines controlled by the transport ministry, they tend to be quite expensive, with pressure to buy return fares (one-ways are almost always available).

The more consistent kaïkia links are summarized in the "Travel Details" section following each island account, though inevitably departures depend on the whims of local boat-owners, so the only firm information is to be had on the quayside.

Kaïkia and small ferries, despite appearances, have a good safety record; indeed it's the larger, overloaded car ferries like the *Iraklion* and the *Express Samina* that have in the past run into trouble. EU regulations being what they are, however, it seems that many of these smaller boats are doomed for trivial reasons, such as not having a second lavatory. Likely to survive are the swarms of **taxi boats** which are a feature of Sými, Hálki, Pátmos and Astypálea, among other spots; these exist to shuttle clients on set routes to remote beaches or ports which can be only be reached arduously, if at all, overland. Costs on these are generally reasonable, usually per person but occasionally per boat.

Flights

Olympic Airways and its subsidiary Olympic Aviation (Ⓦwww.olympic-airways.gr) operate most of the **domestic flights** between the Greek mainland (Athens or Thessaloníki) and the Dodecanese and east Aegean islands, as well as a growing network of radial links between these islands. Airline operation has been officially deregulated in Greece since 1993, but the only private airlines to have successfully challenged the state-run carrier are the recently merged Aegean-Cronus Airlines (Ⓦwww.aegeanair.com or Ⓦwww.cronus.gr). Aegean-Cronus has cherry-picked high-volume, high-profit routes such as those between Mytilíni or Rhodes and Athens. Aegean-Cronus prices and service standards tend to be a bit higher than Olympic, though flight frequencies tend to be sparse. This, of course, could change drastically if financially troubled Olympic goes under or is bought up, as is frequently threatened, and a successor offers an inevitably reduced service.

For the moment, Olympic **schedules** can be picked up at their offices abroad (see "Getting There" sections) or through their branch offices and representatives in Greece, which are maintained in almost every town or island of any size; Greek-only small booklets appear twice yearly (typically October and June), while English-language books geared more for an international readership are also published twice yearly (April and October). There are often long gaps in availability, when you'll have to consult the website or closest sales office. Aegean-Cronus has historically produced two booklets per year, in spring and late autumn.

Tickets for airlines are most easily obtained from travel agents (their own high-street outlets are thin on the ground). **Fares** for flights to and between the islands, including the domestic airport tax of about €10, work out around three to four times the cost of a ferry journey, but on certain inter-island hauls that are poorly served by boat (Rhodes–Kastellórizo or Rhodes–Kárpathos, for example), you should consider this time well bought.

Island flights are often full in peak season; if they're an essential part of your plans, it is worth trying to make a **reservation** at least a week to ten days in advance. If a flight you've set your heart on is full, **waiting lists** exist – and are worth signing onto at the airport check-in counter; experience has shown that there are almost always one or two no-shows or cancellations. Domestic air tickets are non-refundable, but you can change your flight, space permitting, as late as a couple of hours before your original departure. Nominally you're supposed to be charged €15 to do this, but in many cases this fee will be waived.

Incidentally, the only surviving Olympic-run **shuttle buses** between the main town and the airport are on Kós, Límnos and Kastellórizo; others have long since been axed as a cost-cutting exercise. In two instances (Híos, Rhodes), municipally run services have picked up the slack, but otherwise you're at the mercy of the taxi-drivers who congregate outside the arrivals gate.

Like ferries, flights are subject to **cancellation** in bad weather, since many services are on small, 50- or 68-seat ATR turbo-prop planes, or even tinier Dornier 18-seaters, none of which will fly in strong winds or (depending on the destination airport) after dark. Despite these uncertainties, a flight on a Dornier puddle-jumper is a highly recommended experience. You can watch the crew, who are often on first-name terms with passengers, flicking switches in the cockpit; virtually every seat has a view, and you fly low enough to pick out every island feature – you might even select beaches in advance.

Size restrictions also mean that the 15-kilo **baggage weight limit** is fairly strictly enforced; if, however, you've just arrived from overseas or purchased your ticket outside Greece, you are allowed the standard international limit (20–25 kilos depending on carrier). All services operated on the domestic network are **non-smoking**.

Transport on the islands

Most islands have some kind of **bus service**, even if it only connects the port with the main town or village, though on larger islands there is usually an efficient and reliable network along the main roads. For visitors, the main drawback is that buses are almost always geared to local patterns and – from the remoter villages at least – often leave punishingly early to shuttle people to school or work. Luckily, it is almost always possible to **rent a vehicle**, be it a bicycle, motor-scooter or, on larger islands, a car or jeep. Even for just one day, this will enable you to take the measure of a medium-sized island, and work out where you want to base yourself.

Buses

Buses on most islands are cream-and-turquoise-green Mercedes coaches, grouped in a nationwide syndicate known as the KTEL (*Kratikó Tamío Ellinikón Leoforíon*). Except for Mytilíni Town, which has a dedicated, off-street terminal in a parking lot, central bus stations – even on Rhodes – are little more than a marked (or unmarked) stop at a major intersection or platía. Nonetheless, services on the major routes are highly efficient; as a rule, scheduled departures are amazingly prompt, so be there in plenty of time. Seating is generally first-come, first-served, with some standing allowed, and **tickets** are either dispensed on board by a peripatetic *ispráktoros* or conductor, or beforehand at ticket windows (where present).

Car rental

Car rental in the Dodecanese and east Aegean starts at €271–291 a week in high season for the smallest, A-Group vehicle from a one-off outlet or local chain, including unlimited mileage, tax and insurance. Overseas tour operators' and international chains' brochures (particularly on Rhodes) threaten alarming rates of €353–391 for the same period but, except in August, no rental company expects to fetch that price for a car; even on pricey Rhodes they will settle for €315 or so. Outside peak season, at the smaller local outfits on less touristed islands, you can sometimes get terms of about €36 per day, all inclusive, with even better rates for three days or more. **Comparison shopping** among agencies in the larger resorts can yield a variation in quotes of up to twenty percent for the same conditions over a four to seven-day period; the most negotiable variable is whether or not kilometres in excess of one hundred per day (a common hidden catch) are free. Open **jeeps**, an increasingly popular extravagance, begin at about €82 per day, rising to as much as €97 at busy times and places.

Note that brochure prices in Greece almost never include tax, **collision damage waiver** (CDW) or personal insurance. CDW in particular is absolutely vital, as the coverage included by law in the basic rental fee is generally inadequate, so check the fine print on your contract. Be careful of the hammering that cars get on dirt tracks; tyres, windshield and the underside of the vehicle are almost always excluded from even supplementary insurance policies. All agencies will want either a credit card or a large cash **deposit** up front; minimum age requirements vary from 21 to 23. Driving licences issued by any European Union state are honoured, but in theory – and, increasingly, in practice – an **International Driving Licence** is required by all other drivers, including Australasians and North Americans. This must be obtained at home before departure, as ELPA (the Greek motoring association) no longer issues IDLs to foreign nationals.

Car-rental agencies

In the UK

Autos Abroad ⓣ0870/066 7788, ⓦwww.autosabroad.co.uk.
Avis ⓣ0870/606 0100, ⓦwww.avisworld.com.
Budget ⓣ0800/181181, ⓦwww.go-budget.co.uk.
Europcar ⓣ0845/722 2525, ⓦwww.europcar.co.uk.
Hertz ⓣ0870/844 8844, ⓦwww.hertz.co.uk.
Holiday Autos ⓣ0870/400 0000, ⓦwww.holidayautos.com.
National ⓣ0870/536 5365, ⓦwww.nationalcar.com.
Thrifty ⓣ01494/751600, ⓦwww.thrifty.co.uk.
Transhire ⓣ01923/834910.

In Ireland

Autos Abroad ⓣ0870/066 7788, ⓦwww.autosabroad.com.
Avis Northern Ireland ⓣ028/9442 3333, Republic of Ireland ⓣ01/605 7555, ⓦwww.avis.co.uk.
Budget Northern Ireland ⓣ028/9442, Republic of Ireland ⓣ01/878 7814, ⓦwww.budgetcarrental.ie or ⓦwww.budget-ireland.co.uk.
Cosmo Thrifty ⓣ028/9445 2565, ⓦwww.thrifty.co.uk.
Europcar Northern Ireland ⓣ028/9442 3444, Republic of Ireland ⓣ01/614 2800, ⓦwww.europcar.ie.
Hertz Northern Ireland ⓣ028/9442 2533, Republic of Ireland ⓣ0903/27711, ⓦwww.hertz.co.uk.
Holiday Autos ⓣ01/872 9366, ⓦwww.holidayautos.ie.
SIXT ⓣ061/453048, ⓦwww.irishcarrentals.ie.

In North America

Alamo ⓣ1-800/522-9696, ⓦwww.alamo.com.
Auto Europe US ⓣ1-800/223-5555, Canada ⓣ1-888/223-5555, ⓦwww.autoeurope.com.
Avis US ⓣ1-800/331-1084, Canada ⓣ1-800/272-5871, ⓦwww.avis.com.
Budget ⓣ1-800/527-0700, ⓦwww.budgetrentacar.com.
Europe by Car ⓣ1-800/223-1516, ⓦwww.europebycar.com.
Hertz US ⓣ1-800/654-3001, Canada ⓣ1-800/263-0600, ⓦwww.hertz.com.
Kemwel Holiday Autos ⓣ1-800/422-7737, ⓦwww.kemwel.com.
National ⓣ1-800/227-7368, ⓦwww.nationalcar.com.
Thrifty ⓣ1-800/367-2277, ⓦwww.thrifty.com.

In Australia

Avis ⓣ13/6333, ⓦwww.avis.com.
Budget, ⓣ1300/362848, ⓦwww.budget.com.
Hertz ⓣ1800/550067, ⓦwww.hertz.com.
National ⓣ13/1908.
Thrifty ⓣ1300/367227, ⓦwww.thrifty.com.au.

In New Zealand

Avis ⓣ09/526 5231 or 0800/655 111, ⓦwww.avis.com.
Budget ⓣ0800/652 227 or 09/375 2270, ⓦwww.budget.com.
Hertz ⓣ09/309 0989 or 0800/655955, ⓦwww.hertz.com.
National ⓣ09/537 2582.
Thrifty ⓣ09/309 0111, ⓦwww.thrifty.com.nz.

In peak season only you may get a better price (and, just possibly, better vehicle condition) by booking through one of the **overseas booking companies** that deal with local firms, rather than arranging the rental once you're in Greece; this may also be the only way to get hold of a car, at any price, at such times. Competitive companies of this sort in Britain include Autos Abroad, Holiday

Autos and Transhire (see opposite). In the Dodecanese and east Aegean, Autorent, Payless, European, Kosmos, National/Alamo, Reliable, Eurodollar and Just are dependable Greek, or smaller international, chains with branches in many towns; all are considerably cheaper than the biggest international operators Budget, Europcar, Hertz and Avis. Specific local recommendations are given in the guide.

In terms of **models**, many of them unfamiliar to UK/US drivers, the more competitive companies tend to offer the Subaru M80 or Vivio, the Fiat Cinquecento or Seisento and the Suzuki Swift 1000 as A-group cars, and Opel (Vauxhall) Corsa 1.2, Fiat Uno/Punto, Peugeot 106, Hyundai Atos, Citroën Saxo, Renault Clio or Nissan Micra in the B group. Any more than two adults, with luggage, will generally require B category; the Hyundai Atos is particularly widespread and is a decent, punchy model. The badly designed, underpowered Suzuki Alto 600 or 800, Fiat Panda 750/900 and Seat Marbella should be avoided if at all possible as A-group cars, and have been phased out by the more reputable agencies. The standard four-wheel-drive option is a Suzuki jeep (1.3- or 1.6-litre), mostly open – great for bashing down rutted tracks to remote beaches.

Driving in Greece

Greece has the highest **accident rate** in Europe after Portugal, and on Lésvos, Kós or Rhodes – especially along the stretch between Ródhos Town and Líndhos – it's easy to see why. At the Malóna bridge, there's a prominent memorial to five Austrians wiped out in a high-speed wreck during July 1999. **Driving habits** amongst both locals and foreigners are atrocious: overtaking is erratic, tailgating and barging out heedlessly from side roads are preferred pastimes, lane markings and turn signals may as well not exist, and motorbikes hog the road, or weave from side to side. **Drunk driving** is also a major problem; Sunday afternoons in rural areas are particularly bad, and for the same reason you should avoid driving late at night at weekends or holidays.

Matters are made worse by the frequently perilous **road conditions**: signposting is absent or badly placed, pavement markings are utterly faded, asphalt can turn into a one-lane surface or a dirt track without warning on secondary routes, and you're heavily dependent on magnifying mirrors at blind intersections in congested villages. Uphill drivers insist on their **right of way**, as do those first to approach a one-lane bridge; **flashed headlights** usually mean the opposite of what they do in the UK or North America, here signifying that the other driver is coming through or overtaking. Even on the so-called motorways of Rhodes and Kós, there is no proper far-right lane for slower traffic, which is expected to straddle the solid white line at the verge and allow rapid traffic to pass.

Wearing a **seatbelt** is compulsory; periodic checkpoints sift for offenders who are liable to a €150 fine. A first-aid kit in the boot is also required (though some rental companies skimp on this), and children under the age of 10 are not allowed to sit in the front seats. It's illegal to drive away from any kind of accident, and you can be held at a police station for up to 24 hours. If this happens, you have the right to ring your consulate immediately to summon a lawyer; don't make a statement to anyone who doesn't speak and write very good English. In practice, once police are informed that there was no personal injury, they rarely come out to investigate.

Tourists with proof of AA/RAC/AAA membership are given free road assistance from ELPA, the Greek equivalent, which runs **breakdown services** on several of the larger islands; in an emergency ring their road assistance service on ⓣ104. Many car rental companies have an agreement with ELPA's equally widespread competitors Hellas Service, Interamerican and Express Service, which also have three- or four-digit nationwide numbers; however, you will always get a faster response if you dial the local number for the province you're stranded in (ask for these in advance). Any breakdown service is prohibitively expensive to summon on your own – over €120 to enrol as an "instant member" for a year.

Buying fuel

Fuel currently costs €0.76–0.90 per litre for either regular unleaded (*amólyvdhi*) or super unleaded; leaded four-star became unavailable on January 1, 2002, but little bottles of additives are available for those engines that can't digest super unleaded. It is easy to run out of fuel after dark or at weekends in both rural and urban Greece; most stations close at 8pm sharp, and nearly as many are shut all day Sunday. There will always be at least one pump per district open on a rota basis, but it's not always apparent which one it is. This is not so much of a problem on the major highways of the biggest islands, but it is a factor everywhere else, despite an ever-increasing number of gas pumps. So always fill up, or insist on full rental vehicles at the outset.

Some stations which claim to be open around the clock are in fact **automated-only after-hours** – you have to use bill-taking machines, which don't give change. If you fill your tank without having exhausted your credit, punch the button for a receipt and get change the next day during attended hours (assuming you're still in the area). Filling stations run by international companies (BP, Mobil, Texaco and Shell) usually take **credit cards**; Greek chains like EKO, Jetoil, Revoil, Mamidhakis and Elinoil usually don't, except in the most touristed areas (and even then only during summer).

Incidentally, a few retro scooters still consume **"mix"** – a red- or green-tinted fuel dispensed from a transparent cylindrical device. This contains a minimum of three percent two-stroke oil by volume; when unavailable, you brew it up yourself by adding to super-grade fuel the necessary amount of separately bottled two-stroke oil (*ládhi dhýo trohón* in Greek). It's wise to err on the generous side – say five percent – or you risk the engine seizing up.

Motorbikes, scooters – and safety

The cult of the **motorcycle** is highly developed in the Greek islands, presided over by a jealous deity apparently requiring regular human sacrifice. **Accidents** among both foreign and local motorbikers are common, with annual fatalities edging into two figures on the busier islands. Some package companies have even taken to warning clients in print against renting motorbikes or mopeds (thereby making a bit extra on organized overland excursions), but with a little of caution and common sense – plus an eye to increasingly enforced traffic regulations – riding a motorbike on an island should be a lot safer than piloting one through London or New York.

Many tourists come to grief on rutted dirt tracks or astride mechanically dodgy machines. In other cases **accidents** are due to attempts to cut corners, in all senses, by riding two-up on an underpowered scooter simply not designed to propel such a load. Don't be tempted by this apparent economy – you won't regret getting two separate mopeds, or one powerful 100cc bike to share – and bear in mind, too, that you're likely to be charged an exorbitant sum for any repairs if you do have a wipeout. Also, verify that any travel insurance policy will cover motorbike accidents.

One worthwhile precaution is to wear a **crash helmet** (*kránio*); many rental outfits will offer you one, and some will make you sign a waiver of liability if you refuse it. Helmet-wearing is in fact required by law, but very few riders (except army conscripts) wear them – or much else for that matter, though compliance is slowly increasing as police set up random roadblocks to catch offenders.

Reputable establishments demand a full **motorcycle driving licence** for any engine over 90cc (the law actually applies to anything over 50cc displacement), and you will usually have to leave a passport as security. For smaller models, any driving licence will do.

Small **motor scooters** with automatic transmissions, known in Greek as *papákia* (little ducks) after their characteristic noise, are good transport for all but the hilliest islands. They're available for rent in most main towns or ports, and at the larger resorts, for €11.80–17.80. This specimen rate-range can be bargained down considerably out of peak season, or if you negotiate for a longer period of rental.

Before riding off, make sure you check the bike's **mechanical state**, since many are only cosmetically maintained. By law dealers are supposed to sell or scrap rental bikes every three years, but you often wonder. Bad brakes and worn or oil-fouled spark plugs are the most common defects; dealers often keep the front brake far too loose, with the commendable intention of preventing you going over the handlebars. If you break down it's your responsibility to return the machine, so take down the phone number of the rental agency in case the bike gives out in the middle of nowhere (keep your mobile phone with you too). Better agencies often offer a free retrieval service.

There are vanishingly few true **mopeds** – motor-driven pedal-cycles – remaining in Greece; one or two models are still sold, but none is rented. As far as **scooters** go, the

Piaggio Vespa or Peugeot were always more comfortable than mopeds for long trips, but still aren't very stable on unpaved surfaces. The latest generation of these models is ultra-trendy and practical enough, but thirsty on fuel; a few still don't have kick-starts as backups to the battery-operated starter button. The Suzuki Address and its rival the Piaggio Typhoon are also popular, fairly reliable models. Bungee cords (a *khtapódi* or "octopus" in slang) for tying down bundles are supplied on request, while capacious baskets are also often a feature.

In the family of true **motorbikes** with manual transmissions, the longstanding workhorse favourites, in descending order of reliability, are the Honda 50, Yamaha Townmate and Suzuki FB Birdie. Three-speed gearboxes are shifted with an easy-to-learn left-foot pedal action, and (very important) they can all be push-started if the starting-crank fails. These can carry two, though if you have a choice, the Honda Cub 70–90cc series gives more power at nominal extra cost, as does the Yamaha 80 Townmate. Best of all is the attractive Honda Astrea 100 and its rival-brand clones, very powerful but scarcely bigger than older models.

Cycling

Cycling on the Greek islands is not such hard going as you might imagine (except in mid-summer), especially on one of the **mountain bikes** that have all but supplanted balloon-tyre bone-shakers at rental outlets; rental prices are rarely more than €6 a day. You do, however, need nerves of steel, as roads are generally narrow, with no verges or bike lanes except on Kós, and many Greek drivers consider cyclists as some lower form of life, on a par with the snakes found run over everywhere.

If you have your own mountain or touring bike, you might consider bringing it with you. Bikes travel free on most airlines, if they fall within your weight limit, and are free to transport on most ferries. You would be wise to bring any small spare parts you might need, however, since the only specialist bike shops will be found in the main towns of the half-dozen largest islands.

Hitching

Hitching carries the usual risks and dangers, especially for solo women, but overall the Greek islands are one of the safer places in which to do it. As ever, the more lightly travelled and remote the road, the greater the possibility of a lift, though increasingly there's the expectation that foreign tourists should be renting their own transport. In the more thinly populated rural areas, you'll see numbers of elderly Greeks waving down a ride – you'll be doing a useful service by picking them up, and reciprocating in some small way for the hospitality which is still often the rule in isolated regions. From most island towns it's just a short walk to the main road out, where numerous trucks and vans are good bets for thumbing. Hitching on commercial vehicles is nominally illegal, so if you're offered a ride in a large van or lorry, don't be offended if you're set down just before an upcoming town and its potential police checkpoints.

Taxis

Greek **taxis** are among the cheapest in western Europe – so long as you get an honest driver who switches the meter on and doesn't use high-tech devices to doctor the reading. Use of the meter is mandatory within city or town limits, where Tariff "1" applies, while in rural areas or between midnight and 5am Tariff "2" is in effect. On certain islands, such as Kálymnos and Léros, set rates apply on specific fixed routes for "collective" taxis – these only depart when full. Otherwise, throughout Greece the meter starts at €0.75, though the minimum fare is €1.50; any baggage not actually on your lap is charged at €0.15 apiece. Additionally, there are surcharges of €0.90 for leaving or entering an airport, and €0.60 for leaving a harbour area. If you summon a taxi by phone on spec, there's a €1.50 charge, while a pre-arranged rendezvous is €1.80 extra; in either case the meter starts running from the moment the driver begins heading towards you. All categories of supplemental charges must be set out on a laminated card affixed to the dashboard. For a week or so before and after Orthodox Easter, and Christmas, a *filodhórima* or gratuity of about ten percent is levied. Any or all of these extras will legitimately bump up the basic meter reading of about €4 per ten rural kilometres.

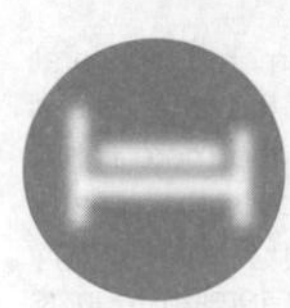

Accommodation

There are huge numbers of beds available for tourists in the Dodecanese and east Aegean islands, so most of the year you can turn up pretty much anywhere and find a room – if not in a hotel, then in a private house or block of rooms (the standard island accommodation). Most of the larger islands have at least one campsite too, which tends to be basic but inexpensive.

Only in the major resorts, during the July–August peak season or around Easter, are you likely to experience problems. At these times, if you don't have accommodation reserved in advance, you'd be wise to keep well off the main tourist trail, turning up at each new place early in the day and taking whatever is available – you may be able to exchange it for something better later on. However, reports indicate that in the wake of poor occupancy levels in recent years, many rooms, blocks and hotels formerly monopolized by north European package operators are again often available to independent, walk-in travellers.

Out of season, you face a slightly different problem: most private rooms – and campsites – operate only from late April or early May to October, leaving hotels your only option. During winter you may have no choice but to stay in the main towns or ports. There will often be very little life outside these places anyway, with all the seasonal beach bars and restaurants closed. On many smaller islands, you will often find just one hotel – and perhaps one taverna – staying open year-round. Be warned also that any resort or harbour hotels which do operate through the winter are likely to have a certain number of **prostitutes** as long-term guests; licensed prostitution is legal in Greece, and the management reckons this is the most painless way to keep the bills paid.

Old-fashioned, 1970s-vintage rooms on the remoter islets, very occasionally still without private bath, tend to fall into the ❶ price category. Standard, en-suite rooms without cooking facilities weigh in at ❷; newer, well-amenitied rooms and self-catering studios occupy the top end of the ❸ niche, along with the more modest C-class hotels, the better among these edging into ❹. The top half of ❹ corresponds fairly well to the better-value B-class hotels and the humbler designer inns on islands like Híos, Sými and Astypálea, while ❺ tallies with most of B-class and the really state-of-the-art restoration projects. ❻ means A- and L-class, and the sky's the limit here – €150 is by no means unheard of these days.

Prices in any establishment should by law be displayed on the back of the door of your room, or over the reception desk. If you feel you're being overcharged at a place which is officially registered, threaten to report it to the tourist office or police, who will generally adopt your side in such cases. A hotelier is free to offer a room at any amount under the

Accommodation prices

Throughout the book we've categorized accommodation according to the following **price codes**, which denote the cheapest available double room in high season. All prices are for the room only, except where otherwise indicated in accounts. Many hotels, especially those in category ❹ and over, include breakfast in the price; you'll need to check this when booking. During low season, rates can drop by more than fifty percent, especially if you are staying for three or more nights. Exceptions are during the Christmas and Easter weeks when you'll pay high-season prices. Single rooms, where available, cost around seventy percent of the price of a double.

❶ Up to €24
❷ €24–33
❸ €34–42
❹ €43–58
❺ €59–72
❻ €73 and upwards

Hot water

A key variable in both rooms and hotels is the **water heating**. Rooftop **solar units** (*iliaká* in Greek), with their nonexistent running costs, are more popular than electric **immersion heaters** (*thermosífona*). Under typical high-season demand, however, solar-powered tanks tend to run out of hot water with the post-beach shower crunch at 6pm, with no more available until the next day. A heater, either as a backup or primary source, is more reliable; proprietors may either jealously guard the **boiler controls** or entrust you with its workings, which involve either a circuit breaker or a rotary switch turned to "I" for fifteen minutes. You should never shower with a *thermosífono* powered up (look for the glow-lamp indicator on the tank) – besides the risk of shock from badly earthed plumbing, it would be fairly easy to empty smaller tanks and burn out the heating element.

official rate, but it's an offence to charge one euro-cent over the permitted price for the **current season**. Depending on location, there are up to three of these: typically October to May (low), June to mid-July, and September (mid) and mid-July through August (high). Small amounts over the posted price may be legitimately explained by municipal tax or out-of-date forms. More commonly you will find that you have bargained so well, or arrived so far out of high season, that you are actually paying far less than the maximum prices – which are in any case optimistically pitched for a few high-traffic days in the year.

Hotels

Hotels in the larger resorts are often contracted out each season by foreign package holiday companies, though there are usually vacancies available (especially in spring or autumn) for walk-in trade. The tourist police set official **categories** for hotels, which range from "De Luxe" down to the rarely encountered "E-class"; all except the top category have to keep within set price limits. There is talk, but so far only just that, of replacing the letter system with a star grading system as in other countries. While they last, letter ratings are supposed to correspond to **facilities** available, though in practice categorization often depends on location within a resort, total number of rooms and "influence" with the tourism authorities – there are so-called E-class hotels with under nine rooms which are plusher than nearby C-class outfits. It is mandatory for D-class hotels to have at least some rooms with attached baths; C-class must additionally have a bar or designated breakfast area. The presence of a pool and/or tennis court will attract a B-class rating, while A-category hotels should have a restaurant, bar and extensive common areas. Often these, and the L outfits (essentially self-contained complexes), back onto a quasi-private beach.

In terms of **food**, C-class hotels are required only to provide the most rudimentary of continental breakfasts – you may choose not to take, or pay, for it – while B-class and above will usually offer some sort of buffet breakfast including cheese, cold cuts, sausages, yogurt, eggs, and so on. With some outstanding exceptions, noted in the guide, lunch or supper at hotel-affiliated restaurants will be bland and poor value.

Private rooms

The most common island accommodation is **privately let rooms** – *dhomátia* in Greek. Like hotels, these are regulated and officially divided into three classes (A down to C), according to facilities. These days the bulk of them are in new, purpose-built, low-rise buildings, but a few are still actually in people's homes, where you'll occasionally be treated to disarming hospitality.

Rooms are almost always scrupulously clean, whatever their other amenities (see the box on p.52 for the full story). At their simplest (now pretty much confined to Ródhos Old Town), you'll get a tiny, almost windowless cell, with a hook on the back of the door in lieu of closet, and toilet facilities down the hall. At the fancier end of the scale, they are modern, fully furnished places with an en-suite bathroom and a fully equipped kitchen shared by guests. Between these extremes there will be a choice of rooms at various prices – owners will usually show you the most expen-

The generic Greek hotel room

After travelling around the Dodecanese and east Aegean for a while, you'll notice that most hotel and *dhomátia* units are so similar from one end of the archipelago to the other (and from the lowest price category to nearly the highest) that you'll eventually be able to find your way around any specimen blindfolded. Thus we describe the typical room now, once and for all, without wasting undue space in the destination accounts.

The **generic Greek hotel room** is entered via a short corridor, with a closet to one side and the en-suite bath on the other. The sleeping area has co-ordinated pine furniture, either depressingly dark-stained (typical of the 1970s) or "natural blonde" (newer units). This will consist of two twin **beds** or (less often) one double bed (*dhipló kreváti*), flanked by one or more **end tables** (*komodhína*). On one of the *komodhína* there will possibly be a telephone, though these are on the wane given the popularity of mobiles. **Televisions** are the Big Thing now, invariably mounted on a bracket high up in the corner, and the remote control will be presented to you at check-in with considerable ceremony. There will be a single ceiling light fixture, with a two-way switch for turning it off just above the headboard, plus a reading **lamp** over each bed (or half of the double bed), and probably one more over the dressing table. There will rarely be enough **power points/outlets**, sometimes just one in the whole room; if this drives you crazy, invest in a multi-socket adapter (they can be had for under €2 at many shops).

There will often be a sort of **latticed rack** for resting your baggage, and a small **dressing table** with two drawers, a mirror and a chair. The **closet** will either be freestanding or a built-in unit, of the same wood (or more likely veneered MDF) and shade as the rest of the furnishings. Inside will be an assortment of cheap hangers, while in the cupboard above you'll find an extra synthetic-fibre pillow or two and a like number of cheap acrylic extra blankets. The **bed linen** itself will be rough but all-cotton sheets, both flat-type, tucked over a lumpy **mattress** due for replacement. The **walls** will be dazzling white (if recent), probably pinky-beige if from the 1970s, institutional green if older. The **floor** varies too: hospital-type linoleum in the 1960s-horror relics, mosaic composition (*terrátso*) from the 1970s, easy-to-clean white or beige tiles for later vintage. The white-tile, white-wall and blonde-pine style is by far the most common, and what we mean by the adjectives "bland", "neutral" or "anodyne". A set of double doors, or possibly a sliding one, will give onto a small **balcony** with some plastic outdoor furniture and a corroding railing that's handy for anchoring clothes lines. The doors themselves will be hidden by a dingy-coloured pair of **acrylic curtains** which you pull to – there's often no cord or proper runner.

The **bathroom**, tiled to head height, will contain a wall-mounting sink with functional chrome fittings (up to the late 1980s), but a sturdier pedestal model thereafter, or in better outfits. A plastic medicine-chest-with-mirror, or a single shelf scarred by numerous cigarette butts, hovers over the sink. As in Britain, it's illegal to have full-strength power points in the bathroom, so you'll have to plug in hairdryers at the dressing table (or sometimes at an outlet just outside the bathroom door); shavers may be accommodated with a low-amp, dual-voltage point in the light fixture over the mirror. Opposite the toilet, a sign in several languages will demand that you throw your used paper in a little plastic **basket or pedal-bin**. The **shower** will consist of a flat floor pan and a cheap **chrome flex** attachment, nicknamed a *tiléfono* ("phone"), meant to be perched on a wall bracket. The chrome flex will invariably be in the process of ravelling and the rubber liner inside splitting, whereupon the management replaces it with a tough, single-layer "garden hose"-type extension – which can't be suspended from the wall-hook. Whether or not the shower corner has a saggy plastic curtain, you will invariably **flood** the entire room (and any clothes you've been so rash as to bring inside) – thus the little drain in the centre of the floor. During the 1970s there was a brief craze for **mini-bathtubs**, with a little ledge to sit on while you scrunch up in foetal position; they're more suited to doing laundry than anything else.

The **better, exceptional** rooms – we indicate which these are in the accounts – might have some or all of the following: split-level air con/heating, recessed halogen lighting, abundant power points, double glazing, full-sized bathtubs, designer sinks and mirrors, marble or terracotta cladding in the bathroom, a well-sealed shower stall, wooden floors, original wall art, orthopedic mattresses, proper armchairs, wrought-iron bed-frames, pastel-patterned bedspreads or curtains, and an economy switch activated with a tab on your room key. But for any of this loveliness you should expect to be paying at least halfway up the range of category ④.

sive first. Some of the cheap places will also have more expensive rooms with en-suite facilities – and vice versa, with singles often tucked under stairways or in other less desirable corners of the building. Price and quality are not necessarily directly linked, so always ask to see the room before agreeing to take it.

Areas to **look for rooms**, along with recommendations of the best places, are included in the Guide. As often as not, however, the rooms find you: owners descend on ferry or bus arrivals to fill any space they have, sometimes waving photos of the premises. In smaller places you'll often see buildings signposted, sometimes in German (*Zimmer*); the Greek signs to look out for are "ENIKIAZÓMENA DHOMÁTIA" or "ENIKIÁZONTEH DHOMÁTIA". In the more developed island resorts, where package holiday-makers predominate, *dhomátia* owners will often require you to stay for at least three days, or even a week. If you can't find rooms in an island town or village, ask at the local **taverna** or kafenío (coffee house). There is very often someone prepared to earn extra money by putting you up, though of course these facilities may not be licensed.

It has become standard practice for room proprietors, like hotel staff, to ask to keep your **passport** – ostensibly "for the tourist police", who do require customer particulars – but in reality to prevent you skipping out with an unpaid bill. Some owners may be satisfied with just taking down your details, as is done in hotels, and they'll almost always return the documents once you get to know them, or if you need your passport for another purpose (to change money, for example).

In **winter**, officially from November until early April, private rooms – except in Ródhos Old Town – are closed pretty much across the board to keep the hotels in business. There's no point in traipsing about hoping to find exceptions – most room-owners obey the system very strictly. If they don't, the owners will find you themselves and, watching out for hotel rivals, guide you back to their place.

Villas and long-term rentals

The easiest – and usually most economical – way to arrange a **villa rental** is through one of the package holiday companies detailed on pp.14–15. They represent some superb places, from fairly simple to luxurious, and costs can be very reasonable, especially if shared between several people. Several of the companies we list will arrange **"multi-centre"** stays on two or more islands.

Ecofriendly tourism

Much has been written lately about the negative **environmental impact** of mass tourism on fragile Mediterranean destinations. As a phenomenon, package travel is here to stay, but following are a few suggestions – endorsed and in some cases suggested by readers or the more sensitive package companies – on how to land more lightly in Greece.

Visiting during the spring or autumn **shoulder seasons** eases pressure on oversubscribed water, power and sewage networks, as well as being a good idea for several other reasons (see "When to Go", p.xii). Speaking of **water**, try to use the same batch twice – for example, use the rinse water when laundering for soaping up the next batch of clothes. Forego those horrible PVC mineral-**water bottles**, which end up littering every beach and roadside, and bring along a permanent canteen/water-bottle; all ferries, hotel bars and restaurants have a tap gushing cold, potable water for serving with oúzo, and staff will gladly top up bottles for customers. (Incidentally, many brands of "mineral" water have been repeatedly shown to be fraudulently filled with ordinary tap water.)

Similarly, decline the automatic dispensing of **nylon bags** for every tiny purchase that will fit in a day pack or the palm of your hand – the wind-blown bags invariably end up on the beach, or submerged next to the PVC bottles. And last but not least, buy when possible locally produced orange and lemon soda sold in **recyclable glass bottles**, rather than international brands or their local subsidiaries such as Ivi. By doing so, you will keep several people in work at island bottling plants (still operating on Lésvos, Híos, Léros, Kálymnos, Kós and Rhodes) and prevent yet more aluminium cans from joining the plastic on the roadside or in the sea.

On the islands, a few local travel agents arrange villa rentals, though they are often places the overseas companies gave a miss or couldn't fill. **Out of season**, you can sometimes get a good deal on villa or apartment rental for a month or more by asking around locally, though in these days of EU convergence and the increasing desirability of the islands as year-round residences, "good deal" means anything under €240 per month for a large studio (*garsoniéra*) or €300 for a small one-bedroom flat.

Camping

Officially recognized **campsites** in the Dodecanese and east Aegean are restricted to Rhodes (one), Kós (one), Léros (one), Astypálea (one), Pátmos (one), Híos (one) and Lésvos (two); see the relevant chapters for full descriptions. The Panhellenic Camping Association publishes an annual booklet covering most officially recognized Greek campsites and the facilities they offer; it's available from many EOT offices, though is remarkably reticent on the sites listed above. Most places cost just under €4 a night per person, slightly less per tent, and €7.50 per camper van, but at the fanciest sites, rates for two people plus a tent can almost add up to the price of a basic room. Generally, you don't have to worry about leaving tents or other equipment unattended at wardened campsites; the Greeks are one of the most honest nations in Europe. The main risk, alas, comes from other campers.

Camping rough outside authorized campsites is such an established element of Greek travel that few people realize that it's officially illegal. Since 1977 "freelance" camping, as EOT calls it, has actually been forbidden by a law originally enacted to harass Gypsies, and regulations are increasingly enforced. Another drawback is the increased prevalence of theft in rural areas, often by marauding bands of refugees from the northern Balkan states. All told, you will feel less vulnerable inside a tent, campervan or even a rock-cave – not that rain is likely during the long Greek summer, but some protection is essential from wind, sun, insects (see p.27) and stray animals raiding your food. You will always need at least a light sleeping bag, since even summer nights get cool and damp at muddy or shady campsites; a foam pad is also recommended for pitching on harder ground.

If you do camp rough, it's vital to exercise sensitivity and discretion. Police will crack down on people camping (and especially littering) around popular tourist beaches, particularly when a large community of campers develops. Off the beaten track, however, nobody is very bothered, though it is always best to ask permission locally in the village taverna or café. During high season, when everything – even the authorized campsites – may be full, attitudes towards freelance camping are more relaxed, even in the most touristed places. At such times the best strategy is to find a sympathetic taverna, which in exchange for regular patronage will probably be willing to guard small valuables and let you use their facilities.

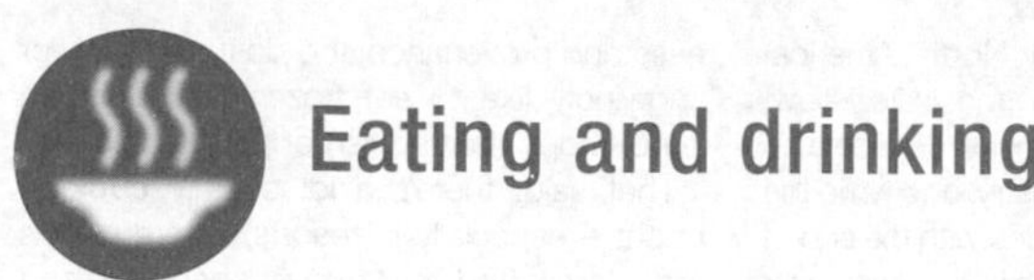

Eating and drinking

Greeks spend a lot of time socializing outside their homes, and sharing a meal is one of the chief ways of doing it. The atmosphere is always relaxed and informal, with pretensions (and expense-account prices) rare outside major resorts on Kós, Pátmos and Rhodes. Greeks are not prodigious drinkers – tippling is traditionally meant to accompany food – though since the mid-1990s a whole range of bars and pubs has sprung up, both in tourist resorts and as pricey music clubs on the outskirts of major towns.

Breakfast, picnic fare and snacks

Greeks don't generally eat **breakfast**, so the only egg-and-bacon kind of places are in resorts where foreigners congregate, or where there are returned North American or Australian Greeks. Such spots can sometimes be fairly good value (€4.50–6.50 for the works, maybe even with "French" filter coffee), especially if there's competition. More indigenous alternatives are yogurts at a *galaktopolío* (milk bar), or cheese pies and pretzel rings from a bakery (see "Snacks", p.56).

Picnic fare

Picnic fare is good, cheap and easily available at bakeries and *manávika* (fruit-and-veg stalls). **Bread**, alas, is often of minimal nutritional value and inedible within a day of purchase. It's worth paying extra at the bakery (*foúrnos* or *psomádhiko*) for *olikís* (wholemeal), *sikalísio* (rye bread), *oktásporo* (eight-grain), or even *enneásporo* (nine-grain), the latter types most commonly baked where large numbers of Germans or Scandinavians are about. When buying **olives**, go for the fat Kalamáta or Ámfissa ones; they're more expensive, but tastier. However, locally gathered olives – especially the slightly shrivelled *hamádhes* or fully ripened, ground-gathered olives – often have a distinctive nutty flavour, compensating for large kernels. The best **honey** in the islands covered is reckoned to be the pure-thyme variety from Límnos, Foúrni or Astypálea – it's about double the price of honeys from Sámos or Lésvos, where the presence of pine trees and their acrid blossoms is considered to make local honey inferior.

Honey is an ideal topping for the famous local **yogurt** which is not confined to the bland stuff of supermarkets. All of the larger island towns have at least one dairy shop where locally produced yogurts are sold in plastic or (better) clay containers of various sizes. Sheep-milk yogurt is richer and sweeter, scarcely requiring honey; cow-milk yogurt is tarter but more widely available. Side by side with these will be *krémes* (custards) and *ryzógala* (rice puddings) in one-serving plastic containers.

Féta cheese is ubiquitous – sometimes, ironically, imported from Holland or Denmark, though the Greeks are clamping down on this legally, as the French do with non-French "champagne" – and local brands are usually better and not much more expensive. The goat's-milk variety can be very dry and salty, so ask for a taste before buying. If you have access to a fridge, leaving the cheese overnight in a plastic container filled with water will solve both problems, though if left too long like this the cheese simply dissolves. This sampling advice goes for other indigenous cheeses as well, the most palatable of which is the expensive gruyère-type *graviéra*.

Despite membership of the EU, plus growing personal incomes and exotic tastes, Greece imports very little garden produce from abroad, aside from bananas and a few mangos. **Fruit** in particular is relatively expensive and available only by season, though in the more cosmopolitan spots it is possible to find such things as **avocados** (light-green ones from Crete are excellent) for much of the year. Reliable picnic fruits include *yiarmádhes*, a variety of giant **peach** available during August and September; *krystália*, tiny, hard green **pears** that ripen a month or two later and are heavenly; and the *himoniátiko*

melon (called casava in North America) which appears at the same time, in its yellow, puckered skin with green flecks. Greece also has a burgeoning **kiwi** industry, and while the first crop in October coincides with the end of the tourist season, availability carries over into the following May. Less portable, but succulent, are the Smyrna **figs** (*boúkhnes*) which are found only on Sámos and Híos; there's a crop of large fruits in May, followed by smaller ones (*boukhnákia*) in August. Salad **vegetables** are more reasonably priced; besides the famous, enormous tomatoes (June–Sept), there is a bewildering variety of springtime greens, including rocket, dill, enormous spring onions and lettuces. Useful **expressions** for shopping are *éna tétarto* (250g) and *misó kiló* (500g).

Snacks

Traditional **snacks** can be one of the distinctive pleasures of Greek eating, though they are being increasingly edged out by an obsession with *tóst* (toasted sandwiches) and other Western junk/fast food at nationwide chains such as *Goody's* (burgers), *Everest* and *Grigoris Mikroyevmata* (assorted nibbles), *Roma Pizza* and *Theios Vanias* (baked pastries) – somewhat less insipid for being Greek-originated. However, independently produced kebabs (*souvlákia*) are widely available, and in most larger resorts and towns you'll find *yíros* – doner kebab with garnish in thick, doughy *píta* bread that's closer to Indian nan bread. To find the closest outlet for such, ask for a *yirádhiko* or *souvladzídhiko* (*souvláki* and *yíros* bars, respectively).

Other common snacks include *tyrópites* (cheese pies) and *spanokópites* (spinach pies), which can usually be found at the baker's, as can *kouloúria* (crispy pretzel rings sprinkled with sesame seeds) and *voutímata* (dark biscuits heavy on molasses, cinnamon and butter).

Restaurants

Greek cuisine and **restaurants** are simple and straightforward. There's usually no snobbery about eating out; everyone does it regularly, and it's still reasonable – €9–13 per person for a substantial (non-seafood) meal with a measure of house wine. Even if the cooking is simple, you should expect it to be wholesome; Greeks are fussy about freshness and provenance and do not willingly or knowingly like to eat frozen New Zealand lamb chops, farmed fish or pre-fried chips.

That said, there's a lot of **lazy cooking** about – especially in resorts, where menus are dominated by pizza, spaghetti and chops. Amongst seasoned Greek travellers, the term "tourist *moussaká*" – the dish heavy with cheap potato slices, and nary a crumb of mince – is shorthand for this kind of low-grade culinary fraud. Sending unacceptable food back is the only potential way to raise the standard of resort dining.

Of late you find growing numbers of what the Greeks call "**kultúra**" restaurants, often pretentious attempts at Greek *nouvelle*, or updated "traditional", cuisine with speciality wine lists, which tend to be long on airs and graces, and (at €17.50–23.50 a head) short on value. The exceptions which succeed have been singled out in the text.

In choosing a restaurant, the best strategy is to go where the Greeks go. And they go late: 2pm to 3.30pm for **lunch**, 9pm to 11pm for **supper**. You can eat earlier, but you're likely to get indifferent service and cuisine if you frequent establishments catering to the tourist schedule. Chic appearance is not a reliable guide to quality; often the more ramshackle, traditional outfits represent the best value. One good omen is the waiter bringing a carafe of refrigerated water, unbidden, rather than pushing you to order bottled stuff.

In busy resort areas, it's wise to keep a wary eye on the **waiters**, who are inclined to urge you into ordering more than you want, then bring things you haven't ordered. Although cash-register receipts are now required in all establishments, these are often only for the grand total, and itemized **bills** will often be in totally illegible Greek script. Where prices are printed on menus, you'll be paying the right-hand (higher) of the two columns, inclusive of all taxes and usually **service charge**, although a small extra tip of about ten percent directly to the waiter is hugely appreciated – and usually not expected.

Bread costs extra, but consumption is not obligatory; unless it is assessed as part of the cover charge, you have the right to send it back without paying for it. You'll be considered deviant for refusing it, but so much Greek bread is inedible sawdust that there's little point in paying extra unless you actually want to use it as a scoop for dips. Good restaurant bread is still so remarkable that its existence is noted in establishment listings; at ouzerís and *kultúra* restaurants on Rhodes and Kós, Italian influence has resulted in the emergence of the more appetizing *skordhópsomo* (garlic bread), the local equivalent of *bruschetta*.

Children are always welcome, day or night, at family tavernas, and Greeks don't mind in the slightest if they play tag between the tables or chase the **cats** running in mendicant packs – which you shouldn't feed, as signs often warn you. They are wild and pretty desperate, and you'll need a doctor's visit and tetanus jab if they whack at a dangled bit of food and claw your hand instead.

Estiatória

There are two basic types of restaurant: the *estiatório* and the taverna. Distinctions between the two are slight, though the former is more commonly found in town centres and tends to have the slightly more complicated casserole dishes known generically as *mayireftá* (literally, "cooked"). With their long hours, old-fashioned-tradesmen's clientele and tiny profit margins, *estiatória* are, alas, something of a vanishing breed.

An *estiatório* will generally feature a variety of such oven-baked dishes as *moussakás*, *pastítsio*, meat or game stews like *kokinistó* and *stifádho*, *yemistá* (stuffed tomatoes or peppers), the oily vegetable dishes called *ladherá*, and oven-baked meat or fish. Choosing these dishes is usually done by going into the kitchen and pointing at the desired steam trays. For a full rundown of common dishes, see p.514 in Contexts.

Batches are cooked in the morning and then left to stand, which is why *mayireftá* are often lukewarm or even cold. Greeks don't mind this (most believe that hot food is bad for you), and dishes like *yemistá* are actually enhanced by being allowed to cool off and stand in their own juice. Similarly, you have to specify if you want your food with little or no oil (*horís ládhi*), but once again you will be considered a little strange since Greeks regard good olive oil as essential to digestion (and indeed it is the healthiest of the vegetable oils, even in large quantities).

Desserts (*epidhórpia* in formal Greek) of the pudding-and-pie variety don't exist at *estiatória*, and yogurt or cheese only occasionally. Fruit, however, is always available in season; watermelons, melons and grapes are the summer standards, and may be offered on the house. Autumn treats worth asking after in more urban restaurants include *kydhóni* or *akhládhi stó foúrno*, baked quince or pear with some sort of syrup or nut topping.

Tavernas and psistariés

Tavernas range from the glitzy and fashionable to rough-and-ready huts set up under a reed canopy, behind a beach. Really primitive ones have a very limited (often unwritten) menu, but the more established will offer some of the main *mayireftá* dishes mentioned above, as well as the standard taverna fare. This essentially means **mezédhes** (hors d'oeuvres) or *orektiká* (appetizers) and *tís óras* (meat and fish, fried or grilled to order).

Psistariés or grill-houses serve spit-roasted lamb, pork or goat (generically termed *soúvla* or *kondosoúvli*), grilled chicken (*kotópoulo skáras*) or *kokorétsi* (grilled offal roulade) – often plonked straight on your table upon a sheet of waxed paper. They will usually have a limited selection of mezédhes, but no *mayireftá* at all.

Since the idea of courses is foreign to Greek cuisine, starters, main dishes and salads often arrive together unless you request otherwise. The best thing is to order a selection of mezédhes and salads to share, in true Greek fashion. Waiters encourage you to take the *horiátiki* **salad** – the so-called Greek salad, including féta cheese – because it is the most expensive. If you only want tomato, or tomato and cucumber, ask for *domatosaláta* or *angourodomáta*. *Láhanokaróto* (cabbage–carrot) and *maroúli* (lettuce) are the typical winter and spring salads respectively.

Vegetarians

If you are **vegetarian**, you may be in for a hard time, and will often have to assemble a meal from various mezédhes. Even the excellent standbys of yogurt with honey, *tzatzíki* and Greek salad begin to pall after a while, and many of the supposed "vegetable" dishes on the menu are cooked in stock or have pieces of meat added to liven them up. Wholly or largely vegetarian restaurants are slowly on the increase in touristed areas; this guide highlights them where appropriate.

The most interesting **mezédhes** are *tzatzíki* (yogurt, garlic and cucumber dip), *melitzanosaláta* (aubergine/eggplant dip), *kolokythákia tiganitá* (courgette/zucchini slices fried in batter) or *melitzánes tiganités* (aubergine/eggplant slices fried in batter), *yígandes* (white haricot beans in vinaigrette or hot tomato sauce), *tyropitákia* or *spanakópites* (small cheese and spinach pies), *revythókeftedhes* or *pittaroúdhia* (chickpea patties analagous to felafel), *okhtapódhi* (octopus) and *mavromátika* (black-eyed peas).

Among **meats**, *souvláki* (shish kebab) and *brizóles* (chops) are reliable choices. In both cases, pork (*hirinó*) is usually better and cheaper than veal (*moskharísio*). The best *souvláki*, though not often available, is lamb (*arnísio*). At *psistariés*, meaty lamb shoulder chops (*kopsídha*) are more substantial than the scrawny rib chops (usually frozen) called *païdhákia*; roast lamb (*arní psitó*) and roast kid (*katsíki stó fournó*) are considered *estiatório* fare. *Keftédhes* (breadcrumbed meatballs), *biftékia* (similar, but meatier) and the spicey, home-made sausages called *loukánika* are cheap and good. *Kotópoulo* (chicken), especially grilled, is widely available but typically battery-farmed in Ípiros or on Évvia. Other dishes worth trying are stewed (*gídha vrastí*) or baked goat (*katsíki stó foúrno*) – goat in general is a wonderfully healthy meat, typically free-range in Greece and undosed with antibiotics or hormones.

As in *estiatória*, traditional tavernas offer fruit rather than sticky **desserts**, though nowadays these are often available, along with coffee, in tavernas frequented by foreigners.

Fish and seafood

Seaside *psarotavérnes* offer **fish**, reckoned by many to be a quintessential part of a Greek holiday experience. For novices, however, ordering can be fraught with peril; see the box opposite, and the species list on p.516 in Contexts, for tips.

Given these considerations, it's often best to set your sights on the **humbler**, seasonally migrating or perennially local species, rather than what you might be familiar with from a UK supermarket fish counter. The cheapest consistently available fish are *gópes* (bogue), *atherína* (sand smelts) and *marídhes* (picarel), eaten head and all, best rolled in salt and sprinkled with lemon juice. Around Rhodes, *yermanós* (leatherback, in Australia) is a good frying fish which appears in spring; *gávros* (anchovy) and *sardhélles* (sardines) are late summer treats, at their best in the northeast Aegean. Also in the north Aegean, *pandelís* or *sykiós* (Latin *Corvina nigra*, in French *corb*) is caught in early summer, and is highly esteemed since it's a rock-dweller rather than a bottom feeder – and therefore a bit pricier than the former. In autumn especially you may encounter *psarósoupa* (fish broth) or *kakaviá* (a bouillabaisse-like stew).

The **choicier** varieties, such as *barboúni* (red mullet), *tsipoúra* (gilt-head bream), *lavráki* (seabass) or *fangrí* (common bream), will be expensive if wild – anywhere from €26.50–41 per kilo, depending on what the market will bear. If the price seems too good to be true, it's almost certainly farmed. Prices are usually quoted by the kilo, and should not be much more than double the street-market rate, so if a type of bream is €14.70 a kilo at the fishmonger's, expect it to be not more than €30 at the taverna. Standard procedure is to go to the glass-fronted cooler and pick your own specimen, and have it weighed (already cleaned) in your presence.

Cheaper **seafood** (*thalassiná*) such as *kalamarákia* (fried baby squid) and *okhtapódhi* (octopus) are a summer staple of most seaside tavernas, and occasionally *mýdhia* (mussels), *kydhónia* (cockles) and *garídhes* (small prawns) will be on offer at reasonable prices. Keep an eye out, however, to freshness and season – mussels in particular are a common cause of stomach upsets or even mild poisoning. The miniature "Sými" shrimps which are also caught around Hálki and Kastellórizo would anywhere else just be used for bait, but here are devoured avidly; when less than a day old, they're distinctly sweet-flavoured.

As the more favoured species have become overfished, **unusual seafoods**, formerly the exclusive province of the poor, are putting in a greater appearance on menus. Ray or skate (variously known as *platý*, *seláhi*, *trígona* or *vátos*) can be fried or used in soup, and are even dried for decoration. Sea urchins (*ahiní*) are also a humble (but increasingly scarce) favourite, being split and emptied for the sake of their (reputedly aphrodisiac) roe that's eaten raw. Only the reddish ones are gravid; special shears are sold for opening them if you don't fancy a handful of spines. Many a quiet beach is littered with their halved carapaces, evidence of an instant Greek picnic.

Fish story

Fresh, wild **fish** is becoming increasingly rare and expensive as prices climb and Aegean stocks are depleted. Dodges used by unscrupulous taverna proprietors to get around this problem are legion: selling inferior Egyptian or Moroccan products as "local", at full price; swishing frozen specimens around in the sea to make them look more "lifelike"; and complying minimally with the legal requirement to clearly indicate when fish is frozen or *katapsygméno* (often only by the abbreviation "kat", "k." or just an asterisk on the Greek-language side of the menu).

Unfortunately, from a tourist's point of view, the greatest variety and quantity of fish is on offer outside of summer. **Drag-net trawling** (the *tráta*) is engaged in between October 1 and May 31, with small local variations dictated by politics; the season really should end April 30, as most baby fish emerge during May. The latest generation of mechanized trawler or *anemótrata* is extremely destructive to the marine environment, indiscriminately hoovering the sea floor, with one monstrous boat having the impact of a half-dozen old-style wooden craft. During summer, lamp-lure (*pyrofáni*) and trident, stationary drift nets, "doughnut" trap (*kýrtos*) and multi-hook line (*paragádhi*) are the only permitted methods. Fish caught during these warmer months tend to be relatively scrawny and dry-tasting, thus requiring the butter or olive oil sauce often served with them.

Most restaurants use imported and/or frozen fish at this time, or rely on *ikhthyotrofía* (fish farms) for a supply of *tsipoúra* and *lavráki* in particular. These **fish farms**, heavily subsidized by EU grants, are a Big Thing on the smaller Dodecanese such as Agathoníssi, Sými, Hálki, Astypálea and Kálymnos, as well as on most of the east Aegean islands, often serving as significant local employers. But quality products are not their strong point – farmed fish subsist exclusively on a diet of pellet food made from low-grade fish meal or even petroleum by-products, giving them an unmistakable muddy taste. The farms are also something of an environmental disaster, as the parasiticide chemicals used to keep them going are highly toxic.

Another peculiar delicacy, frequently available on Rhodes, Kálymnos and several nearby islands, are *foúskes* ("blisters"). These soft-shelled marine molluscs live on rocks at depths of 15–40m, and are gathered by sponge-divers for extra income. They're unprepossessing in the extreme – unfortunately resembling hairy turds – but slice them lengthwise and your opinion will change instantly as you scoop out the liquor and savour the orange-and-yellow innards, which taste much like oysters and cost about the same. Unfortunately they're commonly pickled in beer-bottles of preserving brine, which tends to overpower their delicate intrinsic taste.

Wines

Both *estiatória* and tavernas will usually offer you a choice of bottled **wines**, and many still have their own house variety, kept in barrels, sold in bulk by the quarter-, half- or full litre, and served either in glass flagons or brightly coloured tin "monkey-cups" called *kantária*. Not as many tavernas stock their own wine as once did, but it's always worth asking whether they have wine *varelísio* (**barrelled**) or *hýma* (**in bulk**). You should expect to pay €3.50–5 per litre, with smaller measures priced proportionately. Non-resinated wine is almost always more than decent, though even in the islands' **retsína** – pine-resinated wine, a slightly acquired taste – is popular, usually imported from the mainland (though Sámos and Límnos make their own). Retsína is also available straight from the barrel, though the bottled brands Yeoryiadhi from Thessaloníki, Malamatina from central Greece (often cut with soda water), and Cambas from near Athens, are all excellent and likely to be more consistent in quality.

Among the **bottled wines** available **nationwide**, Cambas Attikos, Boutari Lac des Roches, any white from Zítsa and the Rhodian CAIR products (especially the Moulin range) are good, inexpensive whites, while Boutari Naoussa and Kourtakis Apelia are decent, mid-range reds. If you want a better but still moderately priced red, go for the Merlot of either Boutari and Tsantali, or Averof Katoï from Epirus.

If you're travelling around **wine-producing islands**, however, you may as well go for **local bottlings**; the best available guide to the emerging Greek domaines and vintners is Nico Manessis' *The Illustrated Greek*

Wine Book (see p.503 in *Contexts* for ordering information). Almost anything produced on **Límnos** is decent; the Alexandrine muscat is now used for whites, the local *límnio* grape for reds and rosés. **Sámos** is most famous for its fortified (fourteen to fifteen percent alcohol) dessert wines based on the muscat grape, similar to madeira and still exported in large quantities to France for use as communion wine in church, but the island also has some acceptable premium whites, and some good **rosés**, for example Selana, a blend of the Ritinos and Fokianos varieties. **Ikaría** is just beginning to produce limited bottlings of red from small domaines in the west of the island, with equally patchy success; Afames is reckoned much better than Nikarya label. On **Rhodes**, Alexandhris products from Émbonas are well thought of, as is the Emery label with its Villaré white, and CAIR's dry white "2400".

Curiously, island red wines (except for Rhodes's CAIR Moulin and Emery Cava) are almost uniformly mediocre; in this respect you're better off choosing **reds from the mainland**. Carras from Halkidhikí does the excellent Porto Carras, while Ktima Tselepou offers a very palatable Cabernet-Merlot blend. Antonopoulos Yerontoklima (Pátra), Ktima Papaïoannou Nemea (Peloponnese), and Tsantali Rapsani (Thessaly) are all superb, velvety reds – and likely to be found only in the better *kultúra* tavernas or *káves* (**bottle shops**). Antonopoulos, Tselepos (Mantinia domaine) and Papaïoannou also do excellent **mainland whites**.

The other **premium micro-wineries** on the mainland whose products have long been fashionable, in both red and white, include the vastly overrated Hatzimihali (Atalánti, central Greece), Spyropoulos (central Peloponnese), Athanasiadhi (central Greece), Skouras (Argolid) and the two rival Lazaridhi vintners (Dhráma, east Macedonia), especially their superb Merlots. For any of these you can expect to pay €7–10 per bottle in a shop, double that at a taverna.

Last but not least, CAIR on Rhodes makes its very own **"champagne"** ("naturally sparkling wine fermented *en boteille*", says the label), in both brut and demi-sec versions. It's not Moët & Chandon quality by any means, but at less than €6 per bottle, no one's complaining.

Cafés, cake shops and bars

The Greek eating and drinking experience encompasses a variety of other places beyond restaurants. Most importantly, there is the institution of the **kafenío**, found in every town, village and hamlet in the country. In addition, you'll come across **ouzerís**, *zaharoplastía* (Greek patisseries) and *barákia*.

The kafenío

The **kafenío** (plural, kafenía) is the traditional Greek coffee shop or café. Although its main business is "Greek" (generic Middle Eastern) coffee – prepared *skéto* or *pikró* (unsweetened), *métrio* (medium) or *glykó* (sweet) – it also serves spirits such as oúzo (see below), brandy (usually Metaxa or Botrys brand, in three grades), beer, tea (either the sage-based tea known as *alisfakiá*, or British-style) and soft drinks. Another refreshing drink sold in cafés is *kafés frappé*, iced, jigger-shaken instant coffee with or without milk and sugar – uniquely Greek despite its French-sounding name. Like Greek coffee, it is always accompanied by a welcome glass of cold water. Standard fizzy soft drinks are also sold in all kafenía.

Usually the only **edibles** available are *glyká koutalioú* (sticky, syrupy preserves of quince, grape, fig, citrus fruit or cherry), and the traditional *ipovrýhio*, a piece of mastic submerged in a glass of water like a submarine – which is what the word means in Greek. Peculiar to Níssyros, but sometimes exported to neighbouring islands, is *soumádha*, concentrated almond syrup similar to Italian *orgeat*; diluted four-to-one with cold water, there's nothing more refreshing on a hot day.

Like tavernas, kafenía range from the plastic and sophisticated to the old-fashioned, spit-on-the-floor variety, with marble or brightly painted metal tables and straw-bottomed chairs. An important institution anywhere in Greece, they form the pivot of life in the country villages, especially on Lésvos and Kós. You get the impression that many men spend most of their waking hours there. Greek women are rarely to be seen in the more traditional places – and foreign women may sometimes feel uneasy or unwelcome in these establishments. Even in holiday resorts, you will find that there is at least one coffee house that the local men have reserved for themselves.

Some kafenía close at siesta time, but many remain open from early in the morning until late at night. The chief socializing time is 6pm to 8pm, immediately after the siesta. This is the time to take your pre-dinner oúzo, as the sun begins to sink and the air cools down.

Oúzo, mezédhes and ouzerís

Oúzo is a simple spirit of up to 48 percent alcohol (see box on p.387), distilled from the grape-mash residue left over from wine-making, and then flavoured with herbs such as anise or fennel. There are nearly a score of brands, with the best island ones reckoned to come from Lésvos and Sámos; inferior ones are either weak (such as the Rhodian Fokiali, at forty percent) or spiked with molasses or grain alcohol to "boost" them.

When you order, you will be served two glasses: one with the oúzo, and one full of **water** that's tipped into the latter until it turns a milky white. You can drink it straight, but the strong, burning taste is hardly refreshing if you do. It is increasingly common to add **ice cubes** (*pagáki*), a bowl of which will be provided upon request. The next measure up from a glass is a *karafáki* – a deceptively small 200ml-vial – which will very rapidly render you legless if you don't alternate tippling with snacks.

A much smoother variant of oúzo is *soúma*, found chiefly on Rhodes and Sámos, but in theory anywhere grapes are grown. The smoothness is deceptive – two or three glasses of it and you had better not have any other firm plans for the rest of the day.

Until the 1980s, every oúzo you ordered was automatically accompanied by a small plate of **mezédhes** on the house: bits of cheese, cucumber, tomato, a few olives, sometimes octopus or even a couple of small fish. Unfortunately, these days "*oúzo mezédhes*" is a separate, more expensive option on a price list. Often, however, they are not featured on any formal menu, but if you order a *karafáki* you will automatically be offered a small selection of snacks.

Though they are confined to the better resorts and select neighbourhoods of the bigger island capitals such as Ródhos, Sými, Kós, Léros, Sámos, Híos and Lésvos, one kind of drinking establishment specializes in oúzo and mezédhes. These are called **ouzerís** (same in the Greek plural, we've added "s" to the hybrid) and are well worth trying for the marvellous variety of mezédhes they serve (though lately numbers of mediocre tavernas have counterfeited the name). At the genuine article, several plates of mezédhes plus drinks will effectively substitute for a more involved meal at a taverna (though it usually works out more expensive if you have a healthy appetite). Faced with an often bewilderingly varied menu, you might opt for the *pikilía* (medley, assortment) available in several sizes, the largest and most expensive one usually heavy on the seafood. At other ouzerís the language barrier may be overcome by the waiter wielding an enormous *dhískos* or tray laden with all the current cold offerings – you pick the ones you like the look of. Hot plates are ordered separately, and follow the cold starters.

Eating at an ouzerí is often the best way to get an idea of **regional specialities**, which can be fairly elaborate or incredibly simple. An example of the latter is *krítamo* or rock samphire, mentioned in *King Lear* and offered to the discerning on most of the east Aegean islands. A vitamin- and mineral-rich succulent growing on sea-coast cliffs, it is harvested in June or July by fishermen, pickled in brine, vinegar or wine served unadorned or to jazz up salads.

Sweets, breakfast and western coffee

Similar to the kafenío is the *zaharoplastío*, a cross between café and patisserie, serving coffee, alcohol, yogurt with honey, and sticky cakes.

The better establishments offer an amazing variety of pastries, cream-and-chocolate confections, honey-soaked Greco-Turkish sweets like *baklavás*, *kataïfi* (honey-drenched "shredded wheat"), *loukoumádhes* (deep-fried batter puffs dusted with cinnamon or sesame and dipped in syrup); *galaktoboúreko* (custard pie), and so on.

If you want a stronger slant towards the dairy products and away from the pure sugar, seek out a *galaktopolío*, where you'll often find *ryzógalo* (rice pudding – rather better than the English canned or school-dinner variety), *kréma* (custard) and locally made *yiaoúrti* (yogurt), best if it's *próvio* (from sheep's milk).

Ice cream, sold principally at the gelaterie which have swept over Greece of late, can be very good and almost indistinguishable from Italian prototypes. *Dhodhoni* is the posh local chain, while Häagen-Dazs is also widely available and identical to its north-European profile. A scoop (*baláki*) costs €0.90–1.30; you'll be asked if you want it in a cup (*kypelláki*) or a cone (*honáki*), and whether you want toppings like *santí* (whipped cream) or nuts. By contrast, the mass-produced brands like Delta or Evga are pretty average, with the honourable exception of the Skandalo and Nirvana labels. A sign reading "PAGOTÓ POLÍTIKO" or "KAÏMÁKI" means that the shop concerned makes its own Turkish-style ice cream – as good as or better than the usual Italian version – and the proprietors are probably of Asia Minor or Constantinopolitan descent. On Rhodes, the best ice-cream chain, Stani, is in fact run by Rhodian Turks.

Both *zaharoplastía* and *galaktopolía* are more family-oriented places than the kafenío, and many also serve a basic **continental breakfast** of *méli me voútyro* (honey poured over a pat of butter) or jam (all kinds are called *marmeládha* in Greek; ask for *portokáli* – orange – if you want proper marmalade) with fresh bread or *friganiés* (melba-toast-type slivers). You are also more likely to find proper (*evropaïkó*) tea and non-Greek coffee.

"Nes"(café) has become the generic term for all instant **coffee**, regardless of brand; it's generally pretty vile, and since the mid-1990s there's been a nation-wide reaction against it. Even in the smallest island capital or resort there will be at least one trendy café which does a range of foreign-style coffees – filter, dubbed *fíltros* or *gallikós* (French); cappuccino; and espresso – at overseas prices.

Bars – and beer

Bars (*barákia* in the plural), once confined to the biggest cities and holiday resorts, are now found all over Greece, especially in pedestrianized areas. They range from clones of Parisian cafés or Spanish *bodegas* to seaside cocktail bars, with music or TV running all day. At their most sophisticated, however, they are well-executed **theme venues** in ex-industrial premises or Neoclassical mansions that can hold their own against close equivalents in Spain or London, with western (currently techno, dub or ambient) soundtracks. Formerly **open** from late afternoon until dawn, most *barákia* **shut** between 1 and 3am, depending on the municipality and the day of the week (later on Fri/Sat).

Drinks are invariably more expensive than in a café. Bars are, however, most likely to stock a range of **beers**, mostly foreign labels made locally under licence at just one or two breweries on the central mainland. However, since 1996 several genuinely **local new formulae** have appeared, rapidly capturing a slice of the market: Mythos, a smooth lager in a green bottle, put out by the Boutari vintners; Veryina, brewed in Komotiní and common on the larger islands; Pils Hellas, a sharp pilsner; and last but not least, the resurrected Fix, for years until its demise in 1980 Greece's only beer, though not (according to those who remember) much better the second time around than the first. Kronenbourg 1664 and Kaiser are two of the more common quality **foreign-licence** varieties, with the latter available in both light and dark. Bland, inoffensive Amstel and the increasingly rare, yeasty Henninger are the two cheapies; the Dutch themselves claim that Amstel is better than the one available in Holland, and Amstel also makes a very palatable, strong (seven percent) **bock**. Heineken, still referred to as a "*prássini*" by bar and taverna staff after its green bottle, despite the advent of Mythos, is too harshly sharp for many. Since 1993 a tidal wave of even pricier, genuinely imported German beers, such as Bitburger, Fisher and Warsteiner (plus a few British ones), has washed over the fancier resorts.

Incidentally, try not to get stuck with the one-third litre cans, vastly more expensive (and more of a rubbish problem) than the **returnable** half-litre **bottles** (see the box on Ecofriendly tourism, p.53). On ferry-boats or in remote locales you may not have a choice, however.

Communications: post, phones and the internet

Postal services

Post offices are open Monday to Friday from about 7.30am to 2pm, though the Ródhos Town branch may sometimes have evening and weekend hours. **Airmail letters or postcards** from the islands take three to seven days to reach the rest of Europe, five to twelve days to get to North America, and a bit longer for Australia and New Zealand. Generally, the larger the island (and the planes serving its airport), the quicker the service. Postal rates for up to 20g fall within the normal EU range: €0.60 to Europe, North America or Australasia. For a modest fee (about €3) you can shave a day or two off delivery time to any destination by using the **express service** (*katepígonda*). **Registered** (*systiméno*) delivery is also available for a similar amount, but proves quite slow unless coupled with express service. If you are sending large purchases or excess baggage home, note that **parcels** should and often can only be handled in the main provincial or county capitals. This way, your bundle will be in Athens, and on an international flight, within a day. Always present your box open for inspection, and come prepared with tape, twine and scissors – most post offices will sell cardboard boxes, but nothing to actually close the package.

For a simple letter or card, a stamp (*grammatósimo*) can also be purchased at a *períptero* (kiosk). However, the proprietors charge ten percent commission on the cost of the stamp, and never seem to know the current international rates.

Ordinary **post boxes** are bright yellow, express boxes dark red, but it's best to use only those by the door of an actual post office, since days may pass between collections at other street-corner or wall-mounted boxes. If you are confronted by two slots, "ESOTERIKÓ" is for domestic mail, "EXOTERIKÓ" for overseas. Often there are more: one box or slot for mail into Athens and suburbs, one for your local province, one for "other" parts of Greece, and one for overseas; if in doubt, ask someone.

The **poste-restante** system is reasonably efficient, especially at the post offices of larger towns. Mail should be clearly addressed and marked "poste restante", with your surname underlined, to the main post office of whichever town you choose. It will be held for a month and you'll need your passport to collect it.

Telephones

Making **telephone calls** is relatively straightforward, though the **OTE** (*Organismós Tiliepikinoníon tís Elládhos*, the state-run telecom) has historically provided some of the worst service in the EU. However, since the mid-1990s this has improved drastically, and rates have dropped dramatically, under the twin threats of privatization and competition from thriving local mobile networks.

All land-line exchanges were supposed to become **digital** (*psifiakó*) by 2002, but you may still encounter a few **pulse-analogue** (*palmikó*) exchanges. When ringing long-distance on such circuits, you must wait for a critical series of six electrical crunches on the line after dialling the country or Greek area code, before proceeding. The phone system for Rhodes and the immediately surrounding islands had a state-of-the-art fibre-optic digital system installed in 1993, and it usually works like a dream.

Call boxes, poorly maintained and invariably sited at the noisiest street corners, work only with phone cards; these come in four sizes – 100 units, 200 units, 500 units and 1000 units – and are available from kiosks and newsagents. Not surprisingly, the more expensive cards are the best value in terms of euros per unit. Despite numbers hopefully scribbled on the appropriate tabs, call boxes cannot be rung back; however, green, countertop card phones kept by many hotels can be rung.

If you won't be around long enough to use up a phone card (the cheapest is about €3), it's probably easier to make **local calls** from a *períptero* or **street kiosk**. Here the phone may be connected to a meter (if not, there'll

Phoning Greece from abroad

Dial the international access code (given below) + 30 (Greek country code) + area code/prefix (minus initial 0) + subscriber number

Australia	ⓣ0011	Ireland	ⓣ010	UK	ⓣ00
Canada	ⓣ011	New Zealand	ⓣ00	USA	ⓣ011

Phoning abroad from Greece

Dial the country code (given below) + area code (minus any initial 0) + number

Australia	ⓣ0061	Ireland	ⓣ00353	UK	ⓣ0044
Canada	ⓣ001	New Zealand	ⓣ0064	USA	ⓣ001

Greek phone prefixes

Astypálea ⓣ02430
Athens ⓣ010
Áyios Efstrátios ⓣ02540
Foúrni ⓣ02750
Hálki ⓣ02460
Híos (Town) ⓣ02710
Híos (Kardhámyla-Inoússes) ⓣ02720
Híos (Volissós-Psará) ⓣ02740
Ikaría ⓣ02750
Kálymnos ⓣ02430
Kárpathos ⓣ02450
Kássos ⓣ02450
Kastellórizo ⓣ02460
Kós ⓣ02420
Léros ⓣ02470
Lésvos (Mytilíni) ⓣ02510
Lésvos (Ayiássos-Plomári) ⓣ02520
Lésvos (Kalloní-Sígri) ⓣ02530
Límnos ⓣ02540
Lipsí ⓣ02470
Níssyros ⓣ02420
Pátmos ⓣ02470
Rhodes (Líndhos) ⓣ02440
Rhodes (Town) ⓣ02410
Sámos ⓣ02730
Sými ⓣ02460
Tílos ⓣ02460
Thessaloníki ⓣ0310

Local call rate (like UK's ⓣ0845) ⓣ0801
Mobiles ⓣ093, ⓣ094, ⓣ095, ⓣ097
Toll-free/freefone ⓣ0800

Useful Greek telephone numbers

Ambulance ⓣ166
ELPA Road Service ⓣ104
Express Road Service ⓣ154
Hellas Road Service ⓣ1057
Interamerican Road Service ⓣ168
Fire brigade, urban ⓣ199
Forest fire reporting ⓣ191
Operator ⓣ132 (Domestic)
Operator ⓣ161 (International)
Police/Emergency ⓣ100
Speaking clock ⓣ141
Tourist police ⓣ171 (Athens); ⓣ01 171 (elsewhere)

Phone charge-card operator access numbers from Greece

AT&T USA Direct ⓣ00 800 1311
Australia ⓣ00 800 61 11
Australia (Optus) ⓣ00 800 6121
Bell Atlantic ⓣ00 800 1821
Bell South ⓣ00 800 1721
British Telecom ⓣ00 800 4411
NTL ⓣ00 800 4422
Canada Direct ⓣ00 800 1611
MCI ⓣ00 800 1211
Sprint ⓣ00 800 1411

be a sign saying *móno topikó*, "local only"), and you pay after you have made the call. Local, one-unit calls are reasonable enough (about €0.15 for the first three minutes), but long-distance ones add up quickly.

Other options for calling include a bare handful of **counter coin-op phones** in bars, kafenía and hotel lobbies; these should take small euro coins – probably five-cent, ten-cent, twenty-cent and fifty-cent denominations – and, unlike kerbside phone boxes, can be rung back. Most of them are made in northern Europe and bear instructions in English. You'll probably want to avoid making long-distance calls **from hotel rooms**, as a minimum one-hundred-percent surcharge will be slapped on – we've heard tales of triple and quadruple markups, and since hotels apparently have the legal right to do this, complaining to the tourist police is unlikely to get you anywhere.

For **international** (*exoterikó*) **calls**, it's again best to use kerbside card phones. You can no longer make metered calls from Greek telecoms offices (the OTE) themselves – most keep daytime hours only and offer at most a quieter card-phone or two. Like BT Phoneshops in the UK, they are mainly places to get Greece-based service (including OTE's own mobile network Cosmote), pay your bills, and buy one of an array of phones and fax machines for sale. **Faxes** are best sent from post offices and some travel agencies – at a price; receiving a fax may also incur a small charge. **Reverse charge** (*khréosis toú kalouménou* in Greek) or person-to-person calls, as well as **directory enquiries**, can be made from phone boxes or private subscriber phones using the appropriate operator numbers listed in the box.

Overseas phone calls with a 100-unit card will **cost**, approximately, €0.40 per minute to all EU countries and much of the rest of central Europe, North America and Australia – versus €0.28 per minute on a private subscriber line. There is no particular cheap rate for overseas calls to these destinations, and dialling countries with problematic phone systems like Russia, Israel or Egypt is obviously rather more. **Within Greece**, undiscounted **rates** are €0.16 per minute on a subscriber line, rather more from a card-phone; a twenty-percent discounted rate applies daily from 10pm to 8am, and from 10pm Saturday until 8am Monday.

Charge-card call services from Greece back to the home country are provided in the UK by British Telecom (Ⓣ0800/345144, Ⓦwww.chargecard.bt.com), and NTL Ⓣ0500/100505); in North America, Canada Direct, AT&T (Ⓣ0800/890 011, then 888-641-6123 when you hear the AT&T prompt to be transferred to the 24-hr Florida Call Centre), MCI and Sprint; in Australia, Optus (Ⓣ1300/300937) or Telstra (Ⓣ1800/038000), and in New Zealand Telecom NZ (Ⓣ04/801 9000). There are now a few local-dial numbers with some providers (given in the box opposite) which enable you to connect to the international network for the price of a one-unit call, and then charge the call to your home number – usually cheaper than the alternatives.

Mobile phones

Mobile phones are an essential fashion accessory in Greece, which has the highest per-capita usage in Europe outside Italy – in a population of roughly 11 million, there are claimed to be 6.5 million mobile handsets in use. There are three **networks** at present: Panafon-Vodafon, Telestet and Cosmote. Calling any of them from Britain, you will find that costs are exactly the same as calling a fixed phone – so you needn't worry about ringing them when given as alternative numbers for accommodation – though of course such numbers are pricey when rung locally. **Coverage** country-wide is fairly good, though there are a number of "dead" zones in the shadows of mountains, or on really remote islets. **Pay-as-you-go**, contract-free plans are heavily promoted in Greece (such as Telestet B-Free and Panafon-Vodafon À La Carte), so if you're going to be around for a while, an outlay of €90 or less will see you to a decent apparatus and your first calling card (though you can spend up to €200 for flash models). This lasts up to a year – even if you use up your talk time you'll still have an incoming number, along with a voice-mail service. Top-up calling cards – predicted to be in denominations of €6, €15 and €18 depending on the network – are available at all *períptera*.

Changes to Greek phone codes

All **area codes** in Greece are changed in 2002, owing to the Greek telecoms running out of land lines. A "0" was added to the end of each area code (thus Athens is now 010, Rhódhos Town 02410, Sámos 02730, etc), and – as in France – callers are obliged to dial all digits (the code, essentially now a prefix, plus subscriber number) whether they're in the same code/prefix area or not. In effect this means that there are no more area codes per se in Greece, merely ten-digit numbers. Moreover, late in 2002 the first '0' will become a '2' In the past OTE has been good about placing bilingual recordings on the line advising callers of number changes.

If you want to use your **home-based mobile abroad**, you'll need to check with your phone provider whether it will work. North American users will only be able to use tri-band rigs in Greece. Any GSM mobile from the UK, Australia or New Zealand should work fine in Greece.

In the UK, for all but top-of-the-range price plans, you'll have to inform your service network before going abroad to get international access ("**roaming**") switched on. You may get charged extra for this depending on the terms of your package and where you are travelling to. You are also likely to be charged extra for **incoming calls** when abroad, as the people calling you will be paying the usual rate; discount plans are available to reduce the cost of forwarding the call to you overseas by as much as seventy percent. If you want to **retrieve messages** while you're away, you'll have to ask your provider for a new access number, as your home one (or one-stroke "mail" key) is unlikely to work abroad.

In terms of **call charges**, experience (and examining UK-based bills) has shown that the network that you select out of the three Greek networks available makes little difference: depending on the length of the call, chat back to the UK (including voice-mail retrieval) works out at £0.49–55 per minute; ringing land-lines within Greece is £0.23–0.26 per minute; and calling Greek mobiles ranges from £0.30 to £0.43 per minute – all significantly more than using a card-phone, but worth it to most for the convenience and privacy.

Email and internet

Email and internet use has caught on in a big way in Greece; electronic addresses or websites are given in this guide for the growing number of travel companies and hotels that have them. For your own email needs, you're best off using the various **internet cafés** which have sprung up in the larger island towns – street addresses are given where appropriate. Rates tend to be €4.50 per hour maximum, often less.

Ideally you should sign up in advance for a free **internet email address** that can be accessed from anywhere, for example Yahoo or Hotmail – accessible through Ⓦwww.yahoo.com and Ⓦwww.hotmail.com. Once you've set up an account, you can use these sites to pick up and send mail from anywhere with internet access.

Alternatively, you can lug **your own laptop** around, not such a burden as they get progressively lighter. You will need about 2m of North American-standard cable (UK ones will *not* work), lightweight and easily purchasable in Greece, with RJ-11 male terminals at each end. The Greek **dial tone** is discontinuous and thus not recognized by most modems – instruct it to "ignore dial tone". Many newer hotel rooms have RJ-11 **sockets**, but some older ones still have their phones hard-wired into the wall. You can sometimes get around this problem with a female-female **adaptor**, either RJ-11- or 6P6C-configured, available at better electrical retailers. They weigh and cost next to nothing, so carry both (one is sure to work) for making a splice between your cable and the RJ-11 end of the cable between the wall and phone (which you simply unplug). You will usually have to dial an initial "9" or "0" to get around the hotel's central switchboard for a proper external dial tone.

Compuserve and AOL definitely have **points of presence** in Greece, but more obscure ISPs may also have a reciprocal agreement with Greek-based ISPs like forthnet.gr and otenet.gr, so ask your provider for a list of any available dial-up numbers. **Piggybacking charges** tend to be fairly high, but for a modest number of minutes per day, still work out rather less than patronizing an internet café.

The media

Although the Greek press and airwaves have been relatively free since the fall of the colonels' dictatorship in 1974, nobody would ever propose the Greek media as a paradigm of responsible or objective journalism. Papers are almost uniformly sensational, state-run radio and TV often biased in favour of the ruling party, and private channels imitative of the worst American programming. Most visitors will tune all this out, however, seeking solace in the music of private radio stations, or the limited number of English-language publications.

British **newspapers** are fairly widely available in Greece at a cost of €2–2.50 for dailies, or €3.50–4.20 for Sunday editions. Out on the islands, you'll find one to two-day-old copies of *The Times*, *The Telegraph*, *The Independent* and *The Guardian*'s European edition, plus a few of the tabloids, in all the resorts as well as in major towns. American and international alternatives include the turgid *USA Today* and the slightly more readable *International Herald Tribune*, the latter including as a major bonus a free though heavily abridged English translation of the respected Greek daily *Kathimerini* (online at Ⓦwww.eKathimerini.com; see also below). Among numerous foreign **magazines**, *Time* and *Newsweek* are also widely available.

There are relatively few surviving **locally produced** English-language magazines or papers. The late lamented **magazine** *The Athenian* folded in 1997 after 23 years, with a rather sloppy successor, *Atlantis*, rising less than phoenix-like from the ashes. Marginally better is the expensive, glossy *Odyssey*, produced every other month by and for wealthy diaspora Greeks, and little different from the average in-flight magazine. By far the best of the English-language **newspapers** is the four-colour *Athens News* (daily except Monday, online at Ⓦwww.athensnews.gr; €1.50) with good features and Balkan news, plus entertainment and arts listings on Friday, available in most resorts.

Before setting out from the **UK**, there are two **Greek-specific periodicals** well worth consulting. One is the *Anglo-Hellenic Review* (£2), published twice yearly by the Anglo-Hellenic League; it has excellent essays by renowned scholars, and good reviews of recently issued books on Greek topics. Obtain it either from the Hellenic Bookservice (see p.502) or The Hellenic Centre, 16–18 Paddington St, London W1M 4AS. The other is the Greek London Embassy's almost monthly newsletter, *Greece: Background-News-Information*. Though clearly pro-government to the point of verging on propaganda, it's well written (even humorous), giving a lively overview of events in the country over the past few weeks. To register on their mailing list (free), contact them on Ⓣ020/7727 3071, Ⓕ7727 8960 or email Ⓔofficepress@compuserve.com.

Greek publications

Although you will probably be excluded from the **Greek print media** by the double incomprehensibilities of alphabet and language, you can learn a fair bit about your Greek fellow travellers by their choice of broadsheet, so a quick survey of Greek magazines and newspapers won't go amiss.

Many papers have ties (including funding) with specific **political groups**, so their bias tends to decrease the already low quality of Greek dailies. Among these, only the **centrist** *Kathimerini* – whose former proprietress Helen Vlahos attained heroic status for her defiance of the junta – approaches the standards of a major European newspaper. *Eleftherotypia*, once a PASOK mouthpiece, now aspires to more independence, and has links with Britain's *The Guardian*; *Avriani* has taken its place as the PASOK cheerleading section. *Ta Nea* is a highly popular, MOR tabloid, vaguely similar to London's *Evening Standard* and much loved for its extensive small ads. On the far **Left**, *Avyi* is the

Eurocommunist/Synaspismós forum with literary leanings, while *Rizospastis* acts as the organ of the KKE (unreconstructed Communists). *Ethnos* became notorious some years back for receiving covert funding from the KGB to act as a disinformation bulletin. At the other end of the political spectrum, *Apoyevmatini* generally supports the **centre-right** Néa Dhimokratía party, while *Estia's* no-photo format and reactionary politics are both stuck somewhere at the beginning of the twentieth century. The ultra-nationalist, lunatic fringe is staked out by paranoid *Stohos* ("Our Goal: Greater Greece; Our Capital: Constantinople").

Among **magazines** that are not merely translations of overseas titles, *Takhydhromos* is the respectable news-and-features weekly; *Ena* is more sensationalist; *Ev* tells the growing yuppie class which exotic vacations, fancy wines and lifestyle accessories they need to burn their cash on; *Klik* is a crass rip-off of Britain's *The Face*; while *To Pondiki* (The Mouse) is a satirical weekly revue in the same vein as Britain's *Private Eye* – its famous covers are spot-on and accessible to anyone with minimal Greek. More specialized niches are occupied by low-circulation titles such as *Adhesmatos Typos* (a slightly rightist, muck-raking journal) and *Andi*, an intelligent bi-weekly somewhat in the mould of Britain's *New Statesman*.

Radio

If you have a **radio** on your personal stereo, playing dial roulette can be rewarding. Greek music programmes are always accessible (if variable in quality), and since abolition of the government's former monopoly of wavelengths, regional stations have mushroomed; indeed the airwaves are now positively cluttered as every island town sets up its own studio and transmitter. The two state-run channels are ER1 (a mix of news, talk and popular music) and ER2 (strictly popular music).

On heavily touristed islands like Rhodes, there will usually be at least one station on the FM band trying its luck at English-moderated programming by and for foreigners. The Turkish state radio's Third Channel is also widely (if somewhat unpatriotically) listened to on border islands for its classical, jazz and blues programmes. The **BBC World Service** broadcasts on short wave throughout Greece; 6.18, 9.41, 15.07 and 12.09 MHz are the most common frequencies. However, it has been announced that short-wave services are to be phased out in many parts of the world, so if you can't live without them consult Ⓦwww.bbc.co.uk/worldservice, which lists all their global frequencies. The **Voice of America**, with its transmitters on Rhodes, can be picked up in most of the Dodecanese on medium wave.

Television

Television first appeared in Greece in 1965, but it only became dominant during the 1967–74 junta, with the ruling colonels using it as a means of social control and to purvey anodyne variety revues, sports events and so on. As in many countries, it transformed the Greeks from a nation of live performers and coffee-house habitués to introverted stay-at-homes, which dovetailed nicely with the junta's "family values".

Greece's centralized, government-controlled **TV stations**, ET1, NET and (out of Thessaloníki) ET3, nowadays lag behind private, mostly rather right-wing channels – Antenna, Star, Alpha and Makedonia TV – in the ratings. Mega is the one possible exception to the rule of private dross, recently taken on by the Boutos family and improved beyond recognition. On NET, news summaries in English are broadcast daily at 6pm. Programming on all stations has evolved little since junta days, tending to be a mix of soaps (especially Italian, Spanish and Latin American), game shows, westerns, B-movies and sports. All foreign films and serials are broadcast in their original language, with Greek subtitles. Except for the nearly-round-the-clock channels Mega, Star, Alpha and Antenna, most channels broadcast from around noon until the small hours. Numerous **cable and satellite** channels are received, including CNN, MTV, Filmnet, Euronews (in English), French TV5 and Italian Rai Due. The range available depends on the area (and hotel) you're in.

Opening hours and public holidays

It is virtually impossible to generalize about Greek opening hours, except to say that they change constantly. The traditional timetable starts at a relatively civilized hour, with shops opening between 8.30 and 9.30am, then runs through until lunchtime, when there is a long break for the hottest part of the day. Most places, except banks and government offices, may then reopen in the mid- to late afternoon.

Tourist areas tend to adopt a slightly more northern-European timetable, with shops and offices, as well as the most important archeological sites and museums, usually open throughout the day.

Business and shopping hours

Most **government agencies** are open to the public on weekdays from 8am to 2pm. In general, however, you'd be optimistic to show up after 1pm expecting to be served the same day, as queues can be long. Private businesses, or anyone providing a service, frequently operate a straight 9am to 5/6pm schedule. If someone is actually selling something, then they are more likely to follow a split shift as detailed below.

Shopping hours during the hottest months are theoretically Monday, Wednesday and Saturday from approximately 9am to 2.30pm, and Tuesday, Thursday and Friday from 8.30am to 2pm and 6 to 9pm. During the cooler months the morning schedule shifts slightly forward, the evening session a half or even a full hour back. But there are so many exceptions to these rules by virtue of holidays and professional idiosyncrasy that you can't count on getting anything done except from Monday to Friday, between 9.30am and 1pm. It's worth noting that **delis** and **butchers** are not allowed to sell fresh meat during summer afternoons (though some flout this rule); similarly **fishmongers** are only open in the morning until they sell out (usually by noon), as are **pharmacies**, which additionally are shut on Saturday (except for the duty pharmacist).

All of the above opening hours will be regularly thrown out of sync by the numerous public holidays and festivals – or the equally numerous strikes, which can be general or profession-specific. The most important holidays, when almost everything will be closed, are listed in the box below.

Ancient sites and monasteries

All the major **ancient sites** are now fenced off and, like most **museums**, charge **admission**

Public holidays

January 1
January 6
March 25
First Monday of Lent (48 days before Easter; see below)
Easter weekend (variable April/May; see below)
May 1
Pentecost or Whit Monday (50 days after Easter; see below)
August 15
October 28
December 25 & 26

Variable religious feasts

Lenten Monday

2002	March 18
2003	March 10
2004	Feb 23

Easter Sunday

2002	May 5
2003	April 27
2004	April 11

Whit Monday

2002	June 24
2003	June 16
2004	May 31

fees ranging from a token €1.50 to a whopping €6, with an average fee of around €2.40. At most of them reductions of twenty-five to thirty percent apply to senior citizens, and fifty percent to students with proper identification – students from the EU with proper ID will often get in free. In addition, entrance to all state-run sites and museums is **free** to EU nationals on Sundays and public holidays from November to March – non-EU nationals are unlikely to be detected as such unless they go out of their way to advertise the fact.

Opening hours vary from site to site. As far as possible, individual times are quoted in the text, but bear in mind that these change with exasperating frequency, and at smaller sites may be subject to the whim of a local *fýlakas* or site guard. Unless specified, the times quoted are generally summer hours, in effect from around late May to the end of September. Reckon on similar days but later opening and earlier closing in winter. Note also that the **last admission ticket** is typically sold fifteen to twenty minutes before the cited closing time.

Along with your ticket most sites and museums will provide a little colour **folding pamphlet** prepared by the *Tamío Arheoloyikón Porón* or TAP (Archeological Receipts Fund); they usually include an accurate if potted history and site or gallery plan, and we've found them to be uniformly excellent, in stark contrast to the often miserable labelling of the sites or galleries themselves. Serious students will therefore want to invest in **site guides** or **museum catalogues**, which have often been expertly compiled by the excavating archeologists or curators.

Smaller sites generally close for a long lunch and **siesta** (even where they're not supposed to), as do **monasteries**. The latter are generally open from 9am to 1pm and 5 to 8pm (3.30 to 6.30pm in winter) for limited visits. Most monasteries impose a fairly strict **dress code** for visitors: no shorts on either sex, with women expected to cover their arms and wear skirts; the necessary wraps are sometimes provided on the spot for the "indecently attired".

It's free to take **photographs** of open-air sites, though museum photography or the use of tripods or video cameras anywhere requires an extra fee and a written permit. This must be arranged well in advance and in writing with the relevant Department of Antiquities (*Eforía Arheotíton*). For Rhodes and all of the Dodecanese, it's best to fax requests to Ⓕ02410/31 048; for Sámos, to Ⓕ010/32 51 096; and for Lésvos, Híos and Límnos, to Ⓕ02510/20 745. It's also worth knowing that Classical studies students can get a free annual pass to all Greek museums and sites by presenting themselves at the office on the rear corner (Tossítsa/Bouboulínas) of the National Archeological Museum in Athens – take documentation, two passport-sized photographs and be prepared to say you're a teacher.

Festivals and cultural events

Many of the big Greek festivals have a religious basis, so they're observed in accordance with the Orthodox calendar. Give or take a few saints, this is similar to the regular Catholic liturgical year, except for Easter, which can fall as many as five (but usually one or two) weeks to either side of the western festival – in 2001 the two coincided (a very rare event).

Easter

Easter is by far the most important festival of the Greek year – infinitely more so than Christmas – and taken much more seriously than it is anywhere in western Europe, aside from Spain. From Wednesday of Holy Week until the following Monday, the state radio and TV networks are given over solely to religious programmes.

The **festival** is an excellent time to be in Greece, both for its beautiful religious ceremonies and for the days of feasting and celebration that follow. The remote village of Ólymbos on **Kárpathos** or Pyrgí on **Híos**, and the monastery of Ayíou Ioánnou Theológou on **Pátmos**, are the prime Easter venues among the islands in this guide, but unless you plan well in advance you have no hope of finding accommodation at that time.

The first great public ceremony takes place on **Good Friday** evening as the Descent from the Cross is lamented in church. At dusk the **Epitáfios**, Christ's funeral bier, lavishly decorated with flowers by the women of each parish (in large villages there will be more than one, from each church), leaves the sanctuary and is paraded solemnly through the streets. In many places this is accompanied by the burning of effigies of Judas Iscariot.

Late Saturday evening sees the climax in a majestic **Anástasis** Mass to celebrate Christ's triumphant return. At the stroke of midnight all the lights in every crowded church are extinguished, plunging the congregation into the darkness that envelops Christ as He passes through the underworld. Then there's a faint glimmer of light behind the altar screen before the priest appears, holding aloft a lighted taper and chanting *"Avtó to Fós . . ."* ("This is the Light of the World"). Stepping down to the level of the parishioners, he touches his flame to the unlit candle of the nearest worshippers, intoning *"Dhévteh, láveteh Fós"* ("Come, take the Light"). Those at the front of the congregation and on the aisles do the same for their neighbours until the entire church – and the outer courtyard, where it's standing room only for latecomers – is ablaze with burning candles and the miracle reaffirmed.

Even the most committed agnostic is likely to find this moving. The traditional greeting, as an arsenal's worth of fireworks explode around you in the street (and up in the sky at wealthier villages), is *"Khristós Anésti"* ("Christ is risen"), to which the response is *"Alithós Anésti"* ("Truly He is Risen"). In the week up to Easter Sunday you should wish people *"Kaló Páskha"* (Happy Easter); on or after the day, you say *"Khrónia Pollá"* ("Many Happy Returns").

Worshippers then take the burning **candles** home; they are said to bring good fortune on the house if they arrive still burning. On reaching the front door it is common practice to make the sign of the cross on the lintel with the flame, leaving a black smudge visible for the rest of the year. The forty-day **Lenten fast** – still observed by the devout and in rural areas – is traditionally broken early on Sunday morning with a meal of *mayerítsa*, a soup made from lamb tripe, rice, dill and lemon. The rest of the lamb will be roasted on spits for Sunday lunch, and festivities often take place through the rest of the day.

The Greek equivalent of **Easter eggs** are hard-boiled eggs (painted red on Holy Thursday), which are baked into twisted, sweet bread-loaves (*tsouréki*) or distributed on Easter Sunday. People rap their eggs against their friends', and the owner of the last uncracked one is considered lucky.

The festival calendar

Most of the other Greek festivals are in honour of one or another of a multitude of **saints**, the most important of which are detailed in box pp.72–73. A village or church bearing a saint's name is a fair guarantee of some observance – sometimes a lively festival right across the town or island, otherwise quiet, local and consisting of little more than a special liturgy and banners adorning the chapel in question. Saints' days are also celebrated as **name days**; if you learn that it's an acquaintance's name day, you wish them *Khrónia Pollá* ("Many Years", as in "Many Happy Returns"). Also listed are a few more **secular holidays**, most enjoyable of which are the pre-Lenten carnivals.

In addition to the specific dates mentioned, there are literally scores of **local festivals** (*paniyíria*) celebrating the patron saint of the village church. With hundreds of possible name-saints' days (liturgical calendars list two or three, often arcane, for each day) you're unlikely to travel around Greece for long without stumbling on something.

It is important to remember the concept of the *paramoní*, or **eve of the festival**. Most of the events listed overleaf are celebrated on the night before, so if you show up on the morning of the date given you will very probably have missed any music, dancing or drinking.

Other Festivals

January 1
New Year's Day (*Protokhroniá*) in Greece is the feast day of Áyios Vassílios (St Basil), and is celebrated with church services and the baking of a special loaf, *vassilópitta*, in which a coin is baked that brings its finder good luck throughout the year. The traditional New Year greeting is "*Kalí Khroniá*".

January 6
Epiphany (*Áyia Theofánia*, or *Fóta* for short), when the *kalikántzari* (hobgoblins) who run riot on earth during the twelve days of Christmas are rebanished to the nether world by various rites of the Church. The most important of these is the blessing of baptismal fonts and all outdoor bodies of water. At seaside locations, the priest traditionally casts a crucifix into the deep, with local youths competing for the privilege of recovering it.

Pre-Lenten carnivals
These – known in Greek as *Apokriátika* – span three weeks, climaxing during the seventh weekend before Easter. Amongst the islands covered in this guide, Lésvos (Ayiássos) and Kárpathos (Ólymbos) have the most elaborate festivities. *Katharí Dheftéra* (Lenten Monday) of the last carnival week is always seven weeks (48 days, to be precise) before Easter Sunday.

March 25
The feast of the **Annunciation** (*Evangelismós* in Greek) is both a religious and a national holiday, with, on the one hand, military parades and dancing to celebrate the beginning of the revolt against Ottoman rule in 1821, and, on the other, church services to honour the news being given to Mary that she was to become the Mother of Christ. There are major festivities at any locality with a monastery or church named Evangelístria or Evangelismós.

April 23
The feast of **Áyios Yeóryios** (**St George**), the patron of shepherds, is a big rural celebration, with much dancing and feasting at associated shrines and towns. If April 23 falls before Easter, ie during Lent, the festivities are postponed until the Monday after Easter.

May 1
May Day is the great urban holiday when townspeople traditionally make for the countryside for picnics and return with bunches of wild flowers. Wreaths are hung on their doorways or balconies until they are burnt in bonfires on St John's Eve (June 23). There are also large demonstrations by the Left, claiming the *Ergatikí Protomayiá* (Working-Class First of May) as their own.

May 21
The feast of **Áyios Konstandínos** (St Constantine) and his mother, **Ayía Eléni** (St Helen), widely observed as the name day for two of the more popular Christian names in Greece.

May/June
The **Monday of Áyio Pnévma** (the Holy Spirit, Whit Monday) marks the descent of the same to the assembled disciples, fifty days after Easter. Usually only a modest liturgy celebrated at rural chapels of the Holy Spirit, gaily decked out with pennants, but this is the major festival day at Pagóndhas, Sámos, with live music on the preceding evening.

June 29–30
The joint feast of **Áyios Pétros and Áyios Pávlos** (saints Peter and Paul), two of the more widely celebrated name days, is on the 29th. Celebrations often run together for the Gathering of (all) the Holy Apostles (Áyii Apóstoli), on the 30th.

July 17
The feast of **Ayía Marína**: a big event in rural areas, as she's an important protector of crops. The eponymous port town on Léros will be en fête, as will Ayía Marína village on Kássos. Between mid-July and mid-September there are religious festivals every few days, especially in rural areas, and between these and the summer heat, ordinary business slows or even halts.

July 20
The feast of **Profítis Ilías** (the Prophet Elijah) is celebrated at the countless hilltop shrines of Profítis Ilías, notably the ones on Rhodes and Sámos, where folk keep all-night vigils.

July 22
The feast of **Ayía Markélla** (St Marcelle – not

the same one as in the Catholic calendar). The major festival of northern Híos.

July 26
The feast of **Ayía Paraskeví**; celebrated in parishes or villages bearing that name, for example on Lésvos and Sámos.

July 27
The feast of **Áyios Pandelímon** (St Pantaleon); liveliest and longest festival at the eponymous monastery on Tílos, with a smaller bash on Agathoníssi.

August 6
Metamórfosis toú Sotíros (Transfiguration of the Saviour) provides another excuse for celebrations, particularly at Khristós Ráhon village on Ikaría, at Plátanos on Léros, and on Psará. On Hálki the date is marked by messy food fights with flour, eggs and squid ink, so beware.

August 15
Apokímisis tís Panayías (Assumption or Dormition of the Blessed Virgin Mary). This is the day when people traditionally return to their home village, and in many places there will be no accommodation available on any terms. Even some Greeks will resort to sleeping in the streets. There are especially major festivities at Ayiássos on Lésvos, at the Panayía Kyrá monastery on Níssyros, at Ólymbos on Kárpathos and at several locations on Kálymnos. Curiously, Lipsí celebrates its own Marian festival on the 23rd–24th.

August 29
Apokefálisis toú Prodhrómou (Beheading of John the Baptist). Popular pilgrimages and celebrations at Vrykoúnda on Kárpathos, and the namesake monastery near Kéfalos on Kós.

September 8
Yénisis tís Panayías (Birth of the Virgin Mary) sees special services in churches dedicated to the event; at Vourliótes on Sámos, next to Vrondianí monastery, a particularly lively festival takes place the night before. There's also a major pilgrimage of childless women to Tsambíka monastery, Rhodes.

September 14
A last major summer festival, the **Ípsosis toú Stavroú** (Exaltation of the Cross), keenly observed on Hálki, and also Níssyros.

September 26
The feast of **Áyios Ioánnis Theológos** (St John the Divine), observed on Níssyros and Pátmos.

October 26
The feast of **Áyios Dhimítrios** (St Demetrius), another popular name day. In rural areas new wine is traditionally broached on this day, a good excuse for general inebriation.

October 28
Óhi Day, the year's major patriotic shindig – a national holiday with parades, folk dancing and speechifying to commemorate Metaxas's apocryphal one-word reply to Mussolini's 1940 ultimatum: "*Ohi!*" (No!).

November 8
Another popular name day, the feast of the **Archangels Michael and Gabriel** (Mihaïl and Gavriïl, or Taxiárhon), marked by rites at the numerous churches named after them, particularly at Arhángelos village on Rhodes, Asómati village on Kós, the rural monastery of Taxiárhis on Sými, and the big monastery of Mandamádhos, Lésvos.

December 6
The feast of **Áyios Nikólaos** (St Nicholas), the patron of seafarers, with many chapels dedicated to him.

December 25
A much less festive occasion than Greek Easter, **Christmas** (*Khristoúyenna*) is still an important religious feast. In recent years it has acquired all of the commercial trappings of the western Christmas, with decorations, Christmas trees and gifts. December 26 is not Boxing Day as in England, but the *Sýnaxis tís Panayías* (Gathering of the Virgin's Entourage).

December 31
New Year's Eve (*Paramoní Protokhroniá*), when, as on the other twelve days of Christmas, a few children still go door to door singing the traditional *kálanda* (carols), receiving money in return. Adults tend to sit around playing cards, often for money. The *vassilópitta* is cut at midnight (see January 1).

Cultural festivals and cinema

As well as religious festivals, Greece has a full range of cultural events, including a few on the more popular islands. A leaflet entitled *Greek Festivals*, available from GNTO offices abroad, includes details of smaller, local festivals of music, drama and dance which take place more sporadically. The major festivals falling within the scope of this guide are the **Rhodes Festival** (Aug–Oct), the **Ippokrateia** events on **Kós** (Aug), and the up-and-coming **Sými Festival** (July–Sept) – including events on surrounding islands – as well as the more low-key Manolis Kalomiris and Wine festivals on Sámos (July–Aug) and the Lesviakó Kalokéri/Lesbian Summer on Lésvos.

Greek **cinemas** show a large number of fairly recent American and British movies, always in the **original language**, with Greek subtitles. **Indoor** screenings are highly affordable, currently €5–7 depending on location and plushness of facilities; they shut from mid-May to late September unless they have air conditioning. Accordingly in summer numbers of **outdoor** cinemas set up shop; an outdoor movie (marginally cheaper) is worth catching at least once for the experience alone, though it's best to opt for the earlier screening (about 9pm) since the soundtrack on any later show tends to be turned down or even off to avoid complaints from adjacent residences. Summer cinemas are found on Lésvos, Híos, Ikaría, Sámos, Kálymnos, Astypálea, Kós and Rhodes; winter cinemas operate on Límnos Lésvos, Híos, Sámos, Kálymnos, Kós and Rhodes. Playbills and programmes from October to May tend to be in Greek only.

Watersports

The Greek seashore offers endless scope for watersports, with windsurfing boards for rent in most resorts and, less reliably, waterskiing and parasailing facilities.

The years since the mid-1980s have seen a massive growth in the popularity of **windsurfing** in Greece. The country's bays and coves are ideal for beginners, and boards can be rented in literally hundreds of resorts. Particularly good areas, most with established schools, include the coasts of Sámos (Kokkári), Lésvos (Pétra, Skála Kallonís), Kós (Kamári and Tingáki), Kárpathos (Afiárti) and Rhodes (Prassoníssi and the west coast). You can almost always find a beginner's course of instruction, and rental rates are very reasonable – about €10 an hour.

Waterskiing is available at a number of the larger resorts, such as Faliráki on Rhodes, and a few of the smaller ones. By the crippling rental standards of the ritzier parts of the Mediterranean it's a bargain, with twenty minutes' instruction often available for around €13–16. At many resorts, **parasailing** (*parapént* in Greek) is also possible; rates start at €18 a go.

A combination of steady winds, appealing seascapes and numerous natural harbours have long made the Greek islands a tremendous place for **sailing**. Holiday companies offer all sorts of packaged and tailor-made cruises (see pp.14, 17 & 18). Locally, small boats and dinghies are rented out by the day at many resorts. Larger craft can be chartered by the week or longer, either bare-boat or with skipper, from several marinas in the Dodecanese and the east Aegean. Rhodes is by far the busiest (see Ródhos Town "Listings" for local agencies), and justifiably so given the garland of small, interesting islands less than a day's sail away. Kálymnos is also a major sailing centre, while marinas have been completed or are under construction at Kós and Sámos. There is relatively little sailing activity north of Sámos owing to the enormous distances of open sea between the east Aegean islands, and the relatively poor anchorage when you finally arrive.

Spring and autumn are the most pleasant and least expensive times; *meltémi* winds

Public beaches, sunbeds and umbrellas

Not many people realize that all **beaches** in Greece are public land; that's understandable, given the extent to which luxury hotels encroach on them, and the sunbeds and umbrellas that carpet entire strands. Greek **law**, however, is very clear that the shore from the winter high-tide mark down to the water must be freely accessible, with a right of way provided around hotels or resorts, and that no permanent structures be built in that zone. Accordingly, you should resist pressure to pay rental for unwanted **sunbeds** or **umbrellas**, particularly the latter, which are often anchored with permanent, illegal concrete lugs buried in the sand. Beaches entirely or relatively free of such obstacles are noted in the guide.

make for pretty nauseating sailing between late June and early September, and summer **rates** for the same craft can be three times as high as shoulder-season prices. For more details, contact the Hellenic Yachting Federation, Akti Navárhou Koundourióti 7, 185 34 Pireás ⓣ010/41 37 351, ⓕ41 31 119.

Because of the potential for pilfering submerged antiquities, **scuba diving** is severely restricted around the Dodecanese and the east Aegean. Its legal practice is confined among these islands to short stretches of coast off Rhodes, Kálymnos and (best of all) Léros. For an update on the situation – permitted areas are slowly being added since a liberalization in policy was announced by the Ministry of Culture – contact the Union of Greek Diving Centres (ⓣ010/92 29 532 or 41 18 909), or request the sporadically available information sheet *Regulations Concerning Underwater Activities* from the nearest overseas branch of the GNTO.

Trouble, crime and sexual harassment

As in the past, Greece remains one of Europe's safest countries, with a low crime rate and a deserved reputation for honesty. If you leave a bag or wallet at a café, you'll most likely find it scrupulously looked after, pending your return. Similarly, Greeks are relatively relaxed about leaving possessions unlocked or unattended on the beach, in rooms or on campsites. The biggest hazards on beaches, oddly, are free-ranging goats – who will eat just about anything left accessible – and the wake of passing cruise ships or ferries, which can wash all your possessions out to sea with little or no warning.

In recent years, however, there has been a large increase in **theft** and **crimes against persons** (blamed largely on Albanian and Romanian refugees) throughout the country, so it's wise to lock things up and treat Greece like any other European destination. Following are also a few pointers on offences that might get you into trouble locally, and some advice on sexual harassment – still a lingering fact of life given the classically Mediterranean machismo of Greek culture.

Specific offences

The most common causes of a brush with authority are nude bathing or sunbathing, camping outside an authorized site and taking photographs in forbidden areas.

Nude bathing is legal on only a very few beaches (most notably on Rhodes, Sámos and Lésvos), and is deeply offensive to the more traditional Greeks – exercise considerable sensitivity to local feeling and the kind of place you're in. It is, for example, very bad etiquette to swim or sunbathe nude within sight of a church, of which there are many along the Greek coast. Generally, if a beach has become fairly well established as naturist, or is well secluded, it's highly unlikely that the police are going to come charging in. Where they do get bothered is if they feel a place is turning into a "hippie beach" or nudity is getting too overt on mainstream tourist stretches. Most of the time, the only action will be a warning, but you can officially be arrested straight off – facing up to three days in jail and a stiff fine.

Topless (sun)bathing for women is technically legal nationwide, but specific locales often opt out of the "liberation" by posting signs, which should be heeded.

Very similar guidelines apply to **camping rough**, which has been theoretically illegal nationwide since 1977 (see p.54). Even for this you're still unlikely to incur anything more than a warning to move on. The only real risk of arrest is if you are told to clear off and fail to do so. In either of the above cases, even if the police do take any action against you, it's more likely to be a brief spell in their cells than any official prosecution.

The well-publicized experience of twelve British plane-spotters who languished in Greek jails for over a month in late 2001 on absurd espionage charges – despite having been invited to the military air show in question – should serve as ample incentive to **take no pictures at all in and around airports or military installations**. The latter are usually well festooned with international 'NO PHOTOS' pictographs, and post-September 11 the army is apt to be extra twitchy about this. "No pictures at all" includes farewell snaps of your loved ones on the runway; you just don't know what the authorities will claim is in the background of your viewfinder, and indeed many island civilian airports double as airforce bases.

Incidentally, any sort of **disrespect** towards the Greek state or Orthodox Church in general, or Greek civil servants in particular, may be construed as offences in the most literal sense, so it's best to keep your comments on how things are working (or not) to yourself. Every year a few foreign louts on Rhodes and Kós find themselves in deep trouble over a drunken indiscretion. This is a society where verbal injuries count, with a consistent backlog of court cases dealing with the alleged public utterance of *malákas* (wanker).

In the non-verbal field, ripped or soiled clothes and untucked-in shirts are considered nearly as insulting. Don't expect a uniformly civil reception if dressed in **grunge attire**, since Greeks will interpret this in one of two possible ways, neither reflecting well on you. Poverty is an uncomfortably close memory for many, and they may consider that you're making light of hard times. More to the point, the cult of *la bella figura* is developed to near-Italian levels in Greece; if you clearly have so little self-respect as to appear slovenly and dishevelled in public, why should any Greek respect you?

The hours **between 3 and 5pm**, the mid-day siesta, are sacrosanct – one does not make phone calls, visits to people you're not acquainted with, or any sort of noise during this time. **Quiet** is also enforced **between midnight and 8am**; construction crews are obliged to observe this, and they do so punctiliously, commencing hammering next door to your lodgings at 8.01am (or even 7.59am). There is nothing you can do about this, as they are within their rights.

Drug offences are treated as major crimes, particularly since there's a mushrooming local use and addiction problem. The maximum penalty for "causing the use of drugs by someone under 18", for example, is life imprisonment and an astronomical fine. Theory is by no means practice, but foreigners caught in possession of even small amounts of grass do get long jail sentences if there's evidence that they've been supplying the drug to others. Moreover, you could be inside for well over a year awaiting a trial date, with little or no chance of bail being granted.

If you get arrested for any offence, you have a right to contact your **consulate**, who will arrange a lawyer for your defence. Beyond this, there is little they can, or in most cases will, do. There is an honorary British consulate on Rhodes, but otherwise the closest bona fide UK/North American/Australian diplomatic representation to the islands covered is in Athens or Thessaloníki.

In an emergency, dial ⓣ100 for the police; ⓣ166 for an ambulance; ⓣ191 to report a forest fire; and ⓣ199 for the urban fire brigade. These calls should all be toll-free from a card-phone.

Sexual harassment

Thousands of women travel independently around the Dodecanese and east Aegean without being **harassed** or feeling intimidated. Greek machismo, however, remains strong, if less upfront than in, for example, southern Italy. With the recent sea change in local mores – specifically, a vast increase in the "availability" of young Greek women to young local men, up to and including living together before marriage – much of the impetus for trying one's luck with foreign girls has faded. Any hassle you do get is likely to be from a dwindling minority of professionally single Greek men, known as *kamákia* (fish harpoons), who migrate in summer to the beach bars and discos of the main resorts and towns, specifically in pursuit of "liberated, fun-loving" tourists. Indigenous Greeks, who become increasingly protective of you as you become more of a fixture in any one place, treat these outsiders with contempt; their obvious stakeouts are waterfront cafés, beach bars and dance clubs. Words worth remembering as unambiguous responses include "*pápsteh*" (stop it), "*afísteh meh*" (leave me alone) and "*fíyeteh*" (go away), the latter intensified if followed by "*dhrómo!*" (road, as in "Hit the road!").

Hitching is not advisable for lone women travellers, but **camping** is generally not a problem, though away from recognized sites it is often wise to attach yourself to a local family by making arrangements to use nearby private land. In the more remote islands you may feel more uncomfortable travelling alone. The intensely traditional Greeks may have trouble understanding why you are unaccompanied, and might not welcome your presence in their exclusively male kafenía – often the only place where you can get a drink. Travelling with a man, you're more likely to be treated as a *xéni*, a word meaning both (female) stranger and guest.

Lone men need to be aware of one long-established racket in the port towns of the more populous islands. You may be approached by dubious gents asking the time, or your origins, and then offering to take you for a drink in a nearby bar. This is invariably staffed with hostesses (who may also be on the game) whose main job is to convince you to treat them to drinks. At the end of the night you'll be landed with an outrageous bill, some of which goes towards the hostess's "commission"; physical threats are brought to bear on reluctant payers.

Work

Since Greece's full accession to the European Union in early 1993, a citizen of any EU state has (in theory) the right to work in Greece. In practice, however, there are a number of bureaucratic hurdles to overcome. Formerly, the most common job for foreigners was teaching English in the numerous private cramming academies (*frondistíria*), but lately severe restrictions have been put on the availability of such positions for non-Greeks, and you will more likely be involved in a commercial or leisure-oriented trade. The influx, since 1990, of between 800,000 and a 1.1 million (estimates vary) Albanians, Ukrainians, Bulgarians, Pakistanis, Moldovans, Russians, Somalis, Filipinos and others has resulted in a surplus of unskilled labour and severely depressed wages for casual labour.

Tourism-related work

Most women working casually in Greece find jobs in **bars** or **restaurants** around the main resorts. Men, unless they are "trained" chefs, will be edged out by Albanians even when it comes to washing up.

If you're waiting or serving, most of your wages will probably have to come from tips but you may well be able to get a deal that includes free food and lodging; evening-only hours can be a good shift, leaving you a lot of free time. The main drawback may be the machismo and/or chauvinist attitudes of your employer. (Ads in the local press for "girl bar staff" are certainly best ignored; see "Sexual Harassment" above.) Rhodes, with its big British slant, is an obvious choice for bar work; Kós, Kálymnos, Sámos and Lésvos are also promising. Start looking, if you can, around April or May; you'll get better rates at this time if you're taken on for a season. On a similar, unofficial level you might be able to get a sales job in **tourist shops**, or (if you've the expertise) helping out at one of the **windsurfing** schools that have sprung up all around the coast.

Perhaps the best type of tourism-related work, however, is that of courier/greeter/group co-ordinator for a **package holiday company**. All you need is EU nationality and language proficiency compatible with the clientele, though knowledge of Greek is a big plus. English-only speakers are pretty well restricted to places with a significant British package trade, namely Rhodes, Sámos, Kós and Lésvos.

Many such staff are recruited through ads in newspapers issued outside Greece, but it's by no means unheard of to be hired on the spot in April or May. A big plus, however you're taken on, is that you're usually guaranteed about six months of steady work, often with use of a car thrown in, and that if things work out you may be re-employed the following season with contract and foreign-currency wages from the home company, not from the local affiliate.

Documentation for legal employment

If you plan to work professionally for someone else, you first visit the nearest Department of Employment (in Rhodes, on the Street of the Knights, Odhós Ippotón) and collect two forms: one an **employment application** which you fill in, the other for the formal offer of work by your prospective employer. Once these are vetted, and revenue stamps (*hartósima*, purchased at kiosks) applied, you take them to the Alien's Bureau (Ypiresía Allodhapón) or, in its absence, the central police station, to support your application for a **residence permit** (*ádhia paramonís*). For this, you will also need to bring your passport, six photographs, more *hartósima* and a stable address (not a hotel). Permits are given for terms of one year (green triptych booklets), or five years (white booklets) if they've become well acquainted with you.

You should allow four to six weeks for all the formalities to be completed; the bottleneck is usually the required **health examination** at the nearest public hospital. There you will be chest X-rayed for signs of TB, blood-tested for hepatitis B & C, HIV and a couple of other nasties, and have a (farcical) evaluation by a neurologist or psychiatrist for signs of mental disorder; this is all done at a reasonable cost. Usually some crucial consultant is on holiday, delaying the proceedings; once you've assembled all the results, you'll have to trot these over yourself to the local public health office, where a periodic (once weekly at best) meeting of its administrative council will vet and endorse these, and issue you with a certificate of approval. Finally you take this to the local police or Alien's Bureau, which should have your permit ready, free of charge other than for a few more *hartósima*, within three working days.

As a **self-employed professional**, you must satisfy the requirements of the Greek state with equivalent qualifications to native Greeks plying the same trade. You should also befriend a good accountant, who will advise you on which of the several varieties of incorporation are to your advantage; trading under a corporate name is vastly more expensive tax-wise than doing business as a private person. You will need to sign on with **TEBE**, the Greek National Insurance scheme for self-employed people (analogous to Class 2 National Insurance contributions in the UK). If you are continuing to contribute to a social insurance scheme in a country which has reciprocal agreements with Greece (all EU states do), this must be proved in writing – a tedious and protracted process.

Once you're square with TEBE, visit the tax office or *eforía* to be issued a **tax number** (abbreviated "ah-fi-mi" in Greek, similar to a UK Schedule D number) which must be cited in all transactions. To be issued one of these, you need to bring a birth certificate which shows the full unmarried names of *both* your parents. You will be required to prepare receipt and invoice books with your tax number professionally printed on them, or have a rubber stamp made up for applying that number to every sheet. The tax office will also determine which rate of **VAT** (the "fi-pi-ah") you should pay for each kind of transaction; VAT returns must be filed every two months, which is where a friendly accountant comes in handy again.

The self-employed tend to be issued five-year residence permits. **EU nationals** who do not wish to work in Greece but still need a residence permit (eg property-owners needing to set up a bank account) will still get a "white" pass gratis, but must present evidence of financial solvency; personalized pink exchange receipts, travellers' cheques or credit cards are all considered valid proofs.

At present, undocumented **non-EU nationals** who wish to work in Greece do so surreptitiously, with the ever-present risk of denunciation to the police and instant deportation. Having been forced to accept large numbers of EU citizens looking for jobs in a climate of rising unemployment, Greek immigration authorities are cracking down hard on any suitable targets, be they Albanian, African, Swiss or North American. That old foreigners' standby, teaching English, is now available only to TEFL certificate-holders – preferably Greeks, non-EU nationals of Greek descent, and EU nationals in that order. If you are a non-EU foreign national of Greek descent, you are termed *omólogos* (returned Greek diaspora member) and in fact have tremendous employment, taxation and residence rights and privileges – you can, for example, open your very own *frondistírio* without any qualifications, something starkly evident in the often abysmal quality of language instruction – and disseminated printed material – in Greece).

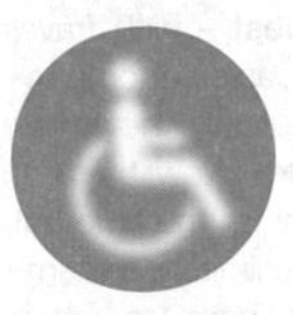

Travellers with disabilities

It is all too easy to wax lyrical over the attractions of Greece: the stepped, narrow alleys, the ease of travel by bus and ferry, the thrill of clambering around the great archeological sites. It is almost impossible, on the other hand, for the able-bodied travel writer to see these attractions as potential hazards for anyone who has difficulty in walking, is wheelchair-bound or suffers from some other disability.

However, don't be discouraged. It is possible to enjoy an inexpensive and trauma-free holiday in Greece if some time is devoted to gathering **information** before arrival. Much existing or readily available information is out of date – you should always try to double-check. A number of addresses of contact organizations are published below. The Greek National Tourist Office is a good first step as long as you have specific questions to put to them; they publish a useful questionnaire which you could send to hotels or owners of apartment/villa accommodation.

Contacts for travellers with disabilities

In the UK and Ireland

Access Travel 6 The Hillock, Astley, Lancashire M29 7GW ⓣ01942/888844, ⓦwww.access-travel.co.uk. A tour operator that can arrange flights, transfer and accommodation. This is a small business, personally checking out places before recommendation. They can guarantee accommodation standards on Rhodes in particular. ATOL bonded, established since early 1990s.

Disability Action Group 2 Annadale Ave, Belfast BT7 3JH ⓣ028/9049 1011. Provides information about access for disabled travellers abroad.

Holiday Care 2nd floor, Imperial Building, Victoria Rd, Horley, Surrey RH6 7PZ ⓣ01293/774535, Minicom ⓣ01293/776943, ⓦwww.holidaycare.org.uk. Provides free lists of accessible accommodation abroad – European, American and long-haul destinations – plus a list of accessible attractions in the UK. Information on financial help for holidays is available.

Irish Wheelchair Association Blackheath Drive, Clontarf, Dublin 3 ⓣ01/833 8241, ⓕ833 3873, ⓔiwa@iol.ie. Useful information provided on travelling abroad with a wheelchair.

Tripscope Alexandra House, Albany Rd, Brentford, Middlesex TW8 0NE ⓣ08457/585641, ⓦwww.justmobility.co.uk/tripscope. This registered charity provides a national telephone information service offering free advice on UK and international transport for those with a mobility problem.

In US and Canada

Access-Able ⓦwww.access-able.com. Online resource for travellers with disabilities.

Directions Unlimited 123 Green Lane, Bedford Hills, NY 10507 ⓣ1-800/533-5343 or 914/241-1700. Tour operator specializing in custom tours for people with disabilities.

Mobility International USA 451 Broadway, Eugene, OR 97401 Voice and TDD ⓣ541/343-1284, ⓦwww.miusa.org. Information and referral services, access guides, tours and exchange programmes. Annual membership $35 (includes quarterly newsletter).

Society for the Advancement of Travelers with Handicaps (SATH) 347 5th Ave, New York, NY 10016 ⓣ212/447-7284, ⓦwww.sath.org. A non-profit educational organization that has actively represented travellers with disabilities since 1976.

Travel Information Service ⓣ215/456-9600. Telephone-only information and referral service.

Twin Peaks Press Box 129, Vancouver, WA 98661 ⓣ360/694-2462 or 1-800/637-2256, ⓦwww.twinpeak.virtualave.net. Publisher of the *Directory of Travel Agencies for the Disabled* ($19.95), listing more than 370 agencies worldwide; *Travel for the Disabled* ($19.95); the *Directory of Accessible Van Rentals* ($12.95) and *Wheelchair Vagabond* ($19.95), loaded with personal tips.

Wheels Up! ⓣ1-888/389-4335, ⓦwww.wheelsup.com. Provides discounted airfare, tour and cruise prices for disabled travellers, also publishes a free monthly newsletter and has a comprehensive website.

In Australia and New Zealand

ACROD (Australian Council for Rehabilitation of the Disabled) PO Box 60, Curtin ACT 2605 ⓣ02/6282 4333; 24 Cabarita Rd, Cabarita NSW 2137 ⓣ02/9743 2699. Provides lists of travel agencies and tour operators for people with disabilities.

Disabled Persons Assembly 4/173–175 Victoria St, Wellington, New Zealand ⓣ04/801 9100. Resource centre with lists of travel agencies and tour operators for people with disabilities.

Planning a holiday

There are **organized tours** and **holidays** specifically for people with disabilities; many companies in Britain will advise on the suitability of holidays or villas advertised in their brochures. If you want to be more independent, it's perfectly possible, provided that you do not leave home with the vague hope that things will turn out all right, and that "people will help out" when you need assistance. This cannot be relied on. You must either be completely confident that you can manage alone, or travel with an able-bodied friend (or two).

It's important to become an authority on where you must be self-reliant and where you may expect help, especially regarding transport and accommodation. For example, while the new Athens airport has lifts between arrivals and the departures concourse, and the Athens metro also has lifts for wheelchairs in every station, you cannot assume that every express bus between the arrivals exit and the first metro stop will be of a "kneeling" design.

It is also vital to **be honest** – with travel agencies, insurance companies, companions and, above all, with yourself. Know your limits and make sure others know them. If you do not use a wheelchair all the time but your walking capabilities are limited, remember that you are likely to need to cover greater distances while travelling (often over tougher terrain and in hotter weather) than you are used to. If you use a wheelchair, it's advisable to have it serviced before you go, and carry a repair kit.

Read your **travel insurance** small print carefully to make sure that people with a pre-existing medical condition are not excluded. And use your travel agent to make your journey simpler: **airlines** or bus companies can cope better if they are expecting you, with a wheelchair provided at airports and staff primed to help. A **medical certificate** of your fitness to travel, provided by your doctor, is also extremely useful; some airlines or insurance companies may insist on it.

Make a **list** of all the facilities that will make your life easier while you are away. You may want a ground-floor room, or access to a large elevator; you may have special dietary requirements, or need level ground to enable you to reach shops, beaches, bars and places of interest. You should also keep track of all your other special needs, making sure, for example, that you have extra supplies of drugs – carried with you if you fly – and a prescription including the generic name in case of emergency. Carry spares of any kind of drug, clothing or equipment that might be hard to find in Greece; if there's an association representing people with your disability, contact them early in the planning process.

Senior travellers

Travellers over sixty are accorded every respect in Greece; you are, for example, rather less likely to be grumbled or shouted at by the famously irate Athens bus drivers or island harbour officials. As previously noted, seniors are entitled to discounts at state-run attractions of twenty-five to thirty percent; without making much effort to publicize the fact, Olympic Airways (and quite possibly its new private competitors) also offers discounts off full fares on domestic flights. Keep proof of age to hand for all these benefits.

Contacts for senior travellers

In the UK

Saga Holidays ⓣ01303/771111, ⓦwww.sagaholidays.com. The country's biggest and most established specialist in tours and holidays aimed at older people.

In the US

American Association of Retired Persons 601 E St, NW Washington, DC 20049 ⓣ1-800/424-3410, membership hotline ⓣ1-800/515-2299 or 202/434-2277, ⓦwww.aarp.org. Can provide discounts on accommodation and vehicle rental. Membership open to US and Canadian residents aged 50 or over for an annual fee of US $10 or $27 for three years. Canadian residents only have the annual option.

Elderhostel 75 Federal St, Boston, MA 02110 ⓣ1/877-426-8056, ⓦwww.elderhostel.com. Runs an extensive worldwide network of educational and activity programs, cruises and homestays for people over 60 (companions may be younger). Programmes generally last a week or more and costs are in line with those of commercial tours.

Saga Holidays 222 Berkeley St, Boston, MA 02116 ⓣ1-877/265-6862, ⓦwww.sagaholidays.com. Specializes in worldwide group travel for seniors. Saga's Smithsonian Odyssey Tours, which include Greece, have a more educational slant.

Vantage Travel ⓣ1-800/322-6677, ⓦwww.vantagetravel.com. Specializes in worldwide group travel for seniors.

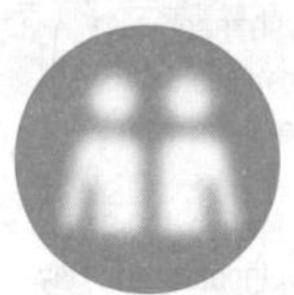

Gay and lesbian travellers

The term "Greek love" may still evoke titters from those educated in British public schools of a classicizing persuasion, but in modern Greece overtly gay behaviour in public remains taboo for men in rural areas. There is, however, a sizeable gay contingent in Athens, Thessaloníki and Pátra, plus a fairly obvious scene at certain resorts like Ídhra, Rhodes or Mýkonos, still the most popular European gay resort after Ibiza. Skála Eressoü on Lésvos, the birthplace of Sappho, is (appropriately) an international mecca for lesbians. Homosexuality is legal over the age of 17, and (male) bisexual behaviour common but rarely admitted. Greek men are terrible flirts, but cruising them is a semiotic minefield and definitely at your own risk – references in gay guides to "known" male cruising

grounds should be treated sceptically. "Out" gay Greeks are rare, and "out" local lesbians rarer still; foreign same-sex couples will be regarded in the provinces with some bemusement but accorded the standard courtesy as foreigners. The gay movement in Greece is represented by Akoe Amphi, PO Box 26022, 10022 Athens ⓣ010/77 19 221.

Contacts for gay and lesbian travellers

In the UK

ⓦwww.gaytravel.co.uk Online gay and lesbian travel agent, offering good deals on all types of holiday. Also lists gay- and lesbian-friendly hotels around the world.

Dream Waves Redcot High St, Child Okeford, Blandford, DT22 8ET ⓣ01258/861149, ⓔDreamwaves@aol.com. Specializes in exclusively gay holidays, including skiing trips and summer sun packages.

Madison Travel 118 Western Rd, Hove, East Sussex BN3 1DB ⓣ01273/202532, ⓦwww.madisontravel.co.uk. Established travel agents specializing in packages to gay- and lesbian-friendly mainstream destinations, and also to gay/lesbian destinations.

Respect Holidays 74 Haverstock Hill, London NW3 2BE ⓣ020/7485 8855, ⓦwww.respect-holidays.co.uk. Offers exclusively gay packages to all popular Europan resorts.

Also check out **adverts** in the weekly papers *Boyz* and *Pink Paper*, handed out free in gay venues.

In US and Canada

Damron Company PO Box 422458, San Francisco, CA 94142 ⓣ1-800/462-6654 or 415/255-0404, ⓦwww.damron.com. Publisher of the *Men's Travel Guide*, a pocket-sized yearbook full of listings of hotels, bars, clubs and resources for gay men; the *Women's Traveler*, which provides similar listings for lesbians; and *Damron Accommodations*, which provides detailed listings of over 1000 accommodations for gays and lesbians worldwide. All of these titles are offered at a discount on the website. No specific city guides – everything is incorporated in the yearbooks.

Ferrari Publications PO Box 37887, Phoenix, AZ 85069 ⓣ1-800/962-2912 or 602/863-2408, ⓦwww.ferrariguides.com. Publishes *Ferrari Gay Travel A to Z*, a worldwide gay and lesbian guide; *Inn Places*, a worldwide accommodation guide; the guides *Men's Travel in Your Pocket* and *Women's Travel in Your Pocket*, and the quarterly *Ferrari Travel Report*.

International Gay/Lesbian Travel Association, 4331 N Federal Hwy, Suite 304, Ft Lauderdale, FL 33308 ⓣ1-800/448-8550, ⓦwww.iglta.org. Trade group that can provide a list of gay- and lesbian-owned or friendly travel agents, accommodation and other travel businesses.

In Australia and New Zealand

Gay and Lesbian Travel ⓦwww.galta.com.au. Directory and links for gay and lesbian travel in Australia and worldwide.

Gay Travel ⓦwww.gaytravel.com. The site for trip planning, bookings, and general information about international travel.

Parkside Travel 70 Glen Osmond Rd, Parkside, SA 5063 ⓣ08/8274 1222 or 1800/888501, ⓔhwtravel@senet.com.au. Gay travel agent associated with local branch of Hervey World Travel; all aspects of gay and lesbian travel worldwide.

Pinkstay ⓦwww.pinkstay.com. Everything from visa information to finding accommodation and work around the world.

Silke's Travel 263 Oxford St, Darlinghurst, NSW 2010 ⓣ02/9380 6244 or 1800/807860, ⓔsilba@magna.com.au. Long-established gay and lesbian specialist, with the emphasis on women's travel.

Tearaway Travel 52 Porter St, Prahan, VIC 3181 ⓣ03/9510 6344, ⓔtearaway@bigpond.com. Gay-specific business dealing with international and domestic travel.

Travelling with children

Children are worshipped and indulged in Greece, arguably to excess, and present few problems when travelling. As elsewhere in the Mediterranean, they are not segregated from adults at meal times and early on in life are inducted into the typical late-night routine. So you'll see plenty of kids at tavernas, expected to eat (and, up to their capabilities, talk) like adults. Outside of certain all-inclusive resorts, however (see "Contacts" below) there are very few amusements specifically for kids – certainly nothing like Disney World.

Most ferry-boat lines and airlines in Greece offer some sort of **discount** for children, ranging from fifty to hundred percent depending on their age; hotels and rooms won't charge extra for infants, and levy a modest surcharge for "third" beds which the child occupies by him/herself.

Baby foods and nappies/diapers are ubiquitous and reasonably priced; private rooms establishments and luxury hotels are more likely to offer some kind of **babysitting** service than the mid-range, C-class hotels.

Contacts for travellers with children

In the UK and Ireland

Club Med ⓣ0700/258 2633, ⓦwww.clubmed.com. Specializes in purpose-built holiday resorts, with kids' club, entertainment and sports facilities on site; has a village at Kós in the Dodecanese.

Mark Warner Holidays ⓣ020/7761 7000, ⓦwww.markwarner.co.uk. Holiday villages with children's entertainment and childcare laid on; has a village on Límnos in the east Aegean.

Simply Travel ⓣ020/8541 2280, ⓦwww.simply-travel.com. Upmarket tour company offering villas and hotels in the less touristy parts of Greece. May be able to provide qualified, English-speaking nannies to come to your villa and look after the children.

In the US

Travel With Your Children, 40 Fifth Ave, New York, NY 10011 ⓣ212/477-5524 or 1-888/822-4388. Publish a regular newsletter, *Family Travel Times* ⓦwww.familytraveltimes.com, as well as a series of books on travel with children including *Great Adventure Vacations With Your Kids*.

Directory

ADDRESSES In Greece streets are cited in the genitive case, usually with no tag like "Street" or "Avenue"; the number always follows. Thus something described as 36 Venizelos Avenue in Roman-alphabet letterhead comes out at Venizélou 36, and it's this convention which we've adopted throughout the book. Postcodes are five-digit, nationwide, and precede the municipality concerned, eg 81100 Mytilíni, on Lésvos.

BARGAINING This isn't a regular feature of touristic life, though you'll find it possible with private rooms and certain hotels out of season. Similarly, you should be able to negotiate discounted rates for vehicle rental, especially for longer periods. Services such as shoe, watch and camera repair don't have iron-clad rates, so use common sense when assessing charges (advance written estimates are not a routine practice).

DEPARTURE TAX This is levied on all international ferries – currently €4.50–6 per person *and* the same again for any car or motorbike – within the EU, ie to Italy. To non-EU states (Turkey, Egypt and Israel), it's €11.80–14.70 per person, sometimes arbitrarily levied twice (on entry and exit). There's also an aggregate airport departure tax of €12 for destinations within the EU/EEA (including Greece), €22 for all other destinations, but it's always included in the price of the ticket – there's no collection at the airport itself. Additionally, all flights out of Athens Spáta airport are surcharged €12.50 for international flights, €8.50 for domestic flights, plus a €1.52 "security charge"; again, it's collected at time of ticket purchase if applicable.

ELECTRICITY Voltage is 220 volt AC throughout the country. Wall outlets – seldom abundant enough – take double round-pin plugs as in the rest of Continental Europe. Three- to two-pin adaptors should be purchased beforehand in the UK, as they can be difficult to find in Greece; standard 5-, 6- or 7.5-amp models permit operation of a hairdryer or travel iron. If necessary, you can change the fuse to a higher rating back in the UK; beware, they're physically smaller than the 13-amp ones popped into all three-prong plugs, and you may have to go to a specialist electrical dealer for them. Unless they're dual voltage, North American appliances will require both a step-down transformer and a plug adapter (the latter easy to find in Greece).

FILM Fuji and Agfa print films are reasonably priced and easy to have processed – you practically trip over "One Hour Foto" shops in some resorts. APS film is also widely sold and processed. Fuji and Ektachrome slide film can be purchased, at more or less UK prices, on the larger islands, but cannot be processed there – whatever you may be told, exposed rolls will be sent to Athens for handling, so best wait until you return home.

FOOTBALL (Soccer) This is by far and away the most popular sport in Greece. The most important (and most heavily sponsored) teams are Panathanaïkós and AEK of Athens, Olympiakós of Pireás, and PAOK of Thessaloníki; the islands covered in this book have no teams of major standing.

HIKING Greeks are just becoming used to the notion that anyone should want to walk for pleasure, yet if you have the time and stamina it is probably the best way to see many of the Dodecanese and east Aegean islands. This guide includes descriptions of a number of hikes (see p.501 in "Contexts" for specialist hiking guides). For essential advice on maps, see p.33.

LAUNDRIES *Plindíria*, as they're known in Greek, are prominent in the main resort towns; sometimes an attended service wash is available for little or no extra charge over the basic cost of €5–5.50 per wash and dry. Self-catering villas or *dhomátia* will usually be furnished with a drying line and a selection of plastic wash-tubs (*skáfes*) or a bucket (*kouvás*). In hotels, laundering should be done in a more circumspect manner; management can freak out if you use bathroom wash-basins – Greek wall-mounting being what it is – or do no more than a few socks and undies. It's best to use the flat pans of showers for both washing and hanging to dry; if you haven't come with a universal flat plug, wadded-up toilet paper can be quite effective in stopping the drain hole.

PERÍPTERA These are street-corner kiosks, or sometimes a hole-in-the-wall shopfront. They sell everything from pens to disposable razors, stationery to soap, sweets to condoms, cigarettes to plastic crucifixes, yogurts to milk-in-cartons – and are often open when nothing else is.

TIME As throughout the European Union, Greek summertime begins at 2am on the last Sunday in March, when the clocks go forward one hour, and ends at 2am the last Sunday in October, when they go back. Be alert to this, as the change is not well publicized, leading scores of visitors to miss planes and ferries every year. Greek time is thus always two hours ahead of Britain. For North America, the difference is seven hours for Eastern Standard Time, ten hours for Pacific Standard Time, with again an extra hour plus or minus for those weeks in April and October when one place is on daylight saving and the other isn't. Greece is eight hours behind Australian Eastern Standard Time (with a one hour variation plus or minus during daylight savings), and six hours behind Perth. New Zealand Standard Time is ten hours ahead of Greek time (eleven hours during daylight savings in NZ, nine hours during Greek summer). A recorded time message (in distinctly slow Greek, 24-hour convention) is available by dialling ⓣ141.

TOILETS Public ones in towns are usually in parks or squares, often subterranean. Except in areas frequented by tourists (such as Ródhos Town), public toilets tend to be pretty filthy – it's best to use those in restaurants and bars. Note that throughout Greece you drop toilet paper in the adjacent wastebins, *not* in the bowl.

USEFUL THINGS TO BRING A high-quality, porcelain-lined canteen or drinking-water bottle; a small alarm clock for early buses and ferries; a flashlight if you're camping out; sunscreen of high SPF (25 or above, tricky to find and/or expensive in Greece); pocket knife (Swiss Army type or similar), with tweezers, mini-screwdriver and other similar accessories (these are now widely sold in Greece at hunting/fishing shops); ear plugs for noisy ferries or hotels; and good-quality tea bags.

guide

guide

1

Rhodes

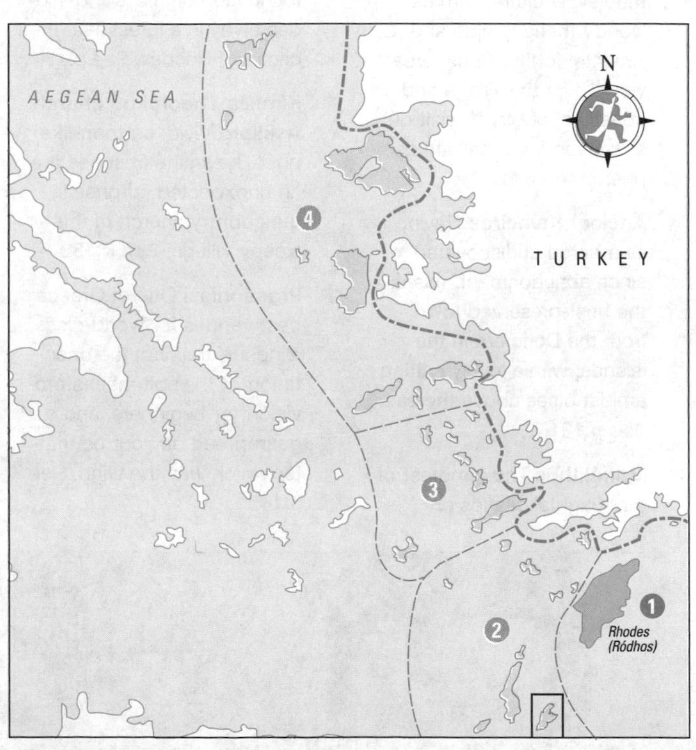

CHAPTER 1 Highlights

* **Ródhos old town** Superbly preserved pebble-mosaic streets and sandstone buildings are inextricably linked with the Knights of St John, who ruled here for over two hundred years. See p.98

* **Lindos acropolis** A pleasing blend of ancient and medieval culture, with its Doric Athena temple and Knights' fortifications; great views over the village and coastline, but try to visit out of season for better atmosphere. See p.126

* **Ancient Kameiros** Having slumbered undiscovered since abandonment, this is the best-preserved town from the Doric era in the islands, with a lovely setting amidst pines above the sea. See p.131

* **Monólithos** The remotest of the Knights' castles on Rhodes presides over the spectacular forested scenery of Mt Akramýtis, Rhodes' wildest mountain, and the secluded beaches of Foúrni far below. See p.133

* **Thárri monastery** Subtle, well-restored Byzantine frescoes in the oldest religious foundation on the island, hidden away in a forest near the centre of Rhodes. See p.136

* **Kímisis Theotókou church, Asklipió** Vivid, cartoon-like post-Byzantine frescoes are an unexpected surprise in the country church of this sleepy village. See p.138

* **Prassoníssi** One of Greece's best venues for world-class windsurf training; the orientation of the spit means provision for beginners, and a guaranteed day out no matter which way the wind. See p.140

Rhodes

It's no accident that **Rhodes** (Ródhos) is, after Crete, the most visited of the Greek islands. Not only is its east coast lined with numerous sandy beaches, but the capital's kernel is a beautiful and remarkably preserved medieval city, a legacy of the crusading Knights of St John who used the island as their main base from 1309 until 1522. Add to this cheap charter flights available over an eight-month season with three hundred sunny days annually, and you have all the ingredients for touristic success. The only quibble might concern its precise nature: dozens of battery-farm hotels lining the "Golden Mile" between the airport and main town hardly bode well for any degree of good taste, nor does the fact that certain guests wear T-shirts inscribed "Sex 90%, Love 1%, Relax 9%, This is Rhodes 100%" or "Ten reasons why a beer is better than a woman/man" without apparent embarrassment. If you're so inclined, you can find the commercialized Rhodes without a guidebook, but those of a more enquiring nature will discover a hilly, partly forested interior big enough to get lost in, remote castles and Byzantine churches, pleasant ridges and stream canyons, as well as peaceful villages still living at least partly from agriculture.

Rhodes has an official population of about 110,000, well over half the inhabitants of the entire Dodecanese. As for the transient and foreign population, several thousand permanent expats are joined in a good year by over one million tourists. Of the foreigners, Germans, Brits, Swedes, Italians (especially in August) and Danes predominate, usually in that order; accordingly, smorgasbord, fish fingers and pizza jostle alongside *moussakás* on tourist menus. Numerous Greeks also frequent the better hotels as Rhodes is heavily promoted domestically as a chic weekend destination. All the proceeds of tourism sloshing about have engendered a notably decadent, mock-Athenian lifestyle among the townspeople, reflected in expensive *gelaterie* and clothing shops featuring the latest designer glad rags. By way of balance there is also, especially during the cooler months, a lively programme of cinema, Greek-language theatre and other events, courtesy of the local student contingent.

Some mythology and etymology

According to legend, the sun god Helios (then personified separately from Apollo) was away doing his daily rounds when Zeus apportioned the world among his fellow Olympian deities. To make amends, he promised Helios any part of the earth that had not yet emerged from the sea. As it happened, Helios had spied the nymph Rodon, daughter of Poseidon and Amphitrite, under the water off Asia Minor; concentrating his rays, he induced her to rise

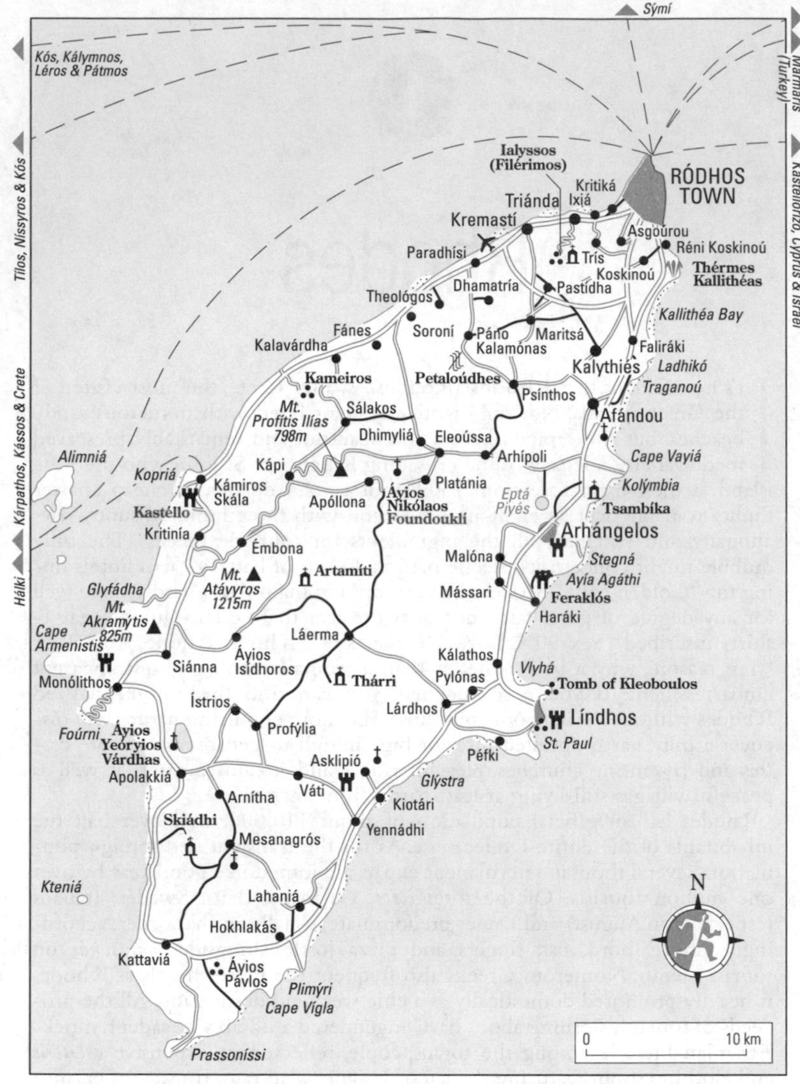

to the surface, whereupon he married her. In its essentials, this pretty myth deviates little from the Father Sky/Mother Earth prototypes common to many early cultures, though in the case of Rhodes it seems the tale evolved to explain the presence of fossilized seashells up in the Rhodian hills, for indeed the island was thrust up from the sea floor aeons ago by earthquakes and plate tectonics.

The real derivation of the **name** "Rhodes" remains controversial: the tourist board claims that it stems from the ancient Greek word for "rose", though neither the domesticated nor the wild *Cistus* rock species, however abundant now, are native to the island. It is more likely a corruption of *ro(i)di* or pomegranate, and ancient coins with a pomegranate on one side and the sun god's head on the other are well documented. A recent, ingenious theory has it that the "rose" is really the hibiscus, which also grows here in profusion, but again is not native.

A brief history

Blessed with an equable climate and strategic position, the island of Rhodes was important from earliest times, despite a paucity of good harbours. The best natural port spawned the ancient town of Lindos, which, together with the other city-states Kameiros and Ialyssos, united in 408 BC to found the new capital of Rhodes at the northern tip of the island. At various moments the cities allied themselves with Alexander, Persians, Athenians or Spartans as prevailing conditions suited, generally escaping retribution for backing the wrong side by a combination of seafaring audacity, sycophancy and burgeoning wealth as a trade centre. Following the **failed siege** of Demetrios Polyorketes in 305 BC (see box on p.94), Rhodes prospered even more, displacing Athens as the major venue for rhetoric and the arts in the east Mediterranean. The ancient town, which lies beneath virtually all of the modern city, was initially laid out by early urban planner Hippodamus of Miletus according to a grid layout much in vogue at the time, with planned residential and commercial quarters. Its perimeter walls totalled nearly 15km, enclosing roughly double the area of today's city, and the Hellenistic population exceeded 100,000, a staggering figure for the ancient world.

Decline set in when Rhodes became involved in the **Roman civil wars** and Cassius sacked the town; by late imperial times, it had become a backwater, a status confirmed by numerous barbarian raids during the Byzantine period. The **Byzantines** were compelled to cede the island to the **Genoese**, who in turn (after a three-year resistance) surrendered it to the Knights of St John (see box pp.102–103). The second great siege of Rhodes, during 1522, saw Ottoman **Sultan Süleyman the Magnificent** oust the stubborn knights, who retreated to Malta; town and island once again lapsed into relative obscurity, though they were heavily colonized and garrisoned until the Italian seizure of 1912.

After 1923 and the Treaty of Lausanne, Fascist-ruled **Italy** selected Rhodes to be the crown jewel of its "Aegean Empire", and lavished great sums on road building, waterworks, reforestation and the first inklings of a mass tourism industry. More controversially, the Italians engaged in excavation and restoration of archeological sites, as well as indulging their tastes in new civic structures and restoration of medieval monuments. The Greek Orthodox population benefited little from this, on the contrary, enduring sustained cultural persecution after 1928 (see "History" in Contexts). In autumn 1943, the Italians capitulated, and certainly the Jews of the Dodecanese must have preferred the relative leniency of their rule to that of the Germans, under whom they suffered almost total annihilation. The British administered the island from mid-1945 until the institution of Greek military rule in April 1947 (prior to the official March 1948 unification with Greece), thus beginning a long-standing love affair between the UK and Rhodes. Only now are the worst memories of Fascist rule fading, as those who directly experienced it pass away, and grudging acknowledgement is finally being made of the comprehensive and partly still-useable infrastructure inherited from the Italians.

The first siege of Rhodes

The first great siege of Rhodes in 305 BC, considered the most noteworthy military campaign of ancient times, resulted from power struggles between the generals and deputies of Alexander the Great following his death. Because of their close trade links, Rhodes sided with Egypt, then ruled by Ptolemy. Rival Macedonian general Antigonus ordered Rhodes to attack its ally on his behalf; when the islanders refused, Antigonus, furious at this rebuff, sent his son Demetrios to discipline the defiant Rhodians. Nicknamed "Polyorketes" (Besieger of Many Cities) and fresh from the capture of Salamis on Cyprus, Demetrios was one of the military geniuses of his day, with intimidating resources to draw upon: 200 warships, nearly as many supporting craft, and 40,000 seasoned infantrymen. Against these forces the Rhodians could muster just 8000 citizen-soldiers, perhaps 2000 Cretan volunteers and Egyptian mercenaries, and 15,000 slaves who were bought up by the municipality and promised their freedom in the event of successful resistance. Additionally, the government guaranteed funerals with full honours for the fallen, plus perpetual subsidy to their surviving relatives. These wise strategies boosted morale, strengthened social cohesion and probably influenced the battle's outcome, as no significant instance of treason was recorded throughout the long siege.

Having blockaded the city with his fleet, Demetrios initially targeted the apparently vulnerable harbour walls, launching projectiles from a pair of ingenious "tortoises": armoured carapaces slung between two ships and protected by booms to repel ramming attacks by the Rhodians. In a daring sortie, these floating weapons were sunk by the Rhodians, whose cause was further helped by the destruction in a storm of a new, land-based siege tower, and the arrival of fresh reinforcements from Ptolemy.

In the light of these reverses, Demetrios changed tactics, devoting his attentions to the landward walls and ordering the construction of the so-called Helepolis or "Overthrower of Cities", the largest siege tower the world had seen. Sheathed in metal and animal hides, it measured 27 metres on each side at the base, tapering slightly over a nine-storey height, with windows for launching missiles and drawbridges for depositing commandos on top of the walls; over three thousand men were required to arm and move this wheeled, 125-tonne behemoth. In response, the tenacious Rhodians doubled their walls and mounted successful forays to break the Macedonian blockade, while Demetrios' numerous enemies surreptitiously arranged to replenish the city's food supplies. The Helepolis repeatedly damaged the city's fortifications, but the Macedonians failed to gain entry; in one nocturnal raid, the Rhodians almost succeeded in setting the tower alight. Following stalled peace negotiations sponsored by other Hellenic cities, Demetrios opted for a decisive charge on the weakest spot, in conjunction with a general attack along the entire length of the perimeter walls. Some 1500 of his men managed briefly to establish a foothold inside the city, near the theatre, but were surrounded by the Rhodians and cut down almost to a man.

By now the siege had been going on for almost a year, with both sides nearly exhausted; Demetrios' father, Antigonus, and Ptolemy began urging their respective protégés to come to honourable terms, as nobody would gain if the wealthiest city in the Aegean were reduced to rubble. This final truce was in fact prompted by an ingenious act of sabotage: a Rhodian engineer directed a team of sappers to tunnel past the walls and undermine the usual path of the Helepolis, causing it to founder and collapse. Demetrios, finally convinced of the islanders' resolve, confirmed Rhodes as an independent city-state, requiring it only to contribute ships towards Macedonian military expeditions as long as hostilities were not directed against Ptolemy, and to provide one hundred noble hostages as security against any breach of the agreement. He also left all his war machinery with the Rhodians to play a crucial role in the saga of the Colossus (see box p.109).

Ródhos Town

RÓDHOS TOWN, built around the second best natural harbour on the island (after Líndhos), is very much the main event on Rhodes, and deservedly so for its exquisite medieval city. Air arrivals miss out on the majestic approach by ferry, usually in the morning light, which shows to advantage a fair amount of the old town's five-kilometre ramparts, their contours softened by gardens and accented by turrets. Once the apotheosis of military architecture, today they are merely a decorative backdrop, dividing the town into two unequal parts: the relatively compact walled quarter, and the sprawling modern neighbourhoods surrounding it on three sides.

The separation of new town from old dates from the Ottoman occupation; the Greeks, forbidden to reside in the walled city built by the Knights of St John, founded several suburb villages or **marásia** in the environs. The churches of Áyios Ioánnis, Áyii Anáryiri, Ayía Anastasía, Mitrópolis and Áyios Yeóryios were initially established due south of the Turkish cemeteries which grew up outside the walls, while Neohóri (sometimes "Niohóri") – synonymous with the sharp promontory to the northwest – was settled last. Since the Italian era they have all merged into one cement-laced conurbation, but the above-named churches still exist, as do the narrow lanes and older houses immediately around them. Even with this filling-in of previously empty spaces, modern Ródhos is still far smaller in both dimensions and population than its Hellenistic precursor.

Tourism is predominant in much of the old town and throughout the Neohóri district west of Mandhráki yacht harbour, where the few buildings that aren't hotels serve as souvenir shops, bars and car rental or travel agencies – easily sixty to seventy in each category. Locals mostly live south and southwest of the walled city, in the older parishes, with students from one of the main campuses of the University of the Aegean supplementing the permanent population of about 50,000.

Arrival, information and transport

The **airport**, expanded in the mid-1990s but still barely coping with high-season traffic, lies 13km southwest of town, conveniently near the village of Paradhísi. Any public **city bus** coming from Paradhísi, Theológos, Kalavárdha or Sálakos will stop up on the road opposite the northerly car-park entrance (look for the wood-and-perspex shelter and signposting opposite the little chapel), and services from the airport to Ródhos Town run fairly frequently from 6am to almost midnight (see "Travel Details" on p.144 for outbound services). The bus fare to town is currently €1.50, versus over €10 for **taxis**, the latter figure (including bag and airport supplements) increasing to nearly €20 between midnight and 5am; standard fares to the most popular resort destinations are displayed on a placard outside the terminal. Those flying in at an unsociable hour might consider arranging **car rental** in advance of their trip, though at slow times you may be able to get something affordable on arrival from the chains (Alamo/National, Drive, Budget, Sixt, Holiday, Hertz, Avis and Europcar) which have booths at the airport.

At the time of writing, all international and inter-island **ferries** drop anchor in the middle one of Rhodes' three ports, the so-called commercial harbour, more properly known as **Kolóna**. In the distant future, some traffic may be diverted to a new terminal planned for the easternmost port, Akándia, but barring a massive influx of EU funds this is unlikely to ever happen. Local boats to and from Sými, plus east-coast excursion boats, currently use the south quay of Mandhráki yacht harbour, while **hydrofoils** dock at the west quay; a plan to move their base of operations to the small jetty in Kolóna where the slow *Nissos Kalymnos* and *Dodekanisos Express* catamaran now call has been postponed indefinitely.

Information and maps

Between the east-coast bus stop and the Mandhráki taxi rank there's a fairly useless **municipal tourist office** (theoretically June–Sept Mon–Sat 9am–8pm, Sun 9am–1pm; ⓣ02410/35 945), while 200m up Papágou, on the corner of Makaríou, is the more helpful and reliably open **EOT office** (Mon–Fri 7.30am–3pm; ⓣ02410/23 255, ⓔeot-rodos@otenet.gr), a good source of information on bus and ferry timetables, archeological sites and the like. Situated next to the EOT, the multilingual **tourist police** (24hr; ⓣ02410/27 423) deal with serious service-related complaints; officers wear a badge or flag indicating languages spoken.

The free island **maps** supplied by tourist offices or car-rental firms are as good as any you can buy, with the exception of the excellent 1:100,000 one produced by Road Editions (about €4.50) which use topographic maps as sources; all others are based on the work of the same Athenian cartographer, Tsopelas. Maps of Ródhos Town, however, are another matter; accept no substitute for the A-to-Z-type mini-atlas "Map of Rhodes Town", which includes an overview poster-map, or "Rhodes, Map of the Old Town", another art-format map of the medieval city, that's nonetheless the most accurate available. Both were prepared in 1994 by long-time resident Mario Camerini, and updated again in 1998.

Local buses

KTEL **buses** for all points along the east coast (except for Koskinoú and Kallithéa) leave from, and arrive at, a terminal on Papágou, just above Platía Rimínis, aka "Sound and Light Square"; they're typically orange and cream (as opposed to the usual Greek green and cream), though a number of all-turquoise or all-red, air-conditioned vehicles have begun appearing. Identically coloured coaches run by RODA depart for the west coast (plus Koskinoú and Kallithéa) from a stop just around the corner on Avérof, under the sidewalk arcades of the so-called New Market; RODA also runs relatively infrequent city routes from the same terminal, with both services severely reduced on Saturday and Sunday. Tickets for the long-distance RODA buses are sold on board, and those for the numbered city routes both on board (€0.80) or from special kiosks (€0.75), in either case subsequently cancelled in the bus.

Taxis and traffic control

Taxi ranks are numerous and shown on the town maps with a circled "T"; the cars themselves are either slate-coloured or midnight blue with white tops, rather than the typical Hellenic grey. Even by the standards of Greek tourist resorts, Rhodian **taxi drivers** can be a source of grief for the inexperienced. Resist their initial gambits to deposit you at inconveniently remote beach-strip hotels, which pay kickbacks to the drivers, and also treat with scepticism any reports that particular hotels or pensions in the old town are "full", "dirty", "closed", "burnt down", etc. If you are luggage-laden, drivers are obliged by law to take you to the door of your chosen accommodation, even if it is in the old town, which is otherwise off-limits to non-residents' vehicles. In the event of any trouble, refuse to pay until delivered to your destination, and if necessary note down licence numbers. **Problems** with Rhodian taxis are so rife that the EOI office has seen fit to print and distribute a sheet with legal fares on one side and on the other a minuscule incident complaint form to send to the Division of Transport and Communications. You may get more satisfaction if you go to the in-town tourist police (see opposite), who are always happy to investigate such incidents.

As noted above, all wheeled **traffic** is banned within the medieval walls, except for residents' cars and scooters; this law is strictly enforced eighteen hours a day in high season by a warden manning a swivel-bar or chain at each gate. **Parking** within any reasonable distance of the old town is a challenge, and the closest most will get is along Filellínon or Ayíou Anaryíron, both streets just outside the Ayíou Athanasíou gate. At night, there may also be space along the walls facing Kolóna harbour, or just inside on Platía Sýmis. Neohóri, the northern extension of the new town, is a nightmare, though surprisingly you can sometimes find a parking spot along Platía Eleftherías, the western esplanade at Mandhráki, or "100 Palms Square" (officially Platía Gavriél Harítou). Even if you find a space, most of these spots are subject during business hours to pay-and-display schemes – either short-term hourly tickets or, more commonly, long-term spaces (*makrís dhiarhías* in Greek) with reloadable cards. If you don't see a ticket machine for hourly windscreen chits, don't park there – the traffic police are very industrious.

Accommodation

Inexpensive pensions abound in the **old town** and are found almost entirely in the area bordered by Omírou on the south, Sokrátous on the north, Perikléous on the east and Ippodhámou on the west; in addition, there are some more hotels in the heart of the old Jewish quarter, east of Perikléous. Anyone arriving without a reservation in peak season or late at night might be prudent to accept the offers of proprietors meeting the ferries and change base next day if necessary – as it frequently is since, on closer acquaintance, many of the unlicensed "rooms" touted turn out to have facilities (and hygienic standards) little changed since the age of the Knights. Establishments recommended below are those most likely to have firm beds, consistent hot water, relatively restrained decor, nocturnal calm and no cockroaches.

The **new town** offers modern, purpose-built hotels, less likely to be open in winter, as well as a limited number of colourful pensions installed in former Italian villas or traditional vernacular houses. Few of the hotels have vacancies for independent travellers, and many are plagued by after-hours noise from the dozens of bars lining nearby streets – though uninterrupted sleep is unlikely to be a priority of many among the hotel clientele. The establishments listed on p.98 have been selected for value and relative peace.

The old town

Andreas Omírou 28d Ⓣ02410/34 156, Ⓕ74 285, Ⓦwww.hotelandreas.com. Perennially popular (reservations needed) and under new dynamic management, this is one of the more imaginative old-house restoration pensions, refurbished in 2000. Rooms vary from doubles to family-size and most are en suite. Terrace view-bar for breakfast and evenings, two-night minimum stay, credit cards accepted, indeed vital for advance booking. Open mid-March to end of Oct. ❸–❹

Apollo Omírou 28c Ⓣ02410/63 894. Basic – cold-water sinks in rooms, baths in halls – but clean and friendly rooms place, under new management in 2001 and lightly refurbished; the self-catering kitchen makes it good for longer stays. ❶

Casa de la Sera Thisséos 38 ⓣ02410/75 154. Best of several Jewish-quarter renovations, with wonderful floor tiles in the fair-sized en-suite rooms and a ground-floor breakfast bar. Proprietor tends to wait up for late arrivals. ③

La Luna Menándhrou 21 ⓣ & ⓕ02410/25 856. Clean, wood-trimmed if plain (no en suites) pension in a converted old Turkish house, complete with still-functioning *hamam* (Turkish bath) on the top floor. Garden bar for breakfast, by the citrus and banana trees. Open year-round. ④

Marco Polo Mansion Ayíou Fanouríou 42 ⓣ & ⓕ02410/25 562, ⓦwww.marcopolomansion.web. Superb 1999 conversion of an old Turkish mansion, again with a *hamam* on site, but all rooms en suite and exquisitely furnished with antiques from the nearby eponymous gallery, plus cotton pillows and handmade mattresses. Large buffet breakfasts included and provided by ebullient manageress Efi; adjoining café after-hours. One-week minimum stay, advance booking required, part open in winter. ⑥

Niki's Sofokléous 39 ⓣ02410/25 115. Some rooms can be on the small side, but almost all are en suite, and upper-storey ones have fine views (including 3 with balconies). There's a washing machine, common terrace and friendly management to round things off. ③

Pink Elephant/Roz Elefandas Officially Irodhótou 42 but actually on Timahídhas, just off Omírou ⓣ & ⓕ02410/22 469. Simple but clean rooms occupying several levels of a modernized old building; roof deck with sunning and covered sections, variable plumbing arrangements. Right by the traditional red-light district, but the "ladies" won't bother you. Offers discount for singles. ③

S. Nikolis Ippodhámou 61 ⓣ02410/34 561, ⓕ32 034, ⓦwww.s-nikolis.gr. A variety of restoration premises in the west of the old town. Hotel/honeymoon-suite rates include rooftop-served breakfast, TV and air con; Sotiris and Marianne's self-catering apartments (⑤–⑥) are among the finest restoration results in the old town, and interconnect to accommodate groups/families. Booking essential, and accepted only with credit-card number or pre-posted travellers' cheques. Open April–Nov; closed otherwise, except by special arrangement. ⑥

Spot Perikléous 21 ⓣ & ⓕ02410/34 737, ⓔspothot@otenet.gr. Yet another old-town hotel under a new generation of management, this modern building has cheerfully painted en-suite rooms of varying formats with textiles on the walls, and air con or fans, representing superb value. Internet facilities, free luggage storage. Open March–Nov. ③

Youth hostel Eryíou 12 ⓣ02410/30 491. Both 3- to 5-bunk dorms and doubles (①) in this courtyarded house with kitchen facilities; €7.50 for a bunk; non-YHA-affiliated.

The new town

Anastasia 28-Oktovríou 46, Neohóri ⓣ02410/28 007, ⓕ02410/21 815. A pension with high-ceilinged, en-suite rooms housed in an interwar building; garden bar. ③

Best Western Plaza Ieroú Lóhou 7, Neohóri ⓣ02410/22 501, ⓕ22 544, ⓦwww.rhodes-plaza.com. Renovated in 1997, this is probably the best A-class hotel within Rhodes city limits, in the heart of Neohóri. Pool, sauna, jacuzzi, buffet English breakfast, heating/air con. It's open all year and, particularly between Nov and April, offers discounts off published rates. ⑥

Capitol Dhilberáki 65–67 ⓣ & ⓕ02410/28 645. Another old-house hotel with fairly large, en-suite, terrazzo-floored rooms; some family-size quads upstairs. Breakfast served in the back garden by young managing (Greek–German) couple. ④

Casa Antica Amarándou 8 ⓣ02410/26 206. Double and quad studios in a made-over 150-year-old house, with clean, white-tile decor, courtyard, roof terrace. Close to some of the better Neohóri tavernas. ④

Esperia Yeoryíou Gríva 7, Neohóri ⓣ02410/23 941, ⓕ0241/23 164, ⓔesperia@esperia-hotels.gr. Well-priced, well-run B-class hotel, with pool, in a quiet location overlooking a little tree-studded plaza. Small to medium-sized salubrious and tasteful rooms with showers. Open all year. ④

New Village Inn Konstandopédhos 10 ⓣ02410/34 937, ⓕ30 733, ⓔnewvillageinn@rho.forthnet.gr. Whitewashed, somewhat grotto-like en-suite rooms arranged around a small courtyard; they're "refreshed" yearly, with air conditioning planned. Friendly Greek and American management; singles available at a good rate. Open most of the year. ③

Spartalis Nikoláou Plastíra 2, Neohóri ⓣ02410/24 371, ⓕ20 406. Reliable, 1970s-vintage C-class, with east-side rooms overlooking a playground-park that's peaceful after dark, most others glimpsing the sea. Medium-sized rooms, lightly refurbished in 1999, en suite with baths. ⑤

The old town

Simply to catalogue the principal monuments and attractions cannot do full justice to the infinitely rewarding **old town**. There's ample gratification to be

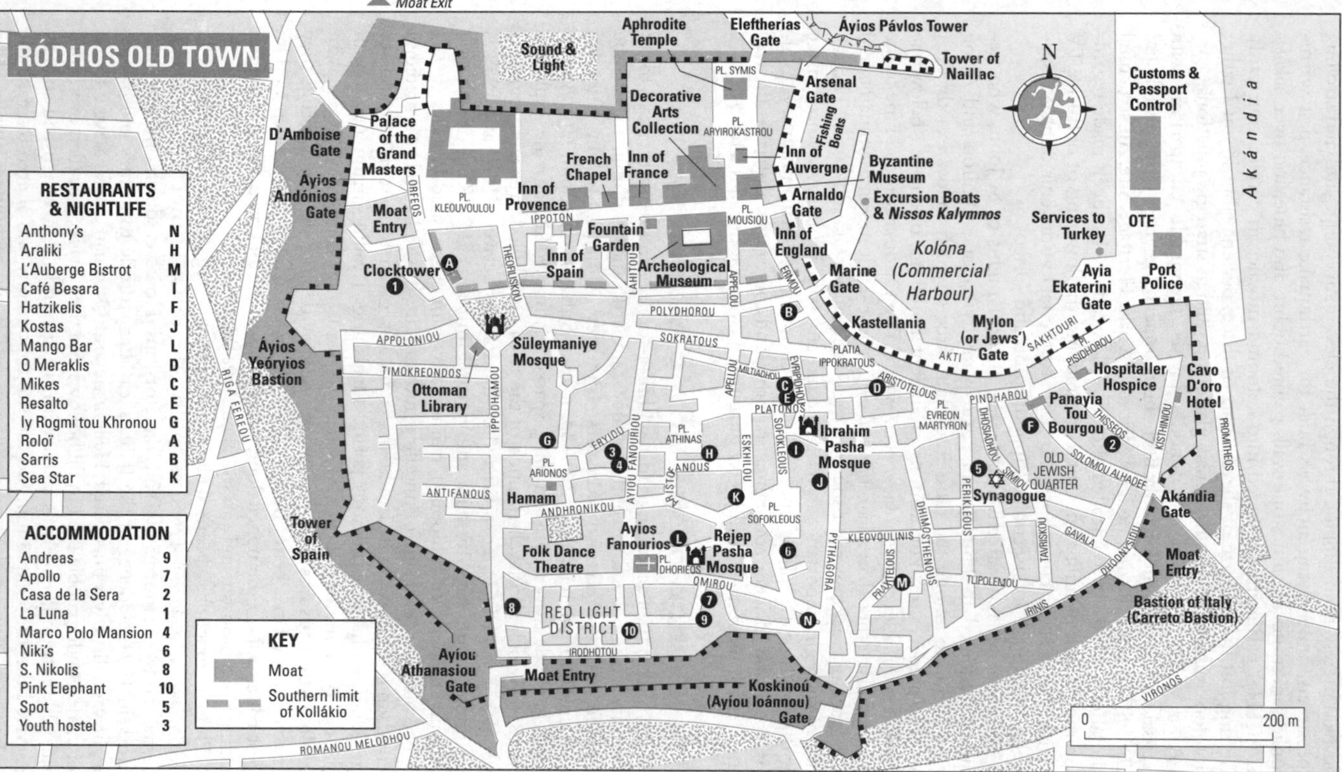
RÓDHOS OLD TOWN
RESTAURANTS & NIGHTLIFE
Anthony's N
Araliki H
L'Auberge Bistrot M
Café Besara I
Hatzikelis F
Kostas J
Mango Bar L
O Meraklis D
Mikes C
Resalto E
Iy Rogmi tou Khronou G
Roloï A
Sarris B
Sea Star K
ACCOMMODATION
Andreas 9
Apollo 7
Casa de la Sera 2
La Luna 1
Marco Polo Mansion 4
Niki's 6
S. Nikolis 8
Pink Elephant 10
Spot 5
Youth hostel 3
KEY
Moat
Southern limit of Kollákio
Moat Exit
Sound & Light
Aphrodite Temple
Eleftherías Gate
Áyios Pávlos Tower
Tower of Naillac
Arsenal Gate
Fishing Boats
Decorative Arts Collection
PL. SYMIS
PL. ARYIROKASTROU
Inn of Auvergne
Byzantine Museum
Arnaldo Gate
Excursion Boats & Nissos Kalymnos
Inn of England
Marine Gate
Kolóna (Commercial Harbour)
Services to Turkey
Customs & Passport Control
OTE
Port Police
Ayia Ekaterini Gate
Akándia
D'Amboise Gate
Palace of the Grand Masters
Áyios Andónios Gate
Moat Entry
French Chapel
Inn of France
Inn of Provence
PL. KLEOUVOULOU
ORFEOS
IPPOTON
Fountain Garden
Inn of Spain
Archeological Museum
PL. MOUSIOU
Clocktower
THEOFILISKOU
LAHITOU
APPELOU
ERMOU
POLYDHOROU
SOKRATOUS
Kastellania
Mylon (or Jews') Gate
AKTI
SAKHTOURI
PL. PISIDHOROU
Hospitaller Hospice
Cavo D'oro Hotel
PROMITHEOS
KISTHINIOU
Áyios Yeóryios Bastion
RIGA FEREOU
APPOLONIOU
Süleymaniye Mosque
TIMOKREONDOS
Ottoman Library
IPPODHAMOU
PLATIA IPPOKRATOUS
MILTIADHOU
EVRIPIDHOU
ARISTOTELOUS
PL. EVREON MARTYRON
PINDHAROU
Panayia Tou Bourgou
THISSEOS
PLATONOS
Ibrahim Pasha Mosque
DHOSIADHOU
SIMIOU
OLD JEWISH QUARTER
SOLOMOU ALHADEF
Synagogue
Akándia Gate
ERYIDU
AYIOU FANOURIOU
PL. ATHINAS
ANOUS
ESKHILOU
SOFOKLEOUS
PL. ARIONOS
ANTIFANOUS
Hamam
ANDHRONIKOU
ARISTOF
PL. SOFOKLEOUS
PERIKLEOUS
DHIMOSTHENOUS
TAVRISKOU
GAVALA
DHODNYSIOU
Tower of Spain
Ayios Fanourios
Rejep Pasha Mosque
PL. DHORIEOS
Folk Dance Theatre
OMIROU
PYTHAGORA
KLEOVOULINIS
PRAXITELOUS
TIPOLEMOU
IRINIS
Moat Entry
Bastion of Italy (Carreto Bastion)
RED LIGHT DISTRICT
IRODHOTOU
Ayíou Athanasiou Gate
Moat Entry
Koskinoú (Ayíou Ioánnou) Gate
VIRONOS
ROMANOU MELODHOU
0
200 m
N

derived merely from slipping through the eleven surviving gates and strolling the streets, under flying archways built for earthquake resistance, past warm-toned sandstone and limestone walls painted ochre and blue, and over *hokhláki* (pebble) pavements, arranged into coloured mosaics in certain courtyards. Getting lost in the maze of alleys is part of the experience, but if you'd rather not, look out for the accurate map-placards posted at strategic junctions.

As a walled medieval city, Rhodes invites favourable comparison with Jerusalem, Carcassonne or Ávila; both the European Heritage Commission and UNESCO agree, having designated it as a World Heritage Site. All structural alterations are strictly controlled, though little headway has been made regarding the placing of utility lines underground and the lowering of obtrusive TV aerials. No such strictures apply, however, to the tacky souvenir displays, especially around the intersection of Ippodhámou and Orféos.

The town today is effectively a legacy of the Knights of St John, who frequently adhered to Hippodamus' grid-plan: Pythagóra, Omírou and Ayíou Fanouríou are among the most important streets which follow exactly their ancient predecessors. Foundations of ancient buildings, often well below the present ground level, are on view everywhere. The Ottomans added little to the urban fabric other than a bare handful of purpose-built mosques, minarets and the graceful clocktower just south of the Palace of the Grand Masters. Though not of strategic importance in itself, the old city suffered heavy bomb damage at the hands of the Allies from 1943 to 1945 owing to German military installations in the adjacent commercial harbour, and the eastern district – the former Jewish quarter – is still pretty dilapidated over five decades later.

The Palace of the Grand Masters

The Kollákio (Collachium), or fort-within-a-fort, lies in the northern sector of the city's originally fourteenth-century ramparts, and is dominated by the **Palace of the Grand Masters** (summer Mon 2.30–9pm, Tues–Fri 8.30am–9pm; winter Mon 12.30–3pm, Tues–Sun 8.30am–3pm; €6). Almost completely destroyed by a lightning-sparked gunpowder magazine explosion in 1856 (which also levelled much of the town and killed over eight hundred people), it was hastily reconstructed by the Italians between 1937 and 1939 as a summer home for Mussolini and Victor Emmanuel III ("King of Italy and Albania, Emperor of Ethiopia"), neither of whom ever visited Rhodes.

The building's exterior, of middling authenticity, is based largely on medieval engravings and accounts. Inside, free rein was given to Fascist delusions of grandeur, with the ponderous period furnishings rivalling many a European palace. A monumental marble staircase leads up to rooms paved with **Hellenistic mosaics** from Kós; while one may deplore their plundering, they have certainly fared better here than if they had remained in the open air. The best panels, all on the upper floor, which you tour clockwise, are of a nymph riding a sea monster, and the so-called *Nine Muses of Kos*.

Though much has been made of its vulgarity (eg, in Lawrence Durrell's *Reflections on a Marine Venus*, see p.491), the palace interior is in fact fairly restrained by the norms of 1930s dictatorships. However, during maintenance work in 1994, evidence of the Italians' cavalier attitude to history and of outright vandalism was uncovered: Hellenistic and Ottoman artefacts were found discarded under rubble used to fill hollows and then bricked or tiled over; considerable artistic licence was taken with the ground floor, which had actually survived the 1856 explosion; and the site topography was altered to make the palace more imposing. Moreover, the materials and techniques employed by

△ Italian-restored turrets, Palace of the Grand Masters, (Ródhos) Old Town

the Italians are not destined to last anywhere near as long as the original ones; much of the masonry is cladding rather than structural, with the wall-cores consisting of low-quality, reinforced concrete, whose iron mesh is already causing tremendous problems owing to corrosion and expansion.

The Medieval Exhibit and "Ancient Rhodes, 2400 Years"

Adjacent to the Palace, the **Medieval Exhibit** and "**Ancient Rhodes, 2400 Years**" (same hours and admission ticket as Palace), are far and away the best presented and interpreted museums on Rhodes. The medieval collection highlights the enduring importance of Christian Rhodes as a trade centre, with exotic merchandise placing the island in a trans-Mediterranean context. Superimposed illuminated colour overlays on one exhibit show how Ródhos Town has shrunk since ancient times to the compact ensemble of today. The Knights are represented with a display covering their sugar-refining industry and a gravestone of a Grand Master; precious manuscripts and books precede a wing of post-Byzantine icons, moved here permanently from Panayía Kástrou (see p.104). A snack bar, well placed at the far end of the exhibits, provides seating looking out onto the Palace courtyard.

From the snack bar, cross the courtyard to reach the entrance to "Ancient Rhodes, 2400 Years", which occupies the ground floor and basement vaults of the north wing. This outstanding, well-labelled collection completely eclipses the "official" archeological museum in terms of explaining the everyday life of the ancient city, by arranging the exhibits according to topic (beauty aids, toys, cookware, worship, burial customs, etc). Highlights include votive offerings from ancient cult shrines; a Hellenistic floor mosaic of a comedic mask; a rare, triple-faced household idol of Hecate, goddess of the occult arts; a lead casket from an early Roman grave; and a Dali-esque mound of "failed" clay amphorae, deformed and discarded during firing.

The city walls

On Tuesday and Saturday afternoons, there's a one-hour **tour** of the **city walls** (starting 2.45pm; separate €6 admission), beginning from a gate next to the Palace and traversing the western and southern reaches as far as the Koskinoú Gate. The tour is the only permitted access to the walls, and worth the expense for unique views of an exotic skyline punctuated with minarets, palm trees and the brooding mass of the Palace. Peering down into seldom-traversed alleys and overgrown gardens, you appreciate just how villagey and – since the World War II bombardments – occasionally crumbled the old town really is. The limestone fortifications, at certain points over 12m thick, date in their present form almost entirely from extensive refurbishment following the siege of 1480 (disregarding modern repairs); the various gates and bastions divided the curtain walls into eight sections, one for each of the Order's "Tongues" or nationalities.

The Knights of St John and the Second Siege of Rhodes

The **Order of the Knights Hospitallers of St John** was established in eleventh-century Jerusalem as a nursing order tending sick Christian pilgrims. But since their original charter involved protecting as well as ministering to Christians, not a great conceptual leap was involved in them becoming a more militant order after the First Crusade. The Knights were compelled to leave Palestine in 1291 after losing their principal strongholds to the Saracens and a competing chivalric order, the Knights Templar.

Cyprus proved unsatisfactory as a new home, so the Hospitallers migrated further west to Rhodes in 1306, which they captured from the Genoese after a three-year war. Once in possession, the Knights began modifying and contracting the relatively flimsy Byzantine town fortifications; adequate funds were ensured when their rivals the Templars were suppressed in 1312 and most of their European assets made over to the Hospitallers by Pope Clement. Despite their origins, the Knights became a seafaring Order, aggrandizing themselves with frequent raids on non-Christian shipping. A huge fleet was fitted out for this purpose, its flagship the Grand Carrack, an eight-decked galley equipped for six months of continuous sailing by hundreds of men.

There were three classes of membership in the Order, each sworn to quasi-monastic vows of chastity, poverty and obedience that were honoured more often than not. Fully fledged **knights**, never numbering more than 650, were recruited only among the nobility, while **brothers**, who served as soldiers or nurses, could be commoners. **Chaplains** were assigned to each of the seven, later eight, nationalities or "**Tongues**": France, Auvergne, Provence, Italy, Spain, Germany and England. Each tongue was headed by a **prior** and the priors chose from among them a **Grand Master** or general prefect, elected for life, though in theory subject to a council of the priors. Of the nineteen Grand Masters, fourteen were French, a reflection of the three Francophone contingents, and the fact that French (with Latin) was one of the two official languages of the Order. During the fourteenth century, Spain managed to divide her contingent into the inns of Aragon and Castile, in a ploy to increase Spanish-speaking influence.

After the fall of Constantinople in 1453, the Knights were the only significant obstacle to further Ottoman expansion in the Aegean, as well as a continuing nuisance to their shipping. Although Rhodes withstood two brief Ottoman sieges in

Their masonry had become pretty bedraggled from exposure to six centuries of salt air, so the stonework is currently being refurbished with EU funding. Already this aid has had a beneficial effect on the **moat**, much of which has been landscaped with lawns and shrubbery, and which is open for free walking tours (unrestricted access from several points), shown on the old-town map on p.99.

The "Street of the Knights"

The Gothic "**Street of the Knights**" (Ippotón) leads due east from Platía Kleovoúlou, in front of the Palace. Once the main thoroughfare of the Kollákio, it was heavily restored by the Italians, who stripped the facades of their wooden, Ottoman balconies and repaired extensive 1856 blast damage. The **Inns** lining it housed most of the Knights of St John (see box below), according to linguistic/ethnic affiliation – those for England and Auvergne are one block away on Apelloú and Platía Aryirokástrou respectively – and their ground floors served as stables for the Knights' horses. Today the Inns (not generally open to the public) contain government offices and foreign cultural institutions vague-

1444 and 1480, Grand Masters Pierre d'Aubusson and Aimerie d'Amboise decided to embark on a fortification programme to resist any technological advance in Ottoman artillery.

In the spring of 1522, Sultan Süleyman the Magnificent, determined to stamp out the Knights' piracy, landed on Rhodes with a force of 100,000. For six months the Knights and their auxiliaries, outnumbered thirty to one, resisted until the Ottomans were ready, like Demetrios before them, to concede defeat. But a traitor among the Knights, piqued at not being elected Grand Master, sent word to the Sultan that the garrison was at the end of its tether and could withstand only a few more concerted attacks. The consequent Turkish offensives in October and November ensured victory, following which Süleyman granted unusually magnanimous terms: the 180 surviving Knights were allowed to take all their moveable property and ships with them on New Year's Day 1523, as well as any civilians who preferred not to live under Muslim rule.

For seven years the Knights searched for a new base in the Mediterranean, before settling on Malta, where they successfully repulsed another, four-month Ottoman attack in 1565, and provided crucial aid for the defeat of the Ottomans at Lepanto six years later. However, the English "Tongue" had been dissolved in 1534 by Henry VIII, and subsequently the Knights proved to be an anachronism: large, unified states of the sixteenth century could commission and outfit armadas far more efficiently, and the opening of trade routes to the New World and the Far East lessened the importance of controlling Mediterranean trade. The French branch of the Order was dissolved during the Revolution, and its assets confiscated; Napoleon met little resistance in 1798 when he annexed Malta in a minor diversion en route to Egypt, and dispersed the remaining Knights, apparently for good.

The English "Tongue" was revived in 1831 and reorganized as the St John Ambulance Brigade in 1888. The oldest visible traces of the Order in London's Clerkenwell district are the medieval gate on St John's Lane, all that survives of the twelfth-century priory where English Knights were recruited, and the crypt of the later church facing St John's Square, with a Maltese cross visible outside. In July 1995, today's worldwide Order – also active in Sweden, the Netherlands, Germany and Italy – held its annual four-day convention on Rhodes, with gala events centred (of course) on the Palace of the Grand Masters.

ly appropriate to their past. Although commercialization is forbidden on this street, the whole effect is predictably sterile and stagey (indeed, nearby streets were used in the filming of *Pascali's Island* in the late 1980s, based on the Barry Unsworth novel and starring Ben Kingsley). The only hint of life, about halfway up on the south side, is an iron-gated garden where a Turkish fountain, surrounded by cannon balls, gurgles – a startling sound amidst the absolute silence prevailing here at night. Directly opposite stands the most ornate of the Inns, that of France, embellished with the coats of arms of several Grand Masters.

The Archeological Museum

At the very foot of Ippotón, the Knights' Hospital has been refurbished as the **Archeological Museum** (Tues–Sun 8.30am–3pm, may open until 7pm and on Mon in peak season; €3), though the building, with its arches and echoing halls, rather overshadows the contents. An appallingly labelled and presented collection consists largely of painted pottery dating from the sixth and seventh centuries BC, enlivened at one point by Bronze Age grave jewellery from Ialyssos. Rather more accessible is the Hellenistic statue gallery, located behind the second-storey sculpture garden, where visitors pose for photos with a not very naturalistic porpoise-head sculpture. In a rear corner stands *Aphrodite Thalassia*, the so-called "Marine Venus" beloved of Lawrence Durrell, lent a rather sinister aspect by her sea-dissolved face; in the adjacent wing crouches a friendlier *Aphrodite Bathing* or, more precisely, wringing out her tresses. Opposite are earlier, fine works of the Rhodian sculpture academy, such as Hygea feeding her familiar serpent and Asklepios leaning on his staff.

The Decorative Arts and Byzantine museums

Near the Archeological Museum, on Platía Aryirokástrou, with its Byzantine fountain from Arnítha village, is the **Decorative Arts Collection** (Tues–Sun 8.30am–3pm; €1.50), gleaned from old houses across the Dodecanese. As at the neighbouring museum, there's not much in the way of explanation, but the fine Iznik and Kütahya ceramics, costumes, embroidery and folk pottery are fairly self-explanatory. The most compelling artefacts are carved cupboard doors and chest lids painted in naïve style with mythological or historical episodes.

Across the way stands the **Byzantine Museum** (Tues–Sun 8.30am–3pm; €1.50), housed in the old cathedral of the Knights, who adapted the Byzantine shrine of Panayía Kástrou for their own needs. Numerous medieval icons and frescoes lifted from crumbling, insecure chapels on Rhodes and Hálki, as well as photos of art still *in situ*, constitute the exhibits. Despite transfers of some of the best items to the Palace of the Grand Masters, this museum is still well worth a visit, since most of the Byzantine churches in the old town and outlying villages are locked; highlights of the permanent collection are a complete cycle from the domes and squinches of Thárri Monastery (see p.137) dating from 1624, lifted in 1967 to reveal much older work beneath. In the north courtyard, with its geometric mosaic panels, a barred stairway leads down to the original Byzantine *ayíasma* or sacred well, built over shortly after the Knights seized the island.

Ottoman Rhodes

If you head south from the Palace of the Grand Masters, it's hard to miss the most conspicuous Turkish monument in Rhodes, the rust-coloured **Süleymaniye Mosque**. Rebuilt in the nineteenth century on foundations three hundred years older, it's currently closed and under scaffolding, like most local Ottoman monuments, though soon to emerge from its lengthy refit in all its candy-striped glory. The old town is in fact well sown with mosques and *mescids* (the Islamic equivalent of a chapel), many of them converted from Byzantine shrines after the 1522 conquest, when the Christians were expelled from the medieval precinct. Among these, the **Ibrahim Pasha Mosque** (1531), in the old bazaar quarter off Sofokléous, retains an ornate portico and is still occasionally used for worship, while on Platía Dhoriéos, the **Rejep Pasha Mosque**, close to collapse until recent first aid, was built in 1588 from fragments of earlier churches.

The Ibrahim Pasha Mosque is still occasionally used by the sizeable Turkish-speaking minority here (see box on p.107), but in general, physical evidence of the four-hundred-year-long Ottoman tenure in Rhodes is neglected and closed to the public, with (until recently) neither the funds nor the political initiative to repair even those mosques reconsecrated for Christian use since 1912. The Süleymaniye Mosque's minaret was declared unsafe in 1989, pulled down, and never replaced.

However, during 1998, six small **Byzantine churches** in the old town – Ayía Paraskeví, Ayía Ekateríni, Áyios Athanásios, Áyios Ioánnis and two named Ayía Triádha – were refurbished, and they are sometimes open unpredictable hours (Tues–Sun; free) for visits. One church that is typically open, and hasn't had the accretions of recent centuries removed, is unprepossessing **Áyios Fanoúrios**, near the south end of the eponymous street. Fanoúrios is a rather popular saint, much resorted to now as in the past by both Rhodian Greeks and Turks for retrieving lost objects (and persons) – or winning the affections of hitherto oblivious lovers. Custom dictates that if you get what (or whom) you were seeking, you must bake a cake, have it consecrated by the priest at Áyios Fanoúrios and distribute it to your neighbours.

Directly opposite the Sülemaniye Mosque stands the **Ottoman library** (Mon–Fri 8.30am–2.30pm & 6–9pm, Sat & Sun 9am–noon; tip custodian if they're around), dating from 1794 and endowed with a rich collection of early medieval manuscripts and Korans; two specimens from the fifteenth century, jointly worth about £400,000, went missing in 1990, but were found at a London auctioneer's and returned in 1994 with appropriate ceremony.

The hamam (Dhimotiká Loutrá)

The Ottomans' most enduring civic contribution is the imposing **hamam** or Turkish baths, marked as the *Dhimotiká Loutrá* ("Municipal Baths"), on Platía Ariónos up in the southwest corner of the old town (subject to prolonged closures for "repairs", but specimen hours Tues 1–6pm, Wed–Fri 11am–6pm, Sat 8am–6pm; admission €1.50, but €0.90 Wed & Sat). Originally constructed in 1558, it was renovated by the builder of the adjacent Mustafa Pasha Mosque in 1765, badly damaged during the last war and restored afterwards.

In their prime, the Rhodes baths were considered among the most elegant in the Aegean, and are now the last working ones in Greece outside Thrace (and, shortly, Mytilíni; see p.382). They are capable of holding about two hundred people at any given time, and supposedly consume a tonne of olive wood daily in the process of heating the water, which courses through pipes under the floor as well as out of the "hot" taps. There are separate facilities for each sex, men (typically) getting the grander central section, with its lofty dome pierced by star-shaped skylights, and the actual washing facilities tucked into smaller, marble-lined rooms off the main hall. The clientele consists principally of old-town Greeks, who use the *hamam* as a social occasion, supplemented by a smattering of tourists and local Turks.

Platía Ippokrátous, Ródhos Old Town

The Turks of Rhodes

The **Turkish community** of Rhodes dates from 1522, when an Ottoman garrison and civil servants took control of the island, settling principally in and around the main town. They were supplemented between 1898 and 1913 by Cretan Muslims fleeing intercommunal troubles on their native island. These Cretan refugees founded the now-dilapidated suburb of Kritiká, not far from the airport.

Some old-town Turks can still trace their ancestry to the sixteenth-century conquest, and will proudly tell you that they have every right to be considered native Rhodians. Not surprisingly such a stance fails to impress the Greek authorities, and their bureaucratic treatment tends to function, as in western Thrace on the mainland, as a barometer of the current state of relations between Greece and Turkey. Recent decades have seen a sharp decline in the local Turkish population (though it is now stabilizing at about 3000); for example, while there were once four Turkish jewellers at the base of Sokrátous, there is now just one, Tzivelek. Although it's still possible to spot Turkish names on the marquees of various sandalmakers, kebab stalls, and kafenía, local "Muslim Hellenes" (their official designation) generally maintain a low public profile, gravitating towards service trades such as delivery, auto-repair, wholesale catering, confectionery and a few restaurants in the new town, where they're less likely to come into contact with outsiders.

Unlike *hamams* in Turkey, no towels or sundries are included in the admission price, so bring everything you need; you'll be assigned a free locker for your clothes. Beyond the weighted doors is the cool room, from which you proceed to the steam room, directly above the heating pipes. Massages may be available, performed on the stone platform that's the focus of any *hamam*. In the bathing rooms you sluice yourself down by dipping a bowl into the stone font. In another contrast with Anatolian practice, bathers strut around stark naked. And although the baths are cleaned scrupulously at closing time, don't be too surprised if you glimpse the odd cockroach – their name in Turkish, after all, means "*hamam*-bug".

The old Jewish quarter

Heading downhill from the Süleymaniye Mosque, **Sokrátous**, once the heart of the Ottoman bazaar, is now the "Via Turista", whose multiple fur and jewellery stores swarm with tourists – conspicuous among them, as one reader memorably put it, "the blue-rinse set off the cruise ships vying for gold by the inch".

Beyond the tiled centrepiece fountain in Platía Ippokrátous, where broad steps lead up to the Kastellania or medieval traders' tribunal and stock exchange, Aristotélous leads to the **Platía ton Evréon Martýron** (Square of the Jewish Martyrs), renamed in memory of the local community that was almost totally exterminated in 1944.

Of the four **synagogues** that once stood in Ródhos Town, only **Kal Kadosh Shalom**, on Simíou, 100m to the south (three doorways past Dhosiádhou 16 – look for the Star of David in relief if a sign's not up; daily 10am–5pm), survives today. This ornate structure features a beautiful *hokhláki* floor and eight arcaded columns supporting the roof. Rarely used for religious services, it's maintained essentially as a memorial to the approximately 1800 Jews of Rhodes and Kós deported to Auschwitz; plaques commemorating the dead are mostly in French, the preferred language of educated Jews in the east Aegean at the beginning of the twentieth century. There are more such memorials in the Jewish section of the city cemetery behind Zéfyros beach (see p.114).

The Jews of Rhodes

As in much of the rest of Greece, **Jews** had dwelt in Rhodes since at least the first century AD, and during the Ottoman era were permitted – unlike the Orthodox Greeks – to live inside the walled city, in the easternmost quarter allotted them by the conquerors. Neither did the local Jews suffer especially under Italian rule – their population even recovering from medieval vicissitudes to around four thousand by the 1920s.

Thereafter, the *Rodesli* (as Rhodian Jews and their descendants call themselves) began to emigrate in large numbers, travelling on Italian passports to what was then the Belgian Congo, Rhodesia, Egypt, South America and the US (especially the Deep South and the Pacific Northwest). By the time restrictive anti-Semitic laws were promulgated and enforced late in the 1930s, and hostilities commenced between Italy and the Allies shortly thereafter, some two thousand had managed to flee overseas, thus avoiding the fate of the 1673 Rhodian and about 120 Koan Jews deported to Auschwitz by the Nazis in June 1944.

Of these, barely eighty survived, while today there are fewer than forty in Ródhos Town, mostly elderly Jews from Vólos, Kardhítsa and Lárissa on the mainland, who resettled here after 1948 on the orders of Greece's head rabbi so that a living Jewish presence would remain on the island. The caretaker, Loukia Modhiano, is an exception, a Rhodian woman who survived Auschwitz and – like so many of her generation – speaks Greek, Ladino (a language spoken by Sephardic Jews from mainly Greece and Spain), Italian and French, but little English. The community is too tiny to support a rabbi, so one comes annually from Belgium or France to conduct Yom Kippur services.

At the rear of the synagogue, a one-room **museum**, well labelled in English, was set up in 1997 by Aron Hasson, a Los Angeles attorney of *Rodesli* descent (see box above). It functions primarily as a resource centre and meeting point for diaspora *Rodesli* – who can be seen photographing photos of ancestors, and copying documents – but is also of general interest for its translations of tombstone inscriptions, some elaborately poetic, and photos of diaspora life in such far-flung spots as Alabama and Buenos Aires.

The traditional red-light district

Prostitution is legal and licensed in Greece, yet some folk are distinctly surprised to stumble onto the traditional **red-light district**, which has dominated the same corner of the old town – a series of lanes between Timahídha, Omírou and Irodhótou by the Ayíou Athanasíou gate – for as long as anyone can remember. There are just a dozen women, each occupying a single house, with a name-plaque, the proverbial red light over the door, and sometimes even "visiting hours" posted. The area is busiest and most obvious when the US Sixth Fleet is anchored offshore – bound to be a less frequent occurrence in the wake of the September 2001 terrorist attacks.

The new town

Nobody comes to Rhodes especially to admire Italian town planning and civic architecture, but it's difficult to avoid noticing some of the choicer examples of Art Deco and later Fascist International scattered about Neohóri. Prominent among these are the town hall and prefecture opposite, the law courts and post office further along Platía Eleftherías, the reconstructed **Basilica of**

Evangelismós (speculatively modelled on that of St John opposite the Palace of the Grand Masters, blown up in 1856) in between, and the rotondas of the nautical club and aquarium on their respective promontories. The Franciscan order also contributed two more modern churches: Áyios Frangískos (San Francesco), just outside the Ayíou Athanasíou gate and still used, and the fine Art Deco church and monastery of Santa Maria della Vittoria (still occupied), ironically in one of the more touristy corners of Neohóri. The irregularly heptagonal **New Market** or *Néa Agorá* still (just) functions as a produce and fish vendor's, though the shops, cafés and *souvláki* stalls within are touristy and not especially good value; honourable exceptions include the no-name bakery (look for the sign reading *Pratirio Artou* in Greek), with wonderfully dense yeastless bread from Triánda, and the resolutely local hangout *Paradhosiako Kafenio Iy Symi*, founded by natives of that adjacent island.

A less than complete separation of old and new towns is most obviously demonstrated by the **Áyios Nikólaos fortress** at the end of relentlessly contemporary Mandhráki harbour's east jetty, itself of ancient vintage and studded with sixteenth-century windmills (one recently restored to working order). The fortress (currently shut) was built by the Knights after the first Turkish siege of 1480, and last saw service as a World War II gun emplacement; it now supports a modern lighthouse.

The entrance to Mandhráki is also the sentimental favourite candidate-site for the **Colossus of Rhodes** (see box below), an ancient statue of Apollo built to celebrate the end of the 305 BC siege; today, two columns surmounted by bronze deer, adopted as the island's mascots (see box on p.113), are less overpowering replacements.

The Colossus of Rhodes

Reproduced ad nauseam on maps, posters, tea towels and T-shirts as the symbol of the island, the **Colossus of Rhodes**, one of the Seven Wonders of the ancient world, has not actually stood intact for over two millennia. According to legend, Demetrios Polyorketes, upon conceding defeat in 305 BC (see on p.94), suggested that his siege paraphernalia be sold and the proceeds used to erect a statue commemorating the campaign. Originally, the Peloponnesian sculptor Lysippos was commissioned to fashion a massive Chariot of the Sun, but subsequently gave the job to a local student, Khares of Lindos, who chose to cast a bronze effigy dedicated to the island's patron deity Apollo Helios. This took twelve years to complete, near the end of which time Khares supposedly killed himself in shame upon noticing a serious design flaw, leaving the final phase to a certain Lakhes.

Ancient travellers described the Colossus as being 35m high and weighing in at an estimated 125 tonnes, though their texts are coy on the all-important issue of where and in what pose the statue was placed. This has not prevented medieval and modern artists from depicting him standing astride the mouth of Mandhráki harbour with ships sailing between his legs. Our only clue is that the Colossus collapsed on land, not into the sea, sundered at the knees by an earthquake in 227 BC. The story goes that the sun god, via his oracle at Delphi, forbade the restoration of the Colossus, and for nearly nine centuries the remains lay untouched. In 654 AD, they were finally purchased by a Jew from Edessa and supposedly hauled away on the backs of nine hundred camels (debunkers say ninety), only to return (according to yet another debatable legend) in the form of Turkish cannonballs during the 1522 siege. Every so often, purported statue fragments are found on the sea bed near Mandhráki, but these have always turned out to be more recent metallic debris.

RÓDHOS TOWN

ACCOMMODATION

Anastasia	6
Best Western Plaza	5
Capitol	4
Casa Antica	3
Esperia	1
New Village Inn	2
Spartalis	7

Hydrofoil docking	H
Yacht docking	Y
Excursion boats	E
Catamaran	C

0 200 m

RESTAURANTS & NIGHTLIFE

Anatolikes Nostimies	M
Blue Lagoon Pool Bar	I
Chalki	D
Christos' Garden	G
Colorado	C
El Divino	K
Felicia	H
Kebap House	R
Khristos (O Vlahos)	W
O Makis	T
Metaxi Mas	X
Minuit	A
Niohori	B
O'Reilly's	E
Palia Istoria	U
Rock Style	N
Sakis	S
7.5 Wonder	F
Sheftalies	V
Stani	Q
To Steki tou Tsima	P
To Steno	O
Sticky Fingers	J
Studio Gas	I
Vassilis	L

N

Aquarium
Hotel Rodon (Casino)
Murad Reis Mosque
Élli Beach
Nautical Club
Villa Cleobolus
Santa Maria della Vittoria
Municipal Theatre
Provincial Government
Áyios Nikólaos Tower
Town Hall
Basilica of Evangelismós
Olympic Airways
Port Police
Mandhráki
Windmills
NEOHORI
New Market
Roda Bus Stop
KTEL Bus Stop
Sound & Light
Kiriakoulis Hydrofoils
Ferry Mooring Points
Hospital
Commercial Harbour (Kolóna)
Customs

KOS
NISSYROU
ASTYPALEAS
KALYMNOU-LEROU
TILOU
GAVRIEL HARITOU
PATMOU
HALKIS
KASTELLORIZOU
PAPANIKOLAOU
KATHOPOULI
IOANNI
KAZOULI
GRIVA
NIKIFOROU
DHRAGOUMI
MANDILARA
AMARANDOU
POLITEHNIOU
G. EFSTATHIOU
IERO LOHOU
IRODON
AMERIKIS
PL. KOUNDOURIOTI
DHODHEKANISION
25-MARTIOU
AKTI MIAOULI
KRITIS
YEORYIOU LEONDOS
APOLLONIOU RODHIOU
DHILBERAKI
OREANIDHOU
28-OKTOVRIOU
IONOS
FANOURAKI
PL. AKADHEMIAS
THEMELI
LAMBRAKI
AMMOHOSTOU
ETHELONDON
MAKARIOU
PLESSA
PL. ELEFTHERIAS
PLASTIRA
PL. KYPROU
GALIAS
KARPATHOU
PAPAGOU
PL. PSAROPOULA
ALEXANDHROU DHIAKOU
S. VENIZELOU
ZERVOU
AKTI KANARI
VALAORITOU
METAXA
ERYTHROU STAVROU
EL. VENIZELOU
PAPALOUKA
LASKOU
VORIOU IPIROU
RIGA FEREOU

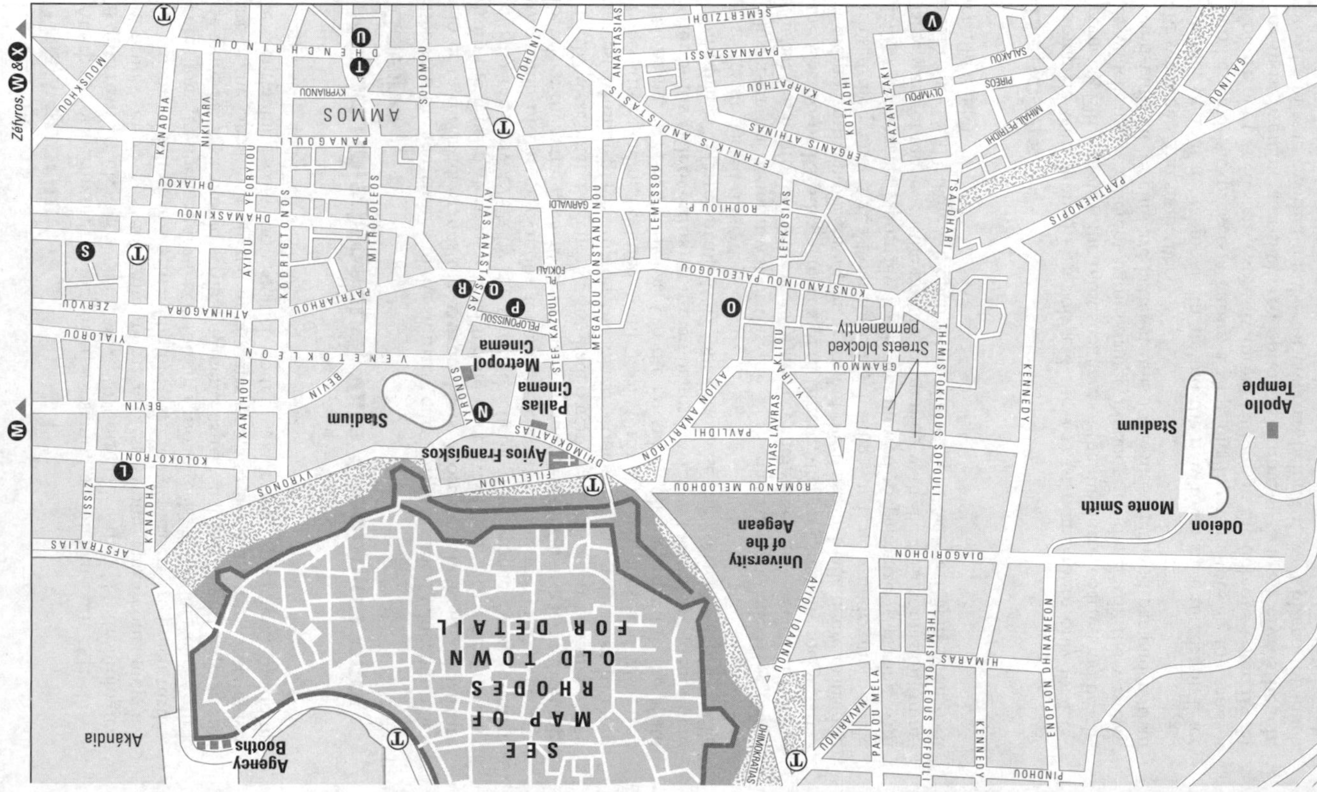
SEE MAP OF RHODES OLD TOWN FOR DETAIL
Akándia
Agency Booths
Áyios Frangískos
Stadium
Pallas Cinema
Metropol Cinema
University of the Aegean
AMMOS
Streets blocked permanently
Monte Smith
Odeion
Stadium
Apollo Temple
Zéfyros, W & X
M
Cemeteries
Rodhíni Park & Líndhos, Asgoúrou, Koskinoú
Airport
AFSTRALIAS
ISSIZ
KANADHA
KOLOKOTRONI
BEVIN
YIALOROU
ZERVOU
MOUSKHOU
NIKITARA
XANTHOU
VYRONOS
ATHINAGORA
AYIOU
YEORYIOU
DHAMASKINOU
DHIAKOU
KODRIGTONOS
PATRIARHOU
VENETOKLEON
MITROPOLEOS
PANAGOULI
KYPRIANOU
DHENDHRINOU
SOLOMOU
AYIAS ANASTASIAS
PELOPONISSOU
STEF. KAZOULI
PL. FOKIALI
GARIVALDI
LINDHOU
FILELLINON
DHIMOKRATIAS
MEGALOU KONSTANDINOU
ANASTASIAS
ETHNIKIS ANDISTASIS
LEMESSOU
RODHIOU P.
KONSTANDINOU PALEOLOGOU
AYION ANARYIRON
ROMANOU MELODHOU
PAVLIDHI
AYIAS LAVRAS
Y. IRAKLIOU
LEFKOSIAS
GRAMMOU
ERGANIS ATHINAS
KARPATHOU
PAPANASTASSI
SEMERTZIDHI
KOTIADHI
KAZANTZAKI
OLYMPOU
PIREOS
SALAKOU
MIHAIL PETRIDHI
TSALDHARI
THEMISTOKLEOUS SOFOULI
KENNEDY
PARTHENOPIS
GALINOU
AYIOU IOANNOU
NAVARINOU
PAVLOU MELA
HIMARAS
DIAGORIDHON
ENOPLON DHINAMEON
PINDHOU
L
S
T
U
V
N
O
P
Q
R

The Aquarium

At the northernmost point of the island, an Italian-built Art Deco **Aquarium** (daily 9am–9pm; €1.80), officially the "Hydrobiological Institute", displays a subterranean maze of sea-water tanks containing live specimens of Rhodian sea life. The biggest crowd-pleasers are green turtles, enormous groupers and wicked-looking moray eels; if nothing else, a dusk or rainy-day visit should settle arguments as to what the English equivalents are of the Greek fish offered in tavernas (see also box on p.59). Upstairs is a less enthralling collection of half-rotten taxidermic specimens, including sharks, seals and even a whale.

Murad Reis Mosque, Villa Cleobolus and Casino

Between the aquarium and the similarly curvilinear Nautical Club, but much closer to the latter, stands the **Murad Reis Mosque**, which, in a departure from the usual pattern of official indifference, was fitted with a new minaret during the early 1990s by the Greek Archeological Service. Next to this is the tomb of the eponymous admiral, who died during the 1522 siege, and between them the *hokhláki* courtyard of the caretakers' ramshackle dwelling. To the west extends a eucalyptus-shaded cemetery, the oldest and one of the largest Muslim graveyards on the island, containing several rather battered *türbe*s (freestanding, domed tombs) of Ottoman worthies and also one belonging to a Shah of Persia. On the far side, a plaque affixed to the **Villa Cleobolus (Kleovoulos)** commemorates Lawrence Durrell's residence here from spring 1945 to spring 1947, but otherwise the cottage – hardly a villa – seems neglected these days.

Just a few paces northwest of this, the 1928-built Albergo delle Rose (*Hotel Rodon*) was refurbished after years of neglect and pressed into service in 1999 as the **Casino of Rhodes**, Greece's third largest. After an extremely rocky start – it did not turn a profit for a year or so, and the Russian-Mafia figure managing it used the premises as a front for drug-dealing – it is now under more stable Italian stewardship. Unusually, locals are allowed to patronize it, parting with large sums of money in the process, beginning with the €15 admission (minimum age 23, ID required; open Mon–Thurs 3pm–6am, Fri 3pm–Mon 6am continuously).

Beaches

Complete with sunbeds, parasols and showers (standing room only for latecomers), **Élli beach** is the most sheltered of the mediocre, coarse-sand beaches which, under different names, fringe Neohóri to the north; the westerly, wind-buffeted beaches are better haunts for windsurfers and paragliders than for swimmers and sunbathers.

Other options for taking a dip around the new town are limited: you'll see families, and backpackers awaiting a ship, digging their toes in the sand at Kolóna, but posted signs expressly forbid bathing in the dubious water. By far the most hygienic and sheltered option is southeast-facing **Zéfyros beach**, broad and sandy, with a number of tavernas behind it, well placed for lunch (see p.115). There's no bus service, and it's a hefty 25-minute walk from the southerly gates of the old town, so your best option is to take a scooter or a taxi.

Monte Smith: Hellenistic Rhodes

About 2km southwest of Mandhráki, the sparse, unenclosed remains of the Hellenistic acropolis perch atop **Monte Smith**. Formerly Áyios Stéfanos, this hill was rather bizarrely renamed after the British admiral Sydney Smith, who used it as a watchpoint during the Napoleonic wars. Dating from the third and second centuries BC, the ruins include a restored, garishly marble-clad *odeion* to one side of the more subdued, 200-metre stadium, a peaceful, tree-flanked spot. Above the *odeion* loom the three re-erected columns and pediment of an **Apollo temple**; visits are most rewarding at sunset, when both temple and town are shown to advantage, with Turkey and Sými visible on the horizon.

Infrequent #5 city buses run from the New Market if you're not keen on the walk, though from the Ayíou Athanasíou gate of the old town it's not much more than fifteen minutes on foot. Other conspicuously signposted reminders of the ancient city are the foundations of an **Aphrodite temple** in the old town's Platía Sýmis; gauging the distance between there and the acropolis gives you a fair idea of ancient Rhodes' vast extent.

Rodhíni Park

Monte Smith is popular enough with joggers and strollers, but for summer shade and greenery the best spot is probably the 1996-spruced-up **Rodhíni park** (free admission), nearly 2km south of town on the road to Líndhos, and served by city bus route #3. This wooded area, known as Zimboúli in Ottoman times, lines either bank of a natural ravine spanned by an aqueduct of indeterminate age. The ravine's watercourse is fed by natural springs and is home to ducks and peacocks. A short distance upstream, separate, adjacent enclosures contain large numbers of Rhodian deer (see box below) and Cretan ibex.

Hellenistic rock-cut **tombs** at the south end of the park, rather dubiously attributed to the Ptolemies, constitute a final possible attraction. A signposted, 700-metre access road winds through a man-made rock tunnel, crosses the top of the ravine, and skirts a football pitch; on the south side of this, beside a subterranean pumping station, stands a hollowed-out natural monolith, constituting the tombs in question (permanently locked).

The deer of Rhodes

The miniature **deer** found on Rhodes, *Dama dama*, are not actually indigenous to the island. They were first introduced in ancient times at the behest of the Delphic oracle in response to islanders' entreaties as to how best to quell an eruption of snakes. Accounts differ as to how the reptiles were dispatched: the deer either repelled them with the odour of their urine, or impaled the serpents on their antlers. The deer themselves subsequently died out and had to be reintroduced by the Knights; the Italians did likewise, after the deer were hunted almost to local extinction during Ottoman rule.

For some years, many specimens lived in the dry moat between the inner and outer walls of the old town. However, eight were killed by feral dogs in 1994, prompting a debate on the future of those remaining. A proposal to release them into the wild south of the island was vetoed for fear of poachers; instead some thirty deer are currently housed in a pen at Rodhíni park, pending a move to a much larger enclosure near the Ptolemaic tombs. Until then, these attractive beasts can be seen hunkered down at midday on straw beds, chewing the cud.

The cemeteries

The giant **municipal cemeteries** at Korakónero, just inland from Zéfyros beach, might not immediately strike one as a hot tourist destination, but if you have any interest in Rhodes' recent past, they prove strangely compelling. For one thing, this is one of the very few remaining spots in the Balkans – certainly the only one in Greece – where the dead of four faiths lie in proximity, albeit separated by high walls. The easterly **Greek Orthodox section** is, of course, the largest and holds the fewest surprises. The small **Catholic section** is not only the last home of various north European expatriates, but also demonstrates that – contrary to received wisdom – a fair number of Italians elected to accept Greek nationality and stay on after the 1948 unification with Greece, and that a few native Greeks had succumbed to temptation and renounced the Orthodox faith. The **Jewish section** – shown erroneously transposed with the Muslim one on virtually all maps – has, for reasons made clear in the box on p.108, seen little activity since 1944, and is full of memorials in French to those who were deported. Immediately opposite its gate, across the busy road, is a small **Allied War graves** plot with 142 burials from 1941 to 1946, some moved here from inconvenient sites on other Dodecanese islands; as ever, there's admirable documentation and a guest register to sign by the gate. Just south of the Jewish section, the "**Muslim**" **section** (ie Turkish) is the most heavily used and best maintained of the three minority cemeteries – perhaps indicating that the Turkish population of Rhodes has stabilized after years of decline, and that the government does not blatantly interfere with the activities of the Rhodian *vakuf* or Islamic benevolent foundation.

Eating and drinking

Finding good-value **tavernas** in and around Ródhos Town is a challenge, though by no means an insurmountable one. The place is large enough that certain economies of scale apply: tradespeople and students have to eat somewhere, and if you're setting your sights a couple of notches higher, it's possible to find carefully prepared, even exotic, meals at not overly inflated prices. Neohóri fare tends to be more western and snacky, while restaurants in neighbourhoods south of the old city offer a serious Greek feed. As a general rule, the more you escape the crowds and the further south you go, the better value you'll find.

Cafés and bakeries

Kringlan Swedish Bakery Íonos Dhragoúmi 14, Neohóri. The stress is on brioches, pizzas, cakes, sandwiches and rich filter coffee. Closed Sun evening.

Ömer Omírou, cnr Pythagora, Old Town. Turkish bakery selling wholegrain bread and fine cakes.

Stani Ayías Anastasías 28, cnr Paleón Patrón Yermanoú, south of the Koskinoú Gate. Most central outlet of a chain of Rhodian Turkish confectioners, scooping out two dozen flavours of the best ice cream on the island, publicity for rival *Mike's* notwithstanding.

Tsirillos Ippodhámou 41, Old Town. Plenty of turnovers suitable for snacks; the last wood-fired bakery in town and, as such, worth supporting.

Restaurants

The old town

Anthony's Souvlaki on Coals cnr Omírou and Pythagóra. Exactly as the sign says, superbly executed for a mostly local clientele. A few salads and starters too; supper only; inexpensive.

Araliki Aristofánous 45. Bohemian expatriates and travellers tired of standard resort grub seek out this old-style kafenío on the ground floor of a medieval house. Small plates of exquisitely original mezédhes are provided by Italian proprietors Miriam (the savouries) and Valeria (the sweets), from a perennial menu and (often more compelling) daily specials. Count on €16.50 per person with drinks, which include Nissyrot *soumádha* or mainland wine. Open March–Dec Mon–Sat from 11.30am until late; also shut two random weeks July–Aug.

L'Auberge Bistrot Praxitélous 21 ☎02410/34 292. Popular, genuine French-run bistro with excellent Frenchified food: allow €18 per person for three hefty courses plus wine from a well-selected Greek list; jazz soundtrack included. Summer seating in the courtyard of this restored medieval inn – inside under the arches during cooler months. Open late March–late Dec for supper daily except Mon; reservations suggested.

Hatzikelis Solomoú Alhadhéf 9, just in from the Panayía Gate beyond the bombed-out shell of Santa Maria del Borgo church. Creative salads, seafood and mezédhes, at fairly reasonable prices. Open most of the year.

Kostas Pythagóra 62. Perennial all-rounder and backpackers' favourite, on this site since at least the 1970s, run by three generations of men. Fish, grills, good *horiátiki*; budget €11 each.

O Meraklis Aristotélous 30. One of the last Rhodian rough edges not yet filed smooth, this *pátsatzídhiko* (tripe-soup kitchen) trotter caters for a pre-dawn clientele of post-club lads, Turkish shopkeepers, prostitutes, pimps, nightclub singers and travellers just stumbled off an overnight ferry. Great free entertainment, including famously rude staff, and the soup's good, too: the traditional Greek working man's breakfast and hangover cure. Open 3–8am only.

Mikes (pronounced "mee-kess") nameless alley behind Sokrátous 17. Inexpensive (for Rhodes, anyway) hole in the wall, serving absolutely nothing but grilled fish, salads and wine.

Sarris (aka *To Magazi tou Sarri*), Platía Evdhímou. An extensive menu, strong on seafood, premium wines (don't ask for *hýma*), foreign beers, proper nappery and winning service are this popular indoor/outdoor taverna's strong points. The quality is decent, but portions small; you can get out for €15 a head, but best budget €19.

Sea Star (aka *Pizanias*) Sofokléous 24, corner of the square. A three-decades-old institution, where colourful Pizanias mans the grill himself. Not only fresh scaly fish – staff show you the pink gills – but shellfish like *kydhónia* (cockles) and *petalídhia* (limpets), grilled octopus and squid. With two bottles of expensive wine, starters and loads of seafood, four can eat for €85–88 – elsewhere in the Old Town it'd be double that. Reservations suggested on ☎02410/22 117.

The new town

Anatolikes Nostimies Kapodhistríou 60, Akándia port. The name means "Anatolian Delicacies", and that's what's on offer at this Rhodian Turkish-run grill: Turkish-Middle Eastern dips and starters, plus sixteen variations of kebab. Not much atmosphere, but friendly and reasonable; post-prandial hubble-bubble provided on request. Open 11am–midnight.

Chalki (aka *Pavlos'*) Kathopoúli 30, Neohóri. Supper-only *mezedhopolío* that's a bit more expensive, elaborate and quirky than nearby *Niohori*.

Felicia Aktí Miaoúli 4–6, just off Platía Psaropoúlou. Genuine, reasonably priced Italian trattoria, specializing in pasta and pizza; congenial decor, a few sea-view tables outside in a wind-proof conservatory.

Kebap House Cnr Ayías Anastasías and Paleón Patrón Yermanoú, opposite *Stani* confectioners. As expected, doner kebap but also *lahmacun* (Turko-Arabic pizza) and roast chicken straight out of the domed oven; pleasant sidewalk-conservatory seating.

Khristos Ouzeri Inomayerio (O Vlahos) Klavdhíou Pépper 165, at the big bend, Zéfyros Beach. As the name implies, both ouzerí fare – marinated fish or peppers, *gávros*, great *tzatzíki* – accompanying a vast oúzo list, plus vegetable-strong *mayireftá* (cuttlefish with spinach, fish soup, eggplant *imam*) that sell out quickly. Not as cheap (€10.50–12 each) or big-portioned as formerly, but still worth the trek out.

Psistaria O Makis Dhendhrinoú 69, Ámmos district. Every conceivable cut of roast beast here, including *kokorétsi* (offal kebab) and *kefalákia* (sheep's head, if you dare); considered by some to be better value for money than *Palia Istoria* across the way (see below).

Metaxi Mas Klavdhíou Pépper 116, Zéfyros Beach. No sign or menu in English – look for the elevated boat – at this seafood ouzerí purveying various exotic titbits (*foúskes, kydhónia*, etc); count on €32.50–35.50 per couple with booze, slightly cheaper per person in a group – but still 25 percent less than in the old town. Daily lunch and dinner except Sun lunch only.

Niohori Ioánni Kazoúli 29, Neohóri, by the Franciscan monastery. Also known as "Kiki's" after the jolly proprietress, this homey, inexpensive local serves lunch and supper; best for grills, sourced from their own butcher/farm.

Palia Istoria Mitropóleos 108, cnr Dhendhrínou, Ámmos district. Reckoned to be the best *kultúra* taverna in town, but predictably expensive for such dishes as cauliflower *yiovétsi*, peppered testicles, celery hearts in egg-lemon sauce and scallops with mushrooms and artichokes, washed down by a hundred-strong wine list. Mon–Sat dinner only; reservations essential on ☎02410/32 421.

Sakis Ipsilándou 27, Áyios Nikólaos. Genuine taverna with pleasant patio seating, equally popular with Rhodians and savvy expats. Excellent seafood and starters; it's possible to have three courses (including modest fish like *yermanós*) and a beer for €11.50. Supper only, all year.

Sheftalies Tsaldhári 21, south of Monte Smith past Marinopoulos Supermarket. Direct antithesis to *Palia Istoria*, since you can fill up for €7.50. Zero atmosphere, but a genuine charcoal griller featuring the namesake *sheftaliés*, dioxin-free chicken (some find this too peppery) and *kokorétsi*, plus a few daily *mayireftá* plates.

7.5 Wonder Dhilberáki 15, Neohóri ☎02410/39 805. Swedish chefs blend French, Mediterranean and Far Eastern classics in startling ways. Their motto is: "Food, drink and party hats since 292 BC" (the year the Seventh Wonder went up). Despite the gimmick, well regarded. Open March–New Year's, dinner only, shut Sun & Mon.

To Steki tou Tsima Peloponnísou 22, around corner from *Stani* (see p.114). Very reasonable seafood ouzerí, with the stress on aficionados' shellfish titbits (*foúskes*, *spiníalo*) and small fish not prone to farming. No airs or graces, just patently fresh materials, and open Sun too.

To Steno Ayíon Anaryíron 29, 400m southwest of the old town. As the name ("narrow" in Greek) implies, this is a small, and unusually in Ródhos Town, a genuinely welcoming ouzerí, with outdoor seating in the warmer months. The menu is limited (sausages, chickpea soup, *pitaroúdhia* or courgette croquettes, salads with caper sprigs), but superbly executed and eminently reasonable in price.

Vassilis (Kova) Kolokotróni, 80m east of Kanadhá, south of Akándia commercial port. Another place to go when you're down to your last euro: a friendly working-man's canteen, busiest from noon to 2pm, with several *mayireftá* dishes to choose from and shady glass-conservatory seating between the auto-repair shops. Also opens evenings.

Nightlife and entertainment

The old town formerly had a well-deserved reputation for being tomb-silent at night; this has changed drastically since the late 1990s, with an entire alley (Miltiádhou) off Apéllou given over to half a dozen loud music **bars and clubs**, frequented almost exclusively by Greeks; their names and proprietors change yearly, but the locations remain the same. This is just an appetizer for the estimated two hundred foreigner-patronized bars and clubs in Neohóri, where theme nights, drinks-with-cover and various other gimmicks predominate. They are found mostly along the streets and alleys bounded by Alexándhrou Dhiákou, Orfanídhou (aka "Skandi Street", after the latter-day Vikings), Lohagoú Fanouráki and Nikifórou Mandhilará.

Sedate by comparison, Ministry of Culture-approved folk dances (June–Oct Mon, Wed & Fri 9.20pm; €10.30) are presented with live accompaniment by the **Nelly Dimoglou Company**, performed in the landscaped "Old Town Theatre" off Andhroníkou, near Platía Ariónos. As these things go, they're amongst the best of their kind, but it's perhaps wise to remember the caveat of the late Hellenophile Kevin Andrews: "for the tourist (there are) the official folk-dances, the open-air productions – carefully resurrected, costumed in a way that we shall never again see in any village, flawlessly executed and dead as mutton. Folk do their dancing when drunk or otherwise exalted, or when they feel the earth moving upward through their bodies."

More of a technological extravaganza is the **Sound and Light** show, spotlighting sections of the city walls, staged in a garden just off Platía Rimínis. There's English-language narration nightly except Sunday, with screening time varying from 8.15pm to 10.15pm (€3.50).

Thanks to a large contingent from the local university, there are several year-round **cinemas** in the new town showing first-run fare indoors or open air according to season and air-conditioning capabilities. Choose from among the summer-only outdoor cinema by the Rodon Municipal Theatre, next to the town hall in Neohóri; the Metropol multiplex, at the corner of Venetokléon and Výronos, southeast of the old town opposite the stadium, refurbished in 2001; and the nearby Pallas multiplex on Dhimokratías, refurbished in 1999.

Bars and music venues

The old town

Café Besara Sofokléous 11–13. Congenial breakfast café/low-key boozer run by an Australian lady, with interesting mixed clientele and live music some nights.

Mango Bar Platía Dhoriéos 3. Piped music and a variety of drinks at this durable bar on an otherwise quiet plaza; also a good source of breakfast after 8am, served under a plane tree.

Resalto Plátonos 6, opposite the mosque. Live Greek *rebétika* and *laïkó* sounds, rather cheaper and more acoustic than nearby rival *Café Chantant*. Typically open Wed–Sun night, but weekends only in low season; free entry but pricey drinks.

Iy Rogmi tou Khronou Platía Ariónos. Taped music at a reasonable level and a congenial crowd make this new (2001) bar worth a look.

Rolóï Orféos 1. The Baroque clocktower erected by Ahmet Fetih Pasha in 1857 is now the focus of possibly the most exclusive café-bar in the old town. Admission charge to climb the tower, and steeply priced drinks, but you are paying for the terrific view.

The new town

Blue Lagoon Pool Bar 25-Martíou 2, Neohóri. One of the better theme bars, in this case a "desert island" with palm trees, waterfalls, live turtles and parrots, a shipwrecked galleon – and taped music. Open 8.30am–3am March–Oct.

Christos' Garden/To Dhiporto Dhilberáki 59. This combination art-gallery/bar/café occupies a carefully restored old house and courtyard with pebble-mosaic floors throughout. Incongruously classy for the area.

Colorado Entertainment Centre Orfanídhou 57, cnr Aktí Miaouli. Triple venue: "pub" with live in-house band (rock covers), "club" with taped sounds, and quiet upstairs chill-out bar.

El Divino Alexándhrou Dhiákou 5. Very classy, Greek-frequented "music bar" with garden seating and the usual range of coffees and alcohol. Open June–Oct.

Minuit Kastellorízou 4 (off "100 Palms Square"). Reasonably priced venue with dancing to international taped music, after live nightly Greek "floor show".

O'Reilly's Apolloníou Rodhíou 61. Irish theme pub with live music almost nightly, and Irish draught beers.

Sticky Fingers Anthoúla Zérvou 6. Long-lived music bar with reasonably priced drinks; live rock several nights weekly from 10pm onwards, Fri & Sat only off season.

Studio Gas 25-Martíou 2. Considered the best disco on Rhodes; cool off in the adjacent *Blue Lagoon* (see above). Open 10pm until dawn.

Listings

Airlines Aegean-Cronus Airlines, Ethelondón Dhodhekanisíon 20 ☎02410/24 400 or 25 444; Olympic, Iérou Lóhou 9 ☎02410/24 571.

Airport information Call ☎02410/83 214 or 82 300 for the latest on (often delayed) flight arrivals and departures.

American Express c/o Rhodos Tours, Ammohóstou 23 ☎02410/74 022 or 21 010. Refund agents for lost/stolen cheques; open Mon–Sat, standard shop hours.

Animal Welfare Society Tsaïri district, Rhodes–Líndhos road, opposite army base ☎02410/37 727 or 69 224. They keep a kennel for mistreated small animals, conduct patrols looking for animal abuse and rely totally on volunteer donations.

Bookshop Second Storey Books, Amarándou 24, Neohóri, has a large stock of used English paperbacks; open all year, normal shop hours. Other than this, you won't get much printed foreign-language joy on Rhodes.

Car rental Prices at non-international chains are fairly standard at €41–44 per day, but can be bargained down to about €32–35 a day, all-inclusive, out of peak season and/or for long periods. More flexible outfits, all in the new town, include Alamo/National, 28-Oktovríou 18 ☎0241/73 570; Drive, Avstralías 2, Akándia port

☎02410/35 141, or 5km out on Líndhos road ☎02410/68 243; Just/Ansa, Mandhilará 70 ☎02410/31 811; Kosmos, Papaloúka 31 ☎02410/74 374; Orion, Yeoryíou Leóndos 36 ☎02410/22 137; and Payless/Olympic, Íonos Dhragoúmi 29 ☎02410/26 586.

Consulates UK, Pávlou Melá 3 ☎02410/27 247; Ireland, Amerikís 111 ☎02410/22 461; Netherlands, c/o Ialyssos Tours, Alexándhrou Dhiákou 25 ☎02410/31 571. All other English-speaking nationals are represented only in Athens.

Environmental protection The Association for the Protection of the Environment of Rhodes, PO Box 253, ☎02410/23 647, fights unequal battles with the developers and attempts to get choice tracts of land set aside as reserves; worth contributing to their National Bank account.

Exchange Most conventional bank branches are grouped around Platía Kýprou in Neohóri, plus there are various exchange bureaux keeping long hours. At other times use the cash dispensers of the Commercial Bank (branch in the old town at lower end of Ippotón), Alpha Bank, or National Bank (also in the old town, next to Panayía Kástrou).

Ferry agents DANE, Avstralías 92 ☎02410/43 150, to Pireás via select Dodecanese; Dodhekanisos Navtiliaki, Avstralías 3, by Shell station ☎0241/70 590, for the *Dodekanisos Express* catamaran to most Dodecanese; Kyriakoulis Maritime, Neoríon dock ☎0241/78 052, for hydrofoils to most of the Dodecanese, Inspiration, Aktí Sakhtoúri 4, base of main ferry dock, ☎02410/24 294, for most G&A boats to Dodecanese and Cyclades, plus DANE sailings; Kouros, Karpáthou ☎02410/24 377, and Kydon, Ethelondón Dhodhekanisíon 14 ☎02410/23 000, between them handle both companies plying to Cyprus; LANE, Alexándhrou Dhiákou 38 ☎02410/33 607, to Crete via Hálki, Kárpathos, Kássos. Weekly tourist office departure-schedule handouts are deeply unreliable, typically having even the agency addresses wrong; authoritative sailing information is available at the *limenarhío*, ☎02410/22 220 or 28 666, on Mandhráki esplanade near the post office.

Internet cafés The most central and competitive of several are *Rock Style*, Dhimokratías 7, opposite the stadium (Ⓦwww.rockstyle.gr), and *Mango Bar* (see "Nightlife" p.117, Ⓔkarelas@rho.forthnet.gr).

Laundries House of Laundry, Erythroú Stavroú 2, Neohóri; Star, Kostí Palamá 4–6, behind New Market; Wash & Go, Plátonos 33, Old Town.

Motorbike rental Low-displacement scooters won't get you very far on Rhodes; sturdier Yamaha 125s, suitable for two people, start at about €20 a day. In the old town, Mandar Moto at Dhimosthénous 2, cnr Platía Evréon Martýron, has a large stable of medium-sized scooters suitable for short jaunts. Recommended outlets in Neohóri include Margaritis, Ioánni Kazoúli 23, with a wide range of late models up to 500cc, plus mountain bikes; or (to roll out in style) Rent a Harley at 28-Oktovríou 80 – classic models for two riders start at a whopping €97 per day.

Post office Main branch with outgoing mail and poste restante on Mandhráki harbour, open Mon–Fri 7.30am–8pm; mobile office on Orféos, in the old town (theoretically daily 7.30am–2pm, but service occasionally suspended).

Scuba diving Waterhoppers ☎ & Ⓕ02410/38 146, Trident ☎02410/29 160 and Dive Med ☎02410/33 654, Ⓕ23 780, all tout for business at Mandhráki quay; however days out are expensive (€40 for boat transfer and one dive, €20.50 for second dive); see box on p.120 for the full story.

Thomas Cook c/o Ialyssos Travel, Sofokléous Venizélou 6, Neohóri ☎02410/35 672. Refund agents for lost/stolen travellers' cheques; Thomas Cook cheques cashed commission-free.

Travel agencies Recommended in the old town is Castellania, Evripídhou 1–3, cnr Platía Ippokrátous ☎02410/75 860, Ⓔcastell@otenet.gr, which can arrange all domestic air tickets, both domestic and international ferries, and also discount scheduled and charter flights abroad. In Neohóri, Visa Travel Club at Grigóri Lambráki 54 ☎02410/33 282, Ⓦwww.visatravelclub.gr and Contours at Ammohóstou 9 ☎02410/36 001 are aiso worth contacting. There is no central outlet for hydrofoil tickets to Marmaris in Turkey – comparison shopping is recommended (see "Travel Details" for the specimen prices to match or beat).

Yacht charter Yacht Agency International, Výronos 1, cnr of Kanadhá, Akándia port ☎02410/22 927, Ⓕ23 393, Ⓦwww.yachtagency.com are the biggest operators; you might also try Vernicos Yachts at Platía Neoríon, Mandhráki ☎02410/30 215, Ⓕ30 838, and Kronos, nearby ☎02410/78 407, Ⓕ21 529, Ⓦwww.kronosyacht.gr. These venues will all probably shift if and when the new yacht port near Zéfyros beach, more or less completed but still unused, opens.

Around the island

While it's conceivable to spend an entire vacation within the confines of Rhodes Town, that would certainly be inadvisable. The enormous, diamond-shaped island offers ample scope for two weeks of excursions, and if you're not on an all-inclusive, one-centre package, it's highly recommended that you change your overnight base at least once; distances are considerable and, despite ongoing improvement programmes, road conditions often leave much to be desired.

With perennially rich soil and wetter winters than it's been getting lately, Rhodes could easily feed itself if mass tourism were not such a lucrative distraction; the island could also keep its population inebriated indefinitely, with ten million litres of wine produced annually. Unhappily, much of the scenery inland – predominantly arid, scrubby sand-hills in the east and south – has been made that much bleaker by fire-scorched areas extending from Profitis Ilías in the centre to Mesanagrós in the far south.

With the exception of the coast between Líndhos and Yennádhi, tourist facilities are still concentrated in the upper third of Rhodes. What the Italians began, the 1967–74 junta continued, monstrous hotels on the northwest coast between the town and airport being their contribution to posterity. Only during the late 1970s did attention shift to the naturally better-endowed east coast. The process continues slowly as bank loans and official permits allow, with facilities spreading towards the southern tip of the island.

The east coast

Heading down the **east coast** from the capital, you have to proceed some distance before you escape the crowds from local beach hotels at Réni Koskinoú and all along Kallithéa Bay, their numbers swollen by visitors using the regular buses from town or on boat tours out of Mandhráki and Kolóna. However, once past the excesses of Faliráki there is surprisingly little development on this side of the island until you reach Líndhos, and a fair number of beaches, most of them sandier and more sheltered than anything on the west coast (see p.129). Incidentally, they face the open Mediterranean, not the windier Aegean, which means that the water tends to be warmer, greener and (usually) cleaner.

Koskinoú

KOSKINOÚ, 7km from Ródhos Town, is famous for the ornate doorways and flower-filled *hokhláki* courtyards of its well-preserved traditional houses. The last bus back, however, is at 9.30pm, so if you've no car you'll have to take a taxi at least one way if you've come out to dine at one of several **tavernas** here, at their best after dark. Doyenne of these is *O Yiannis* at Vassiléos Yeoryíou tou Dheftérou 23, signed in Greek only. To find it approaching from the coast (rather than inland) road, leave your car or scooter at the eastern square, by the church with the wedding-cake belfry, and take the lane adjacent, heading west. Its stock in trade is abundant mezédhes with a Cypriot/Turkish/Middle Eastern flair, washed down with Émbona wine or oúzo; it's extremely reasonable, especially in a group, and claims to be open daily for dinner all year round.

Thérmes Kallithéas and its beaches

Nostalgia buffs might care to look in at the long-abandoned Italian-built spa of **Thérmes Kallithéas** (unrestricted access until refurbishment complete), in a palm grove 3km south of Réni Koskinoú. This is haphazardly signposted, but easy enough to find at the base of a cliff bristling with antennae; look for a road down through pines, which veers off as soon as the hotels lining Kallithéa Bay heave into sight. If visiting by bus, be sure *not* to get onto a vehicle serving sound-alike Kalythiés – this is an inland village reached by an entirely different road.

Formerly (and possibly in the future) illuminated at night, the spa is hugely enjoyable as a bit of kitsch mock-orientalia. A pair of swooping staircases, venue in the past for occasional advertising shots, bracket a six-pillared cupola over a now dried-up pool. The springs here were celebrated in antiquity, since Hippocrates of Kós (see p.235) recommended them; whether they have ceased flowing from a natural process or just neglect is unclear. Over a million pounds equivalent in EU funds have been earmarked for restoration of the spa, which is currently swaddled in scaffolding and rather unaesthetic while it endures plasterers' attentions; works seem to have been stalled since 1999, with no definite date set for completion.

Immediately southeast are several signposted coves, each named after the snack bars which sit just inland of large patches of sand with sunbeds; the catch is you must cross through or over evocative rock formations to get to the water. *Nikolas* and *Tassos*, the two most southerly, are the most popular and attractive.

Faliráki

FALIRÁKI, at the south end of Kallithéa Bay, may once have been a fishing village, but today it's Rhodes' biggest youth-oriented package playpen, firmly in the mould of a Spanish costa resort. An overwhelmingly British and German clientele's typical nicknames for the place are "Fairly Rocky" or "Feely-Fucky", the latter pretty much reflecting the main interest of those in attendance. This, unfortunately, sometimes extends to indecent assaults, as Faliráki has acquired an unsavoury reputation and there have been reported rapes of female tourists.

Scuba diving on Rhodes

Thérmes Kallithéas proper overlooks two small, sandy coves, the southerly one (below the spa entrance) with a snack bar, and the northerly one the usual venue for local **scuba diving** programmes. Three competing outfitters (see Ródhos Town, "Listings") run daily dive-trips here in season, departing Mandhráki at about 9.15am, arriving an hour later, and heading back by 4pm. On offer are a shallow water, guided "try dive" for the inexperienced, or two deeper dives for those previously certified – count on about €60 for a two-dive day, including boat transfer. The more advanced dive, to a depth of just over twelve metres, explores a cave and tunnel system on the north side of the bay.

As the dives tend to be short and relatively shallow, and the day long, there could easily be scope for a third dive, but the scuba instructors confess that two plunges just about exhaust the legal territory of exploration – the confines of this little bay are the sole permitted dive area around Rhodes until further notice. Out of season, at some risk to all concerned, advanced dives at a remote offshore wreck are undertaken by special arrangement.

Snacks (not included) are available on the dive boat or at the spa *kantína* noted above, but it's best to bring some food and drink of your own. Diving tends to finish by 2.30pm, but you're more or less stuck here waiting for the boat back as there's no bus service down to Kallithéa spa and it's a hot, twenty-minute walk up to the coast highway (half-hourly bus service once you get there).

As a local free paper once said, if it's possible or imaginable to do it in, on or over the water, rental equipment is available here. Of late you can "do it" in the air as well, since the ungainly towers of two "sky-surfing" outfits dominate the skyline. Bungee jumping, ringo-ing and banana rides are Big Things, not to mention go-karting, water slides, boardsailing and jet-boating; watersports centres along the beach offer waterskiing and parasailing and also rent out windsurf boards, canoes and pedalos.

So-called "Faliráki North" – where monstrous hotels, and stone-clad, baroquely kitsch shopping malls keep sprouting at a rate of knots – is smarter and geared more towards families. The south end of the developed strip is frowsier (but the only bit with a shadow of local character), while there's also a fair amount of less desirably positioned development on the inland side of the busy highway. In slight mitigation, most of this is predominantly low-rise and still fairly low-density, leaving plenty of greenery and low-lying ground in which the local mosquitoes breed. There's even an unofficial nudist beach at the far south end of matters, in secluded coves beyond a headland. From around here a signposted trail leads to "Anthony Quinn" beach (see below), about forty minutes' walk away.

Practicalities

Given such a self-explanatory, home-from-home environment, specific recommendations for rooms or restaurants are generally pretty futile. If you decide to take advantage of all the creature comforts by staying here, you may as well be hung for a sheep as a lamb, and splash out at mid-beach-front **hotels** like the *Esperides* (Ⓣ02410/85 543, Ⓕ85 079, Ⓔesperides@esperia-hotels.gr; ❻), an affiliate of the *Esperia* in Ródhos Town, with particularly good facilities for children, or the nearby *Apollo Beach Hotel* (Ⓣ02410/85 513, Ⓕ85 823, Ⓦwww.helios.gr/hotels/apollo-beach; ❻), with lush gardens and recently renovated bathrooms.

When it comes to **eating out**, most establishments are predictably plastic and "Europeanized", but for approximately Hellenic grills you might try *O Kandas*, near the *Hotel Columbia Beach*, or *Akti* and *Maria's*, just behind the excursion-boat jetty and small-craft harbour at the far south end of the strip. More exotic possibilities include *La Strada*, near the junction of the main coast highway and the side street down to the bus turnaround area, for high-quality Italian food, including wood-fired pizza, or *Pagoda*, just a few paces north along the main highway, for Thai-slanted Chinese specialities.

Entire inland streets are devoted to fairly obvious **nightlife** at such bars as *Slammers*, *Kelly's Irish Pub* and *The Tartan Arms*, which can reportedly get a bit rough in the small hours; Faliráki is about the only locale in this book with any pattern of punch-ups and muggings. If you've raved all night, *Eden Pool Bar* (near the go-karts) is good for pre-dawn breakfasts. If you're too pissed or hungover to drive anywhere, a little **fake train** – the latest Greek catch-all planning solution, after pedestrianization – shuttles folk up and down the "strip" at regular intervals.

Ladhikó and Afándou

The peninsula closing off Faliráki to the south is called **Cape Ladhikó**; the almost-landlocked, north-facing cove, proclaimed as "**Anthony Queen**" (sic) on certain excursion boat marquees, was a location for the 1961 film *The Guns of Navarone*, and the late Quinn supposedly bought coastal property here. Up close it proves to be harshly pebbly if scenic, with sunbathers staking out odd patches on rock monoliths and availing themselves of a single, limited-fare *kantína* on the clifftop by the car park. Nearly as crowded, the small, sand-and-gravel cove to the south has a full-menu fish taverna; both bays offer fair to good snorkelling.

The island's only surviving **campsite**, *Faliraki Camping* (Ⓣ02410/85 358), a medium-sized compound, is just south of the Ladhikó headland, on the downgrade towards Afándou Bay. It's pitched largely at caravanners, but it's well appointed, with a pool, restaurant and bar. Most guests will find the *Cathryn Hotel/Bungalows* (Ⓣ02410/85 881, Ⓕ85 624; ⑤), well placed on a pass in the Ladhikó access road, more their idea of a holiday base.

South of the Ladhikó headland extends the sweeping pebble-and-sand expanse of **Afándou Bay**, the most undeveloped large beach on the east coast, with just a few stretches of sunbeds and umbrellas. Inland spreads an eighteen-hole **golf course**, the only one in the Greek islands aside from Corfu's, and beyond the coast highway lies Afándou ("the Invisible") village, unobjectionable if not especially memorable. Spare a moment, heading down the main access road to mid-bay, for the atmospheric sixteenth-century **church of Panayía Katholikí**, paved with a *hokhkláki* floor throughout and incorporating fragments of a much older basilica. This ancient monument is currently in disgraceful condition, with swallows nesting inside, though very fine frescoes are slowly being cleaned of accumulated mould and grime, with a fume hood installed over the votive candles (the main culprit in fresco deterioration).

The most interesting bit is the far north end of Afándou Bay immediately south of the Ladhikó headland, known as **Traganoú** beach (and signposted as such from the main highway). Beyond the army officers' R&R post of Erimókastro, which overlooks the protected gravel-pebble cove here, are the Traganospília, a trio of **caves** with both land and sea entrance, and freshwater seeps which make the sea cooler than you'd expect. Showers, sunbeds and snacks are offered by a single *kantína*.

Near the south end of Afándou Bay, you'll find a good **fish restaurant**, *Reni Avantis* (shut Nov–Dec), set back from the beach amongst tamarisks; it's resolutely simple, and not cheap for all that, but highly regarded by the islanders for reliable freshness and preparation. Just beyond here, the ominous-looking radio-mast farm belonging to the Voice of America (and others) bars you from going any further; to reach Kolýmbia (see below) you must detour through a maze of paved inland lanes.

Kolýmbia and Eptá Piyés

Some 5km south of Afándou on the main highway, a dilapidated church is your first hint of **KOLÝMBIA**, developed as a model farm scheme by the Italians to house colonists during the late 1920s. Strange, identical villa-farmhouses with outsized chimneys and exterior ovens – now much done over by post-1948 occupants – dot the coastal plain to the north of the three-kilometre side road. This avenue, lined with around two dozen uninspiring hotels and rows of eucalyptus planted by Italians to drain the marshes here, runs east arrow-straight to **Cape Vayiá**. Frankly, the eucalyptus trees lend the place most of its character; otherwise it's a fairly tatty resort pitched at Germans, Swiss and Austrians, made all the more so by forlorn shopping precincts decimated by a run of poor tourist seasons, and bulldozer scrapings or rubble-piles everywhere (many Greeks seem not to make any cause-and-effect connection between the two). Upon reaching the sea, a left fork quickly ends at the edge of Afándou beach, with sweeping views north to Ladhikó point; bearing right at this T-junction takes you past a small, rocky cove with a taverna to the more picturesque and protected south beach at the base of Tsambíka promontory (see below), dominated by the *Golden Odyssey* hotel, with at least two more under construction. The more modest and congenially designed, adjacent *Relax* ⓣ02410/56 220, ⓕ56 245, ⓦwww.helios.gr/hotels/relax; ④) and *Mistral* (ⓣ02419/56 346, ⓕ56 293, ⓦwww.mistralhotel.gr; ⑤) **hotels** are also within easy walking distance of the sand.

Eptá Piyés

Heading inland from Kolýmbia junction on the main highway, it's a four-kilometre walk or drive to **Eptá Piyés** (Seven Springs), a superb oasis with a tiny dam created by the Italians to irrigate their Kolýmbia colony. It is also accessible by a marked path/mountain bike track from the village of Arhángelos (see below). A **taverna** with shaded streamside seating, in operation since just after World War II and immensely popular at weekends with islanders and visitors alike, serves hearty grills (€13 per person for goat or turkey chops, beer and *pitaroúdhia*) in a setting enlivened by geese, ducks and shrieking peacocks – though expect changes in style in the wake of a 2001 refit.

A trail and a rather claustrophobic Italian **aqueduct tunnel** both lead from the vicinity of the springs to the reservoir. The 186-metre tunnel is strictly one-way, with just a single widened passing point and air vent about halfway through – not for claustrophobes. The reservoir at the far end is more of a deep pond, with no prohibitions (as yet) against diving in.

Tsambíka: monastery and beach

The enormous, Gibraltar-like mass of **Tsambíka**, 26km south of Ródhos Town, is actually the eroded flank of a once much-larger mountain. From the highway, a steep, 1500-metre-long, cement-paved side road terminates at a small car park and taverna, from which 297 concrete steps lead up to the summit monastery of **Panayía Tsambíka** (300m elevation), offering unrivalled views along some fifty kilometres of coastline. It's unremarkable except for the happier consequences of the September 8 festival, when barren women make the climb – sometimes on their hands and knees – to pay homage to an eleventh-century icon and (later) ingest a small piece of the wick from one of the shrine's lamps. Any children born afterwards are called Tsambikos or Tsambika, names that are particular to the Dodecanese – and common enough to confound sceptics. At any time of the year the little chapel is crammed full of waxen and metal *támmata* (*ex votos*) in the shape of infants, left by those desirous of offspring – and the wall festooned with snaps of the resulting toddlers.

From the top you survey Kolýmbia just to the north, and shallow **Tsambíka Bay** on the south side of the headland; of all Rhodian beaches, this warms up earliest in the spring. The entire area appears to have been protected by the forest service from any development other than the paving of the road down to the bay, and a single, permanent **taverna** to complement the seven or eight *kantína* caravans which between them stake out most of the bay. Although there's no public transport to this excellent beach, it teems all summer with waterskiers and people sheltering under their rental umbrellas. On the sea bed at the wilder, southern end of the sand, hundreds of hermit crabs scuttle about in their appropriated shells.

Arhángelos and Stegná

More substantial facilities can be found at **ARHÁNGELOS**, a large citrus-farming village just inland, 29km from Ródhos Town. The place is overlooked by a crumbling fifteenth-century castle, and is home to a dwindling leather-crafts industry, much touted in tourist literature but hard to find on the ground; there's more evidence of flat-weave rug weaving (most of it garishly dreadful) and, at festival times, musical prowess. The courtyard of the main church, with an enormous *hokhláki* dating back to 1845, is the only remarkable sight. Though you might explore the warren of alleys between the main road and the citadel, Arhángelos is now firmly caught up in German package tourism, with a full quota of "mini-markets" and jewellery stores, as well as a **bank** and **post office**. Most commercial life occurs along the single thoroughfare, in the form of a few bars and six **tavernas** – none superlative, but all rather less expensive than in the coastal resorts. The preferred hangout seems to be the **bar** and grill of *George Mavrios*, under the mulberry trees. Recommended local C-class **hotels**, both well out of Arhángelos but with views over it, are *Katerina* (Ⓣ & Ⓕ02440/22 169; ❷) and *Anagros* (Ⓣ02440/22 248, Ⓕ22 857; ❷).

Stegná, three rather steep kilometres by road below Arhángelos, is the closest **beach**, in the throes of a touristic boom, with lots of new **rooms** pitched at Germans beginning to outnumber the summer cottages for locals that straggle along for a kilometre or so. The road-fringed beach is sand-and-gravel but punctuated with rock outcrops; among **eateries**, *Psarotaverna Kozas* – where the access road hits the shore – and *Ouzeri Pitropos* further along get some islander clientele.

Haráki and Ayía Agáthi

A more convenient, slicker overnight base on this stretch of coast is **HARÁKI**, the pleasant, if undistinguished, two-street fishing port of inland Malóna village, overlooked by the stubby ruins of Feraklós castle. Originally a Byzantine fortress, this served as the Knights' initial toehold on Rhodes in 1306, later as a POW compound, and was the last of their strongholds to fall to the Ottomans. **Accommodation** here consists of about twenty self-catering studio outfits overlooking the pedestrianized esplanade, with various UK package companies maintaining a conspicuous presence; quieter establishments more likely to have on-spec vacancies include *Savvas* (Ⓣ02440/51 287; ❸) and *Voula* (Ⓣ02440/51 381; ❸), or the *Yeoryia* (Ⓣ02440/51 170; ❸), at the south end of things near the *Argo Restaurant*.

Speaking of which, most local tavernas are fairly unmemorable; marginally the best in this area is *Efterpi*, 200m south of Haráki at so-called **Mássari beach**, next to the army camp; here you can sample such delicacies as Smyrna-style eggplant and *mýdhia sagánaki* at a price.

There's swimming off the reasonable town beach if you don't mind an audience from the row of waterfront cafés and tavernas, but most people head north to the secluded **Ayía Agáthi** beach. Contrary to expectations, this cannot be accessed from the castle road: you have to backtrack 700m out of the village to a separate, signposted dirt side road, and then proceed another 800m to the short but broad sandy bay, full of hermit crabs, overlooked by the chapel of Ayía Agáthi on the far (north) hillside. The beach here is no secret by any means – there's a *kantína* or two, sunbeds and watersports on offer – but more permanent development seems to have come a cropper, with numerous unfinished and abandoned building sites on the adjacent hillsides.

Líndhos

LÍNDHOS, the island's number-two tourist attraction, erupts from barren limestone surroundings 12km south of Haráki. Like Ródhos Town, its charm is heavily undermined by commercialism and crowds of up to half a million visitors in a typical year. At midday dozens of coaches park nose-to-tail on the narrow access road, with even more on the drive down to the beach. Back in the village itself, those few vernacular houses not snapped up by package operators have, since the 1960s, been bought up and refurbished by wealthy British – including the likes of the late newspaper astrologist Patric Walker, Pink Floyd stars David Gilmore and Roger Waters – plus numerous Italians. The old *agorá* or serpentine high street presents a mass of fairly indistinguishable bars, creperies, mediocre restaurants and travel agents. Although high-rise hotels have been prohibited inside the municipal boundaries, it's still a relentlessly mercenary theme park, especially hot and airless in August, and quite ghostly in winter since the village has scarcely any life apart from tourism. Local house-owners have long since converted or sold off their homes for touristic purposes and moved to nearby Péfki, appearing only by day to milk the cash cow of tourism.

Rhodian village houses

Vernacular rural houses on Rhodes, and to a great extent those on the nearby islands of Tílos, Hálki, Níssyros and Kós, share certain basic characteristics. These are due to the matrilineal system of inheritance, still common in the Dodecanese, whereby the eldest daughter traditionally got the family house upon marriage. The father was also obliged to build similar houses for any younger girls; this made it inadvisable to build costly, involved structures when so many might be required.

In its simplest form, the surviving **Rhodian village house** interior is a single, undivided, one-storey rectangle or *monóhoro*, built of stone and earth, usually with a corner fireplace indicated from outside by a beaked chimney. Opposite the fireplace, along the rear wall, is a raised sleeping platform or *soufás*, with storage cupboards underneath and an embroidered curtain or *spervéri* around it. This longer wall is usually devoted to racks displaying the celebrated Rhodian collections of decorative plates, both imported and locally made. Depending on room size, the space is often divided either width-wise or length-wise by a soaring arch; this helps support a flat roof, traditionally made of cedar beams resting on the wall tops. The gaps in between are filled with successive layers of wild olive or oleander shoots, calamus reeds, seaweed and, finally, hard-packed special earths called *aspropília* or *patélia*, with the walls extending up to form a low surrounding parapet or *koumoúla*.

In wealthier villages, such as Koskinoú and Lahaniá, the basic *monóhoro* unit, often used only on formal occasions, is found at the rear of an enclosed courtyard. Auxiliary buildings, such as kitchens, ovens, stables, olive presses and (built much later) toilets, also face onto the courtyard which is paved in *hokhláki* or pebble mosaic and entered via a *pyliónas* or ornate doorway. Líndhos represents the most elaborate development of this trend, with considerable money and effort expended on the *hokhláki* paving (often present inside the rooms as well), ceilings with painted planks as well as shrub branches or reed canes, and exceptionally ornate *pyliónes* adorned with braided relief work reflecting Frankish or Arab influences. Directly above the *pyliónes* can often be found the so-called "captain's room", from which the master of the house used to watch activity at the north harbour, or scan the horizon for pirates. Though of course such elaborate houses are no longer being built, locals cherish their pebble-courts, which need periodic maintenance – and there are still enough of them around to keep a number of mosaic craftsmen in regular employment.

However, all is not gloom and doom, as recent developments have conspired to force Líndhos to partially reinvent itself. Several tour companies cut back their presence in the late 1990s, and as a result the place has moved marginally more upmarket. Partly empty aeroplanes also mean that Líndhos is currently a good spot to snag one-way tickets back to the UK for £100 equivalent or less; availability is often posted in travel agency windows (see p.129). And if you arrive before or after peak season (or peak hours – before 10am, after 4pm), when the pebble-paved streets between the immaculately whitewashed houses are relatively empty of people, you can still appreciate the beautiful, atmospheric setting of Líndhos.

The **post-Byzantine church** with its recently reconstructed belfry is covered inside with well-preserved eighteenth-century frescoes. The most imposing fifteenth- to eighteenth-century **captains' residences** (see box p.125) are built around *hokhláki* courtyards, their monumental doorways or *pyliónes* often fringed by intricate stonework, with the number of braids or cables supposedly corresponding to the number of ships owned. Several are open to the public, most notably the **Papakonstandis Mansion**, which is the most elaborate and now home to an unofficial museum. Entrance to the "open" mansions is free, but you'll probably come under some pressure to buy something, especially the lace and embroidery for which the place is noted.

The acropolis – and its history

On the 115-metre bluff looming above Líndhos, reached via cypress-shaded rampways, the **acropolis** (summer Mon 12.30pm–7pm, Tues–Sun 8am–7pm; rest of year Tues–Sun 8.30am–3pm; €6) represents a surprisingly felicitous blend of ancient and medieval culture, though the Knights of St John destroyed a considerable quantity of the surviving Hellenistic structures by quarrying them for use in fortification. Danish scholars were the first to excavate sympathetically here, from 1902 until 1913; subsequent Italian work here was (as in Ródhos Town) slipshod, introducing lots of destructive ironwork, and the ongoing Greek-run restoration programme is set to run until 2008.

Once through the tower-gate and associated structures built by the Knights, you ascend two flights of monumental steps separated by the photogenic colonnade of a **Hellenistic stoa** before reaching a high platform with the rudiments of a propylaia or monumental gate, and the far more substantial **Doric Temple** of Athena Lindia, assiduously restored since the early 1980s and back under scaffolding after a brief, picturesque time free of it. The unusual southwest-to-northeast orientation was dictated by the limited triangular area of flat ground on the summit, here tapering to its apex. Visiting sites as close as possible to dawn or dusk is always good advice, and here even more so for the sake of sweeping views: north to Tsambíka and Fáraklos, south to the gaunt cliffs hemming in St Paul's Bay.

Before the founding of ancient Rodos in 408 BC, Lindos with its 16,000 inhabitants was the most important settlement on the island, thanks to its natural defences – the acropolis is a sheer drop on all sides except the north approach – and the two excellent harbours nestling beneath the cliffs. The surrounding craggy countryside was as infertile then as it is now, and the population was forced to look to the sea for a living, with an enormous fleet trading as far as present-day Spain; the local tradition of boat-building continued well into the nineteenth century. As if in corroboration, a fifth-century BC (some say Hellenistic) relief of a trireme clings to the rock face, on the left at the base of the stairs leading up to the castle gate.

Though the ancient city of Lindos and its original temple date from at least 1100 BC, the first stone temple was erected by the tyrant Kleoboulos in the sixth century BC and replaced by the present structure after a 342 BC fire. The word "tyrant" had not then assumed its modern, perjorative overtones; Kleoboulos was actually revered as one of the Seven Sages of antiquity, and to him was attributed the Delphic inscription "Moderation in All Things", usually rendered as "Nothing in Excess". The only other easily found trace of the ancient town is a tiny **theatre** at the south end of the modern village, on the way to the northerly St Paul's beach, carved into the living rock on the southwest slope of the acropolis.

A 45-minute walk east of town, starting from the lane just below *Mavrikos Restaurant*, brings you to the headland and chapel of **Áyios Emilianós**. The latter was originally a round, stone-built tomb, purportedly that of Kleovoulos but actually dating from the first century BC.

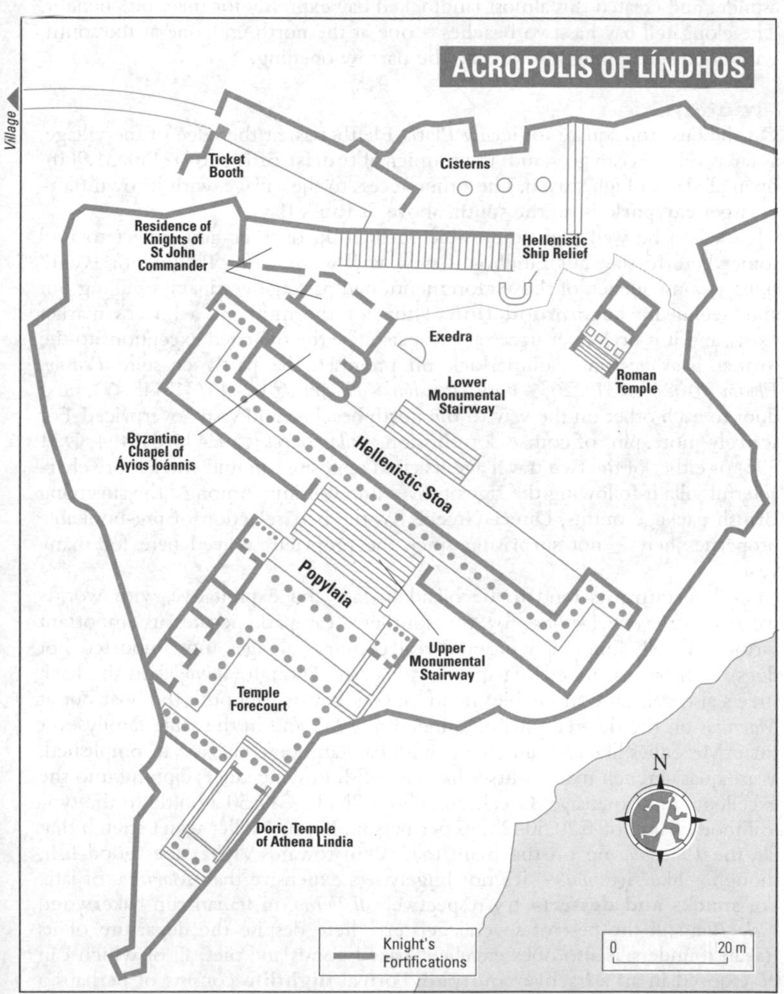

Local beaches

Líndhos' principal **north beach**, once the main ancient harbour, is overcrowded in season and possibly less than one hundred percent salubrious until the sewage treatment plant, courtesy of the EU, is completed at St Paul's Bay. Guaranteed cleaner and quieter swimming is to be had one cove beyond at **Pállas** beach (with a nudist annexe around the headland), or 5km north at **Vlyhá Bay**, where the luxurious *Steps of Lindos* hotel, on the hillside just above, is recommended for self-pampering (ⓣ02440/31 062 or 32 009, ⓕ32 007; ❻).

At the southern flank of the acropolis huddles the small, phenomenally well-sheltered harbour and sandy beach of **St Paul**, where the apostle is said to have landed in 58 AD on a mission to evangelize the island. According to legend, the ship bringing Paul to Rhodes was threatened by a storm and was unable to find the main, north harbour; a miraculous bolt of lightning split the rocks asunder and created this almost landlocked bay expressly for the saint's benefit. The elongated bay has two beaches – one at the north end, one at the south, with good snorkelling just outside the narrow opening.

Practicalities

On the bus-stop square (officially Platía Eleftherías) at the edge of the village, as far as vehicles can go, stands the municipal **tourist office** (ⓣ02440/31 900), open all day in high season. The other access to the village, with its own (fairly large) **car park**, is on the south, above St Paul's Bay.

It used to be well nigh impossible to turn up on spec and expect to find somewhere to stay, but Líndhos is now well sown with "Rooms for Rent" signs, a consequence of those aforementioned package companies pulling out and freeing up **accommodation**. Thus, for the moment, a buyer's market exists, and it is no longer necessary to patronize the oft-cited exceptions to the former package-tour hammerlock on premises: the partly en-suite *Pension Electra* (ⓣ02440/31 226; ❸) and *Pension Katholiki* (ⓣ02440/31 445; ❹), next door to each other on the way to the north beaches, and vastly overpriced. For scarcely more, plus of course commission, *Pallas Travel* (ⓣ02440/31 494, ⓕ31 595) or either of the two travel agents cited opposite can find you a more characterful villa if following the signs proves unrewarding. Amongst the surviving British package outfits, Direct Greece has the best selection of pre-bookable properties here – not surprising since the proprietress lived here for many years.

Local **restaurants** tend to be bland in fare and exploitative, with world-weary staff; even *Agostino's* by the southerly car park negates its important virtues of bulk Émbona wine and real country sausages (not imported hot dogs) with bits of tinned veg speckling its rice. Though *Aphrodite* in the back streets also gets an honourable mention, you may as well push the boat out at *Mavrikos* on the fig-tree square, founded in 1933 and in the same family ever since. Mezédhes like *manoúri* cheese with basil and pine nuts are accomplished, as are quasi-French main courses like cuttlefish in wine sauce; dipping into the excellent (and expensive) Greek wine list will add €17.50 a bottle to the typical food charge of €20.50–23.50 per person. If your wallet won't stretch that far, the *Panorama* up on the main road, 2km towards Vlyhá, does good fish, though – like *Agostino's* – it's not hugely less expensive than *Mavrikos* of late. For **snacks and desserts**, try respectively *Il Forno*, an Italian-run bakery, and *Gelo Blu*, still the best of several gelaterie here despite the departure of its Italian founders; it also does excellent baked goods and pies, all of which can be enjoyed in an attractive courtyard. Formal **nightlife** consists of perhaps a half-dozen music bars on the main high street; no point in citing names, as these tend to change every season.

Local **car rental** rates tend to be 25 to 30 percent less than in Ródhos Town, though accordingly choice and roadworthiness may not be so good. There are two proper **banks** (Commercial and National), both with cash dispensers, whose presence has had a salutary effect on the cost of exchange facilities offered by local **travel agents**. Among the more useful of these are Líndhos Suntours (Ⓣ02440/31 333, Ⓕ31 353), with metered phones (call boxes tend to have huge queues) and a nice line in charter seats back to the UK, as does Village Holidays (Ⓣ02440/31 486). At last look there were three cafés with **internet** facilities in Líndhos, all on or just off the "high street".

The west coast

Rhodes' **west coast** is the windward flank of the island, so it's damper, more fertile and more forested; windmills, first introduced by the Italians, irrigate crops from the high water table. Most beaches along the often steep, cliff-hemmed shoreline are exposed and decidedly rocky, but this hasn't deterred touristic development; as in the east, the first few kilometres of the busy coast road southwest from the capital have been surrendered entirely to industrial tourism. From Neohóri's aquarium down to the airport, the shore is fringed by periodic clusters of 1970s-vintage mega-hotels, though such places as Triánda (8km from the city centre), Kremastí (12km along) and Paradhísi (15km) are still nominally villages, and appear so in their centres.

This was the first part of the island to be favoured by the package operators, and tends to be frequented in summer by a decidedly sedate clientele that often can't be bothered to stir far from the pool. Several local de luxe hotels remain open during the winter, coining a few extra euros from the convention and seminar trade. But for more enterprising tourists, neither the fierce prevailing winds – beach umbrellas consistently point seaward – the planes buzzing over Paradhísi, nor the giant, exhaust-billowing power plant at Soroní offer much inducement to pause here.

Ixiá and Triánda

If it weren't for Ródhos' town-limits sign, you wouldn't be able to tell when you'd left the capital – on the coast road at least – and entered **IXIÁ**, where most of the island's de luxe **hotels** cluster. Of these, the *Miramare Wonderland* (Ⓣ02410/96 251, Ⓕ95 954, Ⓔmamtour@otenet.gr; ❻; open late March–Oct), 5km along, is the most idyllic (and expensive), consisting of recently constructed fake-vernacular bungalows in a landscaped setting just behind the beach lawn. They're painted in traditional red, ochre and *louláki* (powder blue), with tasteful mock-antique furnishings and jacuzzis in some tubs. The complex is so huge that a private mini-railway salvaged from a British mine shunts guests from one end to the other.

Among local **tavernas**, *Ta Kioupia*, 3km inland at Trís hamlet (Ⓣ02410/91 824 for reservations; closed Sun), attracts a clientele of foreigners and Athenians, particularly well-heeled celebrities, who tend to go into ecstasies over its cuisine (arty mezédhes, no fish); however there's long been a feeling that it's overrated and – at about €24 minimum per head – overpriced. In Ixiá proper, opposite the *Hotel Roma*, *To Tzaki* offers mezédhes and barrel wine, often with live music entertainment.

In similarly developed **TRIÁNDA**, confusingly (and officially) called Ialyssós (but see below), the beach – harsh shingle – could be better. The accordingly misnamed *Sandy Beach Taverna* is a popular and very reliable lunch stop, if a bit hard to find at the cul-de-sac end of Fereníkis, the beachfront road (follow signs to *Electra Palace*). The food's not extraordinary – a bit overfried – but abundant and well priced for the area; what makes the place is the pleasant managing family, the peaceful environment out back, and the untouristy Greek soundtrack. Another good local option is *Tempo*, with genuinely friendly staff and all the Greek standards – well above the average tourist fare. Windy Triánda has a number of **windsurfing** outfitters; on the same road you'll find Oxbow (ⓣ02410/91 666), with Fun Surf (ⓣ02410/95 819) also nearby.

Ancient Ialyssos and around

At the central junction in Triánda, you can make a detour inland for the five-kilometre ride up to the site of **ancient Ialyssos** (Tues–Sun 8am–7pm; €3) on flat-topped, pine-covered Filérimos hill; Filérimos means "lover of solitude" and is named after the Byzantine hermits who founded a monastery here in the tenth century. Though only 267m above sea level, this has always been a strategic point; the Knights installed themselves here during their campaign to oust the Genoese, and from its Byzantine castle Süleyman the Magnificent also directed the 1522 siege of Rhodes.

Foundations of third-century **temples to Zeus and Athena**, built atop a far older Phoenician shrine, sprawl just west of the monastery church, while below, further towards the car park, lies the partly subterranean church of **Aï-Yeórgis Hostós**, a simple, barrel-vaulted structure containing fourteenth- and fifteenth-century frescoes. These are unfortunately not as vivid or well preserved as those at Thárri or Asklipió (see p.137 & p.138), but scenes from the life of the Virgin are just discernible on the right vault, while ones from the life of Christ, such as the *Scourging and Mocking*, appear opposite. Just southeast of the parking area, a hillside Doric fountain with a columned facade was only revealed by subsidence in 1926 – and is now off limits owing to another landslip which has covered it again.

Filérimos monastery

Heavily damaged during fighting between Italians and Germans in autumn 1943, the **Filérimos monastery** on view today is for once not just an Italian job, but also the result of postwar restoration. Despite the questionable authenticity of the original Italian work, the existing structure is beautiful, consisting of an asymmetric chapel built in stages. Behind several rib-vaulted chambers lies a small, low-slung cloister overgrown with bougainvillea, while an early cruciform baptismal font embossed with the Cross of the Knights is sunk in the open space south of the belfry. The northernmost chamber (rear far left as you enter the church) features a faint Paleo-Christian mosaic floor, contemporary with the font outside.

As a concession to the Rhodian faithful, the church alone *may* be open to pilgrims after hours, but as the guards make clear, you are to light your candles, drop your coins in the box, pay reverence to the icon of the Virgin and make a swift exit.

The cross of Filérimos

Southwest of the monastery and archeological zone, a "**Way of the Cross**", its fourteen Stations marked out by copper plaques in the Italian era, leads to an enormous concrete crucifix. This has replaced the original, which the Italians erected in September 1934, and destroyed seven years later to prevent Allied airmen using it for navigation during air raids. Today's cross, built in 1995 at a cost of 20 million drachmas (about £50,000 then), is almost identical to the original, standing just under 18m tall with a narrow staircase inside; you're allowed to climb out onto the cross-arms for a supplement to the already amazing view. Illuminated at night, the crucifix is clearly visible from the island of Sými and – perhaps more pertinently – "infidel" Turkey across the straits.

Kremastí, Paradhísi and Theológos

KREMASTÍ, back on the coast and 4km beyond Triánda, is notable for its gargantuan church and schoolhouse, funded by expatriate Rhodians in America, and for its festival on August 15–23, one of the biggest in the Dodecanese, with a street fair, amusement park, and dancing on the last day. At other times you might prefer to avoid this large village, as it's home to the biggest military barracks on the island.

The airport village of **PARADHÍSI**, literally just outside the terminal, is often visited when departing flights get delayed. You might even have to – or want to – **stay** the night, especially if catching a typically early-morning flight to Kássos or Kastellórizo. Two *dhomátia* places, both within a 500-metre walk of the airport car park, are *Anastasia* at Alexándhrou Ipsilándou 3 (Ⓣ02410/81 810; ❷) or *Yiordanis Kladhitis* in the next side street parallel (Ⓣ02410/81 224 or 81 101; ❶). Several **tavernas** operate on or just off the through road, mostly at night.

The relatively calm village of **THEOLÓGOS**, 6km beyond Paradhísi and then 1km inland, has a growing beach-resort annexe consisting of a dozen or so **hotels**, best equipped of these being the A-class *Alex Beach* (Ⓣ02410/82 422, Ⓕ82 424, Ⓔalexb@hol.gr; ❻), at the end of the developed strip and indeed the southernmost hotel on this coast. About the only independent **eatery** hereabouts is *Mezedhopolio Alliotiko*, between Theológos beach district and the Soroní power plant.

Ancient Kameiros

Just over 12km southwest of Theológos, the important archeological site of **Kameiros** was, together with ancient Lindos and Ialyssos, one of the three Dorian powers that united late in the fifth century BC to found the powerful city-state of Rodos. Soon eclipsed by the new capital, Kameiros was abandoned; only in 1859 was it rediscovered, then completely excavated after 1929. As a result, it is a particularly well-preserved Doric townscape, doubly worth visiting for its beautiful, pine-clad hillside location (Tues–Sun: summer 8am–7pm; winter 8.30am–3pm; €3). While none of the individual remains are spectacular, you can pick out the foundations of two small temples, the re-erected pillars of a Hellenistic house, a late Classical fountain, and the stoa of the upper agora complete with archaic water cistern. This upper terrace gives the best overview of the site, much of which is now off limits – pathways tend to go around rather than through it. Kameiros had no fortifications, nor was there an acropolis – partly owing to the gentle slope of the site, and also to the likely settlement here of peaceable Minoans, specifically the half-legendary prince Althaemenes. Unlike Rodos, Lindos and Ialyssos, Kameiros was primarily a town of farmers and craftsmen, a profile borne out by rich finds now in the Rhodes archeological museum and the British Museum.

Practicalities

RODA public buses (see "Travel Details" at the end of the chapter) provide minimal links in season from Ródhos Town, dumping you at the base of the short but steep access road. If arriving under your own steam (more likely), be sure to park so that you won't be hemmed in by the phalanxes of tour coaches which inevitably show up later. On the beach below ancient Kameiros there are several **tavernas**; they're very commercialized, but ideally placed if you're waiting for one of the two daily buses back to town. If you're willing to walk 4km east to **KALAVÁRDHA**, you'll find departures rather more frequent, since besides having its own service, this is where the bus routes descending from Sálakos meet the west coast road. Kalavárdha also has the best, sandiest **beach** on the west coast, though this isn't obvious from the highway – a short side road goes there.

Kámiros Skála and Kástro Kritinías

There are more restaurants clustered 15km south at **KÁMIROS SKÁLA** (occasionally rendered Skála Kámiros or the more pedantically grammatical Skála Kamírou). This tiny anchorage is somewhat inexplicably the hapless target of coach tours in search of an "authentic fishing village" – as credit card stickers in the restaurant windows attest. For a better meal, skip the circus at the five tavernas here and proceed 400m southwest to off-puttingly named **Paralía Kopriá** ("Manure Beach"), where *Psarotaverna Johnny's* has good non-farmed fish and *orektiká*, especially on Sundays when home-made *dolmádhes* and (seasonally) squash blossoms may be on the menu with the usual standards; it's been "discovered" and pricier than before, but still worth a stop.

Less heralded is the daily **kaïki to Hálki**, which leaves Monday to Saturday at 2.30pm, weather permitting, and returns early the next morning; on Wednesdays and Sundays, day-trips depart at 9am and arrive back at 4pm. The Wednesday services tend to be packed out by package transfers between the two islands (see "Travel details" on p.144 for information on return departures). A bus service from Ródhos Town's west-side terminal, shortly before 1.30pm, is designed to dovetail with kaïki departures, ie they're supposed to wait for the arrival of the bus.

Kritinía: castle and village

A couple of kilometres south of Skála, the local castle, officially signposted as **Kástro Kritinías** but locally known as "Kastéllo", is from afar the most impressive of the Knights' rural strongholds; its access road, though paved from both approaches, is too narrow and steep for tour buses. With only a chapel and a rubbish-filled cistern more or less intact inside, Kástro Kritinías proves close up to be no more than a shell – but a glorious shell, with fine views west to assorted islets and Hálki. You make a "donation" to the formidable (not to say aggressive) old woman at the car park booth, in exchange for fizzy drinks, seasonal fruit or flowers if she's in the mood.

KRITINÍA itself, 3km east, is a quiet hillside village of white houses, with a few rooms and tavernas signposted around a central sea-view square, below the main church. The name stems from its supposed foundation by emigrants from Crete (*Kríti* in Greek). An interesting **folklore museum** full of rural oddments and costumes stands just north of the village on the main bypass road, housed in a grandiose, purpose-built round structure (unpredictable hours; free).

Around Mount Akramýtis

Beyond Kritiniá, the main road winds south through dense forest on the lower slopes of **Akramýtis**, Rhodes' second highest and arguably most beautiful mountain ridge; along with Atávyros peak, just northeast, it has been proposed since 1994 as a nature reserve by the local Association for the Protection of the Environment. Non-walkers can make a road circuit of the mountain, by using the dirt track signposted for the rural chapel and festival grounds of Zoödhóhou Piyís – keep going until you emerge on the Monólithos–Foúrni road (see below).

Siánna and Glyfádha

SIÁNNA, just below the 825-metre summit, claims to be the most attractive mountain settlement on the island; the village is less controversially famous for its aromatic pine-and-sage honey and *soúma*, a grape-residue distillate similar to Italian *grappa* but deceptively smooth. This is produced in most Greek wine-making districts with varying degrees of legality – typically distillation is allowed for just 48 hours per year, in October; on Rhodes its manufacture remains legal owing to an Italian-era licence which continues to be honoured. Bus tours call in at the church on the main square, which contains heavily restored eighteenth-century frescoes. Several **tavernas** on the through road announce themselves conspicuously.

Despite their touristic inclination, they're probably a better bet for a meal than anything at **Glyfádha**, reached by a twisty, six-kilometre side road heading seaward about 1500m before Siánna. The ride is green and scenic, arrival a thumping anticlimax: a grubby shingle shoreline presided over by a ruined medieval tower, the power company's cables making a dive for their trip to Hálki, and a pair of cheap and grumpy, down-at-heel **tavernas** purveying stale seafood.

Monólithos and around

The tiered, flat-roofed farmhouses of **MONÓLITHOS**, 4km southwest of Siánna at the end of the public bus line, are scant justification for the long trip out here. Food at the four tavernas tends to be indifferent owing to undemanding tour-group trade, but the view over the bay is striking, and you could use the village as a base by staying in advertised **rooms** or at the *Hotel Thomas* (☎02410/22 741 or 02460/61 291; ❷), its fair-sized rooms belying a grim exterior, and due for a refit in 2002.

Diversions in the area which make showing up worthwhile include yet another **Knights' castle** 2km west of town (unrestricted access), photogenically perched on a 200-metre-high pinnacle (the "monolith" of the village name) but enclosing even less than Kastéllo Kritinías. A few sand-and-gravel beaches at **Foúrni** are hidden five paved but curvy kilometres below the castle, the 800-metre extent of the main cove unadorned except for a drinks *kantína* which appears to have permanently closed down – come equipped. Beyond a headland, to the left as you face the water, are some **caves** that were hollowed out by early Christians fleeing persecution; slippery, well-worn steps lead down to them.

The interior

Inland Rhodes is hilly and still mostly wooded, despite the recent depredations of arsonists. You'll need your own vehicle to see its highlights, especially as enjoyment resides principally in getting away from it all; no single site justifies the tremendous expense of a taxi or the inconvenience of trying to make the best of the sparse-to-nonexistent bus schedules.

In retrospect it will probably be the soft-contoured, undulating scenery which stands out, along with the last vestiges of agrarian life in the villages, some barely mustering three-digit populations. Most people under retirement age are away working in the tourist industry, returning only at weekends and during winter. The young that do remain behind stay largely to help with the grape harvest in late summer. If you have time to spare, and a bit of Greek at your command, traditional hospitality in the form of a drink at the kafenío, or perhaps more, may still be found.

Petaloúdhes: the "Butterfly Valley"

The only highly publicized tourist "attraction" in the island's interior is **Petaloúdhes** or the "Butterfly Valley" (May–Sept daily 8.30am–sunset; spring & autumn €1.50, mid-June to mid-Sept €2.20). Actually a rest-stop for Jersey tiger moths (*Panaxia quadripunctaria*), during July and August it might more accurately be christened the "Valley of the Tour Buses".

In all of Greece, only here and at a similar valley on Páros island do the moths come to live out the final phase of their life cycle, attracted for unknown reasons by the abundant oriental sweetgum (*Liquidamber orientalis*) trees that flourish in this steep-sided canyon. Peak arrival time is July to mid-September, when the moths roost in droves on the trees in order to conserve energy for mating; they cannot eat during this stage of their lives, and die of starvation soon afterwards. Against the tree trunks, the moths are a well-camouflaged black and yellow, but flash cherry-red overwings in flight. On no account should you clap or shout to scare them into flight, as this causes stress and interferes with their reproduction.

Visiting the valley

Petaloúdhes is reached by a seven-kilometre paved side road bearing inland from the west coast road between Paradhísi and Theológos. The canyon is divided into two roughly equal sections by a road crossing it, with an admission booth for each – one ticket is valid for both parts.

Whether the "butterflies" are abundant or not, it's worth visiting just for the sake of the peaceful valley; the Rhodians certainly think so at weekends, packing out the fairly reasonable **taverna** by the parking area just below the lower section. Seats beside the pond-side café, just below the upper section of ravine, are also at a premium. An enjoyable trail threads the length of the valley shaded by conifers as well as the sweetgum trees, repeatedly crossing a non-potable stream on rough-hewn wooden bridges. It's a surprisingly brisk 45-minute walk in total; flip-flops or similar footwear won't do.

Above the highest reaches of the canyon stands the tiny monastic church of **Kalópetra**, built on 1782 foundations, but not really worth the extra ten- to fifteen-minute walk beyond the trail system on forestry tracks. The five-kilometre road from the lower taverna to Psínthos passes the monastery anyway, with asphalt pavement resuming just beyond. Tucked into a depression in the hills, **PSÍNTHOS** – where the Italians decisively defeated the Turks on May 17, 1912 – offers a number of **tavernas** suitable for lunch. Far and away the best and most reasonable (around €12 each) of these, at the edge of the village, is the friendly *Piyi Fasouli*, serving excellent grills (goat, *soúvla*, etc) and appetizers as well as a few *mayireftá* of the day, with tables overlooking plane trees and the namesake spring.

Around Profítis Ilías

At an elevation of 798 metres, **Profítis Ilías** is Rhodes' third highest summit, and its most lushly forested. The Italians endowed the area with a number of their typical follies, and several villages in the surrounding foothills also merit brief halts.

From Psínthos, you can proceed 14km southwest via Arhípoli – the road badly deteriorated – to **ELEOÚSSA**, nestled in the shade of the dense forest at the east end of Profitis Ilías' ridge. The square is flanked by the grandiose former summer residence of the Italian governor, now derelict, plus a huge Italian-built church, among other arcaded structures now used as a high school and military post; at the outskirts of town, heading west, is an enormous circular Art Deco pool with a fountain in the middle.

Two other villages, both with **tavernas**, hug the southeast slopes of the mountain: **PLATÁNIA**, retaining a few brightly coloured houses, glimpses the sea but unfortunately also overlooks the start of an extensive burnt-out area recovering only minimally from 1992–93 blazes; **APÓLLONA**, further west, is surprisingly touristed despite a dull layout enlivened only by domed outside ovens, still in use.

Most people, however, head directly west out of Eleoússa for 3km to the late Byzantine, four-apsed church of **Áyios Nikólaos Foundouklí** (St Nicholas of the Hazelnuts). Locals descend in force for picnics at weekends at the partly shaded site adjacent, with a fine view north over cultivated valleys; the frescoes inside, dating from the thirteenth to fifteenth centuries, have been blurred by damp and could use a good cleaning, but various scenes from the life of Christ are recognizable.

Continuing west beyond the church along the mostly paved main road brings you finally to **Profitis Ilías** itself, where a pair of Italian-built chalet-hotels, the *Elafos* and the *Elafina* (now used exclusively as children's summer camps), hide in deep woods below the road running just north of the summit; a café-snack bar across the road is generally open in summer. The **monastery** of Profitis Ilías in the walled compound next to the ex-hotels does not itself exactly hum with traffic except around the day of the annual festival; over the gateway, a relief plaque shows Elijah being fed in the wilderness by a raven.

Local walks and Sálakos

The peak of Profitis Ilías itself is an off-limits military watchpoint, but there's still scope for an hour-long loop-walk on its slopes, using graded and stepped paths originally laid out by the Italians, with fine views north to Sými and Turkey. For a satisfying **ridge walk**, leave vehicles at the westerly sign announcing the "hamlet", and take the track leading up to another pair of Italian-era buildings: the governor's summer villa and a ransacked church. From behind the latter, a stepped trail leads up to the watershed in about fifteen minutes. Turn left or northeast (right dead ends outside the military installation) and proceed until, at the first glimpse of an OTE installation ahead, the stair-path dips down and left. You continue to follow the ridge, more or less, gradually losing altitude, until you swerve back southwest just before reaching the telecoms installation, passing a ruined barracks en route to the two follies.

Another popular local walk follows the zigzagging path that begins next to the chapel of Áyios Andónis, below the Profitis Ilías monastery, and descends within 45 minutes to the upper edge of **Sálakos** village. However, this route is much easier to find going up; the departure point is well signposted near the western edge of town. There's just one critical left fork, about 200m uphill from the point where you leave a cement drive, and faint red paint splodges put you right thereafter; allow an hour going uphill.

The heart and soul of friendly **SÁLAKOS** is a small, pedestrianized roadside platía, where an Italian fountain shares space with the tables of several "café-snacks"; the most traditional of these is Mihalis Svourakis' *To Steki*. During the mid-1990s, the village attempted to capitalize on its Nymph brand of spring water; an old Italian mansion adjoining the bottling plant was revitalized as the *Nymph Hotel Restaurant Café* (☎02460/22 206 or 22 346), though it rarely seems to be open, and you shouldn't count on so much as a coffee here, let alone a room, outside of July or August. The Profitis Ilías area can also be easily approached from Kalavárdha on the west-coast road, via Sálakos.

Around Mount Atávyros

All tracks and roads west across Profitis Ilías converge upon the road up from Kalavárdha bound for **ÉMBONA**, a large and architecturally nondescript village backed up against the north slope of 1215-metre **Mount Atávyros**, roof of the island. Émbona, with its two *dhomátia* outfits and rather meat-oriented tavernas (of which *Savvas* is the least likely to be swamped by groups), is more geared to handling tourists than you might expect from its unprepossessing appearance, since it's the venue for summer "Greek nights" and daytime wine-tasting excursions from Ródhos Town.

The village lies at the heart of the island's most important grape-growing and **wine-producing** districts, owing to a combination of granitic soil and cooling sea breezes. CAIR – the vintners' cooperative originally founded by Italians in 1928 – produces a variety of acceptable mid-range wines at its two plants near the capital, the most ubiquitous being the white Ilios and the red Chevalier de Rhodes. However, products of the smaller, family-run Emery winery (☎02460/41 208; daily in season 9am–4.30pm; free tours and tastings) at the village outskirts are much more highly esteemed, in particular the Granrosé rosé, the Mythiko red and white, and the premium Villaré white and Cava Emery red.

To see what Émbona would be like without tourists, carry on clockwise around the mountain past modern, nondescript **Artamíti monastery** (population three or four young monks) – its name a corruption of "Artemis" after a pagan temple in the forests nearby – to less-celebrated **ÁYIOS ISÍDHOROS**. This has as many vines and tavernas as Émbona (try *Café Restaurant Atavyros*), a more open feel, and the trailhead for the five-hour return ascent of 1215-metre Atávyros.

This path, beginning at the very northeastern edge of the village, is the safest and easiest way **up the mountain**; sources advocating the steep, cross-country scramble up from Émbona should be disregarded. Look for the wooden placard reading "Arhí Monopatioú" (Start of Path) at the beginning of a bulldozer track; follow this about 200m to the first hairpin turn, where the trail begins obviously behind a crude, wire-fastened gate in the fence. The route has been consolidated and marked with the occasional red-paint arrow or splodge. Most of the mountain itself is bare, except for some enormous oaks on the lower slopes, but dense, unburnt forests extend to the east, beyond Artamíti. Your reward for reaching the summit, besides the expected views, are extensive foundations of an ancient Zeus temple.

Láerma and Thárri monastery

The road from Áyios Isídhoros to Siánna is paved, as is the twelve-kilometre stretch (being widened) from Lárdhos on the east coast to Láerma, but not the fairly appalling track that curves for 12km east from Áyios Isídhoros to Láerma, though even the latter is worth enduring if you've any interest at all in Byzantine monuments and Orthodox monasticism.

LÁERMA itself is an attractive inland village with a handful of **tavernas**, including a *psistariá* under two plane trees in the square. But the area's main attraction is **Thárri monastery**, lost in pine forests four well-marked kilometres south. The oldest religious foundation on the island, this was re-established as a community of monks (currently 20, including some English-speaking ones) in 1990 by the charismatic abbot Amfilohios, educated at Pátmos. Since then he has built up a miniature ecclesiastical empire, centred on several repopulated nunneries and monasteries in southern Rhodes, which actively train monks for service in other islands and nations (especially Africa). Somewhat less admirably, the apostolic mission includes the fanatically Orthodox television station THARRI, whose programming seems to consist largely of nationalistic drama series, video footage of monastic churches and interviews with His own Beatitude.

Most visitors will find the striking **katholikón** (open daily, all day; smocks provided for the "indecently" attired), consisting of a long nave and short transept surmounted by barrel vaulting, of more immediate interest. Various cleanings during the 1990s restored formerly damp-smudged **frescoes** dating from 1300 to 1450 to their former exquisite glory. Currently the most distinct are those in the transept depicting the Evangelists Mark and Matthew (in the south squinches) plus the Archangel Gabriel in *The Annunciation* (north), while the nave boasts various acts of Christ, including such rarely illustrated scenes as the *Storm on the Sea of Galilee* (north side of vault), *Meeting the Samaritan at the Well* and *Healing the Cripple* (both south).

The monastery, dedicated to the Archangel Michael, supposedly takes the name "Thárri" from its foundation legend, as related by an elderly caretaker. A princess, kidnapped and abandoned here by pirates, was visited in a dream by the Archangel, who promised her eventual deliverance. In gratitude, she vowed to build as many monasteries in his honour as the gold ring cast from her hand travelled in cubits. This she did but, upon being reunited with her parents, the ring was lost in some bushes. Thus "Thárri" is derived from *tharévo*, "I hazard/wager/guess", after the family's futile search for the heirloom. In their pique, apparently only this one community was founded.

The far south

South of a line connecting Monólithos and Lárdhos, you could easily begin to think you had strayed onto another island – at least until the still-inflated prices brought you back to reality. Gone are most of the five-star hotels, and with them the bulk of the crowds; lacking too are most other tourist facilities and public transport. Only one or two weekday buses (in season) serve the exceptionally depopulated villages here (though Yennádhi has better service), approaching along the east coast, where deserted beaches are backed by sheltering dunes. Seasonal tavernas grace the more popular stretches of sand, but aside from the growing package resorts of **Lárdhos**, **Péfki** and **Kiotári**, there are still few places to stay. A new auxiliary airport long mooted for the area apparently won't be built after all; the cancellation should act as a damper on runaway development.

Lárdhos and Péfki

Second airport or not, new beachfront development mushrooms to either side of **LÁRDHOS** village, solidly on the tourist circuit despite an inland position between Láerma and the peninsula culminating in Líndhos. Numerous **shops** and **tavernas** flank the central three-way junction where roads head off towards Láerma and the coast. Situated downstream from some of the most fire-ravaged territory on Rhodes, the village endured catastrophic floods during rainy winters following the 1980s blazes. The beach 2km south of Lárdhos is coarse gravel and dull; it's better to continue another 3km to **Glýstra** cove, a small but delightful crescent of dark sand speckled with fine gravel, umbrellas and a snack bar.

Four kilometres east of Lárdhos, on the coastal road to Líndhos, **PÉFKI** (Péfkos on some maps) began life as the garden annexe and overflow for the latter, but is now a fully fledged package resort in its own right, popular with both short- and long-term foreigners who prefer the natural beauty and open vistas to the perceived claustrophobia of Líndhos. The sea is cleaner than at Lárdhos, with a largish main beach as well as small, well-hidden coves which are getting harder to find with all the clifftop development. **Accommodation**, predominantly in villas, is almost totally controlled by UK-based package operators such as Direct Greece (see "Basics" p.14). When **eating out**, nowhere offers particularly memorable meals here, though some people like *Sophia's*, at the Lárdhos end of things.

Asklipió and Kiotári

Nine kilometres beyond Lárdhos, a paved side road heads 3.5km inland to **ASKLIPIÓ**, a sleepy village guarded by a crumbling **Knights' castle** and graced by the Byzantine church of **Kímisis Theotókou** (open daily 9am–6pm). The building dates from 1060, with a ground plan nearly identical to Thárri's, except that two subsidiary apses were added during the eighteenth century, supposedly to conceal a secret school in a subterranean crypt.

The **frescoes** in the nave here are in far better condition than those at Thárri, owing to the drier local climate; they are also a bit later, though some sources claim that the final work at Thárri and the earliest here were executed by the same artist, a master from Híos. Their format and subject matter, though common on nearby Cyprus, are rare in Greece: didactic "cartoon strips" which extend completely around the church in some cases, featuring extensive Old Testament stories in addition to the more usual lives of Christ and the Virgin. On the upper right of the vault, there's a complete sequence of Genesis episodes, from the *Creation* to the *Expulsion from Eden*; note the comically menacing octopus among the fishes in the panel of the Fifth Day, and Eve subsequently being fashioned from Adam's rib. On the lower left, the career of the Prophet Daniel is elucidated, complete with lions' den. A seldom-encountered *Apocalypse of John the Divine* takes up most of the east transept, and *hokhláki* flooring decorates both the interior and the vast courtyard.

Two adjacent buildings (formerly the priest's quarters) now house separate **museums** (open same hours): a small exhibit of ecclesiastical treasures (donation requested) and a folklore gallery crammed with rural oddments, including a *rakí* still, an olive press and the largest wood planes you're ever likely to see. Asklipió's other concession to tourism is the **restaurant-bar** *Agapitos* overlooking the central car park and church; they also have a few **rooms** (Ⓣ02440/43 235; ❷) for those not requiring a coastal base.

Kiotári

Just beyond the detour for Asklipió, the beachfront hamlet of **KIOTÁRI** was in fact Asklipió's original site, until Byzantine-era piracy compelled the residents to retreat inland. For years it was virtually unknown to outsiders – partly because it wasn't even shown on most maps – but during the mid-1990s the Orthodox church elected to sell off its vast landholdings here, and Kotári rapidly became the southernmost outpost of (mostly German and Italian) mass tourism. Luxury mega-**hotels** such as the *Rodos Princess* (Ⓣ02440/47 102, Ⓕ47 267; ❻) and *Rodos Maris* (Ⓣ02440/47 000, Ⓕ47 051; ❺) sprout behind the broad, sandy beach of Kiotári "**North**". Kiotári "**South**", reached by following the shore frontage road or its own "exit" from the main highway, still just clings to a Stegná-like identity as a summer annexe for locals, who've built simple cottages here. The beach is resolutely gravelly but fine for a dip; rock formations and a small offshore reef lend the coast a bit of definition. But even here a half-dozen **tavernas** are resolutely commercialized and a German influence is shown by the number of obscure German beers on tap; the best are probably *Il Ponte* in Kiotári "North", and *Lighthouse* at Kiotári "South".

Yennádhi

At **YENNÁDHI**, 4km further south, a featureless dark-sand-and-gravel beach extends for kilometres in either direction. It's clean and serviceable, with sunbeds and rudimentary watersport gear available, plus three **tavernas** just behind the most central and accessible part of the shoreline, reached by a paved access drive signposted as "Yennádhi Beach". Best of these is *Klimis*, with good house wine, *mayireftá* cooked by his wife in the morning, and occasional fish grills. The rather drab outskirts – including a derelict brick factory – of the village mask the older village core inland, which offers various **amenities** (especially to the numerous soldiers stationed nearby): a post office, car rental, café-bars and some **accommodation** – *Betty Studios* by the pharmacy; (Ⓣ02440/43 020; ❷), or *Effie's Dream Apartments* at the northern end of things, (Ⓣ02440/43 410, Ⓕ43 437; ❷).

Lahaniá and southeast beaches

South of Yennádhi, you'll see more fine if lonely beaches, often marked just by isolated "taverna-rooms" which function in peak season only. Some 10km from Yennádhi, then 2km inland along a side road, invisible from the sea and thus pirate-safe **LAHANIÁ** village, with its smattering of rooms, is a possible base. Nearly half of the 140 inhabitants are bohemians from Munich and Berlin, who since the 1980s have opened craft shops and restored many handsome houses – abandoned after a postwar earthquake – lining the hilly streets in exchange for long-term rent-free occupation. On the main square, strangely sited at the lower, eastern end of the village, *Taverna Platanos* offers eminently reasonable and appetising **meals** – fish, two starters and a beer for €15 or under – with seating under the trees between the church and two wonderful fountains, one retaining an Ottoman inscription. The alternative, up on the village through road, is the *Akropol Chrissis Taverna*, run by the bear-like, amiable priest Papa Yiorgos, and offering good mezédhes; he also rents out **rooms** or even entire **restored houses** (Ⓣ02440/46 033, Ⓕ46 032; ❷–❸).

You can go directly from Lahaniá to the junction-hamlet of Hokhlakás, which straddles a paved side road leading south to **Plimýri**, a well-protected, sandy bay backed by dunes, whose only facility is a single, indifferent **taverna** (*Plimirri Beach*) serving a limited menu dominated by farmed fish. Rather more compelling is the **church of Zoödhóhou Piyís**, adjacent, which has ancient Corinthian columns upholding the groin vaulting in its west porch. Beyond the concrete jetty, which in the distant future may shelter a yacht marina, a 1980-vintage wreck attracts expert scuba divers.

Áyios Pávlos, 5km beyond Hokhlakás, is not even a hamlet, merely another Italian-era model farm, complete with belfried church, now utterly derelict. From here an unmarked fair-quality dirt road leads southeast just over 5km to an unnamed but pristine beach, extending for 2km south of **Cape Vígla**. Beyond the dunes and low junipers stretches a broad, gently shelving bay, one of the last turtle-nesting sites in the Dodecanese; hopefully it will soon benefit from some official protection – for the moment, crude signs ask you to avoid the area at night.

Kattaviá and Prassoníssi

Shortly beyond Áyios Pávlos the road threads through low stands of wind-tormented dwarf juniper before entering **KATTAVIÁ**, nearly 120km from the capital, marooned amidst fields of wheat or barley which are the only crops that thrive locally. Several **tavernas**, pricier than you'd expect, preside over the junction, shaded by sycamore figs, that doubles as the square; the most interesting of these is brightly coloured *Martine's Bakaliko/Mayeriko* (closed Thurs), run by folk from Lahanía, which has some vegetarian dishes and attempts to use local organic ingredients when possible. A vital **filling station** – the first since Lárdhos – and a few **rooms/studios** to rent, aimed mostly at windsurfers (read on), complete the list of facilities. Like so many villages in the far south, three-quarters of the houses here are locked up and vacant, their owners having emigrated to find work in Australia or North America.

From Kattaviá a paved road leads through a frequently used military exercise area to **Prassoníssi**, Rhodes' southernmost extremity and a mecca for European **windsurfers**. The sandspit which tethers Prassoníssi ("Leek Island") and its lighthouse to Rhodes was partially washed away by storms early in 1998, but enough remains to create flat water on the east side and up to two-metre waves on the west, ideal for different ability levels. Of the two windsurfing centres operating here, Swiss-run Procenter (April–Oct; ⓣ02440/91 045, ⓔprocenter.prasonisi@EUnet.at) is the more professional, with hourly rates from €13.50, and a ten-hour card (valid over several days) from €112. They're geared for one-week packages, including jeeps, and lodged in rooms (ⓣ02440/91 030; ❷) above the *Lighthouse/Faros Restaurant*, one of a half-dozen food and accommodation outfits here; the agent in the UK is Sportif (ⓣ01273/844919, ⓔSportif@compuserve.com). There aren't really enough rooms to go around during peak season, when the scrubby junipers rustle with tents and caravans despite signs forbidding the practice – and a complete lack of facilities.

Mesanagrós and Skiádhi Monastery

From Lahaniá, an alternative route heads 9km northwest along a narrow but paved road to the picturesque hilltop village of **MESANAGRÓS**. This already existed in some form by the fifth century AD, if the foundations of a ruined basilica at the village outskirts are anything to go by. Within this vast area, amid patches of mosaic flooring, squats a smaller but equally venerable thirteenth-century chapel; any previously existing frescoes are long gone, but there's a *hokhláki* floor and stone barrel arches to admire. You can fetch the key from nearby *Kafenio O Mike*, and buy a candle and/or a coffee as a donation.

The monastery of Skiádhi

The onward road to the **monastery of Skiádhi**, 6km distant, is shown incorrectly on most maps. Take the Kattaviá-bound road initially, then after about 2km bear right onto an unsigned dirt track; these last 4km are quite badly surfaced, but even a puny Category A rental car can get through in dry conditions.

Known formally as Panayía Skiadhení, the monastery – despite its undistinguished modern buildings – was originally founded in the thirteenth century to house a miraculous icon of the Virgin. In the fifteenth century a heretic stabbed the painting, allegedly causing blood to flow from the wound in her cheek; the fissure, and suspicious brown stains around it, are still visible. As in all such legends, the offending hand was instantly paralyzed.

Except on September 7–8, the festival of the icon, you can usually **stay** overnight upon arrangement with the caretaker priest, although the monastery is not continuously staffed so enquire locally before setting out the final distance. The immediate surroundings of Skiádhi are rather dreary since a comprehensive fire in 1992, but the views west are stunning. Tiny **Khténia islet** is said to be a petrified pirate ship, transformed into stone by the Virgin in answer to prayers from desperate locals about to succumb to yet another raid.

The southwest coast and Apolakkiá

West of Kattavía, the island loop road – completely paved by the mid-1990s, notwithstanding old maps – emerges onto the deserted, **southwest coast**; Skiádhi can easily be reached from this side too, as the still-dirt road up from here is better signposted than from Mesanagrós. This coast is "deserted" because the beaches here are poor and rubbish-strewn, with crashing waves and often a strong undertow; the only amenity is a single taverna about 4km south of Apolakkiá.

The nearest inland village, 7km north of the Skiádhi turning, is nondescript, agricultural **APOLAKKIÁ**, set amid plastic greenhouses and its famous watermelon patches, and also equipped with a few **shops** and tourist facilities. There's a bona fide **hotel** with pool – the *Amalia* (Ⓣ02440/61 365, Ⓕ61 367; ③), convenient if you're mountain-bike touring – plus several reasonable **tavernas** and kafenía surround the central junction, where there always seem to be a few stopped motorists scratching their heads over maps. Northwest leads to Monólithos, due south back to Kattaviá (past a **filling station**), while the northeasterly bearing is a good, paved road cutting quickly back to Yennádhi via Váti – and the ruins of pine forests done for by blazes of the late 1980s and early 1990s.

Áyios Yeóryios Várdhas

A few hundred metres along the northeast road to Yennádhi, a signposted, paved side road heads north to a new irrigation reservoir absent from most maps, oddly scenic as these things go and plainly visible from Siánna overhead. But the best reason to detour here is to visit the tiny country chapel of **Áyios Yeóryios Várdhas**, arguably the finest remote Byzantine monument on Rhodes. After 3km, with the dam looming overhead, bear left onto a dirt track, veer left again when you see an electricity substation, and then almost immediately right again up a steep turning. After a total four-kilometre journey from the main road, you'll see the shed-like chapel (always open) by the roadside. Its thirteenth-to-fourteenth-century frescoes, smudged but wide-eyed and warmly naïve in style, include a fine *Entry to Jerusalem* and *Presentation* on the right (south) wall, a *Panayía Glykofiloússa* (Virgin Kissing the Christ Child) on the left wall, plus what seems to be a personification of Faith, Hope and Charity on the left of the apse.

Greek script table

Ródhos (Town/Island)	Ρόδος	ΡΟΔΟΣ
Afándou	Αφάντου	ΑΦΑΝΤΟΥ
Akándia	Ακάντια	ΑΚΑΝΤΙΑ
Akramýtis	Ακραμύτης	ΑΚΡΑΜΥΤΗΣ
Apolakkiá	Απολακκιά	ΑΠΟΛΑΚΚΙΑ
Apóllona	Απόλλωνα	ΑΠΟΛΛΩΝΑ
Arhángelos	Αρχάγγελος	ΑΡΧΑΓΓΕΛΟΣ
Arhípoli	Αρχίπολη	ΑΡΧΙΠΟΛΗ
Arnítha	Αρνίθα	ΑΡΝΙΘΑ
Asgoúrou	Ασγούρου	ΑΣΓΟΥΡΟΥ
Asklipió	Ασκληπιειό	ΑΣΚΛΗΠΙΕΙΟ
Atávyros	Ατάβυρος	ΑΤΑΒΥΡΟΣ
Ayía Agáthi	Αγία Αγάθη	ΑΓΙΑ ΑΓΑΘΗ
Áyios Emilianós	Άγιος Αιμιλιανός	ΑΓΙΟΣ ΑΙΜΙΛΙΑΝΟΣ
Áyios Isídhoros	Άγιος Ισίδωρος	ΑΓΙΟΣ ΙΣΙΔΩΡΟΣ
Áyios Nikólaos Foundoukli	Άγιος Νικόλαος Φουντουκλή	ΑΓΙΟΣ ΝΙΚΟΛΑΟΣ ΦΟΥΝΤΟΥΚΛΗ
Áyios Pávlos	Άγιος Πάυλος	ΑΓΙΟΣ ΠΑΥΛΟΣ
Áyios Yeóryios Várdhas	Άγιος Γεώργιος Βάρδας	ΑΓΙΟΣ ΓΕΩΡΓΙΟΣ ΒΑΡΔΑΣ
Dhimyliá	Διμυλιά	ΔΙΜΥΛΙΑ
Eleoússa	Ελεούσα	ΕΛΕΟΥΣΑ
Émbona	Έμπωνα	ΕΜΠΩΝΑ
Eptá Piyés	Επτά Πηγές	ΕΠΤΑ ΠΗΓΕΣ
Faliráki	Φαλιράκι	ΦΑΛΙΡΑΚΙ
Filérimos	Φιλέριμος	ΦΙΛΕΡΙΜΟΣ
Foúrni	Φούρνοι	ΦΟΥΡΝΟΙ
Glyfádha	Γλυφάδα	ΓΛΥΦΑΔΑ
Haráki	Χαράκι	ΧΑΡΑΚΙ
Hokhlakás	Χοχλακάς	ΧΟΧΛΑΚΑΣ
Ialyssós	Ιαλυσός	ΙΑΛΥΣΟΣ
Ixiá	Ιξιά	ΙΞΙΑ
Kalamónas	Καλαμώνας	ΚΑΛΑΜΩΝΑΣ
Kálathos	Κάλαθος	ΚΑΛΑΘΟΣ
Kalavárdha	Καλαβάρδα	ΚΑΛΑΒΑΡΔΑ
Kalythiés	Καλυθιές	ΚΑΛΥΘΙΕΣ
Kameiros (ancient)	Κάμειρος	ΚΑΜΕΙΡΟΣ
Kámiros Skála	Κάμειρος Σκάλα	ΚΑΜΕΙΡΟΣ ΣΚΑΛΑ
Kápi	Κάπι	ΚΑΠΙ
Kattaviá	Κατταβιά	ΚΑΤΤΑΒΙΑ
Kiotári	Κιοτάρι	ΚΙΟΤΑΡΙ
Kollákio (Collachium)	Κολλάκιο	ΚΟΛΛΑΚΙΟ
Kolóna	Κολόνα	ΚΟΛΟΝΑ
Kolýmbia	Κολύμπια	ΚΟΛΥΜΠΙΑ

Koskinoú	Κοσκινού	ΚΟΣΚΙΝΟΥ
Kremastí	Κρεμαστή	ΚΡΕΜΑΣΤΗ
Kritiká	Κρητικά	ΚΡΙΤΙΚΑ
Kritinía	Κρητηνία	ΚΡΗΤΗΝΙΑ
Ladhikó	Λαδικό	ΛΑΔΙΚΟ
Láerma	Λάερμα	ΛΑΕΡΜΑ
Lahaniá	Λαχανιά	ΛΑΧΑΝΙΑ
Lárdhos	Λάρδος	ΛΑΡΔΟΣ
Líndhos	Λίνδος	ΛΙΝΔΟΣ
Malóna	Μαλώνα	ΜΑΛΩΝΑ
Mandhráki	Μανδράκι	ΜΑΝΔΡΑΚΙ
Maritsá	Μαριτσά	ΜΑΡΙΤΣΑ
Mássari	Μάσαρη	ΜΑΣΑΡΗ
Mesanagrós	Μεσαναγρός	ΜΕΣΑΝΑΓΡΟΣ
Monólithos	Μονόλιθος	ΜΟΝΟΛΙΘΟΣ
Mónte Smith	Μόντε Σμίθ	ΜΟΝΤΕ ΣΜΙΘ
Neohóri	Νεοχώρι	ΝΕΟΧΩΡΙ
Paradhísi	Παραδείσι	ΠΑΡΑΔΕΙΣΙ
Pastídha	Παστίδα	ΠΑΣΤΙΔΑ
Péfki	Πέυκοι	ΠΕΥΚΟΙ
Petaloúdhes	Πεταλούδες	ΠΕΤΑΛΟΥΔΕΣ
Platánia	Πλατάνια	ΠΛΑΤΑΝΙΑ
Plimýri	Πλημμύρι	ΠΛΗΜΜΥΡΙ
Prassoníssi	Πρασονήσι	ΠΡΑΣΟΝΗΣΙ
Profítis Ilías	Προφήτης Ηλίας	ΠΡΟΦΗΤΗΣ ΗΛΙΑΣ
Profylía	Προφυλία	ΠΡΟΦΥΛΙΑ
Psínthos	Ψίνθος	ΨΙΝΗΘΟΣ
Pylónas	Πυλώνας	ΠΥΛΩΝΑΣ
Réni Koskinoú	Ρένι Κοσκινού	ΡΕΝΙ ΚΟΣΚΙΝΟΥ
Rodhíni	Ροδίνι	ΡΟΔΙΝΙ
Sálakos	Σάλακος	ΣΑΛΑΚΟΣ
Siánna	Σιάννα	ΣΙΑΝΝΑ
Skiádhi Monastery	Μονή Σκιάδι	ΜΟΝΗ ΣΚΙΑΔΙ
Soroní	Σορωνή	ΣΟΡΩΝΗ
Stegná	Στεγνά	ΣΤΕΓΝΑ
Thárri Monastery	Μονή Θάρρι	ΜΟΝΗ ΘΑΡΡΙ
Theológos	Θεολόγος	ΘΕΟΛΟΓΟΣ
Thérmes Kallithéas	Θέρμες Καλλιθέας	ΘΕΡΜΕΣ ΚΑΛΛΙΘΕΑΣ
Triánda	Τριάντα	ΤΡΙΑΝΤΑ
Tsambíka	Τσαμπίκα	ΤΣΑΜΠΙΚΑ
Váti	Βάτι	ΒΑΤΙ
Vlyhá	Βλυχά	ΒΛΥΧΑ
Yennádhi	Γεννάδι	ΓΕΝΝΑΔΙ

Travel details

Island transport

Buses

With some important exceptions just southeast of Ródhos Town, RODA buses serve mostly points on the west coast, while KTEL buses ply the east coast. The schedules below, keyed to workdays, are sharply reduced at weekends. Fares are usually €1.50–3.50 one way, and never more than €5.60. Journey times vary from 10 to 15 minutes for Koskinoú to almost 2hr for Kattaviá in the far south.

RODA

New Market (Néa Agorá) to: airport (Paradhísi; 23 daily 5am–11pm); Apóllona (2 daily at 1.30 & 3.40pm); Émbona (1 daily at 2.45pm); Kalavárdha (8 daily 5am–9.30pm); Kallithéa hotel zone (half-hourly 8am–10.30pm); Kámiros Skála, for Hálki ferry (2 daily at 10am & 1.30pm); Koskinoú (10 daily 5.45am–9pm); Kritinía (Mon–Fri 1 daily at 1.30pm, Sat 2 daily at 8am & 2pm); Monólithos (1 daily Mon–Fri at 1.30pm, returns following morning); Petaloúdhes (1 daily at 9.30am, returns 12.15pm); Sálakos (5 daily 7am–9.30pm); Theológos (12 daily 5am–9.30pm).

KTEL

Platía Rimínis (aka "Sound & Light Square") to: Afándou (15 daily 6.45am–11pm); Arhángelos (14 daily 6.45am–11pm); Asklipió (2 daily Mon–Fri); Faliráki (12 daily 7.30am–11pm); Haráki (2 daily at 10am & 2.15pm); Kattavía (Tues & Thurs at 2.30pm); Kolýmbia (7 daily 9am–9.15pm); Láerma (1 daily Mon–Fri at 1pm, returns immediately); Lárdhos (9 daily 6.45am–7.30pm); Líndhos (14 daily 8.30am–7.30pm); Mássari (4 daily 9am–2.30pm); Mesanagrós (Thurs only at 2.30pm); Péfki (8 daily 8.30am–7.30pm, involves change of bus in Líndhos); Psínthos (4 daily 1.30–9.15pm); Yennádhi (9 daily 6.45am–7.30pm).

Inter-island transport

Key to ferry and hydrofoil company abbreviations

ANES	*Anónymi Navtiliakí Etería Sýmis* (Symian Shipping Company)
DANE	*Dhodhekanisiakí Anónymi Navtiliakí Etería* (Dodecanesian Shipping Company)
G&A	G&A Ferries
LANE	*Lasithiotiki Anónymi Navtiliakí Etería* (Lasíthi Shipping Company)
NEL	*Navtiliakí Etería Lésvou* (Shipping Company of Lésvos)
NK	*Nissos Kalymnos*
KR	Kyriakoulis Maritime
LZ	Laoumtzis Hydrofoils

Kaïkia, small ferries and excursion boats

Kámiros Skála to: Hálki (1 daily at 9am Sun, at 2.30/2.45pm all other days; 1hr 15min).

NB The kaïki carries two or three cars (not that you need one on Hálki). The Wed departure in either direction may occasionally be fully booked by Hálki package clients and thus unavailable to independent travellers. The boat waits for the arrival of the bus from Ródhos Town, which is usually delayed in traffic.

Mandhráki to: Sými (1 daily at approximately 9am on one or more excursion boats or small catamarans, returning 3.30–4pm; or 4 weekly in season – currently Mon, Wed, Sat & Sun – at 6pm on the *Symi I* or *Symi II* run by ANES; 2hr).

NB It is now fairly easy to get a one-way ticket on an excursion boat (*ekdhromikó*) in either direction; count on €7.40–8.80. *Epivátiko* or scheduled passenger sailings cost about half that; current information on *epivatikó* sailings of the *Symi I* or *II* are available from the ANES office at Avstralías 88 ⓣ02410/37 769.

Ferries

Rhodes Commercial Harbour (Kolóna) to: Alexandhroúpoli (1 weekly on NEL; 27–28hr); Astypálea (1–2 weekly on G&A or DANE; 8hr); Crete (2 weekly on LANE to Áyios Nikolaos &/or Sitía; 10hr 15min/12hr 45min); Foúrni (2 weekly on G&A; 9hr 30min); Hálki (2 weekly on LANE; 2hr); Híos (1 weekly on NEL; 11hr 30min); Ikaría (Áyios Kírykos, 2–3 weekly on G&A; 10hr 30min); Kálymnos (10–14 weekly on DANE, G&A or NK; 5hr 30min); Kárpathos (2 weekly on LANE to Dhiafáni & Pigádhia; 4hr 30min–5hr 30min); Kássos (2 weekly on LANE; 6hr 45min); Kastellórizo (2 weekly on NK, 1 weekly on larger boat to be determined; 4–5hr); Kós (12–16 weekly on DANE, G&A, NEL or NK; 4hr–6hr 30min); Léros (at least daily on DANE or G&A; 6hr 30min–7hr); Lésvos (1 weekly on NEL; 16–17hr); Límnos (1 weekly on NEL; 22–23hr); Lipsí (1 weekly on G&A; 8hr); Mílos (2 weekly on LANE; 18hr); Náxos

(1 weekly on G&A; 13hr 30min); Níssyros (3 weekly on NK and either DANE or G&A; 3–5hr); Páros (1 weekly on G&A; 14hr 30min); Pátmos (at least daily on DANE or G&A; 8hr 30min–9hr 30min); Pireás (11–14 weekly on DANE or G&A; 13–19hr); Sámos (2 weekly on NEL or DANE; 8–9hr); Sými (3–4 weekly on NK, and DANE or G&A; 1hr 30min–2hr); Sýros (1 weekly on G&A); Thessaloníki (1 weekly on DANE; 24hr); Tílos (3–4 weekly on NK, and DANE or G&A or NK; 2hr 30min–4hr).

NB The more esoteric connections like Rhodes–Foúrni, Rhodes–Lipsí, Rhodes–Náxos and Rhodes–Ikaría are reliably valid only from late June to mid-September.

Catamarans

There are two high-speed catamarans operating out of Rhodes: the *Dodecanese Express*, also known as *O Spanos* after the supermarket chain which owns it, and the *Sea Star*.

The **Sea Star** does not carry vehicles, and is the less reliable of the two, fitfully serving the line Rhodes–Tílos–Rhodes from June to September, with occasionally Níssyros thrown in. For current information, contact their Ródhos Town agency at Plastíra 9, Mandhráki ☎02410/77 048.

The **Dodecanese Express** can carry 4–5 cars and a slightly larger number of two-wheelers; it's a sleek, 2000-built Norwegian craft, with a limited amount of deck space (but no deck chairs). 2001 was the *Dodecanese Express'* second season and June-to-October departure patterns seem to have settled down as follows: daily 8.30am departure from Rhodes to Kós, Kálymnos, Léros and Pátmos, calling at Lipsí 4 days weekly (usually northbound only) and Tílos and Níssyros once weekly, both inbound and outbound, usually Wed; returning from Pátmos shortly after 1pm, arriving at Rhodes 6.30–7.30pm. During May it may call at Lipsí just twice weekly, serving Sými and Kastellórizo instead twice weekly. It has never called at Astypálea, Agathoníssi, Hálki, or Kárpathos and is unlikely to in the future, though there are rumours that from 2002 on there will be occasional services to Sámos (Pythagório). For current information, contact their head office at Avstralías 3, Ródhos Town ☎02410/70 590, or consult Ⓦwww.12ne.gr.

Hydrofoils

Three hydrofoil companies provide scheduled services out of Rhodes' Mandhráki harbour: ANES, Kiriakoulis and Laoumtzis. **ANES** (see p.187) serves only Sými with the *Aigli*, which leaves Mandhráki at least once daily at 9am or 6pm (sometimes both times), at a cost of about €10. For complete profiles of **Kyriakoulis** and **Laoumtzis** offerings, see "Basics", pp.42–43. For current details, contact Kyriakoulis at ☎02410/78 052; and Laoumtzis (based on Kós) c/o Pulia Tours ☎02420/26 388.

Mandhráki to: Hálki (1 weekly with LZ, 1 weekly with KR; 1hr 10min); Kálymnos (1 daily with KR; 2hr 45min); Kós (2 daily, on KR and LZ; 2hr direct); Níssyros (1 weekly with KR, 1 weekly with LZ, usually Sat/Sun; 3hr); Pátmos (2 weekly with KR; 4hr); Sými (2 weekly with LZ, 1 weekly with KR, typically Mon, Wed, Sat; 1hr); Tílos (1 weekly with LZ, 1 with KR, usually Sat/Sun; 1hr 20min–2hr).

Flights

NB All flights are on Olympic Aviation/Olympic Airways unless otherwise indicated.

Rhodes Dhiagoras Airport to: Athens (5 daily, plus 5 more on Aegean/Cronus; 1hr 10min); Iráklion, Crete (2 weekly April–Oct, plus 1–2 daily on Aegean/Cronus; 1hr); Kárpathos (1–2 daily; 40–70min); Kássos (5 weekly; 40min–1hr 15min); Kastellórizo (1 daily June–Sept, 3 weekly otherwise; 45min); Límnos (2 weekly via Sámos, Lésvos; 4hr); Mýkonos (2 weekly June–Sept; 55min); Santoríni (2–5 weekly; 50min); Thessaloníki (3 weekly, plus 1 daily on Aegean/Cronus; 1hr 25min).

International transport

Ferries and hydrofoils

Ródhos Town to: Limassol, Cyprus (18hr) & Haifa, Israel (39hr), 1 weekly ferry on Salamis Lines & 2 weekly with Poseidon Lines; Marmaris, Turkey (up to 2 daily hydrofoils May–Oct, departing 8am & 5pm; 45min–1hr).

NB Specimen high-season prices for Cyprus and Israel on Poseidon Lines (including taxes but before any applicable student/youth discounts): deck class €80, cheapest cabin €118 to Cyprus, €126.50 deck class and €167.60 cheapest cabin to Israel. Salamis Lines is typically about 25 percent cheaper.

Fares to Turkey with the Greek-run hydrofoil are €29.40 one way, €41.20 return, plus $10 Turkish port tax. There is no longer a regularly scheduled Turkish car ferry; this must be arranged specially and will work out expensive.

Flights

Rhodes Dhiagoras Airport to: Larnaca, Cyprus (1 weekly April–Sept on Olympic; 2 weekly, July–Aug only, on Cyprus Airways).

2

The southern Dodecanese

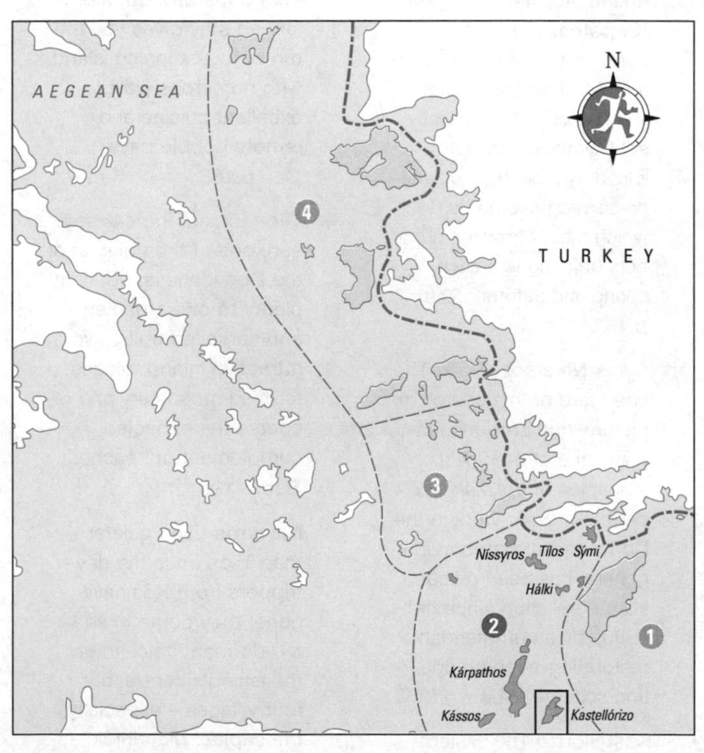

CHAPTER 2 **Highlights**

* **East-coast beaches, Kárpathos** Small, white-sand-and-gravel beaches on the sheltered east coast of Kárpathos approach Caribbean quality with the clarity of their turquoise water. See p.158

* **Hiking, northern Kárpathos** Many of the northern half of the island's remoter bays and villages – in particular dramatically set Ólymbos – are still linked by a network of well-preserved mule paths, which attract growing numbers of foreigners each spring and autumn. See p.162

* **Áyios Nikoláos, Hálki** The courtyard of this church in picturesque Emborió displays one of the finest examples of *hokhláki* or pebble-mosaic work in the Dodecanese; Emborió in general has been rescued from dereliction since the 1980s by a commendable restoration-accommodation scheme. See p.173

* **Kastellórizo** The easternmost Greek territory, with an appropriately end-of-the-line feel, quirky Kastellórizo is for self-entertaining pilgrims to the set of *Mediterraneo*, rather than beach buffs. See p.177

* **Sými** The officially protected harbour and hillside village teem with trippers during the day, but a prolonged stay gives you the run of this stunning island with numerous walks, excellent cuisine and remote pebble bays. See p.185

* **Tílos** Except in peak season, one of the quietest of the Dodecanese, but with plenty to offer: marked and surveyed trails, two attractive inland villages, a fortified monastery and of course the expected complement of beaches. See p.196

* **Níssyros** Even quieter than Tílos once the day-trippers from Kós have gone; they come to see the dormant volcano at the island's centre, but four villages – especially the capital, Mandhráki – are a photographer's mecca. See p.206

2

The southern Dodecanese

The seven **southern Dodecanese islands** closest to Rhodes not only offer ideal escapes when the "big island" begins to pall, but constitute worthy destinations in their own right. An increasing number of visitors effectively skip Rhodes, using a flight-only deal to deposit them at Ródhos Town's harbour, where on any given day in season, hydrofoils, catamarans or ferries are on hand to whisk them off to these surrounding islands. If you have the means, and plan well in advance, this is also an excellent and satisfying group to hop by chartered yacht, starting from Mandhráki harbour.

Rhodes' near neighbours offer a variety of escapes in terms of landscape and amenities. Harshly scenic **Kárpathos** is the only really sizeable island of the southern Dodecanese, with direct charter-flight access from Europe (plus useful local flights from Rhodes), magnificent beaches of all compositions, and an area in the far north of remarkable ethnological interest. Just next door, melancholy **Kássos** will probably appeal only to misanthropes allergic to other tourists.

The more cheerful duo of **Hálki** and **Sými**, which closely bracket Rhodes to the west and north respectively, are essentially one-town limestone outcrops which, like Kássos, have always been forced to make a living from the sea. Sými is greener, more hikeable, better endowed with pebbly beaches, and more geared up for independent travellers – though its spectacular harbour also makes it the most popular day-trip destination from Rhodes among this selection of islands. The houses of Hálki's port town have been comprehensively restored to provide accommodation for a more gentrified package clientele, who tend not to venture much out of sight of the harbour.

The most remote and depopulated isle of the Dodecanese is **Kastellórizo**, which once represented an extreme example of seafaring resourcefulness spurred by the poverty of onshore resources. Today the island serves as an idiosyncratic haven for a non-packaged, slightly alternative crowd willing to brave the long trip out from Rhodes and an utter lack of beaches.

Bare but relatively well-watered **Tílos**, least maritime of all the Dodecanese, combines almost overwhelming tranquillity and excellent beaches with a growing range of creature comforts, though occasionally problematic access

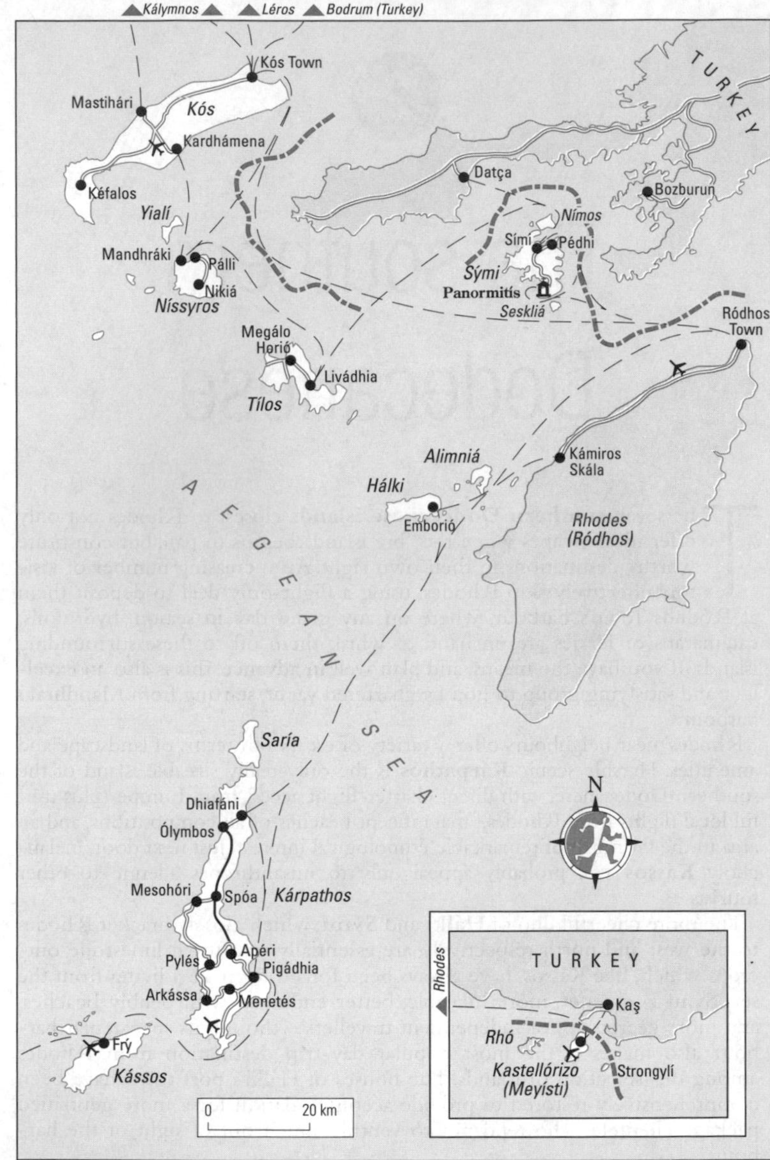

from either Rhodes or Kós could slow further development in the near future. The round volcano-isle of **Níssyros**, dry but fertile, receives regular day-excursions from adjacent Kós, but so far these have scarcely affected the convivial ethos in the main port's many tavernas; nor have they penetrated the picturesque outlying villages or hidden coves.

Kárpathos

A long, narrow island stranded between Rhodes and Crete, wild **Kárpathos** has always been something of an underpopulated backwater, although it is physically the third largest of the Dodecanese, fractionally smaller than Kós. A mountainous spine, habitually cloud-capped as it traps moisture-laden west winds, rises to 1215 metres, dividing the more populous, lower-lying south from an exceptionally rugged north. Despite a magnificent, if windswept, coastline of cliffs and promontories constantly interrupted by little beaches, Kárpathos has succumbed surprisingly little to tourism. This has a lot to do with lingering horrid stretches of road (though the network is much improved since the mid-1990s); the dearth, save two or three exceptions, of really interesting villages; and the surprisingly high cost of food, which offsets reasonable room prices.

Kárpathos doesn't, moreover, always have the most alluring of interiors. The central and northern uplands were badly scorched by 1980s forest fires – a far cry from the days when the island's pines were its most prized asset, valuable for shipbuilding – and agriculture plays a slighter role than on any other Greek island of comparable size. Although there are in fact good oil-bearing olive groves, enough livestock to export and some superb bakeries in villages like Óthos and Voládha, the Karpathians are frankly too well off to bother much with farming and rural crafts. Massive emigration to America and the resulting remittance economy had transformed Kárpathos into one of the wealthiest Greek islands, even before the recent influx of tourists.

Most foreigners come here for a glimpse of the traditional village life that prevails in isolated northern Kárpathos, to hike through the unravaged portions of the interior, and to lounge on numerous superb, secluded **beaches**, among the best in the Aegean. There's an airport (originally Italian-built) which receives several weekly direct charter flights from northern Europe, and visitor numbers – predominantly Scandinavian and German – are on the rise. Since the mid-1990s, package tourism has effectively monopolized Pigádhia and a couple of resorts in the southern half of the island, pushing independent travellers and backpackers into the remote north where facilities are too basic to interest overseas companies.

Although the Minoans and Myceneans established trading posts on the island (then known as Krapathos), Kárpathos' four Classical cities figure little in ancient chronicles. Alone of the major Dodecanese, Kárpathos was held by the Genoese and Venetians after the Byzantine collapse and so has no castle of the crusading Knights of St John, nor indeed any surviving medieval fortresses of consequence. The Ottomans couldn't be bothered to settle or even garrison it; instead they left a single judge or *kadi* in the main town, and made the Greek population responsible for his safety during pirate attacks. Of these there were many, the seas immediately around the island being a favoured haunt.

Getting around the island

For exploring the island as a passenger, there are fairly regular **bus** services to Pylés, via Apérí, Voládha and Óthos, as well as to Ammopí and (in term time only) to Spóa via Mesohóri; the Pigádhia "station" (just a stop with a destination placard) is at the corner of 28-Oktovríou and Dhimokratías, a couple of

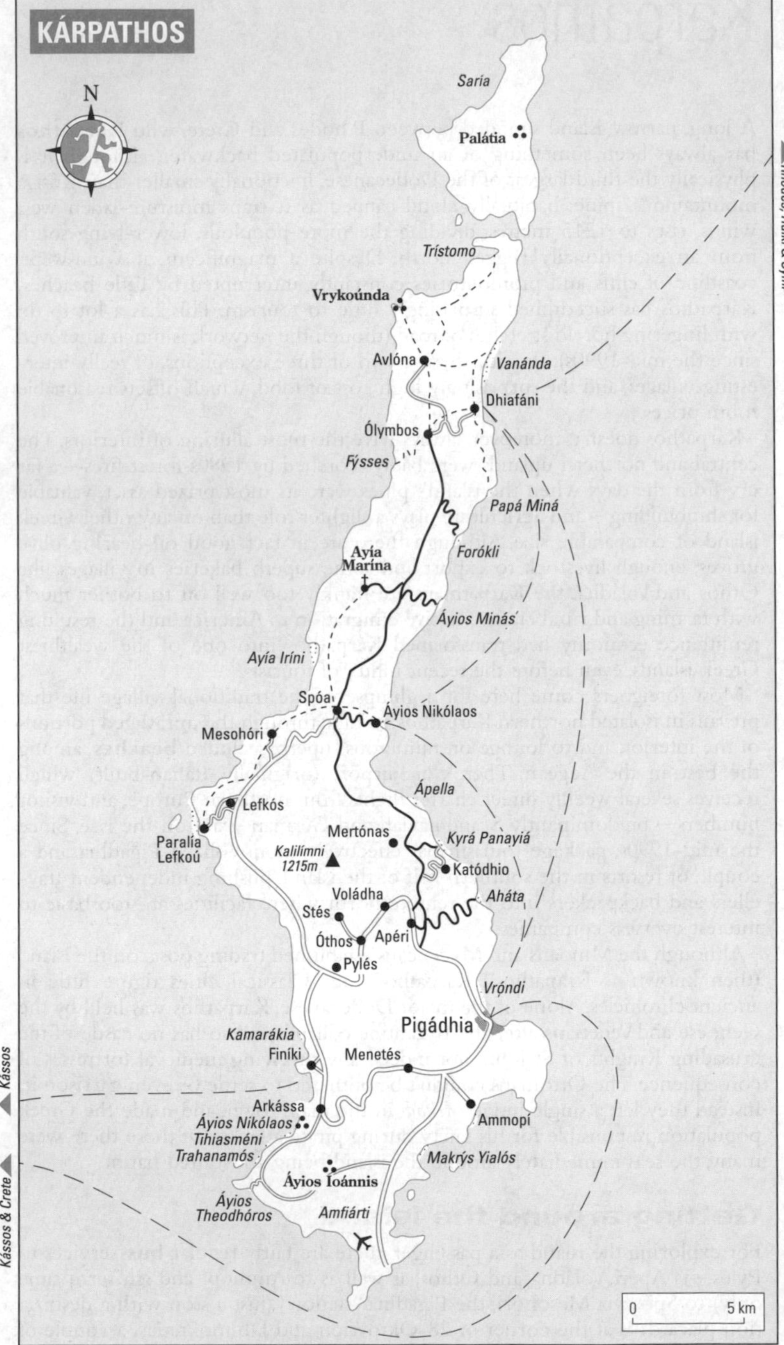
KÁRPATHOS
N
Saria
Palátia
Rhodes, Hálki & Sými
Trístomo
Vrykoúnda
Avlóna
Vanánda
Dhiafáni
Ólymbos
Fýsses
Papá Miná
Forókli
Ayía Marína
Áyios Minás
Ayía Iríni
Spóa
Áyios Nikólaos
Mesohóri
Ápella
Lefkós
Paralía Lefkoú
Mertónas
Kyrá Panayiá
Kalilímni 1215m
Katódhio
Voládha
Aháta
Stés
Óthos
Apéri
Pylés
Vróndi
Pigádhia
Kamarákia
Finíki
Menetés
Kássos
Arkássa
Áyios Nikólaos
Ammopí
Tihiasméni
Trahanamós
Makrýs Yialós
Kássos & Crete
Áyios Ioánnis
Áyios Theodhóros
Amfiárti
0
5 km

blocks back from the front. To be driven anywhere else, you'll have to rely on the set-rate, meterless **taxis** (tables of current fares are posted at strategic points), with a terminal in Pigádhia's municipal car park, a bit further up Dhimokratías. These aren't too expensive for getting to or from the cheerless **airport** (no snacks or diversions to hand) – 17km distant with a huge, NATO-improved runway – or to villages on the paved road network, but they charge a fortune to go anywhere else.

For getting around under your own steam, you can **rent cars** from upwards of a dozen agencies in Pigádhia, though you may have to try every one them to find a free vehicle in high season. Rates are well above the norm, and car condition often leaves a bit to be desired, but available models have improved of late. Among the more reputable are Circle (Ⓣ02450/22 690, Ⓕ23 289), a block from the post office, which may give discounts to clients of *Rose Studios* (see p.154); friendly Avis at the very north end of town (Ⓣ02450/22 702), with good deals for *Hotel Panorama* guests; Trust (Ⓣ02450/81 060, Ⓔtrustgr@yahoo.com), based in Ammopí, which will deliver and collect in Pigádhia; or Billy's (Ⓣ02450/22 921), by the north end of town near *Olympia Apartments*.

For **motorbikes**, Moto Carpathos (Ⓣ02450/22 382), uphill from the *dhimarhío*, has the biggest fleet and on-site service. Be warned that the only **fuel** on the island is found at two pairs of filling stations clustered just to the north and south of town, and that tanks on the small bikes are barely big enough to complete a circuit of the south, let alone head up north beyond Spóa – which is, in any case, expressly forbidden by most outfits. Moreover, local tourist **maps** are among the worst available in the Greek islands, and you won't find anything more detailed or accurate than the one in this book; Road Edition's recently issued #201, "Karpathos-Kasos" is the best of the bunch, but still full of errors. By far the easiest way to reach northern Kárpathos, and some of the more remote east-coast beaches, is by **boat** (for details, see box on p.160).

Pigádhia

The island capital of **PIGÁDHIA**, often known simply as Kárpathos, nestles at the south end of extremely scenic **Vróndi Bay**, whose sickle of sand extends 3km to the northwest. The town itself, curling around the jetty and quay where ferries and excursion boats dock, is as drab as its setting is beautiful; an ever-increasing number of concrete blocks contributes to the air of a vast building site, making the Italian-era port police and county governmental buildings seem like heirlooms by comparison. Although there's absolutely nothing special to see, Pigádhia does offer just about every facility you might need, with a definite package-tourism slant. The name of the main commercial street – Apodhímon Karpathíon ("Karpathians Overseas") – speaks volumes about the pivotal role of emigrants and emigration here, and the wealth they've returned with keeps a plethora of sophisticated boutiques and explicitly touristic shops going, with better-than-average stock.

Among essentials, **Olympic Airways** (Ⓣ02450/22 150) is on Platía 5-Oktovríou, at the west end of Apodhímon Karpathíon, but their hours are so limited that most people buy tickets from either Arriva Travel around the corner (Ⓣ02450/22 110) or Possi Travel on the waterfront (Ⓣ02450/22 235); Possi is also the main ticket outlet for LANE, currently the sole **ferry** company serving Kárpathos. The **post office** is a few paces west of Olympic, up Ethnikís Andístasis, while all three banks have **cash machines**. Pigádhia's main

internet café is *Café Galileo*, two doors down from Olympic on Apodhímon Karpathíon (Ⓦwww.caffegalileo.gr).

Accommodation

Most ferries are met by people offering **self-catering studios** (which tend to be better value than conventional rooms), though in response to protests from aggrieved hoteliers they're no longer actually allowed to tout on the quay itself. Unless you've arranged something in advance, you might consider such offers – the town is small enough that no location will be too inconvenient, though the best place to stay is on the hillside above the bus terminal and central car park. The more expensive, luxurious hotels generally lie north, towards and behind Vróndi beach, to either side of the ruined fifth-century basilica of **Ayia Fotiní**, and tend to be wholly occupied by Nordic package groups; independent travellers will have to make do with humbler, in-town facilities such as those cited below.

Amaryllis Studios Slightly downhill and east of *Rose Studios* (see below) Ⓣ02450/22 375. Not much of a view, but the accommodation comes in enormous, suite-sized units and the management is old-fashionedly polite. ❷

Atlantis Opposite the Italian "palace" Ⓣ02450/22 777, Ⓕ22 780, Ⓔhtatlantis@yahoo.com. Helpful management, a small pool and hot water guaranteed by a boiler are pluses at this C-class hotel; some packages but walk-ins welcome; breakfast included. ❹

Elias Rooms Just above *Hotel Karpathos* Ⓣ02450/22 446. En-suite rooms with a veranda in a converted older house; open June–Sept only. ❶

Karpathos South end of Dhimokratías, at the base of stair-street Ⓣ02450/22 347. Serviceable D-class hotel in a fairly quiet, convenient location; most rooms have air con. ❶

Konaki Near the town hall on 28-Oktovríou, the upper through road parallel to Apodhímon Karpathíon Ⓣ0245/022 908. Rambling, 1970s-vintage backpackers' favourite, now with en-suite rooms. ❶

Panorama In a quiet inland lane at the start of the Vróndi beach road (Ⓣ02450/23 262, Ⓕ23 021. The bar at this C-class hotel is a kitsch masterpiece, but rooms are fair-sized, with fridges, and either orchard or sea views. Some packages, but again a few rooms are kept back for independent trade. ❸

Rose Studios On the hillside behind the *Karpathos* Ⓣ & Ⓕ02450/22 284, Ⓔreservations@mailgate.gr. Well-kept studios and rooms, plus a few basement non-en-suite cheapies, the former with spectacular views; run by a kind family, long resident in Canada and Zimbabwe. Justifiably popular; must be reserved in advance. ❶

Titania Behind the municipal car park Ⓣ02450/22 144, Ⓕ23 307. Not the most inspired location, but another friendly C-class hotel that makes room for on-spec trade; claims to be open all year. ❹

Vróndi beach

Pigádhia's magnificent beach, **Vróndi** ("thunder"), takes its name from an attribute of the sea god Poseidon, who was patron of Pigádhia's ancient precursor Potidaion. The beach improves towards its centre, where the tidal zone has the least amount of rock-reef, though the water everywhere is generally clean and warm. Simple **sports** are engaged in, with windsurfing equipment and canoes rented from beachside lean-tos and tables. While the advancing tide of hotels has yet to fill in all the blank spots, camping rough is definitely a thing of the past. There are just two independent **restaurants**, right behind the sand at the town end: *To Limanaki*, open only for lunch, and *Seaside Snack Bar*, a bit closer to town and open until early evening.

Eating and drinking

Most of Pigádhia's waterfront **tavernas** are undistinguished – *yíros* and chips reign supreme – and overpriced at Rhodes levels; locals mutter about high carriage costs for food, but sheer greed and a not-too-discerning package clientele seem more likely reasons. Happily, bread is generally good, while fresh and (all too common) frozen ingredients are clearly indicated on menus; quality and value improves significantly as you head east towards the ferry dock. Towards the end of the strip are clustered three worthy choices: *To Perigiali*, a fairly genuine ouzerí with home-made desserts; the best all-rounder, *Iy Orea Karpathos*, with good local bulk wine, *trahanádhes* soup, sausages and great spinach pie; and, just beyond by the port police, *To Kyma*, good for non-farmed fish. One block inland, the clear winner is *To Ellinikon*, a *mezedhopolío* that caters all year to a local clientele with hot and cold *orektiká*, meat and good desserts.

Kafenio The Life of Angels (June–Sept), in one of the few surviving old buildings next to the church on Apodhímon Karpathíon, is frequented by a mixed crowd of locals and tourists, drawn by the impromptu nightly live **music** sessions (not, however, the best on the island); the limited evening menu seems a secondary consideration. Among trendier **bars**, *Rocks* and *Escape*, overlooking the bay from perches just below Apodhímon Karpathíon, are perennial favourites, while *Art Café/Bar*, just under one of the banks on Apodhímon Karpathíon, is loud and convivial.

A particularly well-developed Karpathian institution are the half-dozen **cafés** along Apodhímon Karpathíon to either side of the fountain, courtesy of returned USA emigrants. They have been spruced up of late, with egg-and-sausage-fry-up odours banished and ice creams, sweets and fancy coffee purveyed now as well; none cries out for special accolades, though *Kentro Kafe* imports decent gelato from Rhodes.

Southern Kárpathos

The southern extremity of Kárpathos, towards the airport, is flat, extraordinarily desolate and windswept. There are a couple of relatively undeveloped sandy **beaches** on the southeast coast, in the region known as Afiárti (or Amfiárti), but they're only really attractive to windsurfers who come here to take advantage of the prevailing northwest winds. About the nicest of the Afiárti coves is **Makrýs Yialós**, where you'll find *Hotel Poseidon* (Ⓣ02450/22 020, Ⓕ22 603; ④) and at least one windsurfing school offering instruction.

Most people go no further in this direction than **Ammopí**, just 7km from Pigádhia. This, together with development at Arkássa and Paralía Lefkoú (see p.157), is the closest thing on Kárpathos to a purpose-built beach resort: three tree-fringed coves (the northerly pair sandy, the southerly one sand and gravel) overshadowed by the large, nominally C-class *Argo* and *Amoopi Bay* hotels, with the spaces in between being filled up fast by more modest hotels, rooms establishments and tavernas. Germanophone package tourism pretty much has a hammerlock on the area; exceptions include *Rooms Votsalakia* (Ⓣ02450/22 204; ②) above the south beach, or the *Sunflower Studios* (Ⓣ & Ⓕ02450/81 019, Ⓔhotelsunflower@yahoo.com; ③), inland and above from the southerly beach.

Heading west from Pigádhia, rather than south along the coast, the road climbs steeply for 9km up to **MENETÉS**, an appealing village with handsome old hilltop houses, a tiny folklore museum and a spectacularly sited church in the precincts of the ancient acropolis. There are two central **tavernas** (*Ta Dhyo Adhelfia* and *Koula*), both on the through road, and a World War II resistance memorial at the east edge of town by the cemetery, with sweeping views north.

The west coast

Kárpathos' west coast seems far less developed than the east coast, since – with the sterling exception of Paralía Lefkoú – beaches are scanty and exposed, and the shoreline more bleak than dramatic. For a change, the local road system isn't too bad, with un-potholed tarmac connecting all points discussed below and even inching across the island's spine as far as Spóa.

Arkássa and Finíki

Beyond Menetés, the road immediately starts its descent to **ARKÁSSA**, lining the slopes of a ravine draining to the west coast, with excellent views across to Kássos en route. Arkássa's scenic location and smattering of beaches just south of Paleokástro headland have made it a prime target for intensive development, with hotels and restaurants sprouting in clusters along the mostly rocky coastline.

A few hundred metres south of where the ravine meets the sea, a signposted cement side road heads towards the whitewashed chapel of **Ayía Sofía**, five minutes' walk away and built on the spot where **Classical and Byzantine Arkessia** stood. Its visible remains consist of several mosaic floors with geometric patterns, one of which runs diagonally under the floor of a half-buried cistern, emerging from the walls on either side. The headland beyond, known as **Paleokástro**, was the site of **Mycenaean Arkessia**; the walk up is again signposted, but scarcely worth it for the sake of a few stretches of polygonal wall and a couple of tumbled columns.

Much of Arkássa's **accommodation** is aimed squarely at the package market, but independent travellers could try the en-suite *Hotel Dimitrios* (ⓣ02450/61 313, ⓕ61249; ❷), with large common areas and breakfast included, or the pricier bungalows of *Seaside Studios* (ⓣ02450/61 421; ❸) and *Glaros Studios* (ⓣ02450/61 015; ❸), both at **Áyios Nikólaos** beach – 600m of rare sand hereabouts with a single taverna – signposted just south. Most other **tavernas** lie north of the ravine in the village centre, for example the durable *Petaloudha* on the dead-end access street. At the far north end of things, just above the sea, there's the *Alpha Studios* (ⓣ & ⓕ02450/61 352; ❸) – though like its counterparts at Áyios Nikólaos it has contracts with package companies.

Beyond Áyios Nikólaos, the road dwindles to a dirt track as it passes the remote, sandy beaches of **Tihiasméni** and **Trahanamós** en route to the cape of **Áyios Theódhoros**, over 6km from Arkássa. There's a little monastery here, and an equally diminutive, protected beach a steep scramble down in the southeastern lee of the point, but for anyone except misanthropes this won't be worth the bother. Neither will most relish the rough onward track through a giant wind farm and the dreary, abandoned village of Áyios Ioánnis to Kípos hamlet, at Afiárti.

The tiny fishing port of **FINÍKI**, just a couple of kilometres north of Arkássa, offers a minuscule beach, fairly regular excursions to Kássos, half a dozen **tavernas** and several **rooms/studios** establishments. Accommodation includes *Giavasis Studios* (ⓣ02450/61 365; ❷), on the road to the jetty, or for more comfort and value the well-designed and built *Arhontiko Studios* up on the main bypass road (ⓣ02450/61 473, ⓕ61 054; ❸). *Iy Marina* and *To Dhelfini* are currently the most salubrious eateries in Finíki, though there's another well-loved one, *Kostas*, 500m north under two tamarisks at reefy Kamarákia beach.

Paralía Lefkoú and Mesohóri

A paved spur off the asphalt coastal road leads to the attractive resort of **PARALÍA LEFKOÚ**, the beach annexe of inland Lefkós. Unless you rent a car – there are two agencies here now, Lefkos (☎02450/71 057) and Drive (☎02450/71 415) – it's not a particularly convenient touring base, as only three buses a week call here from the island's capital; if you've rented a small motorbike in Pigádhia this is the furthest you can reach and return from without running out of fuel. However, your efforts will be rewarded with a striking topography of cliffs, hills, islets and sandspits surrounding a triple bay, making this a delightful spot for flopping on the beach. On the spit between two more northerly and progressively wilder bays lie the badly crumbling remains of medieval fortifications; indeed the whole area lies within an archeological protection zone, which acts as a healthy brake on development. The single most impressive monument, well signposted off the northerly access road, is a complex of **Roman cisterns** (free, unenclosed), with underground cavities and columns.

There are now over two dozen places to **stay**, and perhaps ten **tavernas**, but package companies have moved in with a vengeance, making it hard to find a room unspoken for between mid-June and September. The access road first passes a stonier, fourth bay to the south, where the *Akroyiali Studios* (☎02450/71 178; ❷) is typical of the half-dozen clustered here and less likely to have groups. At Paralía Lefkoú itself, your best bets are probably on the headlands closing off the bay, where *Fisherman's House* (☎02450/71 170 or 097/4943167; ❶) and *Sunweek*, above *Zorba's Restaurant* (☎02450/71 025 or 71 251; ❶), while both en suite, are too spartan to appeal to the package market. Between the two, *To Steki tou Kalymnou*, with plenty of seafood, is probably the most authentic **taverna** option here; *Le Grand Bleu*, on the far side of the bay, has the most elegant menu and stays open late in the season, while *Blue Sky*, off towards the biggest beach, also gets good marks.

Mesohóri and around

Back on the main road, you climb northeast through one of the few patches of Karpathian pine forest not scarred by fire, eventually reaching Spóa (see p.159) overlooking the east coast. But it's well worth detouring along another side road, leading to attractive **MESOHÓRI**. The village tumbles down towards the sea around narrow, stepped alleys, coming to an abrupt halt at the edge of a flat-topped bluff occupied by "Platía" Skopí, dotted with three tiny, ancient chapels and separated from the village proper by a vast oasis of orchards. These are nurtured by the fountain (with the best water on the island) issuing from underneath the mammoth church of **Panayía Vryssianí**, lodged against the mountainside just east and invisible from the car park at the road's end; a special hall adjacent sees celebrations on September 8–9, beginning on the evening of the 7th. On the stair-street leading to the church is an excellent **taverna**, the *Dhramoundana*, remarkably reasonably priced for Kárpathos, and featuring local caper greens, sausages and marinated "sardines" (really a larger, bonier fish, *menoúla*). If you're seized by the urge to **stay**, there are all-year rooms above *Taverna To Steki* (☎02450/22 159 or 71 349; ❷), near the car park, which gets groups of walkers in spring or autumn; the slightly pricey taverna will do dishes to order in the evening.

As *To Steki*'s seasonal clientele suggests, Mesohóri is a major focus for local **hiking opportunities**. The quickest out-and-back walk, beginning next to Panayía Vryssianí, heads within half and hour to Makrýs Yialós; the walk is satisfying, arrival at the filthy, rocky bay anticlimactic. Well beyond, there's a much sandier, cleaner **beach** at **Ayía Iríni**, accessible only by boat in calm weather; otherwise locals swim at the little headland of Káfkalos just below Mesohóri. Bearing right at the prominent fork early along the Makrýs Yialós trail takes you to Spóa, from where an onward path descends to Áyios Nikólaos on the east coast.

Red paint-dot waymarking also leads you to the south end of Mesohóri and the path to Paralía Lefkoú, a two-hour walk; coming uphill from Paralía Lefkoú, the trail begins near the mini-market. The road cuts it only in one or two spots, and the terrain en route is rolling rather than an unmitigated climb. From the Áyios Yeóryios junction at Lefkós, a path heads up to the 1168-metre Profitis Ilías peak.

Central Kárpathos

The **centre** of Kárpathos supports a quintet of villages blessed with superb hillside settings and ample running water – and a cool climate, necessitating warm clothes even in August, especially if you're on a bike. Nearly everyone here has "done time" in North America, then returned home with their nest eggs. New Jersey, New York and Canadian number plates on huge, imported gas-guzzlers tell you exactly where repatriated islanders struck it rich – in many instances, fabulously so; the area apparently has the highest per capita income in Greece.

A little above the Finíki–Mesohóri road, **PYLÉS** is perhaps the prettiest of these villages, with great views west of the sea and Kássos, a few seasonal snack bars and kafenía on the single "high street", and abundant greenery just downhill – fed, as at Mesohóri, by a spring issuing from the foundations of the central church. **ÓTHOS** lies just below the second most lofty summit of the Dodecanese, 1215-metre **Mount Kalilímni**. The highest (500m) and chilliest settlement on Kárpathos, Óthos is noted both for an ethnographic museum installed in a traditional two-room house, and its sweet, pale-red wine. Much of this comes from vines at the hamlet of **STÉS**, 2km northwest, with yet another church-spring. Among several **tavernas** back in Óthos, try *Toxotis*, basically a bar with mezédhes, a couple of cooked dishes of the day and the excellent bread the village is noted for.

From here you cross a ridge often swirling with cloud to reach **VOLÁDHA**, endowed with a pair of nocturnal **tavernas** (*Klimataria* comes recommended) and a tiny Venetian citadel. Seven kilometres east of Pylés (and 2km from Voládha) lies **APÉRI**, largest, lowest and wealthiest of the four. During the pirate era it served as the island's capital, and is still the seat of the local bishop. In addition to an attractive fountain, the village offers some nondescript snack bars down by the bridge, and a pair of supper-only **tavernas**.

East coast beaches

From Apéri, you can drive 5km east along a very rough side road (thus boat trips from Pigádhia are popular) to isolated **Aháta** beach, a 150-metre, pebble bay in a dramatic setting, with a freshwater fountain and no other facilities (or shade) besides a *kantína* which may do light snacks in high season.

North of Apéri, the main road up the east coast is also extremely rough in places – the islanders have no intention of improving it, preferring the status quo – but this route makes a beautiful drive, passing above beaches again most easily accessible by boat from Pigádhia. The first one encountered is **Kyrá Panayiá**, just below **Katódhio** hamlet, reached via a paved if twisty side road. There are a surprising number of villas, **rooms** and **tavernas** in the ravine behind the 150m of fine gravel. Despite the arduous drive in, most accommodation is contracted out to German companies, though you can try your luck at friendly *Akropolis* (Ⓣ & Ⓕ02450/31 503; ❸ rooms, ❹ studios) up on the south hillside behind the church, with large if plain units and an on-site restaurant. In peak season the beach is hopelessly packed out, understandable given exceptionally clear, turquoise water sheltered from most summer winds, and rock overhangs at each end providing refuge and shade. Kyrá Panayiá can also be reached on foot from the village of Mertónas (sometimes Myrtónas), overhead; it's a fairly popular hike of less than an hour, with the trail emerging onto the lowest curves of the access road.

Continuing north along the main road some 10km past Apéri, another 2500-metre-long, dirt side road leads to **Ápella**, the best of the beaches you can reach by road; from the single taverna-rooms at the dead end you walk a few moments more by trail to the 300-metre sand-and-gravel beach, where shady spots under the pines just behind are at a premium, as is parking at the road's end. The local spring has dried up, so come prepared.

From the Ápella turning it's 5km more to a major junction at the watershed of the island, where you encounter a reliable fountain, ruined windmills (one restored as the high-season-only *Anemomilos* snack bar) and the Mesohóri–Spóa asphalt. **SPÓA** itself, high above the shore just east of the island's summit ridge, has a snack bar (*Folia*) at the end of the southerly village access road, plus the adjacent, more reliably open *Kafenio Akropolis* which does cheap dishes. Any of these might make a better **meal stop** than **ÁYIOS NIKÓLAOS**, 4km below, a small hamlet with an average beach and a single, somewhat overpriced **taverna**, *To Votsalo* (Ⓣ02450/71 205), which also has more reasonable **rooms** (❸) and **studios** (❹). There are also the ruins of a large, if overgrown, early Christian basilica to explore near the fishing port here.

Northern Kárpathos

Although **northern Kárpathos** is connected by a rough, 27-kilometre road with Spóa, the initial southerly 8km falls squarely in the "horrid" category as noted above, and taxis charge a whacking €62 per car for a journey up from Pigádhia. So, much the easiest (and most common) way to get up there is by sea. Inter-island ferries call at **Dhiafáni** thrice weekly in season, and there are smaller excursion or post boats daily from Pigádhia (see box on p.160). These are met at Dhiafáni by buses for the eight-kilometre trip up to the traditional village of **Ólymbos**, the main attraction in this part of Kárpathos.

Ólymbos and around

High above the west coast, remote **ÓLYMBOS** straddles a long ridge below slopes studded with mostly ruined windmills. The village was originally founded during the eighth century AD as a refuge from the pirates that plagued the shoreline settlements at Vrykoúnda and Saría, the now-uninhabited islet that hovers just north of Kárpathos like a ball balanced on a seal's nose. Over the centuries, Ólymbos evolved a Shangri-la-like **self-sufficiency** necessitated by its extreme isolation; during World War II for example, famine was not a threat here as elsewhere in the islands, since the locals had abundant flocks and grain.

Boats to and from the north

Two rival excursion boats are usually moored by the port police in Pigádhia, with inclusive tour-tickets sold on board (and also available at waterfront travel agencies). At a price of €13.20–14.70 (lunch not included) for an all-day tour to Ólymbos, the *Chrisovalandou III* proves more attractive, faster and more stable in heavy seas than the *Karpathos II*. Less well publicized is the fact that you can use these boats for a one-way trip between the north and the south of the island, in either direction, for €5.90. Both craft leave Pigádhia at about 8.30am, returning from Dhiafáni at about 4pm; the only morning departures from Dhiafáni which cater for locals who need to go to "town" are two weekly 8am "post boats", which carry just a few passengers, return from Pigádhia at 3pm, and also charge €5.90 one way. Any of these craft can, depending on sea conditions, take nearly two hours to travel between Pigádhia and Dhiafáni, so if you can coincide with a regular ferry in either direction, you'll save both money (€2.80 fare) and time (1hr 15min journey). Various agents also offer excursions to several isolated east coast beaches which have no (or poor) road access or facilities; enquire as to whether lunch is included, and bring supplies if not.

The area has long been a mecca for foreign and Greek ethnologists who treat it as a living museum of peasant dress, crafts, dialect and music that have long since vanished elsewhere in Greece. Like many remote island communities, it is overwhelmingly endogamous, consenting only occasionally to intermarry with emigrants from the island of Níssyros; someone with one grandparent from even the south of Kárpathos is considered an "outsider".

But Ólymbos is gradually being dragged into the modern era, thanks to the paved road up from Dhiafáni, electricity, and a growing number of tourists; since 1980, the number of day-trippers has increased tenfold to 30,000 annually, to the extent that they often outnumber locals during the day. It's still a very picturesque place, full of (albeit posed) photo opportunities, but traditions are vanishing by the year – or at least they're hard to witness in season, when the inhabitants must certainly get tired of being ogled like animals in a zoo. Nowadays it's only women over about forty, and those working in tourist shops, who wear the striking and magnificently colourful traditional dress (though to their credit they do not take it off once the tourist season ends). This garb is in fact worn throughout the north of the island, specifically Dhiafáni and Ávlona.

After a while you'll notice the dominant role that local **women** play in daily life: tending gardens, carrying goods on their shoulders, or herding goats. Nearly all Ólymbos men emigrate – in particular to Baltimore and Astoria in the US – or work elsewhere on the island, sending money home and returning only on holidays. The long-isolated villagers also speak a unique **dialect**, said to retain traces of its Doric and Phrygian origins; "Ólymbos", for example, is pronounced "Élimbos" locally.

Entering the village, you're obliged to run a gauntlet of **souvenir shops**, from which you can, in high season anyway, expect some persistent if good-natured sales pitches, but beware of Chinese- and Bulgarian-made embroidery touted as "traditional local handicraft". The most genuine articles are unfortunately the least portable: carved wooden doors or furniture, and the flamboyantly painted plaster-relief folk art on houses. Plant and animal, mythic and geometric designs are all represented on balustrades, lintels and eaves, though the most popular motif seems to be the double-headed eagle of the Byzantine Paleologos dynasty.

Deceptively modern-looking, the main **Church of the Assumption** sports seventeenth-century fresco fragments, and the altar screen proved to be gold-leafed after a 1993 cleaning. Two working **windmills** just beyond, restored in the mid-1980s, grind wheat and barley during late summer only, more for show than anything else; one is kept under sail whenever tourists are about. Under one of the mills is tucked a small, inconspicuous **museum** (sporadic hours; free), with such wooden oddities as a fez rack (from the days when such headgear was worn), infants' sling cradles and a vulture trap, baited with carrion, that looks like an oversized garlic press. Nearby, a small shop stocked with local products (honey, oil, wine, herbs) is worth supporting.

Practicalities

The daytime commercialization of Ólymbos provides a good reason for **staying** overnight (especially out of season), when things are more relaxed. The *Rooms Restaurant Olympos* (☎02450/51 252; ❶), near the village entrance, has modern rooms with bath, or others with traditional furnishings, while the two sisters managing the *Café Restaurant Zefiros* keep the en-suite *Hotel Astro* (☎02450/51 378; ❷). *Hotel Aphrodite* (☎02450/51 307; ❷), towards the far edge of the village, offers a like number of en-suite rooms in good condition, with southerly ocean views (but a fair bit of window-rattling from the wind).

Ólymbos – a mild debunking

The apparent exoticism of **Ólymbos** has prompted numerous sensational write-ups in the past, many of them exaggerated, plagiarized from each other, or simply untrue. Much is made of the local matrilineal property inheritance, with houses passing down from mother to eldest daughter – the so-called *kanakára* – upon her marriage, prompting claims of some rediscovered Amazonian realm. However, this custom is prevalent on several other of the Dodecanese; it was apparently a method of dodging taxation or confiscation dating from Ottoman times, when women weren't systematically counted in censuses. Less known is the fact that an oldest son – the *kanakáris*, literally "favourite son" – also inherits all the real property of his father's line; hence the massive emigration of younger brothers, who have literally no prospects in the village.

For at least some of this mystification, the villagers themselves are partly responsible, not being averse to occasional leg-pulling and succumbing to the natural tendency to tell the gullible and the nosey what they want to hear. Amateur anthropologists on flying visits are particularly easy targets: a reporter for the French edition of *GEO Magazine* was once assured by a certain disgruntled, divorced woman shopkeeper that most local men were either homosexual or impotent. This remark subsequently appeared in print, verbatim, without critique or irony, variously causing consternation and hilarity when the news got back to Ólymbos.

Probably the best way to experience Ólymbos at its most authentic involves turning up at one of the seasonal **festivals**, when traditional music is performed by the men; indeed vast crowds descend on August 15 and at Easter. Few outsiders realize, however, that the winter Carnival is nearly as important folklorically; masquers traipse from house to house, performing in return for hospitality and getting thoroughly drunk through straws (no doffing of masks is allowed).

The order of precedence of **musical instruments** is slightly unusual: the *tsamboúna* or bagpipe takes the lead, followed by the *lýra*, or three-string spike fiddle, while the *laoúto*, a relative of the mandolin and principally used for rhythm, defers to both. The *lýra*, with little bells on the curved bow, is unlike the modernized Cretan models, bearing more resemblance to a *politikí* or Pontic *lýra*; for a full description of this and other Dodecanesian music, see p.471 in Contexts.

There are nearly as many places to **eat**; one of the best and most obvious is *O Mylos*, occupying one of the seasonally unfurled mills and offering locally made wine and home specialities. *Parthenonas*, on the square by the church, is also okay if a bit pricey; the lentil soup and *melitzánes imám* are better than their their slightly greasy version of *makaroúnes*, a local dish of home-made pasta with onions and cheese. During springtime, *myrgouátana*, a rock-dwelling marine invertebrate (tastier than it sounds), is served up breaded and sauteed as mezédhes in Ólymbos kafenía, along with *petalídhia* (limpets). Both the *Zefiros* and *Olympos* as noted above are also worth trying. Incidentally, there is no bakery in Ólymbos; the village women make their own bread four or five days a week, at one of several rustic communal ovens. If you need some, you could ask your pension or restaurant proprietor.

Hikes from Ólymbos

Aside from its other attractions, Ólymbos makes an excellent base from which to do some **hiking**, a big plus being that the slopes between Ólymbos, Avlóna and Dhiafáni have retained most of the island's surviving pine-forest cover. There are two competing German-language walking guides to Kárpathos, especially the north, but each has defects – especially in mapping – so always put more trust in on-the-spot oral directions. North Karpathian paths were in good shape until the 1996 completion of the deep-water, car-ferry dock at Dhiafáni; now jeep tracks have been bulldozed, the locals drive everywhere, and as far as the trails are concerned it's a case of use them or lose them as they quickly become overgrown and landslid. Most waymarked walks head generally north from Ólymbos, and are of moderate length and difficulty.

Ólymbos to Fýsses

Fairly quickly if strenuously reached are the boat-sheds and superb, 100-metre sand-and-pebble beach at **Fýsses**, a sharp drop below on the west coast. The path there is deteriorated to nonexistent, with lots of scree, so a stick or walking-pole is useful; begin at the last house of the village, below the school, and allow 35 minutes down (rather less uphill, such is the footing).

Ólymbos to Spóa or Mesohóri

For something more challenging, follow the route from Ólymbos to **Spóa** or **Mesohóri** in the south, a five-hour trek unfortunately made less scenic by a devastating 1983 forest fire (though new trees are now chest-high). The initial two hours or so are on trail, until you meet the Spóa–Ólymbos track; you follow this for a couple of kilometres until adopting another track going west-southwest for the chapel and spring of Ayía Marína, from where an onward trail covers most of the remaining distance to Spóa.

Ólymbos to Dhiafáni

One of the more attractive possibilities, and certainly the easiest, is the hike down to **Dhiafáni**. The path begins just below the two working windmills, well marked with red paint-dots and rock cairns; top up with water at a spring some twenty minutes along. Just under half an hour out of Ólymbos, bear right away from the power lines, briefly down to the stream bed and then up towards the road (the left fork leads to Avlóna; see opposite), and after ten or so minutes, plunge down and left through extensive, unburnt forest, towards the bed of a ravine draining to Dhiafáni. A small stream trickles alongside much of the way, and there's another spring at the one-hour mark; at your approach, snakes slither into hiding and partridges break cover. The entire route takes just under ninety minutes downhill, but unfortunately the final half-hour's approach to Dhiafáni consists mostly of bulldozed riverbed.

Ólymbos to Vrykoúnda

By staying overnight in Ólymbos, you can also tackle the marked trail north to the ruins and beach at **Vrykoúnda**, via the agricultural hamlet of Avlóna; it's best to take ample food and make a day of it. It's just under ninety minutes to Avlóna, mostly on path (locals claim to do it in an hour), though you're forced to road-walk ten minutes over the ridge, past the large white church of Áyios Konstandínos; the trail resumes on the descent. There's another brief stretch of road on the final approach to the sizeable hamlet, overlooking a cultivated plain. **AVLÓNA** supports a mere ten permanent inhabitants (though many more in summer), and a single drinks café at the outskirts, though the management of *Restaurant Olympos* plans to open another taverna-rooms place here in the near future. Only grain – harvested picturesquely in May – is grown locally, since there isn't enough water for market gardens.

From Avlóna it's just over an hour to "Vroukoúnda", as it's pronounced in local dialect, using the initially walled-in path, flanked by fig trees, which takes off from the valley-floor track; there may be a sign up, and the way is cairned and red-dotted. The trail describes a moderate but quite long descent to the attractive bay, often over flagstone steps but also loose scree, and becomes markedly steeper towards the end. A road down to Vrykoúnda is planned, though not atop the path, as much of it dates from Roman times, and the archeological authorities must approve the route.

Visible traces of **Hellenistic/Roman/Byzantine Brykous** (Vrykoúnda), one of Kárpathos' four ancient city-states, consist of masoned wall courses and rock-cut tombs; the main, waymarked trail continues from the vicinity of a prominent tomb-cut monolith to the festival-grounds and remote **cave-shrine of John the Baptist**, on the left-hand promontory closing off the bay. On August 28–29, this turning is busy with locals en route to the saint's celebrations, but at any time it's worth walking at least part way there for sweeping views back down the west coast.

Scrambling down and right from the tomb-monolith brings you to a long pebble-gravel **beach**, which is serviceable enough, though sometimes tar washes up on it. The best cove is off to the left. Retracing your steps to Avlóna, it's an hour and a quarter from the beach to the fountain at the edge of the hamlet; there's no shade en route except for a single boulder equipped with a cement bench. From Avlóna back to Ólymbos, allow another hour-plus (it's slightly downhill).

Avlóna to Trístomo

Don't be too discouraged by the ugly, prominent bulldozer track heading initially northeast out of Avlóna; this has left ninety percent of the old hiking route to **Trístomo** (see overleaf) intact – either beautifully engineered *kalderími* or waymarked path. There's no real beach there, the trip out is the thing. The only bad news is that, contrary to rumours, there is no safe, easy way to angle back towards Vanánda or Dhiafáni from Trístomo; you must return the way you came (3hr one way).

Avlóna to Vanánda

This is perhaps the best walk in northern Kárpathos, and makes possible loops out of Dhiafáni or Ólymbos without using much road or track. Head southeast out of Avlóna, past a water cistern and the last *monastiráki*, then adopt a vehicle track for three minutes, before bearing down and right on a narrow path to reach a prominent *kalderími* on the right bank of the valley here. This climbs gently through pines to a small farm, meeting (25 minutes along) an ugly dirt track going down to Dhiafáni. Go left instead almost immediately onto a faint but marked trail, descending sharply northeast towards now-visible **Vanánda** through pines, under which purple orchids sprout in May. On meeting the stream bed, the path crosses to the north (true left) bank, where it stays for most of the rest of the way (except for the final minutes where you walk in the stream bed itself). Little olive plantations fill terraces, calamus and oleander grow on the banks, and there's even the occasional palm tree for an exotic touch; just overhead, the pines are all bent markedly east, away from the prevailing winds which penetrate even this sheltered valley. It's one hour twenty minutes in total from Avlóna to Vanánda, for more on which see opposite.

Dhiafáni and around

Although its popularity is growing – spurred on by the completion of the ferry dock – rooms in **DHIAFÁNI** are still relatively inexpensive, and the pace of life slow, except in August when it's overrun by Italians and Germans. Most of the settlement only dates from the postwar years, so don't expect much in the way of architectural character; there's a general consensus among travellers that a recent building boom has got out of hand, with cement skeletons sprouting everywhere, vying with the forest which is the place's main asset.

There are numerous places at which to **stay** and eat, several shops, and even a small, somewhat grumpy travel agency, Orfanos Travel (Ⓣ02450/51 410, Ⓕ51 316), which changes money (though there's a free-standing **cash machine** on the quay), and sells ferry tickets. This has its own en-suite hotel, the *Nikos* (❶), though patrons complain that using the showers automatically floods the bedrooms. The obvious *Mayflower Hotel* opposite the quay (Ⓣ02450/51 228; ❷) is to be refurbished for en-suite comfort in 2002; otherwise try the *Rooms Anesis* (Ⓣ02450/51 415; ❶), just up the road towards the *Nikos*, or the non-en-suite *Pansion Delfini* (Ⓣ0245/51 391; ❶), up on the southern hillside, though it ain't the same since life-and-soul of the place Kalliopi Lioreisi, one of Dhiafáni's characters, died in November 2000. Be warned that most other inland rooms have views of nought but piles of construction rubble and the dust raised by passing trucks – the *Hotel Balaskas* (Ⓣ02450/51 309, Ⓕ51 320; ❷) is representative of such, though the rooms are of higher standard than at the *Nikos*.

Back on the front, the most reliable all-season **tavernas** are the *Mayflower*, with such oddities as goat-milk *ryzógalo*, and the Italian-run *L'Angolo-Iy Gorgona*, which is accepted enough to have locals in attendance.

Around Dhiafáni

In season, Orfanos Travel organizes **boat trips** to various nearby beaches, as well as to the Byzantine site at **Palátia** on the east shore of **Saría** islet, just a stone's throw north of the main island; alternative days out involve negotiating a perilously narrow strait to **Trístomo** anchorage and Vrykoúnda.

Saría has a large cave near Palátia that's the focus of a curious tale, reminiscent of the Homeric legend of Odysseus and the Cyclops. Some two centuries ago, a shepherd was repeatedly victimized by pirates who landed and demanded full meals without recompense. One day, the hapless shepherd conceived a plan while stirring milk in a cauldron with an enormous wood ladle. As fifteen or so pirates sat feasting, he blinded them all with a well-aimed arc of scalding milk, then seized their piled-up muskets and did away with the corsairs – and got their beached boat and oars in the bargain.

There are also a few coves within walking distance of Dhiafáni. Closest, though not the best, is **Vanánda**, a frankly stony bay with a lush oasis just inland, whose powerful springs supply Dhiafáni with water. Here you'll find *Sia keh Araxame* (Ⓣ02450/51 288; June–Sept; free tent space if you buy a meal and a drink), a slogan-bedaubed **campsite/snack bar** eccentrically managed by Minas since 1967; it is he who's posted the signs on the beach forbidding absolutely everything that might degrade the local environment. To get to Vanánda, follow the pleasant, signposted path north through the pines and olives, but don't believe the signs that say "ten minutes" – it's over half an hour away. An ugly, more recent dirt road (opened by Minas) cuts the path in two spots, but it's not too obtrusive and the trail is still much quicker.

Much better beaches lie south of Dhiafáni; the boat ride in from Pigádhia is an excellent way of spotting likely coves along this coast, and committing their location to memory. **Forókli** and **Áyios Minás** are the two southernmost, distant enough from Dhiafáni to require arranging a boat shuttle.

Greek script table

Kárpathos	Κάρπαθος	ΚΑΡΠΑΘΟΣ
Aháta	Αχάτα	ΑΧΑΤΑ
Ammopí	Αμμοπή	ΑΜΜΟΠΗ
Ápella	Άπελλα	ΑΠΕΛΛΑ
Apéri	Απέρι	ΑΠΕΡΙ
Arkássa	Αρκάσα	ΑΡΚΑΣΑ
Avlóna	Αυλώνα	ΑΥΛΩΝΑ
Ayía Marína	Αγία Μαρίνα	ΑΓΙΑ ΜΑΡΙΝΑ
Áyios Minás	Άγιος Μηνάς	ΑΓΙΟΣ ΜΗΝΑΣ
Áyios Nikólaos	Άγιος Νικόλαος	ΑΓΙΟΣ ΝΙΚΟΛΑΟΣ
Dhiafáni	Διαφάνι	ΔΙΑΦΑΝΙ
Forókli	Φορόκλι	ΦΟΡΟΚΛΙ
Kyrá Panayiá	Κυρά Παναγιά	ΚΥΡΑ ΠΑΝΑΓΙΑ
Lefkós	Λεφκός	ΛΕΦΚΟΣ
Menetés	Μενετές	ΜΕΝΕΤΕΣ
Mesohóri	Μεσοχώρι	ΜΕΣΟΧΩΡΙ
Ólymbos	Όλυμπος	ΟΛΥΜΠΟΣ
Óthos	Όθος	ΟΘΟΣ
Paralía Lefkoú	Παραλία Λεφκού	ΠΑΡΑΛΙΑ ΛΕΦΚΟΥ
Pigádhia	Πιγάδια	ΠΙΓΑΔΙΑ
Pylés	Πυλές	ΠΥΛΕΣ
Saría	Σαρία	ΣΑΡΙΑ
Spóa	Σπόα	ΣΠΟΑ
Stés	Στές	ΣΤΕΣ
Vanánda	Βανάντα	ΒΑΝΑΝΤΑ
Voládha	Βωλάδα	ΒΩΛΑΔΑ
Vróndi	Βρόντη	ΒΡΟΝΤΗ
Vrykoúnda	Βρυκούντα	ΒΡΥΚΟΥΝΤΑ

The best beach within easy walking distance is attractive **Papá Miná**, 100m or so of small-to-medium pebbles, with some tamarisks for shade. It's just under an hour's hike away, the path starting behind the boatyard area just off the ferry-dock road, prosaically next to the oil-changing bay. As with Vanánda, there's a track to Papá Miná, but the older trail short-cuts it for all except for a five-minute stretch near the harbour, and then for ten minutes about forty minutes along. The trail itself is intrinsically enjoyable, roller coastering in and out of ravines, mixing sharp grades with level progress through olive groves, and heading counterintuitively inland at times.

Kárpathos travel details

Island transport

Buses

Dhiafáni to: Ólymbos (2 daily each way, plus tour coaches).

Pigádhia to: Ammopí (2 daily); Apéri (3 daily); Arkássa (1–2 daily); Finíki (1–2 daily); Mesohóri/Spóa (1 daily Mon–Fri, school term only); Paralía Lefkoú (1 daily Mon, Wed & Sat); Óthos (3 daily); Pylés (3 daily); Voládha (3 daily).

Inter-island transport

Key to ferry companies

LANE *Lassithiotikí Anónymi Navtiliakí Etería* (Lassithian Shipping Company)

Kaïkia

Finíki to: Kássos (irregular service, July & Aug only).

Pigádhia to: Dhiafáni (at least 1 daily June–Sept; 1hr 30min–1hr 45min).

Ferries

Pigádhia/Dhiafáni to: each other (3 weekly on LANE; 1hr 15min); Áyios Nikólaos, Crete (4 weekly on LANE; 7–8hr); Sitía, Crete (3 weekly on LANE; 5hr 20min); Hálki (2 weekly on LANE; 2hr 30min–3hr 30min); Kássos (3 weekly on LANE; 1hr 40min); Mílos (3 weekly on LANE; 15–16hr); Pireás (4 weekly on LANE; 20–21hr); Rhodes (3 weekly on LANE; 4hr 30min–5hr 30min).

Flights

Kárpathos to: Athens (3–5 weekly; 1hr 25min); Kássos (3 weekly; 15min); Rhodes (1–2 daily; 30min–1hr 10min).

NB Flights between Kárpathos and Kássos are not currently subject to airport tax, will often fly in winds which prevent the ferry from docking, and – taxi fare to the airport aside – don't cost vastly more than a ferry or *kaïki* passage. Given the inconvenient Rhodes–Kárpathos–Kássos ferry links – 4am departures from Rhodes are the rule – all local flights are in heavy demand, the tiny Dornier puddle-jumpers used often fill two weeks in advance, and seats should be booked as soon as possible.

Kássos

Like Psará islet in the East Aegean (see p.371), **Kássos** bravely contributed its large fleet to the Greek revolutionary war effort, and likewise suffered appalling consequences. In late May 1824, an Ottoman army commanded by Ibrahim

Pasha of Egypt laid siege to the island; on June 7, aided perhaps by a traitor's tip as to the weak point in Kássos' defences, the invaders descended on the populated north coast plain, slaughtered nearly three-quarters of the 11,000 inhabitants, and put houses, farms and trees to the torch.

Barren and depopulated since then, Kássos attracts few visitors, despite being a regular port of call for large ferries and having reliable air links with Rhodes and Kárpathos. What remains of the population is grouped together in five villages under the shadow of Kárpathos, leaving most of the island deserted, and often accessible only by boat. Though the regulation concrete "box-villas" are beginning to sprout even here, ruining architectural homogenity, there's surprisingly little evidence of the wealth brought to other islands by diaspora Greeks or – since Kássos hasn't much to offer them – by tourists; crumbling houses and disused hillside terraces are poignant reminders of better days.

Kássos is more productive than it appears from the sea, though it's not a fertile island by any stretch of the imagination; as on Psará, wild trees have never taken root again since the holocaust. Sheer gorges slash through lunar terrain, and fenced smallholdings of wind-lashed midget olives provide the only permanent relief. Springtime grain crops briefly soften the usually empty terraces, and livestock manages to get by on a thin furze of thornbush.

Especially after the 1824 events, Kassiots distinguished themselves as skilled pilots (see "Contexts" p.483); the rough, almost harbourless coast here was perhaps the best training-ground imaginable. The sailing tradition endures; you might see a kaïki fetching the largely Kassiot crew from a passing freighter for a three-hour home "furlough". Ironically, in view of Ibrahim Pasha's Egyptian origins, islanders were also instrumental in digging the Suez Canal, and there was for many decades a substantial Kassiot community in Port Said. These days, evidence of emigration to the USA is everywhere: American-logo T-shirts and

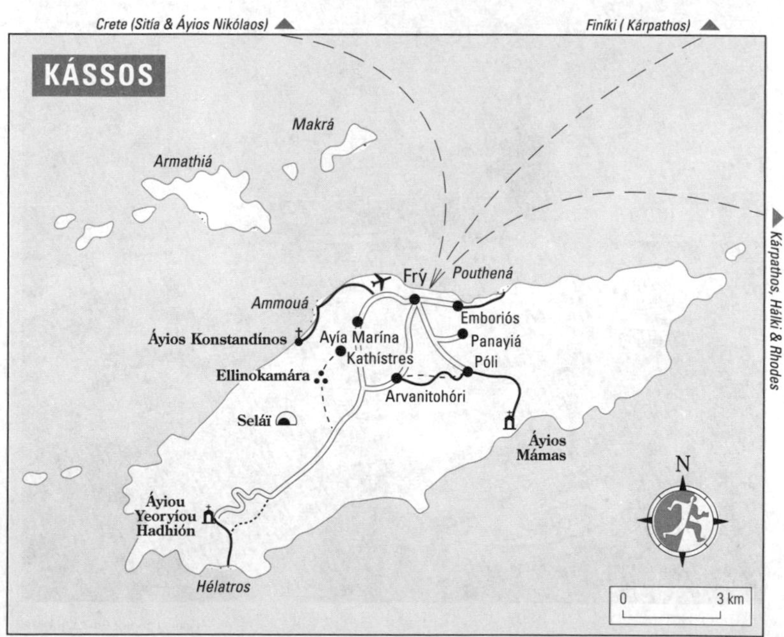

baseball caps are *de rigueur* in summer, and the conversation of vacationing expatriates is spiked with east-coast Americanisms.

Arrival and getting around

Kássos can be a nuisance to reach, and matters are unlikely to improve as two companies have gone bust attempting to build a new jetty east of the existing one, with the third contractor looking to follow suit. Frý's existing jetty, just west of Boúka fishing port, is so poor that passing **ferries** won't stop if any appreciable wind is up. In such cases, you disembark at Kárpathos and fly the remaining distance in light, 19-seater **aircraft**, which are less wind-sensitive. The air ticket plus a taxi fare to Kárpathos airport isn't hugely more than the cost of Finíki (Kárpathos)-based excursion boats which can manoeuvre into Boúka in most weathers. The airport lies 1km west of Frý (pronounced "free"), an easy enough walk (ignore mendacious signs reading "8km"), or a cheap (€1.50) ride in one of the island's three taxis. Except in July and August, when a few rental motorbikes and boat excursions are offered, the only method of exploring the island's remoter corners is by hiking along fairly arduous, shadeless paths and roads. Place-name signposting tends to be in Greek only, and in Kassiot dialect at that – clearly the islanders aren't expecting many non-Kassiot visitors.

Frý and Emboriós

Most of the capital **FRÝ**'s appeal is confined to the immediate environs of the wedge-shaped fishing port of **Boúka**, protected from the sea by the two crab-

Fishing port of Boúka, Kássos

claws of a breakwater and overlooked by the town cathedral of **Áyios Spirídhon**. On June 7, a memorial service for the victims of the 1824 massacre is held here. Inland, Frý is engagingly unpretentious, even down-at-heel; little attempt has been made to prettify what is essentially a scruffy little town that's quite desolate out of season.

Accommodation can be found at the seafront hotels *Anagenissis* (Ⓣ02450/41 495, Ⓕ41 036, Ⓦwww.kassos-island.gr; shared facilities and en suites ❷–❸); it's frankly overpriced, with smallish rooms and (out of season anyway) erratic hot water. Just behind, with fewer views, stands the less expensive, all-en-suite *Anessis* (Ⓣ02450/41 201, Ⓕ41 730; ❷). The manager of the *Anagenessis*, Emmanuil Manoussos, also has a few pricier, higher-standard apartments, and runs the all-in-one travel agency just below the hotel (though Olympic has its own premises two doors down). Both hotels tend to be noisy owing to morning bustle on the waterfront – and the phenomenal number of small but lively fast-food joints and café-bars in town, some right underneath your window. During high season a few, better-value **rooms** operate, for example those owned by Elias Koutlakis (Ⓣ02450/41 363 or 41 284; ❷); these lie towards the suburb of Emboriós (see below), a 500m walk east.

Outside peak season, Frý can support only one full-service **taverna** – *O Mylos*, overlooking the latest intermittent harbour works. Luckily it's excellent and reasonable, with a good variety of daily-special *mayireftá* at lunch and sometimes fish grills by night. From late June to early September you can also try *Iy Oraia Bouka*, perched above Boúka, for Egyptian-influenced dishes, or *To Meltemi* ouzerí, on the way to Emboriós. Of two tavernas in Emboriós itself, only *Ta Tessera Adherfia* by the palm-tree church shows any sign of life outside summer. **Shops** in Frý, including two fruit stalls, are fairly well stocked for self-catering.

Northern beaches

Frý's town **beach**, if you can call it that, is at **Ammouá** (Ammoudhiá), a thirty-minute walk beyond the airstrip along the coastal track. This sandy cove, just before the landmark chapel of Áyios Konstandínos, is often caked with seaweed and tar, but persevere five minutes more and you'll find much cleaner pea-gravel coves. The determined can swim off the little patch of sand at **Emboriós**, along with the half-dozen resident ducks, and there's a more private pebble stretch off to the right. But having got this far it's best to continue ten to fifteen minutes along the shore, first along an old track, then on a path past the last house, for a final scramble to the base of the **Pouthená** ravine, where there's another secluded pebble cove. Otherwise, it's worth shelling out for high-season boat excursions to far better beaches on a pair of islets visible to the northwest. **Armathiá** boasts no fewer than five beaches – two small ones on the southeast flank, plus three larger ones on the more exposed northwest shore; **Makrá** has one large sandy cove at its northeast tip, facing Kássos. There are no amenities (or shade) on either islet, so bring water, a picnic and some sort of sun protection.

Inland villages

Kássos's inland villages cluster at the edges of the agricultural plain just inland from Frý, and are linked to each other by road; all are worth a passing visit, accomplishable by foot in a single day.

Larger in extent and more rural than Frý, **AYÍA MARÍNA**, 1500m inland and uphill, is most attractive seen from the south, arrayed above olive groves; one of its two belfried churches is the focus of the island's liveliest festival, on July 17. Some fifteen minutes beyond the hamlet of Kathístres, a further 500m southwest, the cave of **Ellinokamára** is named for the late Classical polygonal wall completely blocking the entrance; its ancient function – perhaps a cult shrine or tomb complex – is uncertain. To reach it, turn south at the two restored windmills in Ayía Marína, then right (west) at the phone-box junction; carry on, straight and down (not level and left) until you see a red-dirt path going up the hillside to a crude, stone-built pastoral hut. Some modern masonry walls enclose the start of this path, but once at the hut (the cave is more or less underneath it) you're compelled to hop a fence to visit – there are no gates. From Ellinokamára another, fainter path – you'll probably need a guide – continues within ninety minutes in the same direction to the larger, more natural cave of **Seláï**, with impressive stalactites in the rear chamber.

Propaganda to the contrary, walking opportunities on Kássos are poor – trails are few, not marked and in poor condition, with no shade and few reliable water sources. An exception is the forty-minute path from Arvanitohóri to Póli, which is clearly walled in and enjoyable, short-cutting the road effectively – it starts at the base of the village, where two trees occupy planter wells. **PÓLI**, somewhat impoverished and resolutely agricultural, is the site of a badly deteriorated ancient and medieval acropolis – a few stretches of fortification remain – and marks the start of a four-kilometre road leading southeast to **Áyios Mámas**, one of two important rural monasteries and signposted in dialect as "**Áï Mámas**", perched spectacularly overlooking the sea. Alternatively, from Póli you can descend on walled-in path for the first twenty minutes, then dirt track, to **PANAYIÁ**, famous for its now-neglected mansions – many of Kássos's wealthiest ship captains hailed from here – and for the oldest surviving church on the island, the eighteenth-century **Panayía toú Yióryi**. The relatively modern, larger church is the venue for the other major island **festival** on August 15. Just adjacent stands an intriguing Siamese-sextuplet chapel complex, with dedications to six separate saints.

The southwest: Hélatros and Áï Yeóryi

Between Ayía Marína and Arvanitohóri, another paved road veers off southwest from the road linking the two villages; having skirted the narrows of a fearsome gorge, you are unlikely to see another living thing aside from goats, sheep or an occasional Eleonora's falcon. After about an hour, the Mediterranean appears to the south, a dull expanse ruffled only by the occasional ship bound for Cyprus and the Middle East. When you finally reach a fork, adopt the upper, right-hand turning, following derelict phone lines towards the rural monastery of **Ayíou Yeoryíou Hadhión**, (signed as "**Áï Yeóryi**") 12km (3hr on foot) from Frý. This is busiest at its late-April festival time, but during the warmer months there's a resident caretaker who runs a small snack and drinks bar. There are a few open guest cells (ask nicely, donation expected) and cistern water here if you need to fill up canteens; the only other water en route is a well at the route's high point. Since the paving of the road, there's little joy to be had in walking it, certainly not both ways – hire a taxi, rent a bike if available, or hitch a lift in at least one direction.

From the monastery it's another 3km on dirt track – motorbikes can negotiate all but the last 500m – to **Hélatros** (still "Hélathros" on older maps), a lonely cove at the mouth of one of the larger, more forbidding Kassiot canyons. The sand-and-gravel beach itself is small and mediocre, but the water is pristine and – except for the occasional fishing boat – you'll probably be alone. The lower, left-hand option at the fork is the direct track to Hélatros, but this is only 2km shorter and, following severe storm damage in 1995 and 2001, impassable to any vehicle and all but the most energetic hikers; since the paving of the upper road to Áï Yeóryi, it is likely to have become even worse.

Greek script table

Kássos	Κάσος	ΚΑΣΟΣ
Áï Mámas	Άϊ Μάμας	ΑΪ ΜΑΜΑΣ
Áï Yeóryi	Άϊ Γεώργη	ΑΪ ΓΕΩΡΓΗ
Ayía Marína	Αγία Μαρίνα	ΑΓΙΑ ΜΑΡΙΝΑ
Ayíou Yeoryíou Hadhión	Αγίου Γεωργίου Χαδιών	ΑΓΙΟΥ ΓΕΩΡΓΙΟΥ ΧΑΔΙΩΝ
Emboriós	Εμπορειός	ΕΜΠΟΡΕΙΟΣ
Frý	Φρύ	ΦΡΥ
Hélatros	Χέλατρος	ΧΕΛΑΤΡΟΣ
Panayiá	Παναγιά	ΠΑΝΑΓΙΑ
Póli	Πόλι	ΠΟΛΙ
Pouthená	Πουθενά	ΠΟΥΘΕΝΑ

Kássos travel details

Inter-island transport

Key to ferry company

LANE *Lassithiotikí Anónymi Navtiliakí Etería* (Lassithian Shipping Company)

Ferries

Kássos to: Áyios Nikólaos, Crete (3 weekly on LANE; 5hr); Sitía, Crete (3 weekly on LANE; 3hr 30min); Dhiafáni, Kárpathos (3–4 weekly on LANE; 3hr); Hálki (2 weekly on LANE; 4hr 40min); Pigádhia, Kárpathos (3–4 weekly on LANE; 1hr 40min); Mílos (3 weekly on LANE; 13hr 30min); Pireás (3 weekly on LANE; 18hr 30min); Rhodes (3 weekly on LANE; 6hr 30min).

NB In rough seas or adverse winds all ferries will skip the poor mooring at Boúka.

Flights

Kássos to: Kárpathos (1–2 weekly; 15min); Rhodes (5 weekly; 40min–1hr 15min).

Hálki

Hálki, a tiny (20 square kilometres), waterless, limestone speck west of Rhodes, is a fully fledged member of the Dodecanese, though all but about three hundred of the former population of three thousand, including a hundred from the dependency of Alimniá, emigrated (mostly to Rhodes or to Tarpon Springs, Florida) in the wake of a devastating sponge blight during the early 1900s. Despite a renaissance through tourism in recent years, the island is tranquil compared to its big neighbour, albeit with a slightly weird, hushed atmosphere. This has much to do with foreigners vastly outnumbering native islanders for most of the year; the former tend to be invisible during daylight hours, holed up on the verandas of their pricey package villas. The big event of the day is the arrival of the regular afternoon kaïki from Kámiros Skála on Rhodes, since the island is just a bit too remote for the sort of day-trips that plague Sými. Besides people, Hálki is home to about five thousand sheep and goats, plus a thirty-strong fishing fleet which sends most of its catch to Rhodes – together, the only significant economic activity aside from summer tourism.

The first hint of development came in 1983, when UNESCO designated Hálki as the "isle of peace and friendship" and made it the seat of an annual summer international youth conference. (Tílos was approached first but declined the honour.) As part of the deal, some 150 crumbling island houses were to be restored as accommodation for the delegates and other interested parties, with UNESCO footing most of the bill. As of 1987, just one hotel had been completed, by converting the former sponge-processing plant; the only tangible sign of "peace and friendship" was an unending stream of UNESCO and Athenian bureaucrats occupying every available bed and staging drunken, musical binges under the rubric of "ecological conferences". Confronted with an apparent scam, the islanders sent UNESCO packing in 1988 and contracted two UK specialist package operators to complete restorations and bring in paying guests. There is now a third tour company present, and most of the ruins have been refurbished.

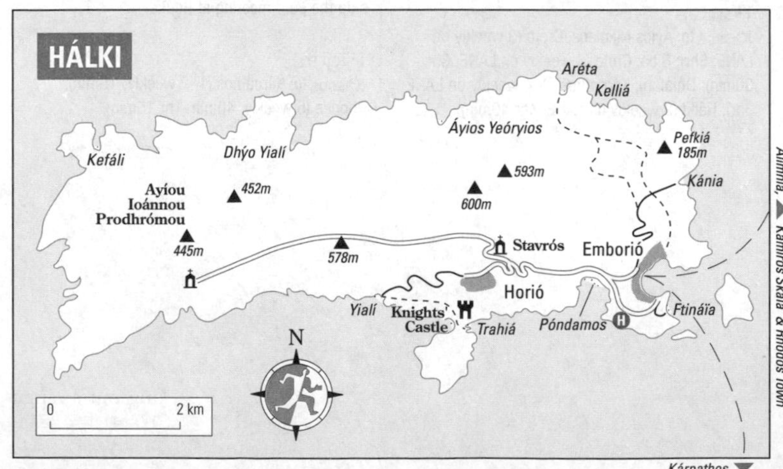

Emborió

All of the restoration villas are in **EMBORIÓ**, the port and only area of habitation, where the waterfront has been paved with fieldstones, prettified and declared off limits to vehicles in season. The skyline is pierced by the tallest free-standing **clocktower** in the Dodecanese, beside the town hall, with each of its four faces permanently stopped at different hours. It's nearly matched in height by the campanile of **Áyios Nikólaos church** below, with its fine *hokhláki* (pebble-mosaic) courtyard.

Accommodation

Most **accommodation** is pretty much block-booked from April to October by the tour companies and occupied by a rather staid, well-mannered, upper-middle class clientele from the British Home Counties. Late July to late September, when the town is often host to consecutive conferences, is pretty well impossible; island-hoppers should avoid Hálki at that time unless they have a reservation. Independent travellers may be lucky to find anything at all, even early or late in the season, and if travelling alone should expect to pay the full double rate. If you're not put off by the above, the following may be able to assist.

The best place to start your hunt is the five-room *Captain's House* (Ⓣ02460/45 201; ❷), a wonderful, quiet spot north of the church and three tiers "up". It has the feel of a French country hotel, where en-suite rooms have fridges and you're in close contact with your hosts, Alex (ex-Greek Navy captain) and Christine Sakelaridhes. Owing to its small size, pre-booking is mandatory, but if they're full, they will point you in other likely directions, perhaps towards include Pension Keanthi (Ⓣ02460/45 334), inland near the school, with bland, pine-furnished rooms (❷) with high ceilings plus a few galleried studios (❸), or the municipally owned Hotel Halki (Ⓣ02460/45 390, Ⓕ45 208; ❸) in the old sponge factory on the south side of the bay, indifferently managed and beset by creeping damp, but likely to have a vacancy.

Eating and drinking

If lodging in the self-catering villas works out relatively expensive, eating out can be surprisingly reasonable, especially compared to any neighbouring isle. Of the half-dozen **tavernas** on Emborió's waterfront, *Remezzo* (aka *Takis*) is excellent for *mayireftá* and pizzas, while *Maria* behind the post office has good grills, and *Houvardas*, near the north end of the quay has proven reliable for *mayireftá* over the years. Less appealing, perhaps, are *Omonia* and *Mavri Thalassa*, where service tends to be slow and portions small.

A similar number of **bars** and **cafés** sit all in a row at mid-quay. *Soula's* (aka "The Parrot Bar" after its resident birds), near the base of the jetty, has puddings and home-made ice cream to die for; *Kostas* is an old standby with good breakfast service, while *To Steki* is usually the most musically active, with a sculpted counter outdoors.

Other practicalities

Other essential facilities include a **post office** (there's no bank), four shops amply stocked for self-catering, a pair of decent bakeries cranking out a range of breads and pies, plus two **travel agencies**: Halki Tours (Ⓣ02460/45 281), the representative of Laskarina Holidays, and Zifos Tours (Ⓣ02460/45 241,

ⓔ zifos-travel@rho.forthnet.gr), which handles Direct Greece and Travel à la Carte properties, and often has a few studio vacancies which they hold back from the UK companies. Both agencies will also **change money** at a pinch – for a two percent commission – while Halki Tours is currently the main ferry-ticket outlet. Last, but not least, a **gym** – popular with locals and visitors alike – operates at the start of the road out of town; one-offs are welcome, at €8.80 per visit, or you can take out a fortnight's membership for €41.10.

The interior

Three kilometres inland, 45 minutes' walk west of Emborió, lies the old pirate-proof village of **HORIÓ**, abandoned in the 1950s. The recent laying down of power lines, and a few restored cottages, suggest that Horió may eventually benefit from the same attentions as Emborió. Except during the August 14–15 *paniyíri*, the liveliest on the island, the church is kept securely locked to protect its medieval frescoes; just behind it a clear path climbs for about ten minutes to the dilapidated **castle**, built largely from ancient masonry. Inside this, traces of Byzantine frescoes still cling to an otherwise ruined chapel – the archeological authorities in Rhodes will eventually spirit these away to safety in their museum. Across the valley, the little monastery of **Stavrós** is the venue for another festival on September 14.

There's little else to see or do inland, though you can spend three hours (each way) on foot following the paved road across the island from Emborió to the monastery of **Ayíou Ioánnou Prodhrómou**. The caretaker there can put you up in a cell (except around August 29, another big festival date), but you'll need to bring supplies. The terrain en route is monotonous, but enhanced by views over half the Dodecanese and Turkey; occasionally an excursion bus trundles along to the monastery, sparing you the dull slog (for a better walk, see opposite). The section of road as far as Stavrós is known as "Tarpon Springs Boulevard", its cement pavement originally donated by the expatriate community in Florida to ensure easy Cadillac access to the Stavrós *paniyíri* grounds. The money might have been better spent on a proper sewage system (finally provided in 1996) and salt-free water supply – like most essentials, fresh water has to be brought from Rhodes by tanker, and often runs out in peak season.

Hálki's beaches

Póndamos, fifteen minutes' walk west of Emborió, is the only sandy beach on Hálki, and even this has been artificially supplemented. Longish but narrow, its sunbeds are completely packed in summer, though you can escape the crowds for some excellent snorkelling. The main facility is the somewhat pricey *Nick's Pondamos Taverna*, open for lunch daily plus four random evenings weekly; a rival snack bar operates at peak season only. A few minutes' walk past the *Hotel Halki*, tiny coves of pebbles along the shore known as **Ftináïa** are also heavily subscribed; here too there's a combination taverna-bar, with a dirt track leading to it.

Small and pebbly **Yialí**, west of and considerably below Horió, is an hour's hike away from Póndamos, down a jeep track. There's absolutely no shade, and the sea can be rough in this exposed setting. Half an hour's walk north of Emborió lies **Kánia**, with a rocky foreshore but sandy bay-bottom; there's no shade in the morning, and a rather industrial ambience from both the power lines coming in from Rhodes, and the island's only petrol pump off to one side. These four coves lie within easy walking distance but are no great shakes, so it's well worth signing on at Emborió's quay for boat excursions to more remote beaches, difficult or impossible to reach by land. More or less at the centre of Hálki's southern shore, directly below Horió's castle, **Trahiá** (or Trahía) consists of two coves on either side of an isthmus, one or the other providing shelter in any wind. You can in fact (just) reach this overland by rough path from Yialí, a trail that's scheduled to be bulldozed into a track soon.

North-coast beaches figuring as excursion-boat destinations (weather permitting) include the pretty fjord of **Aréta**, **Áyios Yeóryios** just beyond, and the remote double bay of **Dhýo Yialí**. Of these, Aréta is the most attractive, and the most accessible overland; directions are given below.

Hike to Aréta from Emborió

To do this with extra confidence you'll want to buy the *Chalki, Island of Peace & Friendship* tourist map, based on Italian-era topographical maps; though the path tracings may not always be reliable, with roads bulldozed over them, the contour lines are correct. The following is the most direct of two possible routes to Aréta.

Begin along the cemented track heading to Kánia; above the municipal cisterns, beyond power lines passing overhead, bear left where a power pole stands at the left verge of the road, near a wrecked white car and a small pastoral shed. Go north through a crude gate, then adopt a path which climbs with a fence to your left until reaching a second gate. Once past this, you're in open country, with the trail fairly well grooved into the surface, and marked by occasional cairns. The route skirts a large stone pen, and levels out briefly as it threads between two terraces of stunted olives; this area is called **Petrólakko**, rendered as "Petrolaco" on the Italian map.

Now the path veers briefly northeast and resumes climbing, right under the island's summit-ridge, here punctuated by overhanging caves. Pointing north again, the path slips through a wall and, about an hour out of Emborió, levels out on a vast plateau inclined slightly to the north. Near a second wall, Tílos pops into view, and a few hundred metres off to the left stands a rock outcrop strongly resembling a pimple or a mole. Once through a third and final wall, the path begins to descend, gradually at first and then more sharply as it gets momentarily fainter. It zigzags just past a livestock corral built into the lee of some rock formations; inside the corral is a cistern, with murky water that might do for emergencies. The most obvious nearby canyon draining to the sea is **Kelliá** ("Cellia" on the Italian map) – stay away from that. The again-distinct correct trail, still cairned, heads northwest, then almost west, to cross the top of the gulch leading down to Aréta. You pass through two gates (often propped open), then curl along the top of the left (west) flank of the canyon, dropping to sea level in easy stages; memorize landmarks here carefully, as it's surprisingly easy to get lost on the way back uphill. The final approach to the beach is a steep "ladder-stair" recessed in the rock-face, manageable by any fit person; you touch down on the small-pebble strand some ninety minutes from Emborió (allow fifteen minutes more if you pause a lot).

Aréta fjord is an impressive place girt by high cliffs where seabirds roost and soar. There's some morning and afternoon shade, but only a brackish well, used by the inquisitive sheep with whom you may share the beach, so it's best to bring plenty of your own water.

Alimniá

One of the more popular trips from Hálki visits the deserted islet of **ALIMNIÁ** (Alimiá), roughly halfway between Hálki and Rhodes, a favourite swimming and barbecuing venue for both islanders and tour clients. Despite more well-water and greenery, and a better harbour than on Hálki, the village here, overlooked by a couple of palm trees and a Knights' castle, was completely depopulated by the 1960s. It is said that the inhabitants were initially deported during World War II after they confessed to assisting British commandos sent in April 1944 to sabotage the German submarines who used the deep harbour here. The seven commandos themselves were captured by the Nazis, bundled off first to Rhodes, then to Thessaloníki, where six of them were summarily executed as spies rather than regular POWs; Kurt Waldheim allegedly countersigned their death sentences.

Despite its historical interest, Alimniá is probably not a place you'd want to be stuck for an entire day. Excursions (out at 10am, back at 4pm) are pricey at €20.50 and up, even considering that this includes a light lunch. Matters begin promisingly enough with anchorage in the lee of diminutive Áyios Minás monastery, but then there's a mad scramble from the usual two docked boats for precious spots on the tiny beaches of the bay's south shore. If you go snorkelling in the outer bay beyond Áyios Minás, you can still glimpse outlines of the submarine pens, while the Italian barracks near the mooring point bear the trace lines of bullet holes. The **old village** sits behind a salt marsh at the head of the bay, consisting mostly of derelict shepherds' huts; near the church a grander house which once served as a taverna contains crude paintings of ships and submarines sketched by bored Italian soldiers. Nowadays just one building is inhabited each season, when Alimniá is used by shepherds grazing livestock; otherwise the place sees life only at the festival of St George in late April. The rather battered **castle** is a 45-minute one-way hike away from the anchorage, with poor paths up, though well worth the climb.

Greek script table

Hálki	Χάλκη	ΧΑΛΚΗ
Alim[n]iá	Αλιμ[ν]ιά	ΑΛΙΜ[Ν]ΙΑ
Aréta	Αρέτα	ΑΡΕΤΑ
Áyios Yeóryios	Άγιος Γεώργιος	ΑΓΙΟΣ ΓΕΩΡΓΙΟΣ
Ayiou Ioánnou Prodhrómou	Αγίου Ιοάννου Προδρόμου	ΑΓΙΟΥ ΙΟΑΝΝΟΥ ΠΡΟΔΡΟΜΟΥ
Dhy 'o Yialí	Δύο Γιαλοί	ΔΥΟ ΓΙΑΛΟΙ
Emborió	Εμπορειό	ΕΜΠΟΡΕΙΟ
Horió	Χωριό	ΧΩΡΙΟ
Kánia	Κάνια	ΚΑΝΙΑ
Póndamos	Πόνταμος	ΠΟΝΤΑΜΟΣ
Stavrós	Σταυρός	ΣΤΑΥΡΟΣ
Trahiá	Τραχειά	ΤΡΑΧΕΙΑ
Yialí	Γιαλή	ΓΙΑΛΗ

Hálki travel details

Inter-island transport

Key to ferry companies

LANE *Lassithiotikí Anónymi Navtiliakí Etería* (Lassithian Shipping Company)

Kaïkia

Hálki to: Kámiros Skála, Rhodes (1 daily on either *Nissos Halki* or the *Nikos Express*; 1hr 30min–2hr).

NB Most days one of these kaïkia leaves Skála at 2.30–2.45pm, returning from Hálki the next morning at 6am. On Sundays, a day-excursion schedule applies, leaving Skála in the morning, returning from Hálki in the afternoon. Wednesday and Sunday, the typical transfer days for tour clients, can be problematic for passage; enquire as to space availability well in advance if you intend to travel on those days.

Ferries

Hálki to: Kárpathos, both ports (2 weekly on LANE; 2hr–3hr 30min); Kássos (2 weekly on LANE; 5hr 30min); Mílos (2 weekly on LANE; 18hr 30min); Rhodes (2 weekly LANE; 2hr).

NB Boats nominally calling at Hálki will skip the island in bad weather, as Emborió's dock is very exposed.

Hydrofoil

1–2 weekly links with Rhodes, provided fitfully by Kyriakoulis and Laoumtzis Hydrofoils.

Kastellórizo

Kastellórizo's official name, Meyísti ("Biggest"), seems more an act of defiance than a statement of fact. While the largest of a tiny local group of islands, it is actually the smallest of the Dodecanese, over seventy nautical miles from its nearest Greek neighbour (Rhodes), but hardly more than a nautical mile from the Turkish coast at the narrowest straits. At night its lights are quite outnumbered by those of the Turkish town of Kaş, about four nautical miles across the bay, with whom Kastellórizo has long had excellent relations.

Some history

Until the early 1900s there were about 14,000 people here, supported by a fleet of schooners that made fortunes transporting goods, mostly timber, from the then-Greek towns of Kalamaki (now Kalkan) and Andifelos (Kaş), on the Anatolian mainland opposite. But the withdrawal of island autonomy after the 1908 "Young Turk" revolution, the Italian seizure of the other Dodecanese in 1912 and an inconclusive 1913–1915 revolt against the Turks sent the island into decline. The French, not the Italians, were masters here between 1915 and 1921 when they needed a staging post for the Syrian front, which made Kastellórizo a hapless target for Ottoman artillery on the Anatolian mainland. On January 9, 1917, the British seaplane carrier *Ben-My-Chree*, among the first such craft ever built, was sunk by a well-aimed Turkish shell while at anchor here.

Kastellorizan ship owners failed to modernize their craft upon the advent of steam power late in the nineteenth century, preferring to sell their fleets to the British for the Dardanelles campaign; the new frontier drawn up between

Kastellórizo and republican Turkey, combined with the expulsion of all Anatolian Greeks in 1923, deprived any remaining vessels of their trade. During the 1930s, Kastellórizo enjoyed a brief renaissance when it became a major stopover point for French and Italian seaplanes en route to the Middle East, but events at the close of World War II put an end to any hopes of the island's continued viability.

When Italy capitulated to the Allies in the autumn of 1943, Kastellórizo was occupied by a few hundred Commonwealth commandos, who left of their own accord during late spring 1944. In early July of that year, a harbour fuel depot caught fire and exploded, taking with it more than half of the two thousand houses on Kastellórizo. Postwar inquiries concluded that, although a small minority of British officers had engaged in some haphazard looting before their departure, it was probably Greek pirates engaged in pillaging of their own who accidentally or deliberately caused the conflagration. The British government, without admitting guilt, agreed during the 1950s to pay compensation

for the missing items; however, the settlement was delayed for three decades, and then only the 850 surviving applicants in Athens were considered eligible for compensation – those who had emigrated to Australia and the few who had chosen to stay on the island after 1945 were inexplicably excluded. As a result, the British are not especially popular here.

Even before these wartime events, most of the population had left for Rhodes, Athens, Australia (particularly Perth) and North America; ironically, when the long-sought union of the Dodecanese with Greece occurred in 1948, there were fewer than seven hundred islanders remaining. Today there are barely three hundred people living year-round on Kastellórizo, largely maintained by remittances from the 30,000-plus emigrants and by subsidies from the Greek government, which fears that the island will revert to Turkish sovereignty should their numbers diminish any further – there was in fact an American-sponsored plan promulgated in 1964 whereby, in return for substantial union of Cyprus with Greece, Greece would cede Kastellórizo to Turkey. With so few inhabitants, life is inevitably claustrophobic, especially in winter when feuds and vendettas are resumed after suspension for the tourist season; some 48 children, presumably outcomes of those boring winter nights, keep the primary school thriving.

Yet Kastellórizo may have a future of sorts, thanks to expat Kassies who have begun renovating their crumbling homes with a view to resuscitating the island as a retirement or holiday venue. Each summer the population is swelled by returnees of Kastellorizan ancestry, a few of whom celebrate traditional weddings in the Horáfia's Áyios Konstandínos cathedral, which incorporates ancient columns pilfered from Patara in Asia Minor. Access to the island has also improved; during the 1980s the government dredged the harbour to accommodate larger ferries and completed an airport for flights to and from Rhodes, though in the wake of the Schengen Treaty, Kastellórizo still isn't an official port of entry, a deficiency – unlike the optimistic sign behind one (not recommended) taverna boldly proclaiming "Europe Begins Here" – not exactly calculated to appeal to the numerous, often Israeli, yachties who drop anchor only to be slapped with exorbitant berthing fees. Legal niceties scarcely concern the hundreds of desperate Kurds fleeing Turkey, who land here, give themselves up and are then sent to refugee camps near Athens.

Perhaps the biggest recent boost for Kastellórizo was its role as the setting for the 1990 film *Mediterraneo*, which has resulted in a tidal wave of Italian visitors; locals routinely chant "*stanze*" (rooms) to all new arrivals, though the island in fact gets a highly varied tourist clientele. Visitors will either love the island and stay a week, or crave escape after a day; its detractors dismiss Kastellórizo as a human zoo maintained by the Greek government for the edification of nationalists, while partisans celebrate an atmospheric, barely commercialized outpost of Hellenism.

Kastellórizo Town

The current population is concentrated in the northern town of **KASTELLÓRIZO** – supposedly the finest natural harbour between Beirut and Fethiye on the Turkish coast – and the little easterly "suburb" of **Mandhráki**. Even in summer, it's the sort of place where, after two strolls up and down the pedestrianized quay, you'll have a nodding acquaintance with your fellow visitors and all the island's characters – such as the bar-crawling priest Papa Yiorgis, who on occasion has been pitched into the water by rowdy yachties.

Most of the town's surviving mansions are ranged along the waterfront, their tiled roofs, wooden balconies and blue or green shutters on tall, narrow windows having obvious counterparts in the originally Greek-built houses of Kalkan and Kaş across the bay. Most recent renovations are in good taste, though there are some startling splashes of blue, purple and maroon amongst the more traditional white and cream housefronts. Just one street back, however, many of the properties are derelict – abandonment having succeeded where 1917 shelling, an earthquake in 1926 and fire in 1944 failed. Sepia-toned and black-and-white postcards and posters on sale of the town in its prime are poignant evidence of its later decline.

Locations used in the filming of *Mediterraneo* have become popular attractions. Locals will be happy to point out the blue-fronted house (now a pension) between the two hotels which hosted the love scenes, or the neglected but beautiful graveyard beyond Mandhráki, whose small non-Orthodox section contains tenants worthy of the movie scenario: a French–Armenian soldier killed in action nearby in 1917, a young French expat who met his end here in 1974, and Riccardo Lazzeri, Milanese house-restorer and island adoptee, who died of a heart attack in 1988.

The fire-blasted hill between the harbour and Mandhráki sports a half-ruined, fourteenth-century **castle of the Knights**, the Greek flag flying from the keep. Reached by steps up from the mosque, the *promáhonas* or outer bulwark once served as the Ottoman governor's quarters and is now home to the local **museum** and its friendly staff (Tues–Sun 7am–2.30pm; free); in the courtyard an old Turkish cistern-fountain still provides potable rainwater. Displays include the old lens from the lighthouse on Strongylí (an islet to the east), plates from a Byzantine shipwreck, seventeenth-century frescoes rescued from the church of Ayíou Nikoláou Kástrou, a reconstruction of an ancient basilica on the site of today's gaudy but derelict Ayíou Yeoryíou Santrapé (in Horáfia district between the port and Mandhráki), plus predictable ethnographic mock-ups. Just below and beyond the museum, in the cliff-face opposite Psorádhia islet, is tucked Greece's only Lycian, fourth-century BC **house-tomb**; it's well signposted from the shoreline walkway, up some stone steps beside the first wooden lamp standard. House-tombs were the common burial places of Lycian nobles and are scattered all along the Turkish coast opposite.

Accommodation

Despite its 1989–1990 strut in front of the cameras, Kastellórizo is not prepared for – nor, outside high season, does it get – more than a dozen visitors per boat arrival. No package holidays operate here, owing to chronically tenuous links with Rhodes and the scarcity of amenities. **Pensions** installed in the old houses have been upgraded up to en-suite status, obviating the need for long climbs up and down stairs to a shared bathroom, and prices have climbed in recent years. For such a waterless island, mosquitoes are a surprising nuisance, breeding in abandoned cisterns.

Pension Asimina Behind the arcaded market ⓣ02460/49 361. Decent, wood-trimmed rooms in a variety of bed formats; fairly quiet considering location. ❷

Pension Caretta Ask at the souvenir shop behind the arcaded market ⓣ & ⓕ02460/49 028, ⓦwww.kastellorizo.de. One of the best budget options a bit inland, with simple but spacious and brightly painted en-suite rooms; they also have a handsomely restored apartment in an old house, suitable for four. Rooms ❷, house ❹

Karnayio Apartments On the northwest quay ⓣ02460/49 225, ⓕ49 266. Well-restored apartments with both studios and family units ④

Kastellorizo Hotel Apartments Opposite the ferry jetty ⓣ02460/49 044, ⓕ49 279, ⓦwww.kastellorizohotel.gr. 2000-built, air-conditioned, quality-fitted studios and galleried maisonettes, some with sea view; small plunge pool and "private" lido. ⑤–⑥

Kristallo ⓣ02460/41 209). Next door to *Pension Caretta*, and of similar standard; a kindly proprietress, but some noise from management's TV. ②

Mediterraneo On the northwest quay ⓣ02460/49 368. Waterfront self-catering pension now under French management and recently renovated, but still recognizable as the house that starred in the film. ③

Eating and drinking

Apart from fish, goat meat and various fig-based sweets, plus whatever fresh produce is smuggled over from Kaş, Kastellórizo must import staple foodstuffs and also drinking water from Rhodes; taverna prices can consequently be slightly higher than usual, with the further pretext of the island's celebrity status.

The two most conspicuous centre-quay **tavernas** have had a long and pernicious acquaintance with the yacht trade – best to continue a few steps to *Mikro Parisi/Little Paris* for reliably fresh and affordable seafood and meat grills. Other good quayside choices include *Iy Ipomoni* (dinner only), two doors left from the arcaded market, featuring simple but hygienic grills and unusual plates like sea snails; *Kaz Bar*, to the right of the Italian market, where Sydney-born Colin and his mother serve up fine grills, vegetable dishes and cold mezédhes nightly except perhaps Thursday in off-season; and the inexpensive but savoury *Akrothalassi*, purveying decent grills and salads near the west end of the quay, by the church.

Trips to (and from) Turkey

Since 1996, it has been possible to arrange a day-trip to Kaş in **Turkey**, on one of several small boats – usually the *Varvara* or the *Ayios Yeoryios* – for the sum of €14.70 return (€11.80 one way), taking care to leave your passport with the port authorities one day before. Monday and Friday, when the islanders go shopping on the mainland, are the most reliable days for a transfer across. Turkey-based boats which used to put in regular appearances, bringing trippers from Kaş have been scared away by the punitive docking fees levied against all non-Greek-registered craft between Turkey and Greece.

What remains nebulous (not to say deliberately obscure) is whether travellers can use Kastellórizo as a one-way entry or exit point to or from Greece, or take a multi-day return trip. Technically, they can: Kaş is a legal port of exit for Turkey, and the Greek authorities cannot unreasonably deny entry to EU nationals, especially if they arrive on a Greek boat. Problems arise from the fact that Kastellórizo does not yet have a fully functioning customs and immigration office, with the necessary stamps to apply to non-EU passports, nor a computerized Schengen database to keep track of miscreants. If you land at Kastellórizo on a non-EU passport, you may be prevented from travelling onwards for a day or two until your personal details are faxed to Rhodes or even Athens and an approval elicited. The Turkish authorities at Kaş, it must be said, will happily stamp you in or out without bothering to check for any Greek stamps. All this, despite a near-farcical situation whereby Kastellorizans themselves must get everything from haircuts to bread to emergency medical care across the way. It's hard to avoid the suspicion that the delays and foot-dragging in inaugurating the necessary facilities serve mostly to protect the lucrative, overpriced operation run by the Rhodes–Marmaris shuttle operators.

Two to recommend **inland** are *Iy Orea Meyisti* and *Ta Platania* (June–Sept only), opposite Áyios Konstandínos in Horáfia, good for daily-changing *mayireftá* and frequently home-made desserts. There are more puddings, and good breakfasts, at *Zaharoplastio Iy Meyisti* back on the waterfront. **Nightlife** spills out of the half-dozen *barákia* lining the quay, occasionally ending up in the water when tipplers overbalance at their tables.

Other practicalities

A single **bank**, with handy cash machine, stands on the east quay; the **post office** is found on the far side of the bay. The Papoutsis travel agency (Ⓣ02460/70 830, Ⓔpaptrv@rho.forthnet.gr) represents all boats calling here, and sells Olympic tickets – providing a better service than rival DiZi Travel. A public transfer van shuttles between town and airstrip at flight times; Damian Mavrothalassitis of *Pension Caretta* is the airport agent and can also sell tickets at a pinch.

The rest of the island

Kastellórizo's austere hinterland is predominantly bare rock, flecked with stunted vegetation; incredibly, two or three generations ago much of the countryside was carefully tended, producing wine of some quality and quantity, as it had since antiquity. A rudimentary paved road system links points between Mandhráki and the airport (and beyond to the rubbish tip), but there are not many specific places to go along it and no scooters to rent (though you'll see plenty of service vans). Additionally, as on many of the lonelier Dodecanese islands, the Greek military presence has been significantly increased on Kastellórizo and its satellites since the Ímia incident (see p.450), with watchpoints or fully equipped army camps at strategic spots. The island is fringed by sheer karst cliffs, and offers no anchorage except at the main town, Mandhráki, and Návlakas fjord (see opposite).

Vathoryáki and Perastá grotto

Swimming options are limited by a total absence of beaches and an abundance of sea urchins and razor-sharp limestone reefs; the safest place to swim near town lies beyond the graveyard and football pitch at **Mandhráki**, or at the tiny, sometimes tar-fouled inlet of **Vathoryáki** just below the little chapel of Áyios Stéfanos, a thirty-minute walk north of town along the obvious trail beginning behind the post office. Many people just dive from the lidos on the northwest quay (incidentally, it's illegal to swim across the harbour mouth – you constitute a navigation hazard). Once you swim away from the shore, you're rewarded by clear waters graced by a rich variety of marine life – and great mounds of amphorae shards offshore from the Mandhráki petrol pump, attesting to the quantity of wine exported in ancient times.

Over on the southeast coast, accessible only by a 45-minute boat ride from town (most reliably arranged with Yiorgos at *Mikro Parisi*), the grotto of **Perastá** (aka Galázia Spiliá) is famous for its stalactites and strange blue light effects; the low entrance, negotiable only by inflatable raft, gives little hint of the enormous chamber within. Splashing about in its depths is magic, though claims of rivalry to Capri's Blue Grotto seem a bit overblown since the blue tint doesn't reflect well on the walls. There is a second cave, inaccessible to humans, to which resident monk seals retire when disturbed by visitors. Two-hour raft trips (€6 each, assuming six passengers) visit the cave, or for €15 minimum you can take it in on a larger kaïki as part of a five-hour tour that includes Rhó islet (see below).

Rural monasteries and ruins

During the infernally hot summer months, you're best off imitating the dozens of cats asleep at midday under the café tables. At cooler times of the day or year, you can hike south up the obvious, zigzag stair-path from town, picked out in whitewash, then through fire-damaged scrub and vineyards to the monastery of **Áyios Yeóryios toú Vounioú**, reached in just over half an hour. The sixteenth- to eighteenth-century church boasts fine rib vaulting and a carved *témblon*, but its highlight is a crypt, with the frescoed, subterranean chapel of **Áyios Harálambos** off to one side; access is via a narrow, steep passage descending from the church floor – bring a flashlight and wear clothes suitable for scrambling. The walled monastery premises are kept locked, so you must first fetch the key from its keeper Kostas, who lives behind the taverna *Mikro Parisi*. From the monastery you can easily continue to Návlakas fjord, partly along a French-built *kalderími*; see below for instructions.

Alternatively, a fifteen-minute track-walk west of the port leads to the peaceful monastery of **Ayías Triádhos**, perched on the saddle marked by the OTE tower – and an army strongpoint which has rendered much of the area off limits. The adjacent monastery of Profítis Iliás is military territory, and shouldn't be confused with its neighbour.

The signposted onward path to the ancient Doric citadel of **Paleokástro** leaves the cemented track just beyond the monastery; after a twenty-minute walk from Ayía Triádha, your arrival is signalled by masonry from Classical to medieval times, a warren of vaulted chambers, tunnels and cisterns (reputedly a hundred, adapted from ancient sarcophagi, with their lining still intact), plus three maroon-roofed chapels with pebble-mosaic courtyards. The best-preserved section of polygonal wall is just behind the lone olive tree. From any of the heights above town you've tremendous views north over sixty kilometres of Anatolian coast and the elephant's-foot-shaped harbour, east to tiny gull-roosts dribbled like batter drops on the griddle of the sea, and west to larger islets, including Rhó (see below).

Návlakas fjord

From Áyios Yeóryios to Vounoú, head southwest on an ugly new bulldozer track – a municipally funded bit of idiocy used by no one – until, about twenty minutes along at the high point of the route, what remains of the magnificent, French-built cobbled way re-emerges on the left. This now descends south in zigzags past the southeast end of the airport runway, finally dropping ever more sharply to **Návlakas**, a multi-lobed fjord that's a favourite with yachts and fishing boats. The only easy way in overland is on the far left, where the path ends as an inconspicuous ramp, now little better than a mud chute; the French opened this route to facilitate offloading supplies here during World War I, out of reach of Ottoman guns. The fjord, uniquely on Kastellórizo, is completely sea-urchin-free, thanks perhaps to cleansing freshwater seeps which also keep the temperature brisk. The south wall has a sharp drop-off to 25-metre depths near the fjord mouth, providing excellent snorkelling. Allow about half an hour either from or to the monastery.

Rhó: Lady and islet

Until her death, *Iý Kyrá tís Rhó* (**The Lady of Rhó**), aka Dhespina Akhladhioti (1898?–1982), resolutely hoisted the Greek flag each day on the islet of that name, in defiance of the Turks on the mainland. In her waning years, an honorary salary, a commemorative postage stamp and television appearances lent her glory and fame which she revelled in; by most accounts she was a miserly curmudgeon, known to have refused passing sailors emergency rations of fresh water.

Should you take a day-trip out to Rhó, the Lady of Rhó's **tomb** is the first thing you see when you dock at the sandy, northwestern harbour; from here a path heads southeast for 25 minutes to the islet's southerly port, past the side trail up to an intact Hellenistic **fortress** on the island's summit. There are no facilities on Rhó – just a few soldiers to prevent Turkish landings or poachings of the hundreds of goats – so bring your own food and water.

Greek script table

Kastellórizo		
Ayías Triádhos	Αγίας Τριάδος	ΑΓΙΑΣ ΤΡΙΑΔΟΣ
Áyios Stéfanos	Άγιος Στέφανος	ΑΓΙΟΣ ΣΤΕΦΑΝΟΣ
Áyios Yeóryios toú Vounioú	Άγιος Γεώργιος τού Βουνιού	ΑΓΙΟΣ ΓΕΩΡΓΙΟΣ ΤΟΥ ΒΟΥΝΙΟΥ
Mandhráki	Μανδράκι	ΜΑΝΔΡΑΚΙ
Meyísti	Μεγίστι	ΜΕΓΙΣΤΙ
Návlakas	Ναύλακας	ΝΑΥΛΑΚΑΣ
Paleokástro	Παλαιοκάστρο	ΠΑΛΑΙΟΚΑΣΤΡΟ
Perastá	Περαστά	ΠΕΡΑΣΤΑ
Rhó	Ρώ	ΡΩ
Vathoryáki	Βαθορυάκι	ΒΑΘΟΡΥΑΚΙ

Kastellórizo travel details

Inter-island transport

Key to ferry companies

G&A G&A Ferries
NK *Nissos Kalymnos*

Ferries

Kastellórizo to: Piréas (1 weekly on G&A via Rhodes and selected Dodecanese; 28hr); Rhodes (1–2 weekly with G&A; 4hr; 2 weekly with NK; 5hr 30min).

NB Kastellórizo has some of the worst ferry connections in the Greek islands; mainline companies like G&A who deign to provide this no-profit link do so under duress, as a condition for receiving government subsidies. Typically G&A provides service only from early July to early September, leaving the island otherwise dependent on the *Nissos Kalymnos*. The municipality has bought a second-hand ferry of its own, the *Agios Raphael* – though this will not be a long-term solution, as this ancient boat will be compulsorily retired within a few years.

Catamaran

Kastellórizo to: Rhodes (1–3 weekly on the *Dodekanisos Express*, typically May–June only; 2hr).

Flights

Kastellórizo to: Rhodes (1 daily mid-June to mid-Sept, 3 weekly otherwise; 45min).

International transport

Kaïkia

Kastellórizo to: Kaş, Turkey (2 weekly minimum or by demand, but see box on p.181).

Sými

Sými's most pressing problem, lack of water, is in many ways also its saving grace. As with so many dry, rocky Dodecanese islands, water must be imported at great expense from Rhodes, pending completion of a reservoir in the distant future. Thus Sými can't hope to support more than a handful of large hotels; instead, hundreds of people are shipped in daily during the season from its larger neighbour, relieved of their money and sent back. This arrangement suits both the islanders and those visitors lucky enough to stay longer. Many foreigners return regularly, and/or own houses here – indeed since the mid-1980s the most desirable dwellings, ruined or otherwise, have been sold off in such numbers that the island has become the Ídhra of the southeast Aegean. The rest remain on sale, at ridiculous prices, and anything with a view of the water has been or is being renovated.

Incredibly, less than a hundred years ago the island was richer and more populous (25,000) than Rhodes, its wealth generated by shipbuilding and sponge-diving, skills nurtured since pre-Classical times. Under the Ottomans, Sými, like many of the Dodecanese, enjoyed considerable autonomy in exchange for a yearly tribute in sponges to the sultan; but the new, Italian-imposed frontier, the 1919–1922 Greco-Turkish war, the gradual replacement of the crews by Kalymniots and (after World War II) the advent of synthetic sponges spelt doom for the local economy. Vestiges of past nautical glories remain in the still-active *karnáyia* (boatyards) at Pédhi and in Haráni district, but today the souvenir-shop sponges come entirely from overseas, and the recent boom notwithstanding, a significant number of the nineteenth-century mansions still stand roofless and empty.

Once beyond the inhabited areas, you'll find a surprisingly attractive island, and ideal walking country in spring or autumn (rather than midsummer, when temperatures are among the highest in Greece). Sými has managed to retain some of its original forest cover of junipers, valonea oaks and even a few pines; lower on the ground there's a thick herbaceous covering of sage, while late spring sees lavender-blossomed thyme and white-flowered oregano. Another prominent feature is dozens of tiny **monasteries** (*monastirákia*) dotting the landscape, most owned by a single family and kept locked except on their patron saint's day – though their cisterns, with a can on a string to fetch water, may be accessible.

Sými Town

SÝMI TOWN, the island's capital and only proper town, consists of two districts: **Yialós**, arrayed around the excellent natural harbour, and **Horió**, which historically led a socially separate existence on the hillside above. The roughly 2500 remaining Symiots are scattered fairly evenly throughout the mixture of surviving Neoclassical and more typical island dwellings; despite the surplus of properties, many outsiders have preferred to build anew rather than restore derelict shells accessible only by donkey or on foot. As on Kastellórizo, a wartime blast – this time set off by the retreating Germans – shattered hundreds of houses up in Horió (see p.480). Shortly afterwards, the official German surrender of the Dodecanese to the Allies was signed here on May 8, 1945: a plaque marks the spot at the present-day *Restaurant Les Catherinettes*, and each year on that date there's a solemn veterans' parade, followed perhaps by some music and folk dancing. Of late, however, this has been overshadowed by the events of the July to September "Sými Festival", which is rapidly becoming one of Greece's more interesting small summer events.

Sými's **port**, an architecturally protected area since the early 1970s, is deceptively lively, especially between 11am and 3.30pm when the spice-and-sponge stalls and a few jewellery shops throng with Rhodes-based day-trippers, and the several excursion craft disgorging them envelop the north quay with exhaust fumes. To relieve congestion, the south quay is currently being widened to become the future main dock, and flagstones laid to match the rest of the waterfront. In deference to the pedestrian clientele, traffic is banned around the harbour except during siesta hours, enforced by a guard manning a chain-barrier by the bus stop.

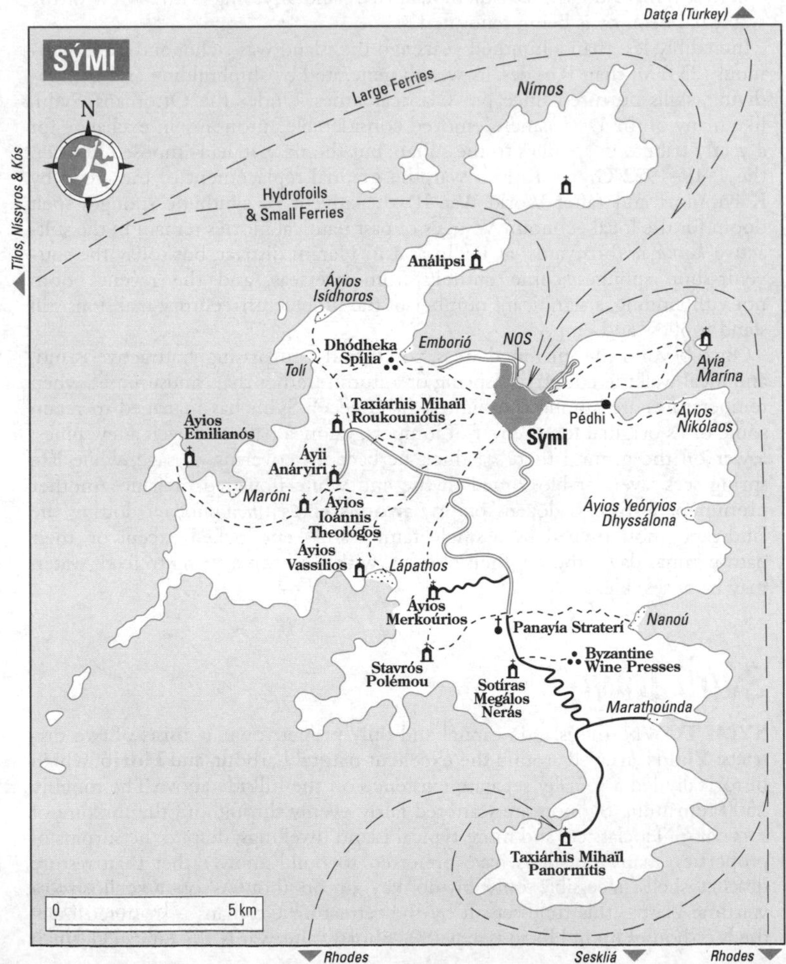

But just uphill, away from the water, the more peaceful pace of village life takes over, with livestock and chickens roaming freely. Two massive stair-paths, the Kalí Stráta and Katarráktes, effectively deter many of the day-trippers and are most dramatic around sunset; huge ruins along the lower reaches of the Kalí Stráta are lonely and sinister after dark, home only to wild fig trees and owls, though these shells too are now scheduled for restoration.

A series of blue arrows through Horió leads you up to the excellent local **museum** (Tues–Sun 10am–2pm; €1.50). Housed in a fine old mansion at the back of the village, the collection concentrates on Byzantine and medieval Sými, with a gallery of medieval icons and exhibits on frescoes in isolated, locked churches. In addition there are antiquarian maps and the inevitable ethnographic wing of costumed mannequins, embroidery and furniture; a cottage in the garden offers a *sandoúri*, old guns and a rusty Victrola. Nearby, the **Hatziagapitos mansion** (may open July–Aug only) has been restored as an annexe to the museum; it dates from around 1800, but seems much older. Wonderful carved wooden chests are the main exhibits, while above various wall niches are traces of wall paintings: the eagle of John the Evangelist, and a female figure (perhaps Learning personified) making a gift of a book to a young lad. As you head back to the village centre, it's worth taking a look at the nineteenth-century **pharmacy**, with its apothecary jars and wooden drawers labelled for exotic homeopathic and herbal remedies; it still functions (after a fashion), in tandem with the adjacent clinic.

At the very pinnacle of things, a castle of the **Knights of St John** occupies the site of Sými's ancient **acropolis**, and you can glimpse a stretch of Classical polygonal wall on one side, as well as the Grand Master's escutcheon. A dozen churches grace Horió; that of the **Assumption**, inside the fortifications of the acropolis, is a successor to the one blown to bits when the Germans detonated the munitions cache there. One of the bells in the new belfry is the nose-cone of a thousand-pound bomb, hung as a memorial. Somehow the islanders have secured permission from the archeological authorities to build another, smaller chapel in stone, on the summit itself.

Arrival, information and getting around

A **catamaran**, a **large kaïki** and a **hydrofoil** run daily to Sými from Mandhráki in Ródhos Town, departing morning and evening on either an *epivatikó* (scheduled service) or *ekdhromikó* (excursion) basis. The hydrofoil *Aigli* leaves Rhodes at 9am or 6pm (sometimes both departures in one day), takes 55 minutes to arrive and costs about €10 one way. Conventional kaïkia like the *Symi I* require just under two hours for the crossing, and cost €7.40–8.80 each way on an excursion ticket, half that as an *epivatikó*; the catamaran *Symi II* is similarly priced, but much quicker. A few times a week there are also mainline ferries as well in either direction, typically the cheapest of all (1hr 40min journey time). ANES, the outlet for *Symi I*/*Symi II*/*Aigli* tickets, maintains a booth on the quay (ⓣ02460/71 100) and an office in the marketplace lanes (ⓣ02460/71 444). Sunny Land, also in the market (ⓣ02460/71 230), is the agent for G&A and the *Nissos Kalymnos*, while DANE Lines and the *Dodekanisos Express* catamaran is handled by Symi Tours nearby (ⓣ02460/71 307).

There's no official tourism bureau but the island's English-language advertiser newsletter, *The Symi Visitor* (free; ⓦwww.symivisitor.com), is literate and has current island gossip alongside informative features. In any season at least one **laundry**, resorted to by those whose hosts forbid clothes washing in rooms, operates in the grid of lanes making up the dwindling market. The **post office** in the official Italian "palace" is open standard hours; of two **banks**, the Alpha is more efficient and has a cash dispenser. During tourist season a small green bus (€0.60 flat fare) shuttles between Yialós and Pédhi via Horió on the hour, returning at the half-hour, until 11pm. There are also six **taxis** (allow €3 between Yialós and Horió with baggage), often clustered near the base of the Kalí Stráta, and one or two outlets for **scooter rental**, though this is steeply priced (€20.50 and up daily) for an island of this size; they know you'll be tempted to take it on the rough road south across Sými, and they cunningly just undercut the price of round-the-isle boat excursions. If unladen, you can happily disregard all this wheeled transport without regret, as Sými is a perfect island for boat and walking excursions.

Accommodation

Accommodation for independent travellers is somewhat limited, though the situation isn't nearly so bad as on Hálki; proprietors tend not to meet arriving boats. Studios, rather than simple rooms, predominate, and package operators control most of these, though curiously you may have an easier time finding spots in July/August than during spring/autumn, considered the most pleasant periods here. Despite asphyxiating summer heat, air conditioning and ceiling fans are rarely found – go for north-facing and/or balconied units when possible. If you're planning in advance, the Symi Visitor website is worth consulting.

Yialós

Albatros Marketplace ⓣ02460/71 707 or 71 829, ⓕ72 257. Partial sea views from this exquisite small hotel; pleasant second-floor breakfast salon, air con, friendly French co-management can arrange similar if full. ❹

Aliki Haráni quay ⓣ02460/71 665, ⓕ71 655, ⓦwww.simi-hotelaliki.gr. A complete overhaul of an 1895 mansion, and Sými's poshest hotel: tasteful rooms with wood floors and some antique furnishings, plus air con and large bathrooms, though only some have sea views. ❻

Anastasia Behind the post office ⓣ02460/71 364. Pleasantly set hotel if limited in harbour views, this has parquet-floored rooms plus a couple of studios, with some package allotment. ❸

Les Catherinettes Above eponymous restaurant, north quay ⓣ02460/72 698, ⓔmarina-epe@rho.forthnet.gr. Creaky but spotless en-suite pension in a historic building with painted ceilings and sea-view balconies for most rooms. ❸–❹

Egli Rooms Base of the Kalí Stráta ⓣ02460/71 392. Basic (non-en suite), but clean enough rooms just a few steps inland from the taxi rank; usually has vacancies when everyone else is full. ❷

Nireus Next to the clocktower ⓣ02460/72 400, ⓕ72 404. Comfortable, balconied sea-view rooms, about half of which have air conditioning. Standard doubles ❺, suites ❻

Symi Gardens Yialós, just up from the basketball courts – no sign, look for the giant arbor vitae ⓣ & ⓕ02460/71 732. Lovely studio apartments with wood trim, mock fireplaces and stone-paved courtyard; lots of packages spring and autumn, but some walk-in vacancies in summer. ❺

Titika Rooms Rear of square, Yialós; enquire at sponge shop left of National Bank, or ⓣ02460/71 501. No views, but quiet and well-equipped rooms with fridge and air con; tiny common kitchen and shared terrace with tables. ❷–❹

Horió

Fiona At the top of the Kalí Stráta ⓣ02460/72 088. Mock-traditional hotel building whose large airy rooms have double beds and stunning views; breakfast in mid-air on common balcony. Does not work with package companies. ❹

Jean Manship c/o Jean & Tonic Bar ⓣ & ⓕ02460/71 819 8pm–1am Greek time. Jean manages two traditional houses in Horió, both suitable for couples and with stunning views. ❸ & ❹

Katerina Tsakiris Rooms ⓣ02460/71 813. Just a handful of rather plain if en-suite rooms with separate self-catering kitchen facilities and a grandstand view over the harbour; reservations essential. ❹

Symi Visitor Accommodation ⓣ02460/72 755, ⓔsymi-vis@otenet.gr. Managed by affable returned Greek-Australian Nikos Halkitis and partner Wendy Wilcox, who offer a variety of houses restored as double-occupancy studios in prime locations of Horió. Rates range from ❸ at *The Cottages* to ❻ at *The Mule House*, by way of ❹ at *The Windmills*; they also have pricier units suitable for 4–5 persons.

Taxiarhis Apartments Edge of Horió overlooking

Pédhi ⓣ02460/72 012, ⓕ02460/72 013. Secluded, well-designed row of studios and one-bedroom apartments with common areas and balconies, though it gets some package groups. Breakfast on request. ❸–❺

Villa Symeria Up the Kalí Stráta (contact *Albatros Hotel*). Restored Neoclassical view mansion comprising two apartments with either air con or fans, suitable for up to four and six persons respectively. ❻

Eating and drinking

You're best off avoiding most **eateries** on the north and west quays of the port, where menus, raw materials, prices and attitudes have been terminally warped by the day-trip trade. Away from these areas, you've a fair range of choice among *kultúra* tavernas, old-style *mayireftá* places, a few genuine ouzerís and even a traditional kafenío or two. Indeed Sými has a tradition of retaining good chefs – either native-born or from elsewhere, many trained at the professional tourism school on Rhodes.

To Amoni Inland side of main platía, Yialós. An excellent, inexpensive, authentic ouzerí, where big helpings of liver, sausage and seafood titbits accompany the usual fried vegetarian starters and mainland bulk wine. Open most of the year, though dinner only low season; seating indoors and out.

Dhimitris South quay, on the way out of town. Excellent, family-run seafood-stressing ouzerí with exotic items such as *hokhlióalo* (sea snails), *foúskes* (mock oysters), *spinóalo* (pinna-shell flesh) and the indigenous miniature shrimps, along with the more usual plates and lots of vegetarian starters.

Ellinikon South side main square, Yialós. The most prominent of the *kultúra* tavernas, where host Nikos Psarros will escort you to the cooled wine cellar to choose from among 140 varieties of top Greek wine. Food portions aren't huge, but recipes – squid-ink pasta, seafood *mousakás*, roasts, ice cream with mulberry sauce – are rich. Budget €25 per head plus the cost of wine.

O Ilios West quay. English-run, with "English" or healthy full breakfasts, plus vegetarian meals and home-made cakes served continuously 8am–10.30pm. Also does picnic hampers for beach outings – notify them the previous day.

To Kantirimi North side main square, Yialós. A good source of pancake or waffle breakfasts under the trees; becomes a snack café-bar later in the day.

O Meraklis Rear of the marketplace. Polite service and fair portions of moderately pricey *mayireftá* and mezédhes make this a reliable bet April–Dec. Sample meal: beans, beets, dips, and roast lamb with potatoes as a tender main course. Allow €13–14 each.

Mythos South quay between bus/taxi stop, Yialós. Superb, supper-only ouzerí that's reckoned among the best, and best-value, cooking on the island. There is a menu, but best let chef Stavros hit you with his Frenchified medley which includes salad, seafood starters (squid in basil sauce), duck with juniper berries, lamb slices, and home-made desserts. Decent wine list; budget €20.50 a head before dipping into that. Roof terrace annexe opening in 2002.

Pahos West quay, beside *O Ilios* (no sign). The old-boys' kafenío, in operation since World War II, and still a classic spot for a sundown oúzo and people-watching.

Yiorgos Near top of Kalí Stráta in Horió. Jolly, much-loved institution maintaining consistent food quality since 1977, with summer seating on a pebble-mosaic courtyard where occasional impromptu live music sessions happen. Service can be slipshod, but perennial recipes include feta-stuffed peppers, spinach-rice, chicken in mushroom-wine sauce, and grilled fish when available. Open random lunchtimes in season, dinner only indoors in winter.

Nightlife

Nightlife, distributed over half a dozen bars in Yialós (plus a few more in Horió), is long and sometimes abusively loud, with a number of bars owned by expatriates. Up in Horió, convivial *Jean & Tonic* is the heart and soul of nightlife, catering to a mixed clientele (visitors and expats until 3am, Greek restauranteurs 3am until dawn) most of the year; *Kafenio Lefteris* is the traditional hangout at the very top of the Kalí Stráta, known for its tender octopus; *Kali Strata*, a bit below, is a low-key place with unbeatable views and excellent, wide-ranging music. Down at Yialós, the *Harani Club* has the nicest interior and a mix of Greek and international music, depending on the crowd, until 2am; its neighbours in the noisy alley nicknamed "the Gaza strip" have lapsed into high-volume aural assaults aimed at empty tables. Elsewhere, *Katoi* on the south quay is a no-touts, no-hassle bar favoured by locals, whilst *The Club* on the platía functions between midnight and dawn, with a pool table.

Around Sými Town: Pédhi to Emborió

Sými has no big sandy **beaches**, but there are plenty of pebbly stretches in the deep, protected bays which indent the coastline. **PÉDHI**, a 45-minute walk from Yialós, retains some of its former identity as a fishing hamlet, with enough ground water in the plain behind – the island's largest – to support a few vegetable gardens. The beach is poor, though, and patronage from yachts and the giant, overpriced but packages-free *Pedhi Beach* hotel (Ⓣ02460/71 981, Ⓕ71 982; ❻) has considerably bumped up prices at the three local beachfront **tavernas**, of which the most reasonable and authentic is *Iy Kamares* at the far south end; you'll recognize it by the stone arches that it's named for, and the fact that it has its feet virtually in the water.

Many will opt for another twenty minutes of walking along a rough but obvious path (sturdy shoes required) along the south shore of almost landlocked Pédhi Bay to **Áyios Nikólaos**. The only all-sand beach on Sými, this offers sheltered swimming, tamarisks for shade, and a mediocre taverna behind its 50-metre extent. Alternatively, a red-paint-splodge-marked path on the north side of the inlet leads in just over half an hour to **Ayía Marína**, where there's a minuscule beach and a larger shingle-and-sunbed lido, with a drinks *kantína*. There is also a monastery-capped islet to which you can easily swim. You might vary the return walk to town by using the onward trail through the gate at the far end of the "beach"; it's waymarked but rough, so allow at least an hour – some of this cross-country – to emerge at the line of windmills at the east end of Horió.

Around Yialós, ten minutes' walk beyond Haráni and its boatyards, you'll find the tiny **NOS (Navtikós Ómilos Sýmis)** "beach", but there's sun here only until lunchtime and it's usually packed with day-trippers. Instead, you can continue along the cement-paved coast road past tiny gravel coves and rock slabs popular with nudists and snorkellers, or cut inland from the Yialós square past the former site of the desalination plant, to appealing **Emborió** Bay (sometimes "Nimborió"), with the well-placed and peaceful *Niriides Apartments* (Ⓣ02460/71 892, Ⓕ71 784; ❺) on the coastal route in, the rather mediocre and overpriced *Metapontis* taverna at one end of the bay, and an artificially strewn sand beach at the other.

Inland from the bay, up a dry ravine and then some steps, a somewhat faded Byzantine **mosaic** fragment lies under a protective shelter, next to Siamese-triplet chapels. Much has been obliterated, but you can discern a man leading a camel, a partridge, and a stag in flight from a boar. Beyond a lone pine beside the chapels, a faint trail marked by painted arrows and letters leads 100m further to a slight rise ringed by a collapsing chain-link fence. Inside the enclosure, a hole in the ground gives access to a subterranean complex known locally as **Dhódheka Spília** (Twelve Caves), either catacombs or the crypt of a basilica which once stood here.

Remote bays and monasteries

Plenty of other more secluded coves are accessible by energetic **walkers** with sturdy footwear. By far the best of two local walking guides is Lance Chilton's *Walks In Symi* (Marengo Publications, UK; also stocked at the Sými Visitor offices). In any event, most interesting island paths have been admirably marked of late with either cairns or paint splodges.

Otherwise, pay a modest sum for the **taxi-boats** moored just opposite the main *agorá* street. These operate daily in season, roughly hourly from 10am to noon, returning from their destinations between 4 and 5.30pm. It must be said that the tourist bureaux associated with the main package companies tend to push expensive, all-day, multi-stop excursions rather than these simple, DIY itineraries. One-way fares on the taxi-boats are quoted only for Emborió, Ayía Marína and Áyios Nikólaos.

The east coast: Nanoú and other bays

You won't necessarily need to use a taxi-boat to get to or from the three bays just cited, but a boat ride remains the easiest way to reach the southeastern bays of **Marathoúnda** and **Nanoú**, and the only method of getting to the spectacular, cliff-girt fjord of **Áyios Yeóryios Dhyssálona**, which served as a location for the 1961 film *The Guns of Navarone*. Dhyssálona lacks a taverna and lies in shade after 1pm or so, while unalluring Marathoúnda is fringed by coarse, slimy pebbles (and can anyway be reached by motorbike), making Nanoú the most popular destination for day-trips. The 200-metre beach there consists of gravel, sand and pebbles, with sunbeds and umbrellas, good snorkelling, a scenic backdrop of rare Symiot pines, and a **taverna** (squid, chips and salad menu) that's probably the most reasonable of Sými's remote eateries.

Hiking to Nanoú

You can reach **Nanoú overland** by a moderately challenging but spectacular three-hour walk from Horió, mostly on path, taking in several of Sými's most interesting rural monasteries en route. As with all island walks, it's best to be equipped with the "Walker's Map of Symi", packaged along with Lance Chilton's *Walks in Symi*.

From the top of the Katarráktes stairway, curl around through the network of village lanes, gaining altitude slightly and turning southwest towards the last, highest houses; paint dots on house corners direct you. Just past the livestock gate at the very western edge of Horió, head up and left at a fork onto a finely engineered *kalderími*. Approaching the asphalt from Horió to island points west and south, you'll find the last 40m of this buried under rubble, necessitating a slippery, steep scramble up to the road. You're obliged to walk on this for about ten minutes along the turning for Panormítis, until you re-adopt it at the first curve; just under half an hour from Horió, you pass Ayía Ekateríni monastery (locked), and then arrive at Panayía Styloú chapel (also shut) after ten more minutes. Here you must leave the *kalderími* (which just goes back up to the road and expires permanently) in favour of a narrower but distinct path, with a few waymarks.

This path initially keeps gloriously high above Áyios Vassílios ravine before slipping over a ridge into a fairly large side canyon draining down to Lápathos and then, just over half an hour from Styloú, entering pine and juniper forest. Some fifteen minutes from the edge of the trees, shun turnings to the right and follow dots left and up to the *monastiráki* of **Áyios Prokópios** (open), which retains some engaging fourteenth-to-fifteenth-century frescoes – *Crucifixion* and *Resurrection* – just right of the door. Ignore bulldozer scrapings in favour of the onward path, starting from the southwest corner of the single outbuilding; it's about twenty minutes from here, up past Panaïdhi monastery (locked) with its two chapels, to the hilltop **Stavrós Polémou** monastery (c. 500m elevation), whose famous views (the earlier in the day the better) are everything they're cracked up to be. Its courtyard kitchen is usually open, with a chained bucket inside for fetching pure cistern water. Return to Panaïdhi, behind which the onward path, partly cemented over, heads northwest, debouching after twenty minutes on the Panormítis road, just shy of a sign pointing along the side track back to Áyios Prokópios. Turn right (south), and within a couple of minutes you should be abreast the chapel of **Panayía Straterí**, up on a cement terrace studded with a flagpole and a blue-and-rust-coloured belfry, west of the road. If you've had an early start and have lots of stamina, you might detour fifteen minutes southeast, initially on *kalderími*, to some moderately interesting Byzantine-era **wine presses**.

But most will be eager to get down to the sea as soon as possible. Immediately opposite Straterí, search bulldozer-tumbled boulders for red-paint arrows and an "X" marking the start of the continuing path; it drops sharply on a scree surface to begin with, then descends more gradually as a corniche trail. This hugs the south flank of a ravine cutting through Sými's thickest forest of junipers and pines, which provide welcome shade. The trail remains distinct throughout, though there are also powder-blue waymarks. It's about 45 minutes downhill from the road to a cistern and then a little chapel, just inland from the Nanoú taverna; line these three landmarks up to reverse the itinerary if necessary, which takes less than an hour uphill – better grip offsets the steep grade. With an early enough start from Horió, you should have plenty of time for lunch and a swim at Nanoú before the last taxi-boat of the day back to Yialós.

Áyios Vassílios

No boats serve the scenic gulf of **Áyios Vassílios** on the southwest coast of Sými, so you'll need to make an easy but satisfying hour-and-a-half trek across the island from Horió through patches of natural juniper forest. The path leaves Horió as for the trip to Panayía Straterí (see above), climbing gradually within half an hour to the paved road arcing out of the village on the Pédhi side; at the second (the first is for Straterí) fork about 25 minutes along, bear left, turn left again when you meet the asphalt and then almost immediately right (south) onto a narrow track, crossing the tree-studded Xissós plateau. Within ten more minutes you pass a few farms and reach the last monastery on the plateau, to the left of which the true path resumes. Hálki appears on the horizon as the trail descends steadily along the west flank of an imposing gorge; there is little or no possibility of getting lost, and Tílos eventually replaces Hálki in your field of view. A final, slithery couloir leads down to the long, gravel-and-small-pebble beach where clothing is optional and the water warm. On the downside, there's a fair amount of washed-up litter, and often afternoon choppiness and turbidity. Perched above the beach, at the top of the final descent, the little **monastery church** of Áyios Vassílios is, unusually, unlocked; it offers a carved wooden *témblon* and tantalizing post-Byzantine frescoes which, if they were ever cleaned properly, would amply reward the trek out here, beach or no.

Áyios Emilianós

The trek to **Áyios Emilianós** at the island's extreme west end takes a minimum of two and a half hours one way, depending on your ability and the route chosen. From Yialós, the most direct way begins along the stair-street beginning inland from the plaza, which becomes a *kalderími* by the highest house; from Horió, begin as for Áyios Vassílios and Panayía Straterí (see opposite), but bear right at the aforementioned second fork. Both routes converge on the ridge west of town, near a clump of eucalyptus trees by the paved road. The main path used to continue from the far side of the road directly west to the little convent of Áyii Anáryiri, but a huge army camp now blocks the way and passage is forbidden.

Thus you make a compulsory detour right, trudging along the paved road, to the conspicuous monastery of **Taxiárhis Mihaïl Roukouniótis**, Sými's oldest (daily 9am–2pm & 4–8pm; €0.75 donation to keepers), its gate shaded by an enormous, 300-year-old juniper in a round planter-well. Inside, the church sports lurid eighteenth-century frescoes by local master Gregory and a peculiar ground plan: the current *katholikón* is actually superimposed on a lower, thirteenth-century structure abandoned after being burnt and pillaged by pirates during the 1400s, though a fine fresco of St Lawrence (Áyios Lavréntios) survives behind the altar screen. Resident, trilingual Father Amfilohios will gladly tell you anything else you might possibly wish to know about the place.

From Roukouniótis you head briefly south along a cemented track to **Áyii Anáryiri** (gate open) to pick up the onward trail rudely interrupted by the army base. A gentle saddle marks the high point of the walk, and then the path enters juniper forests. The view west through the trees to Áyios Emilianós from the rural monastery of **Áyios Ioánnis Theológos** is more than alluring, and you can use the bucket on a rope to fish water out of the big cistern behind the church.

For walkers who feel that the intrusion of the Greek military around Roukouniótis – and it is an eyesore – has compromised the landscape, there's another, alternate way to Áyios Ioánnis Theológos, especially worthwhile from Horió. Proceed as if you were going to Áyios Vassílios, but instead of taking the cement drive south across Xissós, take the paved drive beginning a bit further west, bound for Panayía Myrtariótissa, and find the start of a waymarked path amongst the cottages of a pastoral hamlet on the ridge below this little monastery. After half an hour on this trail you reach the "gentle saddle" noted above to join the lower trail, and arrive at Theológos within 25 more minutes.

However you've arrived, bear right at the fork in the path below Theológos and descend gradually to the vicinity of Maróni cove (indifferent swimming) and the church of Áyios Filímonos (cistern water, a quick 45min from Theológos), where the distinct trail becomes a set of concrete steps down to Skoúmissa cove (poor swimming). From here it's line of sight, with an intermittent path at best, for the final twenty-minute distance north to Áyios Emilianós, perched on an islet tethered to the Kefála headland by a wave-lashed causeway. The monastery's courtyard makes an excellent picnic venue, but alas the kitchen and adjoining cell are no longer kept open, so don't plan on staying the night here. The best flotsam-and-sea-urchin-free swimming hereabouts is roughly halfway between Skoúmissa and the monastery, where eelgrass beds just off a patch of clean pebbles given onto deep water.

Returning, budget just under an hour up to Theológos, another half-hour to Áyii Anaryíri, and another thirty minutes past Roukouniótis to the eucalyptus ridge above the army camp. The wide but scandalously crumbling *kalderími* down to Yialós is easy to find in this direction, bringing the total for the west-to-east traverse to about two and a half hours.

Tolí and Áyios Isídhoros

From near the northernmost point of the asphalt road to Taxiárhis Mihaïl Roukoúniotis, next to the boundary wall of a cottage, a path heads northwest, only briefly skimming or using track systems, to arrive at the secluded and occasionally garbage-strewn cove of Tolí in 45 minutes; in the final minutes you leave the "main" trail in favour of a spur trail ending near an isolated house and giant tree above the beach. **Tolí** is actually a multiple beach divided by a small headland, with the cleanest and most pebbly bit off to the left as you face the sea. After wet winters a small spring, suitable for emergency purposes, surfaces in the ravine staked by oleanders, descending to the northerly half of the cove. If for any reason Tolí doesn't suit, stay with the high inland path for another fifteen minutes to smaller, north-facing **Áyios Isídhoros**, arguably more scenic with its views to islets, and a shallow, sheltered cove offshore, but likely to be dirty onshore.

Rather than return the way you came, make a loop by heading east to Emborió in just under an hour. The track system on the ridge overlooking Tolí heads northeast towards Áyios Yeóryios Kylindhriótis monastery, but don't go all the way there – below and to the right of the track, a poor trail (very indistinct at first) begins through the ravine draining down to the artificially supplemented beach at Emborió.

Taxiárhis Mihaïl Panormítis

At the southern point of the island looms the huge monastery of **Taxiárhis Mihaïl Panormítis** ("Panormítis" for short), Sými's biggest rural attraction and generally the first port of call for the excursion boats from Rhodes (confirm the itinerary if you wish to proceed direct to Yialós – some craft do). These allow you just a quick half-hour tour; if you want more time, you'll have to come by motorbike from Yialós (though the still-unpaved road down from the central escarpment is terrible, with nine hairpin bends), or arrange to stay the night in the **xenónas** set aside for pilgrims. There are large numbers of these in summer, as Mihaïl has been adopted as the patron of sailors in the Dodecanese (and not a few local men bear this name). The only monk permanently in residence, Archimandrite Gavriïl, lived in Australia for a while and so speaks a little English – certainly enough to chat up single women visitors. He is occasionally assisted by novices from the big monastery on Pátmos, of which the place is a dependency. Overnighting is by donation; you'll be chided if you're stingy – €9 is currently the minimum.

Like many of Sými's monasteries, the present Panormítis is of recent (eighteenth-century) construction and was pillaged during the last war, so don't expect too much from the building or its treasures. An appealing pebble-mosaic court surrounds the central *katholikón*, tended by Gavriïl, lit by an improbable number of oil lamps and graced by a fine *témblon*, though the frescoes are recent and mediocre. One of the two small **museums** (€1.50 fee covers both) contains a strange mix of precious antiques, exotic junk (elephant tusks, stuffed crocodiles and koalas), votive offerings, models of ships named *Taxiarhis* or *Panormítis*, and a chair piled with messages in bottles brought here by Aegean currents – the idea being that if the bottle or toy boat arrived, the sender got their prayer answered. Amenities outside the walls include a small beach, a shop/kafenío, a bakery and a **taverna** (*Panormio*) popular with passengers of the many yachts calling in. Near the taverna stands a memorial commemorating three Greeks, including the monastery's abbot, executed in February 1944 by the Germans for aiding British commandos.

Satellite islets

Day boat-trips call at **Nímos**, the satellite islet skirted spectacularly by hydrofoils or ferries approaching Sými from the north, for a beach barbecue and a visit to its monastery; otherwise Nímos is bare and lonely except for grazing goats. By contrast, **Seskliá**, at the far south end of Sými, has greenery and water, and is also a potential target of boat excursions.

Greek script table

Sými	Σύμη	ΣΥΜΗ
Ayía Marína	Αγία Μαρίνα	ΑΓΙΑ ΜΑΡΙΝΑ
Áyii Anáryiri	Άγιοι Ανάργυροι	ΑΓΙΟΙ ΑΝΑΡΓΥΡΟΙ
Áyios Emilianós	Άγιος Αιμηλιανός	ΑΓΙΟΣ ΑΙΜΗΛΙΑΝΟΣ
Áyios Isídhoros	Άγιος Ισίδωρος	ΑΓΙΟΣ ΙΣΙΔΩΡΟΣ
Áyios Nikólaos	Άγιος Νικόλαος	ΑΓΙΟΣ ΝΙΚΟΛΑΟΣ
Áyios Prokópios	Άγιος Προκόπιος	ΑΓΙΟΣ ΠΡΟΚΟΠΙΟΣ
Áyios Vassílios	Άγιος Βασίλειος	ΑΓΙΟΣ ΒΑΣΙΛΕΙΟΣ
Áyios Yeóryios Dhyssálona	Άγιος Γεώργιος Δυσσάλονα	ΑΓΙΟΣ ΓΕΩΡΓΙΟΣ ΔΥΣΣΑΛΟΝΑ
Emborió	Εμπορειό	ΕΜΠΟΡΕΙΟ
Haráni	Χαράνι	ΧΑΡΑΝΙ
Horió	Χωριό	ΧΩΡΙΟ
Marathoúnda	Μαραθούντα	ΜΑΡΑΘΟΥΝΤΑ
Mihaïl Roukouniótis	Μιχαήλ Ρουκουνιότης	ΜΙΧΑΗΛ ΡΟΥΚΟΥΝΙΟΤΗΣ
Nanoú	Νανού	ΝΑΝΟΥ
Nímos	Νίμος	ΝΙΜΟΣ
NOS	___	ΝΟΣ
Pédhi	Πέδι	ΠΕΔΙ
Seskliá	Σεσκλιά	ΣΕΣΚΛΙΑ
Stavrós Polémou	Σταυρός Πολέμου	ΣΤΑΥΡΟΣ ΠΟΛΕΜΟΥ
Taxiárhis Mihaïl Panormítis	Ταξιάρχης Μιχαήλ Πανορμίτης	ΤΑΞΙΑΡΧΗΣ ΜΙΧΑΗΛ ΠΑΝΟΡΜΙΤΗΣ
Tolí	Τολή	ΤΟΛΗ
Yialós	Γιαλός	ΓΙΑΛΟΣ

Sými travel details

Inter-island transport

Key to ferry and hydrofoil companies

DANE *Dhodhekanisiakí Anónymi Navtiliakí Etería* (Dodecanesian Shipping Company)
G&A G&A Ferries
KR Kyriakoulis Hydrofoils
LZ Laoumtzis Hydrofoils
NK *Nissos Kalymnos*

Local kaïkia/speedboat (scheduled services)

Sými to: Rhodes (1 daily, varies from 6–8.30am, always returns 6pm; journey time 1hr on the *Symi II*, 1hr 50min on the *Symi I*).

Catamaran

Sými to: Rhodes, Kós, Kálymnos, Léros (2 weekly, typically May only).

Ferries

Sými to: Kálymnos (1 weekly on DANE, 1 weekly on G&A, 2 weekly on NK; 5hr 30min–7hr); Kastellórizo (1 weekly on G&A, 2 weekly on NK, via Rhodes; 5hr 45min); Kós (1 weekly on G&A, 1 weekly on DANE, 2 weekly on NK; 4hr 30min–5hr 30min); Léros (1 weekly on G&A, 1 weekly on DANE; 7hr); Níssyros (1 weekly on G&A, 2 weekly on NK; 3hr–4hr); Pátmos (1 weekly on G&A, 1 weekly on DANE; 8hr 30min); Pireás (2 weekly on G&A or DANE; 18hr 30min); Rhodes (1 weekly on G&A, 1 weekly on DANE, 2 weekly on NK; 1hr 30min–2hr); Tílos (1 weekly on G&A, 2 weekly on NK; 2hr–2hr 30min).

NB G&A and DANE reliably call at Sými only from early June to mid-Sept.

Hydrofoils

Sými to: Rhodes (daily in season on the *Aigli*, at 7am and/or 4.45pm, returns 9am and/or 6pm; also 1 weekly on KR & 2 on LZ June–Oct); Kós (3 weekly June–Oct, on LZ or KR).

International transport

Sými ranks as an official port of entry to Greece, and in season there are up to 3 weekly kaïki (80min) or hydrofoil (40min) services to Turkey (Datça). The hydrofoil, at €38.20 return including Greek tax (but $12 Turkish tax extra), is cheaper but perhaps not as personable as the kaïki trip (€47 plus Turkish tax). These are sold as day-return excursions and are not really the most practical means of travelling one way to Turkey.

Tílos

The small, blissfully quiet island of **Tílos**, with a population of about five hundred (dwindling to a hundred or so in winter), is one of the least frequented and (outside peak season) worst connected of the Dodecanese, though it can (in theory) be visited as a day-trip from Rhodes by hydrofoil or catamaran a few times a week. Why anyone should want to come for just a few hours is unclear: while it's a great place to rest on the beach or go walking, there is nothing very striking at first glance. After a few days, however, you may have stumbled on several of the seven small castles of the Knights of St John which stud the crags, or have found some of the inconspicuous medieval chapels, often with (locked) frescoed interiors or *hokhláki* courtyards, clinging to the hillsides.

Tílos shares the physical characteristics of its closest neighbours: limestone mountains resembling those of Hálki, plus volcanic lowlands, pumice beds and red-lava sand as on Níssyros. Though rugged and scrubby on its heights, the island has ample water – from springs, or pumped up from the agricultural plains – and clusters of oak and terebinth near the cultivated areas. The climate is exceptionally salubrious, with relative humidity often well below forty percent. From many points on the island there are startling views across to Kós, Sými, Turkey, Níssyros, Hálki, Rhodes and even (weather permitting) Kárpathos.

Stranded midway between Kós and Rhodes, Tílos has always been a backwater, and among all Dodecanese has the least developed nautical tradition. With ample groundwater and rich volcanic soil, the islanders could afford to turn their backs on the sea, and instead made Tílos the breadbasket of the Dodecanese. Until the 1970s, approaching travellers were greeted by the sight of blond, shimmering fields of grain bowing in the wind; today the hillside terraces languish abandoned, evidence of typical small-island depopulation.

Since the late 1980s, Tílos has arrived touristically in a modest way; there are now nearly a thousand guest beds on the island, with four figures to be attained if and when all the rooms blocks and bungalow complexes at foundation or skeleton stage are completed. Laskarina Holidays (see "Basics" p.14) bookings account for just a fraction of this capacity, and the island principally attracts an independent, disparate return clientele. More recently, however, there have been running three-way battles over the direction of future development among northern European visitors who wish to walk and beachcomb in peace, a more raucous crowd (mainly Italians and Greeks), itching to exercise their dirt bikes, 4WD vehicles and shotguns, and some ambitious locals intent on catering to whichever faction will make more lucrative bookings. Though the incumbent mayor has tried to placate the conservationists – Tílos has been a no-hunting zone since 1996, though probably not for much longer – FOTA (Friends of Tílos Association), a Green-ish pressure group of mostly British foreigners, is castigated from various sides as either cultural imperialists or totally toothless, and of late seems to have dwindled to a social-events organizer issuing the occasional newsletter.

Meanwhile, the development boosters are busy reversing the conditions which many visitors have historically come to enjoy; besides the Dodge City atmosphere of Livádhia (see p.198), welts of private and publicly funded **bulldozer tracks** scar almost every mountain and slope in the east of the island. A 1998-vintage road from the telecom-tower hill, heading southeast along the summit ridge, is intended to serve planned fish farms at Áyios Séryios, which will finish that cove as a leisure beach; currently it's paved to the nearby rubbish tip. All is not gloom, however; a half-dozen critical sections of **trail** or **kalderími** in poor condition have been officially surveyed in preparation for cleaning and rebuilding in the near future, so the number of quality **walking opportunities** may have stabilized. Those visitors who come specifically to walk are assisted by the usually accurate **map** prepared by Baz "Paris" Ward and sold at local shops – or by certified walking **guides** Iain and Lyn Fulton (Ⓣ02460/44 128 or 094/6054593, Ⓔfulton@otenet.gr), who may take you on unusual itineraries not described or mapped in existing literature.

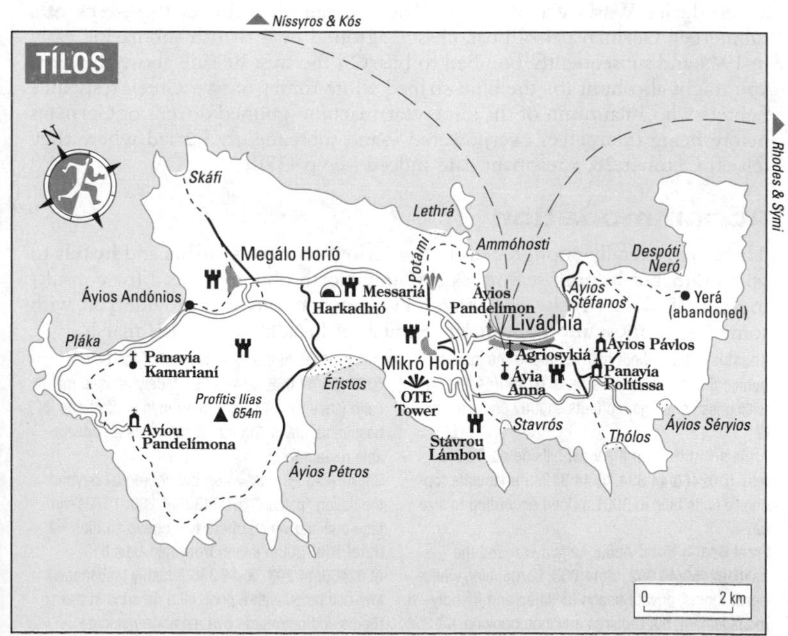

Getting around the island

Tílos's main road, widened and repaved in 1999–2000, runs 7km from Livádhia, the port village, to Megálo Horió, the capital and only other significant habitation. A public **minibus** links the two, and services are theoretically scheduled to coincide with ferry/catamaran/hydrofoil arrivals at the recently improved jetty; at other times the bus makes up to six runs daily along the Livádhia–Éristos stretch. Accommodation proprietors from Éristos, Megálo Horió and the remoter reaches of Livádhia may lay on shuttles to and from the port; there are also two **taxis**, or you can rent a **car** from two outlets in Livádhia (Stefanakis Travel and Tilos Travel). Stefanakis currently has a monopoly on sea tickets; Tilos Travel is arguably the more helpful (Ⓣ & Ⓕ02460/44 294 or 094/6559697, Ⓦwww.tilostravel.co.uk), offering a full accommodation booking service, money exchange, **boat excursions** all season given sufficient passenger numbers, and **scooter rental** (currently the sole outlet as they've merged with the competition). The single **filling station** lies between Livádhia and Megálo Horió.

Livádhia and around

With its unpaved streets, unfinished building sites in every direction and higgledy-piggledy layout, **LIVÁDHIA** makes a poor introduction to the island, but it remains the better equipped of the two settlements to deal with tourists, and is closer to the majority of remaining path-hikes. The long pebble beach, which gets more comfortable to sit on near the middle, is merely adequate at the best of times, and the tidal rocks can get slimy with pollution in high summer when people surreptitiously vent cesspits.

Despite its currently peaceful profile, Livádhia Bay saw a certain amount of action during World War II. At mid-bay, you can snorkel over the wreck of a submerged German patrol boat, chased aground by a British submarine early in 1944 and subsequently bombed to bits. On the west hillside above the jetty, you might also hunt for the blue-striped white tombs of two Greek resistance fighters who, in autumn of the same year, machine-gunned dozens of Germans before being themselves overpowered – and subsequently buried where they fell on October 28, a resonant date indeed (see p.437).

Accommodation

There are generally enough beds in the various **rooms**, **studios** and **hotels** to go around, but in peak season it's certainly worth phoning ahead (or consulting Tilos Travel's website, see above). The better outfits will provide you with some sort of mosquito control, since much of Livádhia is drained marsh.

Anastasia East about halfway along the bay, behind the *Armenon* taverna Ⓣ02460/44 111. A willingness to bargain offsets slightly small rooms. ❶

Anna's Studios On the west hillside above the jetty Ⓣ02460/44 334, Ⓕ44 342. Immaculate top-choice units built in 2001, priced according to size. ❷–❸

Eleni Beach Hotel About halfway around the bayⓉ02460/44 062, Ⓕ44 063. Large, airy, white-decor rooms, private beach facilities and friendly management, but requires advance booking. ❹

Faros Hotel At the extreme end of the bay Ⓣ02460/44 068, Ⓕ44 029. Widely praised for calm (save for an entertaining mynah bird) and its hospitable managing family; also has an acceptable restaurant. ❸

Galini (aka *Paraskevi*) on the shore just beyond the Italian "palace" Ⓣ02460/44 280. 1970s-vintage building which offers two cheap studios. ❷

Hotel Irini 200m inland from mid-beach Ⓣ02460/44 293, Ⓕ44 238.A lushly landscaped low-rise hotel, with a pool, all mod cons in the rooms and patronage by Laskarina package clients, but, even mid-season, individuals can usually secure a vacancy in advance. ❹

Studios Irinna (aka *Kula's*) ☎02460/44 366. Well-appointed studios situated inland, above the ironmonger's which runs it. ❷

Paradise (aka *Stamatia's*) Adjacent to the *Galini*, beyond the Italian "palace" ☎02460/44 341. Very basic rooms at one of the original lodgings on the island. ❶

Pavlos and Nina Overlooking the sea near the *Eleni Beach Hotel* ☎02460/44 011. Very friendly management, well-kept units. ❷

Hotel Tilos Mare Well inland from mid-beach ☎02460/44 100, ⓕ44 105. The top hotel on the island, with attractively colourful and tastefully furnished units in a variety of bed formats, plus courtyard pool, but probably only available outside peak season. ❸ spring/autumn

Eating, drinking and nightlife

There must be a dozen-plus **tavernas** operating around Livádhia in peak season, of which perhaps half merit serious consideration. Among the more authentic spots for a no-nonsense Greek feed are *Irina* (alias *Stefanos and Maria*), doling out inexpensive *mayireftá* (€8 per person) right on the shore near the church, and *Psistaria Kritikos* in the village centre, well regarded by carnivores for its goat chops, sausages and chicken. *To Armenon* (alias *Nikos*'), on the shore road, is an excellent and salubrious beach-taverna-cum-ouzerí, with octopus salad, white beans and the like; turning inland on the way to *Armenon* brings you to *Pantelis Souvla Maria's Pizza* (sic), doing just those things superbly, despite zero atmosphere courtesy of plastic chairs and a purple bug-zapper. The best place for reliably fresh grilled fish with mezédhes is *Blue Sky*, an unmissable eyrie perched above the ferry dock.

For **breakfast** (plus evening pizzas and home-made desserts), Anglo-Italian *Joanna's Café*, just inland from *Kritikos*, is hard to beat, and also features a long list of strong, imaginative cocktails. *Iy Omonia* – under the trees strung with light bulbs, near the post office – is the enduringly popular "traditional" alternative for a sundowner, waiting for a ferry (it's open all afternoon in summer), or breakfast, and also does inexpensive, savoury mezédhes (€7 for two plates and a beer). Livelier organized **nightlife** in or near Livádhia is limited to three bars: *Cafe Ino* on the shore near *Irina* for the trendy set, the *Bozi* at the far east end of bay (nightly in summer, weekends otherwise) and a durable music pub in Mikró Horió (see p.200).

Other practicalities

As throughout the islands, the **post office** no longer changes money other than giro cheques, and there's no bank or free-standing cash machine, so come with sufficient Greek cash or apply to either travel agency with foreign notes (Tilos Travel will do cash advances on plastic for a small commission). A **bakery** off the square does decent *píttes*, and several well-stocked "**supermarkets**" stock a range of produce, as do itinerant pick-up trucks which call regularly from the fertile farms of Éristos. The little gift/souvenir shop opposite *Joanna's Café* may offer basic **email retrieval** facilities (but no surfing the internet).

Walks around Livádhia

Despite ongoing, destructive road-building, there are still enough walks around Livádhia to keep one occupied for a few days. Of the six hiking routes marked out for protection and rehabilitation, four begin in or near the port.

To Lethrá via Ammóhosti

The obvious path on the northwest flank of Livádhia Bay starts at the end of the dirt track bulldozed above the last new villa complexes. This Italian-built thoroughfare leads within an hour, without complications, except for a brief cross-country stretch through trees at the end, to the pebble bay of **Lethrá**. About two-thirds of the way along, you pass the side path to the little red-sand beach of **Ammóhosti**, though in all probability at least one party will have beaten you there. Lethrá is cleanest and most useable at its rightmost cove; from the above-noted trees you can trek uphill through the Potámi canyon to Mikró Horió. The full loop Livádhia–Lethrá–Potámi–Mikró Horió–Livádhia (completed below) is designated as one of the six routes to be conserved, so should not deteriorate any further.

Mikró Horió and Potámi

From Livádhia, a walk southwest along a trail which short-cuts the road system – part of it is fenced in, but you can use two gates to follow the course of a pipeline paralleling the path – takes you within 45 minutes up to the ghost village of **MIKRÓ HORIÓ**. Its 1200 inhabitants left for the island's capital during the 1950s owing to water shortages; the name (meaning "Little Village") is rather a misnomer as it was once more populous than Megálo Horió ("Big Village"). The interesting **ruins**, also accessible by dirt road, include threshing cirques strewn with grain millstones. A sprouting of "IDHIOKTISIA..." ("Property of...") signs on the ruins to deter squatters suggests that the owners have woken up to their potential value once power and water are provided, but thus far, almost the only intact structures are the castle-guarded church (locked, except for the festival on August 15) and an old house which has been restored as a well-publicized, after-midnight **music pub** (July & Aug only). Proportions of Greek and foreign music vary according to tourist numbers, and a shuttle from Livádhia jetty is provided.

From the north end of the village below the castle, a path leads down within twenty minutes to the paved road, meeting it at a double-channelled culvert. Directly below this, the stream bed here has been ploughed under by a recent bulldozer track, though a walled-in path going parallel to it allows you to avoid much of this; some fifteen minutes along either you reach a picturesque, masoned, reliable fountain on the east bank, marked by two poplars – and the end of the track for now. Beyond this point, keep as closely as possible to the bottom of the scenic, steep-sided **Potámi canyon**; do not follow any cairns directing you up and right, as that path merely fizzles out high up on the hillside. By the correct bearing, it's some thirty minutes more down to Lethrá, emerging near the middle of the bay. Going uphill from Lethrá to the spring involves much the same time, as there's some stooping to get through dense vegetation; before June at least, water breaks the surface of the stream bed in several places.

Eastern loop

This half to full-day outing, depending on the number of detours off the basic circuit, takes in most of the territory **east of Livádhia**, and remains popular despite a fair amount of jeep track to be trudged.

Head off east on the ugly recent track beyond Áyios Stéfanos anchorage, past some apartments, to Áyios Ioánnis church where the proper trail (again a candidate for rehabilitation) reappears; some forty minutes along you'll reach a Y-fork. Left leads within half an hour to the abandoned hamlet of Yerá, just inland from the tiny beach and powerful shoreline spring of Despóti tó Neró. From Yerá, the path continues indistinctly northeast along the easternmost headland of Tílos to the island's second highest point at 493m.

Bearing right instead at the fork takes you past another spring to the hamlet of Kalámi, where you meet the end of a bulldozed track. You're obliged to follow this west-southwest through a pass in the hills, with the grounds of Panayía Polítissa below on your right and the now-sullied beach of Áyios Séryios to the southeast, a bulldozer track slowly inching its way down to it. From here it's an easy return northwest, then north down to Livádhia, or you could carry on along the now-paved road some 400m to the next prominent saddle, where Thólos cove beckons to the south and Agriosykiá castle looms to the north.

To Thólos via Agriosykiá

Obviously Thólos can be reached directly from Livádhia. The route, with the more recent road avoidable for quite a way by using the old path running in parallel, begins by the cemetery and the chapel of **Áyios Pandelímon** with its Byzantine *hokhláki* court, then curls around under the seemingly impregnable castle of **Agriosykiá**. Once you're up on the saddle (half an hour out of Livádhia), overlooking the descent to Thólos, a cairned route hairpins back and upwards to the citadel (twenty minutes' walk). Views are wonderful, especially early in the morning, but there no longer seems to be an easy way into the half-ruined castle itself.

From the saddle, a distinct path – again, surveyed in preparation for refurbishment – leads about ten minutes further south, then dwindles to a well-cairned scramble for another half-hour down to the popular sandy beach of **Thólos**. The *thólos* or domed structure itself stands on the east side of the bay; what this is – church, tomb or mine works – seems uncertain.

To Stavrós beach

Stavrós is the closest, cleanest, and arguably the most scenic of the south-facing beaches around Livádhia. Take the track between the *Tilos Mare Hotel* and the *Castellania Apartments* and follow this until it becomes a distinct trail at the highest new house of the "village", more or less as shown on the recommended map. The route curls progressively south, passing a dried-up spring (bring plenty of water) to reach the saddle dividing the Livádhia side from the ravine descending to Stavrós. Cairns guide you through the mess created by the road heading east towards the rubbish tip. Soon the path resumes after a fashion, passing under the crumbled walls of **Stavroú Lámbou castle** on the west, and stays on the right bank of the ravine for the final steepest quarter hour; again surveyor's marks point the way, and over-eager amateur cairning in the bed of the watercourse is best ignored. The **beach** itself, an hour's hike out of Livádhia, turns out to be a hundred-metre crescent of pea-gravel and coarse sand at the head of a cliff-girt inlet; there are sea caves for swimmers to explore on the left, but no shade.

Megálo Horió and around

The rest of Tílos' inhabitants live in or near **MEGÁLO HORIÓ**, and until recently had very little to do with the Livadhians, with whom they were not on the best terms; this all changed when Livádhia's autonomy was abolished in 1998 and the entire island came under the authority of one municipality. The village's simple, vernacular houses, arranged in tiers, enjoy an enviable perspective over a vast agricultural *kámbos* stretching down to the bay of Éristos. Notwithstanding a recent spate of renovations and consequent reduction in derelict dwellings, the village is no metropolis by any standard. But in contrast to Wild West Livádhia, it is well planned and "improved", with an anticlockwise one-way system in effect, plus stone paving and landscaping. Architectural interest is provided by the handsome, post-Byzantine parish **church of Taxiárhis**, built on the site of a temple to Apollo and Athena.

A couple of souvenir shops have sprung up, as well as several kafenía and bars, including the locals' one overlooking the vast *hokhláki* courtyard of Taxiárhis church. Your choices for **accommodation** in the village are the *Pension Sevasti* (☎02460/44 237; ❶) at the lower end of town, the central *Milios Apartments* (☎02460/44 204; ❷) or (best) *Studios Ta Elefandakia* (☎02460/44 213; ❷), among attractive gardens by the car park. Of the two **tavernas**, the *Kali Kardhia*, next to the *Pension Sevasti*, is more reliably open and has the best view; rival *Kastro* tends to be a bit suspicious of outsiders and isn't great value compared to recommendations in Livádhia. There's a traditional **kafenío** by the historic Taxiárhis church and, further up, the Athenian-run *Kafenio Ilakati* (late May to Sept only), with cakes and drinks.

The Knights' castle and the Harkadhió cave

Megálo Horió is overlooked by a vast **Knights' castle**, which encloses a sixteenth-century **chapel** with rather battered frescoes. The castle is reached by a stiff, half-hour climb that begins on the lane behind the Ikonomou supermarket, near the village entrance, and threads its way up through a vast jumble of cisterns, house foundations and derelict chapels – hints of Megálo Horió's much greater ancient and medieval size. A massive gate-tower incorporates Classical masonry, and a block in front of the chapel bearing Greek inscriptions provides additional proof that the *kástro* was built over the ancient acropolis.

From the Knights' castle, two other fortresses are visible across the plain; the easterly one of **Messariá** helpfully marks the location of **Harkadhió cave**, where Pleiocene midget elephant bones were discovered in 1971. Hidden for centuries until exposed by a World War II artillery barrage, the cave is now fenced off while it's being re-excavated, but should eventually be open for visits; meanwhile, a well-signposted dirt road leads to the spring just below it, beside which an attractive amphitheatre has been prepared as the venue for a proposed summer festival. Bones unearthed thus far have been transferred to a tiny **museum** in Megálo Horió, on the ground floor of the *dhimarhío*; the Greek-labelled displays, which also include the skulls of the Áyios Andónios victims (see opposite), aren't exactly compelling, but you can find the English-speaking warden upstairs during civil-service working hours (Mon–Fri 8am–2.30pm; free).

Nearby beaches: Skáfi and Éristos

From Megálo Horió you can reach **Skáfi**, the most easily accessible of Tílos' remote beaches; this lies over an hour's walk away along a path that begins below the Ikonomou supermarket and leads directly up the valley to the north. On a scooter you can get there much quicker by taking the first unmarked dirt track on the right past the helipad and following this over the ridge until it stops (the current end point subject to bulldozer doings), with the bay in sight below. A red-dotted trail resumes here; fork left when given the choice (away from a clump of eucalyptus trees) to arrive at Skáfi after twenty minutes' walk. The main bay is goat- or tar-fouled and rocky, but continue five more minutes over the headland on the right to reach a more idyllic pea-gravel cove, with shelter afforded by overhangs.

South of and below Megálo Horió, signs direct you towards the three-kilometre paved side road to long **Éristos** beach, whose sand hue varies from pink to grey depending on the light; it's allegedly the island's best, though summer rubbish piles from campers can be disconcerting, and a reefy zone must be crossed to enter the water. The far southeast end, where the reef is diminshed, is also a designated nudist zone, as are the two secluded, attractive coves at **Kókkino** beyond the headland (path accessible only).

About halfway down the road on the right amongst the orchards is *Taverna-Rooms Tropikana* (ⓣ02460/44 020; ❶), nothing special in either respect, but the most reliable all-season venue for a snack near the beach. For more comfort, there's the 1998-built *Eristos Beach Hotel* (ⓣ02460/44 024; ❷) – the rooms are good value, though the management can be rather eccentric.

The far northwest

The main road beyond Megálo Horió hits the coast again at dreary **Áyios Andónios**, whose one bright spot is a single **taverna**, the *Dhelfini*, open much of the time for the benefit of local fishermen. A fairly obvious path from the west end of Megálo Horió gets walkers there in twenty minutes. By looking carefully along the exposed, average beach you can find more lava-encased skeletons strung out in a row – human this time, supposedly tide-washed victims of a Nissyrian eruption in 600 BC, and discovered by the same archeologists who found the miniature pachyderms. Other estimates of the age of these relics range from Hellenistic times to the fifteenth century, though most agree that they were "vulcanized" in some way.

There's better swimming and afternoon shade from exotic century plants at isolated **Pláka** beach, 2.5km west of Áyios Andónios. People pitch tents among the olive trees behind, despite a lack of toilet facilities and a brackish well; repeated attempts to transform this area into an official campsite have so far come to nought, though it seems it will be protected from permanent development as a "nature reserve".

Ayíou Pandelímona monastery and around

The paved road finally ends 8km west of Megálo Horió at the fortified monastery of **Ayíou Pandelímona**, founded in the fifteenth century for the sake of its miraculous spring. These days the place is not much frequented except for July 25–27, when long cement tables on the terrace below host the island's biggest festival. Its tower-gate and oasis setting nearly two hundred forbidding metres above the west coast are the most memorable features, though the eminently photogenic inner court boasts a *hokhláki* surface, and the church a fine tesselated marble floor. On the walls of the *katholikón*, an early eighteenth-century fresco shows the founder-builder holding a model of the monastery, while behind the ornately carved altar screen is a possibly earlier fresco of the Holy Trinity.

It used to be that you only had guaranteed access to the monastery if you came on regular Sunday minibus tours from Megálo Horió, but since 2000 a Serbian family has been living on the premises from April until late October; they also run a little drinks café on the festival terrace, and during peak season offer simple meals. The public minibus shows up here perhaps once or twice daily in season, but to heighten the sense of pilgrimage, it's recommended that you arrive on foot from Áyios Andónios. First you've twenty minutes along the shore to the little monastery of Panayía Kamarianí, then through half-abandoned terraces along the old path to the monastery for 45 minutes to a prominent pass with a stone chapel, and then a final twenty minutes down to the monastery gate (the last five minutes on the road). This route is shown correctly on Baz Ward's map.

An advanced trek: Ayíou Pandelímona to Éristos

Committed and experienced hill walkers can tackle the challenging path which curls around the southwest flank of Profítis Ilías (651m), Tílos' highest mountain, finishing three-plus hours later at Éristos. This begins, as signposted, beside the monastery; it's a well-surveyed route – one of the six up for revamping – with no real exposure or sharp drops, and extensive surviving stretches of the old *kalderími* still in place. But there's only one spring along the way, rather demoralizing scree at the start, and the wild feel of a remote traverse on a much larger island. In short, novices need not apply, and it's something best done in a group – in 1996 a lone traveller had to be rescued by helicopter.

The initial scree-slides are so bad that they've obliterated the original course of the trail, as shown on the old Italian ordnance survey maps; the first 25 minutes of the route are thus forced a bit further inland than you'd expect, with a tough climb past or even over the loose scree, until the grade slackens and you get back onto the proper original path. With the worst over, you spend the next twenty minutes threading through three successive, gentle passes; the second is the highest on this part of the route, and you catch a glimpse of the sea swirling around Tílos' southwesterly cape, far below. An hour along should find you at the top of the first little ravine draining down to Limenári; you can see this bay and the claw-like promontory beyond it, but not (yet) the beach at the head of the gulf. Twenty minutes later you reach the lone spring en route, inside a stone enclosure; the water should be potable from the spout, though there's often a dead goat near (or in) the trough. Continue descending, over some less obvious sections, past a dilapidated chapel to cross the bed of the main ravine draining to Limenári, one hour and forty minutes out – before you succumb to the temptation for a detour and swim, remember that you're barely half way to Éristos.

Greek script table

Tílos	Τήλος	ΤΗΛΟΣ
Ammóhosti	Αμμόχωστη	ΑΜΜΟΧΩΣΤΗ
Áyios Andónios	Άγιος Αντώνιος	ΑΓΙΟΣ ΑΝΤΩΝΙΟΣ
Áyios Pétros	Άγιος Πέτρος	ΑΓΙΟΣ ΠΕΤΡΟΣ
Áyios Séryios	Άγιος Σέργιος	ΑΓΙΟΣ ΣΕΡΓΙΟΣ
Éristos	Έριστος	ΕΡΙΣΤΟΣ
Harkadhió	Χαρκαδιό	ΧΑΡΚΑΔΙΟ
Kókkino	Κόκκινο	ΚΟΚΚΙΝΟ
Lethrá	Λεθρά	ΛΕΘΡΑ
Livádhia	Λιβάδια	ΛΙΒΑΔΙΑ
Megálo Horió	Μεγάλο Χωριό	ΜΕΓΑΛΟ ΧΩΡΙΟ
Mikró Horió	Μικρό Χωριό	ΜΙΚΡΟ ΧΩΡΙΟ
Moní Ayíou Pandelímona	Μονή Αγίου Παντελείμωνα	ΜΟΝΗ ΑΓΙΟΥ ΠΑΝΤΕΛΕΙΜΩΝΑ
Panayía Kamarianí	Παναγία Καμαριανή	ΠΑΝΑΓΙΑ ΚΑΜΑΡΙΑΝΗ
Pláka	Πλάκα	ΠΛΑΚΑ
Skáfi	Σκάφη	ΣΚΑΦΗ
Stavrós	Σταυρός	ΣΤΑΥΡΟΣ
Thólos	Θόλος	ΘΟΛΟΣ
Yerá	Γερά	ΓΕΡΑ

Now you climb again in earnest, partly along a revetted corniche path, to the southernmost point of the route at a final saddle, two hours and twenty minutes away from the monastery; bear northeast for the more gradual, final descent to your goal. Just under three hours along, the surveyed route debouches onto a track system, where a little sign cheerily informs those coming the opposite direction that it's three hours to the monastery. This is your last chance for a private swim, at Áyios Pétros bay. The main track system hugs the base of the mountain here; use an obvious side turning to get down to Éristos, three hours and a quarter after leaving Ayíou Pandelímona.

Tílos travel details

Island transport

Buses

The minibus schedule is posted in Livádhia's central square, usually on the door of *Yiorgos' Kafe–Bar* adjacent; however, it's not to be trusted implicitly, so confirm with the driver.

Inter-island transport

Key to ferry, catamaran and hydrofoil companies

DANE	*Dhodhekanisiakí Anónymi Navtiliakí Etería* (Dodecanesian Shipping Company)
G&A	G&A Ferries
KR	Kyriakoulis Hydrofoils
LZ	Laoumtzis Hydrofoils
NK	*Nissos Kalymnos*

Ferries

Tílos to: Kálymnos (1 weekly on G&A, 1 weekly on DANE, 2 weekly on NK; 4hr 15min–4hr 45min); Kastellórizo (1 weekly on G&A, 2 weekly on NK, via Rhodes; 7hr 30min); Kós (1 weekly on G&A, 1 weekly on DANE, 2 weekly on NK; 2hr 45min–3hr 15min); Léros (2 weekly on G&A or DANE; 6hr); Náxos (1 weekly on G&A; 9hr 30min); Níssyros (1 weekly on G&A, 2 weekly on NK; 1hr 15min–1hr 30min); Páros (1 weekly on G&A; 10hr 30min); Pátmos (1 weekly on G&A; 7hr 30min); Pireás (1 weekly on G&A, 1 weekly on DANE; 17–19hr); Rhodes (1 weekly on G&A, 1 weekly on DANE, 2 weekly on NK; 2hr 30min non-stop, 3hr 45min via Sými); Sými (1 weekly on G&A, 2 weekly on NK; 2hr–2hr 30min).

NB DANE or G&A ferries only call reliably from mid-June to late September. From early July to early Aug, the G&A ferry may also stop at Foúrni/Ikaría between Pátmos and Náxos.

Catamarans

The *Dodekanisos Express* serves Tílos at least once weekly (typically Wed) from May to Sept, linking it with Rhodes, Níssyros, Kós, Léros and Pátmos. Northbound departures around 10am, southbound around 6pm. The *Sea Star* typically doesn't start running until June, and while daily connections with Rhodes and Níssyros are promised, 3 weekly is a more realistic figure.

Hydrofoils

Tílos to: Hálki (1 weekly on LZ); Kálymnos (1 weekly on KR); Kós (1 weekly on KR, 1 weekly on LZ); Níssyros (1 weekly on LZ); Rhodes (1 weekly on KR, 1 weekly on LZ).

NB Hydrofoils have historically called here northbound and southbound on Sun and (less reliably) Wed or Sat.

Níssyros

Volcanic **Níssyros** is noticeably greener than its southern neighbours Tílos and Hálki and, unlike them, has proven attractive and wealthy enough to retain over eight hundred of its population year-round (down, though, from 10,000 in 1900, and 2500 just after World War II). While remittances from abroad (particularly Astoria, New York) are significant, most of the island's income is derived from the offshore islet of Yialí, towards Kós, essentially a vast lump of **pumice** slowly being chipped away by a couple of dozen Nissyrian miners. The rent collected by the municipality from Lava Ltd, the company with the quarry concession for Yialí, has engendered a sort of mini-Kuwait situation – the wealthiest per-capita welfare statelet in Europe, complete with publicly run bakery and pharmacy, plus a well-padded civil service. Under the circumstances, the Nissyrians bother little with agriculture other than keeping cows and pigs; the hillside terraces meticulously carved out for grain and grapes lie fallow, and wine is no longer made locally.

The main island's peculiar geology is potentially a source of other benefits: ΔEH, the Greek power corporation, spent the years between 1988 and 1992 sinking exploratory **geothermal** wells and attempting to convince the islanders of the benefits of cheap electricity. The locals rallied against the project, mindful of ΔEH's poor track record on Mílos in the Cyclades, which resulted in noxious fumes, industrial litter and land expropriation. Yet in 1991,

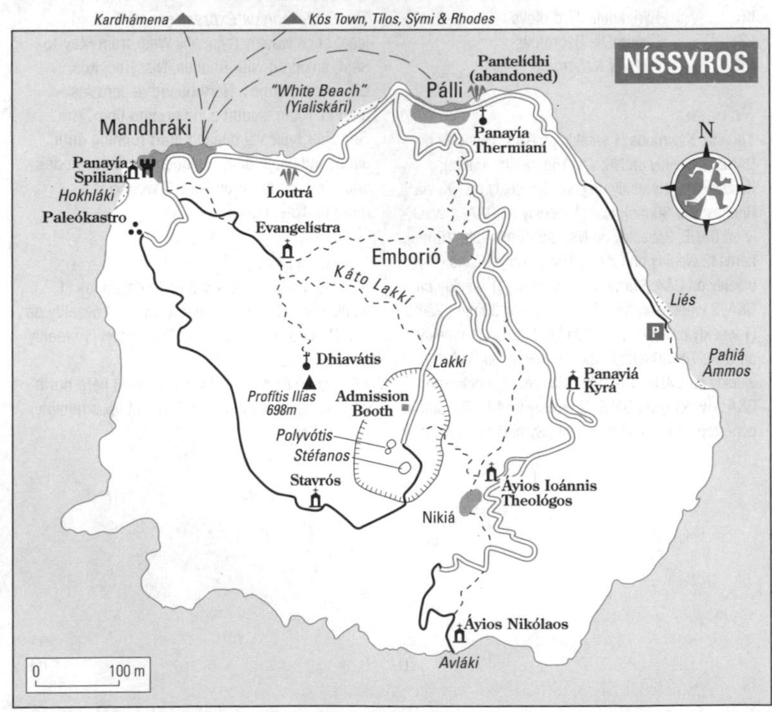

ΔΕΗ persuaded the municipality to bulldoze a new road of dubious necessity around the southwest flank of the island, damaging farmland and destroying a beautiful 700-year-old cobbled footpath (to their credit, many islanders now express considerable regret for this act). Metal debris from unsuccessful test bores also did little to endear them to the local populace.

In 1993, a local referendum went massively against the scheme, and ΔΕΗ, together with its Italian contractor, took the hint and retreated temporarily before returning in 1997 with tempting promises of job offers to locals, and yet another referendum – which again went (narrowly) against. Meanwhile, the desalination plant, reliant on expensive power from the fuel-oil generator, scarcely provides enough fresh water to spur a massive growth in package tourism; rain cisterns remain important. The relatively few tourists who stay the night, as opposed to the day-trippers from Kós, still find peaceful villages with a minimum of concrete eyesores, and a friendly if rather tight-knit population.

Níssyros also offers good **walking** opportunities through a countryside planted with oak or terebinth, on a network of trails fitfully marked and maintained with EU money; wherever you stroll you'll hear the contented grunting of pigs as they gorge themselves on acorns from the many oak trees. Autumn is a wonderful time, especially when the landscape has perked up after the first rains, though the late-January almond blossoming no longer occurs as the nut trees have unhappily died out.

Mandhráki

MANDHRÁKI is the deceptively large port and island capital, with blue patches of sea often visible (and audible) at the end of narrow streets swarming with cats (even by Greek-island standards), and lined with tightly packed houses whose brightly painted wooden balconies and shutters are mandated by law. Except for the tattier fringes near the ferry dock, where multiple souvenir shops and bad tavernas pitched at day-trippers leave a poor first impression, the bulk of the place is ramshackle, villagey and indifferent to tourism, arrayed around the community orchard or *kámbos* and overlooked by two ancient fortresses which protect it somewhat from the prevailing wind.

Into a corner of the nearer of these, the fourteenth-century **Knights' castle**, is wedged the little monastery of **Panayía Spilianí**, built on this spot in accordance with instructions from the Virgin herself, who appeared in a vision to one of the first Christian islanders. The monastery's prestige grew after raiding Saracens failed to discover vast quantities of silver secreted here in the form of a rich collection of Byzantine icons. During 1996–97, the Langadháki area just below was rocked by a series of earthquakes, damaging a score of venerable houses (mostly repaired), and rendering the small folklore museum homeless, though it was never really worth the admission fee for a couple of mannequins in traditional dress. A new combination archeological-ethnographical-historical **museum** has been built on the *kámbos* with money donated by the Nissyrian founder of the Vitex paint company, and should be ready for visitors by 2002.

As a defensive bastion, the seventh-century BC Doric **Paleókastro** (unrestricted access), twenty minutes' well-signposted walk out of Langadháki, is infinitely more impressive than the Knights' castle, and ranks as one of the more underrated ancient sites in Greece. You can clamber up onto the massive, polygonal-block walls, standing mostly to their original height, by means of a broad staircase beside the still-intact gateway.

Accommodation

You'll see a handful of **hotels** on your left as you disembark at the port, convenient (especially for yachties craving a night ashore) but hardly state of the art. Standards in the village itself, all of 400m ahead, are comparable; there's nothing on the island that's really above C-class standard, and you get the feeling that the Nissyrians are happy to keep matters that way.

The port

Polyvotis ⓣ02420/31 011, ⓕ31 204. Municipally run hotel, officially B-class but effectively C-class, which has biggish, neutral-decor rooms with fans and (mostly) knockout sea views. ❷

Romantzo ⓣ02420/31 340. Good-value simple but well-kept rooms with fridges and partial sea views. ❶

Three Brothers On the waterfront, opposite the *Romantzo* ⓣ02420/31 344. Not quite as well kept as its rival, but you do have unobstructed sea views in most cases. ❶

Central Mandhráki

Porfyris ⓣ02420/31 376, ⓕ31 176. Mandhráki's most comfortable hotel accommodation overlooks the sea and *kámbos*, with gardens and a large swimming pool. ❹

Studios Volcano Contacts as for the *Romantzo*. Fully self-catering units about halfway into town. ❸

Sunset/Iliovasilema Near the converted windmill ⓣ02420/31 159 or 097/2141344. Adequate, quiet studios – one of the few places actually on the shore. ❸

Ypapandi In the town proper, ⓣ02420/31 485 or visit *Taverna Panorama*. "Hotel" (really *dhomátia*) that's the main in-town budget option, in a quiet hillside location, but small, very basic and often full. ❶

Eating and drinking

Nissyrian culinary **specialities** include pickled caper greens, honey, *pittiá* (chickpea croquettes), and *soumádha*, an almond-syrup drink widely sold in recycled wine bottles, though it's now made from imported almonds rather than the extinct local bitter almonds, and must be consumed within three months of purchase. When eating out, it's best to give all of the commercialized, shoddy shoreline **tavernas** a miss – simple, old-fashioned *Manolis & Maria Papatsou* is an honourable exception, often with fresh fish – in favour of more genuine haunts inland. Top of the heap is evening-only, musical ouzerí *Iy Fabrika* (closed Thurs), with indoor/outdoor tables by season and family recipes from founder Patti preserved by second owner Manolis, also the miners' chef on Yialí. Fifty years ago this was a *patitíri* (wine press) and wine shop, and the staff have returned it to something like its original function. On their days off, the staff here go eat at summer-evenings-only, resolutely simple *Panayiotis* (no sign) in Langadháki, with lovingly prepared home-style dishes served at a half-dozen outside tables. Pricier runners-up include *Panorama*, with bean and mushroom salad and suckling pig on offer, or *Irini* on lively, ficus-shaded Platía Ilikioméni, with more involved *mayireftá* unavailable elsewhere. Finally, little *Taverna Nissiros*, the oldest eatery in town, is always busy despite predictably average grill quality. Good **breakfasts** can be had at *Tony's*, another exception to the pattern of waterfront tourist traps. Focuses of **nightlife** are Platía Ilikioméni and a string of *barákia* on the shore at Lefkándio district west of *Manolis*, most popular of these is the *Enallax*.

Other practicalities

The most useful of three **travel agencies** is Dhiakomihalis (ⓣ02420/31 459), which acts as a representative for DANE ferries, the *Nissos Kalymnos* and all hydrofoils, rents cars and exchanges money. Kentris, near the town hall, handles G&A ferries and Olympic Airways tickets. There's a **post office** at the port and a single **bank** in town, but this lacks a cash machine and levies stiff commissions, as does Dhiakomihalis. At the base of the jetty is the **bus stop**, with (theoretically) up to four daily departures to the hill villages and five to Pálli; otherwise, there are two set-rate **taxis** and three outlets for **scooter rental**, among which Alfa, or John and John (branch of latter also in Pálli) provide the best service – rates begin at €10.30 per day. There's just one source of **fuel** on the island, between Loutrá and Pálli.

East of Mandhráki: the coast

Beaches on Níssyros are in even shorter supply than water, so much so that excursions are occasionally run to a sandy cove on **Áyios Andónios** islet, opposite the mining machinery on **Yialí**. Closer at hand, the 150-metre, seaweed-strewn beach of **Hokhláki**, behind the Knights' castle, is accessible by a five-minute stroll along the walkway from the northwest corner of town; the black pebbles here get smaller at the far end, where nudism is tolerated near the objets-trouvés folly, though the wind picks up in the afternoon. The town "beach" of **Miramáre** at the east edge of the harbour is merely a lido seasonally filled with sand, and a last resort in any weather.

It's best to head east along the main road, passing the refurbished spa of **Loutrá** (hot mineral-water bath only by doctor's referral) and the smallish "**White Beach**" (properly Yialiskári), 2km along and dwarfed by an ugly, unwelcoming eponymous hotel. The beach name is a bit of a misnomer, as its high percentage of black sand creates a decidedly salt-and-pepper appearance. The Loutrá spa, though itself sporadically shut for restoration, is well worth a stop for its "snack bar" at the far end of the building, really an **ouzerí** with generous portions of reasonably priced salads, fried appetizers, seafood and meat.

A kilometre or so further, 4km in total from Mandhráki, the fishing village of **PÁLLI** makes an excellent hangout at lunchtime, when the port fills with trippers, though the yachts that call here have driven prices up. Tavernas here are multiplying, but stick with the two long-term favourites: the less expensive *Ellinis*, with spit-roasted meat by night, grilled fish in season and simple rooms upstairs (Ⓣ02420/31 453; ❷), or the adjacent *Afroditi* (aka *Nikos & Tsambika*), with big portions of grills and *mayireftá*, Cretan bulk wine and excellent home-made desserts. They've also got a house to rent, all or in part (Ⓣ02420/31 242; €41 for the entire house). The scooter-rental outlet (branch of John and John's), an excellent bakery cranking out rare brown bread and fine pies (branch in Mandhráki on the fountain platía), and modest nightlife east along the quay (try *Captain's House)* also make Pálli worth considering as a base.

A tamarisk-shaded, dark-sand **beach** extends east of Pálli, kept well groomed of late and improving as it goes, to the abandoned Pantelídhi spa, behind which the little grotto-chapel of **Panayía Thermianí** is tucked inside the vaulted remains of a Roman baths complex, now partly open to the sky and with a salt-pool grotto at the rear. To reach Níssyros' best **beaches**, continue in this direction for an hour on foot (or 20min by moped along the partly surfaced road), past an initially discouraging seaweed- and cowpat-strewn shoreline, to the delightful cove of **Liés** (snack bar *Oasis* June 15–Sept 15), just beyond which the now-dirt road ends at a large car park. Walking a further fifteen minutes along a dusty pumice trail around the headland brings you to the idyllic, 300-metre expanse of **Pahiá Ámmos**, with coarse, grey-pink sand heaped in dunes, limited shade at the far end and a large colony of free campers (and naturists) in summer, the only time the place is much frequented. Off season it's so secluded, in fact, that smugglers from Turkey have taken to burying drugs on the beach for their Greek cohorts to retrieve, so it's best not to dig up any suspicious packages.

The interior

The central, dormant **volcano** gives Níssyros its special character and fosters the growth of the abundant vegetation – no stay would be complete without a visit. When excursion boats arrive from Kós, several agency coaches and usually one of the public buses are pressed into service to take customers into the interior. These tours tend to monopolize the crater floor between 11am and 2pm, so if you want solitude, use early morning or late afternoon scheduled buses to Nikiá (two or three daily continue to the crater floor), a scooter or your own two feet to get there.

Emborió and Panayiá Kyrá

The road up from Pálli towards the volcano winds first past the virtually abandoned village and crumbled fortress of **EMBORIÓ**, where pigs and free-ranging cattle (a major driving hazard) far outnumber people, though the place is slowly being bought up and restored by Athenians and foreigners. New owners are often surprised to discover natural saunas, heated by volcanic steam, in the basements of the crumbling houses; at the outskirts of the village there's a signposted public **steam bath** in a grotto, its entrance outlined in white paint. The only other "amenity" is a **taverna** on the little square, *To Balkoni tou Emboriou* (sporadically May–Sept), which has a limited menu but outdoor tables on the namesake balcony overlooking the volcanic caldera.

If you're descending **on foot** to Pálli from here, an old *kalderími*, beginning at the sharp bend below the "sauna", offers an attractive short cut of the four-kilometre road. You can also drop south into the volcanic area along another *kalderími* starting behind *To Balkoni tou Emboriou*, indicated from the platía; in under half an hour this emerges at the last road bend below the village, leaving you with another quarter-hour or so to the craters (see opposite).

About halfway between Emborió and Nikiá, a signposted side road leads down to the island's third major monastery (after Spilaní and Áyios Ioánnis), **Panayiá Kyrá**. Unfortunately, the place is usually locked except around the time of the August 14–15 festival – the island's best – but you can still enjoy the fine setting on fertile terraces overlooking Pahiá Ámmos (to which there is no obvious path down). Over the gate to the courtyard looms a fortification tower; the medieval *katholikón* stands off-centre, on the south side of the compound.

Nikiá and Áyios Ioánnis Theológos

NIKIÁ, the large village on the east side of the volcano's caldera, is with sixty permanent inhabitants more of a going concern than Emborió, and its spectacular situation 14km from Mandhráki offers views out to Tílos as well as across the caldera. There are three places to **drink** (and, modestly, **eat**) here: *Porta* (summer evenings only) and *Platia* on or near the engagingly round *hokhláki* plaza, or *Nikia,* at the entrance to the village.

By the turnaround, signs point to the 45-minute trail, initially a stair-path, descending to the crater floor. A few minutes downhill, you can fork right for the brief detour to the eyrie-like monastery of **Áyios Ioánnis Theológos**, with a shady tree and yet another perspective on the volcano. The picnic benches and utility buildings come to life at the annual festival on the evening of September 25.

Incidentally, it is not worth following signs towards **Avláki**, 5km south of Nikiá. This is an abandoned fishing hamlet of about a dozen houses around the unspectacular monastery of **Áyios Nikólaos**. Its surroundings are dreary and barren, with no beach or easy swimming opportunities, and (after the first four paved kilometres) the road down is rough – the old path from Nikiá short-cuts most of it. Much-touted hot springs in the shallows, off to the left as you face the sea, are tricky to find and (unlike similar ones at Kós and Ikaría) have scant effect on sea temperature: in short, most will reckon the trip down a waste of time and petrol.

The volcano

To **drive** directly to the volcanic area of **Lákki**, 14km in total from Mandhráki, take the signposted road which veers off to the right just past Emborió. Whether you approach from this direction or on foot from Nikiá, a sulphurous stench drifts out to meet you as fields and scrub gradually give way to lifeless, caked powder. The sunken main crater of **Stéfanos** is extraordinary, a moonscape of grey, brown and sickly yellow; there is another, less visited double crater (dubbed **Polyvótis**) to the west, equally dramatic, with a clear trail leading up to it from the access road. The perimeters of both are pocked with tiny blowholes from which jets of steam puff constantly and around which form little pincushions of pure sulphur crystals.

The whole floor of the larger crater seems to hiss, and standing in the middle you can hear something akin to a huge cauldron bubbling away below you. According to legend, this is the groaning of Polyvotis, a titan crushed here by Poseidon under a huge rock torn from Kós. Hardly less prosaic are the facts of a prehistoric **eruption**, when the volcano apparently blew its top Krakatoa-style; the most recent hiccups, which produced steam, ash and earthquakes, occurred in 1422, 1873, 1888 and 1933, and apparently Polyvótis crater, not the more obvious Stéfanos, was responsible for these.

A small, tree-shaded **snack bar** in the centre of the wasteland operates whenever tour groups are around. A €1.50 admission is payable at a small booth, flanking the access road just before you get to the café and staffed during most daylight hours.

Island walks

Since the destruction of the old direct trail between the volcano and Mandhráki, pleasant options for **walking** back to town from the interior are limited and can involve a certain amount of asphalt-tramping. That said, there are still quite a number of worthwhile hikes, many of these indicated on Beate and Jürgen Franke's locally available, GPS-drawn topographical map (free). With the exception of routes beginning from Evangelístra monastery, trailheads are easier to find going downhill – often there are crude, handpainted signposts – so the first step will probably be to take a bus or taxi (€10 per car) to Nikiá or Emborió.

Nikiá to Mandhráki via Stavrós

A few people do still attempt to walk back direct to Mandhráki from Nikiá, a three-hour undertaking. Matters begin well enough along a narrow path exiting the south end of the village, which emerges after 45 minutes at a weather-

Unusual round platía at Nikiá, Níssyros

data station and a rough track linking the caldera with the isolated monastery of **Stavrós**, where a large *xenónas*, or inn, sees tenants only for its September 13–14 festival. You can tramp off west from here through the hills on the jeep track, but it's no comparison to the old *kalderími*, and in season you'll have to contend with lots of speeding yobbos on dirt-bikes.

Nikiá to Emborió

This takes just under ninety minutes, with a short stretch of road walking towards the end, but presupposes experience on easier walks and good orienteering skills, as the trail has been long abandoned and is not shown on the German-made map. Descend from Nikiá towards the volcano and bear right in the direction of Theológos monastery, but then take the left fork by the wooden gate before reaching it. The path ambles along through neglected terraces on the northeast flank of Lákki, without much altitude change, occasionally obstructed by landslide debris and thick vegetation; you'll eventually emerge after 50–55 minutes by some phone and power lines on the modern Emborió-Nikiá road, just opposite the drive serving a small army watchpost. Don't bother hunting for a secondary trail parallel to the road, there isn't one; you must asphalt-tramp for about 1km (15min) to the turnoff for Lakkí, where the onward trail continues conspicuously uphill into Emborió.

The volcano to Mandhráki via Evangelístra

From the admission booth, proceed north along the main crater access road for just over 1km to find the start of a clear, crudely marked path which climbs steeply to a pass, then maintains altitude along the north flank of the small volcanic **Káto Lákki** gulch, and then emerges after ninety minutes at the important monastery of **Evangelístra** with a giant terebinth tree enclosed in a concrete apron just outside. Beyond Evangelístra, you must walk about a kilometre on the access road – now mostly paved – before the old path kicks in for the final half-hour down to Mandhráki. Look sharp at curves to find the old walled-in path which initially just short-cuts the road, and then for quite a long stretch loops above the port well away from the road, finally curling around to emerge on the fourth terrace above the school.

Evangelístra to Profítis Ilías

Evangelístra – where reports of a pilgrim hostel are decidedly premature – also marks the start of the two-hour, round-trip detour up **Profítis Ilías**, at 698m the island's summit. From the pepper-tree roundabout head west about 150m, then left on the start of the rough path. This was cleaned in 1998 and re-marked with cairns and white-painted arrows or crosses, so it's hard to get lost. A few minutes before the shrine on the peak, the farm and chapel of **Dhiavátis**, tucked into a small hollow with huge trees, makes a good picnic spot or emergency bivouac.

Evangelístra to Emborió

Just before arrival at the Evangelístra terebinth tree, coming from the volcano, a paint-splodged path heads right or northeast towards Emborió, mostly along the north flank of Káto Lákki. This route takes 45 minutes and is shown correctly on the German-produced map, though despite haphazard marking and cleaning the trail is still rough or even nonexistent in parts – nonetheless an enjoyable and useful link. You'll enter the village from the top, near the cemetery and small castle; it's marginally easier to find the way in reverse.

Greek script table

Níssyros	Νίσυρος	ΝΙΣΥΡΟΣ
Avláki	Αυλάκι	ΑΥΛΑΚΙ
Áyios Andónios	Άγιος Αντώνιος	ΑΓΙΟΣ ΑΝΤΩΝΙΟΣ
Áyios Ioánnis Theológos	Άγιος Ιοάννης Θεολόγος	ΑΓΙΟΣ ΙΟΑΝΝΗΣ ΘΕΟΛΟΓΟΣ
Emborió	Εμπορειό	ΕΜΠΟΡΕΙΟ
Evangelístra	Ευαγγελίστρα	ΕΥΑΓΓΕΛΙΣΤΡΑ
Hokhláki	Χοχλάκι	ΧΟΧΛΑΚΙ
(Káto) Lakkí	(Κάτο) Λακκί	(ΚΑΤΟ) ΛΑΚΚΙ
Liés	Λιές	ΛΙΕΣ
Loutrá	Λουτρά	ΛΟΥΤΡΑ
Mandhráki	Μανδράκι	ΜΑΝΔΡΑΚΙ
Nikiá	Νικιά	ΝΙΚΙΑ
Pahiá Ámmos	Παχιά Άμμος	ΠΑΧΙΑ ΑΜΜΟΣ
Pálli	Πάλοι	ΠΑΛΟΙ
Panayiá Kyrá	Παναγία Κυρά	ΠΑΝΑΓΙΑ ΚΥΡΑ
Panayía Thermianí	Παναγία Θερμιανή	ΠΑΝΑΓΙΑ ΘΕΡΜΙΑΝΗ
Stavrós	Σταυρός	ΣΤΑΥΡΟΣ
Yialí	Γιαλί	ΓΙΑΛΙ

Níssyros travel details

Island transport

Buses

Mandhráki to: Emborió (4 daily); Nikiá (4 daily); Pálli (5 daily). Departures are well spaced (eg, 7am, 10am, 1.45pm, 5pm) and at least 2 uphill trips tend to include the volcano floor.

Inter-island transport

Key to ferry and hydrofoil companies

KR Kyrakoulis Hydrofoils
LZ Laoumtzis Hydrofoils
DANE *Dhodhekanisiakí Anónymi Navtiliakí Etería* (Dodecanesian Shipping Company)
G&A G&A Ferries
NK *Nissos Kalymnos*

Kaïkia and excursion boats

Níssyros to: Kardhámena, Kós (almost daily in season, 3.30–4pm, or 4–7 weekly to Kós Town at the same time). 2–4 mornings weekly the unpublicized islanders' "shopping" kaïki, the *Chrissula*, departs Pálli at 7am, Mandhráki half an hour later. Unless you're bound for the airport it's not necessarily cheaper to use Kardhámena services when you include the cost of a bus to Kós Town – €7.50 to Kardhámena on an excursion boat, versus €9 to Kós. Journey time to Kardhámena 1hr 30min, to Kós Town 2hr 15min.

Ferries

Níssyros to: Astypálea (1 weekly on DANE, unreliable; 2 weekly on NK via Kálymnos; 2hr 30min–4hr); Kálymnos (1 weekly on G&A, 1 weekly on DANE, 2 weekly on NK; 3hr 45min–4hr); Kastellórizo (1 weekly on G&A, 2 weekly on NK, via Rhodes; 8hr); Kós (1 weekly on G&A, 1 weekly on DANE, 2 weekly on NK; 1hr 45min–2hr); Léros (1 weekly on G&A, 1 weekly on DANE; 4hr 45min); Náxos (1 weekly on G&A; 9hr); Páros (1 weekly on G&A; 10hr); Pátmos (1 weekly on G&A, 1 weekly on DANE; 6hr); Pireás (1 weekly on G&A, 1 weekly on DANE; 16–17hr); Rhodes (1 weekly on G&A, 1 weekly on DANE, 2 weekly on NK;

3hr–4hr 30min); Sými (1 weekly on G&A, 2 weekly on NK; 2hr 15min–3hr); Tílos (1 weekly on G&A, 2 weekly on NK; 45min–1hr).

Catamarans

Níssyros to: Rhodes, Tílos, Kós, Léros, Pátmos, Kálymnos (1 weekly, usually Weds, on *Dodekanisos Express*, May to mid-Sept); Tílos, Rhodes (2–3 weekly on *Sea Star*, June–Sept only).

Hydrofoils

Níssyros to: Hálki, Tílos (1 weekly on LZ); to Kós, Rhodes (2 weekly, on LZ and KR – latter reliably on Sun).

3

Kós and the northern Dodecanese

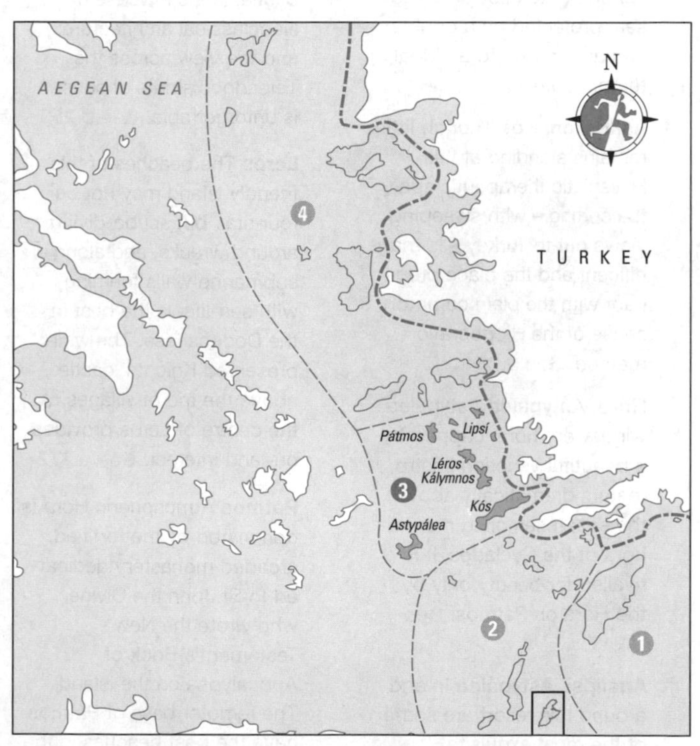

CHAPTER 3

Highlights

* **Dhíkeos range, Kós** The hike up to Khristós peak is increasingly popular; your reward is arguably the most stunning view in all the Dodecanese. See p.237

* **Brós Thermá, Kós** After your alpine exertions, relax in these shoreline hot springs which flow into the sea, protected by a boulder ring and mixing to an ideal temperature. See p.233

* **Asklepion, Kós** Though little remains standing at this Hellenistic therapeutic spa, the setting – with sweeping views out to Turkey – is magnificent and the place pregnant with the plain common sense of the Hippocratic method. See p.234

* **Hóra, Astypálea** Astypálea's windswept hóra, capped by a beautiful Venetian kástro, teeters dramatically above the sea; resembling more a hóra of the Cyclades, it is rivalled for beauty only by the Hóra on Pátmos. See p.249

* **Análipsi, Astypálea** In and around this resort are some of the most exquisite mosaics in the Dodecanese; on the floor of a Byzantine bathhouse, and at a remoter basilica, you can see zodiacal signs and cavorting dolphins. See p.253

* **Kálymnos** The interior of this harshly contoured island offers meaty treks for the well-prepared; the capital of Póthia, despite its big-town bustle, is a showcase of Neoclassical architecture; and the view across the Télendhos straits at sunset is unforgettable. See p.255

* **Léros** The beaches of this friendly island may not be four-star, but scuba-diving around wrecks, and along submarine walls teeming with sea-life, is the best in the Dodecanese. The well-preserved Knights' castle above the trio of villages at the centre of Léros provides on-land interest. See p.272

* **Pátmos** Atmospheric Hóra is dominated by the fortified, arcaded monastery dedicated to St John the Divine, who wrote the New Testament's Book of Apocalypse on the island. The remoter bays of Pátmos have the best beaches in the northern Dodecanese. See p.280

3

Kós and the northern Dodecanese

Compared to teeming Rhodes and its often cosy neighbours, **Kós and the northern Dodecanese** fall somewhere in between. Though by no stretch of the imagination unspoilt, sandy **Kós** feels calmer than Rhodes, partly because in roughly one-third the area of Rhodes, with one-quarter of the population, there's perhaps one-sixth as much going on. However, together with Níssyros it forms an *eparhía* (a Greek county), and it's also the transport hub of the region, with the only international airport in this chapter; all packages arranged on its neighbours are of necessity routed through here. If you choose to spend your entire vacation on Kós, you'll find it has the best beaches of these half-dozen isles, ample creature comforts and distractions, plus surprisingly wild scenery on the slopes of the third-highest mountain in the Dodecanese.

The smaller islands fanning out northwest from Kós, except for **Psérimos** – overrun, like Sými, with organized day-trips – lack the intimacy of the southern Dodecanese, though their larger scale means reliable bus services, consistent scooter rentals, and a wider choice of resorts.

Kálymnos, just across the straits from sandy Kós, could hardly be more different: a limestone-core, seafaring island famous for its sponge-gathering tradition. Only since the late 1980s has it developed a tourist industry at its westerly beaches and on the peacefully car-free islet of **Télendhos** just opposite. **Léros**, a geological continuation immediately northeast of Kálymnos, across an even narrower channel, has long had local tourism inhibited by a sinister institutional reputation, but up close it proves welcoming and varied in its landscapes and townscapes, the latter including some of the best Italian Art Deco buildings in the Dodecanese.

Astypálea and Pátmos, out at the western fringes of this group, are more typical of the adjacent Cyclades archipelago in terms of architecture and general ambience. **Astypálea**, to all intents and purposes synonymous with its stunningly picturesque *hóra*, is protected from blatant exploitation by problematic access and a skeletal road system, while **Pátmos**, with its imposing medieval monuments and excellent beaches, is not surprisingly the most frequented island in this chapter after Kós.

Lipsí, formerly a backwater dependency east of Pátmos, with a single village and a few beaches, has lately awoken to tourism with a vengeance; by contrast,

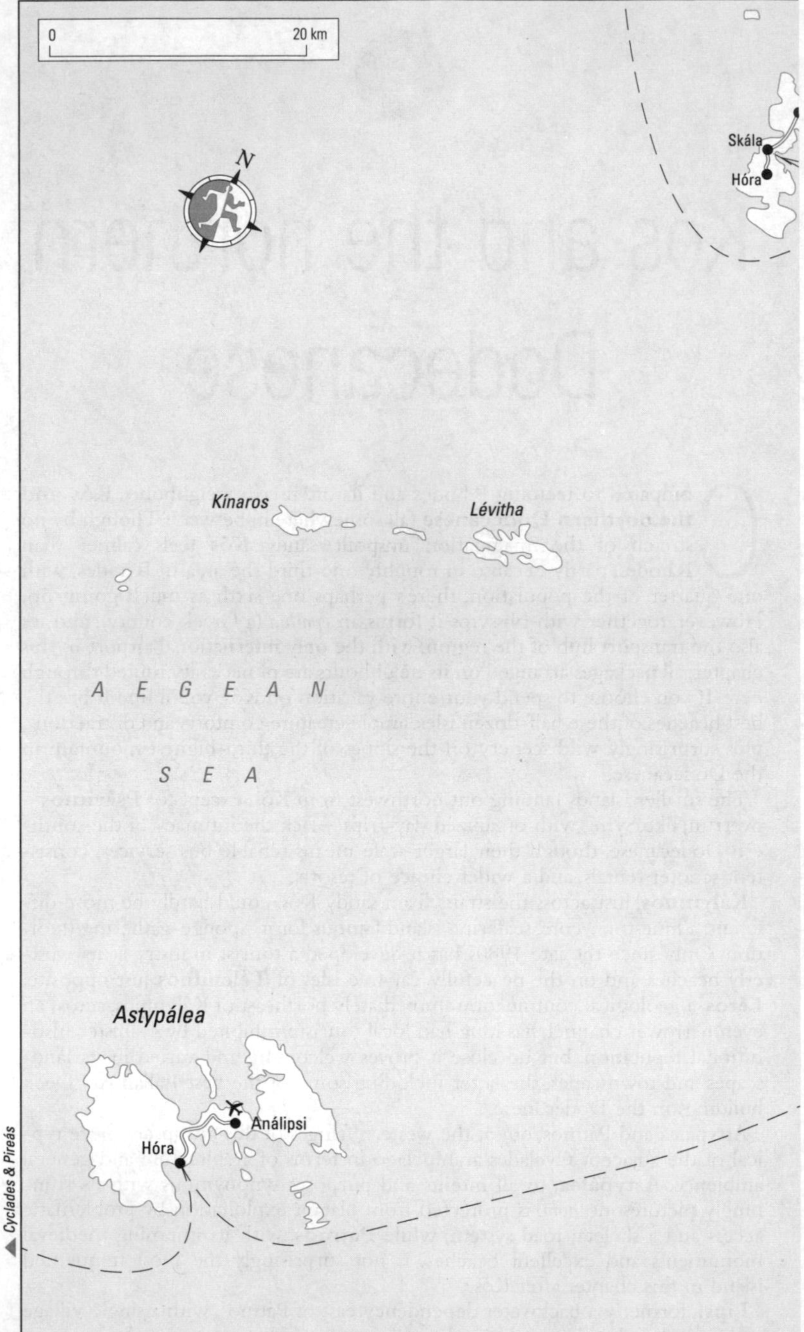
Pireás
0
20 km
N
Skála
Hóra
Kínaros
Lévitha
A E G E A N
S E A
Astypálea
Análipsi
Hóra
Cyclades & Pireás

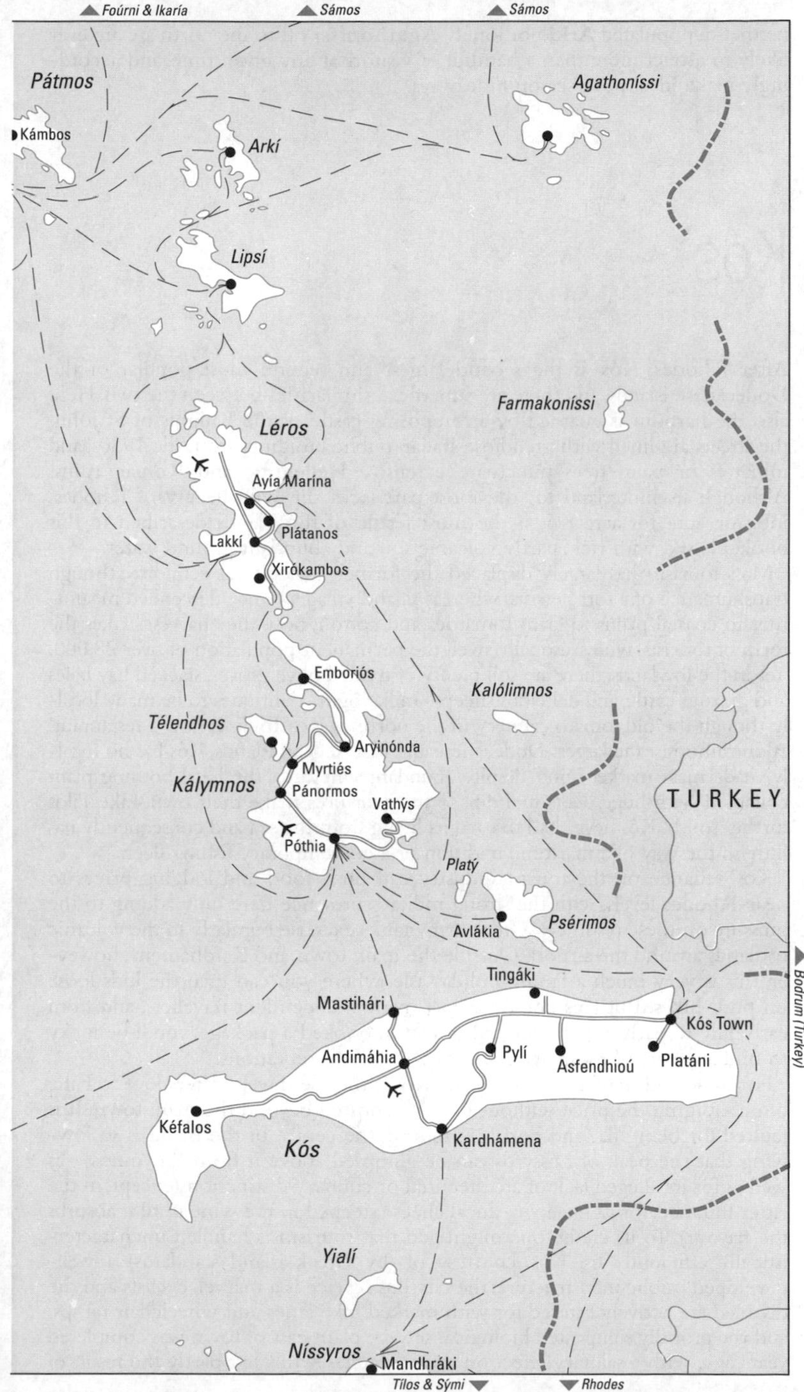
Foúrni & Ikaría
Sámos
Sámos
Pátmos
Kámbos
Arkí
Agathoníssi
Lipsí
Farmakoníssi
Léros
Ayía Marína
Plátanos
Lakkí
Xirókambos
Emboriós
Kalólimnos
Télendhos
Aryinónda
Myrtiés
Kálymnos
Pánormos
TURKEY
Vathýs
Póthia
Platý
Avlákia
Psérimos
Bodrum (Turkey)
Tingáki
Mastihári
Kós Town
Pylí
Asfendhioú
Platáni
Andimáhia
Kéfalos
Kardhámena
Kós
Yialí
Níssyros
Mandhráki
Tílos & Sými
Rhodes

neither depopulated **Arkí** nor lonely **Agathoníssi** off to the north are are ever likely to attract more than a handful of visitors at any given time, and accordingly make ideal peak-season hideaways.

Kós

After Rhodes, **Kós** is the second largest and second most popular of the Dodecanese islands, and there are superficial similarities between the two. Here also the harbour is guarded by an imposing castle of the Knights of St John, the streets are lined with grandiose Italian public buildings from the 1930s, and minarets or palm trees punctuate extensive Hellenistic and Roman ruins. Although its hinterland for the most part lacks the wild beauty of Rhodes' interior, acre for acre Kós is the most fertile of the islands described in this book, blessed with rich, partly volcanic soil and abundant ground water.

Mass tourism has largely displaced the former agricultural economy, though transhumance of a sort persists: whereas inland villagers once descended in summer to coastal plains to farm tomatoes and cotton, now the "harvest" takes the form of tourists, who seasonally swell the permanent population of over 28,000. Yet in the lowlands, there are still plenty of tended olive groves, stacked hay bales and grazing cattle, and delicious sheeps'-milk yogurt continues to be made locally, though the old tomato cannery in the north of Kós Town is now a restaurant. Alone amongst the largest Dodecanese and east Aegean islands, Kós has no locally made mass-market wine, despite abundant vineyards; the local bottling plant collapsed with huge debts in 1998, so most farmers make their own. Like Tílos further south, Kós never had to earn its living from the sea and consequently has little in the way of a maritime tradition or a contemporary fishing fleet.

Kós' reliance on the tourist industry can push food and lodging prices to near-Rhodes levels, with the strong military presence here only adding to the pressure on these resources; Greek army tanks exercise regularly in the volcanic badlands around the airport. Outside the main town and Kardhámena, however, this is very much a family-holiday isle, where you can turn the kids loose on push-bikes. But Kós doesn't attract many independent travellers, and from early July to early September, unless you've booked a package, you'll be lucky to find any sort of room at all without advance reservations.

For these and the following reasons, Kós is the isle travel writers love to hate, often savaging the place without having ventured beyond the main town. It is faulted for being flat and boring – indeed, the centre of the island is so low-lying that the peak of Níssyros can be glimpsed above it from Kálymnos – as well as for its alleged lack of architectural or culinary distinction (except, in the latter instance, for its *krasótyri* – local cheese steeped in red wine until it absorbs the flavour). To its credit, one might add that tourism is handled uncharacteristically efficiently on Kós, courtesy of (by Greek-island standards) a well-developed public infrastructure: the city bus service is a marvel, cyclists and the disabled are actively catered for with marked bike lanes and wheelchair ramps, and the proudly signposted biological sewage plant east of town was completed years ago, with a salutary effect on town beaches – this last partly the result of

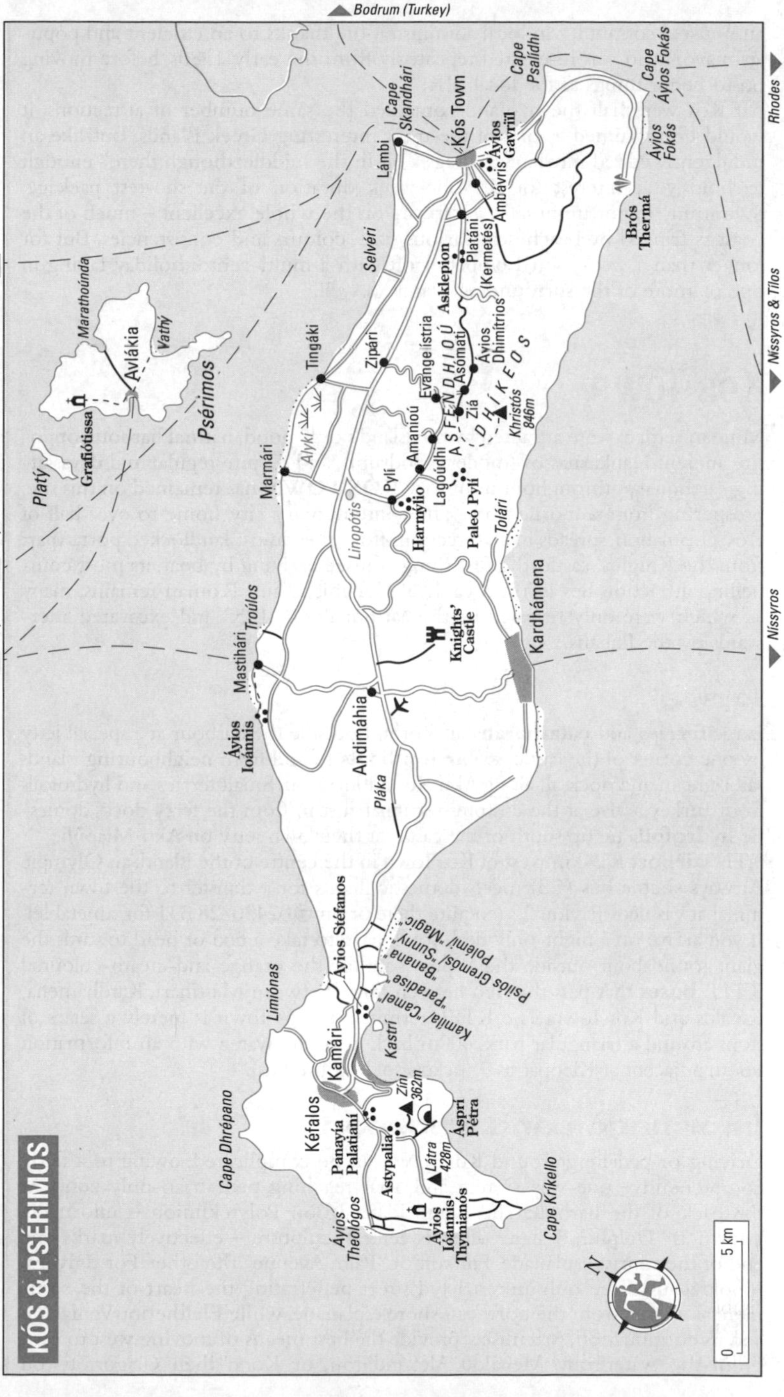

KÓS & PSÉRIMOS

Kálymnos
Kálymnos & Léros
Léros
Platý
Grafiótissa
Marathoúnda
Avlákia
Vathý
Psérimos
Cape Dhrépano
Áyios Ioánnis
Mastihári
Troúlos
Marmári
Limiónas
Kéfalos
Kamári
Áyios Stéfanos
Alykí
Tingáki
Áyios Theológos
Panayía Palatianí
Andimáhia
Linopótis
Selvéri
Lámbi
Cape Skandhári
Bodrum (Turkey)
Zipári
Pláka
Pylí
Astypalia
Zíni 362m
Kastrí
Harmýlio
Amanioú
Evangelístria
Kamíla/ "Camel"
"Paradise"
"Banana"
"Sunny"
Psilós Gremós/ Polémi/ "Magic"
Áyios Ioánnis Thymianós
Látra 428m
Áspri Pétra
Knights' Castle
Lagoúdhi
ASFENDHIOÚ
Asómati
Asklepion
Kós Town
Paleó Pylí
Ziá
DHÍKEOS
Áyios Dhimítrios
Plátani (Kermetés)
Ambávris
Áyios Gavriíl
Tolári
Khristós 846m
Cape Psalídhi
Kardhámena
Cape Kríkello
Brós Thermá
Áyios Fokás
Cape Áyios Fokás
N
0 5 km
Níssyros
Níssyros & Tílos
Rhodes

an unusual continuity in local administration, thanks to an efficient and popular mayor who was re-elected repeatedly from the early 1980s, before moving on to better things as the local MP.

If Kós were half the size and contained the same number of attractions, it would be acclaimed as one of the most interesting Greek islands. But like an indulgently edited movie, Kós drags a bit in the middle, though there's enough to hold your interest for the one-week duration of the shortest package. Swimming opportunities, for a start, are on the whole excellent – much of the coast is fringed by beaches of various sizes, colours and consistencies. But for longer than a week, you'd be better off with a multi-centre holiday, taking in one or more of the surrounding islands as well.

Kós Town

Minoan settlers were attracted by the island's only good, natural harbour, opposite ancient Halikarnassos (modern Bodrum), and despite regular and devastating earthquakes throughout its history, **KÓS TOWN** has remained on this site, prospering from seaborne trade. The contemporary city, home to over half of Kós' population, spreads in all directions from the almost landlocked port. Apart from the Knights' castle, the first thing you see arriving by boat, its most compelling attraction lies in the wealth of Hellenistic and Roman remains, many of which were only revealed by the earthquake of 1933 and excavated afterwards by the Italians.

Arrival

Large **ferries** and **catamarans** anchor just outside the harbour at a special jetty by one corner of the castle; **excursion boats** to and from neighbouring islands sail right in and dock all along Aktí Koundouriótou. Small ferries and hydrofoils from Turkey arrive at the customs terminal, just in from the ferry dock; domestic **hydrofoils** tie up south of the castle, at their own jetty on Aktí Miaoúli.

The **airport** is 24km west of Kós Town in the centre of the island; an Olympic Airways shuttle bus (€3) meets domestic flights for a transfer to the town terminal at Vassiléos Pávlou 22 (enquire there or on ⓣ02420/28 331 for timetable). If you arrive on a flight-only deal, you'll have to take a taxi or head towards the giant roundabout outside the airport gate for the orange-and-cream-coloured KTEL **buses** that pass through here en route between Mastihári, Kardhámena, Kéfalos and Kós Town. The KTEL terminal in Kós Town is merely a series of stops around a triangular park, 400m back from the water, with an information booth adjacent at Kleopátras 7 (tickets sold on the bus).

Information and transport

Driving or pedalling around Kós Town can be complicated, owing to a fairly comprehensive one-way system and a far-reaching pedestrian-only zone. At the back of the harbour, the round Platía Iróön Polytekhníou – informally known as "Dolphin Square" after its central sculpture – effectively marks one end of the tourist esplanade, Finíkon or "Palm Avenue" the other. For **drivers**, Ippokrátous is the only unrestricted street penetrating the heart of the commercial district from the northeast shore esplanade, while Eleftheríou Venizélou and its continuation, Artemisías, provide the best means of moving west to east. From the waterfront, Megálou Alexándhrou, or Koráï then Grigoríou toú

KÓS TOWN

▲ A (100m) & B
▲ C D E & Lámbi (2km)
Campsite (1500m), Psalídhi, Áyios Fokás, Brós Thermá, 9 (200m) & Z (300m) ▶
◀ Villages & Asklepion
Catholic Cemetery ▼
▼ X, Ambávris & Platáni
▼ Y
a 2km

ACCOMMODATION	
Afendoulis	8
Alexis	1
Anna	3
Kamelia	5
Maritina	7
Phaethon	4
Theodhorou	9
M Tselepi	6
Veroniki	2

PLATÍAS	
Ayías Paraskevís	D
Dhiagóras	F
'Dolphin'	A
Eleftherías	C
Kazoúli	B
K. Paleológou	E

RESTAURANTS, CAFÉS & BARS	
Café Aenaos	M
Ambavris	X
Apoplous	Z
Armonia	R
Australia-Sydney	S
Barbas	T
Beach Boys	B
Blues Brothers	L
Central/Kentriko	N
Dell Arte	P
Fashion Club	J
Four Roses	O
Frangoulis	Y
Fresko Gelateria	V
Heaven	E
Hellas	I
Kalua	D
Koakon	H
O Kostas	K
Kyvotos	W
Mavroumatis	a
Mylos	C
Nikolaos O Psaras	F
Noufara	A
Petrino	Q
Pote tin Kyriaki	U
Taurus	G

Old Tomato Cannery
Ferry & Catamaran Dock
Knights' Castle
Hippocrates Park
Port Police
Hellenistic Baths
Excursion Boats
Loggia
Hippocrates' Plane Tree
Hydrofoil Jetty
Turkish Bath (Hamam Bar)
Agora
Old Synagogue
Pórta toú Fórou
Defterdar
Archeological Museum
Winter Cinema
Market
Ancient Stadium
Atik
Turkish Fountain
KTEL
Olympic Airways
Casa Romana
Roman Odeion
Western Excavations
Yacht Marina
Summer Cinema
ITALIAN QUARTER
ITALIAN QUARTER

PAMFYLON
MANDHILARA
THEMISTOKLEOUS
AVEROF
SPETSON
KANARI
NAVARINOU
AMERKIS
SALAMINOS
PIXIOTON
ALIKARNASSOU
ETHNIKIS ANDISTASIS
PSARON
BOUBOULINAS
VERIOPOULOU
IRODHOTOU
OMIROU
KYPROU
25. MARTIOU
ZERVOU
MANDHILARA
PINDHOU
AKTI KOUNDOURIOTOU
RIGA FEREOU
FINIKON
PLESSA
DHIAKOU
AKTI MIAOULI
ELEFTHERIOU VENIZELOU
TSALDHARI
GALIAS
MAKARIOU
VREKOUKIA
25 MARTIOU
FILITA
IFES TOU
KOLOKOTRONI
XANTHOU
IPPOKRATOUS
KLEOVOULOU
MEGALOU ALEXANDHROU
THEOFRASTOU
THEOLOGOU
HRISTODHOULOU
APELLOU
METSOVOU
VASSILEOS PAVLOU
MEROPIDHOS
VYRONOS
ELEFTHERIOU VENIZELOU
KORAI
EPIHARMOU
ARSENIOU
VASSILEOS YEORYIOU
HALKONOS
ARTEMISIAS
ARYIROKASTROU
KORYTSAS
EYILION
ZARAFTOU
VORIOU IPIROU
THEOKRITOU
NISSIRIOU
PISSANDHROU
ANDONIOU IOANIDHI
KLEOPATRAS
KAVAKO POULOU
AYIOU NIKOLAOU
MITROPOLEOS
KOUROUKLI
IOANNIDHI
THIMAKANI
FILIMONOS
THESSALOU
EVRYPYLOU
FENARETIS
XENOFONDOS
ARTEMISIAS
YEORYIOU PAPANDHREOU
HARMYLOU
KARAÏSKAKI
PAPATHEOFANDUS
MAKRIYIANNI
GRIGORIOU TOU PEMPTOU

0 200 m

Pémptou, provide the quickest ways of getting out to the main island trunk road. **Parking** is subject to strict controls (watch for kerbside signs) and fees are payable Monday to Friday, 8am to 9pm; buy hourly scratch-card tickets from kiosks or DEAS, the bus ticket office on the front (see below for address).

The municipally run **tourist information office** at Vassiléos Yeoryíou 3 (July & Aug daily 8am–9pm; May & June, Sept & Oct Mon–Fri 9am–8pm, Sat 8am–3pm; Nov–April Mon–Fri 8am–3pm; ⓣ02420/28 724) is housed in an Italian-era hotel – once an officers' club, then a crèche, and now also home (upstairs) to the local radio station. Staff are reasonably helpful and keep stocks of local maps, bus timetables and specimen ferry schedules (which they stress are not to be trusted implicitly).

The main **taxi** stand lies at the east end of Koundouriótou, near Hippocrates' plane tree. The Kós municipality runs its own efficient **local bus** service, DEAS, through the beach suburbs and up to the Asklepion, with a ticket and information office at Aktí Koundouriótou 7. If you're going to make extensive use of them, it's advisable to pre-purchase bulk ticket packets, as fares are more expensive bought on board. There's also a miniature **fake train** hauling folk up from the waterfront to the Asklepion and back during its opening hours only.

Owing to the island's notorious flatness, **bicycle rental** is a very popular option (see p.231), though there have been complaints about gaps in the bike-lane system which expose cyclists to traffic hazards. Formerly, most islanders got around using this mode of transport too, and the ethos has lingered, despite motor scooters becoming an obligatory fashion accessory for local youth.

Accommodation

If you're just in transit, there's really no viable alternative to staying in Kós Town. But even if you're sticking to the island for one or two weeks, the capital and environs makes an excellent touring base: it offers the broadest range of food and nightlife, the majority of the island's car, motorbike and bicycle rental agencies, and is the hub of public transport. Be wary of the touts which besiege most arriving sea craft – their rooms are apt to be unlicensed, inconveniently remote and of dubious cleanliness.

Most **hotels** are on package operator lists, and relatively expensive; the following establishments are exceptions, geared to walk-in trade even if they reserve a seasonal block of rooms for tours. Except where noted, they operate only between April and late October. Families looking for a beach base in or near Kós Town are best off at calmer, more rural accommodation en route to Cape Psalídhi.

The relatively pricey but well-appointed **campsite** (ⓣ02420/23 275; May to early Oct) also lies 2.5km east towards Cape Psalídhi, and can be reached by either the municipal DEAS service or its own minibus (which meets ferries). You may well find yourself out there unintentionally, since in July and August absolutely every town bed is booked up months in advance.

Centre

Afendoulis About 600m east of the ancient agora at Evripýlou 1 ⓣ02420/25 321, ⓕ25 797. A welcoming C-class hotel under the same management as the *Alexis*; large, cheerful en-suite rooms with fans (no air con), most with balconies. The cool, cave-like basement rooms are a haven in summer. No packages; open April to late Oct. ❸

Alexis Irodhótou 9, corner of Omírou ⓣ02420/25 594. Deservedly popular backpacker's pension in an interwar villa overlooking the Hellenistic baths. Rooms are large and parquet-floored though not en suite. There's a self-catering kitchen and garden terrace, and the management is extremely helpful. Usually open late March to early November. ❶

Anna Venizélou 77 ⓣ02420/23 030, ⓕ23 886. Basic, 1970s hotel in a fairly quiet location well inland, with largish balconies for the en-suite rooms. ❸

Kamelia Artemisías 3 ⓣ02420/28 983, ⓕ27 391. Another friendly, well-placed, family-run hotel, which the *Afendoulis* refers customers to when full; the rear rooms have an orchard view. Supposedly open all year, with winter heating. ❸

Maritina Výronos 19, corner of Venizélou ⓣ02420/23 241, ⓕ26 124. Large, somewhat overpriced businessmen's hotel in a fairly calm mid-town location; its main virtue is year-round operation. See below for their better-value annexe, *Maritina Mare*. ❹–❺

Moustafa Tselepi Metsóvou 8 (enquire at Venizélou 35) ⓣ02420/28 896. These well-furnished rooms, some with cooking facilities, are a good choice for longer stays. ❸

Phaethon Venizélou 75 ⓣ02420/28 901, ⓕ26 902. Virtually next door to the *Anna*, this is another slightly faded, but serviceable, en-suite C-class with air conditioning and without tour groups. Open June–Sept. ❹

Veroniki P Tsaldhári 2 (ⓣ02420/28 122). Another 1970s-vintage C-class hotel in a quiet yet convenient location; open all year. ❹

Psalídhi

Maritina Mare Just before Cape Psalídhi, about 4km from town ⓣ02420/24 803, ⓕ27 444. First impressions suggest this is a cheap and cheerful beach outfit, but the grounds (including pool-bar) are pleasant, the rooms or studios good-sized, plus there's wheelchair access and lifts. Rooms ❷, self-catering ❸

Ramira Beach Psalídhi, 3km from town ⓣ02420/28 489 or 22 891, ⓕ28 489. Well-landscaped mammoth A-class complex, with tennis court, salt water pool and, unusually, direct access to the beach. Units are both in the main original hotel, and two-storey satellite bungalows. Accommodation is on a B&B or half-board basis. The high prices mean there's usually a room to spare even in August. ❻

Seagull Apartments Just past Cape Psalídhi, about 6km out of town ⓣ02420/25 200 or 22 937 for an English-speaker, ⓕ22 514. Low-rise, small-scale apartment complex set in a well-landscaped environment with large pool. Units, including two family suites, are a tad on the small side, but are well maintained and well priced. No packages. Open May–Oct. ❹

Theodhorou Beach Psalídhi, 1.2km from town centre ⓣ02420/22 280, ⓕ23 526. Generous-sized rooms with balconies, attractive common areas and gardens, and a small private patch of beach make this a good choice. Friendly management welcomes walk-ins. Price includes buffet breakfast. ❹

The Town

Despite a population of over 16,000, Kós Town feels remarkably uncluttered, thanks to its sprawling, flat layout. Vast areas of open space alternate with a wonderful hotchpotch of surviving Ottoman monuments and mid-1930s mock-North African, Fascist Internationalist and Art Deco buildings (a good example of which is the old synagogue; see box on p.233). The maze-like Ottoman centre notwithstanding, this is mostly a planned town, with the pines and shrubs planted by the Italians now fully matured, especially in the garden suburb extending east of the central street grid.

The Knights' castle

For most visitors, the obvious first port of call is the **Knights' castle** (Tues–Sun 8am–2.30pm; €2.40), reached by a causeway over its former moat; this has long since been filled in and planted with palms – thus the avenue's Greek name, Finíkon. The original Knights' castle, which stood here from 1314 until 1450, has vanished without trace, replaced by the existing inner castle (1450–78). This in turn nestles within the outer citadel, built to formidable thickness between 1495 and 1514 to withstand new artillery technology following unsuccessful Ottoman sieges in 1457 and 1477.

A fair proportion of ancient Kós, in the form of masonry fragments and tumbled columns, has been incorporated into the walls of both strongholds or, more recently, piled up loose in the southeast forecourt. A bewildering array of escutcheons and coats of arms on the various walls and towers will appeal to aficionados of heraldry, as the period of construction spanned the terms of several Grand Masters and local governors. The south corner of the older castle, for example, bears two Grand Masters' escutcheons, best admired from the massive, most technically advanced southwest bastion, identified with Del Caretto, the Grand Master who finished the job. There are also dozens of cannonballs lying about, few if any fired in anger, since this castle surrendered without resistance in accordance with the terms ending the marathon siege of Rhodes (see p.102). The biggest explosion that ever occurred here was orchestrated for the grand finale of Werner Herzog's first black and white feature, *Signs of Life* (1966), in which a low-ranking Wehrmacht officer goes berserk in 1944 and torches an ammunition dump inside the castle.

At the moment, a tidy sum of EU money is being used to "improve" the castle grounds with walkways, street furniture and spotlights, probably in preparation for using the interior as an events venue.

Hippocrates' plane tree and the Loggia Mosque

Rather sterile steel scaffolding has replaced the ancient pillars that once propped up the sagging branches of **Hippocrates' plane tree**, immediately opposite the causeway leading into the Knights' castle. At seven hundred years of age, this venerable tree has a fair claim to being one of the oldest in Europe, though it's not really elderly enough to have seen the great healer. The trunk has split into four sections, which in any other species would presage imminent demise, but abundant suckers from its roots promise some sort of continuation. Adjacent stand a dried-up hexagonal Turkish pillar fountain, a working one making use of an ancient sarcophagus, and the imposing eighteenth-century mosque of Hassan Pasha, also known as the **Loggia Mosque** after its covered portico on the north side. This three-storey building is locked and still bears the marks of wartime bombardment, especially in the tracery of its upper windows. The ground floor – like that of its near-contemporary the **Defterdar Mosque** on nearby Platía Eleftherías – is taken up by several shops.

The ancient town

The largest single excavated section of ancient Kós is the **agora**, a sunken zone (unrestricted access) reached via steps from either Ippokrátous or Nafklírou. The latter, a pedestrian street (and nightlife mecca, see p.231), leads away from Platía Eleftherías under the **Pórta toú Fórou**, all that's left of the outer city walls built by the Knights between 1391 and 1396.

What you see is confusing and jumbled owing to successive earthquakes in 142, 469 and 554 AD; the most easily distinguishable items are the foundations of a massive double Aphrodite sanctuary roughly in the centre of the site, some columns of a stoa that once surrounded the so-called Harbour Basilica near the Loggia Mosque, plus two re-erected columns and the architrave of the Roman agora itself, in the far west of the archeological zone.

Another, more comprehensible section of the ancient town, the so-called **western excavations** (unrestricted access), abuts the ancient acropolis approximately where Platía Dhiagóras lies today. Intersecting marble-paved **Roman streets** (named Cardo and Decumana), dating from the third century AD, lend definition to this area, as does the **Xystos**, or colonnade, of a covered running track. Inside this the hulking brick ruins of a bath squat alongside the original arch of its furnace room. South of the Xystos stands the restored doorframe of a baptistry belonging to a Christian basilica erected above the baths after 469 AD. The floor of the basilica and of an unidentified building at the northern end of these excavations retain well-preserved fragments of **mosaics**, although the best have been carted off to the Palace of the Grand Masters in Rhodes (see p.100). What remains tends to be under several inches of protective gravel, or – in the case of the famous **Europa mosaic** house, to the north of the east-to-west Decumana street – off limits to visitors. Secreted in a cypress grove just across Grigoríou toú Pémptou is a fourteen-row Roman **odeion**, which at one time hosted musical events associated with the *Asklepieia* festivals (see p.234); it was reclad in rather garish new marble during 1999.

The Archeological Museum

The Italian-built, Fascist Internationalist-style **Archeological Museum**, on Platía Kazoúli (Tues–Sun 8am–2.30pm; €2.40), is a none too subtle propaganda exercise, with a distinct Latin bias in its choice of exhibits. Four rooms containing good, though not superlative, statuary are grouped around a central atrium where a Roman mosaic shows Hippocrates welcoming Asklepios to Kós. The most famous exhibit, a statue thought to portray Hippocrates, is in fact Hellenistic, as is a richly coloured, fragmentary fish mosaic at the rear of the atrium. But most of the other highly regarded works – Hermes seated with a lamb, Artemis hunting, Hygeia offering an egg to Asklepios' serpent, a boxer with his arms bound in rope, statues of wealthy townspeople – are emphatically Roman.

The Ottoman old town: Haluvaziá

Kós heavily touts its medieval "old town", the former Turkish district of **Haluvaziá**, lining either side of a pedestrianized street running from behind the covered produce market on Platía Eleftherías as far as Platía Dhiagóras and the orphaned minaret overlooking the western archeological zone. This begins life as Iféstou, then becomes Apelloú further on. It was long considered an undesirable area, but while all the rickety town houses nearby collapsed in the 1933 earthquake, the sturdily built stone dwellings and shops here survived. Today, they are crammed with thoroughly commercial tourist boutiques and snack bars; one of the few genuinely old things here is a dry **Turkish fountain** with an inscription, found where the walkway cobbles cross Venizélou, though it's often obscured by trinket stalls. Another juts out from the wall of the barber shop at the corner of Hristodhoúlou and Passanikoláki, lodged next to the minaret-less but still-functioning **Atik Mosque**.

Continuing in the same direction, you can make a detour west of Platía Dhiagóras to Nikíta Nissiríou 3, site of the **Anatolia Hamam**. During the Ottoman period this was the mansion of a local pasha, whose descendants emigrated to Izmir in 1950; the small Turkish bath inside (the *hamam* of the name) functioned as the neighbourhood spa until 1970 or so, after which the premises operated sporadically as a brothel before falling into complete disrepair. Since 1992, new leaseholders have restored the original cedar floors and painted ceilings and have made the tiny *hamam* the inner sanctum of an expensive restaurant-bar.

The Casa Romana

The Greeks have apparently attempted to dampen Italian "public relations" by signposting the **Casa Romana** (Tues–Sun 8.30am–3pm; €1.50), on Grigoríou toú Pémptou at the rear of town, as "Restored House of Kós, 3rd Century AD". Already the 1930s reconstruction work on this palatial Roman house is beginning to deteriorate, providing grist for future archeology; during World War II it was used as an infirmary by the Italians – you can still see faint red crosses painted on the exterior to deter Allied bombers.

This building, devastated by the 554 AD earthquake but apparently abandoned long before, was evidently the villa of a wealthy family, and is arrayed around three atria with **tesselated marble or mosaic floors**. The smallest one, by the ticket booth, features panthers attacking a stag; the largest courtyard to the south is flanked by rooms, on opposite sides, showing another panther and a tiger; while the pool of the third atrium is surrounded by dolphins and more fierce felines, plus a damaged nymph riding a horse-headed sea monster, possibly a representation of Poseidon. On your way out, spare a glance for the laundry room in the corner, complete with stone-carved basins.

Eating

Despite an overwhelming first impression of Euro-bland cuisine, it is easy to **eat** well, and sometimes even reasonably, in Kós Town. Virtually all the better-value places are a few blocks inland, and scattered fairly evenly across the town grid; you can pretty much write off most of the waterfront tavernas.

Cafés, breakfast and desserts

See also "internet cafés" in Listings, p.232.

Café Aenaos Platía Eleftherías, right by the ablutions fountain of the Defterdar Mosque. Join the largely Greek crowd here, and people-watch while you refill your Greek coffee from the traditional *bríki* used to brew it up.

Central/Kentriko Platía Ayías Paraskevís, behind the municipal produce market off Vassiléos Pávlou. Best of a handful here, offering American-pancake breakfasts, hot drinks, fruit salads and fresh juices served under giant Indian fig trees.

Fresko Gelateria Café Cnr Kleopátras and Ioannídhi. Crêpes and waffles in the morning, sticky cakes or decadent home-made ice cream later on, served in a giant "tent" abutting the sidewalk.

Kyvotos Voríou Ipírou 16, within sight of the Roman *odeion*. Bills itself as a "teahouse" specializing in herbal teas and less expensive pastries, but it's also a thriving nocturnal café popular with the local trendy set.

Restaurants

Central

Armonia Khristodhoúlou, corner Theológou. Ouzerí with some taverna dishes; sidewalk seating, rather less expensive than *Petrino* across the way.

Australia-Sydney Vassiléos Pávlou opposite the post office. Hole in the wall with a limited menu of daily dishes where two can eat for about €15.

Barbas Evripýlou, opposite *Hotel Afendoulis*. A *psistariá* much improved under new management from Tríkala; tops for chicken and *kondosoúvli*.

Dell Arte Hálkonos 3. The best Italian all-rounder among several contenders: big salads, pasta dishes, wood-oven pizzas, calzone. Slightly pricey at €30 for two; open April–Nov.

Petrino Theológou 1 ⓣ02420/27 251. Kós' best *kúltoúra* taverna, and accordingly expensive at €32 each for the works, booze extra. You can push the total down a bit by sticking to *orektiká* and the house wine. Extensive garden seating, and indoor salon, allows all-year operation; large groups should reserve.

Pote tin Kyriaki Pissándhrou 9 ⓣ02420/27 872. Characterful, ten-table ouzerí which neither wants nor gets many tourists (Greek-only sign). Brief, Greek-only menu – let proprietor Angelos recite it for you – that offers excellent value in the basics: *hórta*, *gávros*, chunky *mýdhia saganáki* and good Rapsáni rosé in bulk. Book ahead if your Greek is up to it, and enjoy the company and taped rebétika as well as the food. As the name suggests, closed Sun all year, open Thurs–Sat in winter when it moves indoors.

Northwest of the port

Hellas Psarón 7, corner Amerikís. All the usual *mayireftá* dishes in a slightly touristy environment, but well executed; they serve fried *orektiká* and grills too.

Koakon Ieroú Lóhou, near corner Amerikís. An experienced chef set up on his own in a new, salubrious location: classic *mayireftá* for a local clientele, without multinational flags or silly photo-menus.

O Kostas Bouboulínas 34. Kós' *patsatzídhiko* or traditional, after-hours offal kitchen: *patsás* (tripe soup), *podhári* (whole trotter) and *glóssa* (boiled tongue) for a pre-dawn clientele of post-clubbers and just-awakened construction workers.

Nikolaos O Psaras/Nick the Fisherman Cnr of Alikarnassoú and Avérof. The most genuine fish taverna in Kós Town, with good *orektiká* preceding mildly pricey seafood; mostly sidewalk seating, open lunch/dinner May–Oct, shut Mon.

Noufara Kanári 67. Carnivore heaven, with roast chicken, *kondosoúvli*, etc; considered the best grill in town. Indoor and outdoor seating. Open most of the year.

Suburbs

Ambavris In the eponymous hamlet, 800m south of the Casa Romana (follow the ruined Ottoman aqueduct by the roadside). Impeccable recipes and fair portions in one of the best tavernas on Kós. Don't order from the rather perfunctory English-only à la carte menu, but take the hint about the house's seasonally changing "Mezedes": *pinigoúri* (bulgur pilaf), *pikhtí* (brawn), little fish, stuffed squash flowers and *fáva* are typical – but won't much exceed €19 for six plates, drinks extra. Outdoor seating in the courtyard of this converted farmhouse; open dinner only May–Oct. Booking required for large parties on ⓣ02420/25 696.

Frangoulis Kakó Prinári district. To get there, exit mid-town on Papatheofánous – one street east of Evripýlou – and keep going about 1500m to the intersection with Aristónos. Well-loved neighbourhood hole in the wall, its outdoor tables always packed. Grilled meat (and occasionally fish) is its strong point, with a few oven dishes and average bulk wine thrown in. Not superlative cuisine, but decent portions, friendly and very reasonable for Kós – two can easily drink (abstemiously) and eat for €20.

Mavromatis Yeoryíou Panandhréou 15, about 2km out on the coast road towards Cape Psalídhi. Despite a plethora of off-putting window stickers, offers good-value, hybrid western-Greek cuisine (ie stuffed chicken breast washed down with imported beer), and outdoor seating overlooking the beach and Turkey. Open May–Oct.

Drinking and nightlife

For loud (120-decibel) **nightlife**, you need look no further than "Bar Street", officially Nafklírou and Dhiákou, two roughly parallel pedestrian lanes joining Platía Kazoúli and the Loggia Mosque. Every address is a bar, just choose according to the crowd and the (techno and house) noise level. Near the end, by the main taxi rank, *Hamam Bar* occupies a genuine converted Turkish bath, and is the most reliable establishment; all others tend to change identity every season (if not more often). It is sobering (though not literally) to reflect that in Ottoman and Italian times this was a gritty bazaar quarter, domain of the blacksmiths and socially on a par with Haluvaziá; today it is your eardrums, not your hooves, that will get a hammering after 10pm.

Off "Bar Street"

Beach Boys Dance Bar Kanári 57. Inexpensive drinks, often accompanied by free nibbles, and a tiny dance floor; people spill out onto the pavement.

Blues Brothers Café Aktí Koundouriótou, corner of Iróön Politekhníou (Dolphin Square). Doyen of the waterfront bars, with rock-and-blues soundtrack, though it has hit a lean patch since the late 1990s, with not quite the crowd of yore.

Four Roses Cnr Arseníou and Vassiléos Yeoryíou. One of the longer-lived "dancing bars", attracting a slightly older clientele.

Mylos Lámbi. Tables on the sand and more of a Greek than foreign crowd.

Discos and live venues

Apoplous By the Theodhórou Beach Hotel, towards Psalídhi. Where most live Greek and foreign acts perform; ⓣ02420/21 916 reserve.

Fashion Club North side of the port, Kanári 2. The most impressive indoor venue, famous for its light shows.

Heaven 2km northwest of the town centre in Lámbi. Outdoor, garden venue, so open June–Sept only.

Kalua Aktí Zouroúdhi, Lámbi. Another outdoor venue, with swimming pool and live acts, adjacent to *Heaven*.

Listings

Air tickets Aeolos Travel, central branch at Annétas Laoumtzí 8 ⓣ02420/26 203, is the representative for a number of UK package companies and thus a good source of one-way charter tickets back to Britain.

Banks and exchange No fewer than six banks in town with cash machines, or failing these plenty of licensed moneychangers amongst travel agencies.

Bike rental Out of a huge number of establishments, most of them north or northeast of the port, try Sernikos-Ideal at Irodhótou 19–21 ⓣ02420/23

670 for bicycles and scooters, or the misnamed Moto Harley at Kanári, corner of Neomartýrou Khrístou, with a large fleet of well-kept larger bikes. Expect to pay €10–15 in high season for a decent scooter, about €4 for a top-end mountain bike, still less for a balloon-tyre pedal-bike, with or without gears.

Bookshops Newsstand, at Ríga Feréou 2, corner Platía Kazoúli, or the bookshop inside the Politistiko Polykendro (Cultural Multi-centre) at the corner of Korytsás and Aryirokástrou; both have a sizeable stock of English-language titles.

Car rental Not absolutely essential on smallish, mostly flat Kós unless there's a group of you; rates start at about €26.50 per day. Try Marion, at Vassiléos Yeoryíou 1 ☎02420/26 293; Alpha, Bouboulínas 23 ☎02420/22 488; Deals on Wheels, Bouboulínas 7 ☎02420/27 393; or (especially recommended for good car condition) Autorent/Helen's, at Vassiléos Pávlou 31 ☎02420/28 882 or 094/4500062, or in Psalídhi at both the *Ramira* and *Okeanis* hotels in Psalídhi.

Cinemas Municipally supported Orfeas screens a varied Oct–May programme in an Art Deco building diagonally opposite the archeological museum in winter, in summer (June–Sept) in premises on Fenarétis at the east end of Halkónos. Programmes (summer hilariously bilingual versions, winter Greek-only) are widely available; the play list tends to be fairly current first-run fare. The indoor venue also hosts concerts and other special events.

Ferry/catamaran/hydrofoil tickets Many, though not all, ferry and excursion boat agents cluster within 50m of each other at the intersection of Vassiléos Pávlou and the waterfront. Among these, Python Tours at Vassiléos Pávlou 1 ☎02420/22 247, specializes in trips to Turkey; Pulia Tours nearby at no. 3 ☎02420/21 130 or 26 388, is the Laoumtzis Flying Dolphins outlet; Kyriakoulis Maritime is at Harmýlou 2 (☎02420/25 920), though more conveniently available from Adris Nissia at no. 2. Agents elsewhere include Exas at Andinavárhou Ioanídhi 4 (☎02420/29 900), for G&A ferries and the *Dodekanisos Express*, and Rhodos Tours Traveland, the central DANE outlet on Platía Iróön Polytekhniíou ("Dolphin Square") (☎02420/26 732). Stefamar, at Avérof 23 ☎02420/26 388, deals strictly with day excursions to neighbouring islands; tickets for the *Nissos Kalymnos* are best bought in the harbour terminal building before departure.

Internet cafés *Café del Mare*, Megálou Alexándhrou 4, is the best equipped; *Taurus* at Mandhilará 9 also has a few terminals squeezed in between its multiple sports screens.

Laundries Happy Wash at Mitropóleos 20; Laundry Center on Mandhilará 56; Laundromat Center, Alikarnassoú 124.

Map Road Editions' 1:60,000 map no. 205. Failing that, the most accurate locally sold map, for both the island and the town, is that published by Pandelis Vayianos; don't be put off by its 3D matchbox art.

Post office Vassiléos Pavlou 14. Open normal weekday hours, no weekend opening.

Scuba outfitters Dive operators are easiest found at their boats, moored along the excursion-craft quay. Note, however, that all diving takes place at a single, authorized area off southern Kálymnos – so nearly three hours is spent getting there and back. Give it a miss and do any diving from Kálymnos.

Around Kós Town

All coastal points between Lámbi, to the north of Kós Town, and Áyios Fokás, to the east, are connected by the DEAS bus line; alternatively you can rent a bicycle and take advantage of the designated cycle paths extending as far east as Cape Psalídhi.

The closest beaches that answer to the description are at and beyond **LÁMBI**, 3km north towards Cape Skandhári with its military watchpoint, the last vestige of a vast army camp which has deferred to the demands of tourism. However, north-facing beaches beyond the point are not among the island's best: narrow, scrappy and closely hemmed by a frontage road.

East of Kós Town, the strands extending to and beyond Cape Psalídhi are grey-gravel and uninspiring; however this hasn't stopped virtually the entire shoreline, from the tourist information office east almost as far as the campsite, from being parcelled out amongst various umbrella-and-sunbed concessions. Possibly more interesting hereabouts are a few re-erected columns of the fourth-century **basilica of Áyios Gavriïl**, just inland from the road as you clear the edge of the urban grid. Similar beaches, functional at best (except for the excellent cove between the military watchpoint and the *Dimitra Beach* complex), line Cape Áyios Fokás well to the southeast, whose focal point is the purpose-built resort areas at Áyios Fokás, 8km from Kós Town.

The unusual and remote hot springs of **Brós Thermá** emerge from volcanic cliffs 5km beyond Áyios Fokás, and though periodically served by DEAS bus (last service 6pm), they are most easily reached by rented vehicle; the final kilometre lies along a rough dirt track heading down and left at a little drinks *kantína* just before the end of the asphalt, where the bus leaves you. The scalding springs issue from a tiny grotto, flowing through a trench to mingle with the sea at comfortable temperatures inside a giant corral of boulders. Winter storms typically disperse the boulder wall, rebuilt every April, so that the pool changes shape from year to year. It's free, and immensely popular with tourists and locals alike, especially by night during the cooler months. Just adjacent, the long-running *Psarotaverna Therma* does affordable seafood – especially parrot fish, swordfish and tuna – though the rest of the menu, with limited, sometimes inedible fried *orektiká*, seems strictly incidental.

Platáni

The Greek–Turkish village of **PLATÁNI** lies 2km south of Kós Town, on the road to the Asklepion, and is served by DEAS bus from 8am until late. Until 1964 it was most commonly known as Kermetés (*Germe* in Turkish), and the Turkish community had its own primary school, but in the wake of the Cyprus crises of that year, the village was officially renamed and education provided compulsorily in Greek only. Subsequent emigration to Anatolia caused Turkish numbers on the island to drop from around three thousand to less than a thousand. Only those Turks owning real estate and businesses have stayed but, as on Rhodes, the long-term outlook is bleak.

The Jews of Kós

Jews had lived on Kós since antiquity, but it seems that the Knights of Rhodes exiled the bulk of the Greek-speaking Jewish community to Nice in 1306. Following the Ottoman conquest, Sephardic Jews settled here, their dwindling numbers reinforced early in the 1900s by co-religionists from Izmir in Anatolia.

Despite this long history, there are just two tangible traces of the Jewish community. Just outside Platáni on the road back to the harbour, a **Jewish cemetery** stands in a dark conifer grove, 300m from the Muslim graveyard. Dates on the headstones, inscribed in a mix of Hebrew and Italian, stop ominously after 1940, after which presumably none was allowed the luxury of a natural death at home. The remaining local community of about 120 was transported to Rhodes in summer 1944 by the Nazis, and thence, together with the Rhodian Jews, to Auschwitz for extermination. Just one Koan Jew, who died in the early 1990s, survived the war; in accordance with Jewish communal law, he inherited all the real estate of his deceased co-religionists, which was sold for a tidy sum when mass tourism reached Kós in the 1970s.

The former **synagogue**, disused since 1944, is a marvellously orientalized, post-earthquake Art Deco building in Kós Town, at Alexándhrou Dhiákou 4, between the ancient agora and the waterfront; it was refurbished in 1991 as a "municipal multi-purpose hall".

Platáni's older domestic architecture is strongly reminiscent of styles in rural Crete, from where some of the village's Muslims came between 1898 and 1913; there's even a working Ottoman fountain near the crossroads. This junction is dominated by several excellent, Turkish-run tavernas: *Arap* (summer only); the slightly less touristy *Asklipios* and *Sherif* across the way (ditto) and *Gin's Palace* (all year), each offering Anatolian-style mezédhes (fried vegetables with yogurt, *ambelofásola*, *bourekákia*, and so on) and kebabs. Any is better than most eateries in Kós Town, and are best enjoyed in a group, when you can pass the various platters around.

The Asklepion

Native son **Hippocrates** is justly celebrated on Kós; not only does he have a tree, a street, a park, a statue and a new international medical institute named after him, but the Hellenistic **Asklepion** (Tues–Sun 8am–7pm, earlier closure in winter; €2.40), 4km south of town, one of just three in Greece, is a major

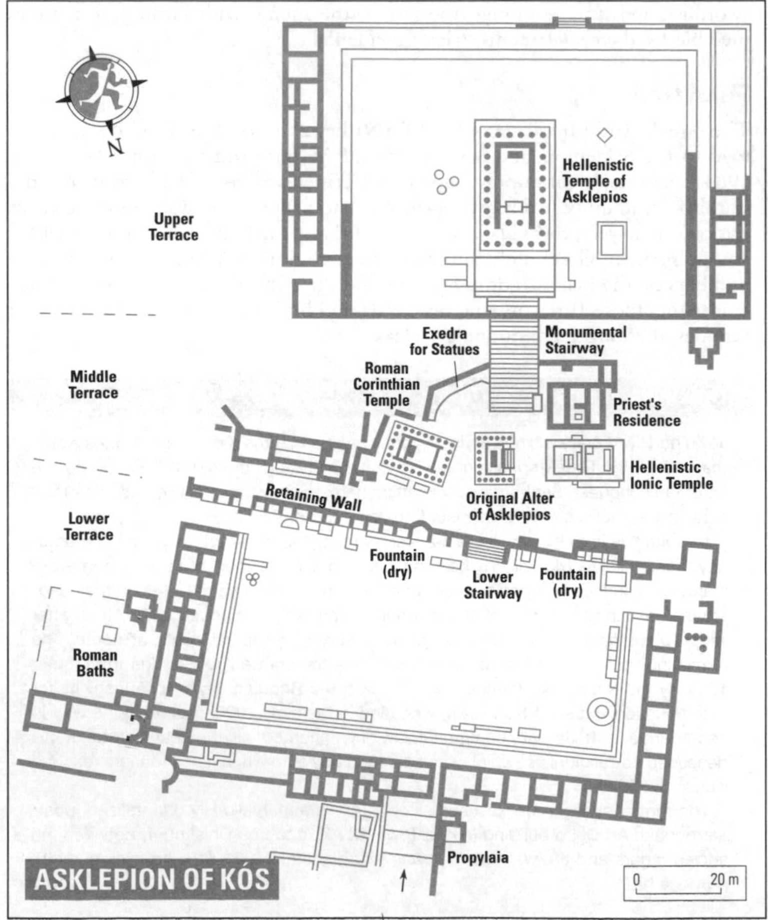

ASKLEPION OF KÓS

Hippocrates

Hippocrates (c. 460–370 BC) is generally regarded as the father of scientific medicine, and still influences doctors today through the Hippocratic oath – which probably has nothing to do with him and is in any case much altered from its original form. Hippocrates was definitely born on Kós, probably at Astypalea near present-day Kéfalos, but other details of his life are few and disputed. What seems certain is that he was a great physician who travelled throughout the Classical Greek world, but spent part of his career teaching and practising at the Asklepion on his native island. A vast number of medical writings have been attributed to Hippocrates, only a few of which he could actually have written; *Airs, Waters and Places*, a treatise on the importance of environment on health, is widely thought to be his, but others were probably a compilation from a medical library kept on Kós, which later appeared in Alexandria during the second century BC. This emphasis on good air and water, and the holistic approach of ancient Greek medicine, now seems positively contemporary.

tourist attraction. DEAS buses or the miniature train make the trip via Platáni between 8am and 6pm; otherwise you've a 45-minute walk or a shorter if steepish cycle ride. There's a small snack bar near the entrance, or pause for a meal in Platáni en route.

The Asklepion was actually founded just after the death of Hippocrates, but it's safe to assume that the methods used and taught here were his. Both a temple to Asklepios (god of medicine, son of Apollo) and a renowned curative centre, its magnificent setting on three artificial hillside terraces overlooking Anatolia reflects early recognition of the importance of the therapeutic environment. Until recently, two fountains provided the site with a constant supply of clean, fresh water, and extensive stretches of clay piping are still visible, embedded in the ground.

Today, very little remains above ground, owing to chronic earthquakes and the Knights' use of the site as a quarry. The lower terrace in fact never had many structures, being instead the main venue for the observance of the *Asklepieia* – quadrennial celebrations and athletic or musical competitions in honour of the healing god. Sacrifices to Asklepios were conducted at an **altar**, the oldest structure on the site, whose foundations can still be seen near the middle of the second terrace. Just to its east, the Corinthian columns of a second-century AD **Roman temple** were partially re-erected by nationalistically minded Italians. A monumental **staircase** flanked by *exedrae* (display niches) leads from the altar up to the second-century BC **Doric temple** of Asklepios on the topmost terrace, the last and grandest of a succession of the deity's shrines at this site.

The north coast

Lying well to the southwest of Cape Lámbi, the two neighbouring resorts of Tingáki and Marmári are separated from each other by a salt marsh called **Alykí**, which retains water until June after (increasingly rare) wet winters. Between January and April it's host to hundreds of migratory **birds**, and most of the year you'll find tame terrapins to feed near the outlet to the warm, shallow sea. There's almost always a breeze along this coast, making it a popular destination for windsurfers, who can rent boards at either resort.

Both Tingáki and Marmári are served by KTEL bus from Kós Town, but if you're travelling under your own steam, especially on a bike of any sort, it's safest and most pleasant to take the obvious **minor road** from the southwest corner of town as far as Tingáki; this entire route is paved, and involves about the same distance as travelling the main trunk road and marked turn-off. Shortly before Tingáki, in the district known as **Selvéri**, some 5km from town, a dead-end side road goes to the sea in the vicinity of two enormous boats, abandoned in their slips at a disused shipyard; between them hides the *Blue Diamond* **taverna** (summer only), surprisingly versatile with *mayireftá* like rabbit stew and *moussakás*. The first really attractive beach out of town in this direction beckons just to the west, free of sunbeds and umbrellas, but only two-wheelers can continue in that direction.

Tingáki

TINGÁKI, the shore annexe of the Asfendhioú villages (see opposite), lies 12km west of Kós Town. It's a busy, somewhat higgledy-piggledy resort popular with Brits, with most of its dozen, medium-sized **hotels** scattered inland among fields and cow pastures. One of the better choices, though heavily subscribed to by packages, is *Hotel Constantinos Ilios* (Ⓣ02420/69 411, Ⓕ69 173; ⑤), a well-designed bungalow complex about a kilometre back from the water. The best, still somewhat touristy local **taverna** here is *Ambeli* (dinner only), well signposted 2.5km east of the main beachfront crossroads. Among **car-rental** outfits, Sevi (Ⓣ02420/69 076) can be recommended for good-condition cars, and will even deliver vehicles on request to Kós Town. The **beach** itself is white sand, long and narrow; it improves, and veers further out of earshot from the frontage road, as you head southwest, with the best patches to either side of the drainage from Alykí. The profiles of Kálymnos, Psérimos and Turkey's Bodrum peninsula on the horizon all make for spectacular scenery, especially at sunset.

Marmári

The traditional annexe of Pylí village (see p.239), **MARMÁRI**, 15km from Kós Town, has a smaller built-up area than Tingáki, and the beach itself is broader, especially to the west where it forms mini-dunes. A grid of paved rural lanes links the inland portions of Tingáki and Marmári.

If you want to **stay**, you'll have a hard time squeezing in amongst the various Germanophone tour groups; one worthwhile spot that may have vacancies on spec is the *Esperia* on the main access road down from the island trunk road (Ⓣ02420/42 010, Ⓕ42 012, Ⓔesperiahotelkos@yahoo.gr; ④), with a medium-sized pool in grassy surroundings. To really push the boat out, look no further than the nearby *Royal Park* (Ⓣ02420/41 488, Ⓕ41 373; ⑥), now part of the Grecotel chain and undergoing refurbishment in 2002. As they stand, the garden- or seaview units are a maximum 300m from the beach, with fridges, air con, tubs in the bath and all other mod cons.

For **food**, just inland on the same access road is a pair of adjacent tavernas: *Apostolis*, and the usually superior *Dimitris*, offering *mezedhákia*, seafood and meat grills at reasonable prices. The latter, open noon till late in season, is pitched partly at locals, and so usually opens weekends from November to April. Another attraction in the area is the **Salt Lake Riding Centre** (Ⓣ094/4104446), just back from the sea on the west side of the salt marsh. This has eight horses and ponies available for rides along the beach or up into the hills, at rates varying from €17.60 per hour to ten hours of riding for €117.

Around Mount Dhíkeos

The main interest of inland Kós resides in the villages on **Mount Dhíkeos** (the ancient Oromedon). This handful of settlements, collectively referred to as **Asfendhioú**, nestles amid the island's only natural forest and worth visiting for a glimpse of what Kós looked like before tourism and concrete took hold. They can be reached from the main island trunk road via the extremely curvy side road from Zipári, 8km from Kós Town; a minimally signposted but paved minor road to Lagoúdhi; or the shorter access road to Pylí.

The Asfendhioú villages

The most accessible Asfendhioú village from Kós Town is **EVANGELÍSTRIA**, up the side road from Zipári, where from behind its namesake parish church extends a neighbourhood of low, whitewashed houses, now two-thirds abandoned in the mad rush down to the coast; the remainder are being bought up and restored by outsiders.

LAGOÚDHI, just west of Evangelístria church, is perhaps livelier, with three **kafenía** (two still fairly traditional), a couple of trinket shops, and a hilltop church of its own.

Further up the road from Evangelístria, **ZIÁ**'s spectacular **views and sunsets** make it the hapless target of up to six tour buses per evening, and its daytime tattiness seems to increase by the year as well. A dozen households at most still dwell full-time in the village, but otherwise any building on the main street that isn't a taverna is probably a souvenir shop. Their wares include kitsch throw-rugs in hideous hues and patterns, fortunately unique to the area.

Best of the dozen **tavernas** here, which trade mostly on their position, is the *Olympia*, at the start of the pedestrian walkway up to the church. Since it's the one without much of a view, the food has to be good and reasonably priced to make up for this deficiency. Dishes not usually associated with tourist resorts, like chickpeas, bulgur pilaf (*pinigoúri* in Koan dialect), *spédzofaï* (sausage and pepper stew) and dark bread are washed down with excellent bulk Nemea red or local white. There's also a good *pikilía* of mezédhes "off menu", especially at weekends when a local clientele predominates; it's also open in winter, always a good sign.

East of Ziá the way deteriorates to dirt as it continues to the final pair of Asfendhioú settlements. The first you'll come to is **ASÓMATI**, home to around thirty villagers plus a handful of foreigners and Athenians renovating houses, which steadily come on the market. The place really only comes to life at the November 7–8 festival celebrated around the **church of Arhángelos**, whose spacious courtyard (usually locked) harbours a fine *hokhláki* mosaic.

ÁYIOS DHIMÍTRIOS, 2km beyond Asómati along an exceedingly rough track, is shown on some maps by its old Ottoman name of Haïhoúdhes. It was abandoned entirely during the junta years, when the inhabitants went to Zipári or further afield. Today, just one farmer lives here beside the recently restored namesake **monastery**. Rather than retrace your steps, it's possible to short-cut directly back from Áyios Dhimítrios to the Asklepion, 7km distant (see p.234); bear left and north just outside the hamlet for the first 3.5km on bad track (passable to ordinary cars) before linking up with the paved road descending from the rubbish tip towards the Asklepion.

Up Khristós peak

Ziá (see above) is the preferred trailhead for the ascent to the summit of 846-metre **Khristós** peak, the highest point of the Dhíkeos range, and indeed on

Kós. Taking rather less than half a day, this is within the capabilities of any reasonably fit, properly shod person, and offers what are arguably the best views in the Dodecanese.

From the *Olympia* restaurant (see p.237) you should head up the paved walkway to the small car park in the upper quarter of the village, then continue south up steps past a few houses. At the top of these stone stairs flows a fountain, the outlet of the famous local Kefalóvrysi spring that keeps Ziá and Evangelístria well watered – and still powers a water mill, now the centrepiece of a tourist shop, near the car park. Top up your water bottle here, as the lone spring further up the mountain is unreliable.

Just above this point you follow a narrow track past the *Taverna Kefalovrysi* through a glen, passing the chapel of **Isódhia tís Theotókou** with its vaulted roof, covered porch and bomb nose-cone hung as the bell. Bear right at the junction behind it and head west past the last house in Ziá. Just beyond this, keep an eye out for the start of the path to **Áyios Yeóryios** chapel ahead to the right, which allows you to avoid the track; a fifteen-minute walk above the restaurant, the chapel itself houses a few frescoes in fair condition. The rough onward track, now scarcely passable to vehicles, curls gradually south past isolated farm cottages and sheep pens; another section of path shortcuts a bend in the track.

Just under half an hour out of Ziá you'll reach the true trailhead amid a grove of junipers. The spot is fairly obvious, with the path flanked by red and blue paint splodges, and further along by cairns. The distinct trail zigzags eastwards up the mountainside, leaving the juniper forest within fifteen minutes and arriving in just under an hour out of Ziá at the ridge leading northeast to the summit. The grade slackens, and three or four shattered cisterns, once used by shepherds, are visible north of the path. From the point where the ridge is attained, it's another twenty minutes to the summit along the watershed, usually just to its north; the little pillbox-like chapel of the **Metamórfosis toú Sotírou**, visible most of the time from this point on, stands about 40m northeast of the altitude survey marker, and has a "guest book" where you can sign your name; there's also a small dugout shelter nearby, erected in 1996, for staying the night should the need arise. A generator lights strung-up bulbs for the August 6 festival, while you can ponder the esoteric symbolism of a giant crucifix fashioned from PVC sewer pipes and filled with concrete – clearly Kós has a budding Turner Prize-calibre artist.

Up on top, Turkey's Knidos Peninsula dominates the view to the southeast; Níssyros, Tílos and Hálki float to the south; Astypálea closes off the horizon on the west; Kálymnos and, on a good day, Léros are spread out to the north; and the entire west and north portions of Kós are laid out before you.

The south flank of the Dhíkeos range is a sheer drop to the Aegean, and the summit ridge northeast can only be tackled by technical climbers – there are too many knife-edge saddles and arêtes. So the only viable descent is back the way you came, which takes only about ten minutes less than the climb up, owing to the rough surface – allow two hours twenty minutes minimum for the out-and-back trip from Ziá, without rest stops.

Pylí: new and old

Further along the main island road from the Asfendhioú turnings is **Linopótis**, a sunken pond fed by a permanent spring, always swarming with terrapins, ducks and eels. From the junction here, a signposted access road leads left to contemporary **PYLÍ**, which divides into two districts. In the upper neighbourhood, 100m west of the upper square and church, the unpretentious

Taverna Iy Palea Piyi serves inexpensive but appetizing grills and mezédhes under a giant Indian fig, in a superb setting overlooking trees, a tankful of carp and frogs, and (best of all) a giant, sixteenth-century cistern fountain, the *piyí* of the name, decorated with four carved lion-head spouts.

Pylí's other attraction is the so-called **Harmýlio** (Tomb of Harmylos), sign-posted near the top of the village as "Heroon of Charmylos". This consists of a subterranean vault (alas, fenced off) with twelve niches, probably a Hellenistic family tomb. Immediately above it, traces of an ancient temple foundation have been incorporated into the medieval **chapel** of Stavrós.

Paleó Pylí

Paleó (medieval) **Pylí**, roughly 3km southeast of its modern descendant, was the Byzantine capital of Kós, inhabited from about the tenth century until the Ottoman conquest. Head there via Amanioú, keeping straight at the junction where signs point left to Ziá and Lagoúdhi. In any case, the castle of old Pylí should be obvious on its crag, straight ahead. The road continues up to a wooded canyon, dwindling to a dirt track beside a trough spring built with livestock in mind. Some five minutes' walk uphill from the fountain along the dirt track, the remains of a **water mill** sit in the ravine just west.

From opposite the fountain, a stair-path leads within fifteen minutes to a **Byzantine castle** dating from the eleventh century, whose partly intact roof affords superb views. En route you pass the ruins of the abandoned village, as well as three fourteenth- to fifteenth-century **churches**. That of **Arhángelos**, the first encountered, retains substantial traces of wall art, particularly numerous scenes from the life of Christ. Outside are the remains of a graceful Latin arcade of a type usually only seen on Rhodes or Cyprus. Rectangular **Áyios Nikólaos**, just south of the route to the citadel, has a *Communion of the Apostles* in the apse, while **Ypapandí**, the largest church and nearest the castle, is almost bare inside but impresses with its barrel vaulting supported by reused Byzantine columns.

Central Kós

Near the **centre of the island**, a pair of giant, adjacent roundabouts by the airport funnel traffic northwest towards Mastihári, northeast back towards town, southwest towards Kéfalos, and southeast to Kardhámena. The fairly dry, desolate countryside hereabouts provides ample ammunition for those who would dismiss Kós as dull or unattractive, and additionally the area is well sown with military installations guarding the airport.

Mastihári

The least developed of the northern shore resorts, three-street-wide **MASTIHÁRI**, was a permanent village long before tourist times, as well as the historic summer quarters of Andimáhia (see p.240). Though shorter than those at Marmári or Tingáki, the local beach extending to the southwest is broader, with less frequented dunes (and no sunbeds) towards the far end. A kilometre or so east is the secluded beach of **Troúlos**, reached by a narrow, 300-metre dirt track, though its peaceful days are numbered by a bungalow complex under construction. The fifth-century basilica of **Áyios Ioánnis** lies about 1.5km down the west beach, following the shoreline promenade; it's fairly typical of Kós' numerous early Christian church foundations, results of Paul's evangelizing of the island, with a row of column bases separating a pair of side aisles from the nave, a tripartite narthex, and a baptistry tacked onto the north side of the building.

Mastihári, 25km from the capital by the most direct route, is also the **ferry port** for the shortest crossing to Kálymnos; throughout the year there are morning, late-afternoon and late-evening ro-ro sailings, keyed more or less to the arrival times of Olympic flights from Athens – though KTEL buses to or from Kós Town don't (to the delight of taxi drivers) always dovetail well. Boats can also be full with package clients in high season, so booking in advance during this period is recommended (see "Travel details", p.246).

Practicalities

Mastihári has a much higher proportion of non-block-booked **accommodation** than other coastal resorts on Kós; examples of quieter digs overlooking the west beach include the simple *Hotel Kyma* (Ⓣ02420/59 045; ❶) or the *Hotel Fenareti* (Ⓣ02420/59 024) further up the grade, with rooms (❶) and studios (❷) in a peaceful garden environment. For **eating out**, *O Makis*, one street inland from the centre of the waterfront, and *Kali Kardia*, right at the base of the jetty, are the best of half a dozen **tavernas** here, both well regarded for moderately priced fresh fish, mezédhes and (at *Kali Kardia*) *mayireftá*.

Andimáhia and Pláka

The workaday village of **ANDIMÁHIA**, 5km southeast of Mastihári, straggles over several of the ridges that extend from here to the far southwestern tip of Kós. The only "sight" and concession to tourism is a much-photographed **windmill** on the main street, the last surviving of more than thirty mills that once dotted the ridges here and at Kéfalos. It's now preserved as a working museum (typical daily hours 8.30am–6pm) and unfurls its sails during daylight hours; for a token donation you can climb up to the mast-loft and observe its workings – which incidentally point downwind, not into the wind as popularly imagined.

One worthwhile diversion from the main trunk road, immediately west of the airport and Andimáhia, is **Pláka**, a forested ravine with picnic grounds, a spring and a flock of semi-tame peacocks. The unmarked but paved side road leads off from a small white-and-blue-roofed chapel opposite the forest of radio masts in the airport precinct, and its dirt-surface continuation out of the Pláka vale emerges again on the main road, just before Kós' southwestern beaches.

The Knights' castle

East of Andimáhia, an enormous, triangular **Knights' castle** overlooks the islands of Níssyros, Tílos and Hálki. Access is via a marked, three-kilometre side road that begins next to a Greek army barracks 700m northeast of the twin roundabouts, and ends in an informal parking area with a seasonal snack bar just before it.

Enormous when seen from afar, the fortifications, to which there is currently unrestricted entry, prove less intimidating close up. Once through the imposing double north gateway, surmounted by the arms of Grand Master Pierre d'Aubusson, you can follow the well-preserved crenellated west parapet. The badly crumbled eastern wall presides over a sharp drop to badlands draining towards Kardhámena (see opposite), to which it's around a two-hour walk (best attempted only in cooler weather). Inside the walls stand **two chapels**: the westerly, dedicated to Áyios Nikólaos, retains a surviving fresco of Áyios Khristóforos (St Christopher) carrying the Christ Child, while the eastern one of Ayía Paraskeví, though devoid of wall painting other than a few fragments above the west door, boasts fine rib vaulting. The castle was originally built during the fourteenth century as a prison for misbehaving knights, then modified during the 1490s in tandem with the fortification programme at the citadel in Kós Town. Works are under way to provide electricity and masonry consolidation with an eye towards use of the castle grounds for nocturnal spectacles, so expect opening hours and an admission fee in the future.

Kardhámena

KARDHÁMENA, on the southeast coast, 31km from Kós Town, is the island's second largest package resort after the capital itself, with locals outnumbered in season twenty to one by young visitors (mainly Brits), most of them intent on getting as drunk as possible, as cheaply and quickly as possible. Runaway development has banished whatever redeeming qualities it may once have had, reducing the town to a seething, downmarket mass of off-licences, bars (far more numerous than tavernas), trinket shops and excursion agencies. Darts, bingo and karaoke competitions are staged regularly, pubs sport names like *Black Swan* and *Slug and Lettuce* and dispense imported beer on tap, and you can even get fish and chips at British-run stalls.

A hefty sand **beach** stretches to either side of the town, to the east hemmed in by ill-concealed military bunkers and a road as far as **Tolári**, home to the thousand-bedded *Norida Beach Hotel* all-inclusive complex. By forking left before reaching Tolári you'll reach Pylí after 9km – a useful, paved shortcut.

Practicalities

Kardhámena is most worth knowing about as a place to catch a **boat to Níssyros**. There are supposedly two daily sailings in season: the morning tourist excursion kaïki at either 9am or 9.30am, and another, less expensive, barely publicized one – the *Chrissula* – at 2.30pm, but in practice the afternoon departure (typically Mon, Wed, Thurs & Fri) can occur any time between 1.30pm and 6.30pm, depending on when the Nissyrians have finished their shopping; Kardhamenans are apt to be reticent about its comings and goings. Arrivals from Níssyros coincide fairly well with bus departures to Kós Town.

Except perhaps during August, there are generally a few **rooms** not taken by tour companies. Prices tend to be about fifteen percent cheaper than in Kós Town and are not outrageous (€20–26.50). If you decide – or are compelled – to stay, search out quieter premises west of the riverbed, beyond the *Valinakis Beach Hotel* – not that sleep is a particularly high priority for most holidaymakers here. One name to remember is the simple but en-suite *Milos Pension* (Ⓣ02420/91 413; ❷), at a fairly calm spot about two-thirds of the way northeast along the waterfront, then a block inland. For more comfort, the nominally B-class *Hotel Rio* (Ⓣ02420/91 627, Ⓕ91 895; ❹) can also be recommended.

Restaurants here in general serve predictably mediocre fare, and tend to change hands and format every season. The most Greek and longest-running **taverna** is *Andreas*, right on the harbour; between it and the jetty, the *Kardamos* is the last surviving traditional kafenío, where you can "meet the locals" (as the sign says) over an oúzo and *mezés*. Within sight of the *Milos Pension*, a **bakery** (the way signed with red arrows) offers local yogurt, brown bread and filled pies, while Peter's **rent-a-bike** (Ⓣ02420/91 487), across the street, is one of the more flexible outfits.

Southwestern Kós

The portion of Kós **southwest** of Andimáhia and the airport is the least developed and most thinly populated part of the island, with its permanent inhabitants confined to the lone, blufftop village of **Kéfalos**. Besides being the only area where non-package tourists are most likely to find a vacancy in high season, it also offers the most secluded and scenic beaches on the island, plus a number of minor ancient sites.

South coast beaches

The south-facing **beaches** between the airport and Kéfalos, though shown as separate extents on most tourist maps, are essentially one long stretch at the base of a cliff, interrupted by headlands only between "Paradise" and Áyios Stéfanos. The sections, listed below going from east to west, are given fanciful English names in tourist literature and are mostly provided with sunbeds and a jet-ski franchise, though the official Greek place names have returned to signs marking the individual access roads.

"**Magic**", officially Polémi, is the longest, broadest and wildest section; "**Sunny/Markos**", officially Psilós Gremós, the next along and an easy walk from "Magic", has a seasonal taverna just inland. **Langádha** is the cleanest and arguably the most scenic, with junipers tumbling off the dunes almost to the shore. "**Paradise**" (Tigáni), often dubbed "Bubble Beach" in boat-trip jargon, owing to volcanic gas vents in the tidal zone, is overrated; the sandy area is too small for the hordes descending upon its wall-to-wall sunbeds and two tavernas, while boats attached to the paragliding and banana-ride outfits buzz constantly offshore. "**Camel**" (Kamíla) is the smallest and loneliest of these strands, flanked by weird rock formations (but no humped beasts) and protected somewhat from crowds by an unusually steep drive down.

Limiónas

Just east of the turning for Áyios Stéfanos, a marked, paved side road leaves the main route, bound for **Limiónas** (Limniónas), the only north-facing beach and fishing port in this part of Kós. After 3.5km along the side road, bear right at another narrow but paved road (2.7km), signposted not for Limiónas but for its two rival **tavernas**. Currently much the better of this pair is *Miltos* up on the hillside, with excellent mezédhes, village bread, and very fresh fish justifying the detour out here. Swimming is actually a secondary consideration, though there are two compact patches of sandy **beach** to either side of a peninsula that ends in an islet now tethered to Kós by a breakwater.

Áyios Stéfanos and Kastrí

Uninterrupted beach resumes at **Áyios Stéfanos** and continues 5km west to Kamári (see opposite). This area is overshadowed by a huge, 1970s-vintage **Club Med** complex of well-landscaped bungalows around a less attractive main hotel, all refurbished in 2001. In a reversal of historic policy, you can now get day-use passes for their extensive facilities, or even book overnight stays on the spot (Ⓣ02420/71 311, Ⓕ72 217; ❻, minimum stay in high season 4 nights). The Club Med has its own sewage treatment plant, which is more than can be said for the haphazard development at Kamári; less commendable is the management's past tendency to imply that both local beaches are private.

The badly marked public access road to the westerly beach begins near the bus stop and cuts through the Club Med grounds, fizzling out just before a peninsula crowned with the exquisite remains of two triple-aisled, sixth-century **basilicas**. Though still the best preserved on the island, these have not been faring well recently; several columns have toppled over since the 1980s. The entire floor area, however, is decorated with excellent **mosaics**, most of them under a protective layer of sand. Visible south of the apse, two peacocks perch upon and drink from a goblet; in the north chapel's aisle, next to the baptistry and font, two mosaic ducks can be seen paddling about.

The basilicas overlook the tiny but striking islet of **Kastrí**, sporting a chapel and a distinct volcanic pinnacle. From the sandy cove west of the peninsula it's just a short swim away; in spots, you can even wade across, local water-ski school activity permitting. The sea here warms up early in the year and is shallow enough to stay that way into November. It offers the best snorkelling on an island not otherwise known for it, owing to rock formations cutting across the generally sandy seabed. As at "Paradise", gas bubbles up from the ocean floor.

Kamári

Essentially the shore annexe of Kéfalos (see below), **KAMÁRI** is a sprawling resort of scrappy, rapidly multiplying breeze blocks, pitched a few notches above Kardhámena, though here, too, British tour operators exert a hammerlock on much of the place. The developed strip, a stream of lower-rise rooms, self-catering studios and tavernas, thins out slightly as you head southwest towards the fishing port; in addition to offering all watersports, particularly windsurfing, in season Kamári may serve as an alternative departure point for Níssyros excursions (up to 5 weekly in season).

Independent **hotels** or **dhomátia** that can be recommended here include *Sydney* (Ⓣ02420/71 286; ❷) and the adjacent *Maria* (Ⓣ02420/71 308; ❷), on the seafront west of the junction for the main road up to Kéfalos. *Stamatia*, near the main roundabout, is the oldest and (relatively) most authentic **taverna** hereabouts.

Kéfalos

Forty-three kilometres from Kós Town and the end of the line for buses, the inland settlement of **KÉFALOS** squats on a flat-topped hill looking northeast down the length of Kós. As densely packed as Andimáhia is straggly, Kéfalos has little to attract the hordes from Kamári other than a few shops, the region's only **post office**, a single **bank** with cash machine, and a few basic **tavernas** and "snak bars" (sic) in the centre. Even the **Knights' castle** here, downhill beside the Kamári-bound road, is rudimentary and unimpressive; the Knights must have thought so too, abandoning it in 1504. But for better or worse, the village makes a staging point for expeditions south into the rugged peninsula that terminates at dramatically sheer Cape Kríkello.

Cape Kríkello

The first point of interest on a tour of the south peninsula is Byzantine **Panayía Palatianí**, 1km south of Kéfalos; a marked path east from the roadside leads to this chapel, which incorporates generous chunks of an ancient temple. Some 500m beyond, a less obvious sign reading "Palatia" points through fencing down a broader, shady lane to the site of ancient **Astypalia**, the original capital of Kós until abandoned in 366 BC. The most conspicuous remains here are those of a Hellenistic temple with just its foundation corners intact, and a late Classical amphitheatre with two rows of seats still in place, enjoying a fine prospect over the curve of Kamári Bay – if you can ignore the generous sprinkling of litter underfoot.

Immediately past Astypalia, a paved road leaves the ridge road and heads west towards **Áyios Theológos**, 7km from Kéfalos. Besides the namesake chapel, there's a convenient **taverna**, the *Sunset Wave*, a reliable option for a home-made sweet and coffee, though the fare in recent years has been tending towards the hamburger and chips persuasion. They also rent out **boogie boards** (€6 per day) for taking advantage of the steady surf here. Forays along the dirt tracks to either side – a jeep or dirt bike is advisable – will turn up more secluded sandy coves at the base of low cliffs.

The appealing monastery of **Áyios Ioánnis Thymianós** (7km from Kéfalos), reached by following the paved road to its end, is pretty much the end of the line for non-4WD vehicles (jeeps can reach Áyios Mámas, 4km beyond). Set on a natural balcony under two plane trees, the church is locked except during the festival on August 28–29; it's a fine picnic spot at other times, but there's no reliable drinking water.

Áspri Pétra

Just under 2km further along the paved ridge road from the Theológos turning, you can make another detour to the **cave of Áspri Pétra**, inhabited in Neolithic times. Instead of continuing straight towards Áyios Ioánnis Thymianós, bear left onto a dirt track heading east towards a chapel and telecom tower atop Mount Zíni; a downed sign proclaims these attractions, as well as "Áspri Pétra 1.5" on a very rusty upright placard. After 600m, there's another fork, with the left option going up towards a quarry, and the right going down to a jetty serving it. In the groin of this junction, marked by a red paint dot on a boulder to the left, is a faint dirt track, non-motorable – so leave transport here. Follow this as it dwindles to a path, running more or less parallel to the lower, right-hand road; the path is somewhat overgrown with baby pines and mastic bushes but red dots persist until the vicinity of a distinct, grey limestone outcrop. Here the path splits; adopt the upper, left-hand branch, now marked with green-paint blobs and crosses. Just right of this outcrop stands a natural rock arch, in turn marked by a large green cross visible from a distance. The cave – at most 25 minutes' walk from the second junction – is below and left of this, room-sized and well protected, though quite featureless other than a bit of rock walling built around the entrance.

Psérimos

Psérimos could be an idyllic little island were it not so close to Kós and Kálymnos. Throughout the season, both of these larger neighbours dispatch daily excursion boats, which compete strenuously to dock at the small harbour village of **Avlákia**. In midsummer, day-trippers blanket the main sandy beach curving around the bay in front of Avlákia's thirty-odd houses and huge communal olive grove; even during May or late September you're guaranteed at least a hundred outsiders daily (versus a permanent population of 25). There are a couple of other, remoter beaches to hide away on during the day: clean **Vathý** (sand and gravel), a well-marked, thirty-minute path-walk east, starting from behind the *Taverna Iy Pserimos*, or grubbier, tar-smeared **Marathoúnda** (pebble), a 45-minute walk north on the main trans-island track. Nowhere on Psérimos, including the monastery of Grafiótissa (big festival August 14–15), is much more than an hour's walk away.

Practicalities

Even during the season there won't be too many other overnighters, since there's a limited number of beds available, and your reception at some of the more put-upon snack bars may become warmer once it's clear that you're **staying**. Pick of the several small pensions is *Tripolitis* (Ⓣ02430/23 196; ❶), over English-speaking *Nick and Anna's* café-snack bar, or the rooms above *Taverna Manola* on the opposite end of the beach (Ⓣ02430/51 540; ❶), who also keep the plusher *Studios Kalliston* next door (❷). There's just one small, limited-stock **store**, since most of the island's supplies are brought in daily from Kálymnos. Eating out however, won't break the bank, and there's often fresh fish in the handful of **tavernas**; many of these have contracts with the tour boats, but *Taverna Manola* doesn't, and despite modest appearances proves very adept at ouzerí fare and seafood.

Greek script table

Kós	Κώς	ΚΩΣ
Andimáhia	Αντιμάχεια	ΑΝΤΙΜΑΧΕΙΑ
Asfendhioú	Ασφενδιού	ΑΣΦΕΝΔΙΟΥ
Asómati	Ασώματοι	ΑΣΩΜΑΤΟΙ
Áspri Pétra	Άσπρη Πέτρα	ΑΣΠΡΗ ΠΕΤΡΑ
Áyios Dhimítrios	Άγιος Δημήτριος	ΑΓΙΟΣ ΔΗΜΗΤΡΙΟΣ
Áyios Fokás	Άγιος Φωκάς	ΑΓΙΟΣ ΦΩΚΑΣ
Áyios Ioánnis	Άγιος Ιοάννης	ΑΓΙΟΣ ΙΟΑΝΝΗΣ
Thymianós	Θυμιανός	ΘΥΜΙΑΝΟΣ
Áyios Stéfanos	Άγιος Στέφανος	ΑΓΙΟΣ ΣΤΕΦΑΝΟΣ
Áyios Theológos	Άγιος Θεολόγος	ΑΓΙΟΣ ΘΕΟΛΟΓΟΣ
Brós Thermá	Μπρός Θερμά	ΜΠΡΟΣ ΘΕΡΜΑ
Cape Kríkello	Ακροτήρι Κρίκελο	ΑΚΡΟΤΗΡΙ
Dhíkeos	Δίκεος	ΔΙΚΕΟΣ
Evangelístria	Ευαγγελίστρια	ΕΥΑΓΓΕΛΙΣΤΡΙΑ
Kamári	Καμάρι	ΚΑΜΑΡΙ
Kardhámena	Καρδάμαινα	ΚΑΡΔΑΜΑΙΝΑ
Kéfalos	Κέφαλος	ΚΕΦΑΛΟΣ
Kermetés	Κερμετές	ΚΕΡΜΕΤΕΣ
Khristós	Χριστός	ΧΡΙΣΤΟΣ
Lámbi	Λάμπι	ΛΑΜΠΙ
Lim(n)iónas	Λιμ(ν)ιώνας	ΛΙΜ(Ν)ΙΩΝΑΣ
Marmári	Μαρμάρι	ΜΑΡΜΑΡΙ
Mastihári	Μαστιχάρι	ΜΑΣΤΙΧΑΡΙ
Pláka	Πλάκα	ΠΛΑΚΑ
Platáni	Πλατάνι	ΠΛΑΤΑΝΙ
Psalídhi	Ψαλίδι	ΨΑΛΙΔΙ
Pylí	Πυλί	ΠΥΛΙ
Tingáki	Τιγκάκι	ΤΙΓΚΑΚΙ
Ziá	Ζιά	ΖΙΑ
Zipári	Ζιπάρι	ΖΙΠΑΡΙ
Psérimos	Ψέριμος	ΨΕΡΙΜΟΣ
Grafiótissa	Γραφιότισσα	ΓΡΑΦΙΟΤΙΣΣΑ
Marathoúnda	Μαραθούντα	ΜΑΡΑΘΟΥΝΤΑ
Vathý	Βαθύ	ΒΑΘΥ

Nearly all the **boats** based on Kós and Kálymnos harbour operate triangle tours (approximately €17.50), which involve departure between 9.30am and 10am, followed by a stop for swimming at either Platý islet or adjacent Psérimos, lunch in Avlákia, or Póthia, or Rína, the ports of Kálymnos (or even on board), and another swimming stop at whichever islet wasn't visited in the morning. If you want to spend the entire day on Psérimos, you're much better off departing Póthia at 9.30am daily on the tiny *Nissos Pserimos*, returning at 4pm (€6 round trip). The islanders themselves use this boat to visit Kálymnos for shopping and administrative business; with just a bare handful of children, there is no longer a school on the island.

Kós travel details

Island transport

City (Deas) buses

Kós Town to: Asklepíon (11 daily except Mon, 8am–6pm); Áyios Fokás (roughly every 15min, dawn–midnight); Brós Thermá (9 daily, 10am–6pm); Lámbi (roughly half-hourly, 6.30am–11.30pm); Platani (16 daily, 8am–11.45pm).

Miniature train

Kós Town to: Asklepion (hourly, Mon–Fri). 9am–5pm, returns 1hr 15min later; hourly 8.15am–1.15pm Sat–Sun).

Ktel buses

Kós Town to: Andimáhia, Kardhámena, Kéfalos (6 Mon–Sat, 3 Sun); Marmári (12 Mon–Sat, 7 Sun); Mastihári (5 Mon–Sat, 3 Sun); Pylí (3–5 daily); Tingáki (7–12 daily); Ziá via Evangelístria (3 daily Mon–Sat).

Inter-island transport

Key to ferry and hydrofoil companies

DANE	*Dhodhekanisiakí Anónymi Navtiliakí Etería* (Dodecanesian Shipping Co)
G&A	G&A Ferries
KR	Kyriakoulis Maritime
LZ	Laoumtzis Flying Dolphins
NK	*Nissos Kalymnos*

Small ferries

Kardhámena to: Níssyros (3–4 weekly, nominally at 2.30pm, on *Chrissula*; 1hr). No cars carried.

Mastihári to: Póthia, Kálymnos (3–4 daily most of the year, 9am–10pm, on ANEM – Shipping Company of Mastihári Anonymous; 45min). Departure times are linked vaguely to arrivals of Olympic Airways' flight from Athens (☎02420/59 027 or 59 124 for current information). Several cars carried.

Excursion boats

Kardhámena to: Níssyros (at least 1 daily; 1hr).

Kós Town to: Níssyros (4–7 weekly; 1hr 40min); Psérimos (4 weekly; 50min).

NB These departures, meant primarily to serve day-trippers, are also available on a one-way basis, though fares are relatively expensive.

Large ferries

Kós Town to: Astypálea (1–2 weekly on DANE or G&A, 2 weekly via Kálymnos on NK; 4–5hr); Foúrni (1–2 weekly on G&A; 6hr); Ikaría (3 weekly on G&A; 7hr); Kálymnos (7–14 weekly on DANE or G&A, 2 weekly on NK; 1hr 15min–1hr 30min); Kastellórizo (1 weekly on G&A, 1 on NK, via Rhodes; 9–10hr); Léros (7–14 weekly on DANE or G&A; 2hr 30min); Lipsí (1–2 weekly on G&A; 3hr 15min); Náxos (1 weekly on G&A; 10hr); Níssyros (1–2 weekly on DANE or G&A, 2 weekly on NK; 1hr 30min–1hr 45min); Páros (1 weekly on G&A; 11hr); Pátmos (7–14 weekly on DANE or G&A; 4hr); Pireás (7–16 weekly on DANE or G&A; 12–16hr); Rhodes (7–14 weekly, mostly direct, on DANE or G&A; 4hr); Sámos (2 weekly on NEL or DANE, direct; 8hr); Sými (1–2 weekly on G&A or DANE; 3hr); Thessaloníki (1 weekly on DANE; 20hr); Tílos (1–2 weekly on DANE or G&A; 2hr 30min).

Catamaran

The *Dodekanisos Express* links Kós with the following islands at the following frequencies from July to mid-Sept: Rhodes, Léros (daily); Pátmos (6 weekly); Kálymnos, Lipsí (4 weekly); Níssyros, Tílos (1 weekly). Maximum journey times, with stops, vary from 2hr 30min for Pátmos to 40min for adjacent Kálymnos. During May and June, when hydrofoils may be lacking, the *Dodekanisos Express* may do some unusual runs, serving Sými (3 weekly), Níssyros and/or Tílos twice weekly and islands to the north much less often.

Hydrofoils

Kós Town to: Agathoníssi (1–2 weekly on KR; 3hr 10min); Foúrni (1–2 weekly on KR; 4hr); Hálki (1 weekly on KR, 1 weekly on LZ; 2hr 30min–3hr 30min); Ikaría (1 weekly on KR; 3hr 30min); Kálymnos (at least daily on KR; 45min); Léros (2 daily on KR; 1hr 30min); Lipsí (5–14 weekly on KR; 2hr); Níssyros (1–2 weekly on KR, 1 weekly on LZ; 50min); Pátmos (1–3 daily on KR, 2 weekly on LZ; 2hr–2hr 30min); Rhodes (at least daily on LZ, 2 daily on KR; 2hr–2hr 30min); Sámos-Pythagório (5–17 weekly on KR; 3hr 30min–4hr 30min); Sými (2 weekly on LZ, 1 weekly on KR; 1hr–1hr 30min); Tílos (1 weekly indirectly on KR, 1 weekly on LZ; 1hr 40min).

Flights

Kós to: Athens (3–4 daily; 1hr).

International transport

Kós Town to: Bodrum, Turkey (2–14 weekly; 45min). Greek boat or Laoumtzis Flying Dolphin leaves 9am, returns 4pm; €29.50 return, Greek tax inclusive; no cheap day-return or one ways, no Turkish port tax. Identically priced Turkish boat (*Fahri Kaptan*) or hydrofoil departs Bodrum 9am or so, leaves Kós 4.30pm; this provides the only service in winter (Nov–April). Only the Turkish afternoon boat takes cars.

Astypálea

Geographically, historically and architecturally, **Astypálea** (alias Astropália) would be more at home among the Cyclades – on a clear day you can see Anáfi or Amorgós (to the southwest and northwest respectively) far more easily than any of the other Dodecanese (except western Kós). Astypálea's inhabitants are descendants of medieval colonists from the Cyclades, and the island looks and feels more like the archipelago to the west than its neighbours to the east. Anecdotes relate that Astypálea was mistakenly reassigned to the Ottomans after the Greek Revolution only because the French, English and Russians had such a poor map at the 1830 and 1832 peace conferences.

Despite its evocative butterfly shape, Astypálea does not immediately impress you as the most beautiful of isles. The heights, which offer modest walking opportunities, are bleak and covered in thornbrush or dwarf juniper. Yet the herb *alisfakiá*, made into a tea, flourishes too, and hundreds of sheep and goats manage to survive – as opposed to snakes, which are (uniquely in the Aegean) entirely absent; legend claims that migrating cranes ate them all. Lush citrus groves and vegetable patches in the valleys signal the presence of a relatively ample water supply, hoarded in a reservoir above Livádhia. The various beaches along the bleak, heavily indented coastline often have reef underfoot and suffer periodic dumpings of seaweed.

In antiquity the island's most famous citizen was Kleomedes, a boxer disqualified from an early Olympic Games for causing the death of his opponent. He came home so enraged that he demolished the local school, killing all its pupils. Things have calmed down a bit in the intervening 2500 years, and today Astypálea is renowned mainly for its honey, fish and lobsters; the abundant local catch has only been shipped to Athens since the late 1980s, a reflection of the traditionally poor ferry links in every direction.

These have improved recently with the introduction of extra services towards Pireás via selected Cyclades, and high-season links with Rhodes via a few intervening islets, but outside July or August you still risk being marooned here for a day or two longer than intended. If this happens, you'll find yourself adapting pretty quickly to the back of beyondness of it all; foreign-newspaper delivery is fitful at best, TVs in the café-bars spend – by Greek standards – a fair amount of time switched firmly off, and the locals – including a sizeable contingent of permanent dropouts from Athens – are, if not exactly bone idle, among the most laid-back folk in the islands.

Despite this relative isolation, plenty of people find their way to Astypálea during the short, intense midsummer season (a predictable mid-July to the first September Sunday before school starts), when the 1300 permanent inhabitants (including an elderly, pinioned pelican at the quayside) are all but overrun by upwards of seven thousand guests a day. Most arrivals are Athens-based Astypaleans, French or Italians, and supplemented by large numbers of yachties and foreign owners of restored second homes in the understandably popular Hóra. At such times you won't find a bed without reserving well in advance – camping rough is expressly frowned upon – and the noise and commotion at the densely built port defies belief. There are relatively few English-speakers among the arrivals, especially since Laskarina Holidays deleted the island from their list in 1995, frustrated by chronically unreliable connections to Kós and its airport. Indeed there is no conventional package tourism of any sort, yet passing yachts (and Athenian tastes) ensure the presence of chichi restaurants in the port, poshly stocked bottle shops and a sprinkling of arty souvenir shops that would do London's Covent Garden proud.

Getting around the island

Two **buses** run along the paved road between Hóra, Skala, Livádhia and Analípsi, frequently in July and August from 8am until 11pm, much less regularly out of season – posted timetables are generally reliable. There are only three official **taxis**, far too few to cope with passenger numbers in high season, when you may have to trudge baggage-laden some distance to your arranged lodgings, adding insult to injury caused by the ungodly arrival times of ferries. Several places rent out **scooters and motorbikes**, the most reliable being Lakis and Manolis (Ⓣ02430/61 263), with branches just below the square in Hóra and at Skála dock; they also rent out a few cars and jeeps. The island **map** sold locally is hilariously inaccurate, even by lenient Greek-island standards, though in compensation rural junctions are adequately signposted.

Skála and Hóra

The main harbour of **SKÁLA** or Péra Yialós dates largely from the Italian era; Astypálea was the first Dodecanesian island the Italians occupied in 1912. Most of the settlement between the quay and the line of nine ridgetop windmills is even more recent – and, it must be said, neither terribly attractive nor peaceful in peak season.

Skála's only real bright spot is a 1998-inaugurated **archeological museum** (June–Sept Tues–Sun 8am–2pm & 6pm–midnight; Oct–May closed evenings; free) at the rear of the bay. Into a single, well-lit room are crammed the best local finds spanning all historical periods in chronological order: Late Bronze Age tomb artefacts, a Hellenistic relief of a symposium, a Roman statuette of Aphrodite, marble fragments from early Christian basilicas – and photographs of their mosaics, still left *in situ*, to whet your appetite for cross-country expeditions to find them.

As you climb up beyond the port towards **HÓRA**, the island's official capital and main business district, the neighbourhoods get progressively older and more attractive, their steep streets are enlivened by the *poúndia*, or colourful wooden balconies with staircases of the whitewashed houses, which owe much to the building styles of Mýkonos and Tínos, the origins of the colonists brought to repopulate the island in 1413. The whole culminates in the thirteenth-century **kástro**, one of the finest in the Aegean, erected not by the Knights but by the Venetian Quirini clan on Byzantine foundations and subsequently modified by the Ottomans after 1537. Until well into this century over three hundred people lived inside the kástro, but depopulation and a severe 1956 earthquake combined to leave only a desolate shell today. The fine rib vaulting over the main west gate supports the church of **Evangelístria Kastrianí**, one of two intact here, the other being **Áyios Yeóryios** (both usually locked, though the site warden will encourage you to climb Kastrianí's belfry for amazing views). In contrast to the ongoing renovation activity outside the walls, restoration of the few interior dwellings is theoretically forbidden, as they're now the property of the Byzantine archeological ephorate. Currently the kástro grounds are in the throes of a consolidation and restoration project undertaken by this authority, designed to keep the wind-battered perimeter fortifications from crumbling further.

Accommodation

Skála, and to a lesser extent Hóra, have **accommodation** ranging from spartan, 1970s-vintage rooms to new state-of-the-art studios; proprietors tend not to meet ferries unless arrangements have been made, even if they have vacancies. Owing to high-season harbour noise – particularly the sound of ferries dropping anchor at 3am – you might, if uninterrupted sleep is a priority, prefer accommodation in the Hóra. A small, basic, seasonal (July–Sept) **campsite** (ⓣ02430/61 338) operates amongst calamus reeds and tamarisks behind Dhéftero Marmári bay (see p.253), about 4km along the road to Análipsi, but it can be mosquito-plagued any year after a wet winter (an increasingly rare occurrence).

Skála

Akti Rooms On the east shore of the bay ⓣ02430/61 281. Good-value if slightly snug studios, much better equipped and maintained than adjacent *Karlos*. ④

Studios Antzela On the hillside above the *Akti Rooms* and *Karlos Studios* ⓣ02430/61 561. Pleasant studios also worth trying; vast if unshaded terraces for some units. ④

Aphrodite Studios On the road up to Hóra ⓣ02430/61 478. Reasonably equipped, if not quite up to the standard of *Aktí Rooms*. ③

Astynea ⓣ02430/61 040, ⓕ61 209. Standard port hotel, refurbished in 1993, whose en-suite rooms have seaviews (plus a certain amount of bustle from tavernas just below and opposite). ③

Karlos Studios East shore of the bay ⓣ02460/61 330. misnamed, well-worn if large rooms without cooking facilities, but really only worth it if you get a seaview unit. ③

Paradisos ⓣ02430/61 224, ⓕ61 450. Elderly but fairly well-kept port hotel; all rooms are en suite and have seaviews. ③

Hóra

Kallihoron Studios Start of road to Livádhia from windmills ⓣ02430/61 934, ⓕ61 400, ⓦwww.astypalaia.com/kallichoron-1.htm. Runner-up in the plushness sweepstakes to the *Kilindra Studios*, these tasteful modern units all have views of Hóra and air con/heating. Open all year. Studios ⑤, one-bedroom ⑥

Kilindra Studios Hóra's west slope ⓣ02430/61 966, ⓕ61 131, ⓦwww.astypalaia.com/kilindra. The island's highest-standard and quietest digs are 2000-built, skilfully done mock-traditional units; all luxury amenities including a pool. The smallest fit two, the largest, four. Open all year. ⑥

Kostas Vaïkousis Houses Atmospheric, if firmiy 1980s technology, restored studios or entire houses (⑥ for 2 peak season, but just ② low) at three locations near the top of Hóra; enquire at Kostas' antique shop on the quay or reserve in advance on (ⓣ02430/61 430).

Provarma Studios About halfway along the road to Livádhia ⓣ02430/61 096, ⓕ61 228. Remoter and more affordable than the above two options, these are southwest-facing galleried studios with white-and-pine decor; large balconies, but no air conditioning. Open June–Oct. ④

Eating and drinking

The restaurant scene is quite distorted seasonally; during August, upwards of 25 **tavernas** and beach snack bars operate across the island, few of them memorable and many concerned primarily with turning a quick profit. The following is a selection of the more long-term or locally orientated restaurants.

Among the more reliable Skála options open outside of peak season, *Iy Monaxia* (aka *Viki's* after the proprietress who lived 16 years in Australia), one block inland from the ferry jetty by the old power plant, has excellent home-style cooking and operates year-round. The *Astropalia* (closes end Sept), on the hillside above the road up to Hóra, does good – if somewhat pricey – fish and not much else; there's even better seafood, island wine and superbly prepared own-grown vegetable dishes at the homey *Australia* (open all year), just inland from the head of the bay, where Kyria Maria presides over the oldest (est. 1971) and most wholesome taverna in Skála. Behind the *Hotel Paradhisos*, you'll find more careful cooking, polished presentation (and prices 25% above the norm) at *Aitherio* and *Maïstrali* (both open into Oct); catering somewhat to the yacht set, it's pot luck as to which is better any given night. Under the *Hotel Astynea* you'll find two more worthy choices: *To Steki* for grills, and the *Dapia Café*, the best source of full breakfasts, midday crêpes and home-made ice cream.

Nightlife and entertainment

Most **nightlife** happens up in more atmospheric Hóra, where the level esplanade between the windmills and the base of the *kástro* hill appears to be one solid café-bar. Of these, favourites include the unsigned *Tou Nikola* (*Iy Myli*) on the corner, with the island's characters installed, and home-made *glyká koutalioú* dished out amidst wonderfully kitsch Greek-royalist decor. This spot, along with much of Hóra, served as the location for *Island*, a truly forgettable 1989 film by Paul Cox, with Irene Pappas lending a bit of star gravitas to what was essentially plotless Indo-Euro-Greek nonsense. *Kafenio Ouzeri Aigaion* is the more spacious and trendy alternative across the way, with snacks in season and *alisfakiá* tea on offer. Relatively subdued **bars**, open peak season only, include long-lived *Kastro Bar*, below the north wall of the castle, classiest and best for conversation-level music, or *Artemis*, also with a terrace. For a livelier time there's *Panorama,* where the island's youth hang out until dawn, or *Faros*, a summer-only live-music venue on the road to Análipsi. More formal **entertainment** means an outdoor cinema (July–Aug only) on the southeast flank of the kástro, and a summer **music festival** (late June to early Aug) which attracts a mix of big Athenian names and local amateur acts.

Other practicalities

The **post office** and main **shopping area** are located in Hóra. Astypalea Tours (Ⓣ02430/61 571) in Skála, below the *Vivamare Apartments*, and Paradise Travel (Ⓣ02430/61 256) below the namesake hotel divide most of the **travel agency** business between them, except for *Nissos Kalymnos* tickets, which are sold only outside the port café, which also provides **internet** facilities. Olympic Airways has its own little office (Ⓣ02430/61 588). Next to the port police is a full-service branch of the Emboriki Trapeza/Commercial Bank, complete with **cash machine**. A **laundry** up in Hóra makes itself well known to yachties, plus there's a well-stocked, long-hours **pharmacy** on the road up from Skála.

The southwest

A twenty-minute walk (or a short bus journey) from Hóra brings you to **LIVÁDHIA**, a fertile valley with a popular, good beach, the foundations of the knoll-top **basilica** just to the west, and a variable collection of restaurants and cafés immediately behind. You can rent a **room or studio** just inland – worthy prospects include *Studios O Manganas* (Ⓣ & Ⓕ02430/61 68; ➎), on the frontage road, representing the highest standard here, or *Venetos Studios & Bungalows* (Ⓣ02430/61 490; ➍), on the westerly hillside. Among the half-dozen **tavernas**, *To Yerani* in the stream bed is about the most consistently open (until Oct) and renowned for its excellent *mayireftá*; they also keep simple rooms adjacent (Ⓣ02430/61 484; ➌). If you want full-on beachfront seating,

Iy Astropelos does pretty good fish, though their *mayireftá* is apt to get dried out from overcooking (or microwaving).

Beaches

If the busy, mixed sand-and-gravel beach at Livádhia doesn't suit, continue southwest fifteen minutes on foot to three small pebble coves at **Tzanáki**, packed out with naturists in midsummer. To get there, you can apparently no longer use the old footpath the entire distance – the fence of a mammoth villa with swimming pool blocks the way – but must use the new trail, which plunges straight down from the roadside where scooters tend to park. The three coves in question – the first two easy to reach, the third more difficult – huddle at the base of sculpted cliffs, with end-on views of Hóra.

Beyond the Tzanáki trio, Moúra cove, slimy-rocked and seaweed-strewn, is a complete waste of time; **Papoú**, just beyond, is a rather better 80-metre fine-gravel strand, but is accessible overland only by a horrifically steep side track, and then a final path approach to skirt a jealously fenced-off farm.

However the third bay beyond Tzanáki, **Áyios Konstandínos**, easily reachable by motorbike along 6km of dirt road from Livádhia, is rather more worth the effort. Here you'll find 200m of partly shaded sand and gravel hemmed in by spring-nurtured orchards, as well as a seasonal taverna.

Around Ehíli promontory from Áyios Konstandínos lie two south-facing beaches, Vátses and Kaminákia; both are easiest visited by boat excursions (typically 11am departure), which alternate days with outings to the islets of Koutsomýti and Ayía Kyriakí southeast of Astypálea. By land, **Vátses** has the easier dirt track in, only 6km (twenty minutes' scooter drive) out of Livádhia; it's long (250m), often windy and wild, at the mouth of a fine canyon with headlands framing the view to Anáfi. Vátses is also one of the sandier island beaches, with no dress code when the summer-only *kantína* is shut.

The half-hour drive to **Kaminákia**, arguably Astypálea's best and cleanest beach, begins reasonably enough, but once past the farms and rural monastery at Armenohóri, the route deteriorates to a bone-jarring, steep final descent, though again there are great views of Anáfi island if you dare take your eyes off the "road". Your reward at the bottom of the grade is a very sheltered, 150-metre, southeast facing cove with sunbeds, a seasonal taverna staying open into September, and a sea cave to explore on the left as you face the water. Excursion boats allow you an hour here, or at Áyios Ioánnis cove (see below), according to passenger consensus.

Áyios Ioánnis monastery and waterfall

A favourite outing in the west of the island is the two-hour walk or half-hour motorbike trip from Hóra to the oasis of **Áyios Ioánnis**, just under 10km away. Proceed northwest along the signposted, initially paved road beginning from the windmills, passing high above the reservoir, then keep left when a side track goes right towards the remote monastery of **Panayía Flevariótissa**. Beyond this point the main track (this time ignore a left) curls north at the base of a ridge, where the overflow of two springs may seep across the road. After skirting high above the half-dozen isolated farms in the valley of **Messariá**, you reach a junction with gates across each option. Go through the left-hand one, and soon the securely walled orchards of the uninhabited farm-monastery **Áyios Ioánnis** come into view.

From the balcony of the church, Anáfi can be seen on the horizon, and a steep, faint path leads down to the base of a ten-metre **waterfall**; alas, after several dry years, the bathing pools here dried up in 2001, so don't come specially for that – though the stream should run again for at least a year or two after the deluges of winter 2001–02. Below, a rather arduous, pathless trek down the canyon ends at a fine, pebbly bay, potentially the last stop for southwesterly boat excursions. For walkers who fancy a different route back to Hóra, there's a faint path east towards Armenohóri, where you can join the dirt-track system.

The northeast

Northeast of Skála, a series of three bays nestle in the narrow "body" of the "butterfly"; they're known as **Próto** (First), **Dhéftero** (Second) and **Tríto** (Third) **Marmári** (marked as **Marmári A', B'** and **C'** respectively on some maps). The first is home to the local power plant and boatyards; the next one hosts the island's only organized **campsite** (see p.250); while the third, reasonably attractive bay, is also the start of a path east to the unfortunately named, but perfectly decent, coves of **Mamoúni** ("Bug" or "Critter" in Greek). Beyond Tríto Marmári, **Stenó** takes its name ("Narrow") from the island's width at this point – a mere hundred metres or so; the middle beach east of the isthmus, with sandy shore and shallows, a few tamarisks and a seasonal *kantína*, is the best.

Análipsi (Maltezána) and beyond

ANÁLIPSI, widely known as Maltezána (after medieval Maltese pirates), is a ten-kilometre bus trip or taxi ride from town. Although the second-largest settlement on Astypálea, there's surprisingly little for outsiders besides a narrow, sea-urchin-speckled **beach** (there are better ones east of the main bay) and a nice view south to some islets. Despite this, blocks of **rooms** (open only July & Aug) sprout in ranks well back from the sea, spurred by the proximity of the airport, 700m away. Among a handful of **tavernas**, the most reliably open (Feb–Christmas) is *Analipsi* (aka *Irini's*, after the proprietress) by the jetty, which doubles as the kafenío for the local fishermen and seemingly every passing worker on the island. The food – fish fry-ups, or *kakaviá* (fish soup) for those willing to wait – is simple but excellent and reasonably priced. For a larger outlay, but also top quality, try *Ovelix* a few hundred yards inland, where you have to pre-order your fish (Ⓣ02430/61 260; closes by mid-Sept). On the road to the east bay, there's a **music club**, *Yacht Club*, open in high season only.

Análipsi and its environs boast the best of the island's several Byzantine mosaics, though these are unprotected and shamefully deteriorating. Behind calamus reeds and eucalyptus trees near the fishing jetty lie the colourful floors of the **early Byzantine Tallarás baths**, with somewhat crude mosaics of zodiacal signs, figures representing the seasons and a central androgynous figure (perhaps Time or Fortune personified), holding the cosmic orb. Beyond the *Yacht Club*, where the road becomes dirt, signs point seaward towards the **Karéklis basilica**, ten minutes' trail-walk away; in the border panels of geometric floor mosaics here, two dolphins can be seen cavorting. En route you pass, on the headland, a memorial obelisk commemorating French sailors who died in the act of scuttling the frigate *Bisson*, trapped by the Ottoman navy here on November 6, 1827, during the Greek War of Independence.

Beyond the turn-off for the mosaic and obelisk, the road hits the sea briefly again at **Váï**, an attractively sandy bay that's unfortunately fully exposed to the prevailing winds and garbage-laden currents – only a swimming possibility on calm or southerly-wind days.

Many maps show a fully fledged village at **Kastelláno**, reached by a side road about 8km past Maltezána, while other sources fancifully describe an opulent villa for Mussolini at this spot. This was in fact a 1930s Italian military base, a camouflage-painted two-storey barracks plus a bunker, standing barely tall enough to provide shade for sheep and goats which today are the "garrison".

The motorable dirt track ends 23km from Hóra at **Mésa Vathý** (invariably and erroneously shown on most maps as Éxo Vathý), a sleepy fishing village with a single **taverna** (*Iy Galini*) and superb small-craft anchorage in what's an almost landlocked inlet terminating in a salt marsh, sporadically home to those snake-eating cranes. Frankly, though, it's not really worth the long, bumpy trip out by land – though yachties esteem the place – and to rub salt in the wound, the fish on the menu is usually frozen (if local). Following several accidents, this is no longer the **backup ferry port** in winter, when Skála is buffeted by the prevailing southerlies; foot passengers (but no vehicles) are transferred ashore to the quay at **Áyios Andhréas**, just west of Tríto Marmári. Neither place has lights on the quay nor good anchorage, which can result in Astypálea being effectively cut off for days on end during winter.

Greek script table

Astypálea	Αστυπάλαια	ΑΣΤΥΠΑΛΑΙΑ
Análipsi	Ανάληψη	ΑΝΑΛΗΨΗ
Armenohóri	Αρμενοχώρι	ΑΡΜΕΝΟΧΩΡΙ
Áyios Andhréas	Άγιος Ανδρέας	ΑΓΙΟΣ ΑΝΔΡΕΑΣ
Áyios Ioánnis	Άγιος Ιοάννης	ΑΓΙΟΣ ΙΟΑΝΝΗΣ
Áyios Konstandínos	Άγιος Κωνσταντίνος	ΑΓΙΟΣ ΚΩΝΣΤΑΝΤΙΝΟΣ
Éxo Vathý	Έξω Βαθύ	ΕΞΩ ΒΑΘΥ
Hóra	Χώρα	ΧΩΡΑ
Kaminákia	Καμινάκια	ΚΑΜΙΝΑΚΙΑ
Karéklis	Καρέκλης	ΚΑΡΕΚΛΗΣ
Maltezána	Μαλτεζάνα	ΜΑΛΤΕΖΑΝΑ
Marmári	Μαρμάρι	ΜΑΡΜΑΡΙ
Mésa Vathý	Μέσα Βαθύ	ΜΕΣΑ ΒΑΘΥ
Skála	Σκάλα	ΣΚΑΛΑ
Stenó	Στενό	ΣΤΕΝΟ
Tallarás	Ταλλαράς	ΤΑΛΛΑΡΑΣ
Tzanáki	Τζανάκι	ΤΖΑΝΑΚΙ
Vaï	Βάϊ	ΒΑΪ
Vátses	Βάτσες	ΒΑΤΣΕΣ

Atypálea travel details

Inter-island transport

Key to ferry companies

DANE *Dhodhekanisiakí Anónymi Navtiliakí Etería* (Dodecanesian Shipping Company)
G&A G&A Ferries
NK *Nissos Kalymnos*

Ferries

Astypálea to: Amórgos (3–5 weekly on G&A; 2hr); Kálymnos (1–2 weekly on G&A or DANE, 2–3 weekly on NK; 2hr 30min–3hr 15min); Kós (1 weekly, mid-summer, on DANE; 3hr 15min); Náxos (3–5 weekly on G&A; 4hr); Níssyros (1 weekly, midsummer, on G&A; 4hr 30min); Páros (3–5 weekly on G&A; 5hr); Pireás (5–6 weekly on G&A; 12hr); Rhodes (1–2 weekly on DANE or G&A; 4hr); Sýros (1 weekly on G&A; 6hr 30min).

Hydrofoils

Astypálea to: Kálymnos (nominally 1 weekly, 90-min journey time, usually Sat, late June to early Sept, but this is deeply unreliable and typically weather permits only 4 trips in any summer).

Flights

Astypálea to: Athens (4–5 weekly; 1hr 10min).

Kálymnos

Most of the 17,000-strong population of **Kálymnos** lives in or around the large port of Póthia, a wealthy but not conventionally beautiful town famed for its **sponge industry**. Unfortunately, almost all of the eastern Mediterranean's sponges were devastated by a viral disease in 1986, related to freak warm currents, and only three or four of the fleet of thirty-odd boats – themselves reduced from the 134 active in 1948 – are still in use. In response to this catastrophe (and a smaller repeat outbreak in 1999), the island established a tourist industry – mainly confined to one string of beach resorts – and also converted most of its sponge boats for deep-sea fishing. This last has had disastrous effects ecologically, as crews – licensed by the government to use scuba gear in the process – virtually hoover the sea floor of marine life. Warehouses behind the harbour still process and sell sponges all year round – a few of these from reviving deep-water beds near Sicily and Malta, but most now imported from Asia and the Caribbean. There are also dwindling numbers of elderly gentlemen about who rely on two canes, walking frames or even wheelchairs, stark evidence of the havoc wrought in their youth by nitrogen embolism (the "bends"), long before divers understood its crippling effects. See box on p.257.

The departure of the remaining **sponge fleet**, usually just after Easter, is preceded by a festive week known as *Yprogrós*; the fleet's return, approximately six months later, has historically also been the occasion for more uproarious, male-oriented celebration in the port's bars. If you see musicians playing on Dodecanese ferries at these or other times, it's a fair certainty that they are either natives of Kálymnos or on their way there. With two festival seasons per year guaranteed, the island has preserved a vital and idiosyncratic musical tradition.

Kálymnos essentially consists of two cultivated and inhabited valleys sandwiched between three limestone ridges, harsh in the full glare of noon but magically tinted towards dusk. The **climate**, especially in winter, is alleged to be drier and healthier than that of neighbouring Kós or Léros, since the quick-draining limestone strata, riddled with many caves, doesn't retain as much moisture. The rock does, however, admit sea water, which has tainted Póthia's wells; drinking water must be brought in by tanker truck from the pure bores at Vathý, and there are also potable, public springs at Dhámos, Potamí district of Póthia and Hóra. In the vegetated valleys, mosquitoes can be a problem, so keep chemical or electrical repellents to hand. There are also seasonal plagues of unusually aggressive, brown and yellow wasps around Massoúri and Télendhos.

Despite its hostile geology, the island's position and excellent harbours ensured that it was of some importance from ancient times – especially during the

Byzantine era, as testified to by the presence of more ruined early basilicas here than on any other island in the Dodecanese. Another local Byzantine legacy is the survival of peculiar medieval names (eg, Skévos, Sakellários and Mikés for men, Themélina, Petránda and Sevastí for women), found nowhere else in Greece.

Since Kálymnos is the home port of the very useful local namesake **ferry** (see p.271), a minor hub for Kyriakoulis Maritime hydrofoils, and moreover where long-distance ferry lines from the Cyclades and Astypálea join up with the main Dodecanesian routes, many travellers only pause here en route to other islands. Yet Kálymnos has sufficient attractions to justify a stay of several days – or even longer, as the package industry at the western beaches suggests. Local legend, common to several other spots in Greece, asserts that if you drink island water (salty or otherwise), you'll return to live here one day. And indeed there seems to be an unusually large number of resident foreigners, either married to locals or in business for themselves, perhaps attracted by the unpretentious ethos of the main town.

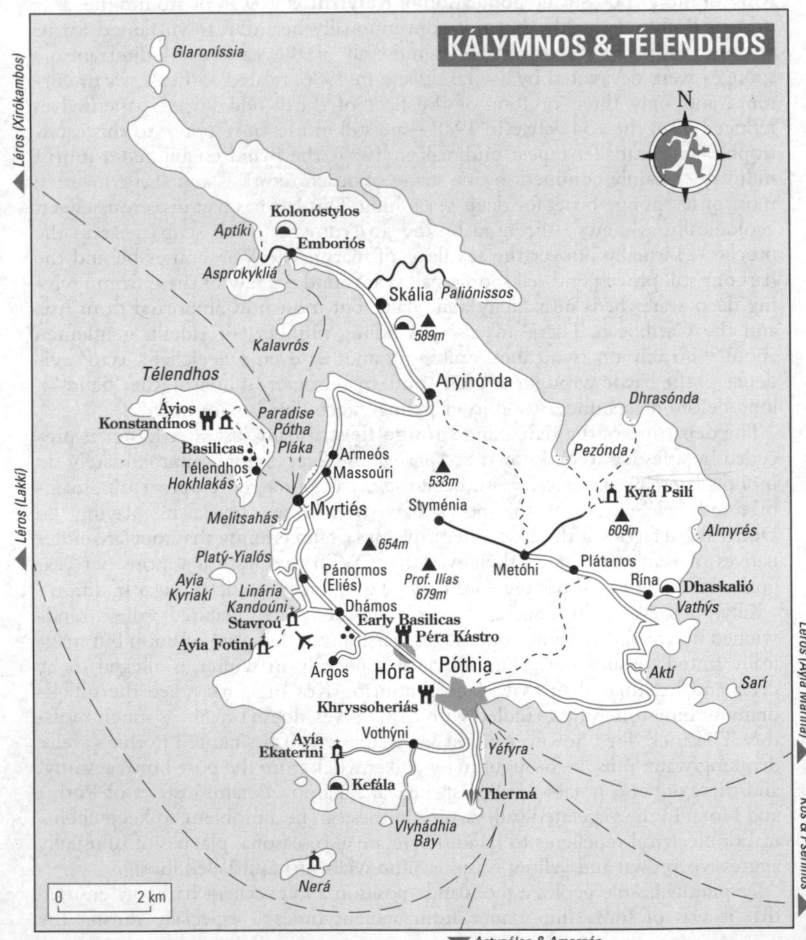

Sponges and sponge diving

Sponges are colonies of microscopic marine organisms which excrete a fibrous skeleton, increasing in size by about thirty percent annually. When alive, they are dark – almost black – in colour, and can be seen throughout the Dodecanese and east Aegean as melon-sized blobs, anchored to rocks in three to ten metres of water. However, these are mostly wild sponges, impossible to clean or shape with shears; Kalymnian divers are after the so-called *ímero* or "domesticated" sponges, which are much softer, more pliable, and dwell at greater depths – typically thirty to forty metres.

Before the late nineteenth century, sponge fishers free-dived for their quarry; weighted with rocks, they descended to the sea bed to hand-collect or spear as many sponges as possible on a single breath of air before being hauled to the surface by a safety line. The industrial revolution signalled momentous changes: divers were fitted with heavy, insulated suits – the so-called *skáfandhro* – and breathing apparatus filled by an air-feed line connected to primitive, hand-operated compressors on board the factory boats. They could now attain depths of as great as 70m, but this resulted in the first cases of the "bends", or nitrogen embolism. Divers working at any depth of over 10m and at pressures of several atmospheres would rise too quickly to the surface, so that the dissolved air in their bloodstream bubbled out of solution – with catastrophic results. From the late nineteenth century until well into the twentieth, roughly half of the sponge divers who left with the fleets in spring never returned in autumn: buried at sea, or in a lonely grave in some remote islet, sometimes while still alive up to his neck so that the hot sand might provide slight relief from the excruciating pain of nitrogen bubbles in the joints.

Not until World War I was the physiological basis of the malady well understood; by then thousands of Kalymnians had died, with many of the "lucky" survivors paralyzed, deaf or blind. The *skáfandhro*, despite being the obvious culprit and having been officially banned in many parts of the Mediterranean, returned to improper use until after World War II, wreaking more havoc. The first decompression chambers, and commercial diving schools imparting systematic knowledge of safe diving practices, were only available in Greece from the 1950s on. Now, new technology enabled the sea bed to be stripped with ruthless, ever-greater efficiency; the sponge fleets were forced to hunt further and further from home, finally ending up in Egyptian and Libyan territorial waters until the Nasser and Gaddafi regimes imposed punitive duties in 1962 and 1972 respectively.

In its natural form, even the "domestic" sponge is unuseable until processed. First the sponges have the smelly organic matter and external membrane thrashed out of them, traditionally by being trodden on the boat deck; next they are tossed in a rotary vat with hot sea water for a day or so, to complete the process. In Póthia you can visit a few workshops (the best is the one on the shore road opposite Ayía Iríni, in Vouvális district) where the sponge vats still spin; in the old days, the divers simply made a "necklace" of their catch and trailed it in the sea behind the boat. A third, optional processing step, that of bleaching the sponges with nitric acid to a pale yellow colour, has been added to accord with modern tastes. But the bleaching process weakens the fibres, so it's best to buy the more durable, natural-brown ones. In line with the risks, and competition from the production of synthetics, natural sponges are not cheap, even on Kálymnos; a good, hand-size bath sponge with a dense network of small holes will cost over €3. The enduring appeal of natural sponges – aside from the mystique of their gathering, and supporting a traditional life-style, however harsh – is that they're simply more durable, softer and absorbent than synthetic products, and lend themselves to a wide range of uses, from make-up artistry to canvas-painting to window-washing.

Trimming sponges for sale, Póthia, Kálymnos

Póthia

Its houses marching up the valley behind and arrayed in tiers up the sides of the mountains enclosing it, **PÓTHIA**, without being stereotypically picturesque, is colourful and authentically Greek. Your first and overwhelming impression will likely be of the phenomenal noise created by exhibitionist motorbike traffic and the cranked-up sound systems of the waterfront cafés. This is not entirely surprising, since with nearly 16,000 inhabitants, Póthia recently overtook Kós Town as the second largest municipality in the Dodecanese, after Ródhos Town. The effects of package tourism are quarantined well away on the west coast, with the only hint of it here being some yacht flotillas at anchor and a tourist agency or two.

Arrival, information and getting around

Kálymnos has an **airport** beyond Árgos village, under construction since 1991 – you can see the scar from the runway grading, above Kandoúni beach – and supposedly set to begin commercial operations late in 2002; private planes and helicopters already land. Olympic Airways has an agency at Patriárhou Maxímou 12 (☎02430/29 265), 200m inland from the quay. All **boat** and **hydrofoil agents**, including the head office of the *Nissos Kalymnos* (☎02430/29 612), line the first 150m or so of waterfront as you bear right out of the pier-area gate; G&A is handled by Mike Magos (☎02430/28 777), while DANE and the Dodekanisos Express are represented by various offices.

The main **taxi** rank is inland on Platía Kýprou, where some of the taxis function as "taxi-buses" (set-route, set-rate, may not depart until full); otherwise you sign on with the dispatcher, who calls out your car number when it's ready. Bona fide green **buses** with a yellow stripe run regularly as far as Aryinónda in the northwest and Vathý in the east, from a stop between the Municipal Nautical and Folklore Museum and the municipal "palace" where schedules are helpfully posted. No tickets are sold on board – buy them from the agent in the adjacent mini-market. Except for the line to the main western resorts, services are not terribly frequent, so for any extended explorations, you might **rent a motorbike** from one of a handful of outlets; Scooteromania (☎02430/51 780 or 097/2834628), just back from the front, near where it bends south, can be recommended for bikes in good condition at fair prices. **Car rental** is also available (eg an Avis franchise, ☎02430/28 990), though the island's compact enough that only families would need one. Incidentally, the locally sold **map** published by Emmanouil Vallas may look amateurish, but in fact is one of the more accurate of Dodecanesian island maps, showing hiking paths more or less correctly.

A minimally helpful municipal **tourist information booth** (sporadic hours) is located at the middle of the excursion/fishing-boat quay. The **post office** lies a good 600m inland from Khristós church, above Platía Kýprou; four **banks** on or just behind the waterfront have cash machines.

Accommodation

Accommodation in town is rarely a problem, since pension proprietors usually meet the ferries (though many of the premises touted are substandard, unlicensed or remote, often all three). The Pothians have so far remained indulgent towards short stays, perhaps realizing that the port won't hold most people's interest for more than a day or two. If you prefer to hunt for yourself, the following establishments are worth contacting in advance.

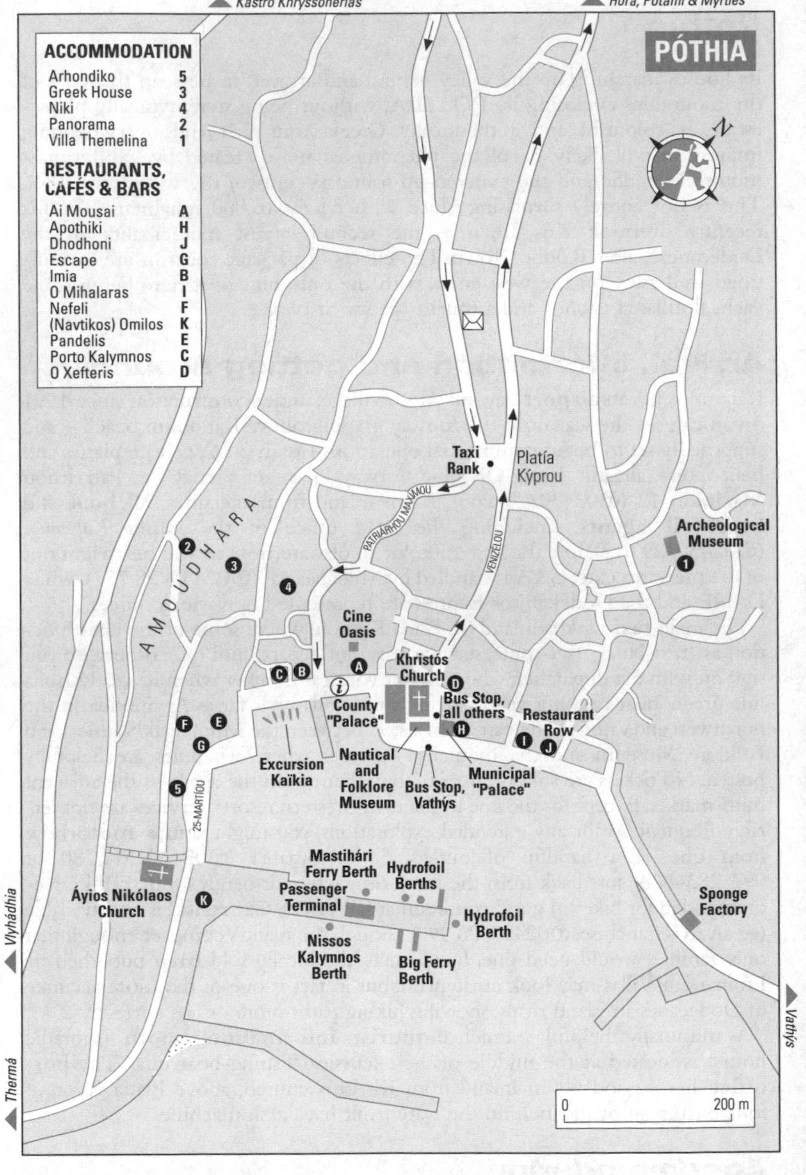

Arhondiko ⓣ02430/24 051, ⓕ24 149. Refurbished mansion just a few paces in from the west quay, but fairly quiet. Small to medium-sized, somewhat plain rooms have TV, fridge and some harbour-view balconies, but promised air con/heating hasn't yet materialized. ❸

Greek House ⓣ02430/23 752 or 29 559. Pension situated in Amoudhára district; if necessary ask directions at the *Flaskos souvláki* stand, at the base of the jetty. Run by a very friendly, voluble proprietress, Ypapandi Flaskou, whose kitsch rooms are all en suite. Best is the "penthouse", up a terrifying spiral staircase. Open most of the year. ❶

Niki ⓣ02430/28 528 or 093/7987403. En-suite pension between Amoudhára and Khristós church, in a fairly quiet spot; run by the friendly management of *Maria's Studios* in Melitsahás (see p.264). ❶

Panorama ⓣ02430/22 917, ⓕ23 138. Well-signposted, well-kept hotel also in Amoudhára, high above *Greek House*. Balconied rooms with views, a pleasant breakfast salon, and studios planned in the future. Open April–Oct. ❸

Villa Themelina ⓣ02430/22 682, ⓕ23 920, ⓦwww.griechenland.com/io2/reisen/302.html. In the quiet Evangelístria district near the archeological museum, this Belle Époque mansion has been converted into Póthia's most elegant hotel, featuring high-ceilinged, wood-floored, bug-screened rooms, many with balconies and English fireplace surrounds. Behind is a large pool, patio-garden where breakfasts are served, and two modern wings in vernacular style, plus a renovated cottage. Unfortuntately the new wings, without air con, can get very hot in summer. Open all year, but no breakfast Oct–Easter. ❸ rooms, ❹ studios

The Town

Perhaps the most rewarding way to acquaint yourself with Póthia is simply to wander its back streets, where elegant Neoclassical houses are surrounded by surprisingly large gardens, or craftsmen ply their trade in a genuine workaday bazaar. The Pothians particularly excel in ironwork, and all but the humblest dwellings in the eastern Evangelístria district are adorned by superbly ornate banisters, balcony railings and fanlights. During the Italian occupation, many houses were painted blue and white to irritate the colonial overlords, and though the custom has all but died out traces of the Greek national colours still appear among more traditional pink and ochre buildings.

The interior of the eighteenth-century **Khristós** cathedral is noteworthy as a sort of impromptu gallery for Kalymnian painters, while the marble *témblon* is by the great, half-mad Tiniot sculptor Yiannoulis Halepas, who died in 1943. Other public artworks, in the form of numerous bronze statues dotted about the town, are the works of contemporary sculptors Mihalis Kokkinos and his daughter Irini.

The only possibility of a swim in or near Póthia is en route to the defunct spa of Thermá, 2km southwest, at the pebbly cove of **Yéfyra**, at the mouth of a small ravine. At **Thermá** itself, there's just a concrete lido and a rather louche restaurant at one end of the crumbling spa building.

The museums

More formal edification is provided by two local museums. Priority should be given to the **Municipal Nautical and Folklore Museum** (Mon–Fri 8am–1.30pm, Sat & Sun 10am–12.30pm; €1.50), on the seaward side of Khristós cathedral. Pause first in front of the large foyer photo showing Póthia in the 1880s: no quay, jetty, roads (the Italians reclaimed most of the foreshore) or sumptuous mansions, with most islanders still living up in Hóra. Then it's on to a miscellany of smaller photos – sponge fishing, shipyards, the Allied liberation of 1945, even a shrine to the crew of a helicopter which crashed during the 1996 Ímia crisis (see p.450). Three-dimensional exhibits include ingenious, dart-shaped nautical-mile logs, dragged off the stern; horribly primitive divers' breathing apparati, all conducive to the bends; and "cages" designed to keep propellers from cutting air lines, a constant fear. The folkloric hall features the *sandoúri*, *laoúto* and *gáïda* beloved of local musicians, plus bread-making equipment and elaborate women's costumes.

The local, somewhat ambitiously titled **Archeological Museum** (Tues–Sun 10am–2pm; guided tours only; free), installed in a grand former residence of the Vouvalis family, is by contrast strictly a time-filler. Nikolaos Vouvalis (1841–1918) made his fortune as the first Greek to export sponges overseas; you're first shown the great man's office, then a room full of Paleolithic and

Bronze Age troves from the island's various caves, and finally the upstairs dining room and salon, furnished in utterly over-the-top Second Empire style.

Eating, drinking and nightlife

When **eating out**, the obvious strategy involves following the waterfront northeast past the Italian-built municipal "palace" to a line of fish tavernas and ouzerís, where the local speciality is octopus croquettes, more tender than you'd expect. However, recent years have seen touts multiply, prices climb and quality dip here, such that you're better off altogether avoiding this "restaurant row". Currently far and away the best seafood and Kalymnian specialities are found at *Taverna Pandelis*, tucked inconspicuously into a cul-de-sac behind the waterfront Olympic Hotel; this features daily, fresh-gathered shellfish like miniature oysters, *foúskes* and *kalógnomes*, plus wild scaly fish at reasonable prices. Fair-value *mayireftá* like *lahanodolmádhes* and bulk retsina can be enjoyed at *O Xefteris*, a traditional taverna (summer courtyard, winter hole-in-the-wall seating), well signposted inland from Khristós church. Excellent wood-fired pizzas are purveyed at equally worthy *Porto Kalymnos* and *Imia*, near each other at mid-quay, while for an inexpensive (if limited menu and not always very inspired) pre-ferry meal, (*Navtikos*) *Omilos* at the base of the ferry jetty is convenient. Sticky-cake fans will want to attend the traditional *Zaharoplastiki O Mihalaras* back on "restaurant row", excellent for *kataïfi*, *baklavás* and *galaktoboúreko*, and worth supporting in the face of inroads made by the local outlet of ice-cream chain *Dhodhoni*.

Most night owls congregate at a half-dozen loud music **cafés** concentrated at the first kink in the harbour quay, opposite the berthing place for the excursion kaïkia. At least two of Póthia's old buildings have been given a new lease of life as **music bars**: *Apothiki* (Warehouse) east of the municipal "palace", and *Escape*, in a hundred-year-old house near the sponge shops and *Taverna Pandelis*. Next door to *Escape*, *Nefeli* is the better equipped of two **internet cafés**. Also worth a look-in is *Ai Mousai* ("The Muses"), a tearoom on the waterfront esplanade with a facade of Corinthian columns which, since its inception in 1904, has served as a local Greek culture-club and reading room, except for a decade or two when the Italians appropriated it. The summer **cinema**, Cine Oasis, operates just inland from *Ai Musai*, with a fairly sophisticated playbill.

Hóra and around

From Póthia, the island's main road leads northwest to its main beach resorts. The first place you come to after 1.2km is a castle of the Knights of St John, **Kástro Khryssoheriás** (unrestricted access), in the suburb of Mýli. Huddled inside the whitewashed battlements are some rock-cut Bronze Age tombs and a small monastery, whose usually locked church contains some battered frescoes. The castle's location permits wonderful views southeast over the town to Kós, and north towards Hóra and Péra Kástro.

The island's old capital, **HÓRA** (aka Horió), 1.5km further along the main road, is still a large village of three thousand or so inhabitants; it guards a critical pass in Kalymnian topography, focus of settlement in every era and perhaps the site of the main ancient town. Steep steps ascend from its highest easterly point to the walled precinct of the Byzantine citadel town **Péra Kástro** (daily May–Oct 10am–2pm; tip to guide), appropriated by the Knights of St John and inhabited until late in the eighteenth century. Inside the imposing gate the former heaps of rubble are slowly being re-pieced together; a guided tour by the keeper visits five well-maintained, whitewashed chapels containing late medieval fresco fragments.

The basilicas

Some 200m past the turning for Árgos and the airport en route to Dhámos, you can detour left to visit two early Byzantine basilicas which are fairly representative, and the easiest to find, of a vast number on the island. Just as the main highway begins to descend, look for whitewashed steps leading over a stone wall to the immediately visible remains of **Khristós tís Ierousalím basilica**, supposedly built by Byzantine Emperor Arcadius during the late fourth century AD in gratitude for his deliverance from a storm off Kálymnos. The apse is fully preserved (if heavily scaffolded), and sections of marble flooring remain; both liberally incorporate masonry, some with ancient-Greek inscriptions, taken from a Hellenistic sanctuary of Apollo whose foundations lie just south, little else remaining above ground other than tumbled blocks. One field east, reached by a separate path from the road, are the larger, three-aisled but less impressive remains of the **Limniótissa basilica**; the east apse is the best-preserved area, and it would appear to have served as a chapel after the rest of the complex was destroyed during the seventh-century Arab raids.

"Brostá": west coast resorts

From the ridgetop basilicas beyond Hóra, the road dips into the pine- and eucalyptus-shaded valley of Dhámos en route to the consecutive **beach resorts** of Kandoúni, Myrtiés and Massoúri. Islanders refer to these collectively as "*Brostá*" (Forward), the leading side of Kálymnos, as opposed to "*Píso*" (Behind), the Póthia area.

Kandoúni and Platý-Yialós

KANDOÚNI, with some 200m of brown, seaweed-strewn, hard-packed sand, is effectively the shore annexe of the inland agricultural village of **Pánormos** (aka Eliés), with all the trappings of the package-holiday industry scattered between the two. The clientele still consists mostly of local and other Greek holiday-makers, who keep summer villas here. The area is unfortunately dominated by an abandoned eyesore of an illegal seven-storey hotel dating from the junta era, which could benefit from some judiciously placed dynamite.

Curiously, there is virtually no **accommodation** overlooking the water except for the package-dominated *Kantouni Beach Apartments* (Ⓣ02430/47 982, Ⓕ47 549; ❺). Of a slightly higher standard, just inland and also usually full of tour clients, is the *Kalydna Island Hotel* (Ⓣ02430/47 880, Ⓕ47 190; ❹), with fridges and bathtubs in the above-average-standard units; the best rooms face the pool-garden. Other good inland choices include *Angelos Apartments* (Ⓣ02430/23 206; ❷), or well north of Pánormos in Kamári district on the ridge overlooking Myrtiés, the family-run *Hotel Kamari* (Ⓣ02430/47 278, Ⓕ48 130; ❷). Cheerful rooms in the front building have seaviews, but there are no frills, such as a pool or sports facilities.

LINÁRIA, a smaller cove at the north end of the same bay, has better sand and is separated from Kandoúni proper by a rock outcrop. Package allotments permitting, you might **stay** at *Skopellos Studios* (Ⓣ02430/47 155; ❷), on the slope below the church. For **eating**, the best option is *Ouzeri Giannis/Ta Linaria* on the shore, with leisurely service but abundant portions of grills and seafood. *To Steki tis Fanis*, occupying an old mansion up on the hillside, offers local specialities such as *merziméli* (salad of greens, *kopanistí* and barley rusks) and ample vegetarian starters, but quality has declined recently and too many frozen ingredients are being used. Further inland on the main highway, just north of the roundabout, *Taverna Marinos* is well regarded for its standard *mayireftá* and grills.

For more abundant **seaview accommodation**, take the side road to **PLATÝ-YIALÓS**, where among a handful of choices for staying on spec, longtime favourite is the Vavoulas family's *Pension Plati Gialos* (Ⓣ & Ⓕ02430/47 029, Ⓦwww.pension-plati-gialos.de), actually overlooking Linária, recently improved with extended balconies, mosquito nets and the breakfast terrace; choose between rooms (❷) or two apartments for four (❹). Alternatives are *Mary-Popi Studios* (Ⓣ02430/47 619; ❶–❷), simple but roomy units at the end of a cul-de-sac – the ground-floor ones are cheapest and coolest in summer – and *Studios Mousselis* (Ⓣ02430/47 757; ❸), which despite heavy package patronage usually has a vacancy, and helpful management. The sandy **beach** itself, though a bit shorter than Kandoúni, is arguably the best on the island: cleaner than its southern neighbours, more secluded, and scenically situated opposite Ayía Kyriakí islet. Those after even more privacy can hunt out tiny, foot-access-only coves in the direction of Melitsahás. A lone **taverna** (*Kyma*) at the base of the cliff behind Platý-Yialós will do nicely for lunch (it shuts at sunset); after dark, *Sea Breeze* at the very top of the grade gets good marks.

For a pleasant walk in the area, best towards sunset, take the obvious 45-minute path from below the large monastery of Stavroú at Kandoúni to the little monastery of **Ayía Fotiní**, tucked under cliffs towards the westernmost point of the island.

Myrtiés, Massoúri and Armeós

The main road, descending in zigzags, finally meets the sea again 8km from Póthia at **MYRTIÉS**, which shares Kálymnos' tourist trade with **MASSOÚRI** and **ARMEÓS**, 1km and 2km respectively to the north but reached by an upper bypass road, part of a giant one-way system. Both have more than their fair share of neon-lit music bars, "spesial menus" (sic), souvenir boutiques and similar accoutrements of a somewhat downmarket package trade.

Possibly this coast's most appealing feature is its position opposite the evocatively shaped islet of Télendhos (see opposite), which frames some of the more dramatic sunsets in Greece. It's also possible to go from Myrtiés directly to Léros aboard the daily early afternoon kaïki (see "Travel Details", p.271). The **beach** at Myrtiés is narrow, pebbly and cramped by development, though it does improve to nearly the same standard as Platý-Yialós as you approach Massoúri. The closest really good beach to Myrtiés lies 500m south, at **Melitsahás** cove, where *Maria's Studios* (Ⓣ02430/48 135 or 093/7987403; ❷) up at the top of the grade is one of the few places to **stay** not block-booked. The spacious units fit three, the furnishings including small ovens. By far the best local **taverna**, with a partly local clientele, overlooks the fishing anchorage; here *Iy Dhrossia* (aka *Andonis*, open all year) is tops for oysters, lobster and shrimp as well as scaly fish at affordable rates. For cultural stimulation, the basilica of **Áyios Ioánnis Melitsahá** stands just up the hill, above the development; the easiest way there is along a signposted track, starting opposite the *Kamari Hotel*.

For other **accommodation** in the area, you'll have a tough time squeezing in amongst the tour allotments. Places to try include the *Oasis Hotel*, on the landward side of the road in Massoúri (Ⓣ02430/47 572, Ⓕ28 856,

Ⓔsponga@klm.forthnet.gr; ❷), or the much remoter *Studios Niki's* (Ⓣ02430/47 201 or 28 575; ❷), up on the bypass road to Massoúri, with great views.

Quality choices are equally limited when it comes to **eating out**; indeed the resort seems to be going through a lean patch, with lots of vacant premises hung with "for sale/for rent" signs. The oft-touted *To Iliovasilema/The Sunset*, supposedly owned by a butcher but purveying pre-processed chips and frozen imported meat, is rather underwhelming. Better to continue to Armeós, where *Tsopanakos* (May to early Sept only) has fresh, island-grazed goat meat, and offers *moúri* (goat or lamb in a clay pot with rice and chopped liver).

Among other amenities, **scooters** and **motorbikes** are available from Lakis (Ⓣ02430/48 039), while Avis has a branch in Myrtiés (Ⓣ02430/47 969). The *Neon Café* in Massoúri has **internet** access.

Télendhos islet

The trip across the strait to the striking, volcanic **islet of Télendhos** is arguably the best reason to come to Myrtiés; little boats shuttle to and fro constantly throughout the day and late into the night. According to local legend, Télendhos is a petrified princess, gazing out to sea after her errant lover; the woman's-head profile is most evident at dusk, before the famous sunsets over the islet and straits. The hardly less pedestrian geological explanation has Télendhos sundered from Kálymnos by a cataclysmic earthquake in 554 AD; extensive traces of a submerged town are said to lie at the bottom of the strait, at a depth of sixteen fathoms.

Home to about fifteen permanent inhabitants, once engaged solely in fishing, Télendhos is car-free and thus blissfully tranquil, though even here increasing numbers of brick and concrete constructions are sprouting up, and package companies have arrived in a big way. As on the main island, early Byzantine ruins are thick on the ground: there's the ruined, three-aisled sixth-century basilica of **Áyios Vassílios** just north of the port, and an even vaster basilica of the same design and vintage, **Ayía Triádha**, excavated only in 1997, at the top of the drop down to Hokhlakás beach (see p.266). Near Áyios Vassílios, there are also a number of cisterns, early Christian tombs and a baths complex to explore. For the more ambitious, a half-day outing takes in the basilica and ruined, fortified Byzantine village of **Áyios Konstandínos** ninety minutes' strenuous uphill scramble to the north. There's no trail as such much of the way, until you intersect with the rough path up from the little shore chapel of Aï Yiórgis; this is the way the islanders go up for the annual festival on May 21.

Practicalities

There are about eight places to **eat** and a roughly equal number of **accommodation** establishments, most (but not all) linked to the tavernas. Establishments that get uniformly positive reviews include *Barba Stathis* taverna en route to Hokhlakás; *Pension Studios Rita* (Ⓣ02430/47 914 or 22 686, Ⓕ47 927; ❷), rooms and renovated-house studios managed by the namesake snack bar/café; the simple but en-suite rooms above the worthy *Zorba's* (Ⓣ02430/48 660; ❶), or, north beyond Áyios Vassílios, the Greek-Australian-run *On the Rocks*. This combines the functions of superbly appointed rooms with double glazing, mosquito nets and so on (Ⓣ02430/48 260, Ⓕ48 261, Ⓦwww.telendos.com/otr; ❹), full-service taverna with lovely home-made desserts, and a bar that's the heart and soul of local **nightlife** (including Mon

& Fri "Greek Nights"). At one corner of the premises you can visit yet another Byzantine monument, the chapel of **Áyios Harálambos**, occupying a former Byzantine bath. If you want more (relative) luxury on Télendhos, you'll have to squeeze in between packages at the *Hotel Porto Potha* (Ⓣ02430/47 321, Ⓕ48 108, Ⓔportopotha@klm.forthnet.gr; ❷), set rather bleakly at the very edge of things but with a large pool and friendly managing family.

A ten-minute walk west along a well-signposted, improved path, past *Zorbas* and *Barba Stathis*, leads over the ridge to scenic if exposed **Hokhlakás** beach and its double bay, with sunbeds for rent and average cleanliness unless the west wind's been up. There's another, sunbed-free cove about ten minutes beyond, towards the rubbish tip. Following instead the coast north from *On the Rocks* brings you to three smaller, more secluded beaches: **Pláka** (with sunbeds), **Pótha** and "**Paradise**" (nudist).

Incidentally, the **straits boatmen** are a law unto themselves; if you pop over to Télendhos for supper, ask them what time their last journey is, regardless of what posted signs say, and treat even this information warily. Télendhos restaurateurs and barkeepers are sympathetic to stranded merrymakers, and may even ferry you back themselves, but it's best not to rely on this.

Northern Kálymnos

The nearly sheer cliffs of northern Kálymnos (and Télendhos) are a magnet for dedicated **big-wall climbers** from Greece, Germany and Britain. If you're in the international climbing fraternity, these formations probably need no introduction; even if not, you can't help but notice the numerous placards which sketch out routes from Armeós north.

Some 5km beyond Massoúri, **ARYINÓNDA** has a clean pebble beach with sunbeds, flanked by a single **rooms** outfit (*Arginonta Beach*, Ⓣ02430/40 000; ❶), with a friendly proprietor, and a few beach **tavernas**. It is also the trailhead for the spectacular trans-island walk to Vathýs (see opposite). **SKÁLIA**, 3km further, has very little to delay you other than an eponymous **cave** that's less famous than the one at Kefála (see p.270); ask in the hamlet for a guide, as you won't find it unaided. Just past Skália, a rough dirt track zigzags east over the ridge to the little anchorage and shingle bay of **Paliónissos**, more usually visited by boat excursion from Vathýs (see opposite).

The end of the paved road is **EMBORIÓS**, 24km from the port. If the twice-daily bus service doesn't suit, there is usually a shuttle boat from Myrtiés at 10am (returning at 4pm). Emboriós offers a gravel-and-sand beach, which improves as you walk west, **accommodation** (much of it taken up by Laskarina Holidays) and a number of **tavernas**, including the long-running *Harry's Paradise*, with attached, air-conditioned garden apartments (Ⓣ02430/40 061; ❸) in bland white-and-pine decor. The conspicuous tavernas down by the jetty tend to give poor value for money.

One cove beyond Emboriós lies goat-patrolled **Asprokykliá** beach, much the same quality as Emboriós'. A dirt track leads high above the beach to *Barba Nikolaos*, which while looking more like a **bar** than a **taverna** actually does reasonable meals on its terrace affording striking views south over a landscape of sea, islets and mountains.

Beyond Emboriós there's another cave, **Kolonóstylos**, with column-like formations after which it's named ("Column-Pillar" in Greek), but of more compelling interest for many are the remote beaches in the island's far northwest.

Follow the rough dirt track above Asprokykliá to the isthmus by the fish farm, then walk fifteen minutes north on a combination of path and abandoned track to **Aptíki**, a smallish but perfectly formed pea-gravel cove; there are other smaller ones en route in the unlikely event it's overcrowded. There's World War II-vintage debris to see when snorkelling, and perhaps moray eels or skates.

Vathýs fjord and valley

Heading east from Póthia, excursions seem initially unpromising, if not downright grim; along the first 4km the road passes Póthia's main boatyard, a power plant, three gas works, two quarries and the local rubbish dump. None of this prepares you for a sudden bend in the road and the dramatic view over Vathýs, a sharp descent below, whose colour provides a startling contrast to the mineral grey and orange elsewhere on Kálymnos. This long, fertile valley, carpeted with orange and tangerine groves, seems a continuation of the cobalt-blue fjord that penetrates the landscape here. A veritable maze of tracks, drives and lanes threads through these orchards, where numerous "for sale" signs suggest that citrus cultivation is no longer as profitable as it was.

Rína

At the little port of **RÍNA**, 8km from Póthia, the modern chapels of Anástasi (south) and Ayía Iríni (north) flanking the head of the fjord sit amidst the ruins of still more Byzantine basilicas – neither very noteworthy but demonstrating the antiquity of settlement here. Near the Anástasi chapel you'll find the best **accommodation** option, the helpful *Rooms Manolis* (Ⓣ02430/41 300; ❶), with cooking facilities; alternatively there's the *Hotel Galini* (Ⓣ 02430/31 241; ❷), overlooking the boatyard. Behind the *Galini*, brackish springs feed a pool haunted by huge fish, before draining to the port.

Some of the five **tavernas** are pricier than you'd expect, owing to patronage from the numerous yachts and excursion boats which call here; currently the best choice, with shambolic service but good grilled fish, is *The Harbor*, first place on the right at the road's end.

The steep-sided inlet has no beach to speak of; people dive from the lido on the far south side of the quay, where yachts moor. The closest strand, about 3km back towards Póthia, is **Aktí**, a functional pebble beach with sunbeds and a single snack bar, reached by a steep cement driveway. Boat excursions from Rína visit the stalactite cave of **Dhaskalió**, out by the fjord mouth and inhabited in Neolithic times, as well as the remote northeast-coast beaches of **Almyrés**, **Dhrasónda** and **Pezónda** (this last also reachable overland, see p.269).

Hikes to and from Vathýs valley

For **walkers**, the lush Vathýs valley immediately behind Rína is the focus of two popular hikes which provide a good transect of the island; however, they pass through the valley considerably inland from Rína. Póthia–Vathýs is easy enough and a favourite outing, Aryinónda–Vathýs a bit more challenging; they can of course be linked back-to-back to make a full day's walking, but attention must be paid to choosing your direction of march – and to public transport links at your destination. You also need to carry at least one, preferably two, litres of water per person, and a sunhat, as there's no water or shade away from the valley floor.

Probably the most sensible strategy would be to do the Póthia–Rína leg, break for lunch, and then take a bus or walk as far as Metóhi, where the path from Aryinónda becomes evident. At the latter you would probably have time for a well-deserved swim before catching the late-afternoon bus from Emboriós back to town. If for any reason this was not forthcoming, you'd have to continue 5km further on foot to Armeós to pick up more regular transport.

Póthia to Vathýs valley

The hike from **Póthia to Plátanos** in the Vathýs valley follows the old *kalderími* used in the days before the coastal road existed. Begin behind the archeological museum and *Villa Themelina* hotel, by the church of Ayía Triádha with its prominent wall sundial; red paint splodges guide you through the highest-positioned houses. Climb sharply in zigzags, past the presumed acropolis of ancient Pothaia, until the town slips out of sight and the cobbled way heads off at a more gentle grade into the bare mountains. Kós and Níssyros are spread out behind you, and in autumn, phalanxes of white sea squill provide the only colour. An hour's walk along, you reach the high point of the route, a 350-metre-elevation pass traversed by power lines, from where it's some forty minutes' descent to the edge of Vathýs' cultivated zone. (If you're following the itinerary in reverse, look for a fenced-in grove of young olives just above two water cisterns in a pipeline system, skimmed by power lines; eight stray older olive trees on the hillside above mark the start of the uphill path proper, difficult to find if you're coming in this direction.)

Descending, the path becomes track by the olives and forces you east and even slightly uphill briefly before turning to cement drive by the highest dwellings. Two hours out of Póthia you hit a cement lane on the valley floor in the Ayía Triádha district of Plátanos hamlet; turn right, but collect water if necessary from the sunken potable spring under the namesake plane tree (*plátanos*) across the road. Another half-hour of unavoidable road walking brings you to Rína where, if you've started early enough, you should have enough time for lunch before catching an early afternoon bus back to Póthia.

Aryinónda to Vathýs valley

An itinerary from **Aryinónda to Metóhi** in the Vathýs valley reverses our recommendation, but is slightly easier to follow. Don't believe sources which show the route emerging at Styménia, and be aware that in the future the local government intends to bulldoze a road from just above the *Arginonta Beach* to Styménia, which may disrupt the first half-hour or so of the trail.

In Aryinónda, the path starts opposite the cistern-spring in the gravel car-park and bus-stop area on the inland side of the road. Thereafter, occasional orange paint splodges guide you up terraces and briefly into a defile where the path is rough, with scree underfoot. You stay fairly high up the south flank of the ravine here, except for one point where you dip down to cross the bed of a side canyon. After about an hour, you attain a gentle saddle, beyond which you'll have your first views over Pezónda bay, and some low junipers tuft the landscape. The trail is fainter here, but resist the temptation to drift down and left – paths toward the sea are difficult to non-existent. The proper way maintains altitude and soon becomes more distinct amidst the vegetation, curling to negotiate the head of a shallow canyon.

About thirty minutes from the first saddle, you'll reach a second, more abrupt, pass with a concrete cistern (dry) and your first good views into the Vathýs valley. Ignore paths going straight ahead – this is a rough traverse to the neighbourhood of Kyrá Psilí – and instead begin the descent down the obvious ravine here towards Metóhi. There are paths on either bank, but the one along the left (east) side is clearer and, with its patches of well-engineered revetment, appears to have been the main one in the old days. About two hours from Aryinónda, you meet the first, highest buildings of Metóhi, including a little church whose courtyard provides some shade but no cistern water. Continue down to the valley floor road and turn left to reach Rína after another hour; en route you will notice extensive stretches of Hellenistic fortification wall, north of the valley floor.

North of Vathýs: Pezónda and Kyrá Psilí

For hikers who prefer out-and-back itineraries, these make excellent destinations, though you'll benefit from having a scooter or bike at first. From Metóhi in the Vathý valley floor, take two-wheelers up the signed, steep cement track to the visible saddle, where it ends beside a bunker-like chapel with a rain cistern (often containing water). Just beyond, the paths to Pezónda bay (down and left) and Kyrá Psilí monastery (straight and up) are indicated by rustic wooden placards.

For the beach, there's an initial ten-minute drop to a ravine bed; once there bear left (northwest) through a livestock pen, gated at each end. Beyond the pen, don't continue further down the ravine centre – the proper path goes up slightly onto the true right (northeast) bank of the canyon, marked by sporadic cairns. Just under half an hour along, you rejoin the now narrow stream bed, and stay in it for a remaining twenty minutes to the scenic fjord of **Pezónda**. Alas, the fine-gravel beach is apt to be dirty with seaborne litter and tar (the bay opens north) and at summer weekends at least you may not even have the consolation of solitude – some family from town has likely got there first on a boat. Snorkelling in the shallows, you'll see a phenomenal amount of rusty World War II debris: shell casings and tips, a bomb, even a giant mine.

Kyrá Psilí hovers tantalizingly in view for much of the fifty-minute return trip to the wooden placards. From there, it's a maximum half-hour round-trip walk to this fortified monastery and *paniyíri* venue (always open), which only sees use on August 15. There's not much else here other than a series of chapels tucked into grottoes of the overhang in the 609-metre mountain above, the second highest on Kálymnos. Accordingly there are superb views northwest at dusk as far as Ikaría and Mount Kérkis on Sámos, taking in intervening islands like Arkí and Foúrni. Incidentally, the name Kyrá Psilí ("The Tall Lady") has nothing to do with the altitude but is an epithet of the Virgin inherited from her predecessors, Aphrodite and Cybele.

Southwestern Kálymnos

Some 6km southwest of Póthia, the small bay of **Vlyhádhia** is reached via the nondescript village of Vothýni, from which a narrow ravine leads down to the sea. The **beach** here, divided into two separate coves (one sand, one shingle), is too unsecluded and often litter-strewn to justify a special trip, and the bay is frankly sumpy; it's mostly islanders who frequent it, and the two lacklustre shoreline tavernas, at weekends. Indeed, foreigners seem to be specifically unwelcome here: a bigoted hermit occupies a *monastiráki* at one end of the beach, emblazoned with placards claiming the place for the Orthodox Christians and anathematizing the topless heterodox heathens – he has also blotted out all Roman-alphabet road signs in the area.

Only if you're interested in **scuba** is the Vlyhádhia area worth a detour, as it's one of the limited number of legal diving areas in Greece. Stavros Valsamidhes, the local divemaster, has also assembled an impressive **Museum of**

Submarine Finds (Mon–Sat 9am–7pm, Sun 10am–2pm; free), which in addition to masses of sponges and shells offers a reconstructed ancient wreck with amphorae and World War II debris. Depending on your ability, dives (arrange in advance on ☎02430/50 662; €30 for one dive, €53 for two) may visit ancient wrecks *in situ*, as well as seal caves.

Kefála cave and beyond

Póthia-based kaïkia make well-publicized excursions to **Kefála cave**, a little to the west ofVlyhádhia.You have to walk thirty minutes from where the boats dock, but the vividly coloured formations are ample reward. The cave was inhabited before recorded history, and later served as a sanctuary of Zeus (who is fancifully identified with a particularly imposing stalagmite in the biggest of six chambers).

Greek script table

Kálymnos	Κάλυμνος	ΚΑΛΥΜΝΟΣ
Aktí	Ακτή	ΑΚΤΗ
Almyrés	Αλμυρές	ΑΛΜΥΡΕΣ
Aptíki	Απτήκι	ΑΠΤΗΚΙ
Aryinónda	Αργυνώντα	ΑΡΓΥΝΩΝΤΑ
Ayía Ekateríni	Αγία Αικατερίνη	ΑΓΙΑ ΑΙΚΑΤΕΡΙΝΗ
Dhaskalió	Δασκαλειό	ΔΑΣΚΑΛΕΙΟ
Dhrasónda	Δρασόντα	ΔΡΑΣΟΝΤΑ
Eliés	Ελιές	ΕΛΙΕΣ
Emboriós	Εμπορειός	ΕΜΠΟΡΕΙΟΣ
Hóra	Χώρα	ΧΩΡΑ
Horió	Χωριό	ΧΩΡΙΟ
Kandoúni	Καντούνι	ΚΑΝΤΟΥΝΙ
Kástro	Κάστρο	ΚΑΣΤΡΟ
Kefála	Κεφάλα	ΚΕΦΑΛΑ
Khryssoheriás	Χρυσοχεριάς	ΧΡΥΣΟΧΕΡΙΑΣ
Kolonóstylos	Κολονόστυλος	ΚΟΛΟΝΟΣΤΥΛΟΣ
Kyrá Psilí	Κυρά Ψηλή	ΚΥΡΑ ΨΗΛΗ
Massoúri	Μασούρι	ΜΑΣΟΥΡΙ
Melitsahás	Μελιτσαχάς	ΜΕΛΙΤΣΑΧΑΣ
Metóhi	Μετόχι	ΜΕΤΟΧΙ
Myrtiés	Μυρτιές	ΜΥΡΤΙΕΣ
Paliónissos	Παλιόνησος	ΠΑΛΙΟΝΗΣΟΣ
Pánormos	Πάνορμος	ΠΑΝΟΡΜΟΣ
Pezónda	Πεζόντα	ΠΕΖΟΝΤΑ
Plátanos	Πλάτανος	ΠΛΑΤΑΝΟΣ
Platý-Yialós	Πλατύ-Γιαλός	ΠΛΑΤΥ-ΓΙΑΛΟΣ
Póthia	Πόθια	ΠΟΘΙΑ
Rína	Ρίνα	ΡΙΝΑ
Skália	Σκάλια	ΣΚΑΛΙΑ
Télendhos	Τέλενδος	ΤΕΛΕΝΔΟΣ
Vathýs	Βαθύς	ΒΑΘΥΣ
Vlyhádhia	Βλυχάδια	ΒΛΥΧΑΔΙΑ
Vothýni	Βοθύνοι	ΒΟΘΥΝΟΙ

The excursion kaïkia also usually schedule a stop at **Nerá** islet, out beyond the mouth of Vlyhádhia bay; there's a **monastery** of Timíou Stavroú (festival Sept 14), and a **taverna** that's apt to make a better fist of lunch than anything at Vlyhádhia.

Kefála can lately also be reached via a broad dirt track from the inland monastery of Ayía Ekateríni, itself just west of Vothýni by paved road. From Kefála it's possible to make an enjoyable trail-trek across the far southwest of the island. First the south-coast path leads past the firmly closed Áyios Andhréas monastery ("*Óhi tourismó stá monastíria*"/No tourism in monasteries" says the sign – the work of the Vlyhádhia hermit), before threading high above the sea, through a boulder-field below impressive cliffs. Next you emerge on a spectacular view over Pithári bay and its remote monastery, with an outsize jetty making it resemble some Bond villain's hideout. From here, a short path inland through a narrow gorge takes you up to the more welcoming monastery of Áyios Konstandínos, in the notch overlooking the plateau of Árgos, which you reach some two hours from Ayía Ekateríni.

Kálymnos travel details

Island transport

Buses

Póthia to: Emboriós (2 daily in season, am and late pm); Kandoúni (5 daily 10am–3.30pm); Myrtiés–Massoúri–Armeós (15 daily, 7am–10pm); Platý-Yialós (2–4 daily); Vathý (4 daily Mon–Sat, 3 Sun); Vlyhádhia (5 daily Mon–Sat, 4 Sun).

NB Above frequencies are for the period mid-June to mid-Sept only – in spring or autumn, only the Myrtiés–Massoúri–Armeós line functions, with reduced frequency (approx. 8 daily).

Inter-island transport

Key to ferry and hydrofoil companies

DANE	*Dhodhekanisiakí Anónymi Navtiliakí Etería* (Dodecanesian Shipping Company)
DodH	Dodecanese Hydrofoils
G&A	G&A Ferries
NK	*Nissos Kalymnos*
KR	Kyriakoulis Maritime

Kaïkia and excursion boats

Myrtiés to: Télendhos (every 10–30min from dawn till long after dark; €1.20 single); Xirókambos, Léros (1 daily at 1pm).

Póthia to: Psérimos (1 daily; 1hr 15min journey; €6 each way).

Small ferries

Kálymnos to: Kós (Mastihári; 3–4 daily, 7am–8 or 11pm, on ANEM).

NB ANEM ferries to Kós have limited space for vehicles on their craft – book in advance (☎02430/22 909).

Large ferries

Kálymnos to: Agathoníssi (2 weekly on NK; 6hr); Astypálea (1 weekly on G&A, 2–3 weekly on NK; 2hr 30min–3hr 15min); Foúrni (1–2 weekly on G&A, summer only; 3hr 30min); Ikaría (1–2 weekly on G&A, summer only; 4hr 30min); Kastellórizo (1 weekly on G&A, 2 weekly on NK, via Rhodes; 13–16hr, including layover on Rhodes); Kós (1 daily on G&A, 5 weekly on DANE, 2 weekly on NK; 1hr 15min–1hr 30min); Léros (1 daily on G&A, 5 weekly on DANE, 2 weekly on NK; 1hr); Lipsí (1 weekly, June to mid-Sept, on G&A, 2 weekly on NK; 2hr–2hr 30min); Náxos (1 weekly on G&A; 7hr 30min); Níssyros (1 weekly, summer only, on G&A, 2 weekly on NK; 2hr 45min–3hr 15min); Páros (1 weekly on G&A; 8hr 30min); Pátmos (1 daily on G&A, 5 weekly on DANE, 2 weekly on NK; 3hr–3hr 30min); Pireás (1 daily on G&A, 5 weekly on DANE; 12hr); Rhodes (1 daily on G&A, 5 weekly on DANE, 2 weekly on NK; 6hr); Sámos–Pythagório (2 weekly on NK; 7hr 30min); Sými (1 weekly on G&A, 2 weekly on NK; 4hr 30min–6hr); Sýros (1 weekly on G&A; 9hr 30min); Tílos (1 weekly on G&A, 2 weekly on NK; 4–5hr).

Catamaran

Kálymnos to: Kós, Rhodes (5–7 weekly, mid-afternoon); Léros, Pátmos (3–4 weekly, morning); Lipsí, Níssyros, Tílos (1–2 weekly); Sými (2–3 weekly, May–June only).

Hydrofoils

Kálymnos to: Agathoníssi (1–2 weekly on KR); 4hr 45min; Astypálea (1 weekly, usually Sat, July–Aug only but unreliable even then, on KR; 1hr 30min); Foúrni (1 weekly on KR; 3hr 15min); Ikaría (1 weekly on KR; 2hr 40min); Kós (2–3 daily on KR; 45min); Léros-Ayía Marína (2–3 daily on KR; 45min); Lipsí (2 daily on KR; 1hr 15min); Pátmos (2–3 daily on KR; 2hr 45min); Sámos-Pythagório (2 daily on KR; 3hr 30min–3hr 45min); Sými (1 weekly on KR; 2hr 30min); Tílos (1 weekly on KR; 2hr).

Léros

Léros is so indented with deep, sheltered anchorages that between 1923 and 1948, it harboured – in turn – the entire Italian, German, and British Mediterranean **fleets**. In a contemporary echo of this, there are enormous dry-docks and marinas for yachts at Parthéni and Teménia. Unfortunately, many of these magnificent fjords and bays seem to absorb rather than reflect light, and the island's fertile valleys and tufts of hillside greenery can seem scraggly and unkempt when compared to the crisp lines of its more barren neighbours. These characteristics, plus Léros' lack of spectacularly good beaches, meant that until the late 1980s just a few thousand foreigners (mostly Italians who grew up on the island), and not many more Greeks, came to visit each August.

Such a pattern is now history, with German, Dutch, Danish and British package-tour operators at the vanguard of those "discovering" Léros and the company of islanders unjaded by mass tourism. Foreign visitor numbers have, however, levelled off since the 1990s, with change unlikely until and unless the tiny airport is expanded to accommodate jets – at present it only takes fifty-seater ATR-42s.

Not that Léros needs, or strenuously encourages, tourism; various **prisons and sanatoriums** have dominated the Lerian economy since the 1950s, directly or indirectly employing about a third of the population of eight thousand. During the junta era the island hosted a notorious detention centre at Parthéni, and today the mental hospital on Léros remains the repository for many of Greece's more intractable psychiatric cases; there is also a home for hundreds of mentally disabled children. The island's domestic image problem is compounded by its name, the butt of jokes by off-islanders, who pounce on its similarity to the word *lerá*, connoting rascality and unsavouriness.

In 1989, a major scandal emerged concerning the administration of the various institutions, with EU maintenance and development funds found to have been embezzled by administrators and staff, and the inmates kept in degrading and inhumane conditions. Since then, an influx of EU inspectors, foreign psychiatrists and extra funding have resulted in drastic improvements in patient treatment, including the establishment of halfway houses around the island and supervised "work internships". Sensational foreign press coverage and a lurid Channel 4 (UK) documentary have ensured that Léros will be a while yet overcoming this additional stigma, though evidence of its institutional identity – despite the recent opening here of one of Greece's main nursing colleges – is not as pervasive as you might expect.

More obvious is the legacy of the **Battle of Léros** on November 12–16, 1943, when overwhelming German forces displaced a British division which had landed on the island following the Italian capitulation. Churchill devoted a page or so of *The Second World War* to this debacle; in a mini-reprise of the Battle of Crete, German paratroopers and supporting aircraft descended on an outnumbered Commonwealth garrison. Bomb nose-cones and shell casings still turn up as gaily painted garden ornaments in the courtyards of churches and tavernas, or have been pressed into service as gateposts. Each year for three days following September 26, memorial services and a naval festival commemorate the sinking of the Greek battleship *Queen Olga* and the British *Intrepid* during the German attack.

Unusually for a small island, Léros has abundant ground water, channelled into potable cisterns at several points, though many ran dry in the long 1996–2001 drought (a giant dam is being built by the airport). All these, plus low-lying ground staked with avenues of eucalyptus trees planted by the Italians, make for a horrendously active mosquito contingent, so come prepared. Some sort of waterproof beach shoes are recommended too, as entry to the sea can often be over foot-bruising rocks.

Léros is sufficiently compact for the energetic to walk around, but there is a reasonably reliable bus service, plus several places renting out motor and mountain bikes, of which Motoland (outlets in Pandélli ⓣ02470/24 103, and Álynda ⓣ02470/24 584) has proven reliable on several occasions. The island is hilly enough to make motorized wheels a better bet, though you could manage with just a mountain bike between Álynda and Lakkí if you're reasonably fit.

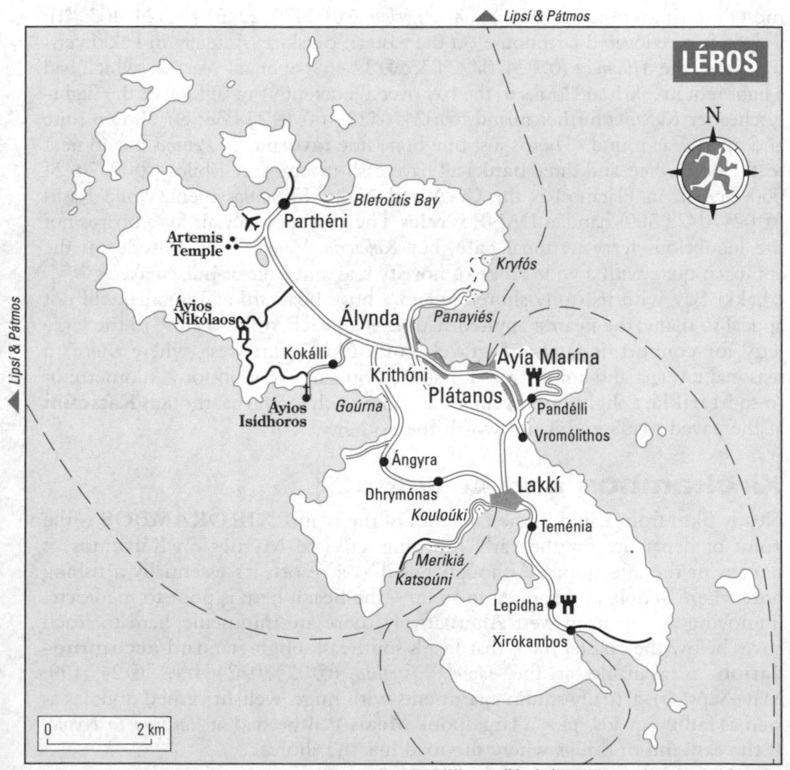

The south: Lakkí to Xirókambos

All medium-sized and large **ferries** arrive at the main port of **LAKKÍ**, once the headquarters of a bustling Italian naval base, which accounts for the extraordinary, rather overdesigned look of the place. Boulevards far too wide for today's paltry amount of traffic are lined with some marvellous Art Deco edifices, including the round-fronted cinema (closed since 1985), the primary and secondary schools, a shopping centre with a round atrium, plus the defunct (but being restored) *Leros Palace Hotel* – all the work of a pair of prominent 1920s architects, César Louis and an associate. Many of these structures have long been allowed to deteriorate when not actually abandoned, this neglect apparently a deliberate policy of the Greeks who would just as soon forget the entire Italian legacy, but since the late 1990s scaffolding for plasterers and painters has appeared. Simultaneously, there's been a decrease in the number of vacant shopfronts which used to accentuate the overall air of depression and a long-gone heyday, as banks, filling stations and supermarkets have slowly realized the benefits of cheap floor space.

Buses don't meet the ferries; instead, **taxis** charge set fares to standard destinations (but if you're willing to walk a few hundred metres out of the harbour confines, you'll get cheaper fares at the official rank). If you're lightly laden and want to ride off immediately on a **rented scooter** immediately, Kostas Koumoulis (ⓣ02740/22 330) on the quay can oblige. Few people stay willingly at any of the handful of moribund **hotels** in Lakkí, preferring to head straight for the resorts of Vromólithos, Pandélli or Álynda (see opposite). If you do get stuck here, the most inspiring choice is the *Xenon Angelou* (ⓣ02470/22 514, ⓕ24 403; ④), lodged in a renovated farmhouse on the eastern outskirts. Actually in Lakkí centre, there's the *Miramare* (ⓣ02470/22 053, ⓕ22 469; open all year; ③), which had a light refit in 2001 and looks to the bay over a (currently) vacant lot, or the slightly cheaper *Katerina* further inland (ⓣ02470/22 460, ⓕ23 038; ③), also en suite and open year-round. There's just one bona fide **taverna**, *To Petrino*, inland next to the post office, and three **banks** all have cash machines. Gribilos (ⓣ02470/24 000, branch in Plátanos) is the G&A and *Nissos Kalymnos* agent, while Kastis (ⓣ02470/22 500) handles DANE **ferries**. The best spot to wait for a boat is not the lugubrious ferry-terminal **café**, but *Kafeteria Morano* a bit outside on the approach quay, with a wide range of novelty teas and fruit or milk shakes.

Lakkí Bay, with its stony shoreline and a busy boatyard at Teménia, will not appeal to many; the nearest approximation of a beach, still too close to the ferry jetty for comfort, is sand-and-gravel **Kouloúki**, 500m west, where there's a seasonal taverna and ample trees for shade. You can carry on for a kilometre or so to **Merikiá**, a slight improvement and also with a taverna, though **Katsoúni** at the paved road's end is not worth the bother.

Xirókambos and Lepídha

Nearly 5km from Lakkí in the far south of the island, **XIRÓKAMBOS** is the point of departure for the early morning kaïki to Myrtiés on Kálymnos (it returns in the afternoon). Although billed as a resort, it's essentially a fishing port where people also happen to swim – the beach here is poor to mediocre, improving as you head west. Alternatively, there are minuscule, hard to reach coves below the coastal track that heads southeast. High-standard **accommodation** is available at the *Hotel Efstathia* (ⓣ02470/24 099, ⓕ24 199; May–Sept; ④), actually studio apartments with huge, well-furnished doubles as well as family quads, plus a large pool. **Meals** can be had at *Taverna To Kyma*, at the east end of things where the road hits the shore.

The village of **LEPÍDHA**, 750m back up the road to Lakkí, also has its own small **castle**; the access road starts 200m north of the campsite (see below). It's visited more for simultaneous views over Lakkí and Xirókambos than for the scanty patches of early Christian mosaics in front of the modern chapel within the castle, or ancient masonry foundations behind.

The **campsite**, shaded by over two hundred olive trees (Ⓣ02470/23 372; late May to early Oct), also doubles as headquarters of one of the better **scuba diving** outfits in the Aegean, the Dutch- and Greek-run Panos Diving Club (Ⓣ094/4238490, Ⓔdivingleros@hotmail.com). They explore Leros' wealth of wrecks from ancient times to World War II, plus natural drop-offs and reefs, in an eight-metre custom dive boat; charges for certified divers vary from €50 for a single dive with rented gear to €470 for a ten-dive package (or a CMAS certificate for the unqualified).

Pandélli and Vromólithos

Just less than 3km north of Lakkí, Pandélli and Vromólithos together form the largest resort on the island – and are certainly two of the more attractive and scenic places to stay, and sometimes eat.

PANDÉLLI is still very much a working port, its modern jetty benefiting local fishermen as well as the increasing numbers of yachts calling here. The shortness of its clean gravel beach is compensated for by a relative abundance of non-package **accommodation**. Close to the water, there's the *Pension Happiness* (Ⓣ02470/23 498; ❷) where the road down from Plátanos meets the sea, or, for a much higher standard, the airy, Aussie-run *Niki Studios* (Ⓣ02470/25 600; ❸), at the base of the road to the castle, with a pool, some air-conditioned units and a package presence. Halfway up the slope, just off the road to the Kástro, four fake but fetching *Windmills* (soon to be six; Ⓣ02470/25 549; ❻) offer characterful self-catering with a view, but again are likely to be booked out in high season. South along the main ridge road from Pandélli to Vromólithos in Spiliá district, *Hotel Rodon* (Ⓣ02470/23 524 or 22 075; ❷) is an excellent choice, its small but well-kept, mostly balconied rooms belying an official E-class rating; the same welcoming family keeps pricier ground-floor studios (❹ for 3 people), with less of a seaview. The peace here may be disturbed only by wafts of music from the *Beach Bar* on a rock terrace below, facing Vromólithos. The other, long-established **bar** is the civilized *Savana*, at the opposite end of Pandélli.

Right next to the *Rodon* is the son's taverna, *Dimitris*, which stays open most of the year and scores highly for its stuffed squash blossoms (in autumn) and chunky, herby Lerian sausages. Back in beachside Pandélli, the soul of the place is the row of waterfront **tavernas**, which come alive after dark. Some are tourist traps, and/or in decline, but two to single out for excellence are *Psaropoula* (alias *Apostolis*), open most of the year with a good balance of fresh seafood and *mayireftá*, and the *Kafenio tou Tzouma*, a combination fishermen's café and characterful ouzerí at the base of the jetty. Don't ask for *fayitó* ("food") here – you get mezédhes and only mezédhes, and well-priced at that – €8 or so for *zargána*, fried red peppers and a *karafáki* of oúzo.

Vromólithos

VROMÓLITHOS offers the best easily accessible **beach** on the island, car-free and hemmed in by hills studded with massive oaks. The shoreline is gravel and coarse sand, and the sea here is clean, but as so often on Léros you have to cross an uncomfortable reef at most points before reaching deeper water. Two **tavernas** behind the beach trade more on their location than their cuisine (which improves when Greek weekenders are about), but the standard of **accommodation** here is higher than at Pandélli, so Vromólithos tends to be dominated by package companies. Exceptions, which keep at least some units back for walk-ins, include *Hotel Glaros* (Ⓣ02470/24 358, Ⓕ23 683; ❺), actually large studios set back and perpendicular to the through road and beach, with garden views, and the *Castle Vigla* (Ⓣ02470/24 083 Ⓕ24 744; ❸–❺) complex of cottages and apartments, perched up on a hill to the south with some of the best views on the island (*vígla* means "watchpoint").

Plátanos and Ayía Marína

The Neoclassical and vernacular houses of **PLÁTANOS**, the island capital 1km west of Pandélli, are draped gracefully along a saddle between two hills, one of them crowned by the inevitable Knights' castle. Known locally as the **Kástro**, this is reached either by a paved but potholed road veering off the Pandélli road, or by a more scenic stair-path from the central square; the battlements, and the views from them, are dramatic, especially at sunrise or sunset. The medieval church of **Panayía toú Kástrou**, inside the gate and originally the powder magazine, houses a small **museum** (daily 8am–12.30pm, Wed, Sat & Sun also 3–6pm; €1.50), though its carved *témblon* and naïve pulpit are more remarkable than the sparse exhibits of icons and other liturgical items.

The other, and more worthwhile, local gallery is the **archeological museum** (Tues–Sun 8am–2.30pm; free), well signposted just off the road between Ayía Marína and Plátanos. Although a bit long on photos and maps of sites and rather short on actual artefacts, it does a comprehensive tour of Lerian history in all eras, from prehistoric obsidian tools, proving contact with Mílos and Níssyros islands, to Byzantine votive-mosaic fragments and assorted church masonry, by way of an Attic *lekythos* with a female head in profile, and Roman amphorae.

Except for *Hotel Eleftheria* (Ⓣ02470/23 550, Ⓕ24 551; ❷), at a peaceful hillside location in town, Plátanos is not really a place to stay or eat, though it's well sown with shops and services. These include Olympic Airways (Ⓣ02470/24 144), south of the turning for Pandélli, and two **banks** (both with cash machines) and the **post office**, down the road towards Ayía Marína. The single **bus** (schedules posted at the central stop, opposite the island's main **taxi** rank) plies several times daily between Parthéni in the north and Xirókambos.

Ayía Marína

Plátanos merges seamlessly with **AYÍA MARÍNA**, 1km north on the shore of a fine bay, and still graced by a small, Italian-built public market building. If you're travelling to Léros on any excursion boat, catamaran or hydrofoil, this (not Lakkí) will be your point of arrival. Helpful Kastis Travel (Ⓣ02470/22 140) sells tickets for all hydrofoils, catamarans and the DANE ferries. There's also a stand-alone **cash machine** on the quay.

Although local **accommodation** is extremely limited – small but clean en-suite rooms above *Ouzeri tou Kapaniri* (Ⓣ02470/22 750; ❶) are convenient if nothing else – Ayía Marína is, however, arguably the best place to **eat** on the island. Start, just west of the police station on the waterfront, with eminently reasonable *Kapaniri* itself, best at night, with plenty – bean soup, Cypriot *hal-loúmi* cheese, *hórta* – for vegetarians, in addition to good seafood and draught beer; they operate all year. Just inland from *Ouzeri tou Kapaniri*, well marked in a little alley, *Ouzeri Kapetan Mihalis* claims to be open all day and offers a range of even more inexpensive local specialities, including various fish *pastós* (marinated in salt); despite the appearance of the dreaded photo-menu, quality seems to have been maintained. Still further west, the *Ouzeri Neromylos* (April–Oct only), out by the sea-marooned windmill, indisputably has the most romantic setting on the island (reservations mandatory July & Aug on ⓣ02470/24 894). Host Takis' specialities include *garidhopílafo* (shrimp-rice) and *kolokythokeftédhes* (courgette patties), as well as the house salad. Back on the main road towards Plátanos, *Giusi e Marcello* (Wed–Sun eves only) offers genuine Italian fare, and is popular with locals as well.

Near *Kapaniri*, the *Elliniko* dishes out the best ice cream on the island, while a fair semblance of **nightlife** is provided by various café-bars, such as *Enallaktiko* behind the Italian "palace", with a few **internet** terminals, and cavernous *Harama* on the quay, also a popular place to wait for a hydrofoil.

Álynda and nearby beaches

ÁLYNDA, 3km northwest of Ayía Marína, ranks as the longest-established resort on Léros, with development just across the road from a long, narrow strip of pea-gravel beach. An **Allied War Graves cemetery**, containing 184 mostly Commonwealth casualties of the November 1943 battle, occupies a walled enclosure near the south end of the beach. Immaculately maintained, and furnished with a guest register and informative booklet inside the gatepost, it serves as a moving counterpoint to the holiday hubbub outside.

The other principal sight at Álynda is the privately run **Historical and Ethnographic Museum** (May–Sept, Tues–Sun 10am–1pm & 6–9pm; €3), housed in the unmistakeable castle-like mansion of Paris Bellinis (1871–1957). Most of the top floor is devoted to the Battle of Léros: relics from the sunken *Queen Olga*, a wheel from a Junkers bomber, a stove made from a bomb casing. There's also a rather grisly mock-up clinic (mostly gynaecological tools) and assorted rural impedimenta, costumes and antiques. A photo collection shows the sad decline of many Lerian monuments: a fine market hall in the square of Plátanos was thoughtlessly demolished in 1903, and a soaring medieval aqueduct linking the far hillside with the Kástro was a casualty of the November 1943 battle.

Practicalities

Álynda is where the first accommodation opens in spring, and (except for Pandélli) the last to shut in autumn. Many of the half-dozen **hotels** and pensions here are block-booked by package companies, but you may have better luck at two outfits overlooking the war cemetery: *Hotel Gianna* (ⓣ02470/23 153; ❸), with fridge-equipped rooms plus a few studios, or the nearby *Studios Diamantis* (ⓣ02470/23 213; ❸) just inland, with large balconied units but somewhat disagreeable management. At **KRITHÓNI**, 1.5km south of the cemetery, more comfort is available at the island's top-flight accommodation: the *Crithoni Paradise* (ⓣ02470/25 120, ⓕ24 680; standard rooms ❹–❻, suites ❻; open all year), a mock-traditional low-rise complex with buffet breakfast, a smallish pool, wheelchair ramps, on-site car rental and all mod cons in the rooms. For more character back at Álynda, try the *Arhondiko Angelou* (ⓣ02470/22 749 or 094/4908182, ⓕ24 403; ❺; June–Sept), a restored 1895 mansion set well inland; rooms, with a "French-style" conversion pre-fab bath in the corner, are a bit creaky, though the orchard setting and outdoor breakfast bar make the place.

Restaurant options at Álynda aren't brilliant, except for *To Steki*, next to the war cemetery, open year-round, whose good grills and mezédhes attract a local clientele. The tiny *Finikas* at mid-beach is okay for a simple meal by the sand.

Panayiés, Kryfós and Goúrna

At the north end of the main Álynda beach strip, you can follow a signposted lane, to **Panayiés**, nearly a kilometre east, past a potable cistern, to a well-situated snack bar overlooking several gravel coves, the most isolated of which is naturist. From there you can continue to pebbly **Kryfós** cove, 20–25 minutes' hard scramble north on a faint path. There's only a cave for shade there, sometimes tar on shore, and no nudism if island families have got there first – which they may have, in a boat.

Otherwise, the road towards the north end of the island takes off from the centre of Álynda; within 1km or so you pass the well-marked turn-off to **Goúrna**. This is Léros' biggest sandy **beach**, hard-packed and gently shelving, with a view west over some islets. But it's also wind-buffeted, often litter-strewn and permanently fringed with construction rubble (lately bulldozed a discrete distance inland) and an impromptu car park. The only facilities are sunbeds, a newish beach **taverna**, and another taverna (the *Iliovasilema*) 1km south along the paved road that loops back over the hills to Lakkí via the tiny hamlets of Ángyra and Dhrymónas.

A separate road beyond the Goúrna turning leads to **Kokálli**, no great improvement beach-wise, but flanked to one side by the scenic islet of **Áyios Isídhoros**, tethered to the body of Léros by a causeway, its eponymous chapel perched on top.

The far northwest

The hills between Panayiés and Blefoútis (see opposite) are a restricted military zone; explorations on foot or scooter are only advisable west of the main road crossing to the north end of the island.

The next turning beyond the one for Kokálli, indicated by a small blue sign (don't continue further to the Toyota dealership) is the start of the rough but motorable track to **Áyios Nikolaos** bay and monastery. The latter is of middling interest, and the single beach here is disappointing, but some walkers find it worthwhile to continue northwest along the rugged coast. Following the track south, then east on a scooter back towards Áyios Isídhoros takes you through country empty except for goatpens and a giant wind farm, erected during 2001, on the ridge above. Immediately south of the wind turbines and livestock corrals are a few little secluded coves, much the best along this coast for swimming.

The Artemis "temple" and Blefoútis

Seven kilometres from Álynda along the main route north, a marked side track leads left to the **"Temple" of Artemis**, atop a slight rise just west of the airport runway – and perilously near the new reservoir works. In ancient times, Léros was originally sacred to the goddess Parthenos Iokallis, who eventually became syncretized with Artemis, but is still recalled in the placename Parthéni. All that remains inside a fenced enclosure (gate open) are some jumbled walls, no more than two masonry courses high; as the archeological museum labelling makes clear, this was an ancient fortress, not a shrine, and indeed the north–south orientation of the ruins is completely wrong for a temple. The real whereabouts of the temple are now unknown, but it seems likely that it was somewhere along the shores of the sumpy, reed-fringed bay below – marshes and river mouths were the usual site of Artemis temples – or perhaps under today's airport runway. Legend asserts that her Lerian sanctuary was inhabited by *meleagrides* or guinea fowl – the grief-stricken sisters of the ancient hunter-hero Meleager, who were metamorphosed thus by Artemis after their brother was killed by the Kalydonian boar.

The onward road skims the shoreline of **Parthéni Bay** before arriving at the eponymous hamlet and army base; in its former capacity as a political prison during the junta era, this must have been a dreary place to be detained, and it's still an unpopular posting for conscripts.

Just over 11km from Plátanos, the paved road ends at **Blefoútis**, a rather more inspiring sight with its huge, virtually landlocked bay backed by greenery-flecked hills. The beach surface and shallows are the Lerian norm – watch your toes getting in – but there are tamarisks to shelter under and a decent taverna, *Iy Thea Artemi*, for a *kalamári*-and-chips-type lunch.

Greek script table

Léros	Λέρος	ΛΕΡΟΣ
Álynda	Άλυντα	ΑΛΥΝΤΑ
Ángyra	Άγκυρα	ΑΓΚΥΡΑ
Ayía Marína	Αγία Μαρίνα	ΑΓΙΑ ΜΑΡΙΝΑ
Áyios Isídhoros	Άγιος Ισίδωρος	ΑΓΙΟΣ ΙΣΙΔΩΡΟΣ
Áyios Nikólaos	Άγιος Νικόλαος	ΑΓΙΟΣ ΝΙΚΟΛΑΟΣ
Blefoútis	Μπλεφούτης	ΜΠΛΕΦΟΥΤΗΣ
Dhrymón(as)	Δρυμών(ας)	ΔΡΥΜΩΝ(ΑΣ)
Goúrna	Γούρνα	ΓΟΥΡΝΑ
Katsoúni	Κατσούνι	ΚΑΤΣΟΥΝΙ
Kokálli	Κοκάλι	ΚΟΚΑΛΙ
Kouloúki	Κουλούκι	ΚΟΥΛΟΥΚΙ
Krithóni	Κριθώνι	ΚΡΙΘΩΝΙ
Kryfós	Κρυφός	ΚΡΥΦΟΣ
Lakkí	Λακκί	ΛΑΚΚΙ
Lepídha	Λεπίδα	ΛΕΠΙΔΑ
Merikiá	Μερικιά	ΜΕΡΙΚΙΑ
Panayiés	Παναγιές	ΠΑΝΑΓΙΕΣ
Pandélli	Παντέλι	ΠΑΝΤΕΛΙ
Parthéni	Παρθένι	ΠΑΡΘΕΝΙ
Plátanos	Πλάτανος	ΠΛΑΤΑΝΟΣ
Vromólithos	Βρομόλιθος	ΒΡΟΜΟΛΙΘΟΣ
Xirókambos	Ξηρόκαμπος	ΞΗΡΟΚΑΜΠΟΣ

Léros travel details

Island transport

Buses

Plátanos to: Parthéni via Álynda in the north, and Xirókambos via Lakkí in the south (4–6 daily).

Inter-island transport

Key to ferry and hydrofoil companies

DANE	*Dhodhekanisiakí Anónymi Navtiliakí Etería* (Dodecanesian Shipping Company)
G&A	G&A Ferries
KR	Kyriakoulis Maritime
ML	Miniotis Lines
NK	*Nissos Kalymnos*

Kaïkia and excursion boats

Léros (Ayía Marína) to: Lipsí (at least 1 daily May–Oct).
Léros (Xirókambos) to: Myrtiés, Kálymnos (1 daily, 7am, May–Oct).

Ferries

Lakkí to: Agathoníssi (2 weekly on NK, 1 weekly on ML; 4hr); Arkí (1 weekly on ML; 3hr); Foúrni (2 weekly on G&A, summer only; 2hr 30min); Ikaría (2–3 weekly on G&A, summer only; 3hr 30min); Kálymnos (5 weekly on DANE, 4–6 weekly on G&A, 2 on NK; 1hr–1hr 15min); Kós (5 weekly on DANE, 5–7 weekly on G&A, 2 on NK; 2hr 30min–3hr); Lipsí (1 weekly on G&A, 1 on ML, 2 on NK; 45min–1hr); Náxos (1 weekly on G&A, summer only; 6hr 30min); Níssyros (1–2 weekly on G&A or DANE; 4hr); Páros (1 weekly on G&A, summer only; 7hr 30min); Pátmos (5 weekly on DANE, 5–7 weekly on G&A, 2 on NK; 1hr 15min–1hr 45min); Pireás (9–12 weekly on DANE or G&A; 12–14hr); Rhodes (5 weekly on DANE, 5–7 weekly on G&A; 6hr 30min–8hr); Samos-Pythagório (1 weekly on ML, 2 weekly on NK; 5hr 15min); Sými (1 weekly on G&A; 5hr 30min); Tílos (1–2 weekly on DANE or G&A; 4hr 30min).

Catamaran

Ayía Marína to: Kálymnos, Kós, Rhodes (4–7 weekly); Pátmos (3–7 weekly); Lipsí (2–4 weekly); Níssyros, Tílos (1 weekly); Sými (2–3 weekly, May–June only).

Hydrofoils

Ayía Marína to: Agathoníssi (1–2 weekly on KR; 1hr 45min); Foúrni (1 weekly on KR; 2hr 15min); Ikaría (1 weekly on KR; 1hr 45min); Kálymnos; 2–3 daily on KR; 45min); Kós (2–3 daily on KR; 1hr 30min); Lipsí (1–2 daily on KR; 20min); Pátmos (2–3 daily on KR; 45min); Sámos-Pythagório (1–2 daily on KR; 1hr 45min–2hr 45min).

Flights

Léros to: Athens (daily mid-June to mid-Sept, 4 weekly otherwise; 1hr).

Pátmos

Arguably the most beautiful and certainly the best known of the smaller Dodecanese, **Pátmos** has a distinctive, immediately palpable atmosphere. It was in a cave here that St John the Divine (in Greek, *O Theologos* or "The Theologian") wrote the New Testament's Book of Revelation and unwittingly shaped the island's destiny. The monastery honouring him, founded here in 1088 by the Blessed Khristodhoulos (1021–93), dominates Pátmos both physically – its fortified bulk towering above everything else – and, to a considerable extent, politically. While the monks inside no longer totally control the

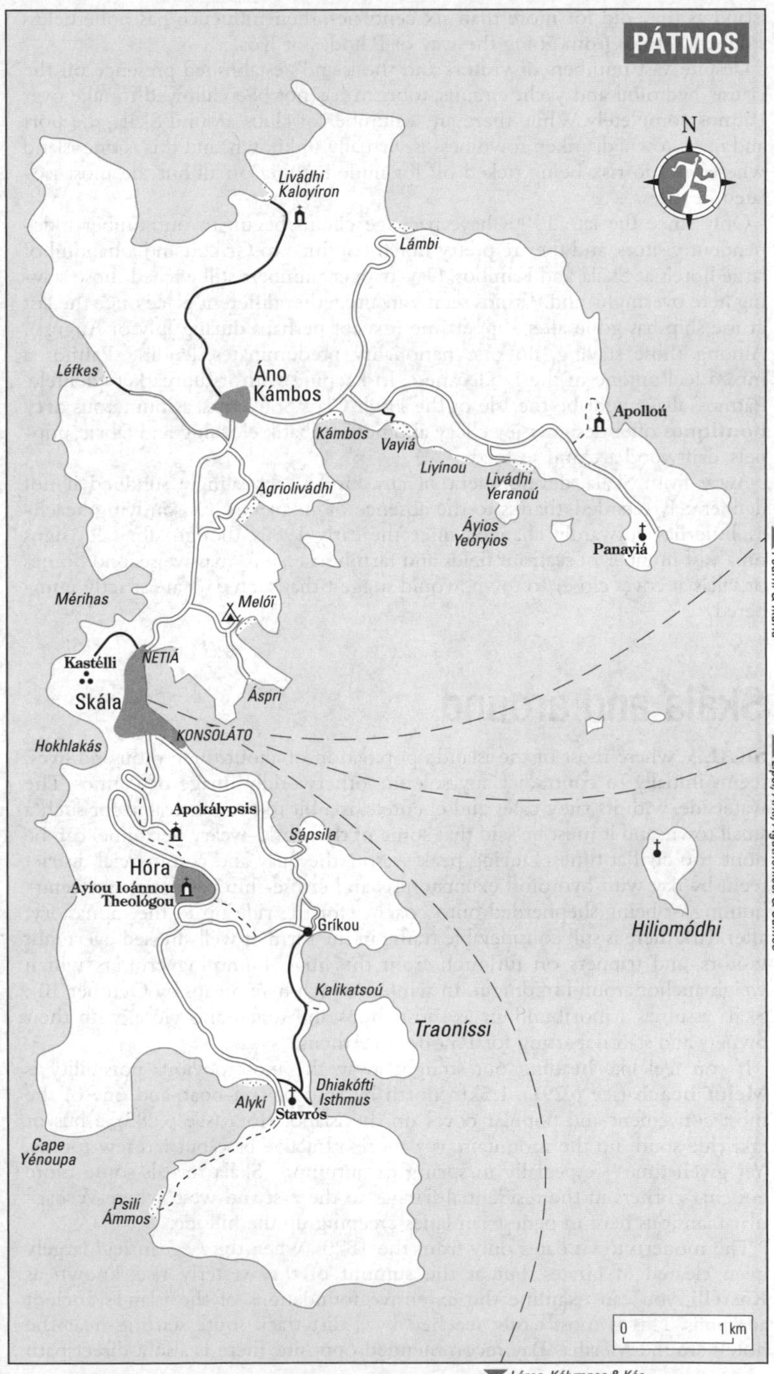
PÁTMOS
N
Livádhi
Kaloyíron
Lámbi
Léfkes
Áno
Kámbos
Apolloú
Kámbos
Vayiá
Liyínou
Livádhi
Yeranoú
Agriolivádhi
Áyios
Yeóryios
Panayiá
Fourni & Ikaría
Mérihas
Melóï
Kastélli
NETIÁ
Skála
Áspri
KONSOLÁTO
Hokhlakás
Lipsí, Arkí, Agathonissi & Sámos
Apokálypsis
Sápsila
Hóra
Ayíou Ioánnou
Theológou
Gríkou
Hiliomódhi
Kalikatsoú
Traoníssi
Dhiakófti
Isthmus
Alykí
Stavrós
Cape
Yénoupa
Psilí
Ámmos
0
1 km
Léros, Kálymnos & Kós

island as they did for more than six centuries, their influence has nonetheless stopped Pátmos from going the way of Rhodes or Kós.

Despite vast numbers of visitors and the island's established presence on the cruise, hydrofoil and yacht circuits, tourism has not been allowed to take over Pátmos completely. While there are a number of clubs around Skála, the port and main town, drunken rowdiness is virtually unknown, and this is one island where you do risk being ticked off for nude bathing on all but the most isolated beaches.

Only since the late 1990s have package clients begun to outnumber independent visitors, and they're pretty much confined to Gríkou and a handful of large hotels at Skála and Kámbos. Day-tripper numbers still exceed those staying here overnight, and Pátmos seems an altogether different place once the last cruise ship has gone after suppertime (except perhaps during July or August). Among those staying, no one nationality predominates, lending Pátmos a mixed feel unique in the Dodecanese. In keeping with its upmarket clientele, Pátmos' alias might be the Isle of the High Class Souvenirs, as numerous **arty boutiques** offer designer jewellery and pottery, batik clothing and fabric, puppets, driftwood art, and so forth.

Away from Skála, development of any kind is appealingly subdued if not deliberately retarded, thanks to the absence of an airport. On outlying beaches, little has outwardly changed since the early 1980s, though "for sale" signs on a vast number of seafront fields and farmhouses, plus massive second homes or villas at coves closer to town, would suggest that such days are strictly numbered.

Skála and around

SKÁLA, where most of the island's population of about three thousand lives, seems initially to contradict any solemn, otherworldly image of Pátmos. The waterside, with its ritzy cafés and clientele, is a bit too sophisticated for such a small town, and it must be said that some of the world-weary personnel can be none too civil at times. During peak season, the quay and commercial district teem by day with hydrofoil excursionists and cruise-ship passengers souvenir-hunting or being shepherded onto coaches for the ride up to the monastery; after dark there is still considerable traffic in the form of well-dressed overnight visitors, and trippers on furlough from the huge, humming cruisers which weigh anchor around midnight. In winter (which here means by October 10), Skála assumes a moribund air as most shops and restaurants close, with their owners and staff departing for Rhodes or Athens.

If you feel like heading out straight away, the most obvious possibility is **Melóï beach** (see p.291), 1.5km north by land or taxi-boat, and one of the most convenient and popular coves on the island. Hóra (see p.285), a bus or taxi ride south up the mountain, is a more attractive base but has few rooms. Yet given time – especially in spring or autumn – Skála reveals some more enticing corners in the residential fringes to the east and west, where vernacular mansions hem in pedestrian lanes creeping up the hillside.

The modern town dates only from the 1820s, when the Aegean had largely been cleared of pirates, but at the summit of the westerly rise, known as **Kastélli**, you can examine the extensive foundations of the island's ancient acropolis. This is most easily reached by a dirt-track route starting near the hotels around Mérihas Bay recommended opposite; there is also a direct path from Skála, beginning from the highest house on the northwest hillside, and passing a double-chapel surrounded by trees. What you find up top – eerily atmospheric at sunset – are several courses of ancient wall enclosing another, higher medieval chapel.

Accommodation

Numerous, persistent "**rooms**" touts meet all ferries and hydrofoils. Their offerings tend to be a long walk distant and/or inland – not necessarily a bad thing, as no location is really remote, and anywhere near the waterfront, which doubles as the main road between Gríkou and Kámbos, will be plagued both by traffic noise and the sound of cruise ships and ferries dropping or weighing anchor at all hours. Bona fide **hotel** proprietors sometimes join the fray on the quayside, though it's wisest to reserve such lodgings in advance.

The calmest areas are to the east at **Konsoláto**, along the relatively quiet road to Gríkou; in the northern district of **Netiá**, near Mérihas Bay, beyond the power plant; and west towards the pebble shore of **Hokhlakás**. Pátmos' vernacular architecture is quite distinctive, but you wouldn't know it from most lodgings: bland if inoffensive rooms thrown up during the 1980s, with institutional (one might even say monastic) furnishings – pitched, in August, at near-Rhodian rates. If you're keen to stay nearer a proper beach, there's a well-run, pleasantly set **campsite** (*Stefanos-Flowers*; ⓣ02470/31 821) at Méloï.

Central Skála

Annetzoula Panayiotaki Less than 10 minutes inland from the quay ⓣ02470/31 447. The kindly hostess sometimes offers little snacks at these modest rooms. ❷

Dhiethnes Inland from centre-quay, in the fields ⓣ02470/31 357. A good compromise both in price and comfort; 1970s-vintage D-class hotel rooms, but in a quiet situation. ❸

Galini In the cul-de-sac beyond the *Rex* ⓣ02470/31 240 or 31 740, ⓕ31 705. C-class hotel that's probably the best value in Skála. High-standard furnishings, full baths and large rooms, most with balconies, approach B-class quality; friendly management usually keeps a few on-spec vacancies despite a package presence. ❹

Rex Just inland from the ferry-dock café ⓣ02470/31 242. This D-class, central, but rather well-worn hotel has en-suite rooms and is a good fall-back if others are full. ❶

Pension Sofia Just off the Hóra-bound road on the left ⓣ02470/31 876. Decent pension often touted at the quay, though you tend to end up in the son's more professional but less welcoming outfit upstairs. ❷

Konsoláto

This area east of the centre takes its name from Pátmos' glory days when its importance justified the presence of a few foreign consulates here. Traffic is minimal and the fishing anchorage is picturesque, but fishermen firing up their motors at 4am may wake you if the small-hours comings and goings of ferries and cruise ships don't.

Blue Bay 150m towards Gríkou from the fishing anchorage ⓣ02470/31 165, ⓕ32 303, ⓔbluebayhotel@yahoo.com. A short distance out of town, this Aussie-Greek-run place is completely free of port-related noise and has the best sea views in Skála, as well as reliable internet facilities, though the rooms are spartan at best. ❺

Byzance A few steps inland from the fishing anchorage ⓣ02470/31 052, ⓕ31 663, ⓔbyzance@hol.gr. Comfortable C-class hotel as premises spread over two buildings – go for the larger rooms with balconies looking onto a garden. ❹

Captain's House At the fishing anchorage ⓣ02470/31 793, ⓕ32 277. Small hotel with well-furnished, but pricey rooms, which come in various sizes with medium-sized balconies; the friendly proprietress rents out cars. ❻

Delfini At the fishing anchorage ⓣ02470/32 060, ⓕ32 061. Rather overpriced hotel and somewhat gruffly managed, but with serviceable balconied rooms. ❺

Netiá

This slightly unglamorous area behind the yacht anchorage and power plant proves attractive up close and far quieter than town, bar the odd grumblings from the dynamo.

Hotel Asteri Near Mérihas cove ⓣ02470/32 465, ⓕ31 347, ⓔpasca@otenet.gr. The highest standard in this area unimproveably set on a knoll overlooking the bay, in a well-landscaped environment that's also a working farm – guests have home-grown produce at breakfast. ⑤

Australis ⓣ02470/31 576, ⓕ32 284. 1970s-vintage hotel, nominally E-class but en suite, owned by a returned Greek-Australian family; full breakfast included in the price and myriad small kindnesses that guarantee an enthusiastic return clientele. ④

Pension Sydney ⓣ02470/31 689. Run by the brother of the *Australis* family, and where overflow tends to be referred to. They all share a scooter-rental business, which save you traipses into town. ③

Villa Knossos ⓣ02470/32 189. Managed by the daughter and son-in-law of the *Australis*'s owners, featuring high-standard self-catering units with balconies. ④

Hokhlakás

Hokhlakás bay is most easily reached by following the main commercial pedestrian street inland and southwest ten minutes from the municipal "palace"; like most of the island's west-facing shore, it's not especially good for swimming, but it is dead quiet out here.

Maria Down in the flatlands ⓣ02470/31 201 or 31 471, ⓕ32 018. Air conditioning and big seaview balconies make up for tiny bathrooms; package presence in peak season may exclude walk-ins. ⑤

Romeos On the southerly slope overlooking the bay ⓣ02470/31 962, ⓕ31 070, ⓔromeos@w12.gr. Skála's top accommodation with a pool, large common areas, and sizeable units numerous enough that there's usually a vacancy despite package patronage. ⑥

Summer On the north hillside ⓣ02470/31 769, ⓕ31 170. Another pleasantly set and landscaped, if somewhat overpriced, C-class hotel. ⑤

Melói

Porto Scoutari Hotel ⓣ02470/33 124, ⓕ33 175, ⓔelinas@12net.gr. A bungalow complex in traditional style, overlooking the beach from a hillside setting, with vehicle access from the main island road. Its enormous, self-catering suites are arrayed around the pool area and have seaview and air con/heating, as well as exquisite, mock-antique furnishings and original art. Arguably the premier establishment on the whole island. Open most of the year. ⑥

Eating and drinking

Despite surges of presumably hungry crowds from the cruise ships, **restaurant options** are surprisingly limited in Skála; there are altogether too many *souvladzídhika* and *yirádhika* joints, as well as pastry-and-crêpe shops, and not enough good-value sit-down places. Another obstacle to dining enjoyment, especially if you're arriving on a ferry (and they all dock late), is that Skála eateries tend to take last orders at the very un-Greek early hour of 10.30pm or so, leaving latecomers with the choice of pizza or fast food.

That said, there are some bright spots. Most durable, inexpensive and distinctive is seafood-only *Ouzeri To Hiliomodhi*, just off the start of the Hóra road on the left, with its vegetarian mezédhes and delicacies such as limpets (served live, be warned), grilled octopus and salted anchovies served out the back at tables on a quiet pedestrian lane.Very nearly as good, newly opened in 2001, is the *Ouzeri Ostria* at the far west end of the inland lane behind the *Arion* and *Astoria* cafés, with big portions of more conventional seafood and smaller platters of salad and *orektiká*; three can eat there, with a modest quantity of drink, for €27–30, and they may well serve you up to about 11.15pm. Honourable mentions go to *Pandelis*, one lane inland behind Astoria Travel, where a wide-ranging menu of reliably good *mayireftá* make up for famously dour – if efficient – service, and *Cactus* on the beach at Hokhlakás, doing nouvelle-minceur Italian snacks (don't show up too hungry) accompanied by Italian wines and aperitifs.

The most reliable **breakfast** venue is on the second, smaller platía beyond the main one, where *La Frianderie* serves hot drinks, yogurt with fruit salad and croissants under medieval arches, and the adjacent bakery turns out terrific turnovers and Greek pastries. The *Astoria Café*, next to the eponymous travel agency on the quay, is good for reasonable ice cream and coffee, plus of course people-watching.

The biggest and most long-lived **café-bar** is the wood-panelled, barn-like *Café Arion* on the waterside, where local youth hang out and play cards. Every year, a few other, livelier clubs try their luck: among the more consistent are *Kafé Aman*, with low-volume music and snacks, and *Konsolato*, a late-night (midnight–dawn) club, both on the shore in Konsoláto district, and *Seline*, at the opposite end of the quay, beyond the town beach. Besides the **internet café** attached to the *Blue Bay Hotel*, there is nominally another, *Millennium*, on the lane bound for Hokhlakás, but in late 2001 it was closed for a "virus" (of a financial nature?) and may not reopen.

Other practicalities

Almost everything of interest can be found within, or within sight of, the Italian-built municipal "palace": large ferries anchor opposite, the port police occupy the east end and the **post office** one of its corners, though the municipal **tourist information** office in the rear of the building was not operating in 2001, and never was of much use anyway. There are two **cash machines**: in front of the Ethniki Trapeza/National Bank, and a stand-alone one (Emboriki/Commercial) on the quay.

Motorbike rental outfits (eg Billis ⓣ02470/32 218) are common, with lowish rates (€10 a day or less) owing to Pátmos' modest size and limited road network. Families or groups can also find **cars** to rent, at Tassos Rent a Car (ⓣ02470/31 753) among others. **Excursion boats** to Psilí Ámmos, Lipsí and Arkí/Maráthi all leave at about 10am from just in front of Astoria Travel (ⓣ02470/31 205) and Apollon Travel (ⓣ02470/31 324), the two most reliable agencies handling **hydrofoil** tickets. G&A Ferries are represented at the back of the central square, while DANE and the *Nissos Kalymnos* share premises (ⓣ02470/32 575) in a lane leading off the same platía. The *Dodekanisos Express* and Miniotis Lines ferries are represented by Kyriaki Liapi in Konsoláto (ⓣ02470/29 303).

The monasteries and Hóra

For all visitors to Pátmos, the first order of business is likely to be the **monastery** of Ayíou Ioánnou Theológou (St John), sheltered behind massive defences in the hilltop capital of **Hóra**. Both this monastery and the monastery of Apokálypsis (see p.287) are on cruise itineraries, becoming hopelessly crowded in the hour or two after the ships have docked, so keep an eye on the harbour and time your visit accordingly. Both public buses and tour coaches make the climb up here, but the half-hour walk along a beautiful old cobbled path shortcutting the road puts you in a more appropriate frame of mind. To find its start, proceed through Skála towards Hokhlakás, and once past the telecoms building, bear left onto a lane starting opposite an ironmonger's; follow this uphill to its end on the main road – immediately opposite you'll see the cobbled path.

In 1088, the soldier-cleric Ioannis "The Blessed" Khristodhoulos was granted a lifetime title to Pátmos by Byzantine Emperor Alexios Komnenos. It had

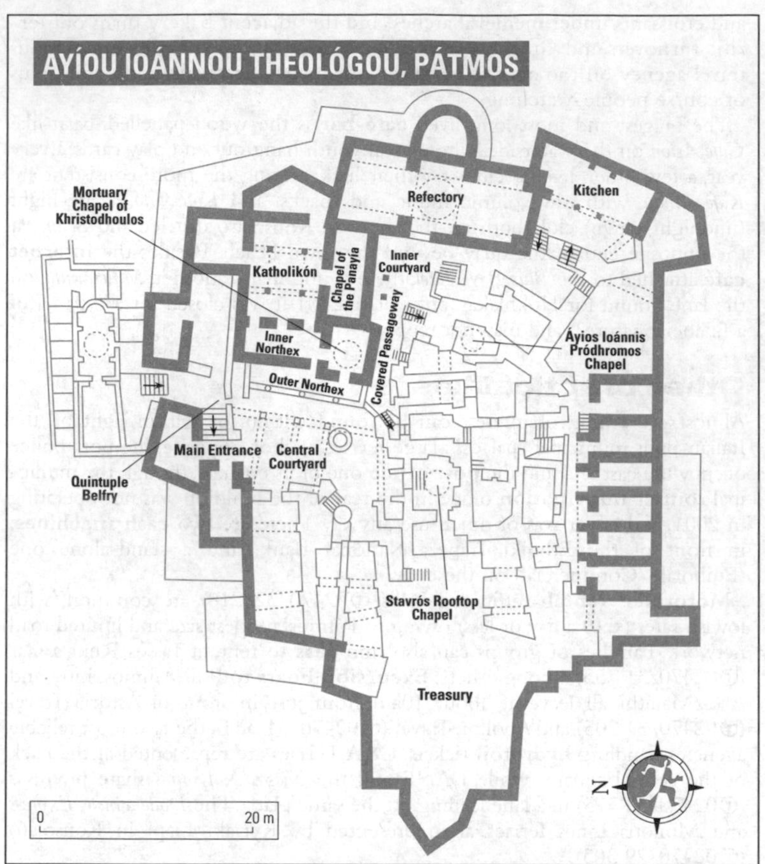

long been Khristodhoulos' ambition to establish a religious community near the site of St John's Revelation, and within three years he and his followers had completed the framework of the monastery now visible, as well as a smaller one around the Grotto of the Revelation. The double threats of piracy and the Selçuk Turks meant that from the outset the main monastery was heavily fortified, with buttresses added later to make its hilltop position virtually impregnable.

The original imperial grant also included provisions for tax exemption and the right of the monks to engage in sea trade, clauses exploited to the full by the monastery and usually respected by later Turkish and Venetian rulers. A commercial fleet and extensive landholdings across the Balkans made the monastic community immensely wealthy, enabling it to steadily augment the library inaugurated by Khristodhoulos, which in its prime contained far more than today's four thousand books and rare manuscripts. During the island's eighteenth-century heyday, local wealth and prestige permitted the foundation of a **theological school** for training clergy; after a century or so of abandonment, this was restored after World War II and now functions once more.

St John on Pátmos

Pátmos has been intimately associated with early Christianity since **John the Evangelist** – later known as John the Divine – was exiled here from Ephesus on the orders of the Roman emperor Domitian, in about AD 95. While John was on Pátmos, supposedly dwelling in a grotto up the hill from the harbour, an otherworldly voice from a cleft in the ceiling bid him set down in writing what he heard. By the time John was allowed to return home, that disturbing finale to the New Testament, the Book of Revelations (or the Apocalypse), had been disseminated in the form of a pastoral letter to the Seven Churches of Asia Minor.

Revelations, whoever really wrote it, belongs squarely within the Judeo Christian tradition of apocalyptic books, with titanic battles in heaven and on earth, supernatural visions, plus lurid descriptions of the fates awaiting the saved and the damned following the Last Judgement. As with other, similar, books in the Old Testament, Revelations is a product of troubled times, when the religion of the elect – whether Judaism or Christianity – was powerless and thus humiliated in secular terms. Some cosmological justification had to be found for this, so emphasis was laid on the imminence of the Last Days. Of all the chapters of the Bible, Revelations is still among the most amenable to subjective application by fanatics, and was in use as a rhetorical and theological weapon within a century of appearing. Its vivid imagery lent itself easily to depiction in frescoes, adorning the refectories of numerous Byzantine monasteries and the narthexes of Orthodox churches, conveying a salutary message to illiterate medieval parishioners.

In addition to transcribing the Apocalypse, John supposedly wrote his Gospel on Pátmos, and also expended considerable effort combating paganism, most notably in the person of an evil local wizard, Kynops. In an episode related by John's disciple Prohoros, Kynops challenged the saint to a duel of miracles; the magician's stock trick involved retrieving effigies of the deceased from the sea bed, so John responded by petrifying Kynops while he was underwater. A buoy near the edge of Skála harbour today marks a submerged rock that is supposedly the remains of the wizard. Mechanical efforts to remove this marine hazard have all failed, and it is claimed that fish caught in the vicinity taste bad. In the far southwest of the island, a foul-smelling volcanic cave has also been identified as a favourite haunt of the magician, whose name lives on as Cape Yénoupa (the modern form of "Kynops").

Forever after in the Orthodox world, heights amidst desolate and especially volcanic topography have become associated with St John, and Pátmos with its eerie landscape of igneous outcrops is an excellent case in point. Other nearby examples include the isle of Níssyros, where one of the saint's monasteries overlooks the volcano's caldera, and Lésvos, where another monastery dedicated to him sits atop an extinct volcano, gazing at basalt-strewn wastelands.

Monastery of Apokálypsis

Just over halfway up the path, pause at the **monastery of Apokálypsis** ("the Apocalypse"; variable hours, but approximately Mon, Wed, Fri & Sat 8am–1pm, Tues & Thurs 8am–1pm & 4–6pm, Sun 8am–noon & 4–6pm; free) built around the grotto where St John heard the voice of God and dictated His words to a disciple, Prohoros – yet again supernaturally, it would seem, since Prohoros apparently lived some centuries after the Evangelist. For many years, a leaflet left for pilgrims pointed out that the "fissure . . . (divides) the rock into three parts, thus serving as a continual reminder of the Trinitarian nature of God" and moreover admonished visitors "to ask yourself whether you are on the side of Christ or of Antichrist". This provocative literature has now vanished, but in the cave wall the presumed nightly resting place of the saint's head is fenced off and outlined in beaten silver.

Monastery of Ayíou Ioánnou Theológou

The grotto compound is merely a foretaste of the **monastery of Ayíou Ioánnou Theológou (St John)** (same hours and admission as Apokálypsis). "Modest" dress is essential, and the monks, fed up with hordes of tourists, can seem brusque, so be discreet. A warren of interconnecting courtyards, chapels, stairways, arcades, galleries and roof terraces (the last regrettably off limits), it offers a rare glimpse of Patmian interior architecture, strongly influenced by the ethos of medieval Crete, owing to the large numbers of Cretans in Khristodhoulos' original working party. Hidden in the walls are fragments of an ancient Artemis temple which stood here before being destroyed by Khristodhoulos. Of the various chapels to your left as you enter the main courtyard, that of **Panayía** has the best preserved and most noteworthy medieval frescoes.

Off to one side, the **treasury** (same hours; separate €3.50 admission) merits a leisurely visit for its magnificent array of religious treasures, mostly medieval icons of the Cretan School – including St John Damascene wearing what appears to be a *keffiyeh* – and liturgical embroidery of the same era, particularly two satin shrouds threaded with gold for the *epitáfios* or bier of Christ, carried in solemn procession on Good Friday. Among the multiple donations of the pious from across the Orthodox world, with Russia particularly well represented, a filigreed cross of incredible delicacy stands out. Yet pride of place goes to the eleventh-century parchment *khrysóvoulos* (chrysobull) of Emperor Alexios Komnenos, granting the entire island to Khristodhoulos; even earlier are various precious manuscripts and an unusual mosaic icon of St Nicholas.

This tallies just a small fraction of the museum's contents; if you get hooked, the well-stocked gift shop at the end offers a catalogue and high-quality reproductions of favourite pieces. The famous **library** is unfortunately off limits to all except credentialled ecclesiastical scholars.

Hóra

The promise of security afforded by Ayíou Ioánnou's stout walls spurred the growth of **HÓRA** immediately outside the fortifications from the late thirteenth century onwards. Despite earthquakes and the Italians' demolition of buildings to create open space, it remains an architecturally homogenous village, with cobbled alleys sheltering dozens of shipowners' mansions, most dating from Pátmos' seventeenth- and eighteenth-century heyday. High, almost windowless walls and monumental wooden doors betray nothing of the opulence within: painted ceilings, *hokhláki* terraces, flagstoned kitchens with carved cistern heads, carved furniture and embroidered bed curtains.

Inevitably a certain amount of touristic tattiness disfigures the main ramps approaching the monastery gate, but away from the principal throughfares you stumble upon passages rarely disturbed by foot traffic, no wider than one person, lined with ruins, blocked by rubble or overgrown with night-fragrant *rodhokaliá* bushes. On summer nights, when the monastery ramparts are floodlit to startling effect, it is tempting to nominate Hóra as the most beautiful settlement in the Dodecanese.

Neither should you miss the **view** from Platía Lódza, named after the remnant of an adjacent Venetian loggia. Easiest glimpsed at dawn or dusk, the landmasses to the north – going clockwise – include Ikaría, Thýmena, Foúrni, Sámos with the brooding mass of Mount Kérkis, Arkí, Lipsí and the double-humped Samsun Dağı (ancient Mount Mycale) in Turkey.

East fortification, Ayíou Ioánnou Theológou monastery, Pátmos

There are over forty "minor" churches and monasteries in and around Hóra, many of them containing beautiful icons and examples of local woodcarving; almost all are locked, to prevent thefts, but someone living nearby will have the key. Among the best are the church of **Dhiasózousa**, the convent of **Zoödhóhou Piyís** (daily 9am–1pm & 4–7pm) well southwest of the village, and the convent of **Evangelismoú**, at the edge of village in the same direction (daily 9–11am); follow the wall-arrows to this last.

Practicalities

Among several **tavernas** in Hóra, *Vangelis* on the inner square has a wonderful old jukebox, friendly service and view seating on various levels (plus the square), but alas the cooking has declined since the late 1990s; you'll probably eat better at either *Balkoni* or the *Ipiros* near the monastery, with views north over the island. Again on the square, *Kafeteria Stoa* is minimally touristy despite its showcase interior, and still functions as the village kafenío. For more organized **nightlife**, there's *Pyrgos*, with a range of snacks and occasionally live touring groups from Athens.

There are, however, almost no places **to stay** on spec; foreigners here are mostly long-term occupants, who have bought up and restored almost a third of the crumbling mansions since the 1960s. Getting a short-term, non-package room can be a pretty thankless task, even in spring or autumn; one strategy is to contact *Vangelis* taverna early in the day for help in arranging private rooms, or phone ahead for reservations at *Yeoryia Triandafyllou* (Ⓣ02470/31 963; ❸) or *Marouso Kouva* (Ⓣ02470/31 026; ❸), both on the south flank of Hóra.

The rest of the island

Pátmos, as a locally published guide once memorably proclaimed, "is immense for those who know how to wander in space and time". Lesser mortals may find it easier to get around on foot or by scooter and bus. There's still scope for **walking**, despite a dwindling network of paths; otherwise the single **bus** offers a surprisingly reliable service between Skála, Hóra, Kámbos and Gríkou – the terminal, with a timetable posted up, is right in front of the main ferry dock.

Southern beaches

After the extraordinary atmosphere and magnificent scenery, **beaches** are Pátmos' main attraction. The closest to town, aside from Melóï, is the north-facing cove of **Sápsila** 2km southeast of Skála, surrounded by farms and holiday real estate – plus the Greek-and-Floridian-run *Benetos* **restaurant** (June–Sept, supper only; reserve on Ⓣ02470/33 089) which, since 1998, has established a reputation as one of the best spots on the island for seafood and generic Mediterranean dishes.

By continuing along the same road, or descending east from Hóra on a separate one (an old path partly shortcuts this), you arrive at the sandiest part of rather overdeveloped **Gríkou** (Gríkos), the main venue for Patmian package tourism – and shut tight as a drum come late September. *Stamatis* at mid-beach is the obvious, and fairly decent, **taverna** choice; hillside *Flisvos* (aka *Floros*) further south, going since the 1960s, has a limited range of inexpensive, savoury *mayireftá*, served on the terrace. They also have simple rooms (❶) and fancier apartments (❹) – reserve on Ⓣ02470/31 380, Ⓕ32 094. Another good **accommodation** option here, open late in the year and not monopolized by packages, is the hillside *Hotel Golden Sun* (Ⓣ02470/32 318, Ⓕ34 019; ❺), with most rooms facing the water. The beach itself forms a thin strip of hard-packed sand giving way to large pebbles as you head south toward the strange volcanic outcrop of **Kalikatsoú**, honeycombed with caves fashioned by Paleo-Christian hermits; at your own risk you can scramble quite high onto this, but you need a head for heights.

A scooter is probably the best mode of transport along the paved roads from Hóra as far as the **Dhiakófti** isthmus with its chapel of Stavrós and some busy boatyards. On the northwest shore of this sprawls **Alykí** beach (no facilities), but most people who've made it out here opt for a thirty minute or less walk along the trail southwest to **Psilí Ámmos** beach. These are, respectively, the best hike and the only pure-sand cove on the island, with shade lent by tamarisks and a good, lunch-only **taverna** that occasionally does freshly roasted goat from the surrounding hills. Cliffs and hills to either side create a dramatic backdrop, though the sea bed itself shelves gently; by tacit consent, the southern third of the beach is resolutely nudist. In summer Psilí Ámmos can also be reached by **taxi-boat**, which departs from Skála at about 10am and returns at 4–5pm depending on the time of year.

Northern beaches

More good beaches are to be found in the north of the island, tucked into the startling eastern shoreline (west-facing bays are uniformly unusable owing to wind and washed-up debris). Most are accessible from side roads off the main route north from Skála, though one or two must be reached on foot in the final moments via stretches of old paths.

Melóï is not only handy – a regular taxi-boat service from Skála makes it more so – but usually quite appealing: there are tamarisks behind the narrow belt of sand, and good snorkelling offshore. It also offers one of the better *mayireftá* **tavernas** on the island, *Meloi* (alias *Stefanos'*): reasonably priced, friendly and open much of the year – in spring or autumn you may find that this is the closest place to Skála that's open for lunch. Just over the hill at **Áspri** cove are two summer-only fish tavernas, *Aspri* and *Kyma* with in your face views of Hóra; the former is reckoned better if pricier, and opens at lunch too.

The first beach beyond Melóï, **Agriolívadho** (Agriolivádhi) has mostly sand at its broad centre, kayak rental, and two tavernas: one at mid-beach, the other (*O Glaros*) on the southern hillside.

The next beach, **Kámbos**, is popular with Greeks, and the most developed remote resort on the island, with seasonal watersports facilities and three tavernas, best of these *Ta Kavourakia*, though the beach's appeal is diminished somewhat by a rock shelf in the shallows and the road directly behind.

ÁNO KÁMBOS, 600m west and uphill, is the only proper village on Pátmos besides Skála and Hóra, the focus of scattered farms in little oases all around. This is the northernmost stop for the bus, which turns around at the cobbled platía beside the church and two **tavernas**, the better being the first one you meet as you enter the village from the south. From Áno Kámbos, you can make a detour northwest to **Livádhi Kaloyíron**, a farming valley that lives oblivious of tourism – perhaps because the road in is rough, and the beach stony, wave-battered and dirty. The little inland monastery here, however, set behind its gardens, is attractive.

East of Kámbos beach, there are several more coves. **Vayiá** (pebbles) and **Livádhi Yeranoú** (sand and gravel) are less visited but arguably more attractive; Yeranoú can offer extensive shade from tamarisks and discreet naturism at the far end, plus an excellent namesake taverna doing simple but hygienic grills and salads. Just offshore lies the small islet of **Áyios Yeóryios**, which you can easily swim out to, with a little beach to rest up on before the lap back.

Between Vayiá and Livádhi Yeranoú, around the Liyínou headland, lie two pebbly coves popular with naturists and accessible by trail only.

From Kámbos you can also travel north to the bay of **Lámbi**, ideal for swimming when the prevailing wind is from the south, and renowned for an abundance of multicoloured volcanic pebbles (mixed with gravel and sand). Lámbi has one of the best **beach tavernas** on the island: *Lambi-Leonidas* (May–Oct), closest to the road's end, serving a range of grilled meat and vegetarian mezédhes like *hórta* and *saganáki*; seafood should be reserved in advance (Ⓣ02470/31 490).

Satellite islets: Lipsí, Arkí, Maráthi and Agathoníssi

Of the various islets to the north and east of Pátmos, **Lipsí** is the largest, most interesting and most visited; ultra-lonely **Arkí**, **Maráthi** and **Agathoníssi** are smaller, far less frequented and more primitive.

Lipsí

Since the early 1990s, **LIPSÍ** has acquired a significant seasonal tourist trade: Germans in early summer, hordes of Italians later on, plus a fair quantity of British package clients (through Laskarina Holidays, see p.14) from spring to autumn, who occupy most of the better lodgings. All of this (helped along by periodic weekend-supplement features proclaiming its "undiscoveredness" and "unspoiltness"), plus the island's regular appearance on both ferry and hydrofoil routes, mean that it's unwise to show up in peak season without a reservation (though rooms proprietors often meet arrivals at other times).

During quieter months, however, Lipsí still makes an idyllic halt, its sleepy pace making plausible a purported link between the island's name and that of Calypso, the nymph who legendarily held Odysseus in thrall for several years. Lipsí in fact ranks as a dependency of the Monastery of Ayíou Ioánnou Theológou on Pátmos, and is as well sown with blue-domed country chapels as any of the larger Dodecanese. Deep wells provide water for many small, well-tended farms and vineyards (which once produced dark, sweet communion wine for the Vatican), but there is only one flowing spring (in the west), and pastoral appearances are deceptive – three times the relatively impoverished full-time population of about seven hundred live overseas (many in Tasmania, for some reason). The homes of most of those who remained behind (or increasingly, return as retirees) cluster around the fine harbour, as does the majority of food and lodging.

Lipsí port

A new freight-loading dock is being built on the south side of the port, and a new breakwater will cut the swell into the fishing anchorage at the east end of the bay, but the **yacht and ferry jetties** will stay where they are, at the northwest end of the quay.

The village doesn't have much in the way of specific sights apart from a hilariously indiscriminate **ecclesiastical museum** (June–Sept only, theoretically Mon–Fri 9.30am–1.30pm & 4–8pm, Sat & Sun 10am–2pm, best real chance of admission 10am–1pm daily; free), featuring such bottled "relics" as oil from the sanctuary on Mount Tabor and water from the Jordan River, as well as archeological finds and two letters from Greek revolutionary hero Admiral Miaoulis.

Accommodation

Aphrodite Hotel Just inland from Liendoú. ⓣ02470/41 000 or 41 394. 1997-built studio and apartment complex designed to house package clients – though they're not averse to walk-ins at slow times. Top-drawer (for Lipsí, anyway). ❺

Flisvos Pension East end of the port ⓣ02470/41 261. Basic, early 1980s, block of rooms, convenient (perhaps too convenient) to a handful of tavernas and cafés. ❸

Apartments Galini Above the ferry jetty ⓣ02470/41 212, ⓕ41 012. A prime budget choice, run by welcoming Nikos and Anna Matsouris, with really large balconied double

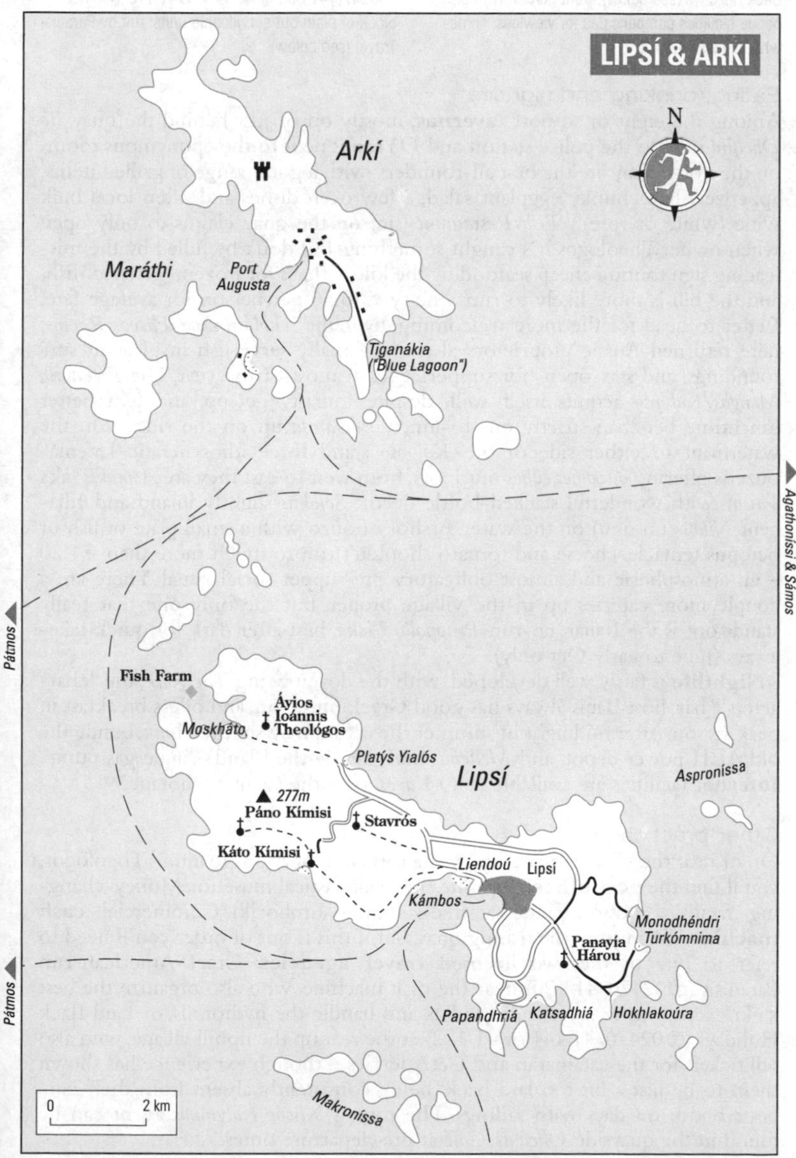

rooms. Nikos is a fisherman and may take groups on kaïki tours on request. ❸

Glaros On hillside behind *Kalypso Hotel/Restaurant* ⓣ02470/41 360. Basic 1980s block of rooms, most with views of the bay. ❷

Studios Kalymnos On the road northeast out of "town" ⓣ02470/41 141, ⓕ41 343, ⓔstudios_kalymnos@lipsi-island.gr. Run by Laid Back Holidays (see below); front garden with barbecue facilities compensates for viewless, somewhat airless, units. ❸

Miramare Studios Back in the fields east of harbour ⓣ02470/41 238. Friendly family keeps these self-catering studios. ❸

Studios Paradise On the ridge north of the *Dhelfini* restaurant ⓣ02470/41 125. Rooms with fridges and hotplates, and some views; enquire at the *Dhelfini*, which manages them. ❸

Rena's Rooms Overlooking Liendoú beach ⓣ02470/41 363 or 41 120, ⓕ41 110. Another block of plain but serviceable units; run by Paradisi Travel (see below). ❷

Eating, drinking and nightlife

Among the eight or so port **tavernas**, mostly on or just behind the quay, *To Dhelfini* next to the police station and *O Yiannis* next to the eponymous rooms on the north quay are the best all-rounders, with a good range of grilled items, appetizers like chunky eggplant salad, a few oven dishes and often local bulk wine (white or rosé). *Fish Restaurant* (sic) on the quay claims to only open when owner Theologos has caught something, but don't be lulled by the misleading sign touting cheap seafood by the kilo – that's for frozen, "generic" fish, and the bill is more likely to run a hefty €16.50 per person for average fare. Better to head for the more welcoming, hygienic *Tholari*, near *Flisvos Rooms*; here returned-Aussie proprietors also occasionally serve fish in pleasant surroundings, and stay open (for supper at least) most of the year. The *Estiatorio Mangos/Kalypso* acquits itself well, despite touristy get-up, and is a better lunchtime bet than strictly out-to-lunch *Barbarosa* up on the ridge. On the waterfront to either side of the *Kalypso* stand three idiosyncratic kafenía-ouzerís offering *ouzomezédhes* outdoors; from west to east they are *Asprakis* (aka *Vasso*), with wonderful stacked-bottle decor; *Sofoklis* slightly inland and adjacent *Nikos* (no sign) on the water. A shot of oúzo with a small plate of fish or octopus tentacle, cheese and tomato shouldn't run to much more than €1.20 – an atmospheric and almost obligatory pre-supper social ritual. There are a couple more eateries up in the village proper, but the only one that really stands out is the Italian co-run *Psitopolio Plaka*, best after dark for quick takeaways (June to early Oct only).

Nightlife is fairly well developed, with the doyen being *The Rock*, the "characters'" bar; host Babis always has good Greek music on, and offers breakfast in peak season. After midnight in summer the action may shift to *Amin*, beside the old ΔΕΗ power depot, and *Meltemi Club*, beside the island's single gas pump. **Internet** facilities are available at *O Kavos*, near the yacht anchorage.

Other practicalities

On or near the village square up by the cathedral of Áyios Ioánnis Theológos, you'll find the **post office**, opposite the ecclesiastical museum. Money-changing facilities now include a free-standing Emboriki/Commercial **cash machine** just in from the fishing quay, but if this is out of order you'll need to refer to one of the two licensed **travel agencies**: Greek-American-run Paradisis (ⓣ02470/41 120) near the cash machine, who also organize the best kaïki excursions to surrounding islets and handle the hydrofoils, or Laid Back Holidays (ⓣ02470/41 141 or 41 102) at the rear up the uphill village, who also sell tickets for the catamaran and G&A ferries – though experience has shown them to be just a bit too laid back, being consistently absent from their harbour booth on days with sailings. The roving *Nissos Kalymnos* agent can be found in the quayside *Okeanis Café* at pre-departure times.

Around the island

From May to October, two **minibuses** run all day on the hour along the route Katsádhia–Harbour–Platýs Yialós, with the town stop very close to the cash machine. Otherwise, there are two **taxis**, and two outfits renting **scooters** (George ⓣ02470/41 340, and the more obvious Markos & Maria ⓣ02470/41 130).

The island's **beaches** are rather scattered, though none is more than an hour's walk (or twenty-minute scooter ride) away. Closest to town, and sandiest, is **Liendoú**, immediately to the northwest, but many visitors prefer the attractive duo of **Katsadhiá** (sand) and **Papandhriá** (pebbles), adjacent small coves about 2km south of the port by paved road. Right above the sea at Katsadhiá you'll find a musical taverna-café-bar, *Dilaila* (June–Sept), which also runs an informal pine-grove campsite (free but you must buy a meal from them daily). By contrast, **Hokhlakoúra**, on the east coast, consists of occasionally grubby shingle with no facilities; nearby **Turkómnima** offers a hundred metres or so of tamarisk-shaded sand, but it's mercilessly exposed to the *meltémi* so often seaweed-caked. A final ten-minute path scramble from a "parking area" at the end of a rough track gets you to **Monodhéndhri** in the far northeast, poor to mediocre as a beach, but very scenic with its photogenic lone juniper tree and the striking rock islets of Aspronissia offshore. There are far superior coves just to the right, past the gated fence, though they get too much shade after noon; clothing is optional everywhere here.

Some 4km of travel along the paved road leading west from town brings you to **Platýs Yialós**, a small, shallow bay with a single taverna. The boulder-studded, sandy beach here isn't up to much, and the bay is ridiculously shallow and exposed, but the **taverna** (*Kostas*) is quite salubrious and popular for lunch (daily June–Sept; May–Oct Wed, Sat & Sun only), with mountainous salads and grills (sometimes including fish).

A bare handful of surviving paths and narrow tracks provide opportunities for genuine **walks** through the undulating countryside, though the well-signposted road network, surfaced or otherwise, seem to increase each year. One of the better surviving treks heads west to the bay of **Kímisi**, where the octagenarian hermit-monk Filippos used to dwell in a tiny monastery just above the shore, next to the single island spring; he is in fact now seriously ill, and living out his last days in a room under the town cathedral. To reach the place, bear left onto the faintly waymarked path taking off from the trans-island road at its high point (some 20min above Liendoú). In as much time again you'll reach the chapel-monastery of Stavrós, tracing the north flank of Lipsi's summit ridge; from there you're obliged to follow an ugly new road, paved except for the final 150m, another twenty minutes to sea level at Káto Kímisi. The beach

The miracle of August 23

Shortly before Hokhlakoúra, just right of the road, stands the appealing, sixteenth-century, triple-apsed church of **Panayía toú Hárou** (The Virgin of Death), focus of a miracle repeated annually since 1943. The church is so named because it once contained an icon of the Virgin cradling the dead Christ, the only such known in the Orthodox world (it is now safely kept in the town cathedral). In gratitude for a favour granted, a parishioner left a sprig of lilies under the glass of the icon; they duly withered, but were found to mysteriously revive only on August 23, the day of the Virgin's reception into Paradise. Each year the island's major festival sees the icon, with rejuvenating flowers, processed with suitable ceremony to its old home and then back to the village square, focus of all-night revelries.

here is decent, with some masonry "improvements" of obscure purpose just behind; you can walk for an extra forty minutes return up a field-stoned and walled path to the neatly kept hermitage of **Páno Kímisi**, preserved as it was before Filippos abandoned this for his lower quarters in the early 1980s. From the shore monastery, an obvious path begins threading high above the coast back towards Liendoú, but the trail is faint to barely existent in the middle, so you'll need good hill-walking skills. At rocky **Eléna** beach a track resumes towards marginally better **Kámbos** cove, and it's just over an hour from Káto Kímisi to Liendoú, for a total (including side trip to Páno Kímisi and a swim at Káto) of just over three hours.

Arkí and Maráthi

About two-thirds the size of Lipsí, **Arkí** is considerably more primitive, lacking drinking water, dynamo electricity (there are solar panels), ferry anchorage or much in the way of a village centre. Just forty permanent inhabitants eke out a living here, mostly engaged in fishing, though catering for yacht parties attracted here by the superb anchorage of Avgoústa ("Port Augusta" on yacht charts) is increasingly important. Arkí is an elective, twice-weekly stop on the Miniotis Lines routes: if you want to disembark here, you must warn the captain well in advance, so he can radio for the shuttle service from the island. Most visitors arrive by the more reliable supply boat from Pátmos (Mon & Thurs sailings guaranteed), which actually docks at the quay. A new jetty capable of accommodating larger ferries and hydrofoils creeps towards completion, but as with all such things in the Aegean, it could take years to happen.

Of the three **tavernas** around the round harbourside platía, the better two – *Nikolas* (Ⓣ02470/32 477) and *O Trypas* (Ⓣ02470/32 230) – each control a handful of **rooms** (both ❷), though in August every vacancy will have been snapped up in advance. *Nikolaos* is more food-orientated, with home-made puddings, while *O Trypas* doubles as the happening music pub, courtesy of the owner's enormous collection of CDs and tapes.

The only "sight" is the scanty remains of the Hellenistic **fortress of Avgoustínis** near the island's summit, the masonry reworked by the Byzantines. You can swim at the "Blue Lagoon" of **Tiganákia** at the southeast tip of the island – all excursions from Lipsí stop there – but there are no real beaches to speak of on Arkí, except for a tiny patch of sand on the west side of Port Augusta.

The nearest tamarisk-shaded, proper sandy beach is just offshore on the islet of **Maráthi**, the only inhabited one of the nine surrounding Arkí, where another pair of **tavernas** cater to day-trippers who come at least several times a week from Pátmos or Lipsí. *Marathi* (Ⓣ02470/31 580 or 32 759; open most of year; ❶), run engagingly by the habitually barefoot Mihalis Kavouras (who looks like a comic-book pirate), is the more traditional, cosy outfit, with waterside seating, local seafood or Mihalis' own free-range goats on the menu, and simple, adequate rooms upstairs. *Pantelis* (Ⓣ02470/32 609; ❷) is plusher but more commercially minded, and only open June to October.

Agathoníssi

The small, steep-sided islet of **Agathoníssi** is still often known by its medieval name Gáïdharo, after its map-outline similarity to a donkey facing east. By contrast its ancient moniker Yetoússa has fallen into disuse; the modern name ("Virtuous-island") was bestowed post-1948 as a tribute to the islanders' supposed sterling qualities. Like Lípsi, it was until 1954 owned outright by the

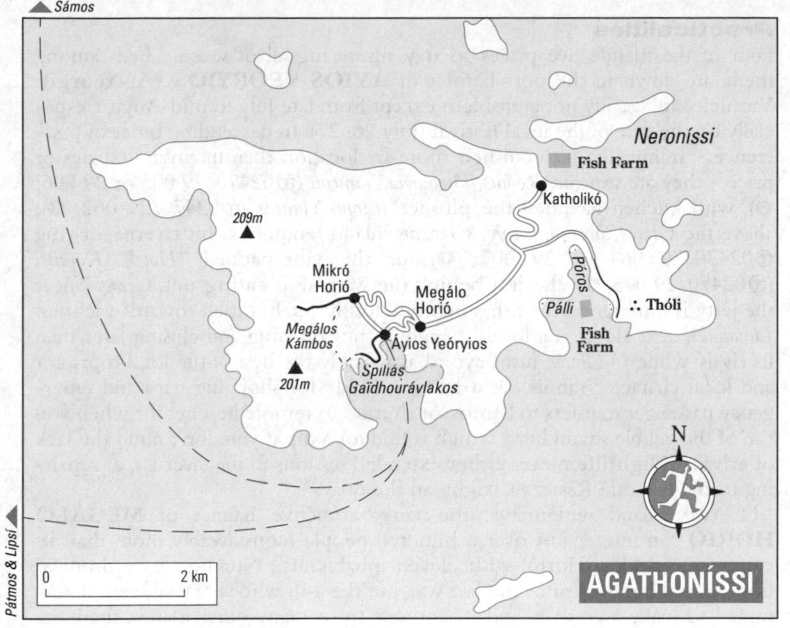

monastery on Pátmos, and it seems the locals are descended from a mix of Byzantine political exiles, pirates and agricultural lay workers dependent on the monastery. It's too remote – much closer to Turkey than Pátmos, in fact – for most day excursions, though some are half-heartedly advertised in Pythagório, Sámos. Intrepid German and Italian backpackers (some of whom return annually) form its main clientele, along with a steady trickle of yachts which dodge the large clan of ducks living in the superbly protected harbour. Even though hydrofoil connections dovetail fairly well with appearances of the *Nissos Kalymnos* or a Miniotis Line boat, you should count on being marooned here for three days, especially if the wind's up. "Marooned" is perhaps too harsh a word, as the island has reasonable swimming, a friendly feel and a numerous enough summer clientele to keep things interesting. The unspoilt character of the place – no tourist-trinket shops yet, for example – is unlikely to be much affected by an orgy of villa construction on the hillside or an increased military garrison whose main task seems to be the apprehension of Kurdish refugees who come ashore here from Turkey.

There are no springs on Agathoníssi, so rain-catchment basins and cisterns are ubiquitous, supplemented by water imported from Rhodes. Nevertheless, the island's thirteen-plus square kilometres are greener and more fertile than they appear from the sea; mastic and carob bushes are interspersed with small oaks on the heights, and two arable valleys lie to the west of Mikró Horió hamlet – the larger of them known accurately enough as Megálos Kámbos (Big Field). Goats, sheep and chickens far outnumber the human islanders for whom they provide the main livelihood, but fresh produce is chronically absent from the single shop, so bring your own. The principal intrusions of the outside world seem to be a helipad, several offshore fish farms, Greek army personnel, and a wonky little power plant – Agathoníssi is one of the last islets with its own dynamo, being too remote from its larger neighours for a cable transfusion.

Practicalities

Four of the island's five places to stay, mustering all of seventy beds among them, are down in the port hamlet of **ÁYIOS YEÓRYIOS (Aï-Yeórgi)**. Vacancies are usually not a problem except from late July to mid-August, especially on the date of the local festival (July 26–27). In descending order of preference – minimally distinguished more by location than intrinsic luxuries or price – they are seafront *Rooms Theoloyia Yiameou* (ⓣ02470/29 005 or 29 006; ❶), with kitchen facilities; the plusher *Rooms Yiannis* (ⓣ02470/29 062; ❷), above the *Glaros Taverna*; *George's Rooms* inland (enquire at his taverna, or ring ⓣ02470/29 064 or 29 007; ❶); or the vine-patioed *"Hotel" Kamitsi* (ⓣ02470/29 003; ❶), also just behind the water. For **eating** out, *George's* near the jetty is quite good for fish, and consciously pitches itself towards yachties; *Limanaki*, next along, is a locals' hangout, thus opening and closing later than its rivals; while *O Glaros*, just beyond, is possibly the best of the lot. Proprietor and local character Yannis has a kaïki available for shopping trips and emergency passenger transfers to Sámos, or shuttles to remote beaches for when you tire of the pebble strand here, which is fine for a dip if you don't mind the lack of privacy. **Nightlife** means either extended sessions in the tavernas, or repairing to the bar-café *Remezzo*, right on the quay.

Of two inland settlements, the fairly attractive hamlet of **MEGÁLO HORIÓ** can muster just over a hundred people (considerably more than its counterpart Mikró Horió, with eleven inhabitants). Numbers have dropped from several hundred since the last war, but the 146 who've stayed seem determined to make a go of it, and in contrast to so many other islands, there are virtually no abandoned or neglected houses here. Just about the entire population turns up in its platía for the island festival on the night of July 26–27, which features live music of varying quality.

Megálo Horió **amenities** consist of just one rather haphazardly stocked shop, the *Kafenio Irini* (light snacks only) and the *Kafenio Dhekatria Adhelfia*, which does generous, home-style lunches, and outside of peak season may be the only place on the island serving food at midday. Not surprisingly, there is no post office or bank here or at the port. A single bakery, on the link road, works mysterious hours, and there are a few cardphones about.

Around the island

Along its south shore, Agathoníssi is nearly as indented as Léros, making it an excellent anchorage for yachts in summer. At the heads of various bays lie numerous small, often stony **beaches**, providing adequate, if not brilliant, swimming opportunities. Boat trips to the more remote coves only operate in peak season; at other times you have to walk – sometimes on roads but often by faint trail – or scramble cross-country.

The closest beach to Áyios Yeóryios is **Spiliás**, a twenty-minute walk southwest along a bulldozed track; this shingle and gravel strand is so named for a small cave at its far end. Despite a lack of fresh water, people camp here. A fifteen-minute scramble southwest over the cave headland on faint paths brings you to rather superior **Gaïdhourávlakos** cove, where nudism goes unremarked on its gravel and sand beach, and there's a water cistern for (dire) emergencies. You can enjoyably vary the return to the port by following a trail up the west bank of the ravine feeding the beach (start at the cistern), ending up at another well and cistern complex at the south end of Megálos Kámbos, and thence along a broader path to join the track at the plateau's eastern edge (some forty minutes along), and finally on to Mikró Horió and the port (a full hour from Gaïdhourávlakos).

Greek script table

Pátmos	Πάτμος	ΠΑΤΜΟΣ
Agriolívadho	Αγριολίβαδο	ΑΓΡΙΟΛΙΒΑΔΟ
Apokálypsi (Apocalypse Monastery)	Αποκάλυψη	ΑΠΟΚΑΛΥΨΗ
Ayíou Ioánnou Theológou (St John Monastery)	Αγίου Ιοάννου Θεολόγου	ΑΓΙΟΥ ΙΟΑΝΝΟΥ ΘΕΟΛΟΓΟΥ
Gríkou	Γροίκου	ΓΡΟΙΚΟΥ
Hokhlakás	Χοχλακάς	ΧΟΧΛΑΚΑΣ
Hóra	Χώρα	ΧΩΡΑ
Kámbos	Κάμπος	ΚΑΜΠΟΣ
Lámbi	Λάμποι	ΛΑΜΠΟΙ
Livádhi Yeranoú	Λειβάδι Γερανού	ΛΕΙΒΑΔΙ ΓΕΡΑΝΟΥ
Melóï	Μελόϊ	ΜΕΛΟΪ
Psilí Ámmos	Ψηλή Άμμος	ΨΗΛΗ ΑΜΜΟΣ
Skála	Σκάλα	ΣΚΑΛΑ
Vayiá	Βαγιά	ΒΑΓΙΑ
Lipsí	Λειψοί	ΛΕΙΨΟΙ
Eléna	Ελένα	ΕΛΕΝΑ
Hokhlakoúra	Χοχλακούρα	ΧΟΧΛΑΚΟΥΡΑ
Kámbos	Κάμπος	ΚΑΜΠΟΣ
Liendoú	Λιεντού	ΛΙΕΝΤΟΥ
Katsadhiá	Κατσαδιά	ΚΑΤΣΑΔΙΑ
Kímisi	Κοίμισι	ΚΟΙΜΙΣΙ
Monodhéndhri	Μονοδένδρι	ΜΟΝΟΔΕΝΔΡΙ
Papandhriá	Παπανδριά	ΠΑΠΑΝΔΡΙΑ
Platýs Yialós	Πλατύς Γιαλός	ΠΛΑΤΥΣ ΓΙΑΛΟΣ
Tourkómnima	Τουρκόμνημα	ΤΟΥΡΚΟΜΝΗΜΑ
Arkí	Αρκιοί	ΑΡΚΙΟΙ
Avgoústa	Αυγούστα	ΑΥΓΟΥΣΤΑ
Maráthi	Μαράθι	ΜΑΡΑΘΙ
Tiganákia	Τιγανάκια	ΤΙΓΑΝΑΚΙΑ
Agathoníssi	Αγαθονήσι	ΑΓΑΘΟΝΗΣΙ
Áyios Yeóryios	Άγιος Γεώργιος	ΑΓΙΟΣ ΓΕΩΡΓΙΟΣ
Farmakoníssi	Φαρμακονήσι	ΦΑΡΜΑΚΟΝΗΣΙ
Gaïdhourávlakos	Γαϊδουραύλακος	ΓΑΪΔΟΥΡΑΥΛΑΚΟΣ
Katholikó	Καθολικό	ΚΑΘΟΛΙΚΟ
Megálo Horió	Μεγάλο Χωριό	ΜΕΓΑΛΟ ΧΩΡΙΟ
Mikró Horió	Μικρό Χωριό	ΜΙΚΡΟ ΧΩΡΙΟ
Spiliás	Σπηλιάς	ΣΠΗΛΙΑΣ
Thóli	Θόλοι	ΘΟΛΟΙ

The cement-paved road heading east out of Megálo Horió leads within 45 minutes (give or take a few trail shortcuts) to **Katholikó**. There's no real beach here, only a partially ruined fishing hamlet of a half-dozen houses under some tamarisks, with an equal number of fishing boats at anchor. A fish farm, owned by an Athenian supermarket chain, floats just offshore in the lee of **Neronísssi**. A gruesome legend attaches to the area: some years ago a kaïki bound for Sámos foundered here, and a woman drowned with her child. The locals buried them in an abandoned lime kiln, without summoning the priest for a proper liturgy; ever since the woman's ghost is said to be heard screaming after dark, and an otherworldly glow envelopes the kiln on moonless nights. Inland to the west are the remains of a Roman dye works, marked by a midden-pile of discarded murex shells.

The closest proper beaches lie twenty minutes' walk south of Katholikó, along **Póros Bay**, accessible via a cemented drive veering southeast a few minutes before Katholikó. The sandy beach at the head of the bay has little shade and is often rubbish-strewn. At the end of the road, an hour's walk from Áyios Yeóryios, is **Thóli**, formerly with good reef-snorkelling but ruined for leisure pursuits by an expanding local fish farm and the debris of its predecessor completely obstructing the pebble beach. The better beach of **Pálli** lies on the far side of the bay, beyond the fish farm, but is usually visited by boat excursion.

Thóli cove takes its name from the internal arcades and vaults of a mysterious late Byzantine or early **medieval structure** just inland, by far the most remarkable sight on the island and (almost) unique in the east Aegean – there's a similar building on Farmakoníssi (see below). It is neither a public bath nor a manor house, and seems to have had no obvious military use; nor does it appear to be part of a monastery, since no church is associated with it. However, its location at the head of a still-used agricultural valley with two threshing cirques just above, plus the discovery of amphorae in the bay below, confirms that this was a trading post and grain warehouse. The architecture matches that of similar Byzantine buildings at Miletus, an important ancient city just out of sight on the Turkish coast.

Other, scantier Roman and Byzantine ruins are found on **Farmakoníssi**, an island lying south of Agathoníssi and often exciting the curiosity of travellers who glimpse it from hydrofoils. Since 1996 and the Ímia crisis, however, it has been taken over by the military and is now off limits to civilians, in particular foreign yachts, so keep well clear. Should the ban ever be lifted, the most noteworthy thing to see here is a series of Roman-era arcades to one side of the little port – supposedly built to house the young Julius Caesar while he was imprisoned here by pirates in 74 BC, in fact more likely to be ancient food warehouses.

Pátmos, Lipsí and Agathoníssi travel details

Island transport

Buses

Skála (Pátmos) to: Gríkou (6–7 daily); Hóra (11 daily, 8am–9pm); Kámbos (4 daily).

Kaïkia

Skála (Pátmos): daily trips to most east-coast beaches, plus Psilí Ámmos.

Inter-island transport

Key to ferry and hydrofoil companies

DANE	*Dhodhekanisiakí Anónymi Navtiliakí Etería* (Dodecanesian Shipping Company)
G&A	G&A Ferries
HF	Hellas Ferries
ML	Miniotis Lines
NK	*Nissos Kalymnos*
KR	Kyriakoulis Maritime
LZ	Laoumtzis Flying Dolphins

Kaïkia and excursion boats

Pátmos to: Arkí (2–7 weekly; 1hr 10min); Lipsí (1 daily); Maráthi (almost daily on demand; 1hr); Sámos (1 daily).
Lipsí to: Ayía Marína, Léros (5–7 weekly May–Oct on *Captain Makis* or *Anna Express*); Pátmos (1 daily May–Oct); Arkí/Maráthi (2–3 weekly on *Rena II*).
Agathoníssi to: Pythagório, Sámos (sporadically, as passenger traffic or grocery shopping demands).

Ferries

Pátmos to: Agathoníssi (2 weekly on NK, 2 weekly on ML; 1hr 30min); Arkí (2 weekly on ML; 45min); Foúrni (2 weekly on G&A; 1hr); Ikaría (2–3 weekly on G&A; 2hr); Kálymnos (2 weekly on NK, 4–5 weekly on DANE, 4–6 weekly on G&A; 2–3hr); Kastellórizo (1 weekly on G&A, via Rhodes;14hr with layover); Kós (5–6 weekly on DANE, 4–6 on G&A; 3hr 30min–4hr); Léros (4–5 weekly on DANE, 4–6 weekly on G&A, 2 on NK, 1 on ML; 1hr 15min–1hr 45min); Lipsí (1 weekly on G&A, 1 weekly on ML, 2 on NK; 45min–1hr); Níssyros (1 weekly on G&A; 5hr 30min); Pireás (4–5 weekly on DANE, 4–6 weekly on G&A; 9–10hr); Pythagório-Sámos (2 weekly on NK, 2 weekly on ML; 3hr); Rhodes (4–5 weekly on DANE, 4–6 weekly on G&A; 8hr); Tílos (1 weekly on G&A; 5hr 30min); Vathý-Sámos (1 weekly on HF; 4hr); Sými (1 weekly on G&A; 6hr).
Lipsí to: Ikaría (1 weekly on G&A; 3hr); Kálymnos (2 weekly on NK; 2hr 15min); Kós (1 weekly on G&A; 3hr 15min); Léros (2 weekly on NK, 1 on G&A; 1hr–1hr 15min); Pátmos (2 weekly on NK, 1 weekly on ML, 1 weekly on G&A; 45min–1hr); Pireás (1 weekly on G&A; 11–12 hr); Pythagório-Sámos (2 weekly on NK, 1 weekly on ML; 4hr); Rhodes (1 weekly on G&A; 8hr); Vathý-Sámos (1 weekly on HF; 5hr).
NB Lipsí service on G&A and HF is only reliable late June to mid-Sept.
Agathoníssi to: Kálymnos, Kós, Léros, Lipsí, Pátmos, Pythagório-Sámos (all 2 weekly on NK; 1hr 30min to Pythagório); 1 weekly on ML to Arkí, Lipsí, Pátmos, Agathoníssi, 1 weekly to Léros (max. journey time 2hr 45min to Agathoníssi).
NB Miniotis Lines services cited above supposedly run most of the year, but may in practice only operate May to December.

Catamaran

Pátmos to: Léros, Kálymnos, Kós, Rhodes (3–7 weekly); Lipsí (1–2 weekly); Níssyros, Tílos (1 weekly high season only); Sými (2–3 weekly, May–June only).
Lipsí to: Léros, Kálymnos, Kós, Rhodes (3–4 weekly); Pátmos (2–3 weekly); Níssyros, Tílos (1 weekly high season only); Sými (2–3 weekly, May–June only).
NB All services provided by the *Dodekanisos Express*.

Hydrofoils

Pátmos to: Agathoníssi (2 weekly on KR; 45min); Foúrni (1 weekly on KR; 1hr 20min); Ikaría (1 weekly on KR; 1hr); Kálymnos (2 daily on KR; 1hr 30min); Kós (2–3 daily on KR, 2 weekly on LZ; 2hr–2hr 15min); Léros (2–3 daily on KR; 45min); Lipsí (1–3 daily on KR, down to 5 weekly low season; 20min); Pythagório-Sámos (3 daily on KR, but 5 weekly low season; 1hr–1hr 30min); Vathý-Sámos (1 weekly on KR; 1hr 45min).
Lipsí to: Agathoníssi (1 weekly on KR; 1hr 30min); Kálymnos, Kós, Léros, Pátmos, Pythagório-Sámos (all 1–3 daily on KR, down to 5 weekly low season; max. journey time 2hr to Kós).
Agathoníssi to: Lipsí (1 weekly on KR; 1hr 15min); Kálymnos, Kós, Léros, Pátmos, Pythagório-Sámos (2 weekly on KR; max. journey time 3hr 15min to Kós).

4

The East Aegean Islands

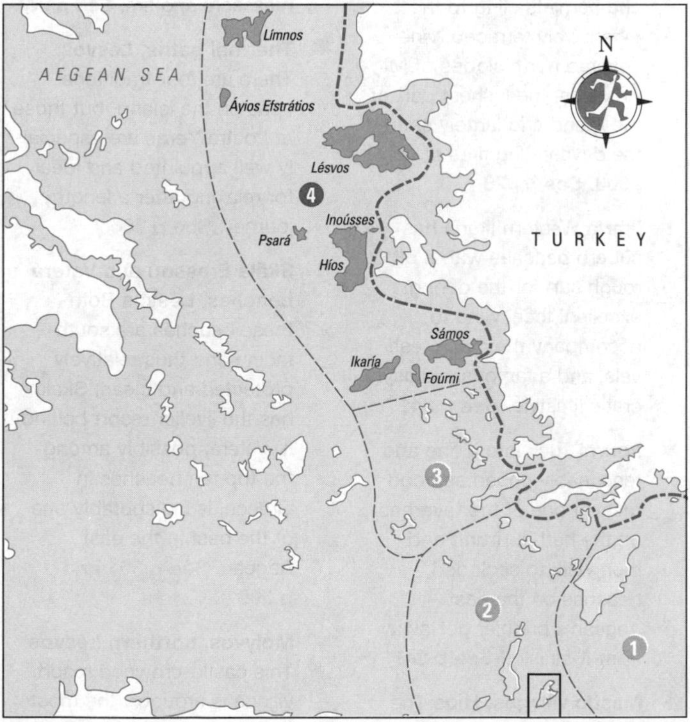

CHAPTER 4

Highlights

* **Vathý, Sámos** Vathý's archeological museum is perhaps the best in the islands of this book; the star is the huge, nearly intact kouros from the local shrine of Hera, but the small-objects collection is also fascinating. See p.314

* **North-coast hill villages, Sámos** A half-dozen villages and hamlets cling to the extensively terraced, vine-covered north slopes of Mt Ámbelos, the lushest part of the island and largely spared the devastating fires of July 2000. See p.328

* **Ikaría** Western Ikaría has superb beaches with a bit of rough surf for the daring, excellent local wine to accompany the many festivals, and a famously idiosyncratic lifestyle. See p.342

* **Foúrni** Tuck into a fine and reasonably priced seafood meal at one of the tavernas on the harbourfront, and then walk to secluded beaches on the east Aegean's premier get-away-from-it-all islet. See p.347

* **Mastic villages, Híos** The architecturally unique *mastihohoriá* (mastic villages) were laid out by the Genoese but have a Middle Eastern feel; Pyrgí is enlivened by *xistá*, while Mestá is the best-preserved community. See p.359

* **Néa Moní, Híos** Particularly noteworthy eleventh-century Byzantine mosaics in an imperial monastery which survived earthquake, massacre and fire. See p.364

* **Thermal baths, Lésvos** There are four traditional spas on the island, but those at Loutrá Yéras are especially well appointed and ideal for relaxing after a lengthy journey. See p.386

* **Skála Eressoú and Vaterá beaches, Lésvos** Both these beaches are south-facing and thus relatively protected and clean; Skála has the livelier resort behind it. Vaterá, possibly among the top ten beaches in Greece, is indisputably one of the best in the east Aegean. See p.391 and p.396

* **Mólyvos, northern Lésvos** This castle-crowned resort village is arguably the most beautiful on the island, if inevitably crowded and twee in season. See p.398

The East Aegean Islands

The five substantial islands and four minor islets scattered off the west Aegean coast of Turkey form a rather arbitrary archipelago. Although there are some passing similarities in architecture and landscape, the strong individual character of each island is far more striking. Despite their proximity to modern Turkey, the members of this "group" (Lésvos excepted) bear few signs of an Ottoman heritage, especially when compared to Rhodes and Kós. There's the occasional mosque, often shorn of its minaret, and some of the domestic architecture betrays obvious influences from Constantinople, Macedonia and further north in the Balkans. But, by and large, the enduring Greekness of these islands is testimony to the 3500-year Hellenic presence in Asia Minor just opposite, which only ended in 1923.

This heritage is regularly referred to by the Greek government in an intermittent propaganda war with Turkey over the sovereignty of these far-flung outposts – as well as the disputed straits between them and the Turkish mainland. Tensions here have often been worse than in the Dodecanese, aggravated by potential undersea oil deposits in the straits between the islands and the Anatolian mainland. The Turks have also persistently demanded that Límnos, strategically astride the sea lanes to and from the Dardanelles, be demilitarized, but so far Greece has shown few signs of giving in other than to reduce the size of its garrison there.

In some respects, this ongoing conflict has given these long-neglected islands a new lease of life, insomuch as their sudden strategic importance has seen infrastructure improvements to support garrisoning, and given a mild fillip to local economies, engaged in providing goods and services to soldiers, something predating mass tourism. Yet, even in spring 1998, the *Guardian* newspaper published the results of an EU-funded study which showed that, in terms of per-capita income, the "northeast Aegean" still ranked along with Epirus on mainland Greece, Apuglia in Italy and Extremadura in Spain as one of the poorest regions in western Europe. At first, this might seem an incredible or sensational judgement, given the lucrative tourist-takings on Sámos or the shipping-based remittance economy of Híos, but forays off the beaten track through the more backward and depressed corners of Ikaría, Lésvos or Límnos will still uncover nineteenth-century lifestyles which are obviously pulling the average down.

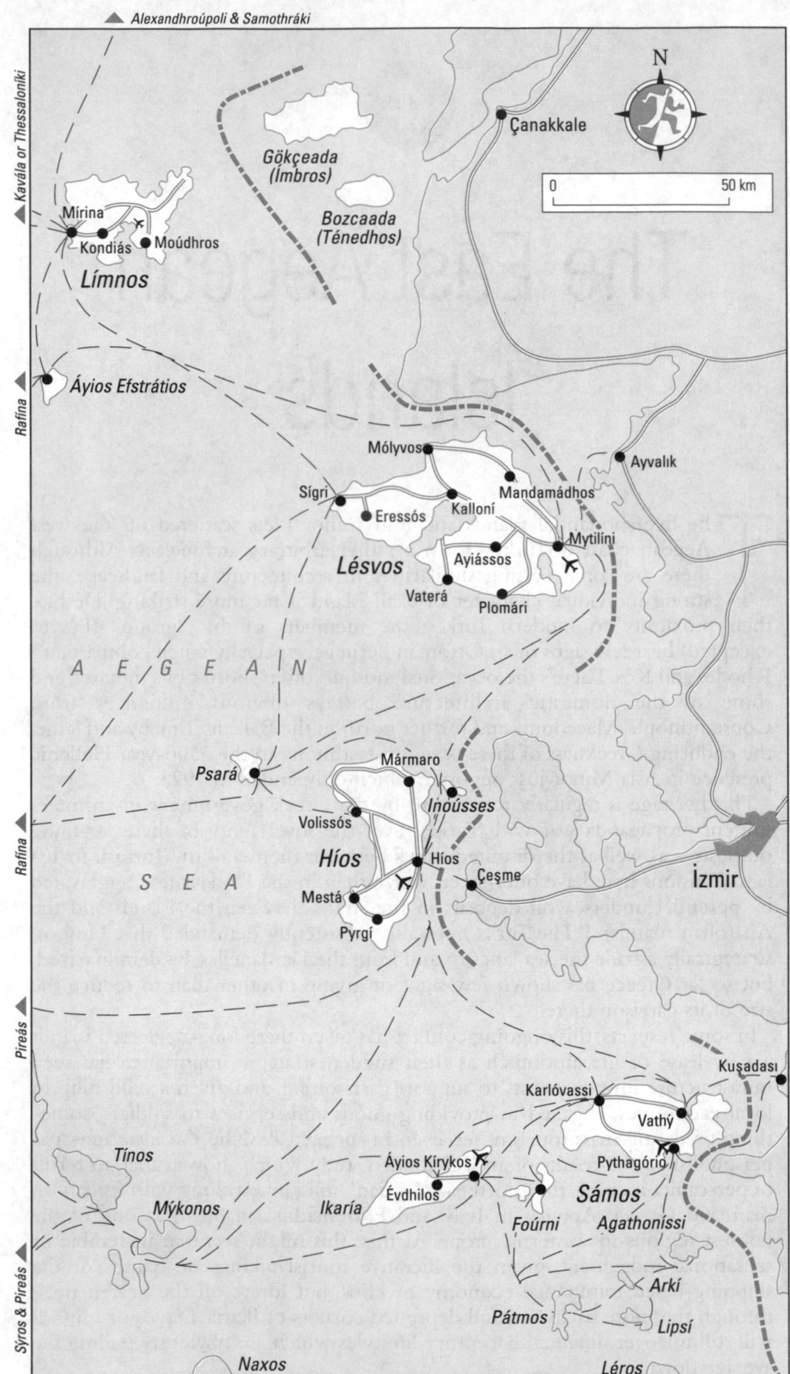
Alexandhroúpoli & Samothráki
Kavála or Thessaloníki
Rafína
Rafína
Pireás
Sýros & Pireás
N
0
50 km
Çanakkale
Gökçeada
(Ímbros)
Bozcaada
(Ténedhos)
Mírina
Kondiás
Moúdhros
Límnos
Áyios Efstrátios
Mólyvos
Ayvalık
Mandamádhos
Sígri
Eressós
Kalloní
Mytilíni
Ayiássos
Lésvos
Vaterá
Plomári
A E G E A N
Mármaro
Psará
Inoússes
Volissós
Híos
Híos
Çeşme
İzmir
S E A
Mestá
Pyrgí
Kuşadası
Karlóvassi
Vathý
Tínos
Áyios Kírykos
Pythagório
Évdhilos
Sámos
Mýkonos
Ikaría
Foúrni
Agathoníssi
Arkí
Pátmos
Lipsí
Naxos
Léros

The heavy **military presence** can be disconcerting, and despite the growth of tourism, large tracts of land remain off limits as military reserves. But, as in the Dodecanese, local tour operators do a thriving business shuttling passengers for inflated tariffs between these islands and the **Turkish coast**, with its amazing archeological sites and bustling resorts. Most of the east Aegean's main ports and towns are not the quaint, picturesque spots you may have become used to in other parts of Greece, but urbanized bureaucratic, military and commercial centres. In all cases you should suppress an initial impulse to take the next boat out, and delve instead into the worthwhile interiors.

Sámos, immediately north of the Dodecanese, ranks as the most visited island of the group but, if you can leave the considerable crowds behind, is still arguably the most verdant and beautiful, even after a devastating July 2000 fire. **Ikaría** to the west remains relatively unspoiled, if a minority taste, with an airport that's too tiny to have much effect on the number of visitors. Nearby **Foúrni** is a haven for determined solitaries (except in August), as are Híos' satellites **Psará** and **Inoússes**, neither of the latter with any package-tour facilities. **Híos** itself offers far more cultural interest than any of its southern neighbours, but its natural beauty has been ravaged by wildfires, and the development of tourism has been deliberately retarded. **Lésvos** may not impress initially, though once you grasp its old-fashioned, Anatolian ambience, you may find yourself amongst the substantial number of return visitors. By contrast, almost no foreigners and few Greeks call in at remote **Áyios Efstrátios**, and with good reason. **Límnos**, the northernmost of this group, is much livelier, but its appeal is confined mostly to the area immediately around the attractive port town.

Sámos

Lush, seductive and shaped like a pregnant guppy, **Sámos** seems to swim away from Asia Minor, to which the island was joined until Ice Age cataclysms sundered it from Mount Mykáli (Mycale) on the Turkish mainland. The resulting 1500- to 2500-metre strait is now the narrowest distance between Greece and Turkey in the Aegean, except at Kastellórizo; accordingly military installations bristle on both sides – though as you ride in from the airport, signs reassuringly announce "Samos unnuclear island" (sic). In its variety of mountainous terrain, beaches and vegetation, Sámos has the feel of a much larger island, and before recent development and wildfires took their toll, it was indisputably among the most beautiful in the Aegean; much of value remains, testimony to its ample natural endowments.

There's little tangible evidence of this now, but Sámos was also once the **wealthiest island** in the Aegean. Under the patronage of the local tyrant Polykrates, it became home to a thriving **intellectual community** which included the philosophers Epikouros (Epicurus) and Pythagoras, the astronomer Aristarkhos (Aristarchus) and the bard Aesop. Decline set in as the star of Classical Athens was in the ascendant, though the island's status improved somewhat during early Byzantine times, when Sámos constituted its own *theme* (imperial administrative district).

Towards the end of the fifteenth century, the Genoese – who controlled Sámos from their base on Híos – evacuated most of the inhabitants, abandoning the island to the mercy of Venetian and Turkish pirates. Following their pillaging and massacring, Sámos remained almost completely **desolate** until 1562, when an Ottoman admiral, Kiliç Ali Pasha, got permission from the sultan to repopulate it with some of the Samians who had fled to Híos with the Genoese, as well as Greek Orthodox settlers recruited from every corner of Greece and Asia Minor. The population was further supplemented after 1923 with an influx of refugees from Anatolia.

The heterogeneous descent of today's islanders largely explains an enduring **identity crisis** and a rather thin topsoil of indigenous culture. Most of the village names are either clan surnames or adjectives indicating origins elsewhere – constant reminders of **refugee descent**. Consequently there is no genuine Samiot music, dance or dress, and little that's original in the way of cuisine and architecture (the latter a blend of styles from northern Greece and the Asia Minor coast). The Samians compensated somewhat for this deracination by struggling fiercely for independence during the 1820s but, despite their accomplishments in sinking a Turkish fleet in the narrow Mycale strait and annihilating a landing army, the Great Powers (Britain, France and Russia) handed the island back to the Ottomans in 1830, with the consolatory proviso that it be **semi-autonomous** and ruled by an appointed Christian prince. This period, referred to as the *Iyimonía* (Hegemony), was marked by a mild renaissance in fortunes, courtesy of the hemp and (especially) tobacco trade. However, union with Greece in 1912, the ravages of a bitter World War II occupation and subsequent mass emigration effectively reversed the recovery until the arrival of tourism during the early 1980s.

Today the Samian economy is increasingly dependent on **package tourism**, with far too much of it in places; the eastern half of the island, and much of the south coast, has almost totally surrendered to the onslaught of holiday-makers, although the more rugged northwestern part has retained most of its undeveloped grandeur. The rather sedate, couples-orientated clientele is overwhelmingly Dutch, Scandinavian, German and Swiss, though lately there are growing numbers of Belgians, Italians, Slovenians and – spurred by a favourable BBC radio feature or two and the efforts of such holiday companies as Laskarina and Sunvil – Brits. The absence of an official campsite on such a large island, tame nightlife a world away from that on Rhodes or Kós and phalanxes of self-catering villas hint at the sort of custom expected.

Not coincidentally, the most heavily developed areas have been most afflicted by **repeated wildfires**, none worse than that which burned for a week in July 2000, ravaging twenty percent of the island's forest and orchards, as well as destroying over ninety dwellings. Now if you mention Sámos to other Greeks, they say *Ah, tó nisí poú kaïke* ("Oh, the island that burned") and, taking into account the other quarter of the island area that had been torched piecemeal since 1987, Sámos has indeed lost about half of its original forest cover. Some stands of magnificent black pines survive on the heights, with Calabrian pine lower down, but in some areas the devastation is total; brace yourself for broad vistas of charred tree-trunks or utterly denuded slopes, and pay heed to fire-damage warnings when deciding where to spend a two-week package. The trees, as ever, will be a half-century in returning, and the tourist market a good few years in overcoming this stigma. Volunteer fire-lookouts, complete with trucks, have now sprouted at critical points, but it does seem a case of locking the stable door after the horse has bolted.

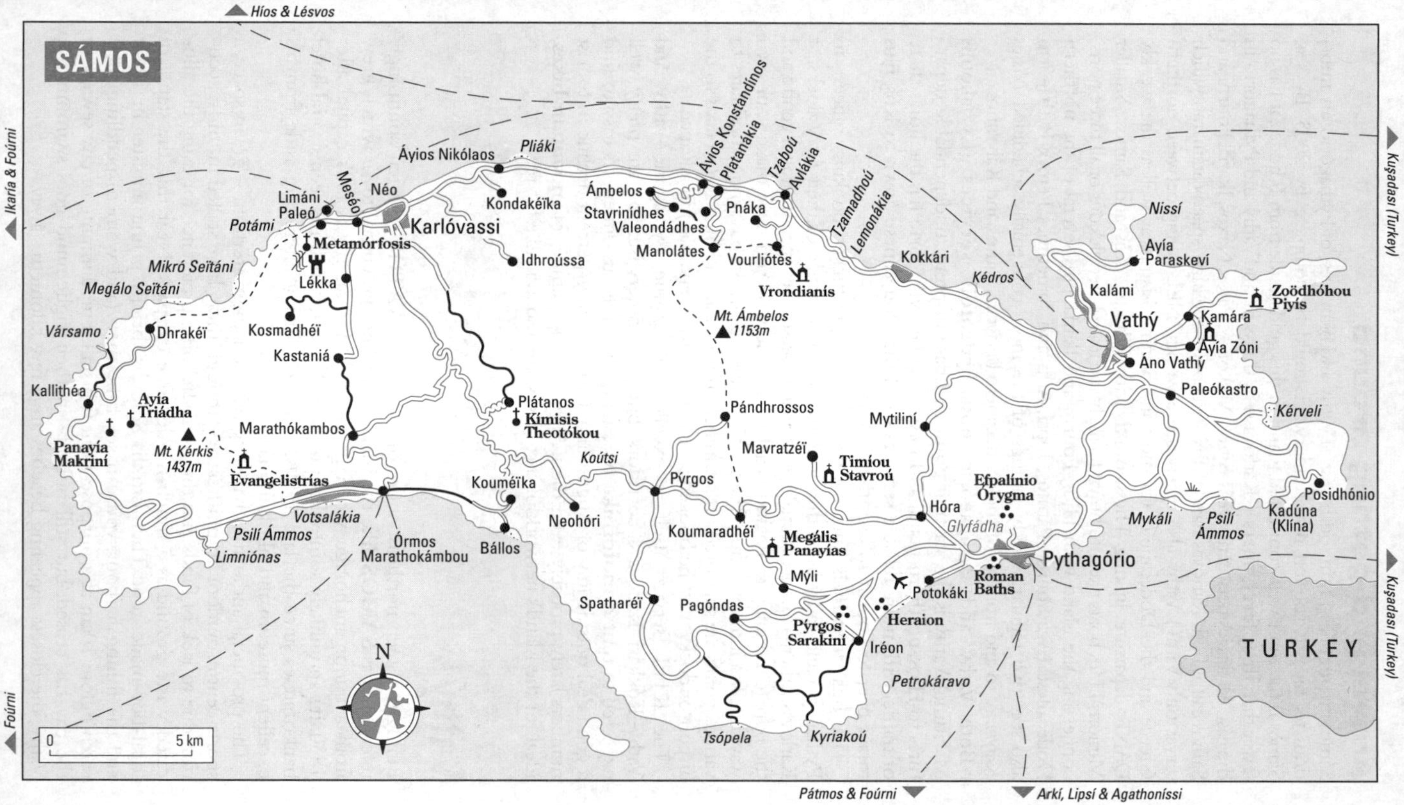

SÁMOS
Kuşadası (Turkey)
Kuşadası (Turkey)
TURKEY
Arkí, Lipsí & Agathoníssi
Pátmos & Foúrni
Foúrni
Ikaría & Foúrni
Híos & Lésvos
0 5 km
N
Posidhónio
Kadúna (Klína)
Psilí Ámmos
Mykáli
Kérveli
Zoödhóhou Piyís
Kamára
Ayía Zóni
Áno Vathý
Vathý
Paleókastro
Kalámi
Ayía Paraskeví
Nissí
Kédros
Kokkári
Lemonákia
Tzamadhoú
Avlákia
Tzaboú
Platanákia
Áyios Konstandínos
Pythagório
Roman Baths
Potokáki
Heraion
Iréon
Petrokáravo
Pyrgos Sarakíni
Glyfádha
Efpalínio Órygma
Hóra
Mytiliní
Tímiou Stavroú
Mavratzéï
Megális Panayías
Mýli
Pagóndas
Spatharéï
Koumaradhéï
Pýrgos
Kyriakoú
Tsópela
Pándhrossos
Mt. Ámbelos 1153m
Vrondianís
Vourliótes
Manolátes
Valeondádhes
Stavrinídhes
Pnáka
Ámbelos
Kondakéïka
Idhroússa
Plátanos
Kímisis Theotókou
Koútsi
Neohóri
Koumeïka
Bállos
Órmos Marathokámbou
Votsalákia
Psilí Ámmos
Limniónas
Evangelistrías
Mt. Kérkis 1437m
Marathókambos
Kastaniá
Kosmadhéï
Lékka
Metamórfosis
Karlóvassi
Néo
Meséo
Paleó
Limáni
Potámi
Plíáki
Áyios Nikólaos
Mikró Seïtáni
Megálo Seïtáni
Várasmo
Dhrakéï
Kallithéa
Ayía Triádha
Panayía Makriní

Arrival and getting around

Sámos **airport** lies 14km southwest of Vathý and 3km west of Pythagório; an ambitious terminal expansion now underway should be complete by 2003. By sea, Sámos is the most well-connected island in this guide, aside from Rhodes; it has no fewer than three **ferry ports** – Karlóvassi in the west, and Vathý and Pythagório in the east. All ferries between Pireás, Sýros, Mýkonos, Páros, Náxos, Ikaría, Foúrni and Sámos call at both Karlóvassi and Vathý (except for the high-speed catamaran which serves only Vathý). Vathý also receives the weekly NEL sailing between northern Greece and the Dodecanese, via most intervening islands, as well as the weekly DANE departure linking Thessaloníki with Rhodes, Kós and Sámos. Smaller Miniotis Lines boats execute bewilderingly intricate schedules out of all three ports, connecting the island with Híos, Foúrni and Ikaría, plus several of the northern Dodecanese (Agathoníssi, Pátmos, Lipsí, Arkí and sometimes Léros). Pythagório also sees two regular weekly sailings of the more congenially scheduled *Nissos Kalymnos* to and from all of the Dodecanese between Sámos and Kálymnos.

Both Vathý and Pythgagório host **hydrofoil services** (Kyriakoulis Maritime): Vathý is the starting point and base of pretty undependable departures to Híos, northern Ikaría and Lésvos, while Pythagório has the lion's share of traffic, with more reliable services to all the Dodecanese down to Kós, plus forays over to Foúrni and southern Ikaría.

The **bus terminals** (no covered stations, just ticket booking offices) in Pythagório and Vathý lie within longish walking distance of their ferry docks; at Karlóvassi, there is an occasional bus service in season between the town centre and the port (continuing to Potámi beach), but otherwise you must make your own way the 3km into town from the port. There is no airport bus service; **taxi** fares to various points are stipulated on prominent placards, and in high season taxis to the airport or docks must be booked several hours (or even a day) in advance.

The KTEL service itself is excellent along the Pythagório–Vathý and Vathý–Kokkári–Karlóvassi corridors, but poor otherwise; you are pretty well expected to **rent a motorbike or car**. With numerous outlets, it's easy to find a good deal outside July or August and, with a twenty-percent decline in tourist numbers lately, probably even then. An increasing number of **mountain bikes**, ideal for the island's network of dirt tracks, are also available for rent.

Vathý

Lining the steep northeast shore of a deep bay, **VATHÝ** – often confusingly referred to as **SÁMOS**, like the island – is a busy provincial town which grew from a minor anchorage when it replaced Hóra as the island's capital after 1830. It's an unlikely, somewhat ungraceful resort, which has seen several hotel bankruptcies since the late 1990s, and is minimally interesting aside from its excellent museum and old hill quarter.

The provincial authorities have big plans for the waterfront – green space, a sports centre, outdoor amphitheatre – though these have stalled in mid-execution due to lack of funds and the overwhelming preference for using the allocated waste ground as a much-needed free car park. Near this, the statue of local-boy-made-good Themistoklis Sofoulis (briefly prime minister in 1948) and the fishing harbour, you can see fishermen (and women) peddling their catch before 10am at a purpose-built fish stall. The dumping of raw sewage in the bay has ceased, but still nobody in their right mind goes swimming at Vathý; the closest appealing beaches are a few kilometres away.

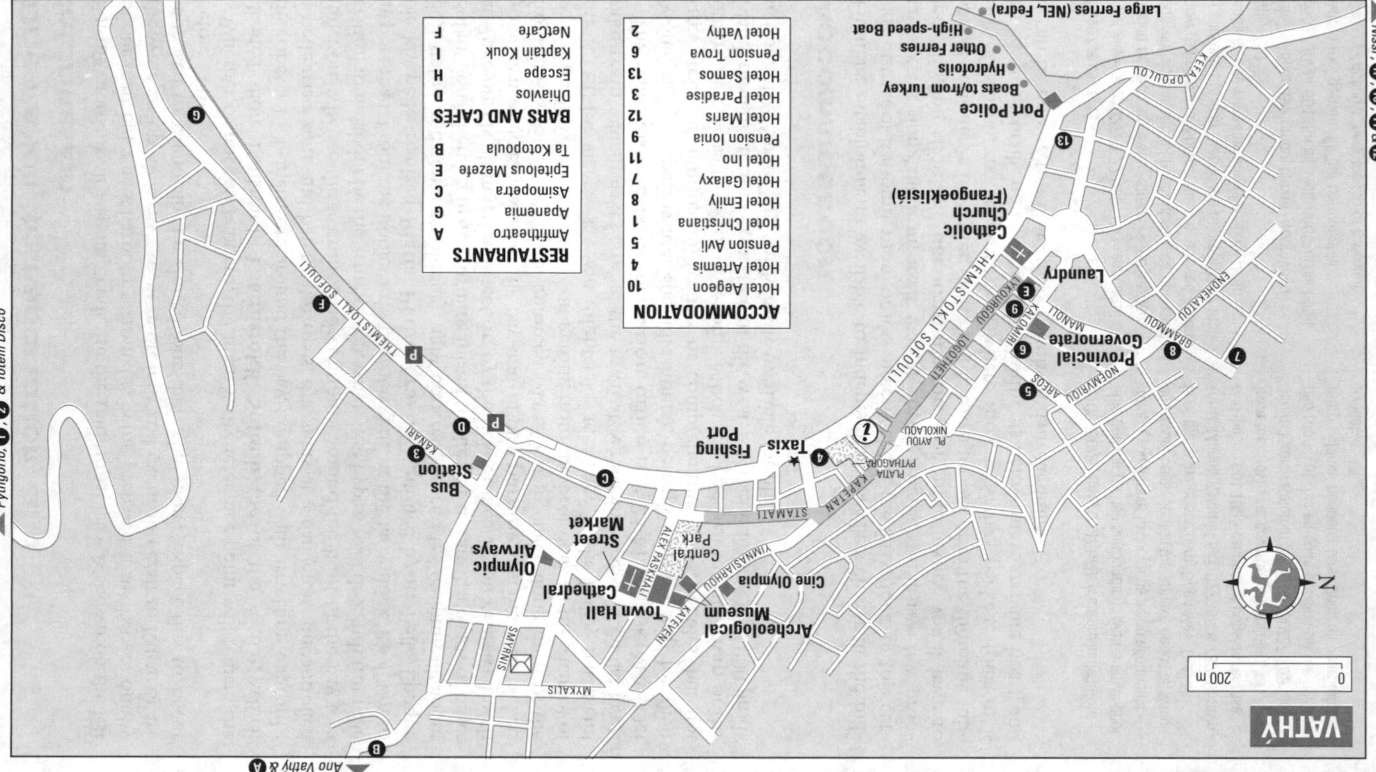
VATHÝ
0
200 m
N
Pythgório, 1, 2 & Totem Disco
Áno Vathý & A
Kokkári I
Nissi, H, 10, 11 & 12
Archeological Museum
Cine Olympia
Town Hall
Cathedral
Central Park
Street Market
Olympic Airways
Fishing Port
Taxis
Bus Station
Catholic Church (Frangoeklisiá)
Laundry
Provincial Governorate
Port Police
Boats to/from Turkey
Hydrofoils
Other Ferries
High-speed Boat
Large Ferries (NEL, Fedra)
THEMISTOKLI SOFOULI
KANARI
SMYRNIS
MYKALIS
KATEVENI
ALEX PASKHALI
YIMNASIARHOU
STAMATI
KAPETAN
PLATIA PYTHAGORA
PL. AYIOU NIKOLAOU
LOGOTHETI
LYKOURGOU
KALOMIRI
MANOLI
AREOS
NOEMVRIOU
GRAMMOU
ENDHEKATOU
KEFALOPOULOU
ACCOMMODATION
Hotel Aegeon 10
Hotel Artemis 4
Pension Avli 5
Hotel Christiana 1
Hotel Emily 8
Hotel Galaxy 7
Hotel Ino 11
Pension Ionia 9
Hotel Maris 12
Hotel Paradise 3
Hotel Samos 13
Pension Trova 6
Hotel Vathy 2
RESTAURANTS
Amfitheatro A
Apanemia G
Asimopetra C
Epitelous Mezefe E
Ta Kotopoula B
BARS AND CAFÉS
Dhiavlos D
Escape H
Kaptain Kouk I
NetCafe F

Orientation, transportation, and information

For the moment, all seagoing craft use the traditional jetty as shown on the left of our map, but a new harbour terminal is being prepared at snail's pace out by the wine co-op; all boats except hydrofoils and excursion craft to Kuşadası are supposed to eventually be shifted out there, but don't expect this to occur before 2004.

Whether or not this happens, the main Vathý reference point will remain the divided shore boulevard, **Themistoklí Sofoúli** (he of the statue), which describes a 1300-metre arc around the bay. Equipped with arty lamp standards, a pedestrian zone and baby palm trees, this splits at a dangerous uncontrolled junction, whence the seafront road continues around the head of the bay to a critical roundabout by the wine co-op, where the bypass road descends from the airport road. From the boulevard's northern end at the ferry dock, it's 400m to bleakly pedestrianized **Platía Pythagóra**, distinguished by its Belle Époque lion statue and some revoltingly ugly concrete-barricade "sculptures"; about 800m along there's a major turning inland to the bus terminal, a chaos of buses at a perennially cluttered intersection by the ticket office. If you've arrived with your own vehicle, beware of the pay-and-display **parking** scheme (strip tickets from kiosks, €0.30 per hour, enforced May–Oct) in effect along most of the waterfront. If you're just intent on getting from the boat dock to the vicinity of the KTEL (or vice versa), you might take advantage of the hokey but useful **fake train** which snakes around the town at regular intervals (€1.20 flat fare).

The municipal **tourist information office** is at 25-Martíou 4 (May–Oct Mon–Fri 9am–2pm; winter sporadic hours), perhaps worth a stop for their large stock of information leaflets or comprehensive bus schedules, but not otherwise especially useful or helpful. Much the best best touring **map** of the island, though far from error-free in the west, is Road Editions' 1:50,000 product no. 210, "Samos"; it's fairly easily available locally.

Accommodation

Humbler establishments available to independent travellers cluster in the hillside district of Katsoúni, more or less directly above the ferry dock, or to a certain extent along the front itself; except during August, you'll have few problems finding affordable **accommodation**. For more luxury you'll have to spread your nets a bit wider, either in the town proper or in the shoreline suburb of Kalámi, to the northwest, where most of Vathý's package tourism is based. Incidentally, none of the establishments below meet arriving boats, and it can be unwise to follow touts to substandard facilities.

Katsoúni

Avli Aréos 2 ⓣ02730/22 939. This wonderful period pension, up a stair-street, is the former convent school of the French nuns (see opposite), now run by genial Spryos. Rooms, arrayed around a courtyard (*avlí* in Greek), are appropriately institutional; one wing has en-suite units. Open May–Oct. ❶

Emily Top of Grámmou, cnr 11-Noemvríou ⓣ02730/24 691. Small, well-run C-class hotel with a roof garden. ❹ but bargainable

Galaxy Angéou 1, near the top of Katsoúni ⓣ02730/22 665, ⓕ27 679. A surprisingly affordable hotel in garden surroundings with a small pool, though you'll have to dodge package allotments – and avoid being sent to the annexe opposite, which is of much lower standard. Open May–Oct. ❹

Ionia Manóli Kalomíri 5 ⓣ02730/28 782. Bottom-end-basic, but 1995-renovated pension, across from the provincial government building. ❶

Trova Manóli Kalomíri 26 ⓣ02730/27 759. Just five rooms at this en-suite pension up the hill from the provincial headquarters. Open all year; kitchen available. ❷

Kalámi

Aegeon Kallistrátou 14, the south-bound shore road, just past the hospital ⓣ02730/22 838. Modestly amenitied but attractively arrayed in tiers, this C-class hotel actively welcomes walk-ins. ❸

Ino Above the hospital on the north-bound one-way road ⓣ02730/23 241, ⓕ23 245, ⓔino@samosnet.com. B-class hotel on a rise with commanding views, recovered from bankruptcy some years back and now expanded into a new wing; has a pool and off-street parking. ❹

Ionia Maris Gangoú beach ⓣ02730/28 428, ⓕ23 108. Vathý's only A-class hotel, with corresponding service and facilities – though the food's a letdown. The other drawback is the low-lying site: despite effectively monopolizing tiny Gangoú beach, there are no views to speak of. Open May–Oct. ❹

Waterfront

Artemis Just off Platía Pythagóra. ⓣ02730/27 792. Extremely humble (E-class) hotel, but with en-suite rooms, some with harbour view. ❷

Samos Themistoklí Sofoúli 11. ⓣ02730/28 377, ⓕ28 482, ⓦwww.samoshotel.gr. The obvious, C-class behemoth at the base of the ferry dock is a firm favourite as a businessmen's hotel, and isn't so bad for all that. Double glazing against traffic noise, rooftop pool-terrace, popular café out front. Open all year, thus popular with Asian tour groups in winter. ❸

Inland

Christiana Potamáki district ⓣ02730/23 084, ⓕ28 856. B-class hotel that's the only accommodation in Áno Vathý, where an attractive ravine setting, huge outdoor pool, friendly management, tie-in (ie discounts) with Budget Car Rental and decent rooms offset rather listless breakfasts. Open April–Oct, but if reception is shut apply to co-managed Budget Car Rental on the waterfront. ❹ Aug, but ❷ most of year

Paradise Kanári 21 ⓣ02730/23 911, ⓕ28 754. Package-dominated B-class hotel with front rooms overlooking the bus stop; side and rear rooms have views of orchards and its pool. Only available to walk-ins May and Oct. ❸

Vathy Neápoli district, below cemetery ⓣ02730/28 124, ⓕ24 045. A bit tough to get to (the managing Mavrelos family will collect you in a shuttle van if you ring in advance), but guaranteed vacancies, great bay views from its hillside setting and a small plunge-pool at this C-class hotel. ❸

The Town

A prominent waterfront curiosity near the ferry jetty is the old French **Catholic church**, labelled "Ecclesia Catolica" but universally known as the **Frangoekklisiá**; it's usually open for visits, with an interesting pamphlet available on the fortunes of the Catholic church in Greece. Since 1974, when the last nuns departed Sámos after having schooled the elite for nearly a century, the church is used at best once weekly, when a priest arrives from Sýros to celebrate mass for interested tourists and the half-dozen or so Samian Catholics. The nun's male compatriots, incidentally, reintroduced the art of wine-making to the island, though the contemporary tipple must bear little resemblance to the ancient stuff acclaimed by Byron ("Dash down you cup of Samian wine..."). The local oúzo – particularly the Yiokarinis brand – is more universally regarded.

Strolls inland can be more rewarding; you might first visit the expensive, higgledy-piggledy **antiquarian and jewellery shop** of Mihalis Stavrinos, just off the "Lion Square", where you can invest in assorted precious baubles or rare engravings. The pedestrianized marketplace just beyond – two-thirds authentic, one-third tourist schlock – and tiers of **Neoclassical houses** on stair-lanes are also of interest. Way up in Neápoli, Miltiades Makris' **antique shop** *Aiones* is as much museum as store; most of the stock is less portable than Stavrinos', but you're assured of a warm welcome from Miltiades.

Áno Vathý

The best target on foot, a twenty-minute walk south and 150m above sea level, is the atmospheric hill village of **ÁNO VATHÝ**, a nominally protected but increasingly threatened community of tottering, tile-roofed houses being steadily replaced by bad-taste blocks of flats. The village's late medieval churches are neglected but still worth a look: the tiny chapel of **Áyios Athanásios** (often locked), immediately behind the municipal offices and crèche, boasts a fine *témblon* and naive frescoes, while the quadruple-domed double church of **Aï Yannáki**, in the vale separating the two hillside neighbourhoods of the village, has an intriguing ground plan that compensates for its scandalously deteriorating condition. Few frescoes have survived the damp, but one – a rare and moving one of the dead Christ in His tomb, known as the "Utter Humiliation" in Orthodox iconography – can be found at the rear left of the unlit interior (bring a flashlight). On an aural level, the more used churches offer (for vespers and Sunday mornings) what must be some of the finest bell concerts in the Greek islands. A 1998-constructed **amphitheatre** and gravel esplanade just above make pleasant vantage points to admire the eighteenth-century structure; the Olympic flame stopped here en route to Sydney in 2000, eulogized by the Australian consul to Greece before being loaded on a Coast Guard boat for the trip to Turkey.

The Archeological Museum

If you're pressed for time, the only must in Vathý is the excellent **Archeological Museum** (Tues–Sun 8.30am–2.30pm; €2.40), set behind the small central park beside the recently restored Neoclassical town hall. One of the best provincial collections in Greece is housed in the old Paskhallion building and the modern wing immediately opposite, the latter specially constructed for the star exhibit: a majestic, five-metre-high **kouros**, discovered – like most of the items – out at the Heraion sanctuary (see p.322). The opening of this wing was delayed for years, since the roof had to be raised twice as more bits of this statue were found; when the building was finally inaugurated in 1987, the president of the German Federal Republic – whose archeological institute controls the Heraion digs – flew out to attend the ceremonies. The *kouros*, the largest freestanding effigy to survive from ancient Greece, was dedicated to Apollo, but found together with a devotional mirror to the Egyptian goddess Mut (syncretized with Hera) from a Nile workshop, one of only two such mirrors discovered in Greece to date.

In the equally compelling collection of small objects in the Paskhallion, more votive offerings of Egyptian design – a hippo, a dancer in Nilotic dress, Horus-as-Falcon, an Osiris figurine – prove trade and pilgrimage links between Sámos and the Nile valley going back to the eighth century BC. The Mesopotamian and Anatolian origins of other artwork confirm the exotic trend at the Heraion, most tellingly in a case full of ivory miniatures: Perseus and Medusa in relief, a kneeling, perfectly formed mini-*kouros* which once adorned a lyre, a pouncing lion, and a *rhyton* or drinking horn terminating in a bull's head. The most famous local artefacts are the dozen or so bronze **griffin-heads**, for which Sámos was the major centre of production in the seventh century BC; mounted on the edge of bronze cauldrons, they were believed to ward off evil spirits. Recently returned from a long sojourn in an Athens basement is an unlabelled **hoard of gold byzants**, imperial coins from the fifth or sixth century AD, found early in the 1980s by a Dutch archeologist wading in the shallows at a remote bay.

Eating and drinking

Vathý's **restaurant** profile is not brilliant, though since the early 1990s chefs from elsewhere in Greece or even overseas have assumed management of formerly stagnating establishments. Skip the obvious rip-off merchants near the dock in favour of more remote tavernas.

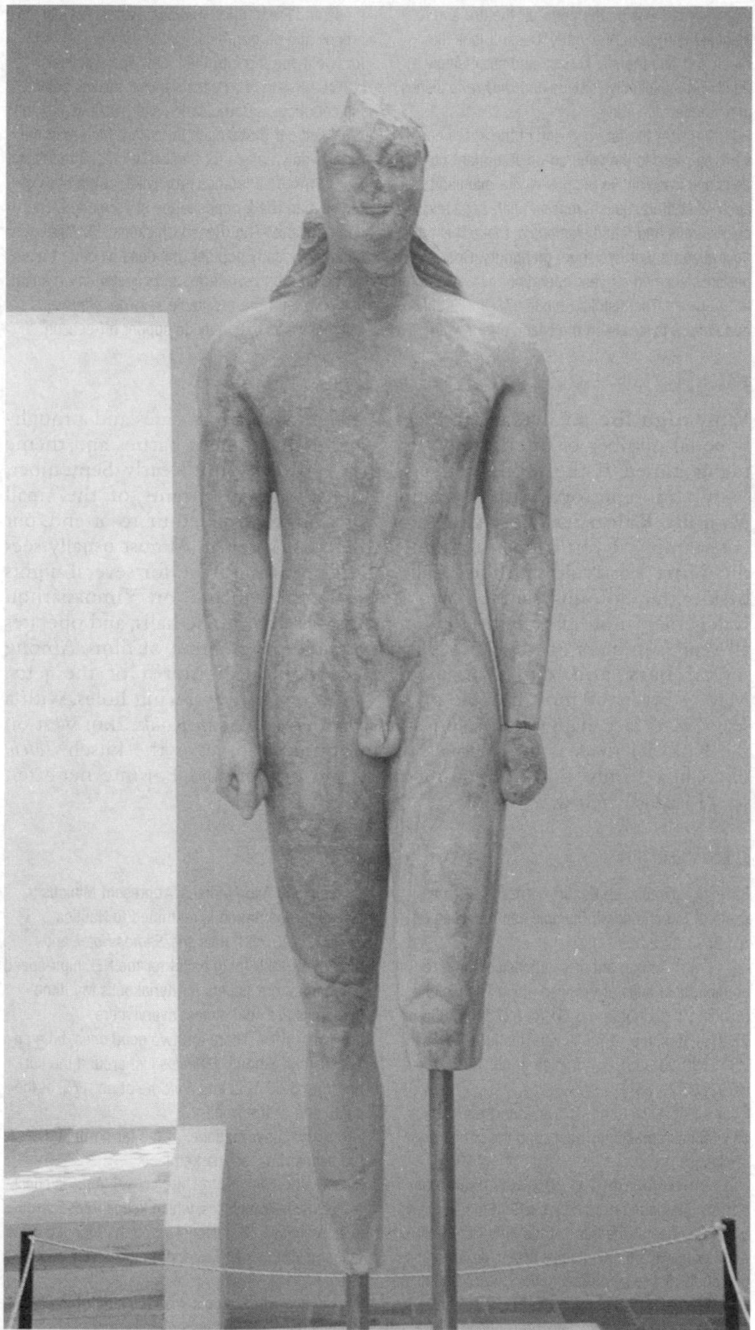

Archaic *kouros*, Archeological Museum, Vathy*, Sámos

Amfitheatro Beside the open-air theatre and Aï Yiannáki church in Áno Vathý. Doesn't look like much, but has friendly service and surprisingly good and inexpensive salads and *mayireftá* dishes in a wonderful setting.
Apanemia At the far west end of the shore boulevard, en route to the wine co-op. Abundant portions and imaginative recipes with a mainland flair, such as stuffed squash, mussel pilaf, *saganáki*, cheese rolls and *katsíki lemonáto*, make this outdoor ouzerí a worthy venue; go hungry. Open supper only, claimed all-year operation.
Asimopetra Themistoklí Sofoúli 97. One of only two *kultúra* tavernas on the island offers well-presented Frenchified *minceur* dishes, novelty breads and an impressive wine list; budget €33 for two if you dip into the latter. Open all year.
Epitelous Mezefé Pedestrianized bazaar, behind the courthouse. Combination sandwich, drinks and breakfast bar that's open from 7am Mon–Sat; the only sit-down place for English or crêpe breakfasts.
Ta Kotopoula Plátanos Prosfiyiká, at the base of the Vlamarí road, opposite the supermarket. The name means "The (Roast) Chickens" but this enduring, locally popular grill does all other meats, raised on their own farm, and vegetarian *orektiká* like *hórta* and the inevitable *revythokeftédhes*. Open all year; may only do supper off-season.

Nightlife and entertainment

Vathý **nightlife** revolves around seven or eight waterfront cafés and a roughly equal number of often pretentious bars, with frequent parties and theme nights aimed at the local clientele. From early July until early September, Vathý (in repertory with Pythagório) hosts various events of the small **Manolis Kalomiris Festival** – not worth making a detour to attend, but entertaining if you happen to coincide. The last week in August usually sees the **Wine Festival**, with food stalls and a live-music stage for several nights beside the Sofoulis statue. The Cine Olympia, inland on Yimnasiárhou Katevéni, is more plushly fitted than many UK/US movie halls, and operates all year (summers on the roof) with a variable programme of films. Among several **bars and clubs**, *Escape* at Kefalopoúlou 9 (north of the jetty, May–Sept) is the most durable of Vathý's more sedate watering holes, with a seaview terrace, happy hours and outdoor videos; *Kaptain Kouk*, 2km west on the Kokkári road, is for serious bopping until dawn, as is the kitsch *Totem* disco, in a grimly industrial setting out on the airport road. For internet cafés, see "Listings" below.

Listings

Airlines Olympic, on Kanári, corner of Smýrnis, south of the cathedral. Olympic can be called on ☎02730/27 237.
Car rental Among ten or so agencies, three recommendable ones are ranged along Themistoklí Sofoúli: try Budget, at no. 31 (☎02730/28 856 or 22 270), Kosmos, at no. 7, near the jetty (☎02730/23 253), or Autoplan at no. 17 (☎02730/23 555).
Banks and exchange At five waterfront banks, all with cash machines accepting the usual range of plastic.
Ferry/travel agents The most useful waterfront one for independent travellers is By Ship, with two branches: one at the base of the jetty (☎02730/80 445), primarily handling ships and hydrofoils, and one about 300m southeast (☎02730/25 065 or 27 337), with an equal stress on air tickets; between them they sell tickets for most ferry lines (DANE, NEL, Hellas Ferries, G&A), as well as for both Olympic and Axon airlines. At present Miniotis Lines representation is restricted to Nautica (☎02730/25 133) near the *Samos Hotel*, and they're also the main outlet for the NEL high-speed catamaran, but tickets for Kyriakoulis Maritime hydrofoils are sold almost everywhere.
Internet cafés There are two good ones, both on Themistoklí Sofoúli: *Dhiavlos* just around the corner from the KTEL, and *NetCafe* at no. 175, at the south end of the front.
Laundries Lavomatique, at the far north end of the pedestrianized marketplace.
Motor- and mountain-bike rental Vathý is chock-a-block with franchises, which keeps rates reasonable. Aramis, on Kefalopoúlou, north of the jetty, has the largest fleet of bikes and a mechanical support team.
Post office On Smýrnis, 200m inland from Olympic Airways; open weekdays only.
Street market Whether or not you're self-

catering, the daily street market or *laïkí agorá*, between the cathedral and OTE headquarters, is one of the largest (and most photogenic) in the islands. Goods on sale include garden produce, honey, wine, dried olives, fish from roving pick-up trucks and garden plants.

Taxi rank Beside the National Bank of Greece; ⓣ02730/28 404.

Around Vathý: eastern Sámos

In the immediate **environs of Vathý**, all around the eastern end of the island, lie some modest beaches and small hamlets with tavernas, all ideal targets for half-day-trips.

Two kilometres east of and above Vathý spreads the vast inland plateau of Vlamarí, devoted to vineyards and supporting the hamlets of **Ayía Zóni** and **Kamára** (plus a rapidly growing number of bad-taste modern villas). Ayía Zóni can offer a fortified monastery with an overgrown courtyard, and a rather listless **taverna** up at the nearby crossroads; if you need a meal, *O Kriton* in Kamára has the edge, with good salads in particular. From Kamára you can head east on the road to the start of the partly cobbled path which climbs to the ridge-top monastery of **Zoödhóhou Piyís** (open at all times) for superb views across the end of the island to Turkey. If you continue into the pines beyond the monastery, you'll find a lovely medieval chapel which has retained its original slate roof.

Heading north out of Vathý, the narrow, tour-bus-clogged street threads through beachless **Kalámi** – formerly the summer retreat of rich Vathyotes, now home to package hotels – before ending after 7km at the pebbly bay and fishing port of **AYÍA PARASKEVÍ** (aka Nissí), with good, if rather unsecluded, swimming. There are, alas, no longer any reliable facilities here other than a fitfully working **snackbar**, *Aquarius* (typically July–Aug only), which also has some **rooms** (ⓣ02730/28 282; ❸).

Kérveli and Posidhónio

As you head southeast from Vathý along the main island loop road, the triple chapel at **Trís Ekklisíes** marks an important junction, with another fork 100m along the left-hand turning. Bearing left twice takes you through the hilltop village of Paleókastro, 3km beyond which is another junction. Forking yet left again, after another 3km you reach the striking bay of **KÉRVELI**, with a medium-sized gravel beach – often packed out in season – and a quiet valley just inland. Of the two waterside **tavernas**, friendly *Sea and Dolphins* has good mezédhes such as egg-based *sgrápa* and pork-based *tiganía*, and *soúma*, the treacherously smooth local firewater, but mains have declined in quality and climbed in price lately. A kilometre back along the access road, *Iy Kryfi Folia* ("The Hidden Nest") is as described: a greenery-shrouded eyrie offering simple but inexpensive (€12 per person) and sustaining fare such as *kalamári* rings, lamb chops and roast goat – ring ⓣ02730/25 194 to order your goat. If you want to **stay**, most local accommodation is firmly in the grip of UK and German package companies, but the B-class *Kerveli Village* hotel (ⓣ02730/23 631, ⓕ23 006, ⓔkerveli@geminia.diavlos.gr; ❺), just above the last road curves descending to the beach, is reckoned one of the best in eastern Sámos – if you can squeeze in.

Bearing right instead at the junction above Kérveli brings you to the road's end at **POSIDHÓNIO** (still known by its Ottoman name of Mulay-Brahim), whose geese-patrolled gravel beach is rather smaller than Kérveli's. Of the two

tavernas here the right-hand *Kerkezos* takes its cooking a bit more seriously – the provincial governors' conference for all Greece has been hosted here – but the seafood, while good, is pricey. Their handful of beach-view self-catering units (ⓣ02730/22 267, ⓕ22 493; ❹) are usually contracted to UK package companies, but there are plenty of other rooms and studios at Posidhónio. Good ones include the misnamed *Sunset Apartments* (ⓣ02730/28 763, ⓕ27 011; ❹), which actually face east, and the *Niota* (ⓣ02730/27 584; ❸), with partial seaviews.

If you decide to base yourself at Posidhónio, it's best to rent wheels elsewhere beforehand; the only other destination within walking distance is the bay of **Klíma**. A paved side road, signposted as "Kaduna", goes there within 2km, but the beach is coarse shingle and the single taverna inconsistent in quality.

Mykáli and Psilí Ámmos

The right-hand option at the second junction just beyond Trís Ekklisíes leads to the beaches of Mykáli and Psilí Ámmos, which draw crowds partly by virtue of their views of Mount Mycale (present-day Samsun Dağı) in Turkey. These are the only spots in this section served by public transport, with a bus service just twice a day in season.

MYKÁLI, a kilometre or so of rather windswept sand and gravel, was developed and fire-scorched in the early 1990s (the two phenomena seem to go together). Winter rains fill a salt marsh just behind, a stopover for migrating flamingos between December and April. If you choose to **stay** out here, the *Sirenes Beach Hotel* (ⓣ02730/24 668, ⓕ25 222; ❹), in a garden setting on the inland side of the road, or the *Saint Nikolas* (ⓣ02730/80 533, ⓕ28 522; ❻), on the beach, are the top two B-class choices, though you may find that only the *Villa Barbara* (ⓣ02730/25 192; ❸), with apartments behind the *Sirenes Beach Hotel*, has vacancies on spec. Far and away the best **eating** on this coast – excellent and well-priced *mayireftá* – is at *Kalypso*, reached by its own dead-end access road off the main Mykáli-bound route.

Psilí Ámmos, further east around the headland, is a sunbed-crowded, sandy cove that's on every local tour operator's signboard. If you show up under your own power, expect to pay for parking. None of the four rather commercialized tavernas here is worth singling out. If you swim out to nearby **Vareloúdhi** islet, a logical target, beware of periodically strong west-to-east currents, which sweep through the narrow straits even in the shallows, and the eelgrass beds which complicate the final approach to the islet.

Pythagório and around

Most traffic south of Vathý heads for **PYTHAGÓRIO**, the island's premier resort – jam-packed and rather tacky in peak season. Formerly known as Tigáni ("Frying Pan"), for reasons that become obvious in midsummer, it was renamed in 1955 to honour native ancient mathematician, philosopher and mystic Pythagoras. The sixth-century-BC tyrant Polykrates established his capital here, now the subject of acres of archeological excavations which have forced modern Pythagório to expand northeastward and uphill. Findings are on display in a minuscule collection in the town hall (Sun & Tues–Thurs 9am–2pm, Fri & Sat noon–2pm; free), on Platía Irínis, just north of the main thoroughfare Lykoúrgou Logothéti. The village core of cobbled lanes and thick-walled mansions abuts a small harbour, which fits almost perfectly into the confines of Polykrates' ancient port and still uses his jetty. Today, however, it's devoted almost entirely to pleasure craft and overpriced cocktail bars.

Sámos' most complete (and recently refurbished) castle, the nineteenth-century *pýrgos* (tower-house) of **Lykourgos Logothetis**, overlooks both the town and the shoreline where that local chieftain, together with a certain "Kapetan Stamatis" and Admiral Kanaris, oversaw decisive naval and land victories over the Turks in the summer of 1824. The final battle was won on Transfiguration Day (August 6), and accordingly the church inside the castle precinct is dedicated to this festival; for many years a huge overhead banner in Greek announced that "Christ Saved Sámos 6 August 1824". Next to the castle are the easily visible remains of an early Christian basilica, occupying the grounds of slightly larger Roman villa.

Accommodation

Except perhaps in August, proprietors of the less expensive grades of **accommodation** tend to assiduously meet incoming ferries and hydrofoils – unlike in Vathý, there's generally no harm in following them. Otherwise it's a matter of tramping the streets unless you've phoned ahead. Many people head straight out, and in truth Pythagório is more the sort of place you stay for just a night prior to catching an early hydrofoil south. The friendly **tourist information** booth, on the left up the main thoroughfare Lykoúrgou Logothéti as you face west (daily June–Sept 8am–10pm; Ⓣ02730/62 274, Ⓕ61 022), can help with finding rooms.

Nocturnal noise can be a problem in Pythagório, so it's worth heading along Pythagóra to its quiet, seaward end, south of Lykoúrgou Logothéti; here you'll find the modest **pension** *Tsambika* (Ⓣ02730/61 642; ❷), while a block west, *Pension Dora* (Ⓣ02730/61 456; ❸) offers higher-standard units occupying an old stone house. Another peaceful area is the hillside north of Platía Irínis, where *Studios Galini* (Ⓣ02730/61 167; winter Ⓣ010/98 42 248; ❹) has high-quality self-catering units with ceiling fans, balconies and kind English-speaking management. Not brilliantly located out by the traffic lights – it's convenient only to the airport – but comfortable, good value and friendly is the *Evelin* (Ⓣ02730/61 124, Ⓕ61 077; ❸), a C-class hotel with a swimming pool, double glazing against noise and on-site motorbike hire.

Eating, drinking and nightlife

Eating out can be frustrating in Pythagório, with value for money often a completely alien concept; multiple tour-company stickers in windows let you know just where reps have been taking kickbacks for steering their charges in that direction. However, aside from the obvious tourist mills there are a few decent alternatives, the only places the islanders themselves will be caught dead or alive in. Away from the water at the top of town on the Vathý road is *Mezedhopolio Lakis*, open most of the year. For dining at the water's edge, you're best off at the extreme east end of the quay, beyond the derelict hotel, at either the courteous *Remataki*, where vegetarians are catered for with such dishes as *anginháres alá políta*, or at adjacent *Psaropoula*, where you get very decent, simple seafood and *orektiká* – don't be scared off by the garish laminated photos and menus. They claim to operate during winter too, in the barrel-lined interior.

Night owls gather at the *Mythos Club* (international sounds) on Platía Irínis, or at *La Nuit*, which features the atrocious Greek aural concoction known as *ellinádhiko*.

Other practicalities

The **bus stop** to get you away is just west of the intersection of Lykoúrgou Logothéti and the road to Vathý. Also on Lykoúrgou Logothéti are two **banks** (both with cash machines) and the **post office**, as well as numerous outlets for car, motorbike and bicycle rental. The flattish country to the west of the town is ideal for bicycle touring, a popular activity. By contrast, **drivers** are penalized by the closing off of the main street to traffic after 5pm, and all but mandatory use of the car park on the hill beside the castle (controlled entrance June–Sept, fees around €1.50 per hour).

Around Pythagório: ancient sites and beaches

Aside from the archeologists' potholes, visible remains of **ancient Sámos** are scattered in a broad zone just beyond the current town limits. Four hundred metres west of Pythagório, just seaward from the main road, lie the remains of the **Roman baths** (Tues–Sun 8.30am–2.30pm; free): fairly dull, though lit up at night to good effect.

Considerably more interesting is the **Efpalínio Órygma (Eupalinian Tunnel)** (Tues–Sun 8.30am–2.30pm; €1.50), a 1040-metre aqueduct bored through the mountain just north of Pythagório. Designed by one Eupalinos of Mégara, and built by slave labour at the behest of Polykrates, it guaranteed the ancient town a siege-proof water supply, and remained in use until late Byzantine times. To get there on foot, take the well-signposted path heading inland off the shore boulevard just west of town; after fifteen minutes' walk you'll meet the access road, and then it's just five minutes' more from here. Visits consist of traversing a hewn rock ledge used to transport the spoil from the water channel far below; there are guard-grilles over the worst drops, lighting for the first 650m, and theoretical plans to open the entire length of the tunnel in the future. Although the work crews started from opposite sides of the mountain, the eight-metre horizontal deviation from true, about halfway along, is remarkably slight, and the vertical error nil: a tribute to the competence of the era's surveyors, and rather better percentage-wise than occurred with the boring of the Channel Tunnel.

You can also climb to the five remaining chunks of the Polykratian **perimeter wall** enclosing the tyrant's hilltop citadel. There's a choice of routes: one leading up from the Glyfádha lagoon, 700m west of Pythagório, past an **ancient watchtower** now isolated from other fortifications; the other approach (easier) leading from the well-signposted monastery of **Panayía Spilianí**, just off the road to the Efpalínion tunnel. The monastery itself, now bereft of nuns and monks, has been insensitively restored and the grounds are crammed with souvenir kiosks, but behind the courtyard, the *raison d'être* of the place is still magnificent: a cool, illuminated, hundred-metre **cave**, at the drippy end of which is a subterranean shrine to the Virgin (open daylight hours; free). It is thought that this was the residence of the ancient oracular priestess Phyto, and a hiding place during the pirate-ridden medieval era.

Potokáki

The main local **beach** stretches for several kilometres west of Pythagório's Logothetis castle, punctuated about halfway along by the end of the airport runway, and the cluster of hotels known as **Potokáki** (not served by public transport). The name, which roughly translates as "A Wee Drop to Drink", comes from the informal, shack-like ouzerís which clustered here until the 1960s. If you don't mind the crowds or occasionally being buzzed by low-

PYTHAGORIO & ANCIENT SAMOS

N

(start)

Efpalínio Órygma

(end)

Ancient watchtower

Artemis temple

Start of the Sacred Way to Heraion

Glyfádha Lagoon (formerly ancient secondary port)

ancient coastline

Airport & Heraion

Early Christian basilica

Roman baths

Roman-Byzantine Aqueduct

Ancient theatre

Panayía Spilianí

course of the ancient walls

Olympic Airways

Ancient agora

Aphrodite temple

Medieval fortification

Lykourgos Logothetis tower

0 200m

Modern Pythagório

Ancient Port

Modern Port

Old harbour wall

Polykrates' original jetty

Ferry Berth

Hydrofoils

Kastrí (Neolithic settlement)

Vathý

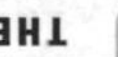

flying jets (and even lower-flying jet-skis), the central zone is equipped with the usual amenities like kayaks and sunbeds. Most of the sand-and-pebble shore here is well groomed, and the water clean. For more privacy, you'll have to head out west towards the end of the road.

Just before the turn-off to the heart of the beach, about 700m from the western edge of Pythagório, sprawls the massive, ultra-luxurious *Doryssa Bay* complex (Ⓣ02730/61 360, Ⓕ61 463, Ⓦwww.doryssabay.gr; ❻), whose accommodation varies from standard rooms in a brutalist 1970s hotel wing (€94), right on the beach, to houses (€161) in a meticulously concocted fake village guaranteed to confound archeologists of future eras. No two of the units, joined by named lanes, are alike; there's even a "platía" with an expensive café, a folklore museum better than many official ones, and Sámos' principal indoor concert and theatre venue, the Aithoussa Sibylla, which hosts an excellent **documentary film festival** the first week of October. More affordable local options, also fringing the beach at Potokáki proper, include the small C-class hotels *Katerina* (Ⓣ02730/61 963; ❷) and *Penelope* (Ⓣ02730/61 601, Ⓕ61 615; ❹).

Ancient Heraion

The Potokáki beachfront road is a dead end, with the main island loop road continuing west from the turn-off for the airport. Along this you'll find signs to the **Heraion Sanctuary** (Tues–Sun 8.30am–2.30pm; €2.40), once linked to the ancient city of Sámos by a five-kilometre Sacred Way that's now buried beneath alluvial mud and quite a bit of the airport runway.

The Samian cult of Hera

The Samian sanctuary of **Hera** was one of only four in ancient Greece, and by far the most important; a fertility goddess of some sort had been worshipped here since Neolithic times. Hera was originally venerated here in the form of a simple wooden board, much like the icons of today's Orthodox Church, though by the start of the first millennium BC this had been supplemented – but not replaced – by a succession of increasingly elaborate cult statues, which became the focus of the annual *Heraia* festival celebrating the goddess' union with Zeus. The original idol was still solemnly paraded in a litter of osiers, a tree sacred to the goddess, to be bathed at the river mouth here, during the annual *Tonaia* festivities, which also commemorated a foiled kidnapping of the image by Argive and Etruscan pirates; having stolen it, they found their ship permanently becalmed offshore, and in panic abandoned their ill-gotten gain on the beach. Just offshore, a suggestively shaped islet – the **Petrokáravo** or "Petrified Ship" is, according to legend, the remains of the thieves' vessel.

From the eighth to sixth century BC, the sanctuary (and ancient Sámos) were both at the height of their prestige and allure; the Heraion, unlike Olympia or Delphi, was effectively owned by the nearby city and shared its fortunes. Accordingly, most of the finds on display at the Vathý museum date from this time and are likely to have been brought by worshipful pilgrims approaching directly by sea, or journeying from the capital along the Sacred Way. But, despite the patronage of Polykrates and the architectural and artistic geniuses at his disposal, two attempts at a stone temple during the sixth century – successors to more rustic, wooden shrines – remained unfinished. The first collapsed owing to earthquake or a design fault; work on the second, a forest of 134 Doric and Ionic pillars, ceased after Polykrates was crucified by the Persians on the shores of Mount Mycale. Byzantine and medieval masons helped themselves to the cut stone, leaving only a single pillar erect as a landmark to mariners. Later, a small basilica was built amidst the ruins, dedicated to what some might see as the latest incarnation of the Mother Goddess – the Virgin Mary.

Much touted in tourist literature, this massive shrine to Hera, the Mother Goddess, assumes humbler dimensions on approach, with just one surviving column and assorted foundations. Yet once inside the fenced precinct you can sense the former grandeur of the largest ancient temple known, never completed owing to Polykrates' untimely death at the hands of the Persians. The site chosen, near the mouth of the still-active Ímvrassos stream, was Hera's legendary birthplace and the spot for her trysts with Zeus; in a far corner of the fenced-in zone you can see a large, exposed patch of the paved processional Sacred Way.

Modern Iréon

Adjacent to Heraion is the modern resort of **IRÉON**, a nondescript grid of dusty streets behind a coarse-shingle beach, attracting a slightly younger and more active clientele than Pythagório. Here you'll find more independent **rooms** and a handful of small **hotels** that might have spur-of-the-moment vacancies, for example *Venetia* (Ⓣ02730/95 295; ❸) and *Faros* (Ⓣ02730/95 262; ❷), both within sight of the water. **Tavernas** tend to come and go by the year; the longest-running and most consistent is *Ireon*, at the west end of the waterfront, just above the fishing anchorage; they also have (very basic) rooms upstairs (Ⓣ02730/95 438, Ⓕ95 361; ❷).

Just inland, about 2km along the road to Mýli village, stands the rather squat **Pýrgos Sarakiní** (locked), and a double-naved church (open). Both were built during the mid-fourteenth century by the Genoese: the tower as a warehouse and defence against pirates, the church to be used by Catholic rulers and Orthodox peasants worshipping side by side – a tolerant arrangement seen elsewhere in Greece only on Náxos (and Plátanos, see p.325).

Hóra and Mytiliní

Three kilometres northwest of Pythagório, the island loop road comes to a junction at long, narrow **HÓRA**, the island's medieval capital. It's still a large, noisy village, though its handful of tavernas have suffered the attentions of too many tour coaches and are no longer worth recommending.

Heading 4km north from the crossroads takes you through a ravine to **MYTILINÍ**, which initially seems an amorphous, workaday sprawl. A brief exploration, however, reveals a fine main square with some atmospheric kafenía, the unmarked, simple *Taverna Dionysos* opposite them, and the well-publicized *Cine Rex*, down a side street. It's reasonably priced for the benefit of the numerous local conscripts, with first-run fare and operation in summer premises.

At the southern edge of town, a local worthy initially endowed a **Paleontological & Natural History Museum** (Mon–Sat 9am–2pm, Sun 10.30am–2pm; €1.50) to house bones recovered from a place nearby where Ice Age animals came to die; it has been expanded, with collections on local flora and butterflies, to justify the "Natural History" tag, though it's still not exactly required viewing.

Southern inland villages

Since the circum-island bus passes through or near the villages only once a day (twice on Tues), you'll need your own vehicle to explore them all.

Some 4km west of Hóra, an inconspicuous turning leads uphill to the still-functioning monastery of **Timíou Stavroú** (Holy Cross), whose annual festival on September 14 is more an excuse for a tatty open-air market than any music or feasting. One kilometre further on, another detour wends its way to **MAVRATZÉÏ**, which lost 49 houses to the July 2000 fire. It's one of two Samian "pottery villages"; this one specializes in the *Koúpa toú Pythagóra* or "Pythagorean cup", supposedly designed by the sage himself to leak onto the wine-drinker's lap if he indulged beyond the "fill" line. More practical wares can be found at three shops in **KOUMARADHÉÏ**, back on the main road, 2km further along.

At Koumaradhéï you can descend a paved road through burnt-off forest to the sixteenth-century monastery of **Megális Panayías** (nominal hours daily 9am–noon & 5–7pm, in practice unreliable), restored early in the 1990s and containing some of the finest frescoes on the island. This route continues to **MÝLI**, a village submerged in citrus groves, also accessible from the Iréon road. Four kilometres above Mýli sprawls **PAGÓNDAS**, a large hillside community with a splendid main square and an unusual communal fountain-house on the south hillside. Though the platía restaurants are festooned with tour-op stickers – it's too close to Iréon to have escaped attention – this is also the venue for one of the better Samian festivals, taking place on **Whit Sunday** eve (Ayíou Pnévmatos in Greek), with live music. Pagóndas is also the subject of a scurrilous island legend which holds that the villagers were formerly much given to buggery, and that no lad reached the age of 15 without being "initiated" by his elders.

From here, a paved road curls 9km around the hill to **SPATHARÉÏ**, a rather poky place – more so since the area was devastated by fire in both 1993 and 2000 – but set on a natural balcony offering the best seaviews this side of the island. From Spatharéï, the road continues 6km till it joins up with the main road at **PÝRGOS**, a friendly village at the head of a ravine draining southwest, and the centre of Samian honey production. A short distance down the gorge, **Koútsi** is a small roadside oasis of plane trees (supposedly 17) shading a gushing spring and an eponymous **taverna** that makes a convenient meal stop; the food is unadorned but sustaining and abundant – the only drawback is its limited opening (June 15–Oct 1 only). From Koútsi, a popular, waymarked **path** leads down the ravine here – which just escaped the July 2000 blaze – to the village of **Neohóri**, which has minimal facilities.

The southern coast

The rugged, now rather scorched, coastline south of the Pagóndas–Pýrgos route conceals a number of largely inaccessible beaches, glimpsed by most visitors for the first and last time from the descending plane bringing them to Sámos. They have been developed in a low-key way, but still suffer nothing like the crowds of the more obvious beaches – and this is even truer since the 2000 fire ruined most of their backdrops.

Kyriakoú

Furthest east of the more accessible coves, the 250-metre sand-and-gravel beach of **Kyriakoú** lies just 5km southwest of Iréon via a well-marked but rough track (jeeps or dirt bikes only). Stavros' "shack" offers grilled snacks, drinks, and a few umbrellas and sunbeds for rent. Though its olive-and-pine hinterland has been incinerated, the water remains pristine, and solitude disturbed only by groups of boat-trippers from Iréon. There is also a slightly longer and less steep but unmarked track in from Pagóndas.

Tsópela

Tsópela, very near the southernmost point of the island, also has marked road access. Matters begin reasonably enough about 4km beyond Pagóndas on the Spatharéï-bound road, but once past the tiny monastery of Evangelistrías, the 6.5-kilometre track deteriorates markedly, though you can now just about wrestle an ordinary car through the fire-ravaged landscape. Your reward for persevering is a highly scenic sand-and-gravel bay at the mouth of a gorge, with views towards the satellite islet of Samiopoúla, rock overhangs under which to shelter, and curious freshwater seeps on the sea bed. A seasonal **taverna** under the pines just to the east, the only bit of local vegetation saved from the 2000 fire, serves cheaper and better fare (including fish dropped off by passing boats) than you'd expect for such an isolated spot.

Kouméïka and Bállos

The western reaches of this shoreline, which suffered comprehensive fire damage in 1994 but are now recovering well relative to the 2000 blaze zone, are approached via the small village of **KOUMÉÏKA**, which has a massive inscribed marble fountain and a pair of kafenía on its plane-tree-shaded square. Below extends the long, pebbly bay at slightly denuded **BÁLLOS**, with sand and a cave; the far east end is reserved for naturists. Bállos itself is merely a sleepy collection of summer houses, several simple places to stay and a few tavernas, all on the shore road. The best **accommodation** for walk-ins is the *Hotel Amfilisos* (Ⓣ0273/31 669, Ⓕ31 668; ❷), while far and away the finest **dining** is found at seafront *Akrogiali* nearby, with an honourable mention for humbler *Iy Paralia* off to the east. Returning towards Kouméïka, the dubious-looking side road just before the village marked "Velanidhiá" is in fact partly paved and useable by any vehicle – a very practical short cut if you're travelling towards the beaches beyond Órmos Marathokámbou (see p.333).

Plátanos

Following the southerly loop road back northeast towards Karlóvassi, it's worth detouring up to **PLÁTANOS**, on the flanks of Mount Karvoúnis; at 520m it's one of the highest villages on the island, with sweeping views west and south. The name comes from the three stout plane trees (*plátanos* in Greek) on its platía, which has retained some of the charm utterly lost at Vourliótes (see p.328); there is also a trio of **tavernas** here – the friendliest is *Sofia* – and a few **rooms** to rent at the outskirts of the village, if you ask around. The only special sight is the thirteenth-century **church of Kímisis Theotókou** (key at house opposite west entrance) in the village centre, double-naved and double-creed like the one at Pýrgos Sarakiní; in this case, however, the Byzantine Nicaean emperors built it, making provision for the spiritual needs of their allies, the Genoese garrison.

Kokkári

Leaving Vathý on the north coastal section of the island loop road, there's little to stop for – other than the reasonably good beach at **Kédros**, 5km west of town – until you reach **KOKKÁRI**, 12km along, the third major Samian tourist centre after Pythagório and the capital. It's also the prime source of nostalgia for Sámos regulars; while lower Vathý and Pythagório had little compelling beauty to sacrifice, much has been irrevocably lost here. The town's profile, covering two knolls behind twin headlands known as Dhídhymi or the Twins, remains unaltered, and one or two families still doggedly untangle their fishnets on the quay. But in general its identity has been transformed beyond recognition, with constant inland expansion over vineyards and the fields of small-bulbed onions that gave the place its name. Since the exposed rocky western beach is buffeted by near-constant winds, Kokkári's mostly German promoters have made a virtue of necessity by developing the place as a successful windsurfing resort.

Practicalities

As at Vathý and Pythagório, a high proportion of Kokkári **accommodation** is block-booked for the season by German and British tour companies. West-beach establishments not completely devoted to package tours include the *Lemos* (ⓣ02730/92 250, ⓕ92 334; ❸), near the north end of the strand, and the *Blue Sea* (ⓣ02730/92 387, ⓕ92 462; ❷). Otherwise Yiorgos Mihelios (ⓣ02730/92 456 or 92 677) has a wide range of rooms and flats to rent (❷–❹). For a guaranteed view of the quiet fishing port, try *Pension Alkyonis* (ⓣ02730/92 225; ❷), or *Pension Angela* (ⓣ02730/92 052; ❷). If you get stuck, seek assistance from the seasonal **EOT post** (ⓣ02730/92 217), housed in a Portacabin near the main church.

Most **tavernas** line the north waterfront and charge above the norm, though they're steadily losing ground to breakfast or cocktail bars. At the extreme eastern end of things, *Ta Adhelfia/The Brothers* is an excellent, unpretentious *psistariá*, run by a friendly local family offering fresh fish, a few oven dishes, home-made chips and bulk wine at normal prices. A few steps west, *To Avgo tou Kokora*, is another good (if pricier) all-rounder, while *Piccolo Porto*, still further along, does excellent Italian dishes, including wood-oven pizzas. The co-managed *Barino*, also here at mid-strip, is the best breakfast place, with fresh-squeezed juices in all flavours, waffles and crêpes. The main focus of **nightlife** is a little square ringed by noisy bars, just west of where the concrete-paved stream (with its family of ducks) meets the sea, but there's also the more elaborate, well-established and musical *Cabana Beach Club* on the west beach, drawing clubbers from across the island.

Other amenities include a **bank** on the through-road (complete with cash machine), a seasonal **post office** in a Portakabin on a lane to seaward, and a long-hours, self-service **laundry** next to that. There are also branches of all the major Vathý travel agents, and a newsstand. Note that almost everything mentioned in this account is closed between mid-October and mid-April, when scarcely a grocery shop stays open in Kokkári.

West of Kokkári: the north coast

The nearest partly sheltered beaches, aside from the more protected easterly town beach, lie thirty to forty minutes' walk west from Kokkári, all with sunbeds and permanently anchored umbrellas. The first beach, **Lemonákia** (2km along), is a bit too close to the road, with an obtrusive café. However, just overhead is perhaps the best hotel on Sámos' north coast, the A-class *Arion*

(Ⓣ02370/92 020, Ⓕ92 006, Ⓦwww.diavlos.gr/samos/arion/arion1.html; ❺–❻), a well-designed hotel-wing and bungalow complex on an unburnt patch of hillside.

One kilometre beyond, the graceful crescent of **Tzamadhoú** (rhyming with Coleridge's "Xanadu") figures in virtually every EOT poster of the island. With path-only access, it's a bit less spoilt than Lemonákia, and each end of the beach (saucer-shaped pebbles) is by tacit consent a nudist/gay zone. Unfortunately, a spring just inland has been fenced off to discourage campers from congregating here, and to encourage everyone to patronize the fairly pricey tavernas signposted up in the vineyards.

There's one more large, pebbly stretch west of Avlákia (a mostly Greek resort 6km from Kokkári) called **Tzaboú**, but unless you're passing by and want a quick dip, this is not worth a special detour as it lies open to the prevailing northwest wind. **AVLÁKIA** itself can offer a few **rooms** and **tavernas**, best of these *Oscar*, which has guaranteed wild, fresh and thus very pricey fish served on a seaside terrace, plus simple rooms upstairs (Ⓣ02730/94 464 to book either tables or rooms; ❷).

Áyios Konstandínos and around

The next spot of any interest along the coast road is **Platanákia**, essentially a handful of tavernas and rooms for rent at a plane-shaded bridge by the turning for Manolátes (see p.328); best of the **tavernas** is *IyApolavsi,* with a limited daily choice of very good *mayireftá*. For **accommodation**, try the *Hotel Iro* (Ⓣ02730/94 013, Ⓕ94 610; ❸), or the *Hotel Apartments Agios Konstantinos* (Ⓣ02730/94 000, Ⓕ94 002; ❸), both on the road down to the sea.

Platanákia is actually the eastern suburb of **ÁYIOS KONSTANDÍNOS**, 1500m distant, a case study in arrested touristic development. The surf-pounded esplanade has been repaved and prettified, but there are no useable beaches within walking distance, so the collection of warm-toned stone buildings (less adulterated than usual by concrete structures) constitutes a peaceful alternative to Kokkári. In addition to modest, 1970s-vintage **rooms**, such as the *Atlantis* (Ⓣ02730/94 329; ❶), or the *Four Seasons* (Ⓣ02730/94 287; ❷), both just above the highway, there's a small, well-designed bungalow complex with a pool, *Apollonia Bay* (Ⓣ02730/94 444, Ⓕ94 090; ❹). **Eating** out, you're spoilt for choice; besides *Iy Apolavsi*, already mentioned, there's *To Kyma* at the east end of the quay (June–Sept), with good bulk wine and *mayireftá*; *To Akroyiali* at mid-quay, where the food's cheaper and better than the plastic photo-menus suggest; or (best of all) the *Aeolos* at the far west end of the esplanade (June–Oct), with terrific, inexpensive fish or grilled meat and a few well-chosen *mayireftá.*

Once past "Áyios", as it's known locally, the mountains hem the road in against the sea, and the terrain doesn't relent until near **KONDAKÉÏKA**, whose kafenío-lined square is worth a visit at dusk for its fabulous sunset views. Afterwards you can descend to its diminutive shore annexe of **ÁYIOS NIKÓLAOS** for excellent fish platters and mezédhes at *Iy Psaradhes* (Easter–Oct), with its terrace lapped by the waves; having appeared (deservedly) in so many guides both Greek and foreign, booking in season is mandatory (Ⓣ02730/32 489), when service can get over-stretched. Though not visible from the upper road, the reasonable pebble-and-sand beach of **Pliáki** lies ten minutes' walk east past the last studio units, perennially occupied by a German clientele in summer. An exception is the *Villa Violeta*, with a small pool, available through Laskarina Holidays (see "Basics", p.14).

Inland from Kokkári: hill villages

Inland between Kokkári and Kondakéïka, an idyllic landscape of pine, cypress and orchards is overawed by dramatic mountains and, except for the slopes below Vrondianís monastery and some streaks of scorched trees reaching the sea between Lemonákia and Tzaboú, the area miraculously escaped the July 2000 fire. Despite ongoing destructive nibblings by bulldozers, a few stretches of the trail system which once comprehensively linked the various **hill villages** remain still intact, and you can walk for as long or as little as you like, returning to the main highway to catch a bus home. Failing that, most of the communities can provide a bed at short notice.

Vrondianís, Vourliótes and Pnáka

The monastery of **Vrondianís** (Vrondá), directly above Kokkári, is the oldest on the island, just predating Megális Panayías (see p.324). However, the lovely trail up from Kokkári was completely destroyed in 1998 and the army used the monastery outbuildings as barracks prior to their severe damage in the 2000 fire, so the place only really comes alive during the September 7–8 festival, when *yiórti* – a special cereal-and-meat porridge – is served. Besides the event at Pagóndas, this is the only really lively and musical Samian celebration, which spills over into the nearby village of Vourliótes.

VOURLIÓTES, 2km north of the monastery, and still accessible by an intact, ninety-minute trail from Kokkári (though the countryside is fire-grim), has beaked chimneys and brightly painted shutters sprouting from its typical tile-roofed houses. Restaurateur greed has ruined the formerly photogenic central square, by cutting down two ancient mulberries and cramming the space with tatty tables, so it's best to pass over the tavernas here in favour of *Iy Pera Vrysi*, at the village entrance, instead; with its enormous plane tree and glimpses of the sea below, this is a popular weekend venue for Athenian Greeks. Even more appealing is the *Piyi Pnaka* taverna, in the idyllic eponymous hamlet of **PNÁKA**, just off the ascending Vourliótes road.

Manolátes and Valeondádhes

MANOLÁTES, an hour-plus walk uphill from Vourliótes via the deep Kakórrema stream canyon, has been gentrified of late with run of the mill and even upmarket trinket shops, and a half-dozen **snack bars** and **tavernas**; of these *Iy Yeoryidhes* by the central fountain is obvious, but by far the best one is *Iy Filia* (lunch only), co-run with *Iy Apolavsi* at Platanákia and occupying a stone-built cottage at the high edge of the village. Here the chef produces a steady stream of carefully concocted *mayireftá*, accompanied by wine from the surrounding vineyards – and the biggest 180-degree eyeful on the island.

Iy Filia sits just below the start of the trail up **Mount Ámbelos** (Karvoúnis), the island's second highest summit; the trek, mostly on trail surface, takes five hours round trip. The trail has been cut perilously in three places by a pointless jeep track a few minutes along, and there are swaths of fire damage, both from a 1995 lightning-started blaze and the 2000 catastrophe, but overall the scenery, including some surviving 25-metre-tall black pines, is still alluring away from the burn zones.

From Manolátes you can no longer easily continue on foot to Stavrinídhes, the next village, but should plunge straight down, partly on a cobbled path, through the shady valley known as "**Aïdhónia**" ("Nightingales", which sing here in May) towards Platanákia (about an hour's walk). At a point shortly downhill from where the path hits the valley floor you'll find the *Hotel Aidonokastro* (Ⓣ02730/94 686 or 097/4666708, Ⓕ94 404; May–Oct; ④), up on the hillside to the west; here the kindly, English-speaking Yannis Pamoukis has renovated about half the abandoned hamlet of **VALEONDÁDHES** as a unique cottage-hotel, each former house comprising a pair of two- or four-person units with traditional touches. Package companies (including Laskarina) have most of the cottages, but Yannis always reserves two or three studios for walk-in customers. The closest alternative accommodation – again with a package allotment, this time Sunvil – is the well-priced, well-managed *Hotel Daphne* (Ⓣ02730/94 003, Ⓕ94 594, Ⓦwww.daphne-hotel.gr; ④), perched on the same slope just a kilometre or so closer to the sea where the valley has opened out, with sweeping views from its pool-terrace.

Stavrinídhes and Ámbelos

STAVRINÍDHES, should you fight your way on foot or by bike through the deplorable mess of bulldozer tracks beyond Manolátes, has little in the way of tourist facilities and much in the way of recent notoriety. To the infinite chagrin of Sámos' archbishop, many local villagers have become Jehovah's Witnesses, a pacifist sect abhorred and actively persecuted in Greece, though they have recently won the right to alternative civilian national service rather than the five years' imprisonment they formerly faced.

Similar conversions have occurred at neighbouring **ÁMBELOS**, more spectacularly perched on a natural balcony above the sea. Its setting has prompted numerous foreigners to buy and renovate houses here, but again there are few specific delights for outsiders other than a nondescript **taverna** at the village outskirts – and, off-season, good mezédhes in one of the kafenía.

Karlóvassi and the northwest coast

KARLÓVASSI, 34km west of Vathý and the second town of Sámos, is decidedly sleepier and more old-fashioned than the capital, despite having roughly the same population. Though lacking much aesthetic distinction, it's popular as a base from which to take a number of rewarding walks or to explore western Sámos' excellent beaches and a smattering of medieval ruins.

The name, incidentally, despite scant evidence of Ottoman legacy elsewhere on Sámos, appears to be a corruption of *karlıova*, Turkish for "snowy plain" – the plain in question being the conspicuous saddle of Mount Kérkis overhead, which is indeed snowcapped in harsh winters.

The town divides into no fewer than four straggly neighbourhoods: **Néo**, well inland, whose untidy growth was spurred by the influx of post-1923 refugees from Asia Minor; **Meséo**, across the usually dry riverbed, tilting appealingly on a knoll; and picture-postcard **Paleó** (or Áno), perched above **Limáni** (or Limín), the small harbour district.

Limáni

The port of **LIMÁNI**, its quay pedestrianized at night, is an appealing place with a working boatyard at the west end. **Ferry-ticket agencies** are scattered within a short distance of each other on the through-road and at the jetty. Just inland from the shorefront road, slightly to the east, sprawls Karlóvassi's branch of the **EOS** (Union of Samian Wine-Producers), open for tours of the production line (and a sample glass) during normal weekday working hours.

Most visitors to the area **stay** in or near Limáni, which has a handful of rooms and several overpriced hotels. The **rooms**, all in the inland pedestrian lane behind the through-road, are quieter: try those of Vangelis Feloukatzis (ⓣ02730/33 293; ❷). Otherwise, the comfortable *Samaina Port Hotel* (ⓣ02730/34 527, ⓕ34 471; ❺), co-managed with the *Samaina Maisonettes* apartments (❺–❻) slightly inland, overlooks the quay.

Tavernas and bars are abundant, though the only remarkable quayside ones are *Rementzo* (April–Oct), tellingly the locals' hangout, with good fish in season plus *mayireftá*, and the more touristy *Boussolas* next door, which does however stay open year-round, with consistent quality. The local university contingent (a maths and computer science faculty is based here) keeps **nightlife** surprisingly active; try the cavernous dance-hall *Popcorn*, in an old stone warehouse opposite the ferry jetty. The summer cinema near the defunct *Hotel Aktaeon* is currently closed for (indefinite) refurbishment, but there's a good October-to-May **movie-house**, the Gorgyra, next to the Agricultural Bank in Néo. July and August also see various musical and theatrical events of the local Karlovassia festival.

Paleó and Meséo

Immediately above Limáni perches the partly hidden hamlet of **PALEÓ**, whose hundred or so houses are draped to either side of a leafy ravine. There are at present no reliable tourist facilities.

MESÉO, just east, could be an alternative to Limáni as a base, with one comfortable **hotel**, the B-class *Aspasia* (ⓣ02730/30 201, ⓕ30 200; ❹), with pool and air con, near the wood-fired bakery, and other rooms scattered along the half-kilometre between here and the sea, including the D-class *Astir* (ⓣ02730/33 150, ⓕ34 074; ❷). On the platía some 200m east of the *Aspasia*, there's a clutch of frequently changing tavernas and bars with a mixed clientele of students and tourists. Following the street linking this square to the waterfront, you pass one of the improbably huge turn-of-the-twentieth-century churches, topped with twin belfries and a blue-and-white dome, which dot the coastal plain here. Just at the intersection with the shore road you'll find the friendly, good-value, sunset-view *To Kyma* ouzerí (April–Oct), where Sudanese proprietress Letekindan Berhane adds a welcome Middle Eastern–East African touch to the broad variety of dishes – most days you'll fight for a table (no reservations taken).

Néo

NÉO has little to recommend it besides a wilderness of derelict stone warehouses and mansions on the east bank of the river mouth, reminders of the extinct leather industry which flourished here during the first half of the twentieth century (the last tannery only closed in the late 1970s). However, if you're staying at Limáni, you'll almost certainly visit one of the three **banks** (cash machines at all of them), the **post office**, or the **bus stop** on the main lower square. A few, though not all, buses from Vathý continue down to the harbour; ask for details. While waiting for a bus, one of two traditional **kafenía** might interest you: recently spruced up *O Kleanthis*, on the lower platía, or *O*

Kerketevs, by the upper square. There are no consistent **eateries** except the popular, year-round *Dionysos Psistaria*, on the west side of town at the start of the Marathókambos road.

Potámi and around

The closest decent **beach** to Karlóvassi beckons at **POTÁMI**, forty minutes' walk via the coast road from Limáni or an hour by a much more scenic, high trail from Paleó, via the minimally interesting grotto-church of Áyios Andónios. This broad arc of sand and pebbles, flecked at one end with tide-lashed rocks (and a hideous clifftop chapel), gets crowded at summer weekends, when seemingly the entire population of Karlóvassi descends here. Near the end of the trail from Paleó stands *To Iliovasilema*, a reasonable and friendly (if oversubscribed) *psistariá* with fish and meat dishes; there are also a very few **rooms** signposted locally, but many individuals camp rough (in defiance of prohibition signs) along the lower reaches of the river that gives the beach its name.

A streamside path leads twenty minutes inland, initially past the exquisite eleventh-century church of **Metamórfosis** – the oldest on Sámos, its dome supported on four early Christian columns – to a point where the stream is squeezed between sheer rock walls. Beyond this point, you must swim and wade 100m further in heart-stoppingly cold water through a series of fern-tufted rock pools (home to harmless freshwater crabs), before reaching a low but vigorous **waterfall**. Of late this enchanting site has become the worst-kept secret of western Sámos, probably worth avoiding in high season when it's included in the "Jeep Safari" trips of certain tour agencies. To cater to their clients, an extended trail – initially very steep and guard-railed – now loops around the narrows to climb up to some pools above the waterfall. A rope has also been affixed at the main, lowest cascade to facilitate abseiling, and the rock walls are now defaced with graffiti down to the water line (though the former piles of litter have been removed).

Just above the Metamórfosis church, another clear if precipitous path leads up to a small, contemporaneous **Byzantine fortress**. There's little to see inside other than a cistern and a badly crumbled lower curtain wall, but the views out to sea and up the canyon are terrific, enhanced in October by a carpet of pink autumn crocus. Some islanders claim that a secret tunnel links the castle grounds with the church just below.

The Seïtáni coves

The coast beyond Potámi ranks among the most beautiful and unspoilt on Sámos; this has been an officially designated refuge for monk seals since 1982, though most recent sightings have been at other points of the island (see box p.332). The dirt track at the west end of Potámi Bay ends after twenty minutes on foot (or five by car), from which you backtrack a hundred metres or so to find the well-cairned start of the side trail running parallel to the water. After twenty minutes' walk along this you'll arrive at **Mikró Seïtáni**, a small pebble cove guarded by sculpted rock walls, with a cave to shelter in. Just under an hour's walk from the trailhead, through partly fire-damaged (but now recovering) olive terraces, will bring you to **Megálo Seïtáni**, the island's finest beach, at the mouth of the intimidating Kakopérato gorge. You'll have to bring food, water and some sort of shade, though not necessarily a swimsuit – there's no dress code at either of the Seïtáni bays, though nudists are prudent to stay away from the summer-cottage end of Megálo.

The monk seals of Sámos

Along with certain remote islets of the Sporádhes in the North Aegean, Sámos is one of the last remaining Greek habitats of the Mediterranean **monk seal** (*Monachus monachus*). Within living memory they were a fairly common sight, even inside Vathý Bay, but their numbers throughout the Aegean began to dwindle alarmingly in the 1960s when steadily reduced fish stocks saw them in increasing competition with humans. Seals can eat nearly their own weight in fish each day and often damage fishnets to get at "ready meals"; aggrieved fishermen have rarely hesitated to kill them, despite their protected status. In addition, the isolated beaches which the seals used to prefer for giving birth have now been invaded by humans, forcing the shy creatures to retire for this purpose to remote sea caves, preferably with a submerged entrance.

Efforts to preserve the severely diminished Samian seal community began in 1979 when the Swiss–English team of Rita Emch and William Johnson, working successively on behalf of Greenpeace and the World Wildlife Fund, attempted to have the area around Megálo Seïtáni declared a natural refuge, with all shoreline construction prohibited. However, the local authorities (in particular the secret police) were unable to reconcile the pair's counter-cultural garb and lifestyle with expensive Zodiac rafts and other sophisticated surveillance equipment, concluding that they were obviously in the pay of a foreign power (ie Turkey). After huge ructions amongst various Greek government ministries, Johnson in particular was declared persona non grata and expelled in October 1982 – ironically just before an official refuge was designated at Megálo Seïtáni. He got his own back in a tendentious but fascinating book chronicling the whole episode (*The Monk Seal Conspiracy*; see p.492 in Contexts).

Conservationists have long feared that the local seals had gone for good – they can swim up to 200km a day if necessary – and that the Seïtáni area would be decommissioned as a reserve and officially opened to roads, power lines and hotels; illegal summer cottages already proliferate at Megálo Seïtáni, and despite strictures from the forest service, dirt roads have crept part of the way down from Kosmadhéï and Dhrakéi villages. So it was with considerable excitement that the spring of 1995 featured several sightings of at least three individuals – including a 1.7-metre-long, several-hundred-kilo adult – basking on pebble coves at the opposite end of the island, near Cape Kótsikas between Vathý and Ayía Paraskeví. Why the seals should have begun surfacing so far from their former haunts is unclear; it may be that they have found inadvertent protection from fishermen's potshots in the regular coastguard patrols mounted to prevent landings of Kurdish refugees from Turkey.

In 2001 a solitary adult was again regularly seen napping on the rocks near the cape, but the local fishermen's attitudes remain hostile, and with Samian seal numbers estimated at fewer than six, the local community is finished as a viable breeding population. If you're lucky enough to see a basking seal, you may find that it will tolerate you from a discreet distance, but on no account should it be touched.

The southwest coast

Heading south out of Karlóvassi on the island loop road, the first place you'd be tempted to stop off at is **MARATHÓKAMBOS**, a pretty, amphitheatrical village overlooking the eponymous gulf; there's a taverna or two, but no short-term accommodation. For that, and most other amenities, you'll have to descend to the coast below, and its several growing resorts.

Órmos Marathokámbou

ÓRMOS MARATHOKÁMBOU, a small harbour 18km from Karlóvassi, has recently been pressed into service as a tourist centre, though some of its original character still peeks through in the backstreets. The port has been improved, with kaïkia offering day-trips to Foúrni and the nearby islet of Samiopoúla, while the pedestrianized quay has become the focus of attention; a curiosity at its west end is one of the island's two sets of traffic lights, controlling entry to a one-lane alley. An indifferent beach extends immediately to the east of the quay, though this improves markedly the further east you go.

The most established place to **stay** here is the seaview *Hotel Kerkis Bay* (Ⓣ02730/37 202, Ⓕ37 372; ❸), also available through Laskarina Holidays; the same company can offer the *Sokratis Apartments* on the jetty, and the hillside *Vigla Apartments* (with a pool). For on-spec, try *Studios Avra* (Ⓣ02730/37 221; ❸), just above the jetty. The four **tavernas** on the quay are pretty indistinguishable – best of these, by a nod, is *Kyra Katina*, with a good range of seafood, if somewhat obsequious service.

Votsalákia

For better beaches continue 2km west to **VOTSALÁKIA** (officially dubbed "Kámbos"), Sámos' most recently "arrived" resort, which straggles a further 2km behind the island's longest (if not its most beautiful) beach. The place's appeal has been diminished in recent years by wall-to-wall rooms, apartments and often rather poor tavernas, plus extensive forest-fire damage of 1993 and 1994, just inland. But for most tastes Votsalákia is still a considerable improvement on the Pythagório area, and the hulking mass of 1437-metre Mount Kérkis overhead rarely fails to impress.

Sunvil and Greek Sun are the main quality British package operators with a presence at Votsalákia. As for on-spec **accommodation**, Emmanouil Dhespotakis (Ⓣ02730/31 258) seems to control a fair proportion of the beds (❸–❹) available here, with most of his premises towards the quieter, more scenic western end of things. Also in the vicinity is *Loukoullos*, an unusual *kultúra* taverna overlooking the sea where all fare is prepared in a wooden oven. Other facilities include branches of nearly all the main Vathý travel agencies, a phenomenal number of **car** and **motorbike rental** outfits (necessary, as only two daily buses call here) and **money exchange**, all catering to an overwhelmingly family clientele.

Psilí Ámmos and Limniónas

If Votsalákia doesn't suit, you can continue 3km further to the 600-metre sandy beach at **Psilí Ámmos** (sometimes Khryssí Ámmos), more aesthetic and not to be confused with its namesake beach in the southeast corner of the island. The sea shelves gently here – ridiculously so, as you're still only knee-deep a hundred paces out – and cliffs shelter clusters of naturists at the east end. Surprisingly, there is as yet little development: just three small studio complexes in the pines at mid-beach, and two tavernas back up on the road as you approach, either of these fine for a simple lunch or supper.

LIMNIÓNAS, a smaller, pea-gravel-and-sand cove 2km further west, is nearly as scenic and more protected; accordingly it's popular with folk messing about in boats, and there seems to always be at least one yacht, cabin cruiser or historic wooden kaïki at anchor. There's a simple **taverna** at the east end of the beach and a smattering of short-term **accommodation**, best of this the

Limnionas Bay Hotel (Ⓣ & Ⓕ02730/37 057; ❸ studios, ❻ 4-person apts, also through Sunvil in the UK), a well-landscaped complex of tiered balconied studio units arrayed around a pool.

Mount Kérkis

A limestone/volcanic oddity in a predominantly schist landscape, **Mount Kérkis** (Kerketéfs) – the Aegean's second highest summit after Mount Sáos on Samothráki – attracts legends and speculation as easily as it does the cloud pennants that usually wreath it. Hermits colonized and sanctified the mountain's many caves in Byzantine times; the *andártes* (resistance guerrillas) controlled it during the last world war; and mariners still regard it with superstitious awe, especially when mysterious lights – presumed to be the spirits of the departed hermits, or the aura of some forgotten holy icon – are glimpsed at night near the cave-mouths.

Greek script table

Sámos	Σάμος	ΣΑΜΟΣ
Ámbelos	Άμπελος	ΑΜΠΕΛΟΣ
Áno Vathý	Άνω Βαθύ	ΑΝΩ ΒΑΘΥ
Ayía Paraskeví	Αγία Παρασκευή	ΑΓΙΑ ΠΑΡΑΣΚΕΥΗ
Ayía Zóni	Αγία Ζώνη	ΑΓΙΑ ΖΩΝΗ
Áyios Konstandínos	Άγιος Κωνσταντινος	ΑΓΙΟΣ ΚΩΝΣΤΑΝΤΙΝΟΣ
Bállos	Μπάλλος	ΜΠΑΛΛΟΣ
Dhrakéï	Δρακαίοι	ΔΡΑΚΑΙΟΙ
Evangelistrías	Ευαγγελιστρίας	ΕΥΑΓΓΕΛΙΣΤΡΙΑΣ
Hóra	Χώρα	ΧΩΡΑ
Iréon	Ηραίον	ΗΡΑΙΟΝ
Kalámi	Καλάμι	ΚΑΛΑΜΙ
Kallithéa	Καλλιθέα	ΚΑΛΛΙΘΕΑ
Kamára	Καμάρα	ΚΑΜΑΡΑ
Karlóvassi	Καρλόβασι	ΚΑΡΛΟΒΑΣΙ
Kérkis	Κέρκης	ΚΕΡΚΗΣ
Kérveli	Κέρβελι	ΚΕΡΒΕΛΙ
Kokkári	Κοκκάρι	ΚΟΚΚΑΡΙ
Koumaradhéï	Κουμαραδαίοι	ΚΟΥΜΑΡΑΔΑΙΟΙ
Kouméïka	Κουμέϊκα	ΚΟΥΜΕΪΚΑ
Koútsi	Κούτσι	ΚΟΥΤΣΙ
Kyriakoú	Κυριακού	ΚΥΡΙΑΚΟΥ
Limniónas	Λιμνιώνας	ΛΙΜΝΙΩΝΑΣ
Manolátes	Μανολάτες	ΜΑΝΟΛΑΤΕΣ
Marathókambos	Μαραθόκαμπος	ΜΑΡΑΘΟΚΑΜΠΟΣ
Mavratzéï	Μαυρατζαίοι	ΜΑΥΡΑΤΖΑΙΟΙ
Megális Panayías	Μεγάλης Παναγίας	ΜΕΓΑΛΗΣ ΠΑΝΑΓΙΑΣ
Mykáli	Μυκάλη	ΜΥΚΑΛΗ

Climbing the peak

Gazing up from a supine posture on the beach, you may be inspired to go and **climb the peak** of Mount Kérkis. The classic route begins at the west end of the Votsalákia strip, along the bumpy jeep track leading inland towards the convent of **Evangelistrías**. After an initial half-hour through fire-damaged olive groves and past charcoal pits (a major industry hereabouts), the proper path begins, more or less following power lines steeply up to the convent. One of four friendly nuns will proffer an oúzo in welcome and point you up the sporadically paint-marked trail continuing even more steeply up to the peak.

The views are tremendous, though perhaps less sweepingly comprehensive than you'd expect since the mountain is rather blunt-topped, and the climb itself is humdrum once you're out of the trees. About an hour before the top, there's a chapel with an attached cottage for shelter in emergencies and, just beyond, a welcome spring that's most reliable after a wet winter. Elation at attaining the summit may be tempered somewhat by the knowledge that one

Mytiliní	Μυτιληνιοί	ΜΥΤΙΛΗΝΙΟΙ
Neohóri	Νεοχώρι	ΝΕΟΧΩΡΙ
Órmos Marathokámbou	Όρμος Μαραθοκάμπου	ΟΡΜΟΣ ΜΑΡΑΘΟΚΑΜΠΟΥ
Pagóndas	Παγώντας	ΠΑΓΩΝΤΑΣ
Paleókastro	Παλαιόκαστρο	ΠΑΛΑΙΟΚΑΣΤΡΟ
Plátanos	Πλάτανος	ΠΛΑΤΑΝΟΣ
Pnáka	Πνάκα	ΠΝΑΚΑ
Pýrgos	Πύργος	ΠΥΡΓΟΣ
Pythagório	Πυθαγόρειο	ΠΥΘΑΓΟΡΕΙΟ
Posidhónio	Ποσειδώνιο	ΠΟΣΕΙΔΩΝΙΟ
Potámi	Ποτάμι	ΠΟΤΑΜΙ
Potokáki	Ποτοκάκι	ΠΟΤΟΚΑΚΙ
Psilí Ámmos	Ψιλή Άμμος	ΨΙΛΗ ΑΜΜΟΣ
Seïtáni	Σεϊτάνι	ΣΕΪΤΑΝΙ
Spatharéï	Σπαθαραίοι	ΣΠΑΘΑΡΑΙΟΙ
Stavrinídhes	Σταυρινήδες	ΣΤΑΥΡΙΝΗΔΕΣ
Timíou Stavroú	Τιμίου Σταυρού	ΤΙΜΙΟΥ ΣΤΑΥΡΟΥ
Tsópela	Τσόπελα	ΤΣΟΠΕΛΑ
Tzaboú	Τζαμπού	ΤΖΑΜΠΟΥ
Tzamadhoú	Τζαμαδού	ΤΖΑΜΑΔΟΥ
Valeondádhes	Βαλεοντάδες	ΒΑΛΕΟΝΤΑΔΕΣ
Vársamo	Βάρσαμο	ΒΑΡΣΑΜΟ
Vathý	Βαθύ	ΒΑΘΥ
Votsalákia	Βοτσαλάκια	ΒΟΤΣΑΛΑΚΙΑ
Vourliótes	Βουρλιότες	ΒΟΥΡΛΙΟΤΕΣ
Vrondianís	Βροντιανής	ΒΡΟΝΤΙΑΝΗΣ
Zoödhóhou Piyís	Ζωöδόχου Πηγής	ΖΩÖΔΟΧΟΥ ΠΗΓΗΣ

of the worst aviation disasters in Greek history occurred here on August 3, 1989, when an aircraft flying out of Thessaloníki slammed into the mist-cloaked peak, with the loss of all 34 aboard. All told, it's a seven-hour outing from Votsalákia and back, not counting rest stops.

Around the mountain

Less ambitious walkers might want to circle the flanks of the mountain, covering part of the way by vehicle and continuing by foot. The road beyond Limniónas to Kallithéa and Dhrakéï, truly back-of-beyond villages with views across to Ikaría, has (except for some short patches before Dhrakéï) been paved the entire distance, making it possible to venture out here on an ordinary motorbike. Bus service is better during school term-time, when these remote spots get visited by a vehicle that departs from Karlóvassi at 1pm every weekday; in summer it operates only two days a week (currently Mon & Fri).

From **DHRAKÉÏ**, the end of the line, a ninety-minute route – almost entirely on waymarked path – descends, with one recovering patch of 1994 burnt forest, to Megálo Seïtáni, from where it's an easy two-hour-plus walk to Karlóvassi. People attempting to reverse this itinerary often discover to their cost that the bus (if any) returns from Dhrakéï at 3pm, compelling them to either retrace their steps or stay overnight at one of two unofficial **rooms** establishments. These are controlled by one or other of the four snack bars/kafenía which may tout assiduously for your custom as you walk through – in particular the priest's wife, Athena Halepi (☎02730/37 861; ❷). For an unusual approach to Mount Kérkis via Zastáni peak, ask for help from the local shepherds.

KALLITHÉA, 7km southwest, can only offer a single, simple *psistariá* on the tiny square and no reliable accommodation at present. From Kallithéa you can follow a newer jeep track (starting beside the cemetery) or walk for 45 minutes along an older trail to a spring, rural chapel and plane tree on the west flank of Kérkis. From here it's a half-hour, path-only walk to a pair of **cave-churches**. **Panayía Makriní** stands detached at the mouth of a high, wide but shallow grotto, whose balcony affords terrific views of Sámos' western extremity. A ten-minute scramble overhead will take you to **Ayía Triádha**, whose structure by contrast is largely composed of cave wall. Just adjacent yawns a narrow volcanic cavern; with a flashlight you can explore some hundred metres into the mountain, perhaps further on hands and knees and with proper equipment.

After these subterranean exertions, the closest spot for a swim is **Vársamo** (Válsamo) cove, 4km below Kallithéa and reached via a well-signposted dirt road. The beach here consists of wonderful multicoloured volcanic pebbles, and there are two caves to shelter in on one side of the bay, plus a single, very welcoming **rooms/snack bar** establishment (☎02730/38 302; ❷) just inland, run by three generations of women.

Sámos travel details

Island transport

Buses

Pythagório to: Iréon (4–5 daily Mon–Sat July & Aug); Karlóvassi (1 daily Mon–Fri, 2 Tues); Pýrgos (1 daily Mon–Fri, 2 Tues).

Vathý to: Iréon (5 daily Mon–Fri); Karlóvassi (7 daily Mon–Fri, 4–5 Sat & Sun); Kokkári (7 daily Mon–Fri, 4–5 Sat & Sun); Mytiliní (2 daily direct, 4 via Pythagório Mon–Fri, 1–2 Sat); Potokáki (5 daily Mon–Fri, 2 Sat–Sun); Psilí Ámmos (2 daily Mon–Fri); Pythagório (12 daily Mon–Fri, 6–7 Sat & Sun).

Karlóvassi to: Dhrakéi (1 daily Mon–Fri Sept–May, Mon & Fri only June–Aug); Votsalákia (3 daily July & Aug, 1 daily June & Sept).

NB All frequencies are for the period June–Sept except where noted.

Inter-island transport

Key to ferry and catamaran companies

DANE	*Dhodhekanisiakí Anónymi Navtiliakí Etería* (Dodecanesian Shipping Company)
G&A	G&A Ferries
HF	Hellas Ferries
ML	Miniotis Lines
NK	*Nissos Kalymnos*
NEL	*Navtiliakí Etería Lésvou* (Lesvian Shipping Company)

Kaïkia and excursion boats

Pythagório to: Agathoníssi (1–2 weekly); Pátmos (4–6 weekly June–Sept); Samiopoúla islet (3–4 weekly June–Sept).
Órmos Marathokámbou to: Foúrni (1–2 weekly in season, by demand).
Karlóvassi to: Foúrni (2 weekly, usually Mon am & Thurs pm)

Ferries

Vathý to: Áyios Kírykos, Ikaría (3–5 weekly on G&A; 3hr); Évdhilos, Ikaría (1 daily on HF; 3hr 30min); Foúrni (2–3 weekly on G&A or HF; 2hr 15min); Híos (2–3 weekly on ML, 1 weekly on HF, 1 weekly with NEL; 3hr 30min–5hr); Kós (1 weekly with DANE; 4hr); Lésvos (1 weekly on NEL, 1 weekly on HF; 7hr); Límnos (1 weekly on NEL; 11hr 30min); Lipsí (1 weekly, peak season only, on HF; 3hr 45min); Mýkonos (5–7 weekly on HF or G&A; 7hr); Náxos (2–3 weekly on G&A or HF; 5hr); Páros (2–3 weekly on HF or G&A; 6hr 15min); Pátmos (1 weekly, peak season only, on HF; 3hr); Pireás (1–2 daily on G&A or HF; 12–14hr); Rhodes (1 weekly with DANE, 1 weekly with NEL; 8hr); Sýros (5–6 weekly on HF or G&A, 1 of these direct; 6–8hr); Thessaloníki (1 weekly on DANE; 16hr).
Karlóvassi: as from Vathý, except no services to Lésvos, Límnos or the Dodecanese with DANE or G&A, but 2 weekly on ML to Foúrni (1hr 30min) and Áyios Kírykos, Ikaría (2hr 30min).
Pythagório to: Agathoníssi (2 weekly on NK, 2 weekly on ML; 1hr 30min); Arkí (2 weekly on ML; 2hr 15min); Kálymnos (2 weekly on NK; 6hr 30min); Léros (2 weekly on NK, 1 weekly on ML; 5hr 30min); Lipsí (2 weekly on NK, 2 weekly on ML; 4hr); Pátmos (2 weekly on ML, 2 weekly on NK; 3hr).
NB From Kálymnos, the *Nissos Kalymnos* provides onward services the following dawn to other Dodecanese islands (see p. 000 for specimen schedule). Miniotis Lines services to Foúrni, Ikária, Lipsí, Arkí, Pátmos and Léros supposedly run year-round, but typically only function May to December.

Catamarans

NEL's *Aeolos Express* links Vathý with Pireás from April to October via a changing repertoire of intervening islands. Total journey time is 6–7hr, depending on the number of stops (if any). Departure from Sámos is either 2pm (autumn) or just after midnight (spring/summer).
Specimen routes:
Vathý–Pireás direct (the most common)
Vathý–Évdhilos–Kéa–Pireás
Vathý–Áyios Kírykos/Évdhilos–Náxos–Páros–Pireás
NB Catamarans do not stop at Karlóvassi, as the harbour there is inadequate.

Hydrofoils

Vathý to: Áyios Kírykos, Ikaría (1 weekly); Évdhilos, Ikaría (1 weekly); Foúrni (1 weekly); Híos (1–3 weekly); Lésvos (1–3 weekly); Pátmos (1 weekly).
Pythagório to: Agathoníssi (2 weekly); Áyios Kírykos, Ikaría (2–4 weekly); Foúrni (2–4 weekly); Kálymnos (3–14 weekly); Kós (3–15 weekly); Léros (3–14 weekly); Lipsí (2–14 weekly); Pátmos (4 weekly to at least 3 daily).
NB All services are with Kyriakoulis Maritime. From Pythagório, during mid-June to late Sept, there will typically be daily morning (7.30–8.15am) and early afternoon (12.30–2pm) services south to the most popular Dodecanese. West- and north-bound services from Vathý are very prone to cancellation.

Flights

Sámos to: Athens (4–5 daily on Olympic, 1hr); Híos (1 weekly; 30min), Lésvos (2 weekly; 1hr); Rhodes (2 weekly, 1hr) Thessaloníki (3 weekly on Olympic; 1hr 20min).

International ferries

Vathý to Kuşadas, Turkey: At least 1 daily, late April to late Oct; otherwise a small Turkish boat only by demand in winter, usually Fri or Sat. Morning Greek boat, 4–5 weekly, takes passengers only; afternoon Turkish boats (usually 2 daily in season) take 2 cars apiece. Rates are €38 one way including taxes on both the Greek and Turkish sides, €43 open return; no day-return rate. Small cars €50 one way. Journey time 1hr 30min. Also occasional (2–3 weekly) services in season from Pythagório, passengers only (journey time 2hr); fares similar to those from Vathý.

NB At present there is no hydrofoil service between Sámos and Turkey.

Ikaría

Ikaría, a narrow, windswept landmass between Sámos and Mýkonos, not surprisingly displays geographical characteristics of both the Cyclades and east Aegean. Except for the forested northwest (now much fire-singed near the shore to clear land for development), it's not a strikingly beautiful island, with most of the landscape being scrub-covered granite and schist put to good use as building material. The mostly desolate **south** coast is fringed by steep cliffs, while the **north** shore is less sheer but furrowed by deep canyons which deflect the road system into terrifying hairpin bends, extreme even by Greek-island standards. Nor are there many picturesque villages, since the rural stone-roofed houses are generally scattered so as to be next to their famous apricot orchards, vineyards and fields, with the community store or kafenío often resolutely inconspicuous.

Though package tourism has arrived at Armenistís, the only resort of consequence, Ikaría overall remains little visited (except by Germans) and invariably dismissed by travel writers who usually haven't bothered to show up. Until the mid-1990s, the islanders resisted most attempts to develop Ikaría for conventional tourism, which still splutters along almost exclusively between July and early September. Though an airport began operating in 1995, with a runway graded across Ikaría's northeast tip to permit approaches in any wind, it wasn't built to accommodate jets – thus no direct charters from overseas.

For years, the only significant tourism was generated by a few radioactive **hot springs** on the south coast, some reputed to alleviate rheumatism and arthritis, others to cure infertility, though a few are so dangerously potent that they've been closed for some time. An unnerving dockside sign, "Welcome to the island of radiation", was replaced late in the 1980s by one proclaiming "Welcome to the island of Ikaros". The island's name supposedly derives from that legendary figure, who fell into the sea just offshore after the wax bindings on his wings melted; as some locals are quick to point out, Ikaría is clearly wing-shaped. (First Test Pilot Icarus has been adopted as the patron of the Greek Air Force – on reflection, a rather inauspicious choice.)

Ikaría, along with Thessaly on the mainland, western Sámos and Lésvos, has traditionally been one of the **Greek Left's strongholds**. This tendency dates from long decades of right-wing domination in Greece, when (as in prior ages) the island was used as a place of exile for political dissidents, particularly Communists; apparently the strategy backfired, as the transportees in their thousands impressed their hosts as the most noble and selfless figures they had encountered, worthy of emulation. At the same time, many Ikarians emigrated to North America, and, ironically, their capitalist remittances help keep the island going. It can be a bizarre experience to receive a lecture on the evils of US imperialism delivered by a retiree in perfect Alabaman English. Of late, the Ikarians tend to embrace any vaguely Left-internationalist cause; posters urge you variously to attend rallies on behalf of Turkish political prisoners, or contribute to funding a Zapatista teacher-training school in Chiapas.

These are not the only Ikarian quirks, and for many outsiders the place is an acquired taste, with loathing and enchantment equally common reactions. Even its most ardent partisans admit that the island hasn't nearly as much to offer as its east Aegean neighbours. If you've spent any amount of time on adjacent Sámos, Ikaría can come as either quite a shock or the perfect antidote, as

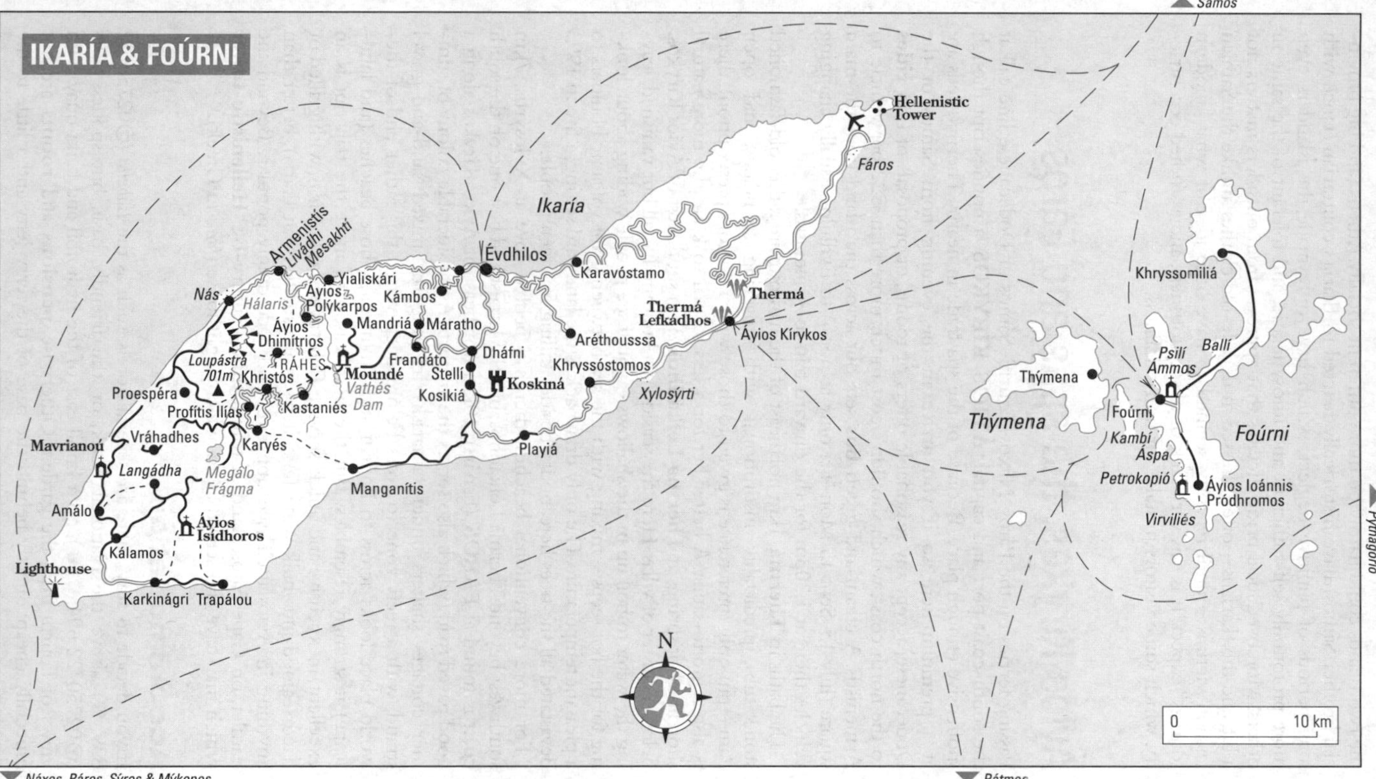

IKARÍA & FOÚRNI
Sámos
Pythagório
Pátmos
Náxos, Páros, Sýros & Mýkonos
Ikaría
Hellenistic Tower
Fáros
Évdhilos
Karavóstamo
Thermá
Thermá Lefkádhos
Áyios Kírykos
Aréthousssa
Khryssóstomos
Xylosýrti
Playiá
Koskiná
Dháfni
Stellí
Kosikiá
Frandáto
Máratho
Mandriá
Kámbos
Yialiskári
Armenistís
Livádhi
Mesakhtí
Nás
Hálaris
Áyios Polýkarpos
Áyios Dhimítrios
RÁHES
Moundé
Vathés Dam
Loupástra 701m
Khristós
Kastaniés
Proespéra
Profítis Ilías
Karyés
Vráhadhes
Mavrianoú
Langádha
Megálo Frágma
Manganítis
Amálo
Áyios Isídhoros
Kálamos
Lighthouse
Karkinágri
Trapálou
Thýmena
Khryssomiliá
Psilí Ámmos
Ballí
Foúrni
Kambí
Áspa
Petrokopió
Áyios Ioánnis Pródhromos
Virviliés
N
0
10 km

the two islands could hardly be more different socially. Athens (and big provincial brother Sámos) have historically reacted to Ikaria's contrarian stance with long periods of punitive neglect, which have only made the islanders even more profoundly self-sufficient and idiosyncratic, and tolerant of the same in others. Moreover, local pride dictates that approval from outsiders matters not a bit, and the Ikarians – often dressed in decade-old clothes, unlike the Samian fashion victims – until recently seemed to have little idea of what "modern tourists" expect. It is this very lack of obsequiousness, and a studied eccentricity, which some visitors mistake for unfriendliness.

Áyios Kírykos, the spas and Fáros

Passing ferries on the Páros–Náxos–Foúrni–Sámos or Dodecanese line call at the south-coast port and capital, **ÁYIOS KÍRYKOS**, a nondescript though inoffensive enough place. Because of the spa trade in nearby Thermá, beds are at a premium here, so if you arrive in the evening from Sámos or the Dodecanese, accept any reasonable offers of rooms, or proposals of **taxi rides** to the north coast, which shouldn't cost much more than €22 per vehicle to Armenistís. A cream-and-green **bus** sets out across the island from the main square (July 15–Sept 15 Mon–Fri only at noon) to Évdhilos, usually changing vehicles there at 1.30pm for the onward trip to Armenistís.

The baths in **Thermá**, 1km northeast of the harbour, are rather old-fashioned stone tubs, predictably institutional with hovering attendants, and open 8am–1pm only (preference is given to those with a doctor's prescription); there is also a grotto-sauna. A better bet for a less formal soak are the more natural shoreline hot springs at **Thermá Lefkádhos**, 3km southwest of Áyios Kírykos, below a cluster of villas. Here the seaside spa building has all but vanished, leaving the water to boil up in the shallows – you'll see people wading about, looking for the hot seeps – mixing with the sea between giant volcanic boulders to a pleasant temperature. The only drawback is the landward setting; a fire in 1993 devastated all the trees hereabouts, besides killing fourteen people.

For more conventional beaches, there's a pebble cove at Xylosýrtis, 7km southwest beyond Thermá Lefkádhos, but the largest and best one on the south coast is found at **FÁROS** (Fanári), 10km northeast of Áyios Kírykos along a good paved road (which also serves the airport). A considerable colony of summer cottages shelters under tamarisks fringing the mixed sand-and-gravel strand, with a reefy zone to cross before deep water; this rather end-of-the-world place looks across to Foúrni and Thýmena, whose beaches (and landscape) it strongly resembles. But the best reason to make the trip out is an excellent, inexpensive and quick-serving **fish taverna**, *Leonidas*, with grilled or fried seafood plus bulk wine (excellent as it usually is on Ikaría), better than anything in Áyios itself (see opposite) and accordingly popular. Beyond the hamlet, on Cape Fáros, stands a round third-century-BC **Hellenistic tower** which may have also served as an ancient lighthouse (*fáros* in Greek).

Accommodation

If you decide to **stay**, there are several hotels, such as the *Isabella* (☎02750/22 839; ❷) above the National Bank, or the friendly, basic but spotless *Akti* (☎02750/22 694; ❶–❸), on a knoll east of the hydrofoil and kaïki quay, with views of Foúrni from the garden. Otherwise, **pensions** and **rooms** are not especially cheap: directly behind the base of the ferry jetty and a little to the west, uphill on Artemídhos, there's the well-appointed *Pension Maria-Elena* (ⓣ02750/22 835, ⓕ22 223; ❸), with sea views. All in a row to the east, the prominently marked *Pension Ikaria* (ⓣ02750/22 804; ❷), the studios (ⓣ02750/22 276; ❸) above the *Snack Bar Dedalos* and the clean *dhomátia* run by Ioannis Proestos (ⓣ02750/23 176; ❷), get noise from the several kafenía and snack bars below. For a full dose of Fellini-esque spa atmosphere, go for the B-class *Marina* (ⓣ02750/22 188; ❸) in a restored older building at Thérma.

Eating and drinking

Eating out, you've even less choice than in lodging. Give the obvious quay-side eateries a miss in favour of the grilled dishes served up at the *Estiatorio Tzivaeri*, just inland from Ioannis Proestos's rooms, or less distinguished *mayireftá* at *Iy Klimataria* (open year-round) just around the corner. The front is more glitzy, with *Casino* the last remaining traditional kafenío; for further entertainment there's a **summer cinema**, the Rex, with first-run fare.

Other practicalities

Hydrofoils, the small Miniotis Lines ferries and kaïkia for Foúrni use the small **east jetty**; large ferries and catamarans dock at the main **west pier**. The three agents for ferry/catamaran/hydrofoil tickets – most useful and comprehensive being Nikos Speis (ⓣ02750/22 397) – can be coy about giving details of the midday kaïki to Foúrni, whose tickets are only sold on board. Three **banks** with cash machines, a **post office** on the road out of town and an Olympic Airways office a few steps back from the quay-esplanade (ⓣ02750/22 214) round up the list of essentials. You can **rent motorbikes and cars** here, too, but there will be better selection and prices in Armenistís.

Évdhilos and around

The twisting, 41-kilometre road from Áyios Kírykos to Évdhilos is one of the steepest and most hair-raising on any Greek island (especially as a taxi passenger), and the long ridge extending the length of Ikaría often wears a coiffure of cloud, even when the rest of the Aegean sky is clear. Karavóstamo, with its tiny, scruffy port, is the first substantial place on the north coast, with a series of three beaches between it and **ÉVDHILOS**. Although this is the island's second town and a daily ferry stop on the Sámos–Mýkonos–Sýros line (tickets from Blue Nice **agency**, ⓣ02750/31572), it's rather less well equipped to deal with visitors than Áyios Kírykos. There are, however, two C-class **hotels** – the smallish *Evdoxia* on the slope southwest of the harbour (ⓣ02750/31 502; ❺), and the low-lying *Atheras* (ⓣ02750/31 434, ⓕ31 926; ❹), with a small pool – plus a few **rooms**, the best of these ones run by Apostolos Stenos (ⓣ02750/31 365; ❶), just west of town. Among several waterfront **restaurants**, the wood-signed *Kafestiatório* between *O Flisvos* and the Blue Nice ticket agency is the most reliable and reasonable option, but for more interesting fare head 1km west of the harbour to **Fýtema** hamlet. Just on the roadside here *To Inomayerio tis Popis* (alias *To Fytema*; Easter–Sept) has lots of options for vegetarians, excellent local wine, low prices and pleasant terrace seating, though portions are on the small side. A **post office** up towards the *Evdoxia*, a pair of **cash machines**, and two good **beaches** just to the east, are also worth knowing about, though the nearer beach will be blighted in the coming years by a new, much-needed harbour jetty.

Kámbos and inland

KÁMBOS, 1.5km west of Fýtema, boasts a small hilltop museum with finds from nearby **ancient Oinoe**, the island's capital in antiquity; the eleventh-century church of **Ayía Iríni** (locked) lies just below, with the remains of a larger fifth-century Byzantine basilica – including mosaic patches, and columns of the carved-stone *témblon* – serving as the entry courtyard. Lower down still are the sparse ruins of a **Byzantine palace** (just above the road), which was used to house exiled nobles, and, last but not least, a 250-metre-long, excellent sandy **beach** with a musical drinks *kantína*. Comfortable, en-suite **rooms** (*Dionysos*) are available by asking at the village store run by Vassilis Kambouris (Ⓣ027 50/31 300 or 31 688; ❷), who also acts as the unofficial but enthusiastic tourism officer for this part of Ikaría, controlling the keys for both the church and a one-room, village-centre museum of finds from Oinoe. Meals are served at a **taverna** that keeps bizarre 10pm to 4am hours (see opposite). More organized **nightlife** consists of the *Petrino* bar above the east end of the beach, with a diet of traditional music at variance with the techno and dub still all the rage in the rest of Greece.

Kámbos is also one possible jump-off point for visits up into the hamlet-speckled valley inland. **STELLÍ** and **DHÁFNI** are attractive examples of the little oases which sprout on Ikaría, while **FRANDÁTO** has a summertime café-bar-ouzerí, *To Anonymo*.

Évdhilos, however, is the start of another, better-marked, route (beginning from the large church) which passes below the Byzantine-Genoese **castle of Koskiná** (Nikariás), just over 15km south. The paved road signposted for Manganítis leads through Kosikiá, just over 9km away, and then for a steeper 2km to a marked side track, along which you can get a sturdy motorbike or jeep to within a short walk of the tenth-century castle. Perched on a distinctive conical hill, this has an arched gateway and a fine, if bare, vaulted chapel in the middle, incorporating ancient masonry.

Beyond this turning, the road creeps over the island watershed and drops precipitously in hairpins towards the south coast; most of this is paved, and with your own vehicle offers an alternative (and far less curvy) way **back to Áyios Kírykos**, in much the same time as via Karavóstomo. It's an eminently scenic route worth taking once for its own sake, the narrow road threading corniche-like through oaks at the pass, and then olives at Playiá village on the steep southern slope of the island; out to sea the islands of Pátmos and Dhonoússa are generally visible, and on really clear days Náxos and Amorgós as well.

Armenistís and around

Most people carry on to **ARMENISTÍS**, 57km from Áyios Kírykos, and with good reason: this little resort lies below Ikaría's finest (if much diminished) forest, with two enormous, sandy beaches battered by near-constant surf – **Livádhi** and **Mesakhtí** – five and fifteen minutes' walk to the east respectively. The sea between here and Mýkonos is perhaps the windiest patch in the Aegean, making this one of the few spots in Greece with anything resembling a consistent surf. The waves – which attract Athenian surfers, boards on cartops – are complicated by strong lateral currents (as signs warn), and regular summer drownings have prompted the institution of that Greek rarity, a lifeguard service. Mesakhtí is so vast that it has no less than three music-bars-cum-drinks-*kantínas* along its length, and on the rare occasions that the sea is calm, the paddling's idyllic.

Armenistís itself is spectacularly set, looking northeast along the length of Ikaría toward sun- and moonrise, with Mount Kérkis on Sámos closing off the horizon on a clear day. A dwindling proportion of older, schist-roofed buildings, plus fishing boats hauled up in a sandy cove, lend Armenistís the air of a Cornish fishing village.

Despite gradual growth it remains a manageable place, reminiscent of similar youth-orientated, slightly "alternative" spots in southern Crete. However, gentrification (and a strong package presence) has definitely set in, and the islanders' tolerance doesn't extend to nude bathing. The long-running, semi-official campsite behind Livádhi beach closed in 2001 – a sign of the times – and probably won't reopen; a few "free-lance" tents still sprout in the river-mouth greenery behind Mesakhtí.

Just east of Messakhtí, the fishing settlement of **Yialiskári** has a handful of tavernas and perhaps half a dozen rooms establishments (look for the signs), with views of a picturesque landmark church on the jetty.

Accommodation

There are easily a score of **rooms** establishments in the Armenistís area, as well as four bona fide **hotels**.

Armena Inn Top of the hill, across the road from Kirki Rooms ⓣ02750/71 320. Spartan, early 1980s block which has private parking, enviable seclusion, unobstructed views and cooking facilities in the rooms. ❸

Atsahas Apartments Far east end of Livádhi beach ⓣ & ⓕ02750/71 226. Cheerful carpeted units with French-windowed balconies offer the best standard and setting outside of the hotels. ❸

Daidalos West edge of Armenistís, start of Nás road ⓣ02750/71 390, ⓕ71 393, ⓔdaidalos@aegean-exodus.gr. The less impersonal and less package-dominated of two adjacent C-class hotels, with an eyrie-pool, unusually appointed, good-sized rooms and a shady terrace for taking the included buffet breakfast. ❺

Erofili Beach Right at the entrance to "town" ⓣ02750/71 058, ⓕ71 483, ⓦwww.erofili.gr. This 1999-built B-class hotel is considered the best on the island; common areas and furnishings are above average (though rooms are not huge, and a tendency to turn the air con off in mid-Sept, whatever the weather, has been reported), and there's a loyal repeat clientele bobbing in a small pool perched dramatically over Livádhi beach. ❻

Kirki Rooms On the town's southeast approach road ⓣ02750/71 254, ⓕ02750/71 083. Pine-and-tile bland but en-suite units, with large private balconies and knockout seaviews. Rooms ❷, studios ❸

Messakhti Village Just above Mesakhtí beach ⓣ02750/71 331, ⓕ71 330, ⓦwww.messakti-village.gr. B-class bungalow complex with a larger pool than Erofili's, and tasteful common areas and large private terraces making up for the slightly minimalist self-catering units suitable for families of three to six. ❻

Paskhalia Rooms Shore lane, village centre ⓣ02750/71 302; winter 010/24 71 411. Rather plain budget rooms are on the small side, but are en suite and good value, with great seaviews (except for two); popular, and usually requiring advance booking. ❶

Eating, drinking and nightlife

Discounting the sweetshops and *souvláki* stalls (a pair each), there are five full-service **tavernas** in Armenistís, of which three have a consistently good reputation. *Dhelfini*, its terrace hovering right above the fishing cove, is the cheap-and-cheerful favourite – come early or very late for a table, and a mix of grills or *mayireftá*. *Paskhalia* (aka *Vlahos* after the helpful managing family), below the rooms noted above, also serves similar fare at its seaview terrace up the hill, and is the most reliable venue for both breakfast and during off-season travel, open until mid-October. Down on the quay itself, *Symposio* is pricier but well worth it for its creative recipes and rich ingredients reflecting the German co-management and chef. Further afield, the *Atsahas*, attached to the namesake apartments, is pretty good as a beach taverna, with generous portions (and bumped-up prices to match) but occasionally undercooked and over-oiled fare. Just east of Mesakthi in the pine-set fishing settlement of **Yialiskári**, there's another cluster of tavernas overlooking the boat-launching slips, of which *Tramountana* and *Kelari* are the most popular, the former purveying superb parrot-fish fry-ups if you strike lucky.

Yialiskári is also home to the area's only **internet café**, Ic@rian-Sea. Several "music bars", often with live Greek gigs, operate seasonally behind Livádhi and at the quay's north end, but for most visitors **nightlife** takes the form of extended sessions in the tavernas and cafés overlooking the central anchorage, or the sweetshops (especially *En Plo*) at the village entrance.

Getting around – and away

Nas Travel and Ikaros Travel are the two main ferry and money-changing agencies. There are now at least four **scooter/mountain-bike rental** agencies in Armenistís; among a like number of **car rental** outlets, Aventura (☎02750/71 117) is the most prominent, with a branch in Évdhilos which could facilitate a self-transfer to east-bound ferries at an ungodly hour (they typically pass by at 4am). Indeed, getting away when you need to is the main drawback to staying in Armenistís, since both taxis and buses can be elusive, though predictability has improved slightly over the years. Theoretically, **buses** head for Évdhilos three times daily mid-June to mid-September, fairly well spaced (typically 7.15am, noon & 7pm, returning an hour or so later), the morning and evening services designed to coincide with west-bound ferries from Évdhilos; Áyios Kírykos has only one through service year-round at 7.15am, though this can be full with school kids in term-time. If you've a ferry or hydrofoil to catch, it's far easier on the nerves to pre-book a **taxi**: ring Kostas Stroupas, ☎02750/41 132, or Yiannis Tsantiris, ☎02750/ 41 322).

Inland: Ráhes and around

Armenistís is actually the shore annexe of four inland hamlets – Áyios Dhimítrios, Áyios Polýkarpos, Kastaniés and Khristós – collectively known as **RÁHES**. Despite the modern, mostly paved, access roads in through the remaining pines (trails shortcut them; see box on p.346), they still retain a certain Shangri-La quality, with mists frequently cloaking the ridges (*ráhes*) of the name, and the older residents speaking a positively Homeric dialect. On an island not short of foibles, **Khristós** (Khristós Rahón in full) is particularly strange, inasmuch as the locals sleep until 11am or so, shop, snack and educate their kids until about 4pm, then have another nap until 9pm, whereupon they rise and spend the entire night shopping, eating and drinking until almost dawn. In fact most of the villages west of Évdhilos adhere to this schedule, defying central-government efforts to bring them into line with the rest of Greece. Not coincidentally, this was one of the main centres of Leftist exile from the 1930s to the 1970s; the irony of daubing "Che", "Lenin" and more elaborate Communist slogans on the rusted shells of East-bloc Wartburgs and Polskis seems to have escaped the locals.

Near the pedestrianized *agorá* of Khristós, paved in schist and studded with gateways fashioned from the same rock, there's a **post office** and a **hotel/restaurant** (☎0275/71 269; ❸), plus asking around will turn up some unlicensed rooms in the ❶ category. After dark up to five other eateries operate, for example *Kapilio* and *Orfeas*, and (in Áyios Dhimítrios) *O Platanos* –

which doubles as the favourite Sunday-afternoon kafenío – but in accordance with the above diurnal schedule, lunchtime can offer pretty slim pickings. The most reliable venue (strictly after 1pm) are the unmarked premises of Vassilis Yiakas, at the far southeast end of the pedestrian way – you'll know it from the enormous antique Victrola and the bare wood floors.

The slightly spaced-out demeanours of those serving anywhere hereabouts – and numbers of old boys shambling nonchalantly about in dirty clothes, with their flies unzipped – may be attributable to over-indulgence in the excellent home-brewed **wine** which everyone west of Évdhilos seems to make: smoky-hued from the *fokianós* grape, organic, strong but not hangover-inducing, and stored in rather off-putting goat-skins. The local festival, with merrymaking and (it is said) controlled substances a-plenty, is August 6, though better ones take place further southwest in the woods at Langádha valley (August 14–15) or at Áyios Isídhoros monastery (May 14).

The **monastery of Moundé**, dating back to the fifteenth century (though the present buildings are 300 years newer), stands 4.5km east of Khristós in a beautiful wooded hollow; take the paved road to Kastaniés hamlet, and continue another couple of kilometres on the dirt road signposted for Frandáto. In summer there will be a warden about, who tends a small **café-snack bar** (10am–7.30pm, no alcohol served) with courtyard seating, and keeps the keys for the triple-aisled church with its interior arcade. Just west, immediately south of the dirt track, lies the little **reservoir of Vathés**, originally dammed in the 1950s and now a designated wildlife reserve for ducks and migratory birds.

Nás

By tacit consent, Greek or foreign hippies and beachside naturists have been allowed to shift 3km west of Armenistís by paved road to **Nás**, a tree-clogged river canyon ending in a small but deceptively sheltered sand-and-pebble beach. This little bay is almost completely enclosed by weirdly sculpted rock formations, but for the same reasons as at Mesakhtí it's unwise to swim outside the cove's natural limits. The crumbling foundations of the fifth-century temple of **Artemis Tavropoleio** (Patroness of Bulls) overlook the permanent deep pool at the mouth of the river. If you continue inland along this, Ikarías' only year-round watercourse, past colonies of "alternative" types defying no-camping signs, you'll find secluded rock pools for freshwater dips.

Back at the top of the stairs leading down to the beach from the road are six tavernas, most of them offering rooms. Among the **tavernas**, *O Nas* doesn't abuse its prime position, operating Easter to October, with a good range of lunchtime *mayireftá*. Among **rooms**, the *Artemis* (☎02750/71 485; ❸) overlooks the river canyon, while all units at *Thea* (☎02750/71 491; ❸) face the sea; both places halve their rates out of season.

The southwest coast

By joining an organized "jeep safari" or renting a sturdy scooter, you can make a tour through several villages at the southwest tip of the island. **VRAHÁDHES**, with two kafenía and a natural-balcony setting, makes a good first or last stop on a tour. A sharp drop below it, the impact of the empty convent of **Mavrianoú** lies mostly in its setting amid gardens overlooking the sea. Nearby **AMÁLO** has two summer-only tavernas; just inland, **Langádha** is not a village but a hidden valley containing an enormous *exohikó kéndro* (rural taverna) used as the venue for the local *paniyíri* on August 14–15, one of the island's biggest.

Walking in western Ikaría

You might well forgo car or scooter rental around Armenistis, as the best of Ikaría lies within a couple of hours' walk from the resort. Since the early 1990s, **walking** between Ráhes and the coast has rocketed in popularity, though as everywhere in Greece, bulldozers and forest fires have reduced the number of attractive possibilities by the year, and additionally on Ikaría paths are poorly marked and used to be jealously guarded as secrets by those with interests in the excursion industry. Since 1998, however, there are at long last locally produced, accurate if somewhat chatty map-guides widely available, as well as a good general touring map (sold in the photo shop at Khristós). The black and white "Road & Hiking Map of Western Ikaria" (€1.20) shows most asphalt roads, tracks and trails in the west-centre of the island; the more closely focused, colour "Round of Ráhes on Foot" (€3) details a loop hike taking in the best the Ráhes villages have to offer. The route sticks mostly to surviving paths, and is well marked; the authors suggest a full day for the circuit, with ample rests, though total walking time won't be more than six hours.

More advanced outings involve descending the Hálaris canyon to Nás, or crossing the island to Manganítis via Ráhes. In either case you'll still need to follow the first portion of the "Round of Ráhes", beginning at the Livádhi road bridge by some discos, climbing up to Áyios Dhimítrios within eighty minutes and to Khristós within 1hr 45min. From Áyios Dhimítrios, it's possible to descend the Hálaris canyon, initially on a steep hillside trail, later along the riverbed, directly to Nás within an hour and a half. From Khristós there's a well-marked trail leading down in forty minutes to a medieval bridge in the Hálaris canyon, where you can fight your way down the stream bed to Nás (some sharp drops, and pools to bathe in), again within ninety minutes.

The main onward path from the bridge, rather intimidatingly signposted "Proespéra 8km, Langádha 22km, Karkinágri 36km", fizzles out in a track system half an hour uphill, on the shoulder of Mount Loupástra. Thus those wishing to traverse Ikaría are best advised to keep on the "Round of Ráhes" route from Khristós a bit further to Karydhiés, from where a historic path crosses the lunar Ammoudhiá uplands before dropping spectacularly southeast to Managanítis on the south coast, a generous half-day's outing from Armenistís.

Other outings for which you'll appreciate an initial vehicle transfer are the hour-plus hike from Vrahádhes to Langádha, visiting 800-year-old troglodytic stone houses en route, or the descent from Áyios Isídhoros monastery to either Karkinágri or Trapálou on the south coast. The trick would be to combine these by closing the short gap between Langádha and Áyios Isídhoros for a proper half-day hike.

It's a sturdy motorbike that gets all the way to **KARKINÁGRI**, at the base of cliffs near the southern extremity of Ikaría, and a dismal anticlimax. One thing that is likely to bring a smile to your lips, however, is the marked intersection of Leofóros Bakunin and Odhós Lenin – surely the last two such forthrightly Communist streets remaining in Greece, not to say all of Europe – at the edge of the village. You'll find two sleepy, seasonal tavernas and a rooms establishment near the jetty. Before the road to Karkinágri was opened (the continuation to Manganítis and Áyios Kírykos has been abandoned at Trapálou, owing to a difficult to dynamite rock face), the village's only easy link with the outside world was by ferry or kaïki. There is in fact still a thrice-weekly post-and-shopping boat from Karkinágri (via Manganítis; Mon, Wed & Fri at 7am, returning from Áyios Kírykos at 1pm), an invaluable facility if you've just made a trek across the island ending here.

Satellite islets: Thýmena and Foúrni

The straits between Sámos and Ikaría are speckled with a mini–archipelago of three islets, of which the inhabited ones are Thýmena and Foúrni. More westerly **Thýmena** has one tiny hillside settlement, at which a regular kaïki calls on its way between Ikaría and Foúrni, but casual visits are explicitly discouraged and there are no tourist facilities.

Foúrni is home to a huge fishing fleet and one of the more thriving boatyards in the Aegean. Thanks to these, and the 1989 improvement of the jetty to receive car ferries, its population is stable at about 1600, unlike so many small Greek islands. The islets here were once the lair of Maltese pirates, and indeed many of the islanders have a distinctly North African appearance.

Apart from the remote hamlet of **Khryssomiliá** in the north, where the island's longest (and worst) road goes, most of Foúrni's inhabitants are concentrated in the **port** and **Kambí**, a hamlet just south. The harbour community is larger than it seems from the sea, with the locals' friendliness adding to a general ambience reminiscent of 1970s Greece.

Getting to Foúrni

The islanders' shopping-and-post **kaïki** leaves Foúrni at 7.30am three days weekly (typically Mon, Wed, Fri) for Ikaría, returning at about 1pm the same day; another twice-weekly kaïki from Karlóvassi (dep 3pm), and the larger car ferries which appear every few days, are likewise not tourist excursion boats but exist for the benefit of the islanders. The only practical way to visit Foúrni on a day-trip is by using the tourist kaïki *Ayios Nikolaos*, which leaves Áyios Kírykos daily in season at 10am, returning from Foúrni at 5pm, or on one of the summer morning **hydrofoils** out of Sámos (Vathý or Pythagório).

Foúrni port

Touts for as many as eight **rooms** establishments meet most incoming craft at the main jetty; however there's nothing stopping you from phoning ahead to reserve space at the more desirable places. About the most popular are the various premises run by Manolis and Patra Markakis (☎02750/51 268; ❶–❷), immediately to your left as you disembark, which offer simple rooms (some with balconies), and superb hilltop studios in a converted old house. If they're full head inland to the plain, 1970s-vintage block of Evtyhia Amoryianou (☎02750/51 364; ❶), whose father Nikos Kondylas meets all boats and is a mine of information about the island, or the bright modern palace of Andonis Ahladhis (☎02750/51 077; ❷), in the westernmost lane.

There are two full-service waterfront **tavernas**: local favourite *Rementzo*, better known as *Nikos'*, where if you're lucky the local *astakós* or Aegean lobster may be on the menu (except from mid-August to January), or the cheaper, less polished *Miltos*, also with good seafood such as the succulent *skathári* or black bream, which thrives in the surrounding waters, or wild (not farmed) *tsipoúra*. For breakfast and home-made desserts, repair to the tamarisk terrace at the Markakis family's café-bar, *To Arhondiko tis Kyras, Kokonas*, under their inn. There's surprisingly lively **nightlife** at a half-dozen musical clubs and ouzerís, often until 5am.

The central "high street", fieldstoned and mulberry-shaded, ends well inland at a handsome square with a traditional kafenío under each of two giant plane trees. Between them stands a Hellenistic sarcophagus that was found in a nearby field, and overhead on the conical hill of Áyios Yeóryios looms the site of the island's nocturnally illuminated ancient acropolis. Nearby is a **post office**, but at time of writing **no functioning bank, cash machine** or any other money-changing facilities – come with lots of cash, or be prepared to make tedious dawn trips to Áyios Kírykos or Karlóvassi with the shopping kaïki. However, shops (including a bakery and pharmacy) are surprisingly numerous and well stocked, so there's no reason to haul in supplies from Foúrni's larger neighbours. Neither is there a need to buy bottled water: the island has plenty of potable stuff from deep well bores, and there are public fountains at each end of the main street. A more worthwhile purchase is the local **thyme honey**: strongly flavoured and very expensive, and likely to be back in production after the heavy rains of 2001–2002.

Southern Foúrni: Kambí and Áyios Ioánnis Pródhromos

A fifteen-minute path-walk south from the port, beginning at the school, skirting the cemetery and then slipping over the ridge with its four restored windmills, brings you to **KAMBÍ**, a scattered community overlooking a pair of sandy, tamarisk-shaded coves which you'll share with chickens and hauled-up fishing boats – and, in season, quite a few other visitors. There are two cheap, comparable and sustaining **tavernas**: Andreas Sklavos' *Kambi* with tables on the sand, and *O Yiorgos* clinging to the side of a valley inland. If you wish to **stay**, try *Studios Rena* (Ⓣ02750/51 364, Ⓕ51 209; ❷), stacked in three tiers on the north hillside.

A path system starting at Kambí's last house continues fifteen to twenty minutes south around the headland to other, more secluded bays of varying sizes and beach consistencies, which like Kambí cove are favourite anchorages for passing yachts. In order of appearance they are sand-and-pebble **Áspa** (with a tiny spring seeping from the rocks just before), **Pelekanía** and **Elidháki** – both coarse pebble. The trail can be slippery and steep in places; some may prefer to arrive on the taxi-boat service occasionally offered from the port. Robust hikers may continue twenty minutes beyond Elidháki to **Petrokopió** (Marmári) cove, so named for its role as a quarry for ancient Ephesus in Asia Minor – you can still see some unshipped marble blocks lying about.

From Petrokopio a faint trail climbs up to the spine of the island, emerging onto the dirt road just south of Theológos chapel. Most of the old ridge path can still be followed south of the chapel, shortcutting the road as it drops to the hamlet and monastery of **Áyios Ioánnis Pródhromos**. There are no facilities whatsoever here except for mineral spring water in the monastery courtyard – and possibly a warm welcome from Papamanolis, the priest. The spring nurtures a tiny oasis, originally planted by a fugitive hermit from Asia Minor late in the nineteenth century, but the monastery itself is lively only around the dates of the local festival (August 28–29).

There are two tiny beaches visible below the hamlet, accessible by steps down to the jetty. Nudists should follow the path uphill from the spring and then down, within fifteen minutes, to secluded **Virviliés** – there may be some goats and tar, but otherwise it's pristine and deserted.

Northern Foúrni: Khryssomiliá and beaches

Heading north from Foúrni harbour via steps, then a trail, you'll find more **beaches**. **Psilí Ámmos**, in front of a derelict fish-processing plant, with a bit of shade and a summer "music bar" at one end, is superior to **Kálamos**, further along the path, which has been ruined by a military watchpoint and the road serving it.

Greek script table

Ikaría	Ικαρία	ΙΚΑΡΙΑ
Armenistís	Αρμενιστής	ΑΡΜΕΝΙΣΤΗΣ
Áyios Isídhoros	Άγιος Ισίδωρος	ΑΓΙΟΣ ΙΣΙΔΩΡΟΣ
Áyios Kírykos	Άγιος Κήρυκος	ΑΓΙΟΣ ΚΗΡΥΚΟΣ
Áyios Polýkarpos	Άγιος Πολύκαρπος	ΑΓΙΟΣ ΠΟΛΥΚΑΡΠΟΣ
Dháfni	Δάφνη	ΔΑΦΝΗ
Évdhilos	Εύδηλος	ΕΥΔΗΛΟΣ
Fáros	Φάρος	ΦΑΡΟΣ
Frandáto	Φραντάτο	ΦΡΑΝΤΑΤΟ
Fýtema	Φύτεμα	ΦΥΤΕΜΑ
Kámbos	Κάμπος	ΚΑΜΠΟΣ
Karavóstamo	Καραβόσταμο	ΚΑΡΑΒΟΣΤΑΜΟ
Karkinágri	Καρκινάγρι	ΚΑΡΚΙΝΑΓΡΙ
Kastaniés	Καστανιές	ΚΑΣΤΑΝΙΕΣ
Khristós	Χριστός	ΧΡΙΣΤΟΣ
Khrysóstomos	Χρυσόστομος	ΧΡΥΣΟΣΤΟΜΟΣ
Koskiná	Κοσκινά	ΚΟΣΚΙΝΑ
Langádha	Λαγκάδα	ΛΑΓΚΑΔΑ
Manganítis	Μαγγανίτης	ΜΑΓΓΑΝΙΤΗΣ
Mavrianoú	Μαυριανού	ΜΑΥΡΙΑΝΟΥ
Moundé	Μουντέ	ΜΟΥΝΤΕ
Nás	Νάς	ΝΑΣ
Playiá	Πλαγιά	ΠΛΑΓΙΑ
Ráhes	Ράχες	ΡΑΧΕΣ
Stellí	Στελί	ΣΤΕΛΙ
Thermá	Θερμά	ΘΕΡΜΑ
Thermá Lefkádhos	Θερμά Λευκάδος	ΘΕΡΜΑ ΛΕΥΚΑΔΟΣ
Trapálou	Τραπάλου	ΤΡΑΠΑΛΟΥ
Vathés	Βαθές	ΒΑΘΕΣ
Xylosýrtis	Ξυλοσύρτης	ΞΥΛΟΣΥΡΤΗΣ
Foúrni	Φούρνοι	ΦΟΥΡΝΟΙ
Áyios Ioánnis Pródhromos	Άγιος Ιοάννης Πρόδρομος	ΑΓΙΟΣ ΙΟΑΝΝΗΣ ΠΡΟΔΡΟΜΟΣ
Ballí	Μπαλλοί	ΜΠΑΛΛΟΙ
Kambí	Καμπή	ΚΑΜΠΗ
Khryssomiliá	Χρυσομηλιά	ΧΡΥΣΟΜΗΛΙΑ
Marmári	Μαρμάρι	ΜΑΡΜΑΡΙ
Petrokopió	Πετροκοπειό	ΠΕΤΡΟΚΟΠΕΙΟ
Psilí Ámmos	Ψιλή Άμμος	ΨΙΛΗ ΑΜΜΟΣ
Thýmena	Θύμαινα	ΘΥΜΑΙΝΑ

At the extreme north of the island, remote **KHRYSSOMILIÁ** still lives in a 1960s time warp, engaged mostly in fishing. It's more usually approached by a daily taxi-boat, as the eighteen-kilometre road in is execrable; only the first 3km out of the port, and the final approach of 2km, are paved. The village, split into a shore district and a hill settlement at the top of a canyon, has a decent beach flanked by better if less accessible ones. Scattered the length of the bay are a pair each of very rough-and-ready kafenía and tavernas; equally simple **rooms** – not more than ten – can be arranged on the spot. It should be said, however, that the locals are pretty suspicious of outsiders and not terribly forthcoming, especially outside of high season.

Should you decide to walk back to town, it's a full three-and-a-half-hour hike from Khryssomiliá to the port. The first two hours are a dreary tramp along the shadeless track, before the old *kalderími* reappears just past the hamlet and isthmus of **Ballí** for the final hour-plus up to the monastery of **Panayía**, which overlooks the town from a ridge to the north. The last section of the path, with two decent beaches in the bay of Ballí below Panayía to the north, are the walk's main redeeming features. Alternatively, you can **rent a bike** (mountain or Enduro) from the one outlet in the port town for the trip, but it's an uncomfortable 75-minute journey riding two-up on an 80cc scooter, and not really worth the effort.

Ikaría travel details

Island transport

Buses

Armenistís to: Évdhilos (3 daily, well spaced, summer only); Ráhes (2–3 daily, summer only).
Áyios Kírykos to: Évdhilos (1 daily Mon–Fri, at noon; connects with 1.30 onward service to Armenistís).
NB Departures can be unreliable except during July & Aug, and schedule times must always be double-checked.

Inter-island transport

Key to ferry, catamran and hydrofoil companies

HF	Hellas Ferries
G&A	G&A Ferries
ML	Miniotis Lines
KR	Kyriakoulis Maritime
NEL	*Navtiliakí Etería Lésvou* (Lesvian Shipping Company)

Kaïkia and excursion boats

Foúrni to: Áyios Kírykos, Ikaría (3 mornings weekly, typically Mon, Wed, Fri; 1hr); Karlóvassi, Sámos (2 mornings weekly, typically Mon & Thurs; 2hr).
Áyios Kírykos to: Foúrni (daily in season, or by demand; 1hr).
Karkinágri/Manganítis to: Áyios Kírykos (3 mornings weekly, typically Mon, Wed, Fri; 2hr).

Ferries

Ikaría (Áyios Kírykos) to: Foúrni (2–3 weekly on G&A or HF, 1 on ML; 45min–1hr); Mýkonos (1–2 weekly on HF or G&A; 3hr); Náxos (2–3 weekly on G&A or HF; 2hr); Páros (2–3 weekly on G&A or HF; 3hr); Piréas (4 weekly on G&A or HF; 8hr 30min–9hr 30min); Pythagório, Sámos (1 weekly on ML; 1hr 15min); Sámos, both northern ports (4 weekly on HF or G&A, 2 weekly on ML; 2hr 30min); Sýros (1 weekly on G&A or HF; 4hr).
NB From late June to early Sept only, G&A provides a service to Rhodes via Foúrni, Pátmos, Léros, Kálymnos and Kós 2–3 times weekly, on one day including an assortment from Níssyros, Tílos and Sými as well. 10–11hr for the full journey.
Ikaría (Évdhilos) to: Foúrni (1 weekly on G&A or HF, low season only; 2hr); Mýkonos (4–6 weekly on G&A or HF; 2hr 30min); Náxos (1–2 weekly on G&A or HF, low season only; 2hr); Páros (1–2 weekly on G&A or HF, low season only; 3hr); Pireás (6–8 weekly on HF or G&A; 7hr 30min–8hr 30min); Sámos, both ports (4–7 weekly on HF or G&A; 2hr 30min); Sýros (1–2 weekly on G&A or HF, low season only; 3hr 30min).
Foúrni to: Áyios Kírykos, Ikaría (2–3 weekly on

G&A or HF, 2 weekly on ML; 45min–1hr); Évdhilos, Ikaría (1 weekly on G&A or HF, low season only; 2hr); Mýkonos (1 weekly on HF or G&A, low season only; 4hr); Náxos (2–3 weekly on G&A or HF; 3hr); Páros (2–3 weekly on G&A or HF; 4hr); Pireás (2–3 weekly on G&A or HF; 10hr); Sámos, both northern ports (2–3 weekly G&A or HF, 2 weekly on ML; 2hr 30min–4hr); Pythagório, Sámos (1 weekly on ML; 2hr 15min); Sýros (1 weekly on G&A or HF, low season only; 5hr).

Catamaran

NEL's *Aeolos Express* calls three times weekly at Évdhilos (c. 10pm–1am) bound for Vathý, Sámos and Pireás, with a stop at Kéa after Sámos once weekly. Alternate days it calls at Áyios Kírykos, bound for the same ports. In the off-season, service may be only west-bound from Évdhilos or Áyios Kírykos, calling at Náxos and Páros prior to Pireás. Journey time to Vathý, 2hr; Náxos, 1hr 15min; Páros, 2hr.

Hydrofoils

Ikaría (Évdhilos) to: Híos, Inoússes, Karlóvassi, Mytilíni; Vathý (1 weekly on KR, unreliably; 4hr to Mytilíni, 1hr 45min to Vathý).
Ikaría (Áyios Kírykos) to: Foúrni (2–4 weekly on KR); Pátmos (2–4 weekly on KR); Kós (1–3 weekly on KR); Léros & Kálymnos (1 weekly on KR, April/Oct only); Pythagório, Sámos (2–4 weekly on KR); Karlóvassi/Vathý, Sámos (1 weekly on KR). Journey times 1hr 20min to Pythagório or Vathý, 4–5hr to Kós (depending on stops).

Flights

Ikaría to: Athens (4–6 weekly; 1hr 20min).

Híos

"Craggy **Híos**", as Homer aptly described his putative birthplace, has a turbulent history and a strong identity. This large island has always been relatively prosperous, in medieval times through the export of mastic **resin** – a trade controlled by Genoese overlords of the Giustiniani dynasty between 1346 and 1566, when they held the island in return for services rendered to the faltering Byzantine Empire, and later by the Ottomans, who dubbed the place *Sakız Adası* ("Resin Island").

Under the Genoese, Hiot prowess in **navigation** was exploited by the scores of ships which called in annually; island legend asserts that Christopher Columbus stayed here for two years, studying with local sea captains, prior to his voyages of discovery. Since union with Greece in 1912, this tradition has re-emerged in the form of several **shipping dynasties** based here, continuing the pattern of wealth. All strata of society participate in the maritime way of life, with many people, including women, serving as radio operators or officers in the merchant navy.

The more powerful ship-owning families and the military authorities did not encourage tourism until the late 1980s, when the combined effect of a worldwide shipping crisis and the saturation of other, more obviously "marketable" islands eroded their resistance. Increasing numbers of foreigners are now discovering a Híos beyond its rather daunting port capital: fascinating villages, important Byzantine monuments and a respectable, if remote, complement of beaches. While unlikely ever to be dominated by tourism, the local scene has a distinctly modernized flavour – courtesy of numerous returned Greek-Americans and Greek-Canadians – and English is widely spoken.

Unfortunately, the island suffered more than its fair share of **catastrophes** during the nineteenth and twentieth centuries. The **Ottomans** under Admiral

Kara Ali perpetrated their most infamous, if not their worst, anti-revolutionary atrocity here in March of 1822, massacring 30,000 Hiots and enslaving or exiling even more. In 1881, much of Híos was destroyed by a violent **earthquake**, and throughout the 1980s the natural beauty of the island was severely compromised by devastating **forest fires**, compounding the effect of generations of tree-felling by boat-builders. Nearly two-thirds of the majestic pines are now gone, with patches of woods persisting only in the far northeast and the centre of Híos.

In 1988, the first charters from northern Europe were instituted, signalling potentially momentous changes for the island. But there are still less than four thousand guest beds on Híos, the vast majority of them in the capital or the nearby beach resort of Karfás and Ayía Ermióni. So far, **tourists** seem evenly divided among a babel of nationalities, including a small British contingent.

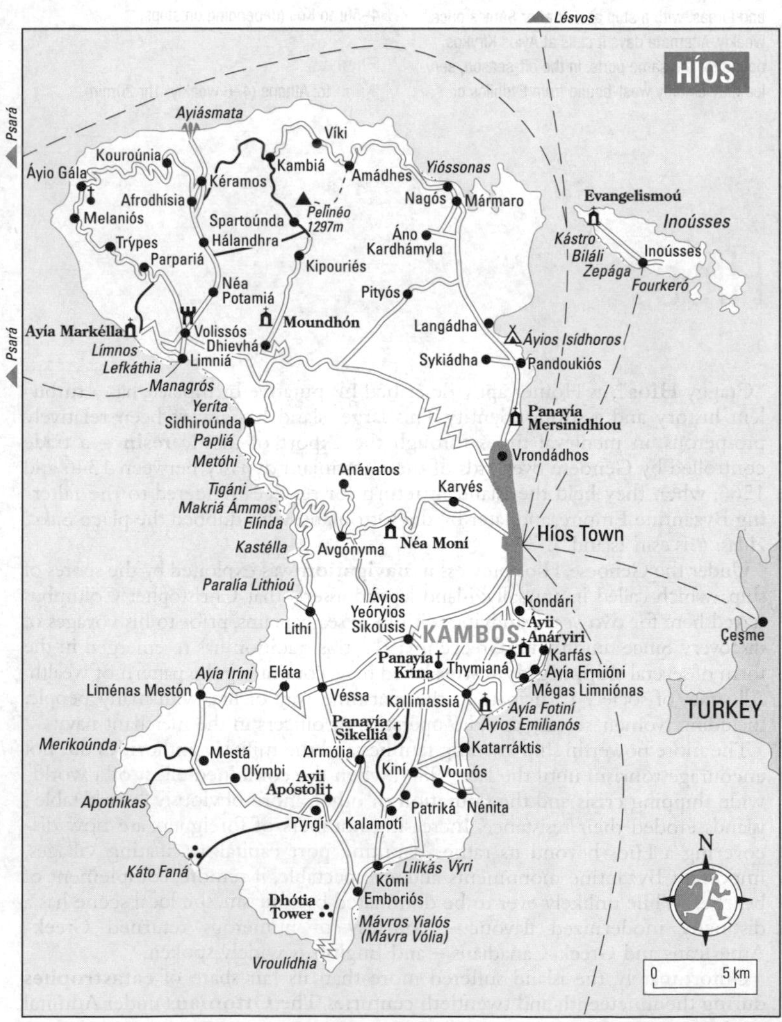

Further expansion has been hampered by the distances and relatively sparse public transport between the port and many of the more interesting villages and beaches, the lack of direct international air links from most countries (including Britain), and the refusal of property owners to part with land for the extension of the airport runway. You often get the feeling, as an outsider, of intruding on the workings of a private club which just happens to have an "open" day. Nonetheless, the provincial authorities have optimistically completed a yacht marina at Vrondádhos, home to many professional seafarers, and existing tourist facilities to date have been pitched at a fairly sophisticated level.

Híos Town

HÍOS, the harbour and main town, will come as a shock after modest island capitals elsewhere; it's a bustling, concrete-laced commercial centre, with little predating the 1881 earthquake. Yet in many ways it is the most satisfactory of east Aegean ports; time spent exploring is rewarded with a large and fascinating marketplace, several museums, some good, authentic tavernas and, on the waterfront, possibly the best-attended evening *vólta* (promenade) in Greece. Old photos show the quay beautifully shaded and paved in red marble; the trees were axed and the marble asphalted over during the 1950s to smooth the rides of imported Cadillacs, but you can still see a few exposed blocks at the water's edge.

Arrival, transport and information

Ferries large and small, plus the infrequent **hydrofoil**, dock at various points as shown on the town map. The **airport** lies 4km south along the coast at Kondári, a €3.50 taxi ride away; otherwise any blue **city bus** labelled "KONDÁRI KARFÁS", departing from the station on the north side of the park, passes the airport gate, opposite which is a conspicuous stop with shelter.

The standard green-and-cream **long-distance KTEL buses** leave from a parking area beside their ticket office on the south side of the park, behind the Omirio Cultural Centre. While services to the south of Híos are adequate, those to the centre and northwest of the island are almost nonexistent, and to explore these areas you'll need to rent a powerful motorbike (*not* a 50cc scooter) or a car (see "Listings" for suggestions). Alternatively, you could share a taxi from the main rank on Platía Vounakioú – they're bright red on Híos, not grey as in most of Greece. **Parking** is a nightmare in town, even where it's not controlled by a pay-and-display scheme; usually the only spaces to be had are northwest of the Kástro walls, along Hándhakos, or at the extreme south end of the harbour, in the side streets behind the *Hotel Kyma.*

The helpful municipal **tourist office** (May–Sept daily 7am–10pm, Oct–April Mon–Fri 7am–3pm; ⓣ02710/44 389) is at Kanári 18, near the Alpha Bank. The conspicuous "Hadzelenis Tourist Information Office" (ⓣ02710/26 743) on the quay can also be helpful, but is a private entity geared primarily towards excursions and accommodation placement. The most accurate **map** of the island available is Road Editions' 1:60,000 product, #211 "Chios", though you're advised to secure it before arrival.

Accommodation

Híos Town has a relative abundance of affordable **accommodation**, rarely completely full, and generally open year-round. Most places line the waterfront or the

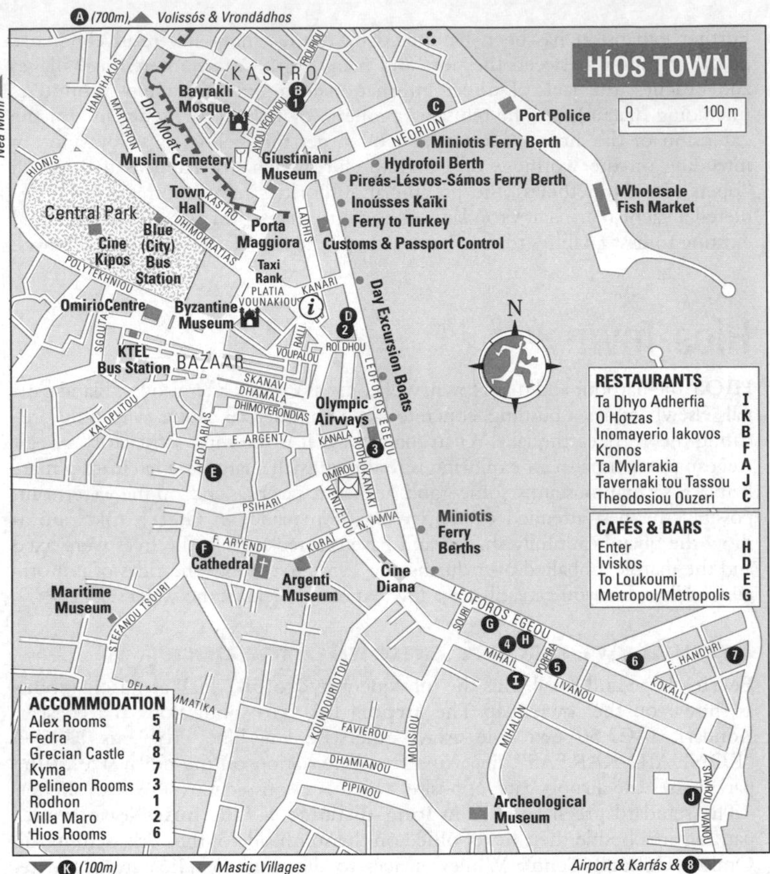

perpendicular alleys and parallel streets behind, and almost all are plagued by traffic noise to some degree – we've focused on the more peaceful establishments.

Alex Rooms Mihaïl Livanoú 29 ⓣ02710/26 054. The friendly proprietor often meets late-arriving ferries; otherwise ring the bell. There's a roof garden above the well-furnished rooms (TV, fans), some en suite. ❶

Fedra Mihaïl Livanoú 13 ⓣ02710/41 130, ⓕ41 128. Well-appointed pension in an old mansion, with stone arches in the downstairs winter bar; in summer the bar operates outside, so ask for a rear room to avoid nocturnal noise. ❹

Grecian Castle Bella Vista shore avenue, en route to airport ⓣ02710/44 740, ⓕ44 052, ⓦwww.greciancastle.gr. Opened in 1996 using the shell of an old factory, and popular with such package tourists as Híos gets, these are Híos Town's top-drawer (A-class) digs. Lovely grounds and a seaview pool, but the smallish main wing rooms, despite their marble floors, wood ceilings and bug screens, aren't worth the rates charged; the rear "villa" suites are far more pleasant. ❻

Hios Rooms Kokáli 1, cnr Egéou ⓣ02710/20 198 or 097/2833841. Wood-floored, high-ceilinged rooms, mostly not en suite but relatively quiet for a seafront location; lovingly restored by proprietors Don (New Zealander) and Dina (Greek), who live on site. ❶

Kyma East end of Evyenías Handhrí ⓣ02710/44 500, ⓕ44 600, ⓦhttp://chios.proodos.gr/kyma. Ensuite B-class hotel rooms in a Neoclassical mansion or modern extension, with TV, huge terraces on the sea-facing side and jacuzzis in some rooms; splendid service and big breakfasts really make the place. The old wing saw a critical moment in modern Greek history in September 1922, when Colonel

Nikolaos Plastiras commandeered it as his HQ after the Greek defeat in Asia Minor, and announced the deposition of King Constantine I. Also available through Greek Sun. ④–⑤

Pelineon Rooms Omírou 9, cnr Egéou ☎02710/28 030. Choose between light, airy and noisy seaview rooms (most en suite), or quiet, poky ones in the back, though we've had complaints about cooking fumes from the *souvláki* bar below. ②.

Rodhon Platéon 10 ☎02710/24 335. The owners can be awkward, and the D-class hotel rooms are not en suite, but it's just about the only place inside the kástro, and pretty quiet. ③

Villa Maro Roïdhou 15 ☎02710/27 003. Modern pension tucked onto a tiny plaza just inland from the water; rear rooms unfortunately overlook the public toilets, but all are en suite, tile-floored and well equipped, plus there's a pleasant breakfast/snack bar on the ground floor. ④

The Town

Although it's a sprawling town of about 25,000 people, most things of interest to visitors lie within a hundred or so metres of the water, which is fringed by **Leofóros Egéou**. When this becomes a pedestrian zone at night, traffic circulates on inland parallel streets such as **Rodhokanáki**, **Venizélou** and **Aplotariás**, the last threading through the main commercial district and off limits to cars by day. **Kanári** links the waterfront with the central park and adjoining main square, officially Plastíra but known universally as **Vounakioú**, to the south and east of which extends the wonderfully lively tradesmen's **bazaar**, where you can find everything from parrots to cast-iron woodstoves. Híos must boast more varieties of **bread** than any other island in Greece – corn, wholewheat, multigrain, "dark" and "village" – and most of these are on sale from the bakers in the marketplace. Like its neighbours Sámos and Lésvos, Híos also makes respectable **oúzo**; the best brand is reckoned to be Tetteris.

The museums

Opposite the Vounakioú taxi rank, occupying the nineteenth-century **Mecidiye Tzamí** (Mosque), the grandiosely titled "**Byzantine Museum**" (Tues–Sun 10am–1pm; free) primarily serves as an archeological warehouse and workshop, awash with marble fragments such as Turkish, Jewish and Armenian gravestones testifying to the island's ethnic diversity in past centuries. Also on view, in the mosque porch, is the top layer of frescoes (1734 vintage) from Panayía Krína (see p.364).

The official **Archeological Museum** on Mihalón (June–Sept daily 8am–7pm, Oct–May Tues–Sun 8am–2.30pm; €1.50) finally reopened in late 1999 after an eight-year overhaul. The wide-ranging and well-lit collection, arranged both thematically and chronologically from Neolithic to Roman times, demands at least an hour or so of one's attention. Highlights include limestone column bases from the Apollo temple at Faná in the shape of lion's claws; numerous statuettes and reliefs of Cybele (the Asiatic goddess was especially honoured here); Archaic faience miniatures from Emborió in the shape of a cat, a hawk and a flautist; terracottas from various eras including a dwarf riding a boar, and figurines (some with articulated limbs) of *hierodouloi* or sacred prostitutes, presumably from an Aphrodite shrine. Most famous of all is an inscribed edict of 322BC from Alexander the Great, commanding local political changes and setting out relations between himself and the Hians.

Near the town centre stands the **Argenti Folklore Museum** (Mon–Fri 8am–2pm, Fri also 5–7.30pm, Sat 8am–12.30pm; €1.50), housed on the top floor of the Koraï Library building at Koraï 2 and endowed by a leading Hiot family. Accordingly, there's a rather ponderous gallery of genealogical portraits, showing – if nothing else – the local aristocracy's compulsion to adopt English dress and artistic conventions in every era. The other wing boasts a hall of costumes and embroidery, kitsch figurines in traditional dress, and carved wooden implements. Among multiple replicas of Delacroix's *Massacre at Hios*, instrumental in arousing European sympathy for the Greek cause, are engravings of eighteenth-century islanders as seen by assorted Grand Tourists.

The **Maritime Museum** at Stefánou Tsoúri 20 (Mon–Sat 10am–1pm; free) consists principally of model ships and oil paintings of various craft, Greek and foreign, all rather overshadowed by the mansion containing them. In the foyer is enshrined the knife and glass-globe grenade of Admiral Kanaris, a native of nearby Psará who commanded the Greek fleet during the events of 1822.

The Kástro

Until the 1881 earthquake, the Byzantine-Genoese **Kástro** was completely intact; thereafter developers razed the seaward walls, filled in much of the moat to the south and made a fortune selling off the real estate thus created around present day Platía Vounakioú. Today the most dramatic entry to the Kástro is via the Porta Maggiora behind the town hall, leading to a little square with an equally diminutive Muslim graveyard (see below). The top floor of a medieval mansion just inside the *porta* is home these days to the **Giustiniani Museum** (minimum Tues–Sun 9am–3pm, may open daily 9am–7pm summer; €1.50, €0.90 Sun), housing a satisfying (and periodically changing) collection of unusual icons and mosaics rescued from local churches. Amongst semi-permanent exhibits are masterly fourteenth-century frescoes of Old Testament prophets from the dome of Panayía Krína (see p.364). Seventy-five Hiot notables were briefly held hostage in the small dungeon adjacent to the museum before their execution by the Ottomans in 1822.

It's well worth having a wander around the old **residential quarter** – formerly the Muslim and Jewish neighbourhoods – inside what remains of the castle walls. Among the wood-and-plaster houses with overhanging second storeys you'll find assorted Ottoman monuments in various states of decay, including a box-like, minaretless mosque, several inscribed fountains, a ruined *hamam* (Turkish bath) and the small **Muslim cemetery** noted above. This contains, among others, the grave of Kara Ali, villain of the 1822 massacres; the rebels had their revenge in June 1822, when a ship under Greek Admiral Kanaris rammed Kara Ali's flagship, blowing it up and killing most of the crew along with the "Butcher Admiral".

Eating

Eating out in Híos Town can be far more pleasurable than the fast-food joints, touristy tavernas and multiple *barákia* on the waterfront (and USA-style pizza parlours inland) would suggest; it is also usually a lot cheaper than on neighbouring Sámos or Lésvos.

Ta Dhyo Adherfia Cnr Mihalón and Mihaïl Livanoú. No-nonsense, competent *mayireftá* and grills, served in the garden during warmer months. Open Sun too.

O Hotzas Yeoryíou Kondhýli 3, cnr Stefánou Tsoúri, off map. Oldest (and arguably best) taverna in town, with chef Ioannis Linos the fourth generation of his family presiding. Menu varies seasonally, but expect a mix of vegetarian dishes (*mavromátika*, cauliflower, stuffed red peppers), and sausages, baby fish and *mydhopílafo* (rice and mussels) washed down by own-brand oúzo or retsina. Supper only, garden in summer; closed Sun; allow €12 each, with local drink as described.

Inomayerio Iakovos Ayíou Yeoryíou Frouríou 20, Kástro. A good balance of well-executed fishy dishes, grilled titbits, cheese-based recipes and vegetables; local white bulk wine or oúzo. Atmospheric garden seating in a vine-cloaked ruin opposite, or inside during winter. Closed Sun, and no lunch Sept–June. Budget €10–12 each; limited seating, so best to book on ☎ 02710/23 858.

Kronos Filíppou Aryéndi 2, cnr Aplotariás. The island's best, with home-made ice cream and nothing but, purveyed since 1929; limited seating or take away.

Ta Mylarakia By three restored windmills in Tambákika district, on the road to Vrondádhos; official address Kaloutá 113 (☎02710/40 412). A large, well-priced seafood selection, every kind of Hiot oúzo and limited waterside seating make reservations advisable in summer. Supper all year, lunch also Oct–April.

Tavernaki tou Tassou Stávrou Livanoú 8, Bella Vista district. Superb all-rounder with creative salads, better-than-average bean dishes, *dolmádhes*, snails, properly done chips, and a strong line in seafood; a bit pricier than usual – allow €15 each – but Tassos' and Tsambika's cooking is worth it. Good barrel wine; open lunch and supper most of the year, seaview garden seating during warmer months.

Theodhosiou Ouzeri Neoríon 33. The genuine article, with a large, reasonable menu, moved in 2001 to large, quieter, arcaded premises from its old spot opposite the main ferry berth. Supper only; closed Sun.

Drinking, nightlife and entertainment

The 1400 or so students at the local technical schools and ecomomics/business management faculties of the University of the Aegean help keep things lively, especially along the portion of the waterfront between the two "kinks" in Egéou. There were once more than a dozen traditional, high-ceilinged, wood-floored, mirror-walled kafenía along the front; now there is just one, the balance replaced by numerous trendy *barákia* more in keeping with the aspirations of younger Hiots.

Cine Kipos In central park from June to mid-September only. Quality/art-house first-run fare, two screenings nightly; watch for flybills around town or enquire at *Pension Fedra*. During winter, the action shifts to **Cine Diana**, under the eponymous hotel.

Enter Just seaward from the *Fedra* hotel. The best-equipped internet café with ten or so terminals upstairs.

Iviskos About halfway along Egéou. This tasteful café is the most popular daytime hangout on the quay, with a range of juices, coffees and alcoholic drinks.

To Loukoumi Alley off Aplotariás 27/c. Old warehouse refitted as a café (8am–2pm), ouzerí (7pm–2am) and occasional events centre. Well executed and worth checking out, but shuts May–Oct & Sun any month.

Metropol/Metropolis Egéou. The longest-lived and most civilized of a string of musical bars on this stretch of the front.

Omirio South side of the central park. Cultural centre and events hall with frequently changing exhibitions; foreign musicians often come here after Athens concerts to perform in the large auditorium.

Listings

Banks/Exchange At least six banks – all with cash machines.

Car rental Three independent, non-chain agencies sit in a row at Evyenías Handhrí 5–7, near *Hotel Kyma*; of these, Vassilakis/Reliable Rent a Car (☎02710/29 300 or 094/4334898, Ⓕ23 205), with a branch at Mégas Limniónas (☎02710/31 728), can be particularly recommended.

Ferry/travel agents Whether for the short hop over to Turkey or long-haul ferries, these cluster to either side of the customs building, towards the north end of Egéou and along its continuation Neórion. NEL (☎02710/23 971) is a few paces south of customs, at the corner of Kanári and Egéou, while Miniotis Lines, at Neoríon 21–23 (☎02710/24 670) or Egéou 11 (☎02710/21 463), operates small, slow ferries to many neighbouring islands. Hiona Travel at Neoríon 13 is the central agent for Hellas Ferries, though these (and the few weekly hydrofoils to Lésvos or Sámos, plus air tickets) are also handled by competent Serafim Travel at Kanári 24 (☎02710/23 558). The Turkish evening ferry to Çesme, as well as the most regular boat to Inoússes (see "Travel details" p.376), is represented by Faros Travel at Egéou 18 (☎02710/27 240).

Olympic Airways On Leoforos Egéou, as shown on map (☎02710/24 515).

Opening hours A Hiot idiosyncrasy is restriction, during summer, of afternoon shopping hours to Mon & Thurs only; on other days, make sure you buy what you want before 2pm.

Nearby beaches: Karfás to Katarráktis

Híos Town itself has no beaches worth mentioning; the closest decent one is at **KARFÁS**, 7km south past the airport and served by frequent blue buses. Since 1988, most of the growth in the Hiot tourist industry has occurred here, to the considerable detriment of the 500-metre-long, minimally shaded beach: massive hotel construction has interfered with natural sand deposition, so that the once gently sloping shore is now steep, rock-studded and seaweedy, except at its far southern end where it broadens out and various watersports are offered.

Karfás practicalities

The main bright spot is a unique and popular **pension**, *Markos' Place* (Ⓣ02710/31 990, Ⓦwww.marcos-place.gr; April–Nov; ❶–❷), installed in the disestablished **monastery of Áyios Yeóryios and Áyios Pandelímon**, on the hillside south of the bay. Markos Kostalas, who leases the premises from Thymianá municipality, has created a uniquely peaceful, leafy environment much loved by special-activity groups. Guests are lodged in the former pilgrims' cells, with a kitchen available; individuals are more than welcome (there are several single "cells"), though advance reservations are strongly recommended, and a minimum stay of four days is required. Also, you should like cats (there are usually about twenty in residence). Virtually the only other establishment shunning package-company contracts is the long-established seaview D-class **hotel**, *Karatzas* (Ⓣ02710/31 180; ❷), midway along the beach, with its own ground-floor terrace-café.

Shoreline **taverna** quality has declined since the late 1990s, so we can make no unqualified recommendations; old favourite *To Tavernaki* at Kondári's scrappy beach, reached from a 90-degree kink in the road at Levkónia district, went under new management in 2001 and may or may not be still be worth a try. On the whole, however, you're better off striking a bit inland. *Ouzeri To Apomero* (open daily), in hillside Spiládhia district west of the airport (go around the runway and follow the many luminous green signs), has lovely terrace seating, live music a few nights weekly in summer, and such delights as cumin pancetta, *garídhes saganáki*, and *sheftalyés* (Cypriot-style meat risolles). Inland, between Thymianá and Neohóri, *Fakiris Taverna* (open all year but weekends only in winter) offers home-marinated aubergine and artichokes, goat baked in tomato sauce and excellent wood-fired pizzas along with well-executed seafood and pork-based *bekrí mezé* in big portions. Until a sign is put up, the easiest way to find it is to head south from Kondári on the road to Kalimassiá and then turn west onto Ayíou Trýfonos road, just before Neohóri, and proceed about a kilometre.

Karfás is well sown with places to rent two- and four-wheelers: just uphill from the beach bus stop, Rabbit Motos (Ⓣ02710/32 501) is recommended for **bikes**, while right across the road MG (Ⓣ02710/31 432, also a branch in Híos Town) is good for **cars**.

Ayía Ermióni, Mégas Limniónas and Thymianá

Some 2km further along the coast from Karfás, **AYÍA ERMIÓNI** is not a beach but a fishing anchorage surrounded by a handful of tavernas and rooms to rent. The nearest beach is a few hundred metres further on at **MÉGAS LIMNIÓNAS**, smaller than Kárfas, shingly and beset by road noise, but more scenic at its south end where cliffs provide a backdrop. Both Ayía Ermióni and Mégas Limniónas are served by extensions of the blue-bus route to either Karfás or **THYMIANÁ**, the nearest inland village. This can offer, at its summit, the atmospheric, untenanted **monastery of Áyii Anáryiri**, with enormous pebble mosaics and thankfully unrestored vernacular architecture. Again, eating options in Ayía Ermióni and Mégas Limniónas aren't brilliant, though in any given season one of the two tavernas overlooking the fishing port is leased to someone fairly competent; during 2001 it was Makarios, who runs the superb wintertime *Pelineo* taverna in Athens.

Ayía Fotiní and Katarráktis

Beyond Mégas Limniónas, the coast road loops up briefly to Thymianá, from where you can (with your own transport only) continue 3km south towards Kalimassiá to the turning for **Ayía Fotiní**, a 700-metre pebble beach with exceptionally clean water. There's no shade, however, unless you count shadows from the numerous blocks of rooms contracted out to Scandinavian tour companies. A few tavernas cluster around the parking area where the side road meets the sea, but there's better eating at the south end of the strand, in the **restaurant** operating in the grounds of **Áyios Emilianós monastery.** Even out of peak season, parking here is mayhem – you'll have to use one of two car parks (one of them free), considerably back from the water. By far the best place to **stay** here is *Apartments Iro* (Ⓣ02710/51 166 or 32 826; ④ in Aug, ② otherwise), large self-catering studios with seaviews.

The last settlement on this coast, 5km beyond Kalimassiá and served by long-distance bus, is **KATARRÁKTIS**, remarkable mainly for its fishing port, pleasant waterfront of balconied houses and handful of **tavernas**. The best of these are at the south end of the quay opposite the boats, where *O Tsambos* is hard to fault for inexpensive fish. Just beyond, on the far side of the dry ravine mouth, *Estiatorio Snack-Bar Meltemaki* is good for *mayireftá*, though out of season the fare tends more towards the snacky end of things. If you're seized by an urge to stay, there's a small, fairly attractive **hotel**, the *Canadian/Kanadhas*, on the front (Ⓣ02710/61 890, Ⓕ61 149; ③), while for a higher standard, go for the *Ostria Studios* a bit inland from the extreme south end of the bay (Ⓣ02710/62 095, Ⓕ62 097, Ⓦwww.ostria.com; ④), with a pool. There are no beaches of any note in the vicinity, but the narrow-alleyed hill villages of **Nénita** (same bus service) and **Vounós**, just inland, are worth exploring.

Southern Híos

Besides its olive groves, the gently rolling countryside in the south of the island is also home to the **mastic bush** (*Pistacia lentisca*). This rather unexceptional plant grows across much of Aegean Greece, but only here – pruned to an umbrella shape to facilitate harvesting – does it produce an aromatic resin of marketable quantity and quality, scraped from incisions made on the trunk during summer. For centuries Hiot mastic was used as a base for paints, cosmetics and the chewable jelly beans that became a somewhat addictive staple in Ottoman harems. Indeed, the interruption of the flow of mastic from Híos to Istanbul by the revolt of spring 1822 was one of the root causes of the brutal Ottoman reaction.

The wealth engendered by the mastic trade supported twenty *mastihohoriá* (**mastic villages**) from the time the Genoese set up a monopoly (the *maona*) in the substance during the fourteenth and fifteenth centuries. However, the demise of imperial Turkey, and the industrial revolution with its petroleum-based products, knocked the bottom out of the mastic market. Now it's just a curiosity, to be chewed – try the sweetened Elma brand gum – or drunk as a liqueur called *mastíha*. Since ancient times it has also been used for medicinal purposes; contemporary advocates claim that mastic boosts the immune system and thins the blood. Whatever the truth about mastic, the *mastihohoriá* today live mainly off their tangerines, apricots and olives.

The villages themselves were the only settlements on Híos spared by the Turks when they put down the local uprising in 1822. Architecturally unique, they were laid out by the Genoese but retain a distinctly Middle Eastern air. The basic plan consists of a rectangular or pentagonal warren of tall stone houses, with the outer row doubling as the town's perimeter fortification and breached by just a few arched gateways. More recent additions, whether in traditional architectural style or not, straggle outside the original defences. All of the *mastihohoriá* lie on the same trunk route, and more or less share a bus service (see "Travel details" on p.376). However, if you're relying solely on public transport, you'll be hard pushed to see the most interesting villages and have a dip at one of the nearby beaches in a single day.

Armólia and Pyrgí

ARMÓLIA, 20km from town, is the smallest and least imposing of the mastic villages. Its main virtues are a **pottery industry** – the best shops are the last two on the right, driving southwest – a free-standing **cash machine**, and the *Psitopolio Klimataria*, open most of the year and most of the day (out of season it can be difficult to find places to eat in the south of the island).

PYRGÍ, 5km further south, is perhaps the liveliest and certainly the most colourful of the communities, with many of its houses elaborately embossed with *xystá*, geometric patterns cut into whitewash, revealing the layer of black volcanic sand underneath; strings of sun-drying tomatoes add a further splash of colour in autumn, when folk also sit at their doorsteps sifting mastic crystals. On the northeast corner of the central square, the twelfth-century Byzantine church of **Áyii Apóstoli** (Tues–Thurs & Sat 10am–1pm) is tucked under an arcade and embellished with seventeenth-century frescoes, with such interesting iconographic deviations as soldiers awake, rather than asleep, in front of the Empty Tomb. The giant Cathedral of the Assumption on the square itself boasts a *témblon* in an odd folk style dating from 1642, and an equally bizarre carved figure peeking out from the base of the pulpit. All this sits a bit incongruously with the vast number of postcard racks and boutiques that have sprung up lately on every thoroughfare, detracting somewhat from the atmosphere.

Pyrgí has a handful of **rooms**, many of them bookable through the Women's Agricultural and Tourist Cooperative (Ⓣ02710/72 496; ❶). In the medieval core you'll find a **bank** (with cash machine), a **post office**, and a few *souvláki* stalls; better to ask at the second storey of the *xystá*-covered kafenío *To Kinotiko* for a mezédhes plate.

Emboriós, Kómi and Vroulídhia

Pyrgí is actually closest to the two major **beach** resorts in this corner of the island. The nearest of these, 6km southeast, is **EMBORIÓS**, an almost landlocked harbour with several decent **tavernas** (*Porto Emborios* has the edge by virtue of such things as *aterína*-and-onion fry-up, local bulk wine and sometimes home-made dessert). The only clue to its former importance as a trading post for the ancient Hiots is a scanty, British-excavated archeological site on the hill to the northeast; though signposted 1km along the road to Kómi, it's

Xistá technique on walls, Pyrgí, Híos

difficult to locate, and all the finds are in Híos Town's archeological museum.

For swimming, follow the road to its end at an oversubscribed car park and obvious beach of **Mávros Yialós** (sometimes called Mávra Vótsala or Mávra Vólia), then continue southwest along an flagstoned walkway over the headland to another, more dramatic pebble strand, partly nudist, twice as long and backed by impressive cliffs. The purply-grey volcanic stones (with the odd orange one thrown in) absorb the sun, reducing reflective sunburn but becoming quite toasty to lie upon.

If you want pure (tan) sand, you'll have to go to **KÓMI**, 3km northeast of Emboriós, also accessible from Armólia via Kalamotí. It's bidding to become a sort of Greek-pitched Karfás, though so far there are just a few **tavernas** (most reliably open out of summer being *Nostalgia* and *Bella Mare*), drinks cafés and summer apartments along the largely pedestrianized beachfront. The *Bella Mare* has some short-term rooms upstairs (Ⓣ02710/71 226; ②), if you fancy **staying**. The bus service is fairly good in season, often following a loop route through Pyrgí and Emboriós. If Kómi's not to your taste, you can head just 2km east to the quieter and more pebbly coves of **Lilikás** or **Výri**.

Coming from Pyrgí, the right fork in the road just before Emboriós leads for 5km past the ruined Genoese Dhótia tower, ending in some hair-raising zigzags down to the 150-metre pea-gravel beach of **Vroulídhia** (sometimes Vourlídhia). The dramatically sculptured volcanic bay, 5km from Emboriós, has views south to the very tip of Híos and Ikaría beyond, but gets packed in summer and has no facilities except for a cistern-spring.

Olýmbi, Mestá and Liménas Mestón

Seven kilometres west of Pyrgí is **OLÝMBI**, the least visited of the mastic villages but by no means devoid of interest. The characteristic defensive tower-keep, which at Pyrgí stands half-inhabited away from the modernized main square, here looms bang in the middle, its ground floor occupied by the community kafenío on one side, and *Estiatorio Pyrgos* on the other, with more elaborate main dishes. The only short-term accommodation is the superbly restored *Chrysanthi Apartments* (Ⓣ02710/76 196, Ⓦwww.chrysanthi.gr), three units suitable for families and available only by the week.

A recently regraded but still unpaved seven-kilometre side road beginning just east of the village leads to the little beach of **Káto Faná**, home to a semi-permanent hamlet of Greek-owned caravans, despite signs forbidding the practice, the stunning averageness of the beach and the lack of any facilities. By the roadside, some 400m above the shore, are the remains of a temple to Apollo, which thus far amount to little more than scattered masonry around a medieval chapel – however, you can see ancient floor paving in the ruins of the baptistry, just below the apse of a larger Byzantine shrine.

The finest example of the *mastihohoriá* is sombre, monochrome **MESTÁ**, just 4km further along the road from Olýmbi. From its main square, dominated by the **church of Taxiárhis** (the largest on the island), a bewildering maze of cool, shady lanes, with anti-seismic buttresses and tunnels, leads off in all directions. Most streets end in blind alleys, except those leading directly to the six gates; the northeast one still has its original iron grate.

If you'd like to stay, there are half a dozen **rooms** in restored traditional dwellings managed by Dhimitris Pipidhis (Ⓣ02710/76 029; ③) and Dhespina Karambela (Ⓣ02710/76 065 or 22 068, or ask at *O Morias sta Mesta* taverna, below; ③). Alternatively, three separate premises managed by Anna Floradhi (Ⓣ02710/76 455 or 28 891; ③) are somewhat more modernized, and like the other two outfits are open year-round, with heating. Of the two **tavernas** on the main platía, *O Morias eis sta Mesta* is renowned for tasty rural specialities like pickled *krítamo* (rock samphire) and locally produced raisin wine: heavy, semi-sweet and sherry-like. However, portions have shrunk of late, wine production is reduced after several years of drought, and *Mesaionas* – whose tables share the square – is better value and has perhaps the more helpful proprietress, Dhespina Syrimis (she also has a room or two, ⓣ02710/76 494 or 76 152, ❸). One or other of these tavernas is open most of the year.

One drawback to staying in Mestá is the dearth of good local beaches. Its harbour, **LIMÉNAS MESTÓN** (formerly Passá Limáni), 3km north, has no beach of any sort and has come down considerably in the world since ferry boats ceased calling here in the late 1980s. There's no longer anywhere to stay short-term, and Limáni is only worth a visit for its two **tavernas**, which have fish in the right season. The closest beach of any description is surf-battered, facility-less **Merikoúnda**, 4km west of Mestá by dirt track; **Apothíkas**, 5km southwest, is more sheltered and a better bet.

Central Híos

The portion of Híos extending west and southwest from Híos Town matches the south in terms of interesting monuments, and good roads (being improved still further with EU funding) make touring under your own power an easy matter. There are also several beaches on the far shore of the island, which, though not necessarily the best on Híos (see "Northern Híos", p.366), are fine for a dip in the course of a day's touring.

The Kámbos

The **Kámbos**, a vast, fertile plain carpeted with citrus groves, extends southwest from Híos Town almost as far as the village of Halkío. This district was originally settled (and planted with orchards) by the Genoese during the fourteenth century, and remained a preserve of the local aristocracy until 1822. Exploring it with a bicycle or motorbike is apt to be less frustrating than going by car, since the web of narrow, poorly marked lanes sandwiched between high walls guarantee disorientation and frequent backtracking. Behind the walls you catch fleeting glimpses of ornate old mansions built from locally quarried sandstone, masoned so that blocks with varying shades alternate. Courtyards are paved either in pebbles or a checkerboard pattern of tiles, most still dominated by a pergola-shaded irrigation pond and a *mánganos* or water wheel used to draw the water from wells up to 30m deep, once donkey-powered but now electrically propelled.

Practicalities

Many of Kámbos' sumptuous three-storey dwellings, constructed in a hybrid Italo-Turko-Greek style unique in the country, have languished in ruins since 1881, but an increasing number are being converted for use as private estates or unique **accommodation**. The best and most consistently attended of these is *Mavrokordatiko* (ⓣ02710/32 900, ⓕ32 902, ⓦwww.mavrokordatiko.com; ❻), about 1.5km south of the airport on Mitaráki, with enormous heated, wood-panelled rooms and breakfast (included) served by the *mánganos* courtyard.

Runner-up is the well-signposted *Perivoli* at Aryéndi 11 (ⓣ02710/31 513, ⓕ32 042; ❷–❹), supposedly open year-round, though generally monopolized by package companies in season. The rooms, no two alike, are mostly en suite and equipped with fireplaces and sofas. The attached garden restaurant has recently gone under new management, with a new dining format, and should be approached tentatively.

Panayía Krína and Panayía Sikelliá

Not strictly speaking in Kámbos, but most easily reached from it en route from Híos Town to the *mastihohoriá*, are two outstanding rural Byzantine monuments.

The eleventh-century Byzantine church of **Panayía Krína**, isolated amidst orchards and woods, is well worth negotiating a maze of paved but poorly marked lanes from the village of Vavýli, 9km out of town. It's closed indefinitely for snail's-pace restoration, but a peek through the apse window will give you a fair idea of the finely frescoed interior, sufficiently lit by a twelve-windowed drum. Works to date consist largely of removing at least two layers of post-Byzantine images to expose the original thirteenth- and fourteenth-century work; some of these later images can be seen in Híos Town's Byzantine and Giustiani museums (see pp.355–356). Specialists and art students can make arrangements for a full visit by contacting archeologist Olga Vassi at the Third Ephorate of Byzantine Antiquities (☎02710/44 238, Mon–Fri 9am–1.30pm), or make initial enquiries at the Giustiniani Museum if your Greek isn't up to it. The cloisonné (alternating brick- and stonework) of the exterior alone justifies the trip here, though architectural harmony is marred by the later addition of a clumsy secondary cupola over the narthex, and the visibly unsound structure is kept from collapse by cable-binding at the roofline.

The monastic church of **Panayía Sikelliá** is much easier to find, visible from afar in its dramatic clifftop setting south of Tholopotámi, beyond which the three-kilometre dirt access road leading to it is well signposted. Roughly contemporaneous with Panayía Krína, Sikelliá is best visited near sunset, when the cloisonné surface of its blind arches acquires a golden tone. There's nothing much to see inside other than a fine, carved *témblon* and a peculiar late fresco of John the Divine, so it's not essential to time your visit to coincide with that of the key-keeper, who may appear at dusk. Except for the festival on September 7–8, you're likely to have the atmospheric premises to yourself; the monastery outbuildings, save for a perimeter wall and a few fortifications above, have long since vanished, but it's worth climbing the latter for views over the adjacent ravine and the entire south of the island.

Néa Moní

Almost exactly in the middle of the island, the monastery of **Néa Moní** was founded in 1042 by the Byzantine emperor Constantine Monomahos IX (The Dueller) on the spot where a wonder-working icon had been discovered. It ranks as one of the most beautiful and important monuments on any of the Greek islands; the mosaics, together with those of Dháfni and Ósios Loukás on the mainland, are among the finest surviving art of their age to be found in Greece, and the setting – high up in still partly forested mountains 15km west of the port – is no less memorable.

Once a powerful and independent community of six hundred monks, Néa Moní was pillaged during 1822 and most of its residents put to the sword; many of its outbuildings have languished in ruins since then, though a recent EU grant has prompted massive restoration work. The 1881 tremor caused comprehensive damage, while exactly a century later a forest fire threatened to engulf the place until the resident icon was paraded around the perimeter wall, miraculously repelling the flames. Today the monastery, with its giant refectory and vaulted water cisterns, is inhabited by just a couple of lay workers; the last tenants, two elderly, frail nuns, died recently, and Néa Moní will reportedly be taken over by monks in the future.

Visiting the monastery

Bus excursions (around €12) are provided by the KTEL on Tuesday and Friday mornings in summer, continuing to Anávatos, Lithí and Armólia; otherwise come by motorbike, or walk from Karyés, 7km northeast, to which there is a regular blue-bus service. **Taxis** from town, however, are not prohibitive at about €15 round trip per carload, including a wait while you look around.

Just inside the main gate (daily 8am–1pm & 4–8pm) stands a **chapel ossuary** containing some of the bones of those who met their death here in 1822; axe-clefts in children's skulls attest to the savagery of the attackers. Further along on the right, upstairs, is a small **museum** (Tues–Sun 8am–1pm; €1.50) devoted to ecclesiastical articles and the history of the monastery.

But you have come principally to see the *katholikón*, whose cupola, resting on an octagonal drum, is of a design seen elsewhere only in Cyprus; the frescoes in the exonarthex are comprehensively damaged by holes allegedly made by Turkish bullets, but the **mosaics** further inside are well preserved. The narthex contains portrayals of the various saints of Híos sandwiched between the *Niptir* (Christ Washing the Disciples' Feet) and *Judas' Betrayal*, in which the critical kiss has unfortunately been smudged out, but Peter is clearly visible lopping off the ear of the high priest's servant. In the dome of the sanctuary (currently obscured by scaffolding), which once contained a complete life cycle of Christ, only the *Baptism*, a partial *Crucifixion*, the *Descent from the Cross*, the *Resurrection* and the evangelists *Mark* and *John* survived the earthquake. But the *Baptism* and *Resurrection* in particular are exceptionally expressive and go a considerable way to justifying Néa Moní's claim to high rank among works of Byzantine art.

Avgónyma and Anávatos

With your own transport, you can proceed 5km west of Néa Moní to **AVGÓNYMA**, a cluster of dwellings on a knoll above the coast; the name means "Clutch of Eggs", an apt description when it's viewed from the ridge above. Since the 1980s, the place has been almost totally restored as a summer haven by descendants of the original villagers, though the permanent population is just seven. A returned Greek-American family runs a reasonable, simple-fare **taverna**/kafenío, *O Pyrgos*, in an arcaded mansion on the main square; co-mananged *To Arhondiko* and *To Asteria* at the outskirts have less reliable opening hours, and uneven food quality. The classiest **accommodation** option here is *Spitakia*, a cluster of small restored houses for up to five people (Ⓣ02710/20 513 or 094/5569787, Ⓕ43 052, Ⓔmissetzi@otenet.gr; ④). Alternatively, *O Pyrgos* also offers a few simpler rooms (Ⓣ02710/42 175; ④, but ③ for longer stays).

A paved side road continues another 4km north to **ANÁVATOS**, whose empty, dun-coloured dwellings, soaring above pistachio orchards, are almost indistinguishable from the 300-metre-high bluff on which they're built. During the 1822 insurrection, some four hundred inhabitants and refugees threw themselves over this cliff rather than surrender to the besieging Ottomans, and it's still a preferred suicide leap. Anávatos can now only muster two permanent inhabitants, and given a lack of accommodation, plus an eerie, traumatized atmosphere, it's no place to be stranded at dusk – though there's a very good **taverna**, *Anavatos*, at the village entrance (lunch most of the year, supper in summer). The ground is too hard to pass pipes through, and the archeological service administers the place, factors which together ensure there will be no renaissance here à la Avgónyma – though for some obscure reason archeologists *are* restoring the summit kástro (open sporadically 10am–2pm daily while works progress).

The west coast

West of Avgónyma, the main road descends 6km to the coast in well-graded loops. Turning right (north) at the junction leads first to the much-advertised beach at **Elínda**, which, though alluring from afar, has a rocky shore and murky waters. You're better off continuing towards the more secluded sand-and-gravel coves of **Tigáni** and **Makriá Ámmos** slightly northwest, probably the best this coast has to offer; there's some reef at the latter, but this drops away as you proceed east along the beach. Just north of here, **Metóhi** bay has an average beach and a seasonal fish taverna; below **SIDHIROÚNDA**, the only village hereabouts (a single **taverna**) with views over the entire west Hian shore thanks to the spectacular hilltop setting, there are more beaches, the most sheltered being **Papaliá** and **Yeríta**.

All along this coast, as far southwest as Limáni Mestón, loom round **watch-towers** erected by the Genoese to look out for pirates; one of these has lent its name to **Kastélla** (officially Trahíli), the first sand-and-gravel cove you reach by turning left from the junction. This is attractive enough, with clean water offshore, but the short side road down is rough and the beach – like the entire area – subject to periodic wasp infestations.

Lithí and Véssa

Sparse, weekday-only bus service resumes 9km south of the coastal junction at **LITHÍ**, a friendly village of whitewashed buildings perched on a forested ledge overlooking the sea. There are tavernas and kafenía near the bus turnaround area, but most visitors head 2km downhill to the hard-packed, often windswept beach of **Paralía Lithioú**, despite its shortcomings a favourite weekend target of Hiot townees. They come mainly for the sake of two adjacent fish **tavernas** at the far end, the better of these *Ta Tria Adherfia*; the other (*Kyra Despina*) has a few **rooms** (ⓣ02710/73 373; ❸).

Some 5km south of Lithí, the valley-bottom village of **VÉSSA** is an unsung gem, more open and less casbah-like than Mestá or Pyrgí, but still homogeneous. Its honey-coloured buildings are arrayed in a vast grid punctuated by numerous belfries; there's a simple taverna (*Snack Bar Evanemos*) installed on the ground floor of a tower-mansion on the main through-road, and you can **stay** at a restored inn, *Nestoras Mereos* (ⓣ02710/25 016 or 73 320; ❹). Your last chance for a swim near Véssa is provided by a series of sandy bays along the sixteen-kilometre road west to Liménas Mestón, but of these only **Ayía Iríni** has a seasonal taverna, and all suffer from exposure to the northerly winds.

Northern Híos

Northern Híos never really recovered from the Turkish massacre, and the desolation left by fires in 1981 and 1987 will further dampen inquisitive spirits. Since the early 1900s, its villages have been all but deserted for much of the year, which means correspondingly sparse bus services. About one-third of the former population now lives in Híos Town, venturing out here only at major festivals or to tend grapes and olives, for at most four months of the year. Others, based in Athens or North America, return to their ancestral homes for just a few intense weeks in midsummer, when marriages are arranged between local families and heritable properties thus consolidated.

The road to Kardhámyla

Blue city buses (labelled "DHASKALÓPETRA" or "Teacher's Rock") run north from Híos Town only up to **VRONDÁDHOS**, an elongated coastal suburb that's a favourite residence of the island's many seafarers. Homer legendarily lived and taught here (thus the bus-front signs), and in terraced parkland just above the little fishing port and pebble beach (mostly local bathers) you can visit what is traditionally claimed to be his lectern, but is more probably an ancient altar of Cybele and is now signposted as such. An adjacent modern amphitheatre amidst the greenery serves as a pleasant venue for summer evening concerts.

If you have your own transport, you can make a stop 2km further along at the monastery of **Panayía Mersinidhíou** (Myrtidhiótissis) – of little intrinsic interest but notable for its photogenic setting overlooking the sea, best at first light. After another 5km, the route swoops down to the tiny bayside hamlet of **PANDOUKIÓS**, bereft of amenities but recently grown in economic importance owing to several offshore fish nurseries. A side road just north leads to stony **Áyios Isídhoros** cove, the rather inconvenient location of the island's only official (and at best sporadically open) **campsite** (ⓣ02710/74 111), though the site itself is shaded and faces Inoússes islet across the water.

Langádha and Pityós

LANGÁDHA, just beyond, is probably the first point on the eastern coast road where you'd be tempted to stop. Set at the mouth of a deep valley, this attractive little harbour looks across its bay to a pine grove, and beyond to Turkey. There is a handful of rooms establishments, but most night-time visitors come for the sustaining seafood at two adjacent **tavernas** at the start of the quay, *Tou Kopelou* (aka *Stelios'*), whose good cooking belies the rather dreary inside decor, and second-choice *Paradhisos*. The rest of the esplanade supports a pair each of bars and fancy cafés of the sort that are now *de rigueur* in Greece. There is no proper beach anywhere nearby; the bay of Dhelfíni, just north, is an off-limits naval base.

Just beyond Langádha, an important side road leads 5km up and inland to **PITYÓS** (formerly Pityoús), an oasis in a mountain pass presided over by a Byzantine tower-keep; people come here from some distance to **dine** at *Makellos* on the west edge of the village, a shrine of local cuisine (daily June–Sept, Fri–Sun eves only Oct–May). Continuing 4km further will bring you to a junction allowing quick access to the west of the island and the Volissós area (see p.370).

Kardhámyla and around

From Langádha most traffic proceeds to **ÁNO KARDHÁMYLA** and **KÁTO KARDHÁMYLA**, the latter 37km out of Híos Town. Positioned at opposite edges of a fertile plain rimmed by mountains, they initially come as welcome relief from Homer's crags. Káto, better known as **MÁRMARO**, is larger, indeed the island's second town, with a bank, post office and a filling station (one of just two in the north of Híos).

Water for Híos: *not* in the pipeline

Travellers may wonder about the silver **pipeline** that runs parallel to most of the road between Híos Town and Kardhámyla. Begun in 1990, this was supposed to solve a chronic **water shortage** in the south of the island by tapping the spring at Nagós. However, nobody bothered to measure the flow volume at Nagós to confirm that it was sufficient for a town of 25,000 (it wasn't); meanwhile, freshwater undersea springs at Pandoukiós, which well up visibly in the bay at a pressure of several atmospheres, were ignored. Second, the pipeline follows the highway rather than the most direct route, so that the contractors could make more on the materials. Finally, the pipes were lined internally with an asbestos-laced resin, which under the typically torrid conditions en route dissolved into the paltry amount of water that trickled through when the tap was finally opened in 1992. Nearly 500 million drachmas (then over £1.5 million) in public funds were wasted on the project, with nothing to show for it but a useless aqueduct that's slowly disintegrating pending bids for the fresh contract to haul the mess away. All in all, it's a sad monument to the debilitating corruption that still besets provincial Greece in particular, years after the fall of the junta and subsequent accession to the EU.

However, there is little to attract a casual visitor other than pastel-painted Neoclassical architecture in the hillside neighbourhoods of Ráhi and Perivoláki: the quay and port, mercilessly exposed to the *meltémi*, is strictly businesslike, and there are few tourist facilities worth mentioning. One exception is the *Hotel Kardamyla* (Ⓣ02720/23 353; ❻ Aug, ❹ otherwise), co-managed with Híos Town's *Hotel Kyma*. It has the bay's only pebble beach, and its restaurant is a reliable source of lunch (July–Aug) if you're touring. Worthwhile independent **tavernas** include *"Snack Bar" Irini Tsirigou*, by the port authority, or *Iy Vlyhadha*, facing the eponymous bay west over the headland, featuring fresh squid and locally produced suckling pig.

Nagós

For better swimming head west – by car from the signposted junction by the church, on foot past the harbour-mouth windmill for an hour along a cemented coastal driveway – to **NAGÓS**, a gravel-shore bay at the foot of an oasis. Lush greenery is nourished by active springs up at a bend in the road, enclosed in a sort of grotto and flanked by a *psistariá*, all overhung by tall cliffs. The placename is a corruption of *naós*, after a large Poseidon temple that once stood near the springs, but centuries of pilfering and orchard-tending, plus organized excavations after 1912, mean that nothing remains visible. Down at the shore the swimming is good, if a bit chilly courtesy of the spring water; here you'll also find two rather mediocre tavernas, plus a few rooms. Your only chance of relative solitude in July or August lies fifteen minutes' walk west at **Yióssonas**, a much longer beach, but less sheltered, rockier and with no facilities.

Northwestern villages

Few outsiders venture beyond Yióssonas, and only two daily summer buses cover the distance between Mármaro and Kambiá village, 20km west. Along the way, Amádhes and Víki are attractive enough villages at the base of 1297-metre **Pelinéo**, the island's summit, most easily climbed from Amádhes – a five-hour round trip. **KAMBIÁ**, overlooking a ravine strewn with the remains of a chapel, has very much an end of the line feel, although a partly paved road heads 5km south towards Spartoúnda, and far worse tracks (jeeps only) venture west through lush valleys to the villages of Kéramos and Afrodhísia. The track heading west from just south of Spartoúnda towards Hálandhra is also pretty horrid, but from Spartoúnda a paved road resumes for the remaining 15km to the intersection with the main trans-island road bound for Volissós. About halfway, well signposted outside the village of **KIPOURIÉS**, there's a superb **psistariá** well placed for a meal stop while touring: *Iy Petrini Platia*, set in a fountain-nourished oasis. It's open daily June to mid-September, but weekends only off season (including winter); ring ⓣ02740/21 672 to make sure, as it's a long trip out.

The monastery of Moundhón

About 5km south of Kipouriés, near the village of Dhievhá, you can make a detour to the engagingly set sixteenth-century **monastery of Moundhón**, second in rank to Néa Moní before its partial destruction in 1822. For admittance to the locked grounds, seek out the warden, Yiorgos Fokas, in Dhievhá itself (ⓣ02740/22 011). The highlight is the *katholikón* with its naïve interior frescoes, the best one depicting the *Ouranódhromos Klímax* (Stairway to Heaven, not to be confused with Led Zeppelin's): a trial by ascent, in which ungodly priests are beset by demons hurling them into the mouth of a great serpent symbolizing the Devil, while the righteous clergy are assisted upwards by angels. In an era when illiteracy was the norm, such panels were intended quite literally to scare the hell out of simple parishioners.

Ayiásmata and around

If you're on foot in Kambiá, ask at one of the kafenía by the main church for directions to the start of a one-hour path across the canyon to the abandoned hamlet of Agrelopó; from the church here a system of jeep tracks leads in another ninety minutes to the tumbledown pier and seaweed-strewn beach at **AYIÁSMATA**. This is one of the strangest spots on Híos, consisting of perhaps twenty buildings (four of them churches), including the miraculous indoor hot springs after which the place is named. The **spa**, a rather soulless, jail-like modern compound, tends to be packed out by unwell islanders for weeks at a time in summer, but is relatively desolate out of season.

Paved roads south from Ayiásmata pass through strikingly beautiful countryside up to the villages of Kéramos and **AFRODHÍSIA**, the latter the more attractive. Here the surfaced road system splits: the southerly turning continues south through Hálandhra and **NÉA POTAMIÁ**, the latter an ugly prefab village built to replace an older one destroyed by landslide. From here it's another 20km to Volissós.

The northwest coast

More worthwhile is the northwesterly turning from Afrodhísia which takes you along a corniche route, running parallel to, but high above the coast, with views out to Lésvos (weather permitting) and Psará. **KOUROÚNIA**, 6km along, is beautifully arranged in two separate neighbourhoods and set amid thick forest.

After 10km more, you reach **ÁYIO GÁLA**, whose claim to fame is a **grotto church** complex, built into a stream-lapped palisade at the bottom of the village. Approaching the village from the south, signs ("Panayía Ayiogaloúsena") point to a lane crossing the water but, for access, except at the festival on August 23, you'll need to find the key-keeper (ask in the village) and descend to the complex from a flight of stairs leading down from a eucalyptus tree. Of the two churches inside the cave, the larger, at the mouth of the complex, dates from the fifteenth century but seems rather newer externally since a 1993 renovation. Inside, a fantastically intricate *témblon* vies for your attention with a tinier, older, freestanding chapel, built entirely within the rear of the cavern. Its fifteenth-century frescoes are badly smudged, except for one in the apse depicting a wonderfully mysterious and mournful Virgin, surely the saddest in Christendom, holding a knowing Child.

Beyond Áyio Gála, bleak scenery is redeemed mostly by fantastic sunset views across to Psará, but overshadowed by a huge, unaesthetic wind farm at **MELANIÓS**, typical of the four scrappy, impoverished villages along the 25-kilometre road to Volissós. At **PARPARIÁ**, roughly halfway between Melaniós and Volissós, there's a single **taverna** on the platía, the *Pagousaina*.

Volissós and around

VOLISSÓS, 42km from Híos Town by the most direct route (but only 2km longer via the much easier itinerary through Avgónyma), was once the market town for the northwestern villages. Its old stone houses still curl appealingly beneath the crumbling hilltop Byzantine fort, whose towers were improved by the Genoese. Volissós can seem depressing at first, with the bulk of its 250 mostly elderly (permanent) inhabitants living in newer buildings around the square, but opinions improve with longer acquaintance. This backwater ethos may not last, however; in its infinite wisdom, the EU has proposed land behind Managrós beach – for years unsold to private developers – as the site of a planned "new town", one of eighteen to be inflicted on Greece, ostensibly intended to reverse local decline. For the moment, the upper quarters are in the grip of a restoration mania, most of it done in admirable taste, with ruins changing hands for stratospheric prices.

Volissós practicalities

Grouped around the square you'll find a **post office**, a stand-alone **cash machine**, two well-stocked shops and three mediocre **tavernas**. There's a better one up in Pýrgos district by the castle car park, the vegetarian *Kafenio E* (April–Sept), run by Nikos Koungoulios; reservations (Ⓣ02740/21 480) are advised. A **filling station**, the only one hereabouts, operates 2.5km out of town; the **bus** only comes out here on Sundays for day-trips, or on Monday, Wednesday and Friday in the early afternoon (unless you care to travel at 4am). **Taxis** from Híos Town are pricey at roughly €27 per carload, versus about €3 per person for the bus (both fares one-way).

You should therefore plan on overnighting – which should cause no dismay, since the area has the best beaches, and some of the most interesting **accommodation**, on Híos. The most reliably available and staffed of a few restoration projects are sixteen old houses restored in the early 1990s, mostly in Pýrgos district, available through Omiros Travel (Ⓣ02740/21 413, Ⓕ21 521; ❸). Units usually accommodate two people – all have terraces, fully equipped kitchens and features such as tree trunks upholding sleeping lofts. Alternatively, lower down by the old school stands the *Arhondiko Zorbas* (Ⓣ02740/21 436, Ⓕ21 720; ❸), a bit more modernized. The final entry in the restoration sweepstakes is Sevasmia Kapiri's *Key to the Castle* (Ⓣ02740/21 863 or 21 463; ❸), a house divided into four studios.

Limniá and local beaches

LIMNIÁ (sometimes Limiá), the port of Volissós, lies 2km south; it's a lively fishing anchorage, with a small Miniotis Lines ferry coming from and going to Psará (theoretically Mon, Wed, Fri most of the year). There is nowhere to stay on the harbour, though there are two **tavernas**: long-established *Ta Limnia* on the jetty, where the emphasis is on *mayireftá*, and summer-only *To Limanaki* at the rear of the cove, which is better for fish.

From Limniá it's not far to the fabled **beaches**. A 1.5-kilometre walk southeast over the headland brings you to **Managrós**, a seemingly endless, undeveloped sand-and-pebble beach where nudism goes unremarked on at the remote south end. More intimate, sandy **Lefkáthia** lies just a ten-minute stroll along the cement drive threading over the headland north of the harbour; amenities at this cove are limited to a seasonal snack-shack on the sand, and Ioannis Zorbas' apartments (Ⓣ02740/21 436; ❸), co-run with the *Arhonidiko* (see opposite) and beautifully set in a garden just before the concrete track joins the asphalt road down from Volissós. This is bound for **Límnos** (not to be confused with Limniá), the next sheltered bay 400m east of Lefkáthia, where *Taverna Akroyiali* provides salubrious food and professional service, and the spruce *Latini Apartments* (Ⓣ02740/21 461, Ⓕ21 871; ❹) are graced with multiple stone terraces.

Ayía Markélla: beach and monastery

Ayía Markélla, 5km further northwest of Límnos, stars in many local postcards: a long, stunning beach fronting a monastery dedicated to the patron saint of Híos. The latter is not especially interesting or useful to outsiders, since its cells are reserved for Greek Orthodox pilgrims. In an interesting variation on the expulsion of the moneychangers from the temple, only religious souvenirs are allowed to be sold within the holy precincts, while all manner of plastic junk is on offer just outside. There's a single, rather indifferent taverna to hand as well, and around July 22 – the local saint's festival and biggest island celebration – "No camping" signs doubtless go unenforced.

Some maps show hot springs at one end of the beach; these, actually twenty minutes' walk north around the headland, turn out to be tepid dribbles into pot-sized cavities, not worth the bother and indicative only of the geological unity of this part of Híos with volcanic Lésvos. Potentially more useful is the dirt track heading north from the monastery grounds, passable (with care) to any vehicle and emerging in Parpariá village with its taverna (see opposite), on the paved road between Melaniós and Volissós.

Satellite islets: Psará and Inoússes

There's a single settlement, with beaches and an isolated rural monastery, on both of Híos' satellite islands, but each is surprisingly different from the other, and of course from their large neighbour. Inoússes, the nearer and smaller (3km by 10km) islet, has a daily kaïki service from Híos Town in season; Psará (11km by 6km) has less regular services subject to weather conditions (in theory daily from either Híos Town or Limniá), and is too remote to be done justice on a day-trip (see "Travel Details", p.376).

Psará

The birthplace of the Greek revolutionary war hero Admiral Kanaris, **Psará** devoted its merchant fleets – the third largest in 1820s Greece after those of Ídhra and Spétses – to the cause of independence, and paid dearly for it. Vexed beyond endurance, the Turks landed overwhelming forces in 1824 to stamp out this nest of resistance. Perhaps three thousand of the thirty thousand inhabitants escaped in small boats and were rescued by a French fleet, but the majority retreated to a hilltop powder magazine and blew it (and themselves) up rather than surrender. The nationalist poet Dionysios Solomos immortalized the incident in famous stanzas:

On the Black Ridge of Psará,
Glory walks alone.
She meditates on her heroes,
And wears in her hair a wreath
Made from a few dry weeds
Left on the barren ground.

Today, it's a sad, stark place fully living up to its name ("the grey things" in Greek), which never really recovered from this holocaust. The Turks burned whatever houses and vegetation the blast had missed, and the permanent population barely exceeds four hundred. The only positive recent development was a 1980s revitalization project instigated by a French-Greek descendant of Kanaris and a Greek team. The port was improved, mains electricity and pure water provided, a secondary school opened, and cultural links between France and the island established, though so far this has not been reflected in increased tourist numbers.

Since few buildings in the east-facing harbour community predate this century, it's a strange hotchpotch of ecclesiastical and domestic architecture that greets the eye on disembarking. There's a distinct southerly feel, more like the Dodecanese or Cyclades, and some peculiar churches, no two alike in style.

Practicalities

Arrival can be something of an ordeal: the regular small ferry from Híos Town can take up to four hours (as against a nominal 3hr 15min) to cover the 57 nautical miles of habitually rough sea. Use the port of Limniá to cross in at least one direction if you have a choice: this crossing takes half the time at just over half the price. Once a week in season there is also a direct large-ferry service from Límnos and Lésvos (Sígri).

If you **stay** overnight, there's a choice between a handful of fairly basic rooms and three more professional outfits: *Psara Studios* (ⓣ02740/61 233, ⓕ61 195; ④), and *Apartments Restalia* (ⓣ02740/61 000, ⓕ61 201; ⑤ Aug, ③), both a bit starkly modern but with balconies and kitchens, or the EOT *xenónas* (ⓣ0274/61 293; ②) in a restored prison. For **eating**, the best and cheapest place is the EOT-run *Spitalia*, housed (as the name indicates) in a restored medieval hospital on the north side of the port. A **post office**, bakery and shop complete the tally of amenities; there's a bank agent, but no full-service bank.

Around the island

Psará's **beaches** are decent, improving the further northeast you walk from the port. You quickly pass **Káto Yialós**, **Katsoúni** and **Lazarétta** with its off-putting power station, before reaching **Lákka** ("narrow ravine"), fifteen minutes' walk from the port, apparently named after its grooved rock formations in which you may have to shelter; much of this coast is windswept, with a heavy swell offshore. **Límnos**, 25 minutes away from the port along the coastal path, is big and pretty, but there's no reliable taverna here, or indeed at any of the other beaches. The one other thing to do on Psará is to walk north across the island – the old track has now been paved – to the **Monastery of the**

Assumption; uninhabited since the 1970s, this comes to life only during the first week of August, when its revered icon is carried in ceremonial procession to town and back on the eve of August 6.

Inoússes

Inoússes has a permanent population of about three hundred – less than half its prewar figure – and a very different history from Psará. For generations this medium-sized islet has provided the Aegean with many of her wealthiest shipping families: various members of the Livanos, Lemos and Pateras clans (with every street or square named after the last-cited family) were born here. This helps explain the large villas and visiting summer yachts on an otherwise sleepy Greek backwater – as well as a **Maritime Museum** (daily 10am–1pm; €1.20) near the quay, endowed by various shipping magnates. At the west end of the quay, the bigwigs have also funded a large nautical academy, engaged in training future members of the merchant navy.

Two church-tipped islets, each privately owned, guard the unusually well-protected harbour (whose jetty is currently being expanded); the **town** itself is surprisingly large, draped over hillsides enclosing a ravine. Despite the wealthy reputation, its appearance is unpretentious and similar to İzmir across the water in Turkey, with the houses displaying a mix of vernacular and modest Neoclassical style.

Practicalities

On Sundays in season can you make an inexpensive **day-trip** to Inoússes from Híos with the locals' ferry *Inousses*; on most other days of the week this arrives from the big island at 3pm, returning early the next morning. One or two days weekly during summer there's an unreliable hydrofoil service as well, leaving Híos at about 9.30am, and returning from Inoússes at about 3pm. Otherwise, during the tourist season you must participate in the pricier excursions offered from Híos, typically on the *Maria*, with return tickets running up to three times the cost of the regular ferry. All that's really possible on a typical six-hour excursion is a look around the single town, a swim at one of Inoússes' attractive beaches and a meal.

Since most seasonal visitors stay in their ancestral or holiday homes, there is just one, fairly comfortable **hotel**, the *Thalassoporos* (Ⓣ02720/51 475; ❷), on the main easterly hillside lane. **Eating out** is similarly limited; every year a few simple ouzerís off towards the nautical academy try their luck, but the most reliable option is the simple good-value *Taverna Pateronissia*, conspicuous at the base of the disembarkation jetty. Otherwise, be prepared to patronize one of the three shops (one on the waterfront, two up the hill), but you may be better off bringing your own picnic food, especially out of season. Beside the museum are a **post office** and a **bank**.

Around the island

The rest of this tranquil island, at least the southern slope, is surprisingly green and well tended; there are no springs, so water comes from a mix of fresh and brackish wells, as well as a reservoir. The sea is extremely clean and calm on the sheltered southerly shore; among its **beaches**, choose from **Zepága**, **Biláli** or **Kástro**, respectively five, twenty and thirty minutes' walk west of the port. More secluded **Fourkeró** (Farkeró in dialect) lies a 25-minute walk east, first along a cement drive to a seaside chapel, then by path past pine groves and over a ridge. As on Psará, there are no reliable facilities at any of the beaches.

Greek script table

Híos	Χίος	ΧΙΟΣ
Afrodhísia	Αφροδίσια	ΑΦΡΟΔΙΣΑ
Amádhes	Αμάδες	ΑΜΑΔΕΣ
Anávatos	Ανάβατος	ΑΝΑΒΑΤΟΣ
Áno Kardhámyla	Άνω Καρδάμυλα	ΑΝΩ ΚΑΡΔΑΜΥΛΑ
Apothíkas	Αποθήκας	ΑΠΟΘΗΚΑΣ
Armólia	Αρμόλια	ΑΡΜΟΛΙΑ
Avgónyma	Αυγώνυμα	ΑΥΓΩΝΥΜΑ
Ayía Ermióni	Αγία Ερμιόνη	ΑΓΙΑ ΕΡΜΙΟΝΗ
Ayía Fotiní	Αγία Φωτεινή	ΑΓΙΑ ΦΩΤΕΙΝΗ
Ayía Iríni	Αγία Ειρήνη	ΑΓΙΑ ΕΙΡΗΝΗ
Ayía Markélla	Αγία Μαρκέλλα	ΑΓΙΑ ΜΑΡΚΕΛΛΑ
Ayiásmata	Αγιάσματα	ΑΓΙΑΣΜΑΤΑ
Áyii Anáryiri	Άγιοι Ανάργυροι	ΑΓΙΟΙ ΑΝΑΡΓΥΡΟΙ
Áyio Gála	Άγιο Γάλα	ΑΓΙΟ ΓΑΛΑ
Áyios Emilianós	Άγιος Αιμιλιανός	ΑΓΙΟΣ ΑΙΜΙΛΙΑΝΟΣ
Áyios Yeóryios Sikoússis	Άγιος Γεώργιος Συκούσης	ΑΓΙΟΣ ΓΕΩΡΓΙΟΣ ΣΥΚΟΥΣΗΣ
Dhaskalópetra	Δασκαλόπετρα	ΔΑΣΚΑΛΟΠΕΤΡΑ
Dhievhá	Διευχά	ΔΙΕΥΧΑ
Elínda	Ελίντα	ΕΛΙΝΤΑ
Emboriós	Εμπορειός	ΕΜΠΟΡΕΙΟΣ
Evangelismoú	Ευαγγελισμού	ΕΥΑΓΓΕΛΙΣΜΟΥ
Fourkeró	Φουρκερό	ΦΟΥΡΚΕΡΟ
Inoússes	Οινούσσες	ΟΙΝΟΥΣΣΕΣ
Kalamotí	Καλαμωτή	ΚΑΛΑΜΩΤΗ
Kambiá	Καμπιά	ΚΑΜΠΙΑ
Kámbos	Κάμπος	ΚΑΜΠΟΣ
Karfás	Καρφάς	ΚΑΡΦΑΣ
Karyés	Καρυές	ΚΑΡΥΕΣ
Katarráktis	Καταρράκτης	ΚΑΤΑΡΡΑΚΤΗΣ
Káto Faná	Κάτω Φανά	ΚΑΤΩ ΦΑΝΑ
Kéramos	Κέραμος	ΚΕΡΑΜΟΣ
Kómi	Κώμη	ΚΩΜΗ
Kondári	Κοντάρι	ΚΟΝΤΑΡΙ
Kouroúnia	Κουρούνια	ΚΟΥΡΟΥΝΙΑ
Langádha	Λαγκάδα	ΛΑΓΚΑΔΑ
Lefkáthia	Λευκάθια	ΛΕΥΚΑΘΙΑ
Lilikás	Λιλικάς	ΛΙΛΙΚΑΣ
Liménas Mestón	Λιμένας Μεστών	ΛΙΜΕΝΑΣ ΜΕΣΤΩΝ

At the end of the westerly road, beyond Kástro, stands the somewhat macabre convent of **Evangelismoú**, endowed by the Pateras family. Inside reposes the mummified body of the lately canonized Irini, whose prayers to die of cancer in place of her terminally ill father Panagos were answered early in the 1960s;

Limniá	Λιμνιά	ΛΙΜΝΙΑ
Límnos	Λήμνος	ΛΗΜΝΟΣ
Lithí	Λιθί	ΛΙΘΙ
Makriá Ámmos	Μακριά Άμμος	ΜΑΚΡΙΑ ΑΜΜΟΣ
Mármaro	Μάρμαρο	ΜΑΡΜΑΡΟ
Mávros Yialós	Μάυρος Γιαλός	ΜΑΥΡΟΣ ΓΙΑΛΟΣ
Mégas Limniónas	Μέγας Λιμνιώας	ΜΕΓΑΣ ΛΙΜΝΙΩΝΑΣ
Melaniós	Μελανιός	ΜΕΛΑΝΙΟΣ
Merikoúnda	Μερικούντα	ΜΕΡΙΚΟΥΝΤΑ
Mestá	Μεστά	ΜΕΣΤΑ
Metóhi	Μετόχι	ΜΕΤΟΧΙ
Moundhón	Μουνδών	ΜΟΥΝΔΩΝ
Nagós	Ναγός	ΝΑΓΟΣ
Néa Moní	Νέα Μονή	ΝΕΑ ΜΟΝΗ
Nénita	Νένητα	ΝΕΝΗΤΑ
Olýmbi	Ολύμποι	ΟΛΥΜΠΟΙ
Panayía Krína	Παναγία Κρήνα	ΠΑΝΑΓΙΑ ΚΡΗΝΑ
Panayía Mersindhíou	Παναγία Μερσινιδιου	ΠΑΝΑΓΙΑ ΜΕΡΣΙΝΙΔΙΟΥ
Panayía Sikelliá	Παναγία Σικελιά	ΠΑΝΑΓΙΑ ΣΙΚΕΛΙΑ
Pandoukiós	Παντουκιός	ΠΑΝΤΟΥΚΙΟΣ
Papaliá	Παπαλιά	ΠΑΠΑΛΙΑ
Parpariá	Παρπαριά	ΠΑΡΠΑΡΙΑ
Pelinéo(n)	Πεληναίο(ν)	ΠΕΛΙΝΑΙΟ(Ν)
Pityós	Πιτυός	ΠΙΤΥΟΣ
Psará	Ψαρά	ΨΑΡΑ
Pyrgí	Πυργοί	ΠΥΡΓΟΙ
Sidhiroúnda	Σιδηρούντα	ΣΙΔΗΡΟΥΝΤΑ
Spartoúnda	Σπαρτούντα	ΣΠΑΡΤΟΥΝΤΑ
Tigáni	Τηγάνι	ΤΗΓΑΝΙ
Vavýli	Βαβύλοι	ΒΑΒΥΛΟΙ
Véssa	Βέσσα	ΒΕΣΣΑ
Víki	Βίκι	ΒΙΚΙ
Volissós	Βολισσός	ΒΟΛΙΣΣΟΣ
Vounós	Βουνός	ΒΟΥΝΟΣ
Vrondádhos	Βροντάδος	ΒΡΟΝΤΑΔΟΣ
Vroulídhia	Βρουλίδια	ΒΡΟΥΛΙΔΙΑ
Výri	Βύρη	ΒΥΡΗ
Yeríta	Γερίτα	ΓΕΡΙΤΑ
Yióssonas	Γιόσωνας	ΓΙΟΣΩΝΑΣ

he's entombed here also, having outlived Irini by some years. The abbess, presiding over around twenty novices, is none other than the widowed Mrs Pateras. Only modestly attired women are allowed admission, and even then casual visits are not encouraged.

Híos travel details

Island transport

NB All frequencies given are for the period June to early Oct.

Buses – Blue City Lines

Híos Town to: Karyés (6 daily Mon–Fri, 7am–3pm, 4 Sat); Kondári (Airport), Karfás, Mégas Limniónas, Ayía Ermióni, Thymianá (14 daily 7am–9pm, often with the order juggled); Vrondádhos, Dhaskalópetra (2 hourly 7am–8.30pm Mon–Sat, 1 hourly Sun).

Buses – green long-distance KTEL

Híos Town to: Anávatos* (Tues & Fri at 9am); Armólia (5 daily Mon–Fri, 3 Sat, 1 Sun); Ayía Fotiní (3 daily); Ayía Markélla* (1 on Sun at 8am); Emboriós (4 daily Mon–Fri, 3 Sat, 1 Sun); Katarráktis (7 daily Mon–Fri, 2 Sat, 1 Sun); Komí (4 daily Mon–Fri, 3 Sat, 1 Sun); Langádha (5 daily Mon–Fri, 3 Sat); Mármaro (5 daily Mon–Fri, 3 Sat); Mestá (6 daily Mon–Fri, 3 Sat, 1 Sun); Néa Moní* (Tues & Fri at 9am); Paralía Lithioú (2 daily Mon–Fri only); Pyrgí (8 daily Mon–Fri, 3 Sat, 1 Sun); Véssa (2 daily Mon–Fri only); Volissós (Mon, Wed, Fri at 4.20am & 1.30pm, Sun* 8am).

NB * indicates that departure or destination is part of a set price, guided KTEL tour taking in other destinations.

Buses – KTEL loop routes and local shuttles

Emboriós–Pyrgí (4 daily Mon–Fri, 3 Sat, 1 Sun); **Kómi–Emboriós** (4 daily Mon–Fri, 3 Sat, 1 Sun); **Kómi–Pyrgí** (4 daily Mon–Fri, 3 Sat, 1 Sun); **Mármaro–Nagós** (3 daily Mon–Fri, 2 Sat).

Inter-island transport

Key to ferry and hydrofoil companies

HF	Hellas Ferries
DANE	*Dhodhekanisiakí Anónymi Navtiliakí Etería* (Dodecanese Shipping Co)
ML	Miniotis Lines
NEL	*Navtiliakí Etería Lésvou* (Lesvian Shipping Co)

Large ferries

Híos to: Alexandhroúpoli (1 weekly on NEL; 17hr); Kavála (1–2 weekly on NEL, summer only; 13hr 30min if no layover on Lésvos); Kós (1 weekly on NEL; 7hr 30min); Lésvos (daily on NEL, 3 weekly on HF; 3hr 30min); Límnos (1–5 weekly on NEL; 9hr); Mýkonos (1 weekly on NEL; 7hr); Pireás (at least daily on NEL, 4 weekly on HF; 9–15hr); Rhodes (1 weekly on NEL; 11hr 30min); Sámos, Vathý only (2 weekly on HF & NEL; 3hr 30 min); Sýros (1 weekly on HF; 5hr 30min); Thessaloníki (1–2 weekly on NEL; 17hr).

Psará to: 1–2 weekly on NEL Lines to Lésvos, Sígri (3hr), Áyios Efstrátios (6hr), Límnos (7hr 30min), Rafina (6hr).

Catamaran

NEL's *Aeolos Kenteris* plies 3 times weekly most of the year to Lésvos (1hr 30min) and Pireás (4hr); typical northbound departure time is 8.30pm, towards Athens 6pm.

Small ferries

Híos Town to: Psará (4 weekly, usually Tues, Thurs, Sat, Sun am on ML; 3hr 30min–4hr); Sámos, both northern ports (2–3 weekly on ML, 3hr 30min–5hr).

Limniá to: Psará, 3 weekly on ML, usually Mon, Wed, Fri 2pm; 1hr 30min).

Psará to: Lésvos, Mytilíni (1 weekly; 3hr).

Kaïkia

Híos Town to: Inoússes (minimum 1 daily Mon–Sat 2pm, not Tues Oct–May, Sun 9am; returns early morning Tues–Sat, 4pm Sun. 1hr journey time). Other excursion boats according to demand.

Hydrofoils

From Híos to: Évdhilos, Ikaría (1 weekly; 1hr 30min); Inoússes (1–3 weekly; 25min); Lésvos (1–3 weekly; 2hr); Sámos, both northern ports (1–3 weekly; 1hr 30min–3hr via Ikaría).

Flights

NB All are on Olympic Airways/Aviation.

Híos to: Athens (4–5 daily; 1hr); Lésvos (1 weekly; 30min); Límnos (1 weekly; 1hr); Sámos (1 weekly; 30min); Thessaloníki (3 weekly, 1 via Lésvos; 1hr 30min–2hr).

International transport

Ferries

Híos to: Turkey (Çesme); 2–13 boats weekly, depending on season. Spring/autumn, about 7 weekly; Thursday evening (Turkish boat) and Saturday morning (Greek boat) services tend to run year-round. Passenger fares on the Greek boat (Miniotis Lines) are €47 one way, €59 open return (no day-return fare), including Greek taxes; no Turkish taxes. These are the "rack rates", which can often be beaten by comparison shopping and bargaining; it's also about twenty percent less expensive to travel *from* Turkey. Turkish boat (typically *Ertürk II*) is usually cheaper going from Híos, at €33 one way, €44 return, Greek taxes inclusive. Small cars €73.50 each way, taken on either morning or evening boats. Journey time 45min.

Lésvos

Lésvos (Mytilíni), the third largest Greek island after Crete and Évvia, is not only the birthplace of Sappho, but also of Aesop, Arion and – more recently – the "naïve" artist Theophilos, the poet Odysseus Elytis and the novelist Stratis Myrivilis. Despite these artistic associations, Lésvos may not at first strike the visitor as particularly beautiful or interesting; much of the landscape is rocky, volcanic terrain, dotted with thermal springs and alternating with vast grain fields, salt pans or even near-desert. But there are also oak and pine forests as well as vast olive groves, some of these over five hundred years old. With its balmy climate – even winter rain obliges by usually falling before dawn – and suggestive contours, the island tends to grow on you with prolonged acquaintance.

Historically, olive plantations, oúzo distilleries, animal husbandry and a fishing industry supported those inhabitants who chose not to emigrate; but with most of these enterprises stagnating since World War II, mass-market **tourism** has made considerable inroads. However, there are still few large hotels outside the capital or Mólyvos, villa-type accommodation just barely outstrips rooms, and the first of two official campsites opened only in 1990. While Lésvos is far more developed touristically than Híos, it is rather less so than Sámos, a happy medium that will accord with many people's tastes. Tourist numbers have in fact levelled off in recent years, the result of a fudged airport expansion, unrealistic hotel pricing and the dropping of the island from several German and Dutch tour operators' programmes. So while a few disused olive-mill grindstones have found a new lease of life as hotel decor, tourism still makes up less than five percent of the local economy, and a healthy surplus in olive oil is sent annually to Spain and Italy for rebottling.

Some history

Lovers of medieval and Ottoman **architecture** certainly won't be disappointed on Lésvos. Byzantine–Genoese castles, many built on early foundations, can be found at the main town of Mytilíni, Mólyvos, Eressós, and near Ándissa; most of these date from the latter half of the fourteenth century, when the island was given as a dowry to a Genoese prince of the Gattilusi clan on his marriage to the niece of one of the last Byzantine emperors.

Apart from Crete and Évvia, Lésvos was the only Greek island where Turks settled appreciably in rural villages (they usually stuck to the safety of towns),

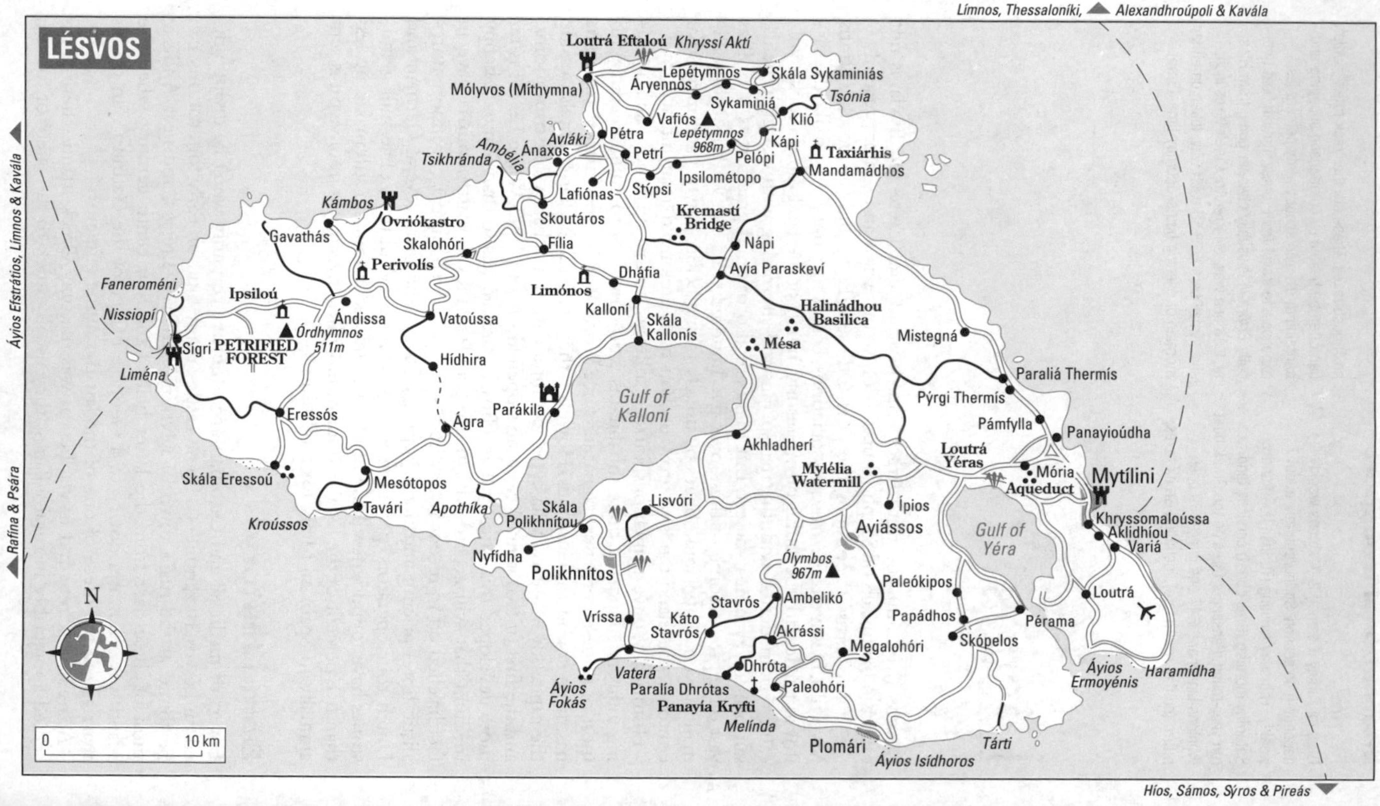

LÉSVOS

Límnos, Thessaloníki, Alexandhroúpoli & Kavála
Áyios Efstrátios, Límnos & Kavála
Rafína & Psára
Híos, Sámos, Sýros & Pireás

Loutrá Eftaloú
Khryssí Aktí
Lepétymnos
Skála Sykaminiás
Mólyvos (Míthymna)
Áryennos
Sykaminiá
Tsónia
Vafiós
Klió
Avláki
Pétra
Lepétymnos 968m
Kápi
Taxiárhis
Ambélia
Ánaxos
Petrí
Pelópi
Tsikhránda
Mandamádhos
Ipsilométopo
Lafiónas
Stýpsi
Kremastí Bridge
Kámbos
Skoutáros
Ovriókastro
Gavathás
Skalohóri
Fília
Nápi
Perivolís
Dháfia
Ayía Paraskeví
Faneroméni
Ipsiloú
Limónos
Kalloní
Halinádhou Basilica
Nissiopí
Ándissa
Vatoússa
Skála Kallonís
Órdhymnos 511m
Mistegná
Mésa
Sígri
PETRIFIED FOREST
Hídhira
Liména
Paraliá Thermís
Gulf of Kalloní
Pýrgi Thermís
Eressós
Parákila
Ágra
Pámfylla
Panayioúdha
Akhladherí
Loutrá Yéras
Mylélia Watermill
Mória
Skála Eressoú
Mytílini
Aqueduct
Mesótopos
Ípios
Skála Polikhnítou
Lisvóri
Tavári
Apothíka
Khryssomaloússa
Kroússos
Ayiássos
Gulf of Yéra
Aklidhíou
Variá
Nyfídha
Polikhnítos
Ólymbos 967m
Paleókipos
Loutrá
Ambelikó
Vríssa
Stavrós
Papádhos
Káto Stavrós
Pérama
Akrássi
Skópelos
Megalohóri
Dhróta
Áyios Fokás
Vaterá
Paleohóri
Áyios Ermoyénis
Haramídha
Paralía Dhrótas
Panayía Kryftí
Melínda
Tárti
Plomári
Áyios Isídhoros
N
0 10 km

which explains the odd Ottoman bridge or crumbling minaret often found in the middle of nowhere. That these have survived at all can be ascribed to the relative tolerance of contemporary islanders; the first two centuries of **Ottoman rule** were particularly harsh, with much of the Orthodox population sold into slavery or deported to the imperial capital – replaced by more tractable Muslim colonists – and most physical evidence of the Genoese or Byzantine period demolished, though many of the major monasteries which still exist today had been refounded by the 1500s.

Again, unusually for the Aegean islands, Ottoman reforms in the late seventeenth and eighteenth centuries encouraged the emergence here of a Greek Orthodox land- and industry-owning **aristocracy**, who built rambling, rural tower-houses, some of which have survived the thoughtless destruction that claimed the rest during the twentieth century. More common are the **bourgeois mansions** of the worthies in Mytilíni town, built from the late nineteenth to early twentieth century on French Second Empire models; many more of these remain, often pressed into service as government buildings or even restored as hotels.

Out in the country, especially at Mólyvos, Turks and Greeks got along, relatively speaking, right up until 1923; the Turkish authorities favoured Greek *kahayiádhes* (overseers) to keep the peons in line. However, large numbers of the lower social classes, oppressed by the Ottoman pashas and their Greek lackeys, fled across to Asia Minor during the nineteenth century, only to return again after the exchange of populations.

Social and economic **idiosyncrasies** persist: anyone who has attended one of the extended village *paniyíria* here, with music for hours on end and outdoor tables piled with food and drink, will not be surprised to learn that Lésvos has the highest alcoholism rate in Greece. Breeding livestock, especially **horses and donkeys**, remains disproportionately important, and traffic jams caused by mounts instead of parked cars are not unheard of – signs reading "Forbidden to Tether Animals Here" are still very much part of the picture, as are herds of apparently unattended donkeys wandering about. Much of the acreage in olives is still inaccessible to vehicles, and the harvest can only be hauled away by those donkeys – who are duly loaded en masse onto pickup trucks to be transported to the point where the road fizzles out.

Until recently, another local quirk was a marked tendency to **vote Communist**, in part a reaction to the late medieval quasi-feudalism here, which lingered on in the share-cropping system which prevailed in the countryside until the 1930s. But lately there's been a shift to the right, with KKE incumbents being chucked out in favour of Néa Dhimokratía candidates (1990), who were in turn supplanted by PASOK (1993), though the KKE clawed back one of three seats in 1996, retaining it in 2001. But whatever their politics, you'll find the islanders fairly religious, with old-fashioned (if occasionally rough-edged) manners and – by Greek-island standards – a strong sense of community. In contrast to certain neighbouring islands, infrastructure improvement projects do eventually get completed (depending on EU or Greek-state grants), and forests are well cared for, with permanent firebreaks backed up during dangerous seasons by 24-hour surveillance crews. As a result, Lésvos has in recent years had only one devastating blaze, attributed to foreign (ie Turkish) saboteurs.

Getting around the island

Public **buses** tend to radiate out from the main harbour for the benefit of working locals, not day-tripping tourists. Carrying out such excursions is next to impossible anyway, owing to the size of the island – about 70km by 45km at its widest points – and the last few appalling roads (most others have been improved, along with their signposting). Moreover, the topography is complicated by the two deeply indented gulfs of Kalloní and Yéra, which means that going from A to B on public transport usually involves an obligatory change of bus at either Mytilíni, on the east shore, or at the town of Kalloní, in the middle of the island. In short, it's best to decide on a base and stay there for at least a few days, exploring its immediate surroundings on foot or by rented vehicle. Scooters or even proper motorbikes make little impact on this huge island, and will certainly go for a spill on some of the rougher dirt roads.

A special word of warning: **road rage** has come to Lésvos in a big way – there were two driving-related killings in 1998 – so avoid provoking locals by impeding them in any fashion.

Mytilíni Town

MYTILÍNI, the main port and capital, home to about 25,000, sprawls between and around two broad bays divided by a fortified promontory, and in Greek fashion often doubles as the name of the island itself. Many visitors are put off by the combination of urban bustle and (in the traditionally humbler northern districts) slight seediness, and contrive to leave as soon as possible; the town returns the compliment by in fact being a fairly impractical and occasionally expensive place to base yourself. However, there are several diversions to occupy you for a few hours, particularly the marketplace and a few museums, all located within a few minutes' walk of the waterfront.

Arrival, orientation and information

There's no bus link with the **airport**, so a shared **taxi** for the 7km into Mytilíni Town is the usual shuttle method; most of the drivers have lived in Australia, and thus speak fluent English (of a sort). As on Híos, there are two **bus stations**: the *iperastykó* (standard KTEL) buses leaving from a small station near Platía Konstandinopóleos at the southern end of the harbour, plus the *astykó* (blue bus) service departing from one corner of the enormous free public **car park** nearby (which you should use if driving, as there are no other easily available spaces in the centre). Elsewhere, the best single parking spot is the currently unrestricted loop-street next to the new archeological museum. Most of the facilities you'll need are located on the waterfront along **Pávlou Koundouriótou**, which wraps itself around the entire south harbour. **Ermoú** begins one block west of this and threads north through the heart of the marketplace. If you're driving, **8-Noemvríou**, starting just behind the ferry quay and passing both archeological galleries, is the quickest way to the northern harbour of Epáno Skála and beyond to the Mandamádhos road.

Before leaving town, you might visit the **EOT** regional headquarters at James Aristárhou 6 (Mon–Fri 8am–2.30pm; ⓣ02510/42 511) to get hold of their excellent town and island maps, plus other brochures. However the best island **map**, spottily available locally, is Road Edition's no. 212 1:70,000 title "Lesbos", though road-surface ratings have not kept pace with ongoing works.

Accommodation

Finding **accommodation** can be initially daunting: the obvious waterfront hotels are noisy and exorbitantly priced, with few singles to speak of. If you

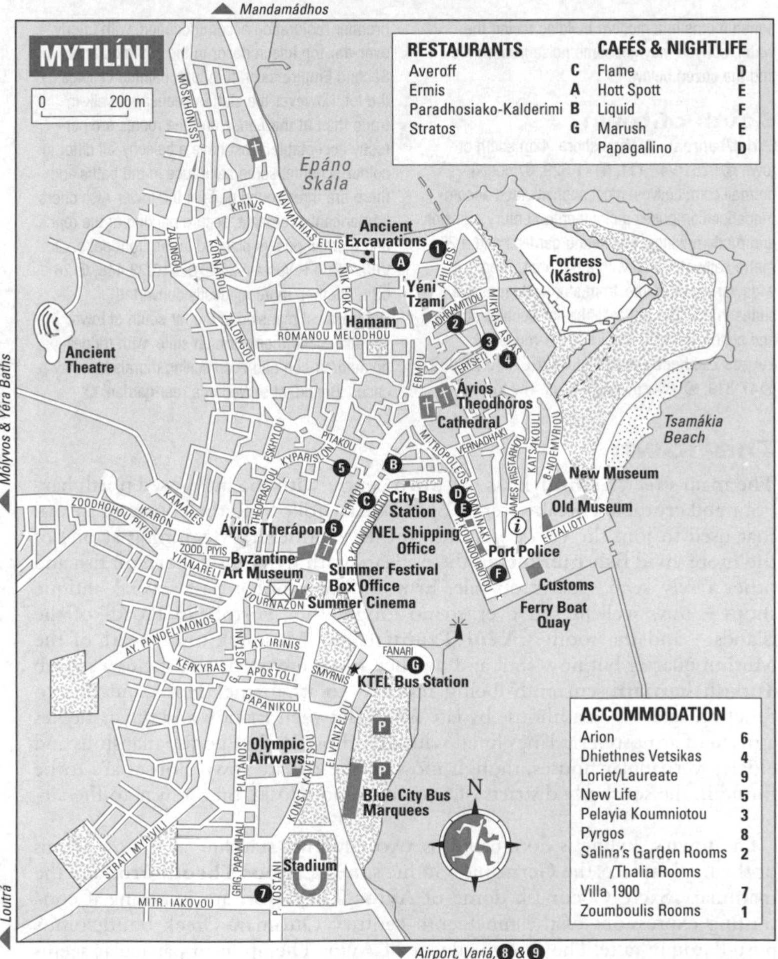

need to stay, it's preferable to hunt down better-value rooms in the backstreets, especially between the castle and Ermoú, with supply usually exceeding demand. For better-value luxury, head towards the south of the town or even beyond city limits, to Variá.

Centre and north of town

Dhiethnes/Vetsikas Yeoryíou Tertséti 1 ⓣ02510/24 968. Relatively comfortable en-suite rooms in a side street off Mikrás Asías. ❷

New Life Rear of Olýmbou, cul-de-sac off Ermoú ⓣ02510/42 650 or 093/2279057. Polished-wood-floored, en-suite rooms in an old mansion, or similarly priced ones, but with bizarre modern murals, in the co-managed **Arion** down the street at Áriono 4. ❸

Pelayia Koumniotou Yeoryíou Tertséti 6 ⓣ02510/20 643. Friendly, basic, non-en-suite rooms establishment that also rents out scooters. ❶

Salina's Garden Rooms Fokéas 7 ⓣ02510/42 073. En-suite and very quiet rooms located near the Yéni Tzamí. ❶

Thalia Rooms ⓣ02510/24 640. Located across the street from *Salina's Garden Rooms* and under the same management – essentially its overflow. ❶

Zoumboulis Rooms Navmahías Ellís 11 ⓣ02510/29 081, ⓕ44 204. En-suite, air-conditioned rooms in a modern building facing the water, but you may get some noise from traffic and the ouzerí below. ❸

South of town

Loriet/Laureate At Variá shore, 4km south of town ⓣ02510/43 111, ⓕ41 629, ⓔloriet@hotmail.com. Lésvos' most sophisticated accommodation comprises a nineteenth-century mansion and modern wings, bracketing gardens and a 25-metre saltwater pool with a bar area. There's a wide variety of rooms, from studios to massive suites in the "Big House"; "basic" doubles studios and suites. Booking required year-round. ❻

Pyrgos Eleftheríou Venizélou 49 ⓣ02510/25 069, ⓕ47 319, ⓦwww.pyrgoshotel.gr. The town's premier restoration accommodation, with utterly over-the-top kitsch decor in the common areas: Second Empire salon furniture, painted ceilings, the lot. However the staff is keener on walk-in trade than at the *Loriet*, and the rooms are perfectly acceptable. Most have a balcony, all differ in colour scheme, some have tubs in the baths and there are three round units in the tower. Also offers "American" breakfast, secure parking at the rear and a small pool is planned in the front patio. ❻

Villa 1900 P. Vostáni 24 ⓣ02510/23 448, ⓕ28 034. Another, more modestly converted Neoclassical mansion in the far south of town; variable-sized rooms are en suite, with fridges, heating/air con and even ceiling murals in a few cases. Breakfast served in a rear garden. ❹

The Town

The main street, **Ermoú**, links the town centre with the little-used north harbour and crumbled breakwater of Epáno Skála, following the course of a canal that used to join the two ports until the Byzantine era. Beginning at one of the more vivid **fish markets** in the Aegean, with flying fish, scorpion fish and other rarely seen species on sale, Ermoú forges north past several antique shops – now well picked over, so no longer the "Portobello Road" of the islands – and the roofless **Yéni Tzamí** (New Mosque), once heart of the Muslim quarter but now shut and derelict. Just a few steps east stands a superb Turkish **hamam**, currently being restored to its former glory and due to function again as a bathhouse by late 2002. Between Ermoú and the castle lies a maze of atmospheric lanes lined with grandiose Belle Époque mansions and elderly vernacular houses, though most of the ornate town houses are to be found in the southerly districts of Sourádha and Kióski, on the way to the airport.

The town's skyline is dominated by two churches standing at opposite ends of the marketplace: the Germanic-Gothic spire of **Áyios Theodhóros** and the mammary, Sacré-Coeur-ish dome of **Áyios Therápon** are imposing if contrasting expressions of the nineteenth-century Ottoman–Greek bourgeoisie's post-Baroque taste. The interior decor of Áyios Therápon in particular seems more appropriate to an opera house than a church, not least because of its chandelier – the most extravagantly ornate in the east Aegean.

The well-lit and well-laid-out **Byzantine Art Museum** (no regular hours at present; apply to church office adjacent Mon–Fri 9am–noon), just behind Áyios Therápon, contains various icons rescued from rural island churches. The most noteworthy exhibit, and the oldest, is a fourteenth-century icon of Christ *Pandokrátor*; other highlights include a sultanic *firmáni* or grant of privileges to a local bishop, a rare sixteenth-century three-dimensional icon of the *Crucifixion* and a canvas of the *Kímisis* (*Assumption*) by Theophilos (see p.385).

On the promontory between the bays sits the Byzantine-Genoese-Ottoman **fortress** (Tues–Sun 8am–2.30pm; €1.50), its mixed pedigree reflected in the Ottoman-Turkish inscription immediately above the Byzantine double eagle at the southern outer gate. Inside you can make out the ruins, variously preserved, of the Gattilusi palace, a Turkish *medresse* (Koranic academy), a dervish cell and a Byzantine cistern. Just below the fortress, at **Tsamákia**, is the mediocre, fee-entry town "beach".

Tucked away on the westerly hill, and assiduously signposted, the **Hellenistic theatre** (unrestricted access, free admission) proves resoundingly anticlimactic on arrival; most of its masonry was pilfered for use in the castle, or reduced to plaster in Ottoman lime kilns.

The archeological museums

Mytilíni's excellent **archeological collection**, and the only real must-see in town, is housed in **two separate galleries** a few hundred metres apart. The newer, upper museum (daily May–Sept 8am–7pm; Oct–April Tues–Sun 8.30am–3pm; €1.50), about 200m up 8-Noemvríou, is devoted to finds from wealthy Roman Mytilene, in particular three rooms of well-displayed mosaics from second and third-century AD villas – highlights are a crude but engaging scene of Orpheus charming all manner of beasts, and two fishermen surrounded by clearly recognizable (and edible) sea creatures. Earlier eras are represented in the older wing (Tues–Sun 8.30am–3pm; same ticket as Roman wing), housed in a former mansion just behind the ferry dock. The ground floor is Neolithic finds from Áyios Vartholoméos cave and Bronze Age Thermí, but the star, late Classical exhibits upstairs include minutely detailed terracotta figurines: a pair of acrobats, two *kourotrophoi* figures (goddesses suckling infants, predecessors of all Byzantine Galaktotrofoússa icons), children playing with a ball or dogs, and Aphrodite riding a dolphin. A specially built annexe at the rear contains stone-cut inscriptions of various edicts and treaties, plus a Roman sculpture of a drunken satyr asleep on a wineskin.

Eating and drinking

Dining options in Mytilíni have improved since a late-1990s nadir, when several of the more characterful old-style ouzerís and tavernas shut down in favour of fast-food joints, and there was hardly a sit-down meal to be had.

Averoff West quay, or back entrance at Ermoú 52. Run by the Kakambouras family since 1925, this is the town's classic *mayireftá* venue, doling out early morning *patsás* (tripe soup) for those straight off a boat, and also where all and sundry have lunch before an afternoon ferry departure.

Ermis Kornárou 2, cnr Ermoú. Much the best of a cluster of ouzerís up at Páno Skála; a recent refit hasn't much affected its century-old decor (panelled ceiling, giant mirrors, faded oil paintings), or its claimed two centuries of purveying titbits to a jolly, mixed crowd in the pleasant courtyard. Better service than *Paradhosiako-Kalderimi* at comparable prices, and open daily (though restricted menu Sun).

Liquid Koundouriótou 79. The handiest place for a proper breakfast straight off the ferry serving omelettes and decent coffees.

Papagallino Koundouriótou 59. Strong on coffees, crêpes and pricey smoothies, plus a magnificent interior atrium occasionally hosting exhibits.

Paradhosiako-Kalderimi Two adjacent premises in the bazaar at Thássou 2. The market-characters' ouzerí, with the big plus its seating under the shade of vines. A large-portioned if plainly presented autumn meal of white beans, sardines and stuffed squash flowers, plus drink, shouldn't exceed €12 per head. Closed Sun.

Stratos Fanári quay, south end of port. The last, and marginally the best, in a series of touristy fish tavernas, and the only one that doesn't tout aggressively; also grills and *mayireftá*.

Nightlife and entertainment

With an important university in residence, Mytilíni can offer decent **nightlife and entertainment**, especially along the northeast quay, which the student contingent have claimed as their own. Here, all in a row between Budget rent-a-car and the NEL agency, you'll find *Flame* (with bowling upstairs), *Papagallino* as described above, *Marush* (with video games), and the durable *Hott Spott* (with music). The closest cavernous dance club is *Quebracho*, 5km north at Panayioúdha. Formal live events constitute the Lesviakó Kalokéri **festival**, held in the castle or other venues from mid-July to late August. The summer **cinema** Pallas lies in between the post office and the park on Vournázon, plus there's a winter venue as well as a weekly cinema club of art films pitched at the university crowd.

Listings

Airlines Olympic offices are southwest of the bay and central park, at Kavétsou 44 (☎02510/28 660); Aegean-Cronus is only at the airport (☎02510/61 120), but their tickets are sold through any on-line travel agent.
Banks and exchange At least five banks along Koundouriótou have cash machines, plus there's a stand-alone one on the quay.
Car rental Most reputable agents cluster at the northeast corner of the harbour, on or just off of Koundouriótou. Especially recommended is Payless/Auto Moto at Koundouriótou 49 (also at the airport; ☎02510/43 555, ⓔautomoto@otenet.gr), for good-condition cars and no surcharges for credit-card use. Alternatively try Budget next door (☎02510/29 600), Egeon at Híou 2 (☎02510/29 820), Just at no. 47 (☎02510/43 080), and Alpha in the alley off Koundouriótou 83 (☎02510/26 113). Off-peak rates for a B-category car should be maximum €30/day for four days or more. You will often find it cheaper to rent at the resort of your choice, but then you may not have the invaluable option of airport or ferry-dock drop-off upon departure.
Ferry/travel agencies All ferry and travel agencies are found along Koundouriótou. NEL has its own outlet at no. 47 (☎02510/28 480), though their tickets (including the catamaran) can also be obtained from Dimakis Tours at no. 73 (☎02510/27 865). Dimakis and adjacent Picolo Travel at no. 73a (☎02510/27 000) are the most reliable venues for any ferries running to Turkey, while Picolo also handles Hellas Ferries and the occasional hydrofoil south.
Post office On Vournázon, a block behind the central park.

Around Mytilíni

If you are based in Mytilíni, there are a few diversions within easy reach; of these, the Variá **museums** and the Loutrá Yéras **spa** are the most worthwhile.

North: Panayioúdha, Mória, Pýrgi Thermís

The coast road heading **north** from Mytilíni towards Mandamádhos (see p.408) follows a rather nondescript coastline, but offers startling views across the straits to Turkey. The most appealing spot en route is **PANAYIOÚDHA**, 8km away, with a church resembling a miniature Áyios Therápon, and waterside **tavernas** buzzing at weekends. Best, most popular and priciest of these is *Kostaras*, one of the first establishments you encounter coming from Mytilíni. At the far end of the flagstoned pedestrian quay, the simple *Akroyiali* is homier and also excellent value.

Just past Panayioúdha you can make a detour to **MÓRIA**, and thence to a valley 1km south, the site of a second-century-AD Roman **aqueduct** that used to bring water from the foothills of Mount Ólymbos; the eleven remaining spans of its 26-kilometre extent are intact to varying degrees, lofty and impressive. A little further along the coastal road at **PÁMFYLLA** and **PÝRGI THERMÍS** you may glimpse various *pýrgi* (tower-mansions), relics of the nineteenth-century gentry. Also near Pýrgi Thermís stands the well-preserved ninth- to fourteenth-century Byzantine church of **Panayía Troulotí**, one of the few Byzantine monuments to escape Ottoman ravages. Just 500m further at **PARALÍA THERMÍS**, the Roman-Byzantine **hamam** has been allowed to decay in favour of an ugly, sterile modern facility adjacent, though it still supplies the hot water, and you can stick your head in to admire the vaulted brickwork. You're a bit far (13km) from town here, but if you fancy staying there's a decent seafront B-class hotel, the *Votsala* (Ⓣ02510/71 231, Ⓕ71 179, Ⓔvotsala@otenet.gr; ④–⑤), with watersports off the somewhat scrappy beach.

South: the Variá museums

Just south of town, on the road to the airport, you glimpse more tower-mansions at Khryssomaloússa and Aklidhíou. But the most rewarding targets in this direction are a pair of unlikely museums in the formerly elegant (and now overbuilt) village of **VARIÁ**, 5km from town; blue urban buses cover the distance every half an hour.

The Theophilos Museum

The **Theophilos Museum** (May–Sept Tues–Sun 9am–2pm & 6–8pm; may omit pm hours Oct–April; €1.50 admission includes key-catalogue), well signposted on the southern edge of Variá, honours this regional painter with five rooms of wonderful, little-known canvases specifically commissioned by his patron Thériade (see box below) during the years leading up to the artist's death. Theophilos' personal experience of pastoral Lésvos is evident in the wealth of accurate sartorial detail found in such elegiac scenes as fishing, reaping, olive-picking and baking. There are droll touches too, such as a cat slinking off with a fish in *The Fishmongers* (Room 2). The *Sheikh-ul-Islam* with his hubble-bubble (Room 2) seems drawn from life, as does a highly secular Madonna merely titled *Mother with Child* (also Room 2). As an ethnographic document, *The Albanian Dancer* (Room 5) is of most value. However, in classical scenes – such as *Sappho and Alkaeos* (Room 5), a landscape series of Egypt, Asia Minor and the Holy Land, and episodes from wars historical and contemporary – Theophilos was clearly on shakier ground; in the painting *Abyssinians Hunting an Italian Horseman* (Room 3), for instance, the subject has been conflated with New World Indians chasing down a Conquistador. The sole concessions to modernity are the aeroplanes sketched in as an afterthought over various island landscapes.

Theophilos Hadzimihaïl (1873–1934): the Rousseau of Greece?

The "naïve" painter **Theophilos** Hadzimihaïl was born and died in Mytilíni Town, and both his eccentricities and talents were remarkable from an early age. After a failed apprenticeship as a shoemaker, he ran away to Smyrna, then to Mount Pílio on the Greek mainland in 1894 after allegedly killing a Turk. Wandering across the country from Pílio to Athens and the Peloponnese, Theophilos became one of the prize eccentrics of turn-of-the-century Greece, dressing up as Alexander the Great or various revolutionary war heroes, complete with *tsaroúhia* (pom-pommed shoes) and *fustanélla* (pleated skirt). A recluse who (it is claimed) neither drank, swore, smoked nor attended church, Theophilos was ill and living in severely reduced circumstances back on Lésvos when he was introduced to Thériade in 1919; the latter, virtually alone among critics of the time, recognized his peculiar genius and ensured that Theophilos was supported both morally and materially for the rest of his life.

With their childlike perspective, vivid colour scheme and idealized mythical and rural subjects, Theophilos' works are unmistakeable. Relatively few of his works survive today, because he executed commissions for a pittance on ephemeral surfaces such as kafenío counters, horsecarts, or the walls of long-vanished houses. Facile comparisons are often made between Theophilos and Henri Rousseau, the roughly contemporaneous French "primitive" painter. Unlike "Le Douanier", however, Theophilos followed no other profession, eking out a precarious living from his art alone. And while Rousseau revelled in exoticism, Theophilos' work was principally and profoundly rooted in Greek mythology, history and daily life.

The Thériade Museum

The **Thériade Museum** (Tues–Sun 9am–2pm & 5–8pm; €1.50), its palatial extent contrasting with the adjacent, cottage-like Theophilos Museum, is the brainchild of native son Stratis Eleftheriades (1897–1983). Leaving Mytilíni for Paris at the age of 18, he Gallicized his name to Thériade and went on to become a renowned avant-garde art publisher, persuading some of the leading artists of the twentieth century to participate in his ventures. The displays here comprise two floors worth of lithographs, engravings, woodblock prints and watercolours by the likes of Miró, Chagall, Picasso, Matisse, Le Corbusier, Léger, Rouault and Villon, either annotated by the painters themselves or commissioned as illustrations for the works of prominent poets and authors – an astonishing collection (albeit slightly depleted by a 1999 burglary) for a relatively remote Aegean island, and one which deserves a leisurely perusal. Highlights include Miró's cheerfully lurid lithos for Alfred Jarry's *Ubu Roi* and *L'Enfance d'Ubu*, Chagall's surprisingly coarse, sometimes Brueghelesque *Biblical Cycle*, and reproductions of illuminated medieval manuscripts from issues of *Verve*, the art quarterly which Thériade published from 1937 to 1971.

Beaches: Haramídha and Áyios Ermoyénis

Beyond the airport and Krátigos village, a paved road loops around 9km more to the pebbly double beach of **Haramídha** (16km in total from town). The eastern bay boasts several **tavernas** – best of these *Theodhora Glava*, aka *Grioules* – and a medium-sized hotel, but the marginally superior western strand has no shade or facilities.

Remote as it seems, the more scenic double beach at **Áyios Ermoyénis**, 3km due west of Haramídha, can get very crowded at weekends with townees. The patron saint's chapel perches on the cliff separating the two small, sandy coves; there's no proper taverna or place to stay, merely a snack-café by the parking area. If you're driving from Mytilíni, the most direct (13km) paved road is via Loutrá village.

Loutrá Yéras

For other pleasant immersions near Mytilíni, it's worth heading for **Loutrá Yéras**, 8km west along the main road to Kalloní. Just the thing after a sleepless night on a malodorous ferry, these **public hot springs** (daily: June–Sept 7am–7pm; Oct & April–May 8am–6pm; Nov–March 9am–5pm; €2) – the best appointed on the island – feature three marble spouts feeding 38°C water into a marble pool in a vaulted chamber; there are separate facilities for each sex (ladies have only two spouts, but pool size is comparable), and skinny-dipping is, unexpectedly in prudish Greece, obligatory. A seasonal café-restaurant (weekends only off season) on the roof of the bath house overlooks the gulf.

Southern Lésvos

The southernmost portion of Lésvos is indented by two great inlets, the gulfs of **Kalloní** and **Yéra**. The former curves in a northeasterly direction, the latter northwesterly, creating a fan-shaped peninsula at the heart of which is pine-cloaked, 967-metre-high **Mount Ólymbos**. Both shallow gulfs are in turn almost landlocked by virtue of very narrow outlets to the open sea, which don't have – and probably never will have – bridges spanning them. This is some of the most verdant and productive territory on Lésvos; the best oil-bearing olives are grown here, and the stacks of pressing mills, many still functioning, are a familiar sight on the skyline.

Pérama

With its mostly abandoned industrial structures dedicated to the olive-oil and tanning trade, **PÉRAMA** is still one of the larger places on the Gulf of Yéra, and has a regular daytime **kaïki-ferry** service (no cars but two-wheelers okay; €0.75 per foot passenger) linking it with Koundoroudhiá and blue city buses to/from Mytilíni on the far side.

A more likely reason to show up is to patronize one of the better **taverna-ouzerís** in the region: *Balouhanas*, northernmost of a line of eateries on the front, with a wooden, cane-roofed balcony jutting out over the water. The name's a corruption of *balıkhane* or "fish-market" in Turkish, and seafood is a strong point, whether grilled or made into croquettes, as are regional starters like *giouzlemés* (cheese-stuffed fried crêpe) and home-made desserts. They're open all year (lunch/supper); count on €15 per head.

Plomári

Due south of Mount Ólymbos and perched on the edge of the "fan", **PLOMÁRI** is the only sizeable coastal settlement in the south, and indeed the second largest town on Lésvos. It presents an unlikely juxtaposition of scenic appeal and its famous oúzo distilling industry; among several local brands, Varvayianni is the most famous but Yiannatsi and Arvanitou are reckoned just as good. They can all be sampled at the phenomenal number of **traditional kafenía** – especially the vine-shrouded one on central Platía Beniamín – interspersed with a few more contemporary bars, which crowd the old marketplace around the central plane tree.

Oúzo!

Oúzo is the Greek version of a grape-mash spirit found across the Mediterranean from Lebanon to France. The fermented residue of grape skins, pips and stalks left after wine-pressing, called *stémfyla* in Greek, is boiled in a copper still. Oúzo was unknown until late medieval times, since before the perfection of copper-sheet technology, such spirits could not be mass-produced. The resulting distillate was known under the Ottomans as *rakí*; its popularity grew during the nineteenth century, when shortages at distilleries in Smyrna, Constantinople and Lésvos tempted the unscrupulous to concoct pseudo-*rakí* by simply dumping pure grain alcohol into flavoured water. This was countered by the official, compulsory addition of dye to incoming alcohol shipments, necessitating distillation to remove it.

The modern term oúzo probably derives from the Italian *uso Massalia*, used to tag early shipments leaving the Ottoman empire for Marseille. Today it means a *rakí* base flavoured with various aromatic spices, usually star anise or fennel; exact flavourings and proportions are closely guarded secrets of each distiller. Bottled oúzo's alcohol content varies from 38 percent to 48 percent, with 44 percent strength considered the minimum for any quality. It is illegal to bottle oúzo at more than 50 percent strength – the risk of explosion is too great – though you may find home-made oúzo in wooden barrels at strengths approaching 60 percent. Mediocre commercial oúzo is often fortified with molasses, or even alcohol as in Ottoman days. Oúzo has the harmless property of turning milky white when water or ice cubes are added; this results from the binding of anethole, an aromatic compound found in both fennel and anise.

The local *paniyíri* season kicks off in mid-July with an **oúzo festival**, and culminates towards the end of the month in celebrations honouring Áyios Harálambos and including such rural activities as horse races (but no longer, apparently, a bull sacrifice).

Practicalities

Plomári is linked to Mytilíni by a direct **bus** route, which runs past the pretty villages of Paleókipos, Papádhos and Skópelos (as well as Áyios Isídhoros resort); if you have your own two-wheeler, you can cut the journey time slightly by using the kaïki-ferry between Koundoroudhiá and Pérama.

Despite a resounding lack of good beaches in the immediate vicinity, Plomári is besieged in summer by hordes of Scandinavian package tourists, but you can usually find a **room** (they are prominently signposted) at the edge of the charmingly dilapidated old town, which fills both sides of the Sidhoúndas ravine. Your best bet for an on-spec vacancy, above the inland Platía Beniamín, is the welcoming *Pension Lida* (Ⓣ & Ⓕ02520/32 507; ❷), a fine restoration inn occupying adjacent old mansions, with seaview balconies for most units. Another quiet, attractive area for budget lodging is the western suburb of **Ammoudhélli**, 1km along the road to Melínda, poised above a church and little fine-gravel **beach**; examples here include *Irini Rooms* (Ⓣ02520/32 875; ❷) and *Marcia Rooms* (Ⓣ02520/32 755; ❸). Most tourists actually stay in **ÁYIOS ISÍDHOROS**, 3km east, essentially a cluster of hotels at the west end of a long, fine-pebble beach. Pick of the **hotels** here, not completely overrun with packages, is the C-class *Pebble Beach* (Ⓣ02520/31 651, Ⓕ31 566; ❺), co-managed by the extroverted, cat-loving Evangelia Saropoulou, who grew up in Connecticut. Most of the large rooms overlook the beach, where a boardwalk crosses a bit of reef; there's also a ground-floor restaurant with pastel-blue and driftwood decor, on-site **car rental**, a saltwater pool and a few sports facilities (including the municipal footie grounds next door).

Prospects for a decent **meal** in or around Plomári are somewhat limited; the supper-only *Platanos* taverna near the central plane tree is often unbearably busy, and nothing special at that, while a string of several waterfront tavernas are uniformly mediocre, with the honourable exception of reliable and long-established *Bacchus* at the east end of the harbour square. Ammoudhélli can offer the shambolic but friendly *To Ammoudhelli*, perched unimproveably over the beach and open at lunch too; skip the touristy printed menu and ask for the dishes of the day (eg *ambelofásola*, sardines) and *orektiká* like *tyrokafterí* and grilled octopus – budget €9 per person. At Áyios Isídhoros you might try *Iy Mouria*, where the road turns inland to cross the creek draining to the long, popular pebble beach, or (1km inland from this) *Tou Panai*, with seating in an olive grove.

Rounding out the list of Plomári's vital amenities are two **banks**, each with a cash machine, and a **post office** on the shoreline road.

Melínda and Tárti

Given the dearth of good beaches within walking distance, tourism supremos in Plomári promote **boat trips** to various better ones along the southwest coast. But of course there's nothing stopping you getting there under your own steam. The closest is **MELÍNDA**, 6km west of Plomári by paved road, a 700-metre sand-and-shingle **beach** at the mouth of a canyon choked with olive trees. It's an alluring place, with sweeping views west towards the Vaterá coast and the cape of Áyios Fokás, and south (in clear conditions) to Mount Pelinéo on Híos and the Turkish Karaburun peninsula. Development in the hamlet just behind consists of three **taverna/rooms** outfits, of which easternmost *Maria's* (Ⓣ02520/93 239; ❶) is an endearingly ramshackle place with simple but reasonably priced food and lodging, with *Paradhisos* (Ⓣ02520/93 220; ❶) of similar standard; *Melinda* (aka Dhimitris Psaros; Ⓣ02520/93 234; ❶), at the west end of the strand by the monolith, has a more elaborate menu and higher quality en-suite rooms.

Even more unspoiled (thanks to a formerly dreadful 10-km side road in, now sixty percent paved), **TÁRTI**, some 22km in total from Plomári, is a 400-metre-wide cove where Lésvos hoteliers and restaurant owners take *their* holidays. Rocky capes gird it to either side, and for once the bay here deserves its blue-flag rating. Of the three beachfront **tavernas** here, two work late into September; **rooms** (eg those of Vangellis Asmanis, Ⓣ02510/83 577; ❷) flank the final approach road should you want to stay.

Ayiássos

AYIÁSSOS, nestled in a remote, wooded valley under the crest of Mount Ólymbos, is the most beautiful hill town on Lésvos, its narrow cobbled streets lined by ranks of tiled-roof houses. Its Shangri La quality is heightened on the more usual northerly approach from Mytilíni Town, 26km away, which gives no clue of the enormous village until you see huge knots of parked cars at the southern edge of town (where the bus drops you).

Don't be put off by the endless ranks of kitsch wooden and ceramic souvenirs or carved "Byzantine" furniture, aimed mostly at Greeks, but continue uphill to the old marketplace, with its kafenía, yogurt shops and butcher stalls. Regrettably, multiple video-game arcades have marred the traditional ambience, but in certain cafés, bands of *sandoúri*, with clarinet, lap-drum and violin, play on weekend afternoons, accompanying spontaneous, inebriated dance performances on the cobbles outside.

The central church of the **Panayía Vrefokratoússa**, internally lit by an improbable number of hanging *kandília* (oil lamps) – now electrified for safety – was originally built in the twelfth century to house a wonder-working icon supposedly painted by the Evangelist Luke. With such a venerable icon as a focus, the local **festival** on August 15 is one of the liveliest in Greece (let alone Lésvos), and vividly illustrates the country-fair element in a traditional *paniyíri*, where pilgrims come to buy and sell as well as perform devotions. Stalls in the foundations of the sanctuary are leased year-round to small businesses – a practice with age-old Greek antecedents, though currently far more common in Turkey. Ayiássos also takes **Carnival** very seriously; there's a club dedicated to organizing it, opposite the post office.

The Mylélia water mill

If you're headed for Ayiássos with your own car, you might consider a stop at the **Mylélia water mill**, whose inconspicuously signposted access track takes off 1km west of the turning for Ípios village. The name means "place of the mills", and there were once several hereabouts, powered by water brought by aqueduct from the same spring at Karíni up-valley that fed the Roman aqueduct at Mória (see p.384). The last survivor (open daily 9am–6pm), restored to working order in the mid-1990s, has thankfully not been twee-ified in the least; the keeper will show you the millrace and paddle wheel, as well as the flour making its spasmodic exit, after which you're free to buy gourmet pastas (somewhat pricey, consider the mark-up a donation) at the adjacent shop.

Practicalities

To reach Ayiássos from Mytilíni you have a choice of several daily **buses**. Access from Plomári is slightly more complicated; there's asphalt road and public transport only as far as Megalohóri, good dirt surface and your own conveyance thereafter. The area between Megalohóri and the summit ridge was severely charred by a forest fire in 1994, and though the road was unaffected, the countryside's appeal has taken a tumble – until you cross the watershed with its military watchpoint, and dense woods of unscathed oak and chestnut take over from scorched pine.

Ayiássos' best **restaurants** are *Dhouladhelli*, on your left as you enter the village from the extreme south (bus-terminal) end, or the idiosyncratic nocturnal ouzerí *To Stavri*, at the extreme north end of main thoroughfare 28-Oktovríou 1944 in Stavrí district, its walls bedaubed with maxims in local dialect. At either of these spots you can eat for a fraction of the prices asked at the coastal resorts.

Polikhnítos and around

A different bus route from Mytilíni leads to the inland village of **POLIKHNÍTOS**, also accessible from Kalloní by a paved shortcut road via the coastguard base at Akhladherí. There are a few grills and *barákia* around the central junction, but these are largely monopolized by conscripts from the huge nearby army camp. The main potential point of interest for outsiders is a 1997-restored **spa** 1.5km east of Políkhnitos (daily July–Aug 6–11am & 3–6pm; spring/autumn 7–11am & 4–6pm; €1.50), with separate, pink-tinted domed bath chambers of iron-laced water for each sex. More attractive are the **hot springs** of **Áyios Ioánnis**, fairly well signposted 3km below the village of **LISVÓRI**, in turn 4km east of Políkhnitos, but also more directly accessible via a poorly marked, 1.5-kilometre dirt road taking off from the main highway just east of an emergency military runway which crosses it. Flanking the eponymous chapel beside the stream here are two pools housed in unlocked, whitewashed, vaulted chambers (the left-hand, easterly one's nicer), with 37°C water and no dress code once inside. Bring candles or a torch at night, though the keeper is usually on hand to switch on the lights (€1.50 fee), and he runs a decent little **taverna** in the modern buildings on the north side of the stream.

Skála Polikhnítou and Nyfídha

From Políkhnitos, a paved road leads 4km northwest to **SKÁLA POLIKHNÍTOU**, a pleasantly scruffy place with an uninspiring beach but an embarrassment of choice in **tavernas** behind its prettified quay, open most of the year. Among a half-dozen of these, *T'Asteria* sits at the north end of things, on the way to the salt works, while the *Exohiko Kendro Tzitzifies*, closest to the jetty and opposite the jujube trees of the name, is actually a delightful seafood ouzerí with a limited but inexpensive menu, a loyal local clientele, a kind family in charge plus no fewer than eight different brands of oúzo on offer. Skála has just one unusual **accommodation** option: *Soft Tourism* run by Lefteris and Erika (Ⓣ02520/42 678 or 093/7925435; ❷), who also have the concession to run the Polikhnítos spa. They generally host special-interest groups from April to June and in September, but especially welcome independent travellers during July and August.

Veering left on the approach road to Skála takes you after 5km to **NYFÍDHA**, which has a better, kilometre-long beach (though periodically beset by north winds) and just a couple of **tavernas**, of which *Ouzeri Yiotis* at mid-beach, and *Exohiko Kendro O Grigoris* are the most reliable.

Vaterá and Vríssa

The actual end of the Polikhnítos bus route, 9km south via the attractive village of Vríssa, and 55km in total from the port, is **VATERÁ**. The seven-kilometre-long, sandy **beach** here, backed by vegetated hills and looking out to Turkey, Híos and Psará, offers some of the warmest, cleanest swimming on Lésvos. A proposed direct coastal road from Vaterá to Melínda will probably never materialize owing to politics in Plomári (they suspect they'd lose all their day trade to Vaterá), rugged cliffs to be blasted and funding difficulties.

The Vaterá area hit the Greek news in 1997 when an Athenian paleontologist, Michael Dermitzakis, confirmed what farmers unearthing bones had long suspected when he announced that the area was a treasure trove of **fossils**, including the bones of two-million-year-old gigantic horses, mastodons, monkeys and tortoises, the latter the size of a Volkswagen Beetle. Until 20,000 years ago, Lésvos (like all other east Aegean islands) was joined to the Asian mainland, and the gulf of Vaterá was a subtropical freshwater lake; the animals in question came to drink, died nearby and were trapped and preserved by successive volcanic flows. In **VRÍSSA**, Dermitzakis and the University of Athens have established a Natural History Collection in the former girl's school (daily 9.30am–7pm; €0.90) dedicated to the paleontological finds – it's not exactly required viewing as presently organized, but a new, more extensive gallery is promised.

Practicalities

Development at Vaterá straggles for several kilometres to either side of the central T-junction; near the west end of the strip is one of the very few consistently attended and professionally run **hotels**, George and Barbara Ballis' C-class *Vatera Beach Hotel* (Ⓣ02520/61 212, Ⓕ61 164, Ⓦwww.our-lesvos.com; open Easter–Oct 15; ❺ but 20% discount for internet bookings), whose well-appointed rooms have fridges and air con. This also has a good attached restaurant with home-grown produce and shoreline tables from where you can gaze out to the cape of **Áyios Fokás**, 3km west, where only foundations and broken column stubs remain of a **temple of Dionysos** with a superimposed early Christian basilica. The little tamarisk-shaded anchorage here has an acceptable **fish taverna**, *Akrotiri/Angelerou*, better than any of the several independent eateries at Vaterá proper but not quite so good as those at Skála Polikhnítou.

The local **campsite** (*Dionysos Club*, Ⓣ02520/61 151; June–Sept), a walled compound with chalets as well as a pool and disco-bar, lies well inland from the portion of Vaterá beach east of the main T-junction, where seasonal villas and apartments for locals predominate. At the extreme eastern end of things, set slightly inland amongst pines, the well-priced C-class *Irini* (Ⓣ02520/61 407, Ⓕ61 410; ❸) is the other recommendable local **hotel**, a bit remote but thus eager to please.

If you intend to stay anywhere in Vaterá you'll certainly want your own transport, since the closest fully stocked shops are at Polikhnítos and the bus appears only a few times daily. You can **rent cars** from Alfa (Ⓣ02520/61 132 or Ⓔalfacar@aias.gr), near the T-junction.

East from Vaterá

Once past the *Hotel Irini*, the beach ends and the seafront road veers inland up a river valley to Káto Stavrós, where the paved road currently ends. Ambelikó, the next village east on the hillside, can be reached via a paved road from the north, but the way in from Káto Stavrós is along a rough dirt track. The onward route to Akrássi and (eventually) Megalohóri is now finally paved, and the stretch down the canyon to Melínda via Paleohóri is under construction. While works remain in progress, count on almost ninety minutes' hard driving to reach Melínda from Vaterá.

From Akrássi, a seven-plus-kilometre dirt track descends to the island's remotest coastal settlement, **Paralía Dhrótas**, a collection of shacks behind a coarse-pebble shore. Electric power arrived here (and in the inland village of Dhróta, 1km before) only in 1996, and it's the sort of place, with its near-Third World squalor, that makes you understand how the northeast Aegean got its poverty rating (see p.305) from the EU. Though the scenery is grand enough, there's no joy here except for a seasonal snack bar that apparently charges what it likes; given the state of the roads, it wouldn't be much slower (one and a half hours) to walk in from Vaterá along the coast – a popular outing. You could continue east towards Melínda, reaching the scenically set cliffside church of **Panayía Kryftí** about halfway along.

Western Lésvos

The main road **west of Loutrá Yéras** is surprisingly devoid of settlement, with little of interest before you glimpse the Gulf of Kalloní. The nondescript, eponymous town at its head is the gateway to a mostly treeless, craggy region whose fertile valleys offer a sharp contrast to the bare ridges. River mouths form little oases behind a handful of beaches which account for the existence of **resorts** like Skála Kallonís, Sígri and Skála Eressoú. A trio of **monasteries** lining the road west of Kalloní, in addition to occasionally striking inland villages, provide architectural interest.

Kalloní and Skála Kallonís

KALLONÍ itself is an unembellished agricultural and market town more or less in the middle of the island, 41km from Mytilíni. You may pause here since it's the intersection of most bus routes and has plenty of shops, including pharmacies and three **banks** with precious cash machines – the only such facilities on the island aside from those at Mytilíni Town, Plomári, Mólyvos and Skála Kallonís.

With time to spare, you might make the three-kilometre detour south to **SKÁLA KALLONÍS**, Lésvos' fifth-ranking package resort. Besides a long, coarse-sand beach on the lake-like gulf, there are a half-dozen **hotels** here, more comfortable than most at either Skála Eressoú or Plomári. This accommodation has been relegated west out of town to the edge of the salt marsh, which attracts hundreds of **bird-watchers** during the March-to-May nesting season. Pick of the **accommodation** here is the human-scale bungalow complex *Malemi* (Ⓣ02530/22 594, Ⓕ22 838, Ⓦwww.hit360.com/malemi; ❺), run by the Kapsalis family, with a variety of units from doubles to family suites, attractive grounds, tennis court and a large pool. **Tavernas** lining the quay with its fishing fleet are generally indistinguishable – though most offer the gulf's celebrated *sardhélles pastés*, or sardines marinated in lemon and salt crystals for a day; the locals themselves tend to favour *Mimi's*, on the square just inland. From late summer through early autumn, you'll find the sardines deliciously grilled fresh. Local **sports facilities** include bicycle rental – ideal for the flat terrain hereabouts – and a small windsurf/Hobie Cat school near the hotel cluster. On the waterfront there's a freestanding **cash machine**.

Mésa temple, Kremastí bridge and Halinádhou basilica

Signposted about 1km east of the Akhladherí shortcut (see p.390), some 14km east of Kalloní, are the traces of an ancient **Aphrodite temple** (Tues–Sun 8am–2.30pm; free) at **MÉSA** (Méson). At the site, marked by two great oaks and ringed by grain fields on a gentle slope, just the original eleventh-century-BC foundations and a few later column stumps remain, plus the ruins of a fourteenth-century Genoese basilica built within; it was once virtually on the sea but a nearby stream has silted things up in the intervening millennia. All told, it's not worth a special trip, but certainly merits the short detour if you're passing by.

Some 7km west of Mésa, back towards Kalloní, lies the turning for **AYÍA PARASKEVÍ**, an intriguing tableau of nineteenth-century bourgeois architecture, with its central crossroads flanked by an inordinate number of kafenía and shops. The place is famed for its **bull-sacrifice rite** on Pentecost Saturday (seven weeks after Orthodox Easter, usually June), a festival also accompanied by less bloodthirsty horse racing.

Another, perhaps more compelling, reason to pass through is to visit the Genoese-built **Kremastí bridge**, the largest and best preserved medieval bridge in the east Aegean. This stands 3km west of Ayía Paraskeví, beside a dirt road taking off from the main paved onward road to Nápi (head straight through the central junction). However, it is slightly easier to find from the Kalloní–Mólyvos road, and since all junctions are unsignposted exact distances are given: head 3.7km south from the turn-off to Stýpsi, bear left (east) onto the unmarked dirt track before the filling station, and then proceed 4.3km – the bridge is obvious just to the north.

An equally worthwhile monument, the early Christian **Halinádhou basilica**, lies just over 5km east of Ayía Paraskeví on a dirt road, patchily signposted from the central crossroads (turn right, coming from the Kalloní road). Nearly a dozen columns of this three-aisled basilica remain standing, some with their capitals – a peaceful spot amidst a wilderness of pines and olives, which prompts speculation as to why it was built just here, as it was clearly never the *katholikón* of a monastery. Naturally the masonry is of a piece with the surrounding basalt boulders on the adjacent, pine-tufted ridge.

The monastery of Limónos

West of Kalloní, the road winds 4km uphill to the monastery of **Limónos**, (re?-)founded in 1527 by the monk Ignatios. It is a huge, rambling complex, with just a handful of monks and lay workers to maintain three storeys of cells around a vast, plant-filled courtyard; the north wing, where Ignatios' cell is preserved as a shrine, is the oldest section. The eighteenth-century *katholikón*, with contemporary frescoes, an elaborately painted carved-wood ceiling and archways, is built in Asia Minor style and is traditionally off limits to women. A sacred spring flows from the church's south foundation wall; men can request a look at the church interior when they visit the ecclesiastical exhibit.

A former abbot established a **museum** (daily 9.30am–6pm, may close 3pm low season; €1.50) on two floors of the west wing. The ground-floor ecclesiastical collection is, alas, the only wing open as of writing, with the more interesting upstairs ethnographic gallery off limits indefinitely. Content yourself with an overflow of farm implements stashed in a corner storeroom below at the northwest corner of the compound, next to a chamber where giant *pithária* (urns) for grain and olive oil are embedded in the floor. Just west, through a gateway, the pilgrims' inn and an old-age home share space with patrolling peacocks and an aviary.

Beyond, the road heading west passes through **FÍLIA**, with its truncated minaret and pre-1923 mosque, where you can turn off for a paved shortcut to Skoutáros and the north of Lésvos. Most traffic continues through to the unusually neat village of **SKALOHÓRI**, with its battered minaret and its houses stacked in tiers at the head of a valley facing the sea and the sunset. From here you can head on to **VATOÚSSA**, the most landlocked but also the most beautiful of the western settlements. Its upper quarter – away from the through road – has a clutch of atmospheric kafenía and ouzerís little frequented by outsiders; try the kafenío of Tryfon for simple mezédhes and sardines. On the lower, more prominent platía, there's *Mihalis*, with an ampler menu of grills and a few *mayireftá*.

The monastery of Perivolís

Some 8km beyond Vatoússa, a short track leads down to the sixteenth-century **monastery of Perivolís** (daily 8am–1hr before sunset; donation, no photos; pull on the bell rope for admission if necessary), built in the midst of a riverside orchard (*perivóli*). Feeble electric light is available to view fine if damp-damaged frescoes in the narthex. On the south wall, in an apocalyptic panel worthy of Bosch (*The Earth and Sea Yield Up Their Dead*), the Whore of Babylon rides her chimera, and assorted sea monsters disgorge their victims; just to the right, towards the main door, the Magi approach the Virgin Enthroned with the Christ Child. On the north side you see a highly unusual iconography of *Abraham, the Virgin, and the Penitent Thief of Calvary in Paradise*, with the mythical Four Rivers of Paradise gushing forth under their feet; just right of this are assembled the Hebrew kings of the Old Testament.

Ándissa and around

ÁNDISSA, 3km beyond Perivolís, nestles attractively under the only pine grove in the west of the island. At the edge of the village a sign implores you to "Come Visit our (Central) Square", not a bad idea for the sake of several kafenía sheltering under three enormous plane trees.

Directly below Ándissa, a paved road leads 6km north towards the fishing hamlet of **GAVATHÁS**, all of 25 buildings, with a narrow, partly sheltered beach and a bare handful of places to eat and stay – principally the *Hotel Restaurant Paradise* (Ⓣ02530/56 376; ❷), serving good fish and locally grown vegetables. A dirt side track leads one headland east to the huge, duney, surf-battered beach of **Kámbos**. You can keep going in the same direction, following signs pointing to "Ancient Andissa", though they actually lead you to **Ovriókastro**, the most derelict of the island's Genoese castles, evocatively placed on a promontory in plain sight of Mólyvos and with a good stretch of coast to either side. The dirty, exposed beaches here are unlikely to appeal, though there is a small snack bar. The locals mistakenly identify the castle with the ancient town, but the latter is actually on the next hillock east, formerly an islet; little remains besides the stubby foundations of its walls.

The monastery of Ipsiloú

Just west of modern Ándissa there's an important junction. Keeping straight leads you past the turning for the monastery of **Ipsiloú**, founded in 1101 atop an outrider of the extinct volcano of Órdhymnos to the south (511m), and still home to four monks. The *katholikón*, tucked in one corner of a large, irregular courtyard, has a fine wood-lattice ceiling, but its frescoes were repainted to detrimental effect in 1992. More intriguing are the bits of Iznik tiles stuck into the facade, and the exquisite double gateway. Upstairs you can visit a fairly rich **museum** of ecclesiastical treasure (sporadically open; donation in exchange for a postcard). Ipsiloú's patron saint is St John the Theologian, a frequent dedication for monasteries overlooking apocalyptic landscapes like the surrounding parched, boulder-strewn hills, some of the most desolate terrain in Greece.

The petrified "forest"

Signposted some 4km west of the monastery is the paved, five-kilometre side road to the main concentration of Lésvos' rather overrated **petrified "forest"** (daily 8am–sunset; €1.50), indicated by placards which also warn of severe penalties for pilfering souvenir chunks. On an east-facing slope, this fenced-in "reserve" of the best specimens can be toured by a total of 3km in walkways. For once, contemporary Greek arsonists cannot be blamed for the state of the trees, created by the combined action of volcanic ash from Órdhymnos and hot springs between 15 and 20 million years ago. The mostly horizontal sequoia trunks average a metre or less in length, though there are a few two to three-metre-long behemoths as featured in promotional posters. Another more accessible (and free) cluster can be found south of Sígri (see below), plus there are a fair number of petrified logs strewn about the courtyard of Ipsiloú.

Sígri

SÍGRI, near the western tip of Lésvos, has an appropriately end-of-the-line feel, accentuated by the general doldrums of tourism throughout the island. At the best of times it had a limited future as a resort, though its use by NATO as a naval base has been scaled down considerably from the early 1990s when battleships could be seen moored here in the superb harbour. The bay is guarded by a small castle and the long island of **Nissiopí**, which stretches across its mouth and acts as a buffer to the prevailing winds. Once or twice a week a NEL ferry calls here on its way between Límnos, Áyios Efstrátios and Rafina on the Greek mainland.

The eighteenth-century Ottoman **castle** sports a *tuğra* (the sultan's monogram) over its entrance; rarely seen outside Istanbul, this was a token of the high regard in which productive Lésvos (and specifically strategic Sígri) was held. The vaguely Turkish-looking **church of Ayía Triádha** overlooking the quay is in fact a converted **mosque**, while the town itself is a somewhat drab mix of traditional and modern cement dwellings. For an exhaustive guide to all the town monuments (including numerous fountains), obtain Roy Lawrance's guide booklet *Where the Road Ends: Sigri* (see "Books" in Context for full details).

The nearest of several **beaches**, south of the castle headland, is somewhat narrow and backed by a little-used road to Eressós; the far superior one of **Faneroméni** lies 3.5km north by a coastal dirt track from the northern outskirts of town. This beach is long and scenic, but there are no facilities to hand, and non-4WD vehicles will founder in the sand of the frontage "road". A shorter but equally good strand, **Liména**, can be found 2km south of Sígri at another creek mouth, just off the rough one-lane, 15-kilometre track to Eressós (use of which saves a bit of fuel but no time – best take a jeep).

Practicalities

Most people staying at Sígri are British clients of Direct Greece, the latest in a succession of small, specialist operators who have tried to make a go of selling holidays here – and who may in fact soon give up as their predecessors have done. At present, there's little **accommodation** that's not contracted out to the company, but you could try *Nelly's Rooms and Apartments* (Ⓣ02530/54 230; ❸), overlooking the castle, and the nearby *Rainbow Studios* (Ⓣ02530/54 310; ❸). Among several **tavernas**, the best all-rounder, just inland, is Italian-run, ultra-hygienic *Una Fatsa Una Ratsa*, with lovely grilled garlicky vegetables, pizza, pasta, grills and an Italian wine list; *Remezzo* further back is good for lobster. *Kavo Doro* opposite the base of the jetty gets first pick of the fishermen's catch, but has become rather pricey in recent years. If you wish to catch the occasional **ferry** (usually at an ungodly hour), ring Ⓣ02530/54 430 for current information.

Eressós and Skála Eressoú

The southerly option of the T-junction between Ándissa and Ipsiloú leads in just under 10km to the inland town of **ERESSÓS**. This is home to a large colony of expatriates who have bought or rented property, and a stroll along lanes flanked by the vernacular houses is rewarding during the cooler hours of the day.

During summer, half the population is down at the idyllic beach resort of **SKÁLA ERESSOÚ**, 4km further south, only resettled halfway through the nineteenth century after medieval piracy prompted the settlement of Eressós. Behind the resort stretches the largest and most attractive agricultural plain on Lésvos, a welcome green contrast to the volcanic ridges above. The three-kilometre beach here, given additional character by an islet within easy swimming distance, runs a close second in quality to Vaterá; despite this, the latter 1990s saw a sharp decline in Skála's fortunes, with few tour operators staying for successive years. Local attempts to boost the place as a family resort have been partly stymied by its reputation as the premier **lesbian watering hole** of Europe, engendered by a purported connection with Sappho and helped along by some titillating documentaries on UK television. Lesbians are the most consistent and loyal customers, so locals are hardly about to bite the hand that feeds, though in autumn 2000 there was considerable annoyance about a tour organized by London gay venue Candy Bar, whose publicity, not exactly intended for island consumption, got "leaked" to the villagers.

All that said, high summer still sees an odd mix of Brits, north Europeans, and Greek families putting in an appearance alongside those of the Sapphic persuasion. In 1998, the *Aeolian Village* luxury complex west of the village was purchased by Cypriot interests, who fly their countrymen in by regular direct flights; already clientele polarization has subsided, as many lesbian visitors occupy some of the hotel units, and much of the nude cavorting on the part of the beach used by the complex seems to have been toned down.

Accommodation

Skála has countless **rooms** and **apartments**, but ones near the sea fill early in the day or are block-booked by tour companies, though often not actually occupied. Other vacancies – like those touted at the bus stop – can be attributed to the fairly appalling standard of some units. In peak season, the best and quietest rooms tend to be inland, overlooking a garden or fields. Even following a recent decline in tourist numbers – Direct Greece has dropped the resort, citing a lack of commitment to "family values" – it's wise to entrust the search to Sappho Travel (Ⓣ02530/52 140, Ⓕ52 000, Ⓔsappho@otenet.gr). Jo and Joanna are switched-on and helpful, also serving as the local Budget car-hire station, ferry agent and air-ticket source; they are happy to place walk-ins in accommodation (❷–❹), but suggest you consult their UK-based website in advance, Ⓦwww.lesvos.co.uk.

Otherwise, there are just three bona fide **hotels** in Skála itself, plus the A-class *Aeolian Village* off to the west (Ⓣ02530/53 585, Ⓕ53 795; ❻, also pricier bungalows), 500m inland from the beach, western Lésvos' only luxury digs and large enough to have walk-in vacancies even in summer. Two establishments – the remote *Antiopi* (Ⓣ02530/53 311; ❶ rooms, ❸ studios), off by itself in the fields behind town, and the seafront *Sappho the Eressia* (Ⓣ02530/53 495, Ⓕ53 174, ⒺSappho_sarani@hotmail.com; ❸), with a cheerful, trendy ground-floor café – are run exclusively by and for lesbians. Others have to make do with the central, air-conditioned *Galini* (Ⓣ02530/53 138, Ⓕ53 137; ❹) slightly inland.

The Town

There's not much to Skála: just a roughly rectangular grid of perhaps five streets by eight, angling up to the oldest cottages on the slope of **Vígla** hill, and including the waterfront pedestrian lane (officially Papanikolí). The café-lined **square** at mid-waterfront is dominated by a bust of Theophrastos (372–287 BC), a renowned philosopher and botanist who hailed from **ancient Eressos**. This was not, as you might suppose, on the site of the modern village, but atop Vígla hill at the east end of the beach; crumbled bits of the remaining citadel wall are still visible from a distance. Once on top, the ruins prove even scantier, but it's worth the scramble up for the views – you can discern the ancient jetty submerged beyond the modern fishing anchorage.

Another famous reputed native of ancient Eressos was **Sappho**, the ancient poetess (c. 615–562 BC) and reputed lesbian. There are usually appreciable numbers of gay women paying homage to her – at the special-interest hotels noted above, certain of the waterfront kafenía, and at the somewhat reduced clothing-optional zone of the beach west of the river mouth.

Ancient Eressos lingered on into the Byzantine era, whose main legacy is the basilica of **Áyios Andhréas**, behind the modern church. The surviving foundations are oddly aligned southwest to northeast rather than the usual west to east; a notable floor mosaic is currently hidden under sand and plastic until a permanent sunshade is built. A one-room archeological museum (Tues–Sun 8am–2.30pm; free), immediately behind the basilica, is of minimal interest.

Other practicalities

Most **tavernas**, with elevated wooden dining platforms, back onto the beach; none is utterly awful – they wouldn't survive the intense competition for falling tourist numbers – but some stand out. The *Blue Sardine* at the far west end of the front is an excellent seafood ouzerí with good bread, clearly identified frozen items, unusual salads and extra touches to the fish. By contrast overpriced *Adonis* adjacent is best avoided in favour of *Soulatsos* a couple doors further east, a good full-service taverna with meat and fish dishes. East of the platía, *Zephyros* makes a good account of itself for grills, while Canadian-run *Yamas* is the place for pancake breakfasts, veggie burgers, wholemeal bread and decadent chocolate desserts – proprietress Linda also sells her art next door. The gay-women's contingent favours *Dhekati Mousa/Tenth Muse*, on the Theophrastos platía, though everyone is made welcome; a summer cinema further inland and west rounds up the nightlife, as does the music club *Primitive*, off in a suitably wild setting west of the river, and going since 1990.

Other amenities include a **post office**, a coin-op **laundry** near the church, and (in the premises of Sappho Travel), a **cash machine**, though it's unwise to rely exclusively on this – come prepared with euros from elsewhere.

Beaches near Skála: Kroússos and Tavári

Excursion boatmen at Skála Eressoú have a hard time convincing customers to leave the beautiful beach here, but if you get restless, there are two potential targets a little further east; both are also accessible by dirt road from Mesótopos (see below).

Kroússos, the first attractive bay along, is medium-sized and sandy, if utterly shadeless; in springtime there's good bird-watching in the reedbeds of the river mouth. From the deceptively simple **kantína** of Kyra-Maria, installed in a derelict KTEL bus on the sand, issues forth a steady, daily-changing stream of lovely *mayireftá* and salad goods grown in the adjacent field, which have made this a cult favourite and required meal stop amongst Greek beach-goers.

Tavári, the next cove along, is by contrast emphatically not worth the extra bother: apart from the stones and sea urchins in shallow water, the frontage road runs right along the beach. It's hard to fathom just why the management of the *Aeolian Village* has bought extensive land holdings here.

East to Kalloní

If you're returning to the main island crossroads at Kalloní, you can complete a loop from Eressós along the western shore of the Gulf of Kalloní via the hill villages of Mesótopos and Ágra; this route is entirely paved, notwithstanding obsolete maps which show it as a track.

The only settlement of any consequence on the Gulf of Kalloní's west shore is **PARÁKILA**, which boasts a ruined mosque (whose minaret non-acrophobes can easily climb in five minutes – but take care of crumbled plaster on the steps), an Ottoman bridge and the majority of Lésvos' limited citrus groves. Nearby beaches are not really worth stopping for, but for the record the best one (relatively speaking) is at **Apothíka**, back near the mouth of the gulf, with a taverna installed in the former kafenío.

Northern Lésvos

The main road north of Kalloní winds up a pine-flecked ridge and then down the other side into increasingly attractive country stippled with poplars and blanketed by olive groves. Long before you can discern any other architectural detail, the cockscomb silhouette of Mólyvos castle indicates your approach to the oldest established tourist spot on Lésvos, and still the island's fourth most populous settlement.

Mólyvos

MÓLYVOS (officially **MÍTHYMNA**), 61km from Mytilíni, is arguably the most beautiful village on Lésvos. Tiers of sturdy, red-tiled houses mount the slopes between the picturesque harbour and the castle, some standing defensively with their rear walls to the sea. Modern dwellings and hotels have been banned from the preserved municipal core, with a two-storey height limit imposed – a powerful watchdog group, "Friends of Molyvos", has seen to that – but this has, not surprisingly, promoted tweeness and steadily drained all the authentic life from the vine-canopied market lanes. Just one lonely tailor still plies his trade amongst souvenir shops far in excess of requirements, and the last locals' kafenío-ouzerí shut down in 1989, its "updated" successor *Salguimi* also folding within a decade.

Having been initially pitched in the 1970s and 1980s as an upmarket resort, there were for many years no smutty postcards or other tacky accoutrements; that's all history, with silly T-shirts and other shoddy souvenirs carpeting every vertical surface, and serving as constant reminders that you are still strolling through a stage-set, however beautiful, for mass tourism.

Arrival and information

If you're driving, beware that cars are banned from the harbour quay and the upper village, with parking limited in any case; there is a single, small **parking** area up by the castle, a larger one opposite the tourist office, just off the road to Eftaloú, and another small one a few hundred metres along Mihaïl Goútou, the road towards the harbour (in peak season cars are usually prohibited from proceeding any further).

The municipal **tourist office** (theoretically daily summer 8am–3pm & 6.30–8.30pm, spring/autumn 8.30am–3pm; ⓣ02530/71 347), by the bus stop, stocks some literature, and can help with accommodation. Immediately around the tourist office are two **cash machines**, a private money-exchange broker, plus several **motorbike and car rental** places; among the latter, Kosmos (ⓣ02530/71 650) and Best (ⓣ02530/72 145) can be recommended, the former with good rates for entry-level Group B cars. The **post office** is near the top of the upper commercial street, Kástrou.

Accommodation

Except in August, visitor numbers have fallen since 1996, yet package tour companies continue to monopolize much of the more comfortable and/or desirable **accommodation**. The principal duty of the tourist office is to provide a no-fee telephone placement service for nearly two thousand more modest rooms (❷–❸) in the village. It's worth taking advantage of this, as staff appear to be relatively unbiased and clued up on current vacancies, and it will save you a fair bit of trudging around.

The olives of Lésvos

No other Greek island is as dominated by olive production as Lésvos, which is blanketed by approximately 11 million olive trees. Most of these vast groves date from after a lethal frost in 1851, though a few hardy survivors are thought to be over five hundred years old. During the first three centuries after the Ottoman conquest, production of olive oil was a monopoly of the ruling pasha, but following eighteenth-century reforms in the Ottoman Empire, extensive tracts of Lésvos (and thus the lucrative oil trade) passed into the hands of the new Greek bourgeoisie, who greatly expanded the industry.

As in most of Greece, olives are harvested on Lésvos between late November and late December, the best ones coming from steep hillside plantations between Plomári and Ayiássos (see p.387 and p.389). Each grower's batch is brought to the local *trivío* (mill) – ideally within 24 hours of picking – pressed separately and tested for quality. Good first-pressing oil, some forty percent of that available in the fruit, is greenish and low in linoleic acid (by EU law, less than one percent acidity is required to earn the label "extra virgin"). The remaining oil, much of it from the kernels and other waste mash, is used for inferior blended oils and for soap production. In general, Greek oil tends to exceed Spanish or Italian in quality, owing to hotter, drier summers which promote low acid levels in the olives.

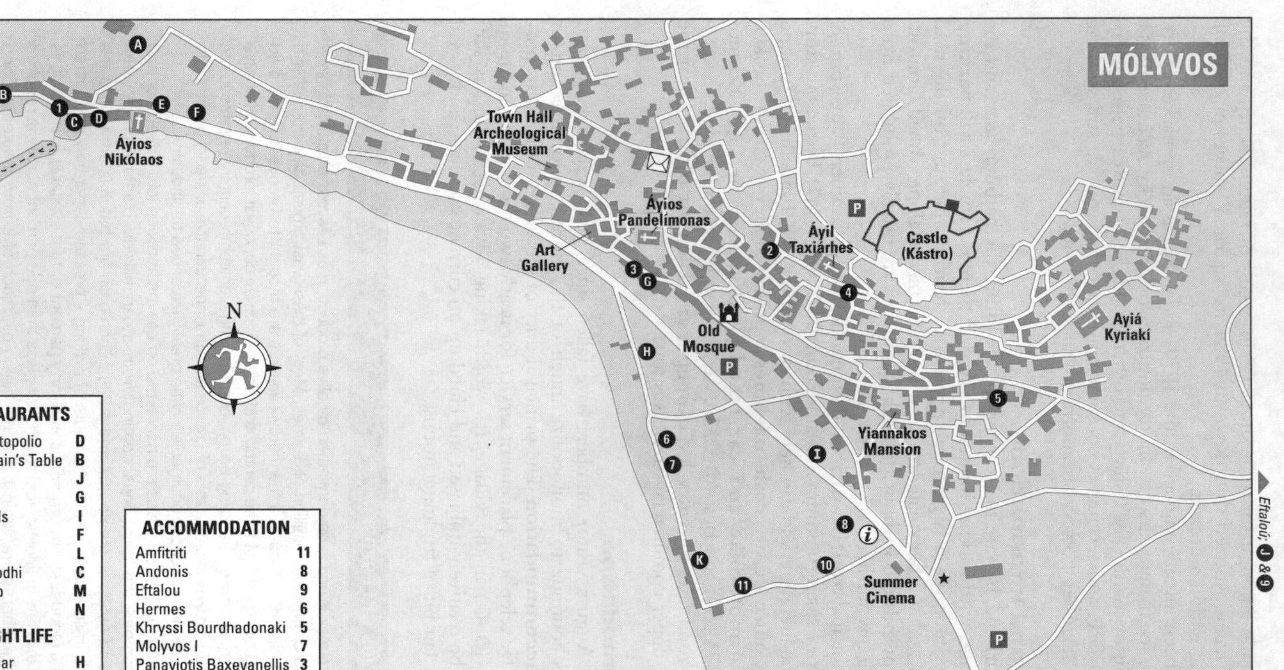
MÓLYVOS
Port
Áyios Nikólaos
Town Hall
Archeological Museum
Áyios Pandelímonas
Art Gallery
Áyil Taxiárhes
Castle (Kástro)
Old Mosque
Ayiá Kyriakí
Yiannakos Mansion
Summer Cinema
N
0
100m
Eftaloú; J & 9
Pétra & O
Vafiós; L, M & N
RESTAURANTS
Babis Psitopolio D
The Captain's Table B
Iy Eftalou J
El Greco G
Fili/Friends I
Galliano F
O Ilias L
To Khtapodhi C
To Petrino M
Vafios N
NIGHTLIFE
Congas Bar H
Gatelousi O
Gatelousi Piano Bar K
Music Bazaar E
Skala Bar A
ACCOMMODATION
Amfitriti 11
Andonis 8
Eftalou 9
Hermes 6
Khryssi Bourdhadonaki 5
Molyvos I 7
Panayiotis Baxevanellis 3
Poseidon 10
Sea Horse 1
Studios Voula 2
Varvara Kelesi 4

If you don't coincide with their opening hours, you could always try ringing ahead the selected listings below, or hunting on the spot – just look for placards with the blue-on-white official EOT logo of a face in profile. Mólyvos **hotels** are all lower down, along or just off the main sea-level thoroughfare, which heads straight past the tourist office towards the harbour; the more modest of these are not yet completely taken over by package allotments. If all else fails, the official **campsite**, *Camping Methymna* (ⓣ02540/71 169; June–Sept), lies 2km northeast of town, on the way to Eftaloú.

Amfitriti Immediately behind the *Olive Press* (see p.404) ⓣ02530/71 741, ⓕ71 744. This B-class hotel has its own pool in a peaceful garden setting, but it's monopolized by packages except during spring or autumn. ❺

Andonis Seaward of Mihaïl Goútou ⓣ02530/71 866, ⓕ71 636. This C-class has heating and is thus the only all-year hotel in Mólyvos; fairly peaceful location below the street. ❹

Eftalou 1.5km along the Eftaloú road ⓣ02530/71 584, ⓕ71 669. A well-managed C-class hotel, with a loyal independent clientele amongst the package groups. Lush gardens, pool, well-regarded restaurant, balconied, tan-tiled rooms with subdued wallpaper, air con and double glazing. ❹

Hermes Shore road ⓣ02530/71 250, ⓕ72 050. Large, airy, en-suite rooms at this C-class hotel, some with seaviews; opens late April, shuts late Oct, and far enough from bars that noise shouldn't be a problem; limited packages. ❹

Khryssi Bourdhadonaki Southeast hillside, towards Ayía Kyriakí district ⓣ02530/72 193. Modern self-catering rooms in an old house, with partial seaviews. ❸

Molyvos I Next door to the *Hermes* ⓣ02530/71 496, ⓕ71 460. Nominally B-class outfit nicely located on the shore, behind the tamarisks and its own stone-paved front terrace; tile-floored rooms in a converted old building. A bit pricey, considering the lack of special amenities, though you do get use of (and shuttle to) the pool and sports facilities at sister, out-of-town hotel *Molyvos II.* ❺

Panayiotis Baxevanellis ⓣ02530/71 558, or visit *El Greco* sweet shop. Rooms with a preponderance of double beds (rare in Mólyvos) and a common kitchen for self-catering. ❶

Poseidon Just seaward from the tourist office ⓣ02530/71 980, ⓕ71 570. Too humbly endowed a C-class to interest the package companies, but not such a bad location, with views to the castle from rear rooms. ❸

Sea Horse Overlooking the port ⓣ02530/71 320, ⓕ71 374. Acceptable C-class hotel if you're not interested in making an early night of it, and somewhat overpriced, but superb location. ❺

Studios Voula Below castle parking lot ⓣ02530/71 305, 72 017 or 71 567 – ask for Theoktisti on last two numbers. Pleasant studios with stunning views (❸), while the adjacent four-person suite in a restored house (❺) is the best spot in town for families.

Varvara Kelesi Near the castle ⓣ02530/71 460. Just three non-en-suite rooms, fairly representative of older rooms places in Mólyvos; pleasant, quiet and very high up, with a kindly proprietress. ❶

The Town

The perimeter walls and highest bastions of the Byzantine–Genoese **castle** (summer Tues–Sun 8am–2.30pm; €1.50) provide interesting rambles and views of Turkey across the straits. Closer examination reveals a dozen weathered Turkish-inscribed fountains along flower-fragrant, cobblestoned alleyways, a reflection of the fact that before 1923 Muslims constituted over a third of the population here and owned most of the finest mansions. You can try to gain admission to the Greek-built **Krallis** and originally Turkish **Yiannakos mansions** (erratic opening times, fine murals in the former) or the municipal **art gallery** (Tues–Sun 8am–2.30pm; free) occupying the former residence of local novelist Argyris Eftaliotis.

The local **archeological museum** (Tues–Sun 8.30am–3pm; free), in the basement of the town hall, features finds from ancient Mithymna, just northwest. Although the collection is well labelled and lit, space is limited and the best bits have inevitably been sent to Mytilíni. Besides numerous sea-life-encrusted amphorae, there's a clutch of blue Roman beads to ward off the evil eye (belief in this affliction is age-old and pan-Mediterranean). Of more contemporary interest are archival photos showing the Greek Army's victorious advance across the island, beginning November 8, 1912; a month later it was all over for the Ottomans, with the last image showing their prisoners being bundled into kaïkia at Mólyvos harbour for transfer to Anatolia.

Until excavations resume (unlikely), the site of Mithymna remains of essentially specialist interest, though a **necropolis** has been unearthed next to the bus stop; it's mainly the use of the Classical name that has been revived. The motivation for this, as so often in the Balkans, is nationalistic; *Mólyvos* ("Graphite", of which there is none locally) is an attempted Hellenization of the Turkish name *Molova*.

Beaches

Despite a plethora of organized activities and sunbeds to rent, the shingly **town beach** is mediocre, with rocks and sea urchins in the shallows, though it improves somewhat as you head towards the south end with its clothing-optional zone. Advertised boat excursions to bays as remote as Ánaxos and Tsónia (see p.404 and p.406) seem a frank admission of this failing; there are also six to eight daily minibus shuttles in season, linking all points between Ánaxos and Eftaloú – schedules are posted on strategic local windows.

Eating and drinking

Choose carefully when **eating out**; the obvious seaview tavernas on 17-Noemvríou climbing up from near the tourist office are all much of a muchness, where you pay primarily for the view rather than miniature portions. Instead, you should head either to Eftaloú, Vafiós village, or down towards picturesque Mólyvos harbour, to where the centre of the village's nocturnal gravity has shifted since the mid-1990s. Note that even tavernas designated "open all day" may shut at lunch during spring or autumn.

Babis Psitopolio Just above the harbour car park. The favourite off-season hangout for carnivores who pile inside; only three balcony tables. Mainly supper.

The Captain's Table Harbour quay, towards the boatyard – look for the green chairs. Theo and Melinda offer reasonable and very fresh seafood, vegetarian mezédhes and meat grills; live music two nights a week. Open all day, and consistent quality since 1995 opening.

Iy Eftalou 4km northeast, just before the eponymous spa. Splendid food, mostly grills, served in the almond- and fig-shaded courtyard at this much-loved *exohikó kéndro* (rural taverna); open most of the year for supper, with a fireplace indoors for the cooler months. Open all day in season.

Fili/Friends Mihaïl Goútou, near tourist office. An excellent *psistariá*, open until the wee hours (and much of the year), where fishermen and Mólyvos restaurateurs go after *they* close up. Chicken nuggets in pitta a speciality.

Galliano Just before the harbour. Great wood-oven pizzas, open for supper only until the small hours.

El Greco On the lower shopping street. Traditional pudding and cake shop; Panayiotis the proprietor is a wonderful raconteur (in several languages) and acts as mother hen to aspiring foreign artists, as the numerous dedicated paintings testify. Open most of the day until late, except mid-afternoon.

O Ilias Vafiós, 5km east, bottom of village. Excellent bread, good bulk wine and genuine atmosphere; fried mezédhes are filling, so go hungry. Open all day.

To Khtapodhi By the entrance to the port. Perched in an unbeatable location, this is the oldest outfit here, housed in the former customs house; atmospheric and popular with locals, who come for the grills, *mayireftá* and mezédhes like *sardhélles pastés*. Supper only.

To Petrino Vafiós village, 5km east. A newish (2000) entrant on the scene here, and compared to its rivals stresses more traditional island mezédhes and grilled meat. Open lunch and supper.

Vafios Vafiós village, 5km east. More extensive menu than its rival *Ilias*, with slicker presentation and less deep-frying, and still popular with Greeks despite reports of inconsistent quality. Worth trying if "Greek Night" coaches haven't descended. Open all day.

Nightlife

In terms of formal events, midsummer sees a short **festival** of music and theatre up in the castle; there's also a well-regarded summer **cinema** next to the taxi rank, with first-run fare. When out **tippling**, be advised that Mólyvos is as expensive in this regard as in everything else, though there are some happy hours.

Congas Bar Below the shore road, beyond the *Molyvos I*. Tropical decor at this crowded, disco-ey young things' hangout.

Gatelousi 3km out on the Pétra road. State-of-the-art outdoor techno-dub-trance disco on a cantilevered platform like a ship's deck. Open mid-June to Aug only.

Gatelousi Piano Bar Behind the *Olive Press Hotel*. A more genteel hangout for older folk, with live or taped music. Open all season.

Music Bazaar Just before the harbour. Popular and long-lived indoor dance bar.

Skala Bar Directly above the harbour, in a former blacksmith's. Live listening music three nights weekly: typically foreign/experimental on Sun, contemporary Greek Wed and Fri.

Pétra

Since there are both practical and political limits to the expansion of Mólyvos, many package companies have shifted their emphasis to **PÉTRA**, 5km south. Accordingly the place is beginning to sprawl untidily behind its broad, sandy beach and seafront square, but this has been partly pedestrianized to exclude idling buses, and the core of old stone houses, many with Levantine-style balconies overhanging the streets, remains.

Pétra takes its name from the giant volcanic monolith located some distance inland and capped by the eighteenth-century church of **Panayía Glykofiloússa**, reached via 103 rock-hewn steps on the northeast side. The walled compound at the top is of little intrinsic interest, but you should climb up at dawn or dusk for superb views of the surrounding agricultural plain. More intriguing local sights include the sixteenth-century church of **Áyios Nikólaos**, at the foot of the rock, sporting three phases of well-preserved frescoes up to 1721, and the intricately decorated and recently restored **Vareltzídhena mansion** (Tues–Sun 8.30am–7pm; may close earlier off season; free), some of whose rooms sport exquisite naïve, late-eighteenth-century murals: courting couples, a bear being trained, sailing ships, and a stylized skyline of Constantinople complete with cannons booming in a naval engagement.

Practicalities

For **accommodation**, there are a few small hotels, most block-booked by tour companies; one that's only partly committed, and one of the best walk-in choices, is the C-class *Michaelia* (Ⓣ02530/41 730, Ⓕ22 067; ❹), on the southerly road towards Ánaxos. With more money to spend, head for the B-class *Clara Hotel-Bungalows* at Avláki, 2km south (Ⓣ02530/41 532, Ⓕ41 535, Ⓦwww.aegeanweb.gr/clara; ❻), the first and still about the best of the luxury complexes near Pétra, with a pool and tennis court. All of the large, tastefully furnished rooms face the sea and Mólyvos; some have bathtubs, all have heating/air con.

Plenty of inexpensive **rooms** are available through the Women's Agricultural Tourism Cooperative (Ⓣ02530/41 238, Ⓕ41 309, Ⓔwomes@otenet.gr), formed by Pétra's women in 1984 to provide a more unusual option for visitors. In addition to operating an excellent, inexpensive, all-day **restaurant** on the square, with both grills and *mayireftá* served indoors or on a seaview roof terrace, they arrange rooms or studios (❶–❷) in a number of scattered premises.

Aside from the co-operative's eatery, most tavernas lack distinction, though some readers have liked *Iy Dhrosia* and *To Khrysso Petalo* behind the beach, despite their commercialization. Further afield at tiny **Avláki** beach, 1500m southwest on the way to Ánaxos and accessible by a marked coastal path or its own signposted driveway, *Estiatorio Avlaki*, really more of an ouzerí, has been going since 1975, and while quality had dipped and prices climbed slightly at last visit, it's still better than most alternatives in either Pétra or Ánaxos.

With the *Gatelousi* disco looming on the hillside to the north, organized **nightlife** in town is understandably very modest. The old olive press on the coast road has been converted into a "dance bar", *Machine*, with the industrial apparatus *in situ* – hence the name. Back in the market lanes, *Magenta* is its more recently opened rival. During August, the municipality typically lays on a **festival**, with music and theatre events at various locales in Pétra and nearby Ánaxos.

In addition to a Ethniki Trapeza/National Bank, with limited opening hours, Pétra's amenities include a **post office**, next to Áyios Nikólaos, and a number of **scooter or car-rental** places such as Homerus (☎02530/41 577) on the north side of town. There's a tiny **internet café** with three terminals in the grid of market lanes, at 4-Dhekemvríou 1912.

Petrí and around

Inland from Pétra, you can drive or walk the steep, partly paved road 3km up to sound-alike **PETRÍ** village, unimproveably set on a natural, west-facing balcony. The main reason to come here is the excellent **taverna** *To Petri* (lunch & supper, May–Oct 15) near the top of the village, with superb *mayireftá* and view-terrace seating. By day, Petrí is the trailhead for the partly waymarked **path to Vafiós**, though the start of this has been confused by bulldozing. It's forty minutes down to the Pigádhos ravine, with its ruined water mill and aqueduct, and thence a further twenty minutes' walk to an abandoned farm with an open irrigation tank among some poplars. From here you've another, tougher hour, sometimes through prickly shrubs, to reach Vafiós.

Drivers will also like to know that the unmarked but paved right turning at the edge of Petrí, by the army camp, emerges on the paved road just west of Stýpsi and knocks a good 8km off the drive there from Pétra on the main road.

Outlying beaches: Ánaxos, Ambélia, Tsikhránda

ÁNAXOS, 3km southwest of Pétra and also reachable via a coast-hugging path from Avláki, is a bit of a higgledy-piggledy mess, but it fringes by far the cleanest beach in the area. The kilometre stretch of sand is dotted with pedalos, sunbeds, and a handful of **tavernas** that are an improvement on the unmemorable snack bars of yore; some readers have liked *Villa Niki*, at the river end of the beach. The blocks of rooms inland are increasingly monopolized by tour companies, making Ánaxos less of a good bet than previously for short-notice accommodation in high season; there may also be mosquitoes from the river mouth. Inexpensive bike or car rental at Billy's (☎02530/41 057) would seem to be the main draw here, along with the beach and the beautiful sunsets behind three offshore islets visible on this stretch of coast.

For something utterly different, drivers can head 1km south, then 3km west along a well-signposted side road (then right at the only fork) to **Ambélia**, an idyllic, 700-metre sand-and-pebble beach that's also reachable by the ongoing coastal trail from Ánaxos. There are some large pebbles in the shallows, and often washed-up seaweed, but generally the place is fairly clean, with an attractive, cultivated valley for a backdrop. Facilities are limited to a single, dubiously hygienic **taverna** (*George's*) which, however, often has fresh fish in season.

Just past Skoutáros village, you can ignore without regret a three-kilometre side road descending to the rather scrappy, exposed pebble beach of **Tsikhránda** – not brilliant, and with two equally undistinguished summer snack bars.

Loutrá Eftaloú

From Mólyvos, the shuttle bus runs 5km northeast to the rustic but recently restored **thermal baths** at **Loutrá Eftaloú**. Insist on patronising the hot pool under the Ottoman-era domed structure, not the sterile modern tub-rooms in the adjacent annexe (daily 8am–noon & 2–6pm; €2.40). The original spa may be too hot (43–46.5°C at source) and shallow to submerge oneself in fully, necessitating frequent cooling dips at the pebble beach (clothing optional) just outside. The shoreline west of this point is seaweed-strewn and unattractive, which means that the hotels and bungalow complexes here all have pools. About 1km east, however, there is a decent little beach, **Khryssí Aktí**, with an equally decent eponymous taverna just above it.

Around Mount Lepétymnos

East of Mólyvos, the villages of 968-metre **Mount Lepétymnos**, marked by tufts of poplars, provide a day or two of rewarding exploration. The main road around the mountain, completely asphalted, first heads 6km east to Vafiós before curling north around the base of the peaks. **VAFIÓS** (for whose taverns see p.402) is the starting point for the most direct **climb** up to the secondary 937-metre peak of **Profítis Ilías**, a three-hour walk there and back; begin in the obvious ravine with an aqueduct behind the village, and then from a plane-shaded spring about half an hour along, angle steeply up to the chapel on the ridge here.

East of the village of Áryennos, and the landslip-ruined derelict village of Lepétymnos, stands the enchanting hill village of **SYKAMINIÁ** (Sykamiá). This is the birthplace of regional novelist Stratis Myrivilis, whose childhood home is identified among the imposing basalt-block houses below the "Plaza of the Workers' First of May", with its two traditional kafenía and sweeping views north to Turkey.

Skála Sykaminiás

A signposted trail from the roadside 800m west of Sykaminiá shortcuts the twisty 2.5-kilometre road down to **SKÁLA SYKAMINIÁS**, easily the most picturesque fishing port on Lésvos. Myrivilis used it as the setting for his best-known work, *The Mermaid Madonna*, and the tiny rock-top chapel at the end of the jetty will be instantly recognizable to anyone who has read the novel (see p.499).

On a practical level, Skála has a few **pensions**, such as the central *Gorgona* (Ⓣ & Ⓕ02530/55 301 or 55 400; ❷), and the quieter, seaview *Rooms Anna* (Ⓣ02530/55 242; ❷), 200m west of the chapel. It also boasts four **tavernas**, the most durable of these *Iy Sykamnia* (aka *Iy Mouria*), with seating under the mulberry tree in which Myrivilis used to sleep on hot summer nights, though newer *Anemoessa* (closest to the chapel) has overtaken it quality-wise, and operates all year. In addition to good seafood, courtesy of the active local fleet – *gávros* (anchovy) in June or July, sardines in August or September – you can try sterling renditions of the island's late-summer speciality of *kolokytholoúloudha yemistá* (stuffed squash blossoms).

The only local **beach** is the extremely stony one of **Kayiá** just east, where *Psarotaverna Kayia* near its east end does lots of dishes besides fish. A fairly rough, roller-coaster track follows the shore west from Skála for 9km back to the baths at Eftaloú, its condition not deterring a steady stream of vehicles and the odd walker.

Klió and Tsónia

Continuing east from upper Sykaminiá, you soon come to **KLIÓ**, whose single main street (marked "kentrikí agorá") leads down to a square with a plane tree, fountain, kafenía and views across to Turkey. The village is set attractively on a slope, down which a six-kilometre dirt road, marked in English and/or Greek and passable with care in an ordinary car, leads to the 600m of beautiful pink volcanic sand at **Tsónia** beach, with just a single taverna and another café at the fishing-anchorage end, and two modern rooms places at the beach end. The jerry-built prefab cottages just inland essentially form the summer annexe of Klió, whose entire population migrates here at weekends in season – a custom still observed to a diminishing degree at all shoreline colonies around the island.

Greek script table

Lésvos	Λέσβος	ΛΕΣΒΟΣ
Akhladherí	Αχλαδερή	ΑΧΛΑΔΕΡΗ
Ambélia	Αμπέλια	ΑΜΠΕΛΙΑ
Ambelikó	Αμπελικό	ΑΜΠΕΛΙΚΟ
Ánaxos	Άναξος	ΑΝΑΞΟΣ
Ándissa	Άντισσα	ΑΝΤΙΣΣΑ
Apothíka	Αποθήκα	ΑΠΟΘΗΚΑ
Ayía Marína	Αγία Μαρίνα	ΑΓΙΑ ΜΑΡΙΝΑ
Ayía Paraskeví	Αγία Παρασκευή	ΑΓΙΑ ΠΑΡΑΣΚΕΥΗ
Ayiássos	Αγιάσος	ΑΓΙΑΣΟΣ
Áyios Ermoyénis	Άγιος Ερμογένης	ΑΓΙΟΣ ΕΡΜΟΓΕΝΗΣ
Áyios Isídhoros	Άγιος Ισίδωρος	ΑΓΙΟΣ ΙΣΙΔΩΡΟΣ
Eressós	Ερεσός	ΕΡΕΣΟΣ
Fília	Φίλια	ΦΙΛΙΑ
Gavathás	Γαβαθάς	ΓΑΒΑΘΑΣ
Haramídha	Χαραμίδα	ΧΑΡΑΜΙΔΑ
Ipsilométopo	Υψηλομέτωπο	ΥΨΗΛΟΜΕΤΩΠΟ
Kalloní	Καλλονή	ΚΑΛΛΟΝΗ
Kápi	Κάπη	ΚΑΠΗ
Klió	Κλειώ	ΚΛΕΙΩ
Kroússos	Κρούσος	ΚΡΟΥΣΟΣ
Lepétymnos	Λεπέτυμνος	ΛΕΠΕΤΥΜΝΟΣ
Lisvóri	Λισβόρι	ΛΙΣΒΟΡΙ
Loutrá Eftaloú	Λουτρά Εφταλού	ΛΟΥΤΡΑ ΕΦΤΑΛΟΥ
Loutrá Yéras	Λουτρά Γέρας	ΛΟΥΡΑ ΓΕΡΑΣ
Mandamádhos	Μανταμάδος	ΜΑΝΤΑΜΑΔΟΣ
Megalohóri	Μεγαλοχώρι	ΜΕΓΑΛΟΧΩΡΙ
Melínda	Μελίντα	ΜΕΛΙΝΤΑ
Mesótopos	Μεσότοπος	ΜΕΣΟΤΟΠΟΣ
Míthymna	Μήθυμνα	ΜΗΘΥΜΝΑ
Mólyvos	Μόλυβος	ΜΟΛΥΒΟΣ
Moní Ipsiloú	Μονή Υψιλού	ΜΟΝΗ ΥΨΙΛΟΥ
Moní Limónos	Μονή Λειμώνος	ΜΟΝΗ ΛΕΙΜΩΝΟΣ
Moní Perivolís	Μονή Περιβολής	ΜΟΝΗ ΠΕΡΙΒΟΛΗΣ

South slope villages

Just south of Klió, the route forks at Kápi, from where you can complete a loop around the mountain by bearing west along a paved road tracing its southern flank. After 5km you reach **PELÓPI**, ancestral village of the unsuccessful 1988 US presidential candidate Michael Dukakis (who finally visited the island in 2000); the main square sports an old mosque now used as a warehouse. Greenery-swathed **IPSILOMÉTOPO**, 5km further along, is punctuated by a minaret (but no intact mosque) and hosts revels on July 16–17, the feast of Ayía Marína. By the time you reach sprawling **STÝPSI**, 13km from Kapí, you're just 4km shy of the main Kalloní–Mólyvos road; consequently there's a sporadic bus service here, as well as a large **taverna** at

Mória	Μόρια	ΜΟΡΙΑ
Mytilíni	Μυτιλήνη	ΜΥΤΙΛΗΝΗ
Nyfidha	Νυφίδα	ΝΥΦΙΔΑ
Ovriókastro	Οβριόκαστρο	ΟΒΡΙΟΚΑΣΤΡΟ
Paleókipos	Παλαιόκαστρο	ΠΑΛΑΙΟΚΑΣΤΡΟ
Pámfylla	Πάμφυλλα	ΠΑΜΦΥΛΛΑ
Panayía Kryftí	Παναγία Κρυφτή	ΠΑΝΑΓΙΑ ΚΡΥΦΤΗ
Panayioúdha	Παναγιούδα	ΠΑΝΑΓΙΟΥΔΑ
Papádhos	Παπάδος	ΠΑΠΑΔΟΣ
Parákila	Παράκοιλα	ΠΑΡΑΚΟΙΛΑ
Paralía Thermís	Παραλία Θερμής	ΠΑΡΑΛΙΑ ΘΕΡΜΗΣ
Pelópi	Πελώπη	ΠΕΛΩΠΗ
Pérama	Πέραμα	ΠΕΡΑΜΑ
Pétra	Πέτρα	ΠΕΤΡΑ
Pýrgi Thermís	Πύργοι Θερμής	ΠΥΡΓΟΙ ΘΕΡΜΗΣ
Plomári	Πλωμάρι	ΠΛΩΜΑΡΙ
Polikhnítos	Πολιχνίτος	ΠΟΛΙΧΝΙΤΟΣ
Sígri	Σίγρι	ΣΙΓΡΙ
Skála Eressoú	Σκάλα Ερεσού	ΣΚΑΛΑ ΕΡΕΣΟΥ
Skála Sykaminiás	Σκάλα Συκαμινιάς	ΣΚΑΛΑ ΣΥΚΑΜΙΝΙΑΣ
Skalohóri	Σκαλοχώρι	ΣΚΑΛΟΧΩΡΙ
Skoutáros	Σκουτάρος	ΣΚΟΥΤΑΡΟΣ
Stavrós	Σταυρός	ΣΤΑΥΡΟΣ
Stýpsi	Στύψη	ΣΤΥΨΗ
Sykaminiá	Συκαμινιά	ΣΥΚΑΜΙΝΙΑ
Tárti	Τάρτι	ΤΑΡΤΙ
Tavári	Ταβάρι	ΤΑΒΑΡΙ
Tsikhránda	Τσιχράντα	ΤΣΙΧΡΑΝΤΑ
Tsónia	Τσόνια	ΤΣΟΝΙΑ
Vafiós	Βαφειός	ΒΑΦΕΙΟΣ
Variá	Βαρειά	ΒΑΡΕΙΑ
Vaterá	Βατερά	ΒΑΤΕΡΑ
Vatoússa	Βατούσσα	ΒΑΤΟΥΣΣΑ
Vríssa	Βρίσα	ΒΡΙΣΑ

the edge of town to which coachloads of tourists descend in season for "Greek Nights".

Like Petrí, Stýpsi also makes a good jump-off point for rambles along Lepétymnos' steadily dwindling network of **trails**; throughout the north of the island you'll see advertisements for **donkey- or mule-trekking**, which in recent years has become more popular than walking. The Mytilíni EOT jumped into the fray during the mid-1990s, marking several long-distance routes across the island with yellow diamonds and documenting them in its brochure "Trekking Trails on Lesvos". However, these rely almost exclusively on vehicle tracks or roads, and are considered locally as something of a bad joke; the most worthwhile and path-like of these are the coastal track from Pétra to Ambélia (it continues rather pointlessly past Gavathás) and the Kápi–Sykaminiá–Skála Sykaminiá traverse. A better printed **guide** is the locally sold, self-published one by Mike Maunder, *17 Walks Around Pétra and Mólyvos*, which details some rambles on the hillsides.

Mandamádhos and Taxiárhis monastery

The main highway south from Klió to the capital runs through **MANDAMÁDHOS**, 6km along. This attractive inland village is famous for its pottery, including the Ali-Baba-style *kioupiá* (olive-oil urns) seen throughout Lésvos, but more so for the "black" icon of the Archangel Michael, whose enormous **monastery of Taxiárhis** (daily: summer 6am–10pm; winter 6.30am–7pm), in a valley just northeast, is the powerful focus of a thriving cult, and a popular venue for baptisms. The image – supposedly made from a mixture of mud and the blood of monks slaughtered in a medieval massacre – is really more idol than icon, both in its lumpy three-dimensionality and in the former mode of veneration which seems a vestige of pagan times. First there was the custom of the coin-wish, whereby you pressed a coin to the Archangel's forehead; if it stuck, then your wish would be granted. Owing to wear and tear on the image, the practice is now forbidden. Instead, supplicants leave enormous votive candles beside a substitute icon by the main entrance.

It's further believed that while carrying out his various errands on behalf of the faithful, the Archangel gets through more footwear than Imelda Marcos. Accordingly the icon used to be surrounded not by the usual *támmata* (votive medallions) but by piles of miniature gold and silver shoes. The ecclesiastical authorities, embarrassed by such "primitive" practices, removed all the little shoes in 1986. Since then, a token substitute has reappeared: several pairs of tin slippers which can be filled with money and left before the icon. Just why his devotees should want to encourage these perpetual peripatetics is unclear, since in Greek folklore the Archangel Michael is also the one who fetches the souls of the dying, and modern Greek attitudes towards death are as bleak as those of their pagan ancestors.

Lésvos travel details

Island transport

Buses

Mytilíni to: Ayiássos (5 daily Mon–Fri, 4 Sat–Sun); Eressós (2 daily Mon–Sat, 2 Sun summer, 1 daily off season); Kalloní (5 daily Mon–Sat, 3 Sun); Mandamádhos (4 daily Mon–Fri, 3 Sat–Sun); Mólyvos (5 daily Mon–Sat, 3 Sun); Pétra (5 daily Mon–Sat, 3 Sun); Plomári (4 daily Mon–Fri, 2 Sat–Sun); Sígri (2 daily Mon–Sat, 1 Sun summer only; 1 daily off season); Vaterá (3 daily Mon–Fri, 2 Sat & Sun).

Inter-island transport

Key to ferry companies

HF Hellas Ferries
NEL *Navtiliakí Etería Lésvou* (Lesvian Shipping Co)
ML Miniotis Lines
KR Kyriakoulis Maritime

Ferries

Lésvos (Mytilíni) to: Alexandhroúpoli (1 weekly on NEL; 13hr 30min); Híos (7–9 weekly on NEL, 4 on HF; 3hr 30min); Kavála (1–2 weekly on NEL; 10hr); Kós (1 weekly on NEL; 11hr); Límnos (3–6 weekly on NEL; 5hr 30min); Mýkonos (1 weekly on NEL; 8hr); Pireás (7–9 weekly on NEL, 4 weekly on HF; 11hr direct, 13hr via Híos, 18hr via Sámos); Psara (1 weekly on ML; 3hr); Rhodes (1 weekly on NEL; 15hr 30min); Sámos, Vathý only (1 weekly on NEL, 1 on HF; 7hr); Sýros (1 weekly on NEL, 1 weekly on HF; 9–13hr); Thessaloníki (1–2 weekly on NEL; 13hr 30min).
Lésvos (Sígri) to: Áyios Efstrátios (1–2 weekly on NEL; 3hr); Límnos (1–2 weekly on NEL; 4hr 30min); Psará (1 weekly on NEL; 3hr); Rafína (1 weekly on NEL; 9hr).

Catamaran

NEL's *Aeolos Kenteris* sails to Híos (1hr 45min) and Pireás (5hr 45min) at least three times weekly, year-round; typical departure time is 4pm.

Hyrofoil

NB All services on KR; unreliably provided owing to weather conditions even in high summer.
Lésvos (Mytilíni) to: Híos (1–3 weekly; 2hr); Ikaría, Évdhilos (1 weekly; 3hr 15min); Inoússes (1–3 weekly; 1hr 40min); Sámos, Karlóvassi/Vathý (1–3 weekly; 3hr 30min–5hr 30min).

Flights

NB All flights on Olympic unless otherwise specified.
Lésvos to: Athens (4–5 daily on Olympic; 55min; 3 daily on Aegean-Cronus; 45min); Híos (1 weekly; 30min); Límnos (4 weekly; 40min); Rhodes (2 weekly; 2hr); Sámos (2 weekly; 1hr); Thessaloníki (6–8 weekly on Olympic, 1 daily on Aegean-Cronus; 1hr 10min–2hr).

International transport

Ferries

Lésvos (Mytilíni) to: Turkey (Ayvalık; 4–8 weekly May–Oct, winter link unreliable). One of two Turkish craft, the *Cunda Express* and the *Jalehan*, departs Mytilíni 8am most days; the *Jalehan* (carries 2 cars) may also do an evening trip Tues, Thurs & Sat. Passenger rates €38 one way, €47 round trip, all taxes inclusive. Small cars €58 each way. Journey time 1hr 40min.

Límnos

Límnos is a sizeable agricultural and garrison island whose remoteness and peculiar ferry connections have until recently protected it from the worst excesses of the holiday trade. Most summer visitors are Greek, particularly from Thessaloníki, though the locals have become increasingly used to numbers of Germans and a smaller British package clientele. Accommodation across the island tends to be comfortable if a bit overpriced, with a strong bias (near the capital at least) towards self-catering units. Having come late to the tourist trade, and saddled with a short tourist season owing to the northerly latitude, the Limnians have skipped the backpacker phase entirely – budget travellers are explicitly discouraged – and gone straight for the **high end of the market**. Indeed, the bucolic island has been getting trendy of late: there are upscale souvenir shops, village houses restored by Thessalonians as weekend retreats, some sort of noon-to-small-hours music bar at every beach, and a significant gay scene.

The conspicuous **military presence** ran to 25,000 soldiers at the nadir of Greco-Turkish relations in the late 1980s, though it is now down to about 10,000; conventional tourism was slow in coming because the islanders made a reliable living off the soldiers and family members coming to visit them. Since the 1960s, the island has been the focus of periodic disputes between the Greek and Turkish governments; Turkey has a long-standing demand that Límnos should be demilitarized, and Turkish aircraft regularly intrude Greek air space overhead, prompting immediate responses from the Greek Air Force squadron based here.

The bays of **Bourniá** and **Moúdhros**, the latter one of the largest natural harbours in the Aegean, almost pinch H-shaped Límnos in two. The west of the island is dramatically bare and hilly, with abundant basalt put to good use as street cobbles and house masonry. Like most volcanic islands, Límnos produces excellent **wine** from westerly vineyards – good dry whites and rosés, some of the best retsina in Greece (unfortunately none of this exported) – plus oúzo from Kondiás. The low-lying eastern leg of the "H" is speckled with seasonal ponds or marshes popular with duck-hunters, while the intervening land is occupied by cattle, combine harvesters and vast cornfields.

The Limnians proudly tout an abundance of **natural food products**, including thyme honey and sheep's milk cheese, and indeed the population is almost self-sufficient in foodstuffs. Despite off-islander slander to that effect, Límnos is not flat, barren or treeless; much of the countryside consists of rolling hills or volcanic crags, the latter forming the backdrop for most of the west coast. There is plenty of **vegetation** except on the heights, with substantial, carefully nurtured clumps of almond, jujube, myrtle, oak, fig, poplar and mulberry trees. The island is, however, extremely dry, with irrigation water pumped from deep wells, and a limited number of potable springs. Yet various terrapin-haunted creeks bring sand to several long, **sandy beaches** around the coast, where it's easy to find a stretch to yourself – though there's no escaping the stingless but disgusting jellyfish which periodically pour out of the Dardanelles (fortunately decreased in recent years) and die here in the shallows. On the plus side, beaches shelve gently, making them ideal for children and quick to warm up early in summer, with no cool currents except near the river mouths.

Mýrina

MÝRINA (Kástro), the capital and port on the west coast, has the atmosphere of a provincial market town rather than a resort. With about five thousand inhabitants, it's pleasantly low-key, if not especially picturesque apart from a core neighbourhood of old stone houses dating from the Ottoman occupation, and the ornate Neoclassical mansions of Romeïkós Yialós. Few explicitly Turkish monuments have survived: a dilapidated octagonal structure, probably the *tekke* or lodge of a dervish order, hides behind the Co-op supermarket on the main harbour platía – though a fountain at the harbour end of Kydhá retains its calligraphic inscription and is still highly prized for its drinking water.

Arrival, transport and information

The sleek new civilian **airport** is 19km east of Mýrina, almost at the exact geographical centre of the island, sharing a runway with an enormous air-force

LÍMNOS
Kavála, Thessaloníki or Alexandhroúpoli
Rafína, Áyios Efstrátios, Lésvos & Híos
0 5 km
N
Pláka
Panayiá
Salt Marsh
Kavírio (Kabireio)
Ifestía (Hephaestia)
Kondopoúli
Kalliópi
Kéros
Bournia Bay
Kótsinas
Repanídhi
Romanoú
Roussopoúli
Kamínia
Polyókhni (Polyochni)
Fyssíni
Áyios Sózon
Skandháli
Allied War Cemetery
Havoúli
Moúdhros
Moúdhros Bay
Lýkhna
Város
Atsikí
Karpássi
Livadhohóri
Kallithéa
Néa Koútali
Pedhinó
Tsimándhria
Dhiapóri
Angariónes
Portianoú
Allied War Cemetery
Áyios Dhimítrios
Dháfni
Katálakos
Sardhés
Kornós
Káspakas
Thermá
Mýrina (Kástro)
Kondiás
Evgátis (Áyios Pávlos)
Thános
Paralía Thánous
Platý
Paralía Platý
Playíso Mólos
Rihá Nerá
Avlónas
Áyios Ioánnis

base; there's still an Olympic-run shuttle bus between town and airport – consult the Olympic office (Ⓣ02540/22 078) for departure times. **Ferries** dock at the south end of the town, in the shadow of the castle and the modern clocktower; there are separate agencies for the sailings of NEL boats (Nikos Vayiakos, Ⓣ02540/22 460) and the *Saos II* (Ⓣ02540/29 571).

The **bus station**, for what little it's worth, is on Platía Eleftheríou Venizélou, near the north end of Kydhá. One look at the abysmally sparse schedules (only a single daily afternoon departure to most points, slightly more frequent departures to Kondiás and Moúdhros) will convince you of the need to **rent your own vehicle**. Cars, motorbikes and bicycles can be had from either Myrina Rent a Car (Ⓣ02540/24 476 or 24 100), Petridou Tours (Ⓣ02540/22 039), Holiday (Ⓣ02540/24 357), Best (Ⓣ02540/22 127), or Auto Europe (Ⓣ02540/23 777); rates for bikes are only slightly above the island norm, but cars are expensive. A motorbike (most obviously from Moto Lemnos, Ⓣ02540/25 002) is generally enough to explore the coast and the interior, as there are few steep gradients but many perilously narrow village streets. For sea-going jaunts, there's a **boat-rental** and general watersports facility, open to the public, at Rihá Nerá beach.

All five **banks** have cash machines; the **post office** and Olympic airlines terminal are adjacent to each other on Garoufalídhou, with a **laundry** across the way by the *Hotel Paris*. There are **internet** facilities at *Excite Club*, just behind the port roundabout, and at *Joy*, by the post office. The Maroula cinema, down the street near the intersection with Frýnis, was refurbished in 2001 as a general indoor events venue.

Accommodation

Despite Límnos' steady gentrification, you may still be met off the boat with offers of a **room**. Romeïkós Yialós has several **pensions** or **small hotels** in its restored houses, most of these plagued to some extent by evening noise from the bars below. Just north of Romeïkós Yialós, the areas of Rihá Nerá and Áyios Pandelímon are good bets for **self-catering units**. There's **no official campsite** on Límnos; Greek caravanners and campers have been banished from their former haunt at the north end of Platý beach, though a few tents still sprout furtively at Paralía Thánous and Kéros (see p.415 and p.418 for these attractions).

Akti Myrina At the north end of Rihá Nerá Ⓣ02540/22 681, Ⓕ22 947, Ⓦwww.ventaglio.com. A self-contained, luxury complex of 110 wood-and-stone bungalows (avoid the horrid modern addition), with all conceivable diversions and comforts, including watersports on the private beach. It is now run by and for Italian interests, and is off limits from late June through August, but during low season (May/Sept) you can squeeze in, with all meals and sports facilities included. ❻

Apollo Pavillion On Frýnis Ⓣ02540/24 315, Ⓕ 23 712, Ⓔapollo47@otenet.gr. Hidden away in a peaceful cul-de-sac about halfway along Garoufalídhou, this offers a variety of accommodation ranging from multi-bed rooms in the basement (❷) to more comfortable studios on the upper floors (❹). All upstairs rooms have balconies, with views of either the castle or the mountains.

Blue Waters Romeïkós Yialós Ⓣ02540/24 403, Ⓕ25 004, Ⓔbwkon@otenet.gr. Slightly higher standard rooms than its near neighbour *Kosmos* (see below). ❹

Ifestos Ethnikís Andístasis 17, Andhróni district, inland from Rihá Nerá Ⓣ02540/24 960, Ⓕ23 623. Quiet, professionally run (something of a rarity in town) C-class hotel, with pleasant common areas. Slightly small rooms have air con, fridges, balconies and again a mix of sea or hill views. Available through Sunvil; otherwise ❹

Kosmos Romeïkós Yialós 21 Ⓣ02540/22 050. Acceptable en-suite and air-conditioned rooms at this waterfront pension above the namesake restaurant. ❹

Lemnos Harbourfront ⓣ02540/22 153, ⓕ23 329. The more cheerful and better appointed quayside C-class hotel, with air con, fridges and balconies offsetting small-hours ferry noise. Available through Sunvil; otherwise ④

Porto Myrina Palace Avlónas beach, 1.5km north of Rihá Nerá ⓣ02540/24 805, ⓕ24 858. Now that the *Akti Myrina* is out of bounds much of the year, this is your best alternative as a beachfront luxury facility. A choice of hotel-wing rooms or freestanding bungalows, one of the largest pools in Greece, and a little temple of Artemis found during construction to lend extra interest. Through Sunvil, or ⑥

Poseidon Apartments Rihá Nerá ⓣ02540/24 821, ⓕ23 982. Set back a little from Romeïkós Yialós beach; somewhat overpriced "studios" with TV and fridge but no cookers. ④

Romeïkos Yialos Sakhtoúri 7 ⓣ02540/23 787. A venerable B-class pension in a Romeïkós Yialós mansion that's quieter than waterfront outfits. ③

The Town

Mýrina is fairly large for an island town, but most things of interest are situated on the main shopping street, **Kydhá/Karatzá** – stretching from the harbour to **Romeïkós Yialós**, the beach and esplanade to the north of the castle – or on its perpendicular, **Garoufalídhou**, roughly halfway along. As town beaches go, Romeïkós Yialós is not at all bad, and its southerly counterpart, **Toúrkikos Yialós**, beyond the fishing port, provides a decent alternative.

On the headland between Romeïkós Yialós and the south-facing ferry dock stands an originally Byzantine **castle** (access unrestricted), quite ruined despite later additions by the Genoese and Ottomans. It's worth climbing at sunset for views over the town, the entire west coast and – in clear conditions – over to Mount Áthos, 35 nautical miles west (also to be glimpsed from any suitable height east of town).

The Archeological Museum

The 1993-overhauled **Archeological Museum** (daily 8am–7pm; €1.50) occupies an Ottoman mansion behind Romeïkós Yialós, not far from the site of Bronze Age Myrina in the suburb of Rihá Nerá. Finds are assiduously labelled in Greek, Italian and English, and the entire premises are exemplary in terms of presentation – the obvious drawback being that the best items have been spirited away to Athens, leaving a collection that's essentially of specialist interest. Because of Límnos' fertility and convenient position near the Dardanelles, it was occupied in prehistoric times; exhibits belong predominantly to the Archaic period and before, since the island became a backwater satellite of Athens during Classical times.

In broad terms, the south ground-floor gallery is devoted to pottery from Polyókhni (Polyochni); the north wing contains more of the same, plus items from ancient Myrina; while upstairs are galleries of post-Bronze-Age artefacts from Kavírio (Kabireio) and Ifestía (Hephaestia). The star upper-storey exhibits, much imitated in local modern jewellery, are votive lamps in the shape of sirens, found in an Archaic sanctuary at Hephaestia. Rather less vicious than the harpy-like creatures described by Homer, they are identified more invitingly as "muses of the underworld, creatures of superhuman wisdom, incarnations of nostalgia for paradise".

There are also numerous representations of the goddess Cybele/Artemis, who was revered throughout the island; her shrine was typically situated at a fauna-rich river mouth – on Límnos at Avlónas, now in the grounds of the *Porto Myrina* resort. Also noteworthy is an entire room devoted to metal objects, including gold jewellery and bronze objects both practical (cheese graters, door knockers) and whimsical (a vulture and a snail).

Eating and drinking

Mýrina's **tavernas** are usually better value than its lodgings. About halfway along the main commercial thoroughfare, on an atmospheric little square hemmed in by old houses and two plane trees, *O Platanos* serves traditional *mayireftá* to big crowds (particularly at lunchtime); for affordable seaside dining, look no further than *Ostria* at the town end of Toúrkikos Yialós beach, which offers a mix of grills, fish and *ouzomezédhes* from noon until late.

Seafood on Límnos is generally excellent (if not bargain-basement cheap), thanks to the island's proximity to the Dardanelles and seasonal migrations of fish through it; accordingly there are no fewer than five tavernas arrayed around the little fishing port. There's little to distinguish their prices or menus, and all the proprietors are related by blood or marriage, though *O Glaros* at the far end is considered the best – and works out slightly more expensive.

Not too surprisingly given the twee setting, the few restaurants and many bars along Romeïkós Yialós are pretty poor value, except perhaps for a drink with views of the nocturnally illuminated castle. The tree-shaded tables of *Iy Tzitzifies* on Rihá Nerá beach, the next bay north, are a far better option; most of the extensive menu of fish, mezédhes and *mayireftá* is likely to be available on any given day.

Other than the venues at Romeïkós Yialós, **nightspots** (except for the aforementioned *Excite* internet bar) are not conspicuous; *Aeras*, a music bar-ouzerí right on the ferry dock, is as good as any.

Western Límnos

For more deserted beaches than those at Romeïkós Yialós and Toúrkikos Yialós, you should strike out 3km north from town, past *Akti Myrina*, to the beach at **Avlónas**. This is unencroached upon except for the *Porto Myrina* luxury complex on the south and coolant-water discharge from the local power plant at the north end. In between the two, the lively, standard-issue Limnian beach bar, currently incarnated as *Kioski*, offers sunbeds to its youthful punters.

Some 3km further on from Avlónas you work your way (until the bypass road is finished) through **KÁSPAKAS**, its north-facing houses arranged in pretty, tiled tiers, before plunging down to **Áyios Ioánnis**. Here the island's most unusual **taverna** (late June to Sept 1) features seating in the shade of piled-up volcanic boulders, with a sandy beach opening to the north, beyond the fishing anchorage. If it's shut, *Taverna Iliovasilemata* to the south is welcoming, with good (if not especially cheap) fish. The beach between the two, however, is rocky and unattractive, often buffeted by southwest winds.

Platý: village and beach

PLATÝ village, 2km southeast of Mýrina, has had its profile spoiled by the kind of modern villa construction that is blighting many Limnian villages lately, but it does have two nocturnally popular **tavernas**. By far the better of these is *O Sozos*, just off the main platía, where you'll have to show up early for a table (groups should reserve ⓣ02540/25 085). Fine *orektiká*, lamb chops, steamed mussels, grilled *biftéki*, *tsípouro* (the north-mainland answer to oúzo) and local bulk wine are strong points; the bill won't exceed €9. The nocturnal activity here makes the handful of **rooms** here a noisy proposition; better to head west beyond the village limits, to Nikos and Soula's *Panorama Studios*

(Ⓣ02540/24 118 or 22 487; ④), well-kept units fitting two to four persons, with seaviews and easy parking.

The long, sandy **beach**, 700m below, is popular and usually jellyfish-free, with watersports on offer at the north end, and crags on the horizon. Except for the unsightly Mark Warner compound at the south end, the area is still resolutely rural, with sheep parading to and fro at dawn and dusk. The single hotel, low-rise *Plati Beach* (Ⓣ02540/23 583 or 094/4965189; ②), has an enviable position in the middle of the beach, but get a room towards the back if you don't fancy noise from the ground floor bar-restaurant; there are more basic **rooms**, with fridges and proper showers, available through *Tzimis Taverna* (Ⓣ02540/24 142; ①), which divides the lunchtime trade with its neighbour *Grigoris* near the south end of the beach, though both lose out in the evenings to the village-centre tavernas. The one night spot at the beach is *Zefyros*, a **café-bar** as popular as any in Mýrina.

The highest standard of **studios** in the area, if not the island, is the tastefully landscaped, well-appointed *Villa Afroditi* (Ⓣ02540/23 141 or 094/5390320, Ⓕ25 031, winter Ⓣ010/96 33 488; ④ or through Sunvil), with a pleasant pool bar, weekly barbecue nights for guests, and one of the best buffet breakfasts in Greece. Hospitable, multilingual Panayiotis and Afroditi Papasotiriou, late of South Africa, also offer a lovely restored house in Kondiás village, with a full kitchen and double glazing, which sleeps four – €73.50 per night for a weeks' stay.

If Platý beach gets too crowded – likely in August – there's another cove, **Playíso Mólos**, less than 2km away, heading south past the Mark Warner complex. The road there turns to dirt, and the water shelves sharply with rocks in the shallows (so it's not great for kids), but the bay is very scenic, with a little islet to give it definition.

Thános and Evgátis beach

THÁNOS, 2km further southeast, seems a bigger, more architecturally characterful version of Platý village, with another well-regarded central-platía **taverna** (evenings only) and high-standard mock-trad **bungalows** at the east edge (Ⓣ02540/23 162; ④). A 1.5-kilometre paved but unsigned road leads down from the east edge of the village to **Paralía Thánous**, perhaps the most scenic of the southwestern beaches, with Áyios Efstrátios island showing clearly on the horizon in the later afternoon. Of the two **tavernas**, one (*Nikos Yiannakaros*; lunch only except Aug) rents out basic **rooms**, probably the cheapest on Límnos (Ⓣ02540/22 787; ①).

Beyond Thános, the road curls over to the enormous beach at **Evgátis** (Áyios Pávlos), flanked by standard-issue volcanic crags to the west and reckoned to be the island's best. A typical terrapin-filled river meets the sea at mid-strand; facilities comprise a few unobtrusive umbrellas and wooden shade-pavilions, a music bar-*kantína* on the sand, and a full-service **taverna** across the road.

Kondiás

Some 3km further along (11km from Mýrina), **KONDIÁS** is the island's third-largest settlement, cradled between two hills tufted with Límnos' only natural pine forest. Stone-built, red-tiled houses combine with the setting to make Kondiás the most attractive inland village, a fact not lost on the urban Greeks restoring old houses with varying degrees of taste. Short-term facilities are limited, and aren't much better at the shore annexe of **Dhiapóri**, 2km east. The beach – backed by a huge, fenced-off minefield – is unappealing, the tavernas listless, with the main interest lent by the narrow isthmus dividing the bays of Kondiás and Moúdhros.

Portianoú war cemetery, Pedhinó and hill villages

From Kondiás it's 11km northeast to the junction with the main trans-island road at Livadhohóri. En route, the first detour worth making is the brief one to visit one of Límnos' two **World War I cemeteries** (see opposite for the other) at **PORTIANOÚ** village, 5km along. Turn left (west) onto a lane marked by a blue-on-white sign reading "ANZAC ST" (and of late, another placard clearly indicating the cemetery), which passes below a large hilltop church. Keep left on a rough lane, avoiding the gated way up to the church, and behind the latter you'll discover the cemetery, surrounded by pines. Amongst the 348 graves here are those of two Canadian nurses and one of the "enemy", a Levantine or Jewish Ottoman officer.

The next potential deviation is right of the road, to **PEDHINÓ**, mostly abandoned since a 1960s earthquake but like Kondiás a magnet for those hunting out weekend houses. The main amenity for short-term visits is an excellent **psistariá**, *To Petrino Horio* (supper only), with all manner of roast beast served at tables on the fieldstoned, shaded platía.

Rather than using the fast but dull main highway west, you can vary the return to Mýrina by continuing northeast to Karpássi, and then bearing northwest towards Atsíki for the entirely paved "high" road back to the port. The villages and scenery en route give a good impression of rural Limnian life, though be prepared to reverse when confronted by giant grain combines or large flocks of sheep.

DHÁFNI, the first village you'll encounter, challenges stereotypical images of the island's flatness with a hillside setting above a wooded ravine. **SARDHÉS**, 2.5km further on, is the highest community on Límnos, providing wonderful views of broody sunsets. Just past Kornós, you rejoin the main road and shortly afterwards pass the easterly turning for **Thérma**, a nineteenth-century Ottoman spa complete with calligraphic plaques. Restored in the mid-1990s, it is again closed; if it's operating again, you bathe in modern bathtubs in odd-sized rooms under the original domes. Unusually for a hot spring, the water is non-sulphurous and the tastiest on the island, so there is always a knot of cars parked nearby under the trees while their owners are filling jerry cans with warm water from a **public fountain** – again with a bilingual Greek-Ottoman inscription.

Eastern Límnos

The shores of sumpy **Moúdhros Bay**, glimpsed south of the trans-island trunk road, are muddy and best avoided. The bay itself enjoyed considerable importance during World War I, when it served throughout 1915 as the staging area for the unsuccessful Allied landings on the Gallipoli peninsula, and later saw Allied acceptance of the Ottoman surrender aboard the British warship HMS *Agamemnon* on October 30, 1918.

Moúdhros and the main Allied cemetery

MOÚDHROS port, the second largest town on Límnos, was (until recently) quite literally a God-forsaken place, owing to an incident late in Ottoman rule. Certain villagers killed some Muslims and threw them down a well on property belonging to the Athonite monastery of Koutloumousioú; the Ottoman authorities, holding the monks responsible, slaughtered any Koutloumousiot brethren they found on the island and set the local monastery alight. Two monks managed to escape to Áthos, where every August 23 a curse was chanted, condemning Moúdhros' inhabitants to "never sleep again"; the Athonite brothers finally relented in July 2001.

Moúdhros is an indisputably dreary place visually, and only a wonderfully kitsch church – looking like a Baroque Iberian church with its two belfries – redeems it. Despite this, there are two **hotels** here, including the frankly overpriced *To Kyma* (Ⓣ02540/71 333, Ⓕ71 484; ④), though its taverna makes a good lunch halt while touring. There is, however, little to prompt an overnight stay; the closest local beach, 4km south by dirt track, is **Havoúli**, mud-sandy and too close to the confines of the bay to be really attractive.

A kilometre or so northwest, on the paved road towards Roussopoúli, you pass the island's main Allied **military cemetery** (unlocked), maintained by the Commonwealth War Graves Commission, its neat lawns and rows of white headstones incongruous in such parched surroundings. Of the 36,000 Allied dead resulting from the disastrous Gallipoli campaign, 887 are buried here (plus the 348 noted opposite at Portianoú) – mainly battle casualties, who died after having been evacuated to the base hospital at Moúdhros. Though the deceased are mostly British, there is also a French cenotaph, and – speaking volumes about imperial sociology – a mass "Musalman" grave for Egyptian and Indian troops in one corner, with a Koranic inscription.

Polyókhni

Indications of the most advanced Neolithic civilization in the Aegean have been unearthed at **Polyókhni** (Polyochni), 3km by paved road from the gully-hidden village of **KAMÍNIA** (two simple grill-tavernas), 7km east of Moúdhros. Since the 1930s, ongoing Italian excavations have uncovered four layers of settlement, the oldest from late in the fourth millennium BC, predating Troy on the Turkish coast opposite; the town met a sudden, violent end from war or earthquake in about 2100 BC. Very little of Homeric or Mycenean vintage has been found yet, though a gold hoard similar to the so-called "Priam's Treasure", rediscovered in Russia in the early 1990s, was uncovered in 1956 inside a clay vase where it had been hurriedly secreted.

The actual ruins (daily 8am–5/7pm; free) are of essentially specialist interest, though a *bouleuterion* (assembly hall) with bench seating, a mansion and the landward fortifications are labelled. During August and September the Italian excavators are about; if they are free to show you around, the place may become that much more engaging. At other times you should obtain the useful TAP brochure entitled "Poliochni" from the Mýrina museum to make any sense of the place. The site occupies a bluff overlooking a long, narrow rock-and-sand beach flanked by stream valleys, the mouth of one of these being the old port; two wells within the fortifications suggest that reliable fresh water or sieges were major preoccupations.

Incidentally, it's not particularly worth continuing south from Kamínia to Fyssíni village and the remote monastery of Áyios Sózon – the final approach, on dirt track, is bleak, and the neglected modern monastery of zero intrinsic interest.

Ifestía and Kavírio

Ifestía and Kavírio, the other significant ancient sites on Límnos, are most easily reached via the village of **Kondopoúli**, 7km northeast of Moúdhros. Both sites are rather remote and only accessible by private transport.

Ifestía

Ifestía (or Hephaestia), in Classical times the most important city on the island, took its name from Hephaistos, god of fire and metalworking. According to legend, he attempted to intercede in a quarrel between his parents Hera and Zeus, and for his troubles was hurled from Mount Olympus by his father. A hard landing on Límnos left Hephaistos permanently lame, but he was adopted by the Limnians and held in high esteem thereafter.

A rough four-kilometre dirt track, well marked from Kondopoúli, leads to the edge of the **site** (unrestricted access), most of which remains unexcavated. Leave vehicles at the edge of the sumpy bay here, and walk ten minutes uphill to view the scant remains of a theatre, a temple dedicated to the god and a cluster of house foundations. All told, it's the most unevocative of the island's three major sites and can be skipped without regret by non-specialists.

Kavírio

Somewhat more rewarding is **Kavírio** (Kabireio), on the opposite shore of Tigáni inlet from Ifestía, and accessed by the same road built to serve the now-bankrupt and derelict Kaviria Palace luxury complex. The **ruins** (daily 8am–5/7pm; free) are of a sanctuary connected with the cult of the Kabiroi on the island of Samothráki just to the north, although the site on Límnos is probably older. Little survives other than the ground plan – aligned unusually southeast to northwest, an orientation dictated by the topography of the headland – but the setting is undeniably impressive. Eleven column stumps stake out a stoa, behind eight spots marked as column bases in the main *telestirio* or shrine where the cult mysteries took place.

More engaging, perhaps, is a nearby **sea grotto** identified as the Homeric **Spiliá toú Filoktíti**, where the Trojan war hero Philoktetes was abandoned by his comrades in arms until his stinking, gangrenous leg had healed. Landward access to the cave is via steps leading down from the caretaker's shelter, though final access (from a little passage on the right as you face the sea) involves some wading.

Kótsinas

Besides these two sites, the only other attraction on the shores of Bourniá Bay, reached via Repanídhi village on the other side of Kondopoúli, is the often dirty, hard-packed beach of **Kótsinas**. The nearby anchorage (follow signs to "Kótsinas Fortress") offers a pair of **tavernas**; the better of these *To Korali* by the water, is reliably open at lunch, with a wide range of mezédhes and affordable fish. Up on a knoll overlooking the jetty looms an oxidized-green, sword-brandishing statue of Maroula, a Genoese-era heroine who delayed the Ottoman conquest by a few years. Also on this hill stands a large church of Zoödhóhou Piyís (the Lifegiving Spring); this itself is nothing extraordinary, but beside it 63 steps lead down through an illuminated tunnel cut into the rock to the potable (if slightly minerally) spring in question, oozing into a cool, vaulted **subterranean chamber**.

Eastern beaches

Certainly the best beach on this part of Límnos is the strand at **Kéros**, 2.5km by dirt road below **KALLIÓPI** (two snack bar/**tavernas**, smart rooms at the edge of town – ☎02540/41 730, ❸), in turn 1km from Kondopoúli. A 1.5-kilometre stretch of sand with dunes and a small pine plantation, shallow water and a certain amount of seaweed, Kéros attracts Greek tourists and Germans with camper vans and windsurfing equipment, but is large enough to absorb most weekend crowds. Near the parking area, a small *kantína*/snack bar operates during July and August only. By contrast, the beaches near the village of **PLÁKA**, at the northeastern tip of the island, are not worth the extra effort; the adjacent hot springs appearing on some maps are actually warm mud baths.

Áyios Efstrátios (Aï Strátis)

ÁYIOS EFSTRÁTIOS ("Aï Strátis" for short) is without doubt one of the quietest and loneliest islands in the Aegean. Historically, the only outsiders to stay here were compelled to do so – it served as a place of exile for political prisoners under both the Metaxas regime of the 1930s and the various right-wing governments that followed the Civil War: up to six thousand of them during the 1950s. Before that, it was only permanently settled in the sixteenth century, after a long period of desertion since ancient times, and its land is still largely owned by three monasteries on nearby Mount Áthos. Despite increasing numbers of summer visitors, it's still unusual for foreign travellers to show up on the island, and if you do, you might be asked why you've come.

Arrival

Large **ferries** between Límnos and Rafina call also at Áyios Efstrátios twice weekly throughout the year; in summer, there's a regular small ferry too, the *Aiolis*, from Límnos, departing every weekday at 3pm, returning early the next morning. The harbour was improved in 1993 to allow large ferries to dock, replacing the lighters which perilously transferred goods and passengers, but it is still a very exposed anchorage, and in bad weather you could end up stranded here longer than you bargained for. If an indefinite stay does not appeal, it may be best to get just a taste of the island through one of the weekly day-trips (typically Sunday) running from Límnos during high season.

The port

ÁYIOS EFSTRÁTIOS port – the sole settlement on the island – must be one of the ugliest habitations in Greece. Devastation caused by an earthquake in February 1968, which also killed half the population, was compounded by the rebuilding plan: the contract went to a company with connections to the colonels' junta, who prevented the survivors from returning to their old homes and used army bulldozers to raze even those structures that could have been repaired. From the northern hillside, some two dozen remaining houses of the old village overlook its replacement, whose grim rows of prefabs, complete with concrete church and underused shopping centre, constitute a sad monument to the corruption of the junta years. If you're curious, there's a pre-earthquake photograph of the village in the kafenío by the port.

Architecture apart, Áyios Efstrátios still functions as a fishing and farming community of about three hundred, with the prefabs set at the mouth of a wooded stream valley draining to the sandy harbour beach. Tourist amenities consist of just three **tavernas** (*Thanassis*, *Andonis* and *Tassos*), plus a total of three **pensions**. Best of these, in one of the surviving old houses, is the *Xenonas Aï-Stratis* (Ⓣ02540/93 329; ③); *Andonis Paneras* (Ⓣ02540/93 209; ③) and *Apostolos Paneras* (Ⓣ02540/93 343; ③) have more conventional rooms out in the prefabs. These relatively stiff prices for such an out of the way place reflect

Aï Stratis' increasing popularity with Greeks, and you may have to ring all three spots for a vacancy in season.

The rest of the island

As you walk away from the village – there are few cars and no paved roads – things improve rapidly. The landscape, dry hills and valleys scattered with

Greek script table

Límnos	Λήμνος	ΛΗΜΝΟΣ
Atsikí	Ατσική	ΑΤΣΙΚΗ
Avlónas	Αυλώνας	ΑΥΛΩΝΑΣ
Áyios Efstrátios	Άγιος Ευστράτιος	ΑΓΙΟΣ ΕΥΣΤΡΑΤΙΟΣ
Áyios Ioánnis	Άγιος Ιοάννης	ΑΓΙΟΣ ΙΟΑΝΝΗΣ
Áyios Pávlos	Άγιος Πάυλος	ΑΓΙΟΣ ΠΑΥΛΟΣ
Dháfni	Δάφνη	ΔΑΦΝΗ
Dhiapóri	Διαπόρι	ΔΙΑΠΟΡΙ
Evgátis	Ευγάτης	ΕΥΓΑΤΗΣ
Havoúli	Χαβούλι	ΧΑΒΟΥΛΙ
Ifestía	Ηφαιστεία	ΗΦΑΙΣΤΕΙΑ
Kallιópi	Καλλιόπη	ΚΑΛΛΙΟΠΗ
Kamínia	Καμίνια	ΚΑΜΙΝΙΑ
Karpássi	Καρπάσι	ΚΑΡΠΑΣΙ
Káspakas	Κάσπακας	ΚΑΣΠΑΚΑΣ
Kavírio	Καβείριο	ΚΑΒΕΙΡΙΟ
Kéros	Κέρος	ΚΕΡΟΣ
Kondiás	Κοντιάς	ΚΟΝΤΙΑΣ
Kondopoúli	Κοντοπούλι	ΚΟΝΤΟΠΟΥΛΙ
Kornós	Κορνός	ΚΟΡΝΟΣ
Kótsinas	Κότσινας	ΚΟΤΣΙΝΑΣ
Livadhohóri	Λιβαδοχώρι	ΛΙΒΑΔΟΧΩΡΙ
Lýkhna	Λύχνα	ΛΥΧΝΑ
Moúdhros	Μούδρος	ΜΟΥΔΡΟΣ
Mýrina	Μύρινα	ΜΥΡΙΝΑ
Pedhinó	Πεδινό	ΠΕΔΙΝΟ
Pláka	Πλάκα	ΠΛΑΚΑ
Platý	Πλατύ	ΠΛΑΤΥ
Polyókhni	Πολυόχνη	ΠΟΛΥΟΧΝΗ
Portianoú	Πορτιανού	ΠΟΡΤΙΑΝΟΥ
Repanídhi	Ρεπανίδι	ΡΕΠΑΝΙΔΙ
Romanoú	Ρομανού	ΡΟΜΑΝΟΥ
Roussopoúli	Ρουσσοπούλι	ΡΟΥΣΣΟΠΟΥΛΙ
Sardhés	Σαρδές	ΣΑΡΔΕΣ
Thános	Θάνος	ΘΑΝΟΣ
Város	Βάρος	ΒΑΡΟΣ

a surprising number of oak trees, is deserted apart from wild rabbits, sheep, an occasional shepherd, and some good beaches where you can camp in desert-island isolation – perhaps the main reason you're likely to visit Áyios Efstrátios. **Alonítsi**, on the north coast, a ninety-minute walk from the village along a track up the north side of the valley (bear right at the only junction), is a two-kilometre stretch of sand with rolling breakers and views across to Límnos.

South of the village, there's a series of greyish sand beaches, most with wells and drinkable water, although with few real paths in this part of the island, getting to them can be quite a scramble. **Lidharío**, at the end of an attractive wooded valley, is the first worthwhile beach but, again, it's a fairly strenuous ninety-minute walk from town, unless you can persuade a fisherman to take you by boat. Some of the caves around the coast are home to the rare Mediterranean monk seal (see box, p.332), but you're unlikely to see one.

Límnos travel details

Inter-island transport

Key to ferry companies

ANES	Saos II
NEL	*Navtiliakí Etería Lésvou* (Lesvian Shipping Co)

Kaïkia/small ferries

Límnos to: Áyios Efstrátios (5–6 weekly June–Sept, 2–3 weekly otherwise; from Mýrina daily Mon–Fri at 3pm, from Áyios Efstrátios 6.30am Mon–Fri; journey time 2hr).

Large ferries

Áyios Efstrátios to: Límnos (1–2 weekly on NEL; 1hr 30min); Psará (1 weekly on NEL; 4hr); Rafína (1–2 weekly on NEL; 6hr 30min); Sígri, Lésvos (1 weekly on NEL; 3hr).

Límnos (Mýrina) to: Alexandhroúpoli (2 weekly on NEL; 4hr 30min); Áyios Efstrátios (2 weekly on NEL; 1hr 15min); Híos (2 weekly on NEL; 11hr); Kavála (3 weekly on NEL, 4 weekly on ANES; 4hr 30min); Kós (1 weekly on NEL; 19hr); Lávrio, Attica (2 weekly on ANES; 8hr 30min); Mytilíni, Lésvos (4 weekly on NEL; 6hr); Pireás (2 weekly on NEL; 17hr); Rafína (3 weekly on NEL; 8–9hr); Rhodes (1 weekly on NEL; 21hr); Sámos (1 weekly on NEL; 15hr); Samothráki (1 weekly on ANES; 2hr 30min); Sígri, Lésvos (1 weekly on NEL; 4hr 30min); Thessaloníki (2 weekly on NEL, 1 weekly on ANES; 7hr 30min).

Flights

Límnos to: Athens (3 daily; 1hr 5min); Híos (1 weekly; 1hr); Lésvos (4 weekly; 35min); Rhodes (2 weekly; 3hr); Sámos (2 weekly, 1hr 30min); Thessaloníki (1 daily; 45min).

NB Because of heavy use by the Greek armed forces, these flights need to be booked well in advance throughout the year.

contexts

contexts

The historical framework

This section serves merely to lend some perspective to travels in the Dodecanese and east Aegean, and is heavily weighted towards more recent centuries. Although these two island groups are the most recent additions to the modern Greek state, their Hellenic identity has been fairly consistent since ancient times – something the kafenío sages will be only too willing to corroborate in political discussions.

Neolithic, Minoan and Mycenean ages: c.5500–1150 BC

It seems that people originally came to the Dodecanese and east Aegean in fits and starts, predominantly from the **Anatolian mainland** just opposite. Settlement of the islands after the sixth millennium BC is fairly well documented by archeological finds, particularly at present-day Thermí, Lésvos; Emboriós, Híos; Líndhos, Rhodes; various sites on Límnos; and in several caves on Kálymnos. In contrast to the exclusively farming communities on the mainland, these were trading posts founded at or near excellent natural harbours.

The years between about **2000 and 1100 BC** were a period of fluctuating regional dominance, based at first upon **sea power**; the Phoenicians in particular lingered briefly at Rhodes en route to Crete from the Middle East. Minoan Crete, which monopolized the eastern Mediterranean trade routes during an era subsequently called the **Minoan Age**, in turn dispatched more permanent colonists during the sixteenth century BC, establishing trading posts at Ialyssos and Kameiros on Rhodes' west-facing Aegean coast.

When the Minoan cities finally succumbed to disaster, natural or otherwise, around 1400 BC, it was the flourishing mainland centre of **Mycenae** that assumed the leading role in these islands, until it in turn collapsed during the twelfth century BC. On Rhodes, the Mycenean invaders left traces of their distinctive **pottery** (which dominates the town's archeological museum), and re-established the cities of Ialyssos, Kameiros and Lindos. By now the island and some of its neighbours (including Kós and Sými) were prominent enough to participate in the semi-legendary **Trojan War**, with their ships included in Homer's roster of those who sailed to Troy.

The Dorian and Archaic eras: c.1150–500 BC

The collapse of the Mycenean (or more properly, Late Bronze Age) civilization has traditionally been attributed to the invasion from the north of a fair-skinned "barbarian" people, the **Dorians**, who devastated the existing culture and initiated the first "**Dark Ages**". Revisionist archeologists now see the influx more in terms of shifting **trade patterns**, though undoubtedly there was major disruption during the **twelfth century BC**.

Out in the islands, this era saw Límnos apparently retain its indigenous, non-Mycenean population, and Lésvos play host to **Aeolians** displaced from mainland Thessaly. Meanwhile, the so-called Dorians took over most islands to the south, including Rhodes, where Ialyssos and Kameiros began to grow. Together with Lindos, Astypalia (on Kós), Knidos and Halikarnassos (the latter two on the Anatolian mainland opposite), these six settlements formed the confederacy known as the **Dorian Hexapolis**.

Two cultural trends are salient in this period: the almost total supplanting of earlier mother goddesses by **male deities** (a process begun under the Myceneans), and the appearance of an **alphabet** still recognizable by modern Greeks, which replaced the so-called "Linear A" and "Linear B" Minoan/Mycenean scripts.

Archaic period

By around **800 BC**, the initially rigorous rule of the Dorians had relaxed on the islands as elsewhere in Greece, perhaps accelerated by the influx from Asia Minor of the so-called Ionians, particularly on the islands of Híos, Ikaría and Sámos. The twelve-town **Ionian League**, centred at the Panionion shrine on Mount Mycale opposite Sámos, included these islands as members.

Here as elsewhere in the Hellenic world, the ninth century BC ushered in the beginnings of the more democratic Greek **city-state** (*polis*). Citizens – rather than just kings or aristocrats – became involved in government and took part in community activities organizing industry, worship and leisure. Colonial ventures by the wealthier cities (including Lindos) increased, as did commercial dealings, and the consequent rise in the import-export trade gradually gave rise to a new class of manufacturers.

Each city-state retained both its independence and a distinctive style, with the result that the sporadic attempts to unite against any external enemy were always pragmatic and temporary. The two most powerful states to emerge on the mainland were **Athens** and **Sparta**, who were to engage in fierce rivalry for the next five centuries. In the Dodecanese and east Aegean, the most important city-states were Lindos on Rhodes, Astypalaia on Kos, Mithymna and Mytilene on Lesbos, and the eponymous island capitals, Hios and Samos. Their heyday was the sixth century BC, when Mytilene, Lindos and Samos were ruled by **tyrants** of distinction – Pittakos, Kleovoulos and Polykrates respectively, with the word "tyrant" yet to acquire all of its modern perjorative connotations.

Each city-state had its **acropolis**, or high town, where religious activity was focused. Worship at this stage was **polytheistic**, grouping the Olympic pantheon under Zeus. The proliferation of references to names and of sanctuary finds on the islands suggests a preference for the divine twins Apollo and Artemis, the latter often merely a thinly Hellenized version of the Anatolian goddess Cybele; Aphrodite and Hera were also well represented – only to be expected, bearing in mind the proximity to Asia with its cults of love goddesses such as Astarte.

The Classical and Hellenistic eras: c.500–166 BC

Of the outside threats faced by the various city-states, none was greater than that of the **Persians**, who under successive kings Darius and Xerxes made repeated attempts to subjugate both islands and mainland. By virtue of their position, as well as innate sympathies, many of the east Aegean and Dodecanesian city-states took the side of the invaders; though Rhodes successfully resisted Darius' first attack in 491 BC, in the year 480 it contributed nearly forty ships to Xerxes' fleet at the **Battle of Salamis**. It was the decisive Greek naval victory (479 BC) in the Mycale straits off Sámos that finally ended the Persian threat. Shortly thereafter the **Delian Confederacy**, an alliance dominated by Athens, was established, in which many island city-states (including those of Rhodes) were enlisted voluntarily or otherwise.

Athens again was the first to elaborate the concept of **democracy** (*demokratia*), literally "control by the people" – at this stage "the people" did not include women or slaves. In Athens there were three organs of government. The **Areopagus**, composed of the city elders, had a steadily decreasing authority and ended up dealing solely with murder cases. Then there was the **Council of Five Hundred**, elected annually by ballot to prepare the business of the Assembly and attend to matters of urgency. Finally, the **Assembly** gave every free man a political voice; it had sole responsibility for law-making and provided an arena for the discussion of important issues. Other "democratic" city-states adopted variations of these institutions, but they were slow to catch on in the eastern islands, where in most cases oligarchies of some sort remained in power.

The power struggles between Athens and Sparta, each allied with various networks of city-states, eventually culminated in the **Peloponnesian Wars** of 431–404 BC. The Dodecanese and east Aegean saw little military action, but because of a Dorian heritage shared with Sparta, city-states there tended to defect to the Spartan side when given the opportunity; Mytilene for example revolted in 428 (partly to spite pro-Athenian neighbour Mithymna), and Rhodes, Kos and Hios changed sides in 412. Only Samos remained a more or less constant Athenian ally to the end of the war. These conflicts (superbly recorded by Thucydides) were nominally won by Sparta, and thereafter the small city-state ceased to function so effectively.

On Rhodes, decline was hastened by the founding in 408 BC of a single city intended to replace the three original centres of Ialyssos, Kameiros and Lindos. The result of this act of union (*synoekismos*) was **Rodos**, at the northeastern tip of the island, endowed with three natural harbours still in use today. The original trio slowly suffered a loss of status over the next few centuries, until only Lindos retained any importance or independence. Quickly growing wealthy from **trade** – particularly the export of wine to Egypt in exchange for grain – Rodos minted its own currency, which gradually replaced earlier coinage from Lindos, Ialyssos and Kameiros.

During this period, the islands of Samos and Hios were at their nadirs, intermittently occupied by the resurgent Persians taking advantage of disorder following the Peloponnesian Wars; Kos effected a *synoekismos* of its own in 366 BC, founding the present-day port and capital. Only the largest of a half-dozen original city-states on Lesbos remained important during the fourth century BC.

The most important factor in the decline of the city-states was emerging on the northern mainland, in the kingdom of **Macedonia**. Based at the Macedonian capital of Pella, Philip II (359–336 BC) was forging a strong military and unitary force, pushing forward into Thrace and establishing control over the southern mainland. His son, **Alexander the Great**, in an extraordinarily brief but glorious thirteen-year reign, extended these gains into Persia and Egypt as well as parts of modern India and Afghanistan. The east Aegean and Dodecanese islands quickly sided with Alexander, especially mercenarily minded Rhodes, which was granted generous commercial concessions in the conqueror's new Levantine territories.

This unwieldy empire splintered almost immediately upon Alexander's death in 323 BC, and was divided into the three Macedonian dynasties of **Hellenistic Greece**. It was not long before the Antigonids in Macedonia, the Seleucids in Syria and Persia, and the Ptolemies in Egypt fell to fighting among themselves. Their conflicts involved Rhodes, whose islanders had understandably refused an "offer" by Antigonus to join him in attacking Egypt, their long-standing ally and trade partner. Enraged at this defiance, in 305 BC Antigonus sent his son Demetrios to bring the Rhodians to heel; the result was a year-long **siege**, one of the great battles of antiquity (see box on pp.94). Having fought each other to a standstill, attackers and defenders agreed to a truce, and Demetrios' abandoned war machinery was sold to defray the costs of the **Colossus of Rhodes** (see box on p.109).

Hellenistic Rodos emerged from the war with redoubled prestige and wealth; poets, philosophers, rhetoricians and artists, both native-born and immigrant, made the city their home during a "**golden age**" that was to last until the middle of the second century BC. During this time Rhodes' sea-going power was such that her **maritime and trading law** became standard across the Mediterranean, and was adapted by Augustus three centuries later for application throughout the Roman Empire.

The Roman and Byzantine eras: 166 BC–15th century AD

Until now, **Rhodes** had proved adroit at avoiding political alliances and keeping commercial criteria paramount, but as the second century BC progressed, she became entangled with an expanding **Rome**. The mainland had been subdued by the Romans in a series of campaigns beginning in 215 BC, and by 190 BC their operations extended to the islands, Anatolia and the Middle East. Rome repaid Rhodes for its military assistance with a grant of authority over lands in Lycia and Caria, but the latter complained repeatedly to the Senate. Matters came to a head in 166 BC, when Rome withdrew the Rhodian concession in these two Anatolian realms, and declared the central Aegean islet of Delos a free port, sending Rhodian prosperity into free fall. Rhodes compounded her error by siding against the assassins of Julius Caesar in 42 BC; in retaliation, Cassius plundered and burnt Rodos city, massacring the citizens and forwarding enormous booty to Rome.

Kos' turn had come in 88 BC, at the hands of the brigand-king **Mithridates of Pontus**, who sacked the port town, relieving it of £1 million equivalent in bank deposits; the island was otherwise known for its wine and silk, both now long since disappeared. **Samos** had taken Mithridates' part and was punished accordingly, though later it was chosen to host the honeymoon of Anthony and Cleopatra. Of all these islands, **Lesbos** was the Romans' favourite for its lively town life and gentle scenery, with money spent on lavish public works, and imperial visits to its academies and theatres. Following a decree by Emperor Augustus, these four cities were designated **venues of banishment** for disgraced notables – not too onerous a punishment given the creature comforts they afforded.

Christianity and Byzantium

Christianity came early to the east Aegean and Dodecanese. The apostle Paul stopped here in the first century to evangelize Rhodes, Kós, Sámos, Híos and Lésvos, and these, plus virtually every smaller island (particularly Kálymnos) have at least two ruined basilicas with mosaic floors, invariably from the fifth or sixth century, often built atop pagan shrines; these early churches were mostly levelled by Arab raids in the seventh century.

The **decline of the Roman Empire** involved its apportioning into eastern and western empires. In 330 AD Emperor Constantine moved his capital to the Greek city of **Byzantium**, and here emerged Constantinople (modern Istanbul), the "new Rome" and spiritual and political capital of the Byzantine Empire. While the last western Roman emperor was deposed by barbarian Goths in 476, this eastern portion was to be the dominant Mediterranean power for some seven centuries; only in 1453 did it collapse completely.

Christianity had an influential advocate in Constantine (who, however, for reasons of state converted personally only on his deathbed), and by the end of the fourth century it was the **official state religion**; its liturgies (still in use in the Greek Orthodox church), creed and New Testament were all written in the **koine**, a form of Greek evolved from the ancient dialect. A distinction was drawn, though, between perceptions of Greek as a language and as a cultural concept. The Byzantine Empire styled itself Roman, or *Romios*, rather than Hellenic, and moved to eradicate all remaining symbols of pagan Greece, for instance by dismantling ancient temples for use as masonry in building churches.

The seventh century saw **Constantinople** besieged by Persians, and later by Arabs, but the Byzantine Empire survived, losing only Egypt, the least "Greek" of its territories. During the ninth to the early eleventh centuries, culture, confidence and security flourished in the core Byzantine domains. Linked to the Orthodox Byzantine faith was a sense of spiritual superiority, and the emperors saw Constantinople as a "new Jerusalem" for their "chosen people". This was the beginning of a diplomatic and ecclesiastical conflict with the Catholic West that was to have disastrous consequences over the next five centuries. In the meantime the eastern and western patriarchs mutually excommunicated each other.

From the seventh through to the eleventh centuries the Dodecanese and east Aegean became something of a provincial backwater, making little mark in the historical record, with islands such as Ikaría and Lésvos used mostly (as under the Romans) to house banished troublemakers; most illustrious of these was the disgraced **Empress Irene**, exiled to Políkhnitos – some say the village of Vassiliká, just east – in 802.

All the islands were ravaged repeatedly by piratical **Saracen raids**, and from these years date numerous castles and watchtowers. Only at the close of this period did two great Byzantine monuments appear: the imperially founded monasteries of **Néa Moní**, on Híos, and **St John the Theologian**, on Pátmos. The latter foundation involved an imperial grant of the entire, previously insignificant island to the abbot Khristodhoulos, with the sanctity of the place curiously respected by most subsequent rulers and invaders.

The coming of the Crusaders

Early in the eleventh century, **Latin Crusaders** began to appear in the region. In 1095 the Normans landed on the Dodecanese, with papal sanction, on their way to liberate Jerusalem. However, these were only a precursor to the rerouted **Fourth Crusade** of 1204, when Venetians, Franks and Germans diverted their armies from the Holy Land to Byzantium, sacking and occupying Constantinople. These Latin princes and their followers, intent on new lands and kingdoms, settled in to divide up the best part of the Empire. All that remained of Byzantium were four small peripheral kingdoms or **despotates**; none of these was based in the islands, though Rhodes was ruled by Leon Gavalas, a wealthy Byzantine governor, for three decades (a street in Ródhos' old town bears his name).

There followed two centuries of manipulation by and struggle between Franks, Venetians, Genoese, Catalans and Turks. In 1261, the **Paleologos** dynasty, provisionally based at Nicaea, recovered the city of Constantinople but little of its former territory and power. Virtually their only Latin Catholic allies were the **Genoese**, whose support came at a heavy price: extensive commercial privileges in the capital itself, and the effective cession, at various moments during the thirteenth and fourteenth centuries, of virtually all the east Aegean and Dodecanese islands to assorted Genoese families.

Within a generation of driving out the Franks the Byzantine Greeks faced a much stronger threat in the expanding empire of the **Ottoman Turks**. Torn apart by internal struggles between their own ruling dynasties, the Paleologi and Kantakuzenes, and unassisted except by the Genoese, they were to prove no match for the Turks. On Tuesday, May 29, 1453, a date still solemnly commemorated by the Orthodox church, Constantinople fell to the forces of **Sultan Mehmet II** after a seven-week siege.

Genoese and Crusader rule: 1248–1478

From the thirteenth century onwards the histories of the Dodecanese and east Aegean islands began to diverge slightly, with often widely varying dates of handover between one conqueror and another, even for neighbouring islands.

Genoese adventurers seized Rhodes from Venetian rivals in 1248, but in 1306 the chivalric order of the **Knights Hospitallers of St John** (see box on pp.102–103), expelled from Palestine and discontent on Cyprus, landed at Feraklós castle on the east coast of Rhodes. After a three-year war they evicted the Genoese from the island; Genoese-held Kós fell to the Knights in 1314, after which their possession – and prominent fortification – of most of the Dodecanese was a foregone conclusion. The main exceptions were Astypálea, Kárpathos and Kássos, which remained under Venetian rule, and the ecclesiastical idiosyncrasy of Pátmos.

From their main bases on Rhodes and Kós, the Knights engaged in both legitimate trade and piracy, constituting a major thorn in the side of the expanding Ottoman empire, and, in the final century of their toehold, the only effective opposition to Ottoman authority in the Aegean. Attempts to dislodge them from these two islands during the fifteenth century were unsuccessful, and it took the Ottoman's acquisition of Kastellórizo as a base in 1512, and then a protracted siege of Rhodes by Sultan Süleyman the Magnificent in 1522 (see box on pp.102–103), to send them packing off to Malta, and for all of the Dodecanese to fall into Turkish hands.

Remote Sámos and Ikaría supported garrisons of Venetians plus sundry other adventurers and pirates from the twelfth century onwards, but the **Genoese** gained undisputed possession of all islands from here north to the Thracian mainland during the fourteenth century. The marriage in 1355 of a Byzantine emperor to the daughter of the **Gattilusi family** resulted in Lésvos passing into the hands of the latter. By all accounts they ran a civilized and enlightened principality, except for the unsavoury last of their line, Nicolò, who was defeated and killed by the Ottomans in 1462. Límnos, briefly taken over by the Venetians, followed in 1478.

Híos was allotted to the **Giustiniani clan** in 1344, who instituted harsh government through a *maona* or holding company, monopolizing the lucrative gum mastic trade until the Ottoman conquest in 1566. Sámos, essentially deserted since the fifteenth century, and adjacent Ikaría were acquired by the sultan or his representatives in the same decade, making these three islands the last to fall under Ottoman suzerainty.

Ottoman occupation: 1478–1912

Under what Greeks refer to as the **Turkokratía** or years of Ottoman rule, the Dodecanese and east Aegean lapsed into rural provincialism, taking refuge in a self-protective mode of village life that endured undisrupted until the 1920s. Only those larger islands with plenty of flat, arable land, such as Rhodes, Kós, and Lésvos, attracted extensive Turkish colonization and garrisoning, and then (except for Lésvos) only in the largest towns, where non-Muslims were forbidden residence in the strategic central citadels. Taxes and discipline from Istanbul were imposed locally through resident judges, tax collectors and military personnel, but large enterprises or estates could remain in the hands of local notables – civilian or military – who often enjoyed considerable independence.

By and large, provincial Ottoman government was lethargic if not downright lackadaisical; travellers reported extensive neglect and deterioration on Rhodes in the eighteenth and nineteenth centuries, with discarded weapons and unrepaired damage both still dating from the 1522 siege.

Greek identity, meanwhile, was preserved through the offices of the **Orthodox Church**, which, despite occasional instances of enforced conversion and intermarriage, and the transformation of some churches into mosques, suffered little interference from the Ottomans. All Orthodox people, Greek or otherwise, were officially grouped as one *millet* or **subject nation**, with the patriarch responsible for the behaviour of his flock, collecting taxes and for administering communal and inheritance law. **Monasteries** organized schools and became the trustees of Byzantine culture; this had gone into stagnation after the fall of the empire, whose scholars and artists emigrated west, adding impetus to the Renaissance.

As Ottoman administration became increasingly decentralized and inefficient, individual Greeks rose to local positions of considerable influence, and a number of communities achieved a significant degree of **autonomy**. Even on tightly governed Lésvos, much of the lucrative olive-oil trade had passed into Greek Orthodox hands by the eighteenth century; Híos enjoyed special privileges by virtue of its continued monopoly on gum mastic; Sámos produced fine tobacco and rope hemp; while the barren, maritime islets of the Dodecanese, such as Hálki, Kálymnos, Sými and Kastellórizo, made fortunes either by diving for sponges, transporting Anatolian goods on their own fleets, or building boats on Turkish commission. The Ottomans, until relatively late in their history, never bothered to acquire much seamanship, preferring to rely on island crews and shipyards.

A typical anecdote relates how the Symians, on hearing of the fall of Rhodes, sought to allay imperial wrath by presenting Süleyman the Magnificent with a load of their finest sponges. Duly impressed, the sultan declared Sými a duty-free port, and gave the islanders the exclusive right to dive for sponges anywhere in the Aegean, in return for a yearly tribute similar to their introductory gift. These and similar indulgences were mostly honoured until after the establishment of a Greek state in 1830 (see opposite), with incremental withdrawal of privileges occurring between 1874 and 1908 in response to continued warfare between the Ottomans and "free" Greece.

The struggle for Independence

By the eighteenth century, opposition to Turkish rule on the Greek mainland was becoming widespread, exemplified most obviously by the *klephts* (brigands) of the mountains. It was not until the nineteenth century, however, that a **resistance movement** could muster sufficient support and firepower to mount a real challenge to the Ottomans. In 1770 a Russian-backed uprising enjoyed considerable success out in the islands, with Sámos and Pátmos in particular occupied by Catherine the Great's favourite, Admiral Orlof, for three years. On the mainland, however, it was easily and brutally suppressed.

Fifty years later, however, the situation had changed. In Epirus, on the mainland, the Ottomans were over-extended, subduing the expansionist campaigns of local ruler Ali Pasha. The French Revolution and its propagandists had provided impetus, rationale and confidence to national freedom movements; the Greek fighters were given financial and ideological underpinning by the **Filikí Etería**, or "Friendly Society", a secret group recruited among the exiled Greek merchants and intellectuals of central Europe. Accordingly, a somewhat motley coalition of *klephts* and theorists launched their insurrection at the monastery of **Ayía Lávra** near Kalávryta in the Peloponnese, where on March 25, 1821, the Greek banner was openly raised by the local archbishop, Yermanos.

The Dodecanese and east Aegean islands participated to varying, often limited degrees in the insurrection; the Aegean was usually not a primary theatre of operations. Pátmos and Sámos had virtually liberated themselves by 1824, though an uprising on Sými was easily quelled and its historic privileges rescinded. At Eressós, on Lésvos, a Turkish frigate was blown up by a kamikaze fire boat, prompting widespread massacre on the island; appalling reprisals were also visited on Híos for rebelling at Samian instigation. Kássos and Psará both harassed Ottoman shipping with their own large fleets, and suffered overwhelming revenge in consequence.

However, even where entire populations (such as on Kós and Rhodes) were restrained en masse by Ottoman garrisons, it was impossible to prevent individual volunteers from slipping away on boats to join the fracas on the mainland – the start of a tradition that was to gather momentum over the next century and a quarter in various struggles involving mainland Greece, commemorated by the Rhodian street Ethelondón Dhodhekanisíon (Dodecanesian Volunteers).

In 1830, the Western powers confirmed **Greek independence** by the Treaty of London, and borders were drawn up at a supplementary conference of 1832. Within these resided just 800,000 of the six million Greeks living within the Ottoman Empire, and the "free" territories were for the most part the poorest of the Classical and Byzantine lands, comprising Attica, the Peloponnese, the Argo-Saronic islands, the Sporades islands and the Cyclades. The rich agricultural belt of Thessaly, Epirus in the west, and Macedonia in the north, remained for the moment in Ottoman hands, as did all of the east Aegean islands and the Dodecanese. Alone among the east Aegean islands, Sámos, in recognition of its war efforts, was accorded special status by the 1832 **Treaty of London**; it ranked as a semi-autonomous Ottoman province overseen by a suitably compliant Christian "prince", who was appointed by the sultan.

The emerging state

From the outset, irredentism was to be the main engine of Greek foreign policy for the next century. The **Megáli Idhéa** (Great Ideal), as it was termed, enshrined the liberation of all ethnic Greek populations residing outside the initially limited Greek state, by expanding its borders to incorporate as much as possible of former Byzantine territories. Among other regions, the east Aegean and Dodecanese were prime targets and beneficiaries of such sentiments.

In 1862, the new king, a Danish prince who would rule Greece as George I, requested that Britain give up their "protectorate" of the Ionian islands as a condition of his accession to the Greek throne. In 1878, Thessaly, along with southern Epirus, was ceded to Greece by the Ottomans; less gloriously, the Greeks failed in 1897 to achieve *énosis* (union) with **Crete** by attacking Turkish forces on the mainland, and in the process virtually bankrupted the state. The island was, however, granted a status similar to Sámos' (here the prince was appointed by France, England and Russia), eventually becoming a de jure part of Greece in 1913.

It was from Crete also that the most distinguished Greek statesman of the twentieth century emerged. **Eleftherios Venizelos**, having led a civilian campaign for his island's redemption, was in 1910 elected prime minister of Greece. Two years later he organized an alliance with Serbia, Romania and Bulgaria to fight the two **Balkan Wars** (1912–13), campaigns that saw the Ottomans all but driven out of Europe and the Aegean islands.

In the east Aegean, the first island to revolt was Ikaría, in July 1912, which in typically idiosyncratic fashion declared itself independent, issuing its own stamps and flying its own flag. This lasted a mere five months, until the Greek fleet showed up in November, en route to landings on Híos, Lésvos and Límnos, where Ottoman troops resisted for only a few weeks. Already by September, members of the tiny Turkish garrison on Sámos had been bundled into kaïkia and sent to Asia Minor after the last prince, deemed collaborationist, had been assassinated. With Greek frontiers extended to include central

Epirus and western Macedonia (with its capital, Thessaloníki), the *Megáli Idhéa* was approaching reality.

One area however that remained outside its scope was the Dodecanese, which had been seized by the Italians in a brief campaign during spring 1912, part of a larger war begun in autumn 1911 to push the Ottomans out of Libya. At first the Italians were acclaimed as Christian liberators by the overwhelmingly Greek Orthodox population, and the invaders in turn undertook not to outstay their welcome. At the outset of **World War I**, however, Italy elected to remain neutral, and was only persuaded to join the Allies by being promised, among other things, that its sovereignty over the Dodecanese would be recognized – duly codified after the war in the 1920 **Treaty of Sèvres** signed by the last sultan; it's this treaty (as well as others) that some Turkish diplomats repudiate today.

Since the Balkan Wars, Venizelos had proved himself a shrewd manipulator of domestic public opinion by revising the constitution and introducing a series of liberal social reforms. Division, however – the fabled *Ethnikós Dhíhazmos* or "**National Schism**" – was to appear with the outbreak of World War I. Venizelos urged Greek entry on the Allied side, seeing in the conflict possibilities for the "liberation" of Greeks in Thrace and Asia Minor. However, the new king, **Constantine (Konstantinos) I**, married to a sister of the German Kaiser, imposed a policy of neutrality. Eventually Venizelos and his adherents set up a revolutionary government in Thessaloníki, provoking a brief civil war which saw royalist Pireás also menaced by Allied battleships; all of the recently liberated east Aegean islands declared for the Venizelists. In 1917, Greek troops entered the war to join the French, British and Serbian armies in the Macedonian campaign. Upon the capitulation of Bulgaria and Ottoman Turkey, the Greeks occupied Thrace, and Venizelos presented at **Versailles** demands for the predominantly Greek region around Smyrna (now Izmir) on the Asia Minor coast.

The Katastrofí and its aftermath

This marked the beginning of one of the most disastrous episodes in modern Greek history, still referred to in Greece as the **Katastrofí** – meaning precisely the same as the English cognate "catastrophe". Venizelos was authorized to move forces into Smyrna in May 1919, but soon afterwards Allied support, except for Lloyd George's Britain, began to evaporate; in particular the Italians, now consolidating their hold on the Dodecanese, had no wish to be hemmed in on three sides by Greek territory. Within Turkey itself, a new nationalist movement – surreptitiously assisted by the French and Italians – was taking power under Mustafa Kemal, or **Atatürk** as he came to be known.

When Venizelos unexpectedly lost the 1920 elections, the Royalist party, along with the recently returned King Constantine, took over. They not only forfeited most support (including financial) from the British, but showed relatively little enthusiasm or competence in pursuing what they considered to be a rash imperialist venture inherited from the Venezelists, and little of the Cretan's skill in foreign diplomacy. Greek forces, now led for the most part by incompetent and corrupt Royalist generals, were ordered to advance upon Ankara in an attempt to crush Atatürk and the Turkish nationalist armies. Greece's Anatolian mandate ignominiously collapsed in late August 1922, when Turkish troops launched a massive attack at Afyon, forcing the Greeks back to the Aegean coast and into a hurried evacuation from Smyrna. After triumphantly entering Smyrna, the Turks systematically massacred a significant fraction of the remaining Armenian and Greek population before burning most of the city to the ground.

Although an entire Greek army remained intact in eastern Thrace, and was prepared to fight on, Greece was compelled to accept Atatürk's own terms, formalized by the **Treaty of Lausanne** in 1923, with Venizelos called back from retirement to salvage what he could from the loser's side of the negotiating table. Among other provisions, the treaty ordered the exchange of religious minorities in each country – in effect, the first regulated ethnic cleansing. Turkey was to accept 390,000 Muslims resident on Greek soil. Greece, mobilized almost continuously for the last decade and with a population of under five million, was faced with the resettlement of over 1,400,000 Christian refugees, some tens of thousands of whom were lodged on the east Aegean islands. Many of these had already read the writing on the wall after 1918 and arrived of their own accord, from Bulgaria and revolutionary Russia as well as Asia Minor. The *Megáli Idhéa* had ceased to be a viable blueprint for action.

Changes were immediate and far-reaching. Within a few years great agricultural estates on mainland Thessaly, as well as Crete, Évvia and Lésvos, were redistributed both to native Greek tenants and refugee farmers, and huge shantytowns grew into new quarters around Athens, Pireás and other cities, a spur to the country's then almost nonexistent industry.

Political reaction was even swifter. By late September 1922, a group of army officers under **Colonel Plastiras** assembled on Híos after the retreat from Smyrna, "invited" King Constantine I to abdicate and, after a November show trial, executed six of his ministers held most responsible for the *Katastrofí*. Democracy was nominally restored with the proclamation of a **republic**, but for much of the following decade changes in government were brought about by factions within the armed forces. Meanwhile, among the urban refugee population, unions were being formed and the **Greek Communist Party (KKE)** was established.

Venizelos' last gasp – and the rise of Metaxas

Elections in 1928 had returned **Venizelos** to power, but his freedom to manoeuvre was severely restricted by the Great Crash the following year. He had also borrowed heavily abroad and was unable to renegotiate loan terms in 1931. Late 1932 saw another, local crash brought on by England's abandonment of the gold standard, with Greek currency devalued sixty percent and Venizelos forced from office. His supporters attempted to reinstate him by means of a putsch in March 1933, but the coup was quashed and Venizelos fled into exile in Paris, where he died in 1936.

By 1936 the Communist Party had enough electoral support to hold the balance of power in an otherwise deadlocked parliament, and would have done so had not the army and the by then restored king decided otherwise. **King George II** had been returned by a plebiscite held – and almost certainly manipulated – the previous year, and so presided over an increasingly factionalized political scene.

In April 1936, George II appointed as prime minister the Germanophile Royalist officer **General John Metaxas**, despite the latter's support from only six parliamentary deputies. Immediately a series of KKE-organized strikes broke out, and the king, ignoring attempts to form a broad liberal coalition, dissolved parliament without setting a date for new elections. It was a blatantly unconstitutional move, and opened the way for five years of ruthless and at times absurdist **dictatorship**.

Metaxas averted a general strike with military force and proceeded to set up a state based on fascist models of the age. Left-wing and trade union opponents were imprisoned or forced into exile, a state youth movement and secret police set up, and rigid censorship, extending even to passages of Thucydides, imposed. It was, however, at least a Greek dictatorship, and while Metaxas admired Nazi organizational methods, he completely opposed German or Italian domination.

Italian rule in the Dodecanese: 1912–43

The **Italian tenure** in the Dodecanese always rested on a flimsy legalistic tissue, which contemporary Turkey has not been slow to criticize in its ongoing dispute with Greece over sovereignty in the Aegean. Briefly, the first **Treaty of Lausanne** (October 1912) stipulated that the Dodecanese were to be returned to the Ottomans when they had evacuated Libya. When Italy and the Ottomans entered World War I on opposite sides, the Italians claimed that this treaty was nullified, to be replaced by the 1915 **Treaty of London** formally acknowledging their possession of the Dodecanese (except for Kastellórizo, occupied by the French for military reasons). Between 1918 and 1923, various conferences agreed that the Dodecanese were to be handed over to Greece, with the exception of Rhodes, but after the beginning of Fascist rule in Italy, and the Greek collapse in Asia Minor, this became progressively more unlikely.

With the rise of **Mussolini and the Fascists**, Italy dropped all altruistic pretences in the Dodecanese, annexing them officially in 1923 as the "**Isole Italiane del'Egeo**" and embarking in upon a gradual, forced **Latinization** campaign. Under the tenure of the first Governor General, **Mario Lago**, land was expropriated for use by Italian colonists, and intermarriage with local Greeks encouraged, though only Catholic ceremonies were recognized. An attempt was made to set up a puppet **Orthodox bishopric**, and when this failed (except for three collaborationist bishops on Kálymnos, Rhodes and Kárpathos), the Orthodox rite, in all local secular institutions, was suppressed completely. Italian was introduced as the compulsory language of education and public life in 1936, when the even harsher governor **De Vecchi** replaced Lago and accelerated all assimilationist measures; as a result anyone in the Dodecanese born before 1928 is probably bilingual in Italian and Greek. In response to these incremental strictures there were riots on Kastellórizo during 1933, and on Kálymnos in 1935 (with stone-throwing women in the front line), resulting in some loss of civilian life.

The Dodecanese were never considered a fully fledged part of metropolitan Italy, and had a status somewhat like Gibraltar vis a vis the UK, or as Puerto Rico is to the US. The islanders were awarded en masse the so-called "**lesser**" **Italian nationality**, with no obligation for military service (and no civic rights), while "major" or **full Italian citizenship** was reserved as a reward for those who collaborated with the Fascist administration in some conspicuous way. Emigration was (just) possible with a "minor" passport, acting as a social safety valve like elsewhere in the Greek world, and indeed the Greek population of many islands dropped by nearly half even before World War II, which could only have pleased the Fascists. However, exit to the USA in particular became progressively more difficult throughout the 1930s – the result of racist anti-immigration laws, the onset of the Great Depression and worsening relations with Italy even before America entered World War II. Pressure groups of expatriated Dodecanesians were formed, especially in New York, Egypt, Australia and England, to lobby anyone who would listen about the Hellenic cause in the Dodecanese.

On the larger islands, massive public works were undertaken to make them the showcases of the "**Italian Aegean Empire**" as Mussolini styled the archipelago; roads, monumental buildings and waterworks were constructed (sometimes with forced Greek labour), sound and not-so-sound archeology engaged in, and the islands accurately mapped for the first time. The first hotels were built on Rhodes and Kós, and the first tourists arrived by boat or seaplane for stays averaging months rather than weeks. However, smaller islands, except for militarily strategic Léros, were neglected and left punitively undeveloped once the requisite Art Deco municipal "palace" had been erected.

World War II and the Greek Civil War

Using a submarine dispatched from a naval base on Léros, the Italians tried to provoke the Greeks into **World War II** by surreptitiously torpedoing the Greek cruiser *Elli* in Tínos harbour on August 15, 1940. This outrage went unanswered, as Greece was ill equipped to fight; however, when Mussolini occupied Albania, and on October 28, 1940, sent an ultimatum demanding passage for his troops through Greece, Metaxas responded to the Italian ambassador in Athens with the apocryphal "*óhi*" (no). (In fact, his wording, in the mutually understood French, was "*Alors, c'est la guerre*".) This marked the entry of Greece into the war, and the gesture is still celebrated as a national holiday.

Galvanized into brief unity by the crisis, the Greeks drove Italian forces from the country, and in doing so took control of the long-coveted and predominantly Greek-populated northern Epirus (southern Albania). However, the Greek army subsequently frittered away its strength in the snowy mountains there rather than consolidate its gains or effectively defend the Macedonian frontier, and proposed co-ordination with the British never materialized.

Occupation and resistance

In April of the following year Nazi columns swept through Yugoslavia and across the Greek mainland, effectively reversing the only Axis defeat to date. By the end of May 1941, airborne and seaborne **German invasion** forces had completed the occupation of all the other islands, including those of the east Aegean (with the exception of Sámos, Ikaría and Foúrni, which were granted to the Italians). Metaxas died before their arrival, while King George and his new self-appointed ministers fled into exile in Cairo; few Greeks, of any political persuasion, were sad to see them go.

The joint Italian-German-Bulgarian **occupation** of Greece was among the bitterest experiences of the European war. Nearly half a million Greek civilians starved to death over the winter of 1941–42, as all food was requisitioned, principally by the Germans, to feed occupying armies. In addition, entire villages on the mainland and Crete were burned and nearly 130,000 civilian residents slaughtered at the least hint of resistance activity.

With a puppet regime in Athens – and an unpopular, discredited Royalist government in Cairo – the focus of Greek resistance between 1942 and 1945 passed largely to **EAM**, or National Liberation Front. By 1943 it had assumed virtual control of most rural areas of the mainland and several islands, working with the British on tactical operations. Initially it commanded widespread popular support, and appeared to offer an obvious framework for a postwar government.

However, most of its highest ranking members were Communists, and British Prime Minister Winston Churchill was determined to reinstate the monarchy.

Even with two years of war remaining it became obvious that there could be no peaceful post-liberation regime other than a republic. Accordingly, in August 1943 representatives from each of the main resistance movements – including two non-Communist groups – flew clandestinely to Cairo to request that the king not return unless a plebiscite had first voted in his favour. Both Greek and British authorities demurred, and the best possibility of averting civil war was lost.

The EAM contingent returned divided, as perhaps the British had intended, and subsequently a conflict broke out between those who favoured taking peaceful control of any government imposed after liberation, and hard-line Stalinist ideologues who forbade participation in any "bourgeois" regime.

In October 1943, with fears of an imminent British occupation following the Italian capitulation of September, **ELAS** (the armed wing of EAM) launched full-scale attacks upon its Greek rivals; by the following February, when a ceasefire was arranged, they had wiped out all rivals except EDES, a rival right-wing grouping suspected of collaboration with the Germans.

The **Italian-occupied** areas of the Aegean fared slightly better, though scenarios on neighbouring islands varied widely. In the Dodecanese it was business as usual, only more so owing to the exigencies of war. On Foúrni, the Italian garrison and the islanders reached an understanding ensuring as calm and amicable an occupation as possible, while on adjacent Sámos an active resistance contingent on Mount Kérkis prompted a mass reprisal execution in one village.

German-occupied Híos was relatively quiet, though Lésvos – in keeping with its Communist sympathies – had like Sámos an active resistance contingent. Kaïkia and other small boats were requisitioned for German use – thus also nullifying their potential for smuggling people and goods between the islands and Turkey – while such fishing boats that continued to work often had a Wehrmacht officer posted on board to expropriate the entire catch. They also, it is claimed, encouraged the practice of dynamite-fishing, which has been a social nuisance ever since. Such measures caused fish to disappear from the civilian diet, and guaranteed widespread malnutrition. Both here and in the Dodecanese, thousands of civilians still managed to escape by kaïki to the Turkish coast, where they spent most of the war years avoiding starvation.

When Italy capitulated in September 1943, a brief free-for-all ensued on the islands it had controlled. As elsewhere in Greece, German troops attacked, disarmed and executed their erstwhile allies, particularly on Rhodes. The British quickly occupied Kós, Kastellórizo, Sámos and Léros, but in insufficient strength to repel German attacks; within two months they had to abandon these positions, with considerable losses. Churchill considered the Dodecanese easy pickings, but in the end was denied adequate resources for the job by the Americans, who refused to risk the already precarious advance through Italy proper. The British were compelled to reconquer the Dodecanese gradually from September 1944 onwards, picking off vulnerable islands one by one, though Rhodes, Kós and Léros were too strongly defended and only evacuated by the Germans after their surrender of May 1945 to the Allies, signed on Sými. These were the last Greek territories to be abandoned by the Axis.

Civil war

As the Germans began to leave in October 1944, most of the EAM leadership agreed to join a British-sponsored "official" **interim government**. This quickly proved a tactical error, however. With almost ninety percent of the countryside under their control, the Communists were given only one-third representation, and a new regular army began to form, relying on right-wing extremists rather than the ELAS officer corps. The king showed no sign of renouncing his claims and, in November, Allied forces ordered ELAS to disarm. On December 3 all pretences of civility or neutrality were dropped; the police opened fire on an EAM demonstration in Athens, killing at least sixteen; within days fighting broke out between ELAS and British troops, in the so-called **Dhekemvrianá** battle. Though ELAS quickly quashed all opposition in the countryside, they failed to drive the British and right-wing Greeks from Athens, thus losing their best chance of seizing power. In their fury at being thwarted, ELAS rounded up their most influential and wealthiest opponents in the largest towns, and marched them out to rural areas in conditions that guaranteed their death.

A truce of sorts was negotiated at Várkiza in February 1945, but this agreement was never implemented. The army, police and civil service remained in right-wing hands and, while collaborationists were often allowed to retain their positions, left-wing sympathizers, many of whom were merely Venizelist Republicans and not communists, were systematically excluded, the mildest aspect of what developed into a veritable "**White Terror**". The elections of 1946 were won by the right-wing parties (the Left, perhaps unwisely, boycotted them), followed by another rigged plebiscite in favour of the king's return. By 1947 guerrilla activity had again reached the scale of a full **civil war**, with ELAS reorganized into the Democratic Army of Greece (**DSE** in Greek).

In the interim, King George had died and been succeeded by his brother Paul (with his consort Frederika), while the **Americans** had taken over the British role and begun implementing the cold-war **Truman doctrine**. In March 1947 they took virtual control of Greece, their first significant postwar experiment in anti-communist intervention. Massive economic and military aid was given to a client Greek government, while official decrees had to be countersigned by the American Mission chief in order to become valid.

In the mainland mountains, US military advisers trained the Nationalist army for **campaigns against the DSE**, and in the cities there were mass arrests, court martials and imprisonments – an extension of the White Terror – lasting until 1951. Over three thousand executions were recorded, including (for their pacifist stance and refusal to swear loyalty oaths) a number of Jehovah's Witnesses, "a sect proved to be under communist domination", according to US Ambassador Grady. To deny the DSE local support, over 700,000 civilians were forcibly evacuated from mountain villages and dumped in squalid internment camps near towns, a move which helped destroy any hope of postwar rural existence. In the east Aegean, Ikaría, Foúrni and Áyios Efstrátios became – as they had been under Metaxas – venues of internal exile for thousands of "dangerous" leftists, who arrived off the boat manacled hand and foot.

In the autumn of 1949, with the Yugoslav–Greek border closed after Tito's rift with Stalin, the last DSE guerrillas finally admitted defeat and retreated into Albania from their strongholds on Mount Grámmos. Atrocities had been committed on both sides, including, from the Left, considerably more than three thousand executions, widespread vandalization of monasteries and the dubious evacuation of children from "combat areas". Such errors, as well as the hopelessness of lightly armed guerrillas fighting an American-backed army equipped with aircraft and heavy artillery, almost certainly doomed the DSE's efforts from the start.

The Dodecanese: union with Greece

The British ruled as an occupation force for approximately 22 months from May 1945, to the considerable unease and resentment of the Greek government, who suspected that they intended to set up a Cyprus-style colonial regime or (worse) hand some or all of the islands back to Turkey. However, the British claim they had always intended to hand the Dodecanese over to Greece at the right moment, not least to present the Nationalists an unqualified success to point to in their propaganda battle with the DSE, and were only holding off pending the **Italian-Greek peace treaty** negotiations of September 1946 to February 1947. In the interim, considerable progress was made in reconstituting the much-depleted Dodecanesian shipping, and the two surviving collaborationist bishops were forced into retirement by the Ecumenical Patriarch in Istanbul.

The main sticking points of the treaty were the offsetting of Greek demands for war reparations against Italian claims of compensation for "improvements" to the Dodecanese (in the end these were held to cancel each other out) and, more seriously, the fate of native Italians, and Greek islanders who had opted for "major" Italian **nationality**. Metropolitan Italians, including those who had married islanders, were given a year from February 1947 to choose between Greek or Italian nationality; if they went for the latter, they were obliged to leave for Italy (a surprising number stayed). Native islanders who had enjoyed "major" Italian citizenship had their cases examined minutely prior to any "renaturalization", and those shown to have obtained this status voluntarily and with enthusiasm could expect to be deported to Italy.

Once the peace treaty was ratified, the Greek Army assumed control of the Dodecanese from the British, on March 31, 1947 – a date responsible for the frequent, half-true assertion that the islands were joined to the mainland in that year. However, military governor **Vice Admiral Periklis Ioannidis** presided over a strict, ten-month regime of lustration – whose primary purposes were sifting through the cases of suspect "major" Italian subjects, and an equally stringent filtering for communists and fellow travellers, either home-grown or arriving from the mainland. Once this was deemed complete, the Dodecanese were **officially annexed** to Greece on January 9, 1948, and the first civilian governor, **Nikolaos Mavris** of Kássos, was appointed to general rejoicing.

Reconstruction American-style: 1950–67

After a decade of war that had shattered much of Greece's infrastructure, it was a demoralized country that emerged into the Western political orbit of the 1950s. Greece was also perforce American-dominated, enlisted into the Korean War in 1950 and NATO the following year. In domestic politics, the US Embassy – still giving the orders – foisted a winner-takes-all electoral system, which was to ensure victory for the Right over the next twelve years. Overt leftist activity was banned (though a "cover" party for Communists was soon founded); those individuals who were not herded into political "re-education" camps on barren islands, or dispatched by firing squads, legal or vigilante, went into exile throughout eastern Europe, to return only after 1974.

The American-backed, highly conservative "**Greek Rally**" party, led by General Papagos, won the first decisive post-civil-war elections in 1952. After the general's death, the party's leadership was taken over – and to an extent liberalized – by **Constantine Karamanlis**. Under his rule, stability of a kind was established and some economic advances registered, particularly after the revival of Greece's traditional German markets. Health and life expectancy improved dramatically, as the age-old scourges of tuberculosis and malaria were finally confronted with American-supplied food, medicine and pesticides. Less commendable was Karamanlis' encouragement of the law of **andiparohí**, whereby owners of small refugee shanties or Neoclassical mansions alike could offer the site of such properties to apartment-block developers in exchange for two flats (out of 8 to 10) in the finished building. This effectively ripped the heart out of most larger island towns like Híos, Sámos and Ródhos, and explains their baleful aesthetics a half-century on.

The 1950s was also a decade that saw wholesale **depopulation** of villages, as migrants sought work in Australia, America and western Europe, or the larger Greek cities. In the east Aegean and the Dodecanese this was especially pronounced – ironically in the case of Rhodes and its neighbours, where the long-sought union with Greece provided merely unhindered freedom to **emigrate**.

By 1961, unemployment, the Cyprus issue and the installation of US nuclear bases on Greek soil were changing the political climate, and when Karamanlis was again elected prime minister, there was strong suspicion of a fraud arranged by the king and army. **Strikes** became frequent in industry and even agriculture, and both King Paul and the autocratic, fascist-inclined Queen Frederika, were openly attacked in parliament and at protest demonstrations. The far Right grew uneasy about "communist resurgence" and, losing confidence in their own electoral influence, arranged the **assassination** of left-wing deputy **Grigoris Lambrakis** in Thessaloníki in May 1963. (The murder, and its subsequent cover-up, was the subject of Vassilis Vassilikos's thriller *Z*, filmed by Costa-Gavras.) It was against this volatile background that Karamanlis resigned, lost the subsequent elections and left the country.

The new government – the first controlled from outside the Greek Right since 1935 – was formed by **George Papandreou's Centre Union Party**, and had a decisive majority of nearly fifty seats. It was to last, however, for under two years as conservative forces conspired to thwart its progress. In this the chief protagonists were the army officers and their constitutional Commander-in-Chief, the new king, 23-year-old **Constantine II.**

Since power in Greece depended on a pliant military as well as a network of political appointees, Papandreou's most urgent task in order to govern securely and effectively was to reform the armed forces. His first minister of defence proved incapable of the task and, while he was investigating the right-wing plot suspected of rigging the 1961 election, "evidence" was produced of a Leftist conspiracy connected with Papandreou's son Andreas (also a government minister). When the allegations grew to a crisis, George Papandreou assumed the defence portfolio himself, a move which the king refused to sanction. Papandreou then resigned to gain a fresh mandate at the polls, but the king would not order new elections, instead persuading members of the Centre Union – chief among them **Constantine Mitsotakis** – to defect and organize a coalition government. Punctuated by strikes, resignations and street demonstrations, this lasted for a year and a half until new elections were eventually set for May 28, 1967. They failed to take place.

The Colonels' junta: 1967–74

It was a foregone conclusion that Papandreou's Centre Union would win the polls against the discredited coalition partners. And it was equally certain that there would be some anti-democratic action to prevent it from reassuming power. Disturbed by the party's leftward shift, King Constantine was said to have briefed senior generals for a coup d'état, to take place ten days before the elections. However, he was caught by surprise, as was nearly everyone else, by the **coup of April 21, 1967**, staged by a group of "unknown" colonels. It was, to quote Andreas Papandreou, "the first successful CIA military putsch on the European continent".

The Colonels' **junta**, having appropriated all means of power, was sworn in by the king and survived the half-hearted counter-coup which he subsequently attempted to mount a few months later. It was an ostensibly fascist regime, absurdly styling itself as the true "Revival of Greek Orthodoxy" against Western "corrupting influences", though in reality its ideology was nothing more than reheated dogma from the Metaxas era with a fair bit of ultranationalism thrown in.

All **political activity** was **banned**, trade unions were forbidden to recruit or meet, the press was so heavily censored that many papers stopped printing or published blank pages in protest, and thousands of "communists" were arrested, imprisoned, and often tortured. Among the persecuted were both Papandreous, the composer Mikis Theodorakis (deemed "unfit to stand trial" after three months in custody), and Amalia Fleming (widow of Alexander). While relatively few people were killed outright – one, dissident lawyer Nikiforos Mandilaras, found mutilated in the sea off Rhodes, has a street named after him on the island – thousands were permanently maimed physically and psychologically in the junta's torture chambers. The best-known Greek actress, Melina Mercouri, was stripped of her citizenship *in absentia*, and thousands of prominent Greeks joined her in exile.

Cultural life was also throttled. The colonels put an end to most popular live music and inflicted ludicrous censorship on literature and theatre, including (as under Metaxas) a ban on production of the Classical tragedies. From this time also the historically gradual, insidious degradation of Greek public discourse accelerated; chief colonel Papadopoulos's rambling, illiterate speeches became bywords for obfuscation, bad grammar and Orwellian Newspeak.

The junta lasted for seven years, opposed (especially after the first two years) by the majority of the Greek people, officially excluded from the European Community, but propped up and given massive **aid by US presidents** Lyndon Johnson and Richard Nixon. To them and the CIA, the junta's Greece was not an unsuitable client state: human rights considerations were then thought trivial, orders were placed for sophisticated military technology, and foreign investment on terms highly unfavourable to Greece was made available to multinational corporations. It was a fairly routine scenario for the exploitation of an underdeveloped nation.

Opposition was from the beginning voiced by exiled Greeks in London, the United States and western Europe, but only in late 1973 did demonstrations break out openly in Greece – the colonels' secret police had done too thorough a job of infiltrating domestic resistance groups and terrifying everyone else into docility. On November 17 the students of **Athens Polytechnic** began an occupation of their buildings. The ruling clique lost its nerve; armoured vehicles stormed the Polytechnic gates and a still-undetermined number of students (estimates range from tens to hundreds) were killed. (Today they are commemorated throughout the east Aegean and the Dodecanese, in leftist municipalities, by streets called Iróön Polytekhníon – "Heroes of the Polytechnic"). Martial law was tightened, and junta chief George Papadopoulos was replaced by the even more noxious and reactionary General Ioannides, until then head of the secret police.

Return to civilian rule: 1974–81

The end of the ordeal, however, came within a year as the dictatorship embarked on a disastrous political adventure in **Cyprus**, essentially the last playing of the *Megáli Idhéa* card. By attempting to topple the Makarios government and impose *énosis* (union with Greece) on the island, the junta provoked a Turkish invasion and occupation of nearly forty percent of the Cypriot territory. The army finally mutinied, and Constantine Karamanlis was invited to return from Paris to again take office. He swiftly helped negotiate a ceasefire (but no durable solution) in Cyprus, withdrew Greece temporarily from NATO, and warned that US bases in Greece would have to be removed except where they specifically served Greek interests.

In November 1974 Karamanlis and his **Néa Dhimokratía (New Democracy) party** was rewarded by a sizeable majority in **elections**, with a centrist and socialist opposition. The latter was the **Panhellenic Socialist Movement (PASOK)**, a new party led by Andreas Papandreou.

The election of Néa Dhimokratía was in every sense a safe conservative option, but to Karamanlis's enduring credit it oversaw an effective and firm return to democratic stability, even legalizing the KKE (Communist Party) for the first time in its history. Karamanlis also held a **referendum on the monarchy**; 59 percent of Greeks rejected the return of Constantine II, so Karamanlis instituted in its place a French-style presidency, a post he himself occupied from 1980 to 1985, and again from 1990 to 1995. Economically there were limited advances, although these were more than offset by inflationary defence spending (the result of renewed tension with Turkey), hastily negotiated entrance into the EC, and the decision to let the drachma float after decades of being artificially fixed at 30 to the US dollar.

Most crucially, Karamanlis failed to deliver on vital reforms in bureaucracy, social welfare and education; while the worst figures of the junta were brought to trial and jailed for life, the ordinary faces of Greek political life and administration changed little. By 1981 inflation was hovering around 25 percent, and it was estimated that tax evasion was depriving the state of one-half of its expected annual revenue. On the foreign policy front, the US bases remained, and it was felt that Greece, back in NATO, was still acting as little more than an American satellite. The traditional right had proved demonstrably unequal to the task at hand.

PASOK 1981–89

"Change" (*Allayí*) and "Out with the Right" (*Ná Fíyi íy Dhexí*) were the watchwords of the election campaign that swept **PASOK** and Andreas Papandreou to power on October 18, 1981.

This victory meant a chance for Papandreou to form the first socialist government in Greek history and break a half-century monopoly of authoritarian right-wing rule. With so much at stake, the campaign had been passionate even by Greek standards, and PASOK's victory was greeted with euphoria both by the generation whose political voice had been silenced in the civil war, and by a large proportion of the young. Their hopes ran naively and perhaps dangerously high.

The electoral margin, at least, was conclusive. PASOK won 174 of the 300 parliamentary seats and the KKE (Communists) – though not a part of the new government – returned another thirteen deputies, one of them composer Mikis Theodorakis. Néa Dhimokratía moved into unaccustomed opposition. There appeared to be no obstacle to the implementation of a **radical programme**: devolution of power to local authorities, the effective nationalization of heavy industry, improvement of the woefully skeletal social services, a purge of bureaucratic inefficiency and malpractice, the end of bribery and corruption as a way of life, an independent and dignified foreign policy following expulsion of US bases, and finally withdrawal from NATO and the European Community.

A change of style was promised, too, replacing the country's long traditions of authoritarianism and bureaucracy with openness and dialogue. Even more radically, given that Greek political parties had long been the personal followings of charismatic leaders, PASOK was to be a party of ideology and principle, dependent on no single individual member. Or so, at least, thought some of the youthful PASOK enthusiasts.

The new era started with a bang. ELAS was officially recognized; hitherto they hadn't been allowed to take part in any celebrations, wreath-layings or other ceremonies commemorating the wartime Resistance. Peasant women were granted pensions for the first time – 3000 drachmas a month (about US$55 in 1982), the same as their outraged husbands – and wages were indexed to the cost of living. In addition, civil marriage was introduced, family law reformed in favour of wives and mothers, and equal rights legislation was put on the statute book.

These quick, no-cost and popular reformist moves seemed to mark a break with the past, and the atmosphere had indeed changed. Greeks no longer lowered their voices to discuss politics in public places or wrapped their opposition newspaper in the respectably conservative *Kathimerini*. At first there were real fears that the climate would be too much for the military, who would once again intervene to choke a dangerous experiment in democracy, especially when Andreas Papandreou, imitating his father, briefly assumed the defence portfolio himself. But he went out of his way to soothe military susceptibilities – increasing their salaries, buying new weaponry, and being fastidious in his attendance at military functions. In reality, the resistance of the Polytechnic students to the 1967–74 junta was constantly mythologized, and PASOK activists could be counted on to form human cordons around party headquarters at the least sign of unrest in the armed forces.

The end of the honeymoon

Papandreou promised a populist bonanza which he must have known, as an academically trained economist, he could not deliver; as a result he pleased nobody. He could not fairly be blamed for the inherited lack of investment, low productivity, deficiency in managerial and labour skills and other chronic problems besetting the Greek economy. However, he certainly aggravated the situation early in his first term by allowing his supporters to indulge in violently anti-capitalist rhetoric and by the prosecution and humiliation of the

Tsatsos family, owners of one of Greece's few profitable businesses (Hercules Cement) for the illegal export of capital, something of which every Greek with any savings was guilty. These were cheap victories, not backed by any rational public investment programme, and the only nationalizations were of hopelessly lame-duck companies.

Faced with a sluggish economy and burdened with the additional expense of (marginally) improved social benefits and wage-indexing, Papandreou's government had also to cope with the effects of **world recession**, which then always hit Greece with a delayed effect compared with northern Europe. **Shipping**, the country's main foreign-currency earner, was devastated. Remittances from emigré workers fell off as they became unemployed in their host countries, and tourism diminished under the dual impact of recession and US President Ronald Reagan's warning to Americans to stay away from the allegedly terrorist-vulnerable Athens airport.

With huge quantities of imported goods continuing to be sucked into the country in the absence of significant domestic production, the **foreign debt** topped £10 billion in 1986, with inflation still at 25 percent and the balance of payments deficit approaching £1 billion. Greece also began to experience the social strains of unemployment for the first time. Not that it did not exist before, but it had always been concealed as underemployment because of numerous family-run businesses and the rural/seasonal nature of the economy – as well as by the absence of reliable statistics.

The second term

A modest spending spree transparently intended to buy votes, continued satisfaction at the discomfiture of the Right and the popularity of his Greece-for-the-Greeks foreign policy gave Papandreou a second term with a **June 1985** electoral victory scarcely less decisive than the first. But his complacent and dishonest slogan was "Vote PASOK for Even Better Days". By October PASOK had imposed a two-year wage freeze and import restrictions, abolished the wage-indexing scheme and devalued the drachma by fifteen percent. Papandreou's fat was pulled out of the fire by none other than his *bête noire*, the European Community, which offered a huge two-phase loan on condition that an IMF-style **austerity programme** was maintained.

The political price of such classic monetarist strategies, accompanied by shameless soliciting for foreign investment, was the alienation of the KKE and most of PASOK's own core constituency. Increasingly autocratic (ironic, given his earlier pledges of openness), Papandreou's response to **dissent** was to fire recalcitrant trade union leaders and expel some three hundred members of his own party. Assailed by strikes, the government stumbled badly, losing ample ground in the municipal elections of October 1986 to Néa Dhimokratía, including the mayoralties of the three major cities – Athens, Thessaloníki and Pátra – the first two retained by them ever since. Papandreou assured the nation that he had taken the message to heart, but all that followed were two successive cabinet reshuffles, which saw the departure of most remaining PASOK veterans; the new cabinet was so unsocialist that even the right-wing press called it "centrist".

Similar about-faces took place in foreign policy. The first-term anti-US, anti-NATO and anti-EC rhetoric had been immensely popular, and understandable for a people shamelessly bullied by bigger powers since 1830. There was some high-profile nose-thumbing, like refusing to join EC partners in condemning Jaruzelski's Polish regime or the Soviet downing of a Korean airliner. The "realistic" policies that Papandreou increasingly pursued during his second term were far more conciliatory towards his big Western brothers. Not least was the fact that **US bases** remained in Greece until 1994, largely due to the fear that snubbing NATO would lead to Greece being exposed to Turkish aggression, still the only issue that unites the main parties to any degree. As for the once-reviled **European Community** (now the European Union), Greece had by now become an established beneficiary, and its leader was hardly about to bite the hand that feeds.

Scandal

Even as late as **mid-1988**, despite the many betrayals and failings of Papandreou, it seemed unlikely that PASOK would be toppled in the following year's elections. This was due mainly to the lack of a credible alternative. Constantine Mitsotakis, a bitter personal enemy of Papandreou's since 1965, when his defection had brought down his father's government and set in motion the events that culminated in the junta, was an unconvincing and unlikeable character at the helm of Néa Dhimokratía. Meanwhile, the liberal centrist parties had disappeared, and the KKE seemed trapped in a Stalinist timewarp under the leadership of Harilaos Florakis. Only the **Ellenikí Aristerá (Greek Left)** or Euro-Communist party spun off from the KKE, seemed to offer any sensible alternative, but they had a precariously small following.

However, a combination of spectacular blunders, plus perhaps a general shift to the Right influenced by the cataclysmic events in Eastern Europe, conspired against PASOK. First came the extraordinary **cavortings of the prime minister** himself. Late in 1988, seventy-year-old Papandreou was flown to Britain for open-heart surgery. He took the occasion, with fear of death presumably rocking his judgement, to make public a year-long liaison with a 34-year-old Olympic Airways hostess, **Dimitra "Mimi" Liani**. Widespread media images of an old man shuffling about after a young, large-chested blonde, to the public humiliation of Margaret, his American-born wife, were not helpful (Papandreou soon divorced Margaret and married Mimi). His integrity was further dented when he missed important public engagements in order to relive his youth in flashy nightspots with Mimi.

The real damage, however, was done by a series of **economic scandals**, ranging from illegal arms deals to fraudulent farm-produce sales by assorted ministers. The most serious of these involved a self-made, Greek-American con man, **Yiorgos Koskotas**, director of the Bank of Crete, who managed to embezzle £120 million (US$190 million) in deposits, distribute it lavishly amongst numerous Greek public figures, and worse still slip through the authorities' fingers on a private jet back to the US, where he had begun his career as a housepainter. Certain PASOK ministers and even Papandreou himself were implicated in the scandal.

United in disgust at this corruption, the other left-wing parties – KKE and Ellinikí Aristerá – formed a coalition, the **Synaspismós**, siphoning off still more support from PASOK.

Three bites at the cherry

In this climate, an inconclusive result to the **June 1989 election** was unsurprising. Less predictable, however, was the formation of a bizarre "**kathársis**" **(purgative) coalition** of conservatives and communists, expressly to cleanse PASOK's Augean stables.

Synaspismós would have formed a government with PASOK but set an impossible condition for doing so – that Papandreou step down as prime minister. In the deal finally cobbled together between the Left and Néa Dhimokratía, Mitsotakis was denied the premiership, too, in favour of **Ioannis Tzanetakis**, a popular former naval officer who had led an unsuccessful mutiny against the junta.

During the three months that the coalition lasted, *kathársis* turned out to be largely a matter of burying the knife as deeply as possible into the ailing body of PASOK. Andreas Papandreou and three other ministers were officially indicted of involvement in the Koskotas affair – though there was no time to try them before the return to the polls. In any case, the chief witness and protagonist, Koskotas himself, was still imprisoned in America, awaiting extradition proceedings.

Contrary to the Right's hope that publicly accusing Papandreou and his cohorts of criminal behaviour would pave the way for a Néa Dhimokratía victory, PASOK actually recovered slightly in the **November 1989 elections**, though the result was again inconclusive. This time the Left refused to do deals with anyone, resulting in a caretaker government under the neutral aegis of Xenophon Zolotas, reluctantly dragged into the prime minister's office from the rectorship of Athens University. His only mandate was to keep the country on the rails while preparations were made for yet another election.

These took place in **April 1990** with the same party leaders *in situ*, and with Synaspismós having completed its about-face to the extent that in the five single-seat constituencies (the other 295 seats are drawn from multiple-seat constituencies in a complex system of reinforced proportional representation), they supported independent candidates jointly with PASOK. Greek communists are good at about-turns, though; after all, composer Mikis Theodorakis, musical torchbearer of the Left during the dark junta years, and formerly a KKE MP, was now standing for Néa Dhimokratía, prior to his resignation from politics altogether.

On the night, Néa Dhimokratía scraped home with a majority of one, later doubled with the defection of a centrist, and Mitsotakis finally realized his long-cherished dream of becoming prime minister. The only other memorable feature of the election was the first parliamentary representation for an independent member of the **Turkish minority** in Thrace, Ahmet Sadiq, and for the Greens in Attica – a focus for many disaffected PASOK voters. Sadiq, who had spent as much time in jail for dissident activities as he was to spend in parliament, was eventually winkled out of office on a technicality and killed in suspicious circumstances on July 24, 1995, in his native Thrace.

A return to the Right: Mitsotakis' tenure

On assuming power, Mitsotakis prescribed a course of **austerity measures** to revive the chronically ill economy. Little headway was made, though given the world recession, that was hardly surprising. Greek inflation was still approaching twenty percent annually, and at nearly ten percent, unemployment remained chronic.

Other measures introduced by Mitsotakis included laws to combat strikes and **terrorism**. This had been a perennial source of worry for Greeks since the appearance in 1974 of a group called **Dhekaeftá Noemvríou** ("November 17", the date of the colonels' attack on the Polytechnic in 1973). Since 1974 they (and one or two copycat groups) have killed 24 industrialists, politicians and

NATO military personnel and have attacked buildings of foreign corporations in Athens; the lack of any significant arrests to date fuels continued speculation that they were and are a rogue faction from within PASOK itself. It hardly seemed likely that Mitsotakis's laws, however, were the solution. They stipulated that the typically long-winded, ideologically contorted statements of the group could no longer be published, which led to one or two newspaper editors being jailed for a few days for defiance – much to everyone's embarrassment. The **anti-strike laws** threatened severe penalties but were equally ineffectual, as breakdowns in public transport, electricity and rubbish collection all too frequently illustrated.

As for the Koskotas scandal, the man himself was eventually extradited and gave evidence for the prosecution against Papandreou and various of his ministers. The trial was televised and proved as popular as any soap opera, given its twists of high drama – which included one of the defendants, Agamemnon "Menios" Koutsoyiorgas, dying in court of a heart attack in front of the cameras. The case against Papandreou gradually lost steam and he was officially acquitted (by a margin of one vote on the tribunal panel) in early 1992. The two other surviving ex-ministers, Tsovolas and Petsos, were convicted, given jail sentences (bought off with a heavy fine) and barred from public office for a time.

The great showcase trial thus went out with a whimper and did nothing to enhance Mitsotakis's position. If anything, it served to increase sympathy for Papandreou, who was felt to have been unfairly victimized. The indisputable villain of the piece, Koskotas, was eventually convicted of major fraud and is serving a lengthy sentence at the high-security Korýdhallos prison.

The Macedonian question

The last thing the increasingly unpopular Mitsotakis needed was a major foreign policy headache. That is exactly what he got when, in 1991, one of the breakaway republics of the former Yugoslavia named itself **Macedonia**, thereby injuring Greek national pride and sparking off vehement protests at home and abroad. Diplomatically, the Greeks fought tooth and nail against anyone's recognizing the breakaway state, let alone its use of the name "Macedonia", but their position became increasingly isolated, and by 1993 the new country had gained official recognition from both the EU and the UN – albeit under the provisional title of the Former Yugoslav Republic of Macedonia (FYROM).

Salt was rubbed into Greek wounds when the FYROM started using the "Star of Vergina" (and of the ancient Macedonian kings) as a national symbol on their new flag, allegedly printed a banknote portraying the White Tower of Thessaloníki (Solun in Macedonian) and retained passages in its constitution referring to "unredeemed" Aegean territories. Greece still refuses to call its neighbour Macedonia, instead referring to it as *Proín Yugoslavikí Dhimokratía Makedhonás*, or *Tá Skópia* after the capital – and for quite some time you couldn't go anywhere in Greece without coming across officially placed stickers proclaiming that "Macedonia was, is, and always will be Greek and only Greek!"

The ongoing argument for legitimacy hinges mostly on whether the ancient Macedonian kings were pure-bred Hellenes (the Greek position), Hellenized barbarians (the neutral conclusion) or proto-Slavs (the Macedonian claim).

The pendulum swings back

The Macedonian problem effectively led to Mitsotakis's political **demise**. Mitsotakis had also been plagued for months by accusations of phone-tapping and theft of antiquities to stock his large private collection in Crete, plus links with a complicated contracts scandal focused around the national cement company. In the early summer of 1993 his ambitious and disaffected foreign minister, **Andonis Samaras**, jumped on the bandwagon of resurgent Greek nationalism to set up his own party, **Politikí Ánixi (Political Spring)**. His platform, still right-wing, was largely based on action over Macedonia, and during the summer of 1993 more **Néa Dhimokratía** (ND) MPs defected, making Politikí Ánixi a force to be reckoned with. When parliament reconvened in September to approve severe new budget proposals, it became clear that the government lacked sufficient support, and early **elections** were called for **October 1993**.

On October 11, Papandreou romped to election victory with 169 parliamentary deputies; in an exact reversal of the 1990 results, Néa Dhimokratía lost in 85 percent of the constituencies (including the entire east Aegean and Dodecanese), though the Synaspismós disappeared from the electoral map, replaced as the third party in parliament by Samaras' Politikí Ánixi and the unreconstructed Communists, now under Aleka Papariga, with nine deputies each. The youthful Miltiades Evert, ex-mayor of Athens, replaced Mitsotakis as head of Néa Dhimokratía, so that – along with ex-KKE head Florakis – two of the "dinosaurs" of post-junta politics had passed from the scene.

The morning after

And so a frail-looking Papandreou, now well into his seventies, became prime minister for the third time. He soon realized that he was not going to have nearly so easy a ride as in the 1980s.

PASOK immediately fulfilled two of its pre-election promises by removing restrictions on the reporting of terrorists' communiques and de-privatizing the Athens city bus company. The new government also set about improving the health system, and began proceedings for Mitsotakis to be tried for his purported misdemeanours, though all charges were mysteriously dropped in January 1995, prompting allegations of an under the table deal between Papandreou and his old nemesis.

The root of popular dissatisfaction remained **the economy**, still in dire straits. Nor could PASOK claim to have won any diplomatic battles over Macedonia, despite a lot of tough posturing. The only concrete move was the imposition in October 1993 of a **trade embargo** on the FYROM, which merely landed the Greeks in trouble with the European Court of Justice – and succeeded in virtually shutting down the port of Thessaloníki. By contrast, alone among NATO members, Greece was conspicuous for its open **support of Serbia** in the wars wracking ex-Yugoslavia, ostentatiously breaking that particular embargo with supply trucks to Belgrade via Bulgaria.

In **October 1994**, for the first time ever in a PASOK-sponsored reform, provincial governors were directly elected, rather than appointed from Athens. In **March 1995**, **presidential elections** were held in parliament to designate a successor to the 88-year-old Karamanlis, who enjoyed just three years of well-deserved retirement before his death in spring 1998. The winner, supported by Politikí Ánixi and PASOK, was Kostis Stefanopoulos, ex-head of the dissolved party DIANA (Democratic Renewal), like Politikí Ánixi a breakaway movement from ND. Untainted by scandal if a bit of a nonentity, he had been nominated by Samaras and accepted by Papandreou in a deal that would allow PASOK to see out its four-year term without ructions.

The prime recurring scandal for 1995 had to do with the high-security **prison of Korýdhallos**, home to Koskotas, the former junta figures – and Colombian-style rackets. Two mass breakout attempts bracketed the discovery of an extensive drug-dealing ring controlled from inside; a call girl was detected in Koskotas's cell, as were large quantities of guns, ammunition and narcotics in the office of the head warden (subsequently jailed). The prison remains a hellhole to this day, largely controlled by foreign (read Albanian and Romanian) prisoners.

In November 1995, Greece **lifted its embargo** on "Macedonia", opening its mutual borders to tourism and trade in return for the Macedonians suitably editing their constitution and removing the offending emblem from their flag. Relations, in fact, were instantly almost normalized, with only The Name still moot; perennial possibilities include "New Macedonia" or "Upper Macedonia", though as of writing the place is still being referred to as FYROM (the Former Yugoslav Republic of Macedonia) by most outsiders.

Islets and the Ímia crisis

The Dodecanese and to a lesser extent the east Aegean are dotted with scores of tiny, uninhabited islets, frequented only by fishermen and yacht passengers. They are, however, cherished and minutely classified by the Greeks themselves, despite their resounding lack of natural endowments. The twin islets of Ímia were, in early 1996, the focus of a major international incident.

A **nisídha** (plural *nisídhes*) is defined as any islet of between four and sixteen square kilometres, which might at some point in the past have supported a small permanent population. Waterless specks smaller than four square kilometres are further subdivided into **vrahonisídhes**, which have enough soil to support a thin covering of thorny vegetation, and **vráhi**, essentially gull-roosts with no soil at all.

As far as the Greeks are concerned, the **sovereignty** of these islets is an open-and-shut case; they were ceded by Italy to Greece in 1947 as part of the same treaty that included the larger Dodecanese. Previously, in December 1932, Italy and Turkey had drawn up a complicated maritime frontier in the straits between the Dodecanese and Anatolia, which assigned most of the islets clearly to one country or another. As the successor state to Italy, Greece feels that she has clearly "inherited" all the islets so allotted at that time. Turkish threats to *vrahonisídhes* are seen as merely the thin end of the wedge, with the Turks deemed intent on graduating to attempted annexation of larger, inhabited islands unless firmly opposed. Memories of Turkey's 1974 intervention in Cyprus, where over one-third of that island was overrun, are still fresh in Greece, and regarded – along with several recent islet incidents – as incontrovertible proof that an inherently expansionist Turkey harbours designs on more of the Aegean.

For their part, some Turks claim lately that the Dodecanese were strictly speaking not Italy's to keep or give away, as their seizure by the Italians in 1912 had never been assented to by Turkey. Moreover, Turkey has never ratified the Geneva Convention of 1958, nor the more recent **Law of the Sea**, whereby a country can claim territorial waters of up to twelve nautical miles around its islands. Various Turkish pronouncements have made it clear that any attempt by Greece to do so, effectively turning the Aegean into a Greek lake, would be considered by Turkey an act of war. Fishing rights and, further north, access to oil deposits are at stake, adding an economic dimension to what is ostensibly a matter of national honour and the reputation of domestic politicians.

In July 1995, the Greek Defence Ministry announced that the **colonization** of numerous uninhabited islets across Greece was to be officially encouraged; applications from "responsible" persons (ie no hippies or dope fiends), both foreign and Greek, were invited, with promised provision of basic shelter, desalinated water, solar electricity and satellite telephones, as well as a long lease. Several of the islets fell within the limits of the Dodecanese, precariously poised between larger islands and the Anatolian mainland. Overseas Greek consulates and embassies were immediately deluged by eager calls from prospective applicants, to the extent that phones had to be put off the hook. As ever in the Balkans, there was an ulterior

However, the emerging critical issue was the 76-year-old Papandreou's obstinate clinging to power despite obvious signs of dotage. Numerous senior members of PASOK became increasingly bold and vocal in their criticism, no longer fearing expulsion or the sack as in the past.

By late 1995, Papandreou was desperately ill in intensive care at the Onassis hospital, dependent on life-support machinery. As there was no constitutional provision for replacing an infirm (but alive) prime minister, the country was

motive behind the Defence Ministry's altruism; by subsidizing resettlement of these long-neglected outposts, it hoped to emphasize their essential Greekness.

The first step in strengthening Greece's territorial claims was to plant Greek flags on these islets, done by Greek navy patrol boats during the latter half of 1995. This was bound sooner or later to provoke a Turkish reaction. In the event, an initial flare-up occurred on January 25, 1996, when a Turkish vessel ran aground in stormy weather on one of two islets, each less than three square kilometres, poised between Kalólimnos (near Kálymnos) and the Bodrum peninsula – if you look carefully you can see the two low-lying islets from any hydrofoil going between Kós and Léros. The skipper refused assistance from a Greek coastguard boat, claiming that the islet was Turkish territory, despite the presence of a Greek flag (planted in this case by the mayor of Kálymnos) and its description as **Ímia** on international nautical charts. For the Turks, this pair of islets was and always had been Kardak, and two days later some Turkish journalists landed by helicopter and replaced the Greek flag with a Turkish one. On January 28, the Greek navy appeared, restoring the Greek colours and leaving a permanent guard.

By January 30, more than twenty heavily armed naval vessels from each side were manoeuvring around each other in the vicinity of the goat-inhabited *vrahonisídhes*, and journalists the world over were rummaging about for large-scale maps – the Ímia duo is simply too minute to show up on conventional atlases. Then a Greek helicopter apparently developed a fault and went down, with three airmen drowned; if it was actually spooked by Turkish aircraft, or even shot down, the fact was concealed so as not to further inflame public opinion. For days the Greek and Turkish media focused almost exclusively on the developing crisis; war fever gripped each country, and provocative statements were issued by both political leaderships. Turkey in particular had just emerged from an inconclusive general election, and the consensus even there was that caretaker Prime Minister Çiller was indulging in a Falklands-style diversionary ploy to rally national opinion behind her.

In the end, open warfare was only averted by intensive, round-the-clock **diplomatic pressure** on both sides; as of January 31, both Greece and Turkey were required to remove their flags and commandos from the islets, and their fleets from the general area, pending mediation. To date, this has not transpired; the proposed civilian resettlement programme has been quietly scrapped, and instead more incontrovertibly Greek islets such as Farmakoníssi have been more vigorously garrisoned to counter periodic Turkish claims that "the Greek state is not there to rule over all of the 132 Aegean rock islets which are really ours" (Turkish President Demirel, August 1998).

The Ímia episode was the worst such scare since a 1987 oil-prospecting dispute in the north Aegean, and hopefully will be the last. Many outside observers still have difficulty believing the earnestness of the conflict, dismissing it as scarcely more than a storm in a teacup that escalated out of control. Unfortunately for the parties involved it was a deadly serious issue, with long historical antecedents and assorted potential implications.

essentially rudderless for two months, until the barely conscious old demagogue finally faced up to his own mortality and signed a letter **resigning** as prime minister (though not as party leader) in January 1996. The "palace clique" of Mimi Liani and cohorts was beaten off in the parliamentary replacement vote in favour of the allegedly colourless but widely respected technocrat **Kostas Simitis**, who seemed to be just what the country needed after years of incompetent flamboyance.

Upon assuming office, Simitis indicated that he wouldn't necessarily play to the gallery as Papandreou had with (for a Greek politician) a remarkable statement:

"Greece's intransigent nationalism is an expression of the wretchedness that exists in our society. It is the root cause of the problems we have had with our Balkan neighbours and our difficult relations with Europe."

These beliefs were immediately put to the test by a tense armed face-off with Turkey over the uninhabited Dodecanese double-islet of **Ímia** (see box on p.450), which very nearly escalated into a shooting war. Simitis eventually bowed to US and UN pressure and ordered a withdrawal of Greek naval forces, conceding "disputed" status to the tiny goat-grazed outcrops – in hindsight a wise decision, but one for which at the time he was roundly criticized in parliament by fire-eating ND MPs and the media.

Andreas finally succumbed to his illness on June 22, 1996, prompting a moving display of national mourning; it was genuinely the end of an era, with only Karamanlis (who died less than two years later) and junta colonel Papadopoulos (who died, still incarcerated, in June 1999) as the last remaining "dinosaurs" of postwar Greek politics. Already Papandreou's canonization process proceeds apace, with a spate of streets renamed to honour him in provincial towns where he was always revered, but the long-term **verdict of history** is likely to be harsher. Papandreou the Younger valued sycophancy over ability, and in his declining years was completely manipulated by the "Palace Clique" around "Mimi" (styled as the Empress Theodora reincarnated by many observers). Alleged Bank of Crete transactions aside, he also enjoyed indubitable success as a "common cheat" (as described by Karamanlis in his tart memoirs), dying with a huge fortune which he could not possibly have amassed on a public servant's salary.

Simitis:2, Néa Dhimokratía:0

Papandreou's demise was promptly followed by PASOK's summer conference, where Simitis ensured his survival as party leader by co-opting his main internal foe, Papandreou's former head of staff, Akis Tsohadzopoulos, with a promise of future high office (first minister of defence, currently minister of development). Following the summer congress, Simitis cleverly rode the wave of pro-PASOK sympathy caused by Papandreou's death and called **general elections** a year early in **September 1996**.

The **results** were as hoped for: 162 seats for PASOK versus 108 for Néa Dhimokratía despite a margin of only three percentage points, the winner's strength artificially inflated by a convoluted electoral law. Given that the two main parties' agendas were virtually indistinguishable, the core issues boiled down to which was better poised to deliver results – and whether voters would be swayed by ND chief Evert's strident Slav- and Turk-baiting nationalism (they weren't). The biggest surprise was the collapse of Samaras's Politikí Ánixi, which failed to clear the three-percent nationwide hurdle for parliamentary representation, but three leftist splinter parties did well: eleven seats and just over five percent for Papariga's KKE, ten seats (including a new Thracian Muslim deputy) with about the same tally for the Synaspismós under new chief Nikos Konstantopoulos, and nine seats at just under five percent for the Democratic Social Movement (DIKKI), founded early in the year by rehabilitated ex-minister Tsovolas to push for 1980s-vintage leftist policies. Evert resigned as ND leader, being succeeded by Karamanlis's nephew Kostas. Néa Dhimokratía was down but by no means out; in the **June 1999** Euro elections the party finished first nationwide and sent forty percent of Greece's Euro MPs to Strasbourg.

Simitis' first-term problems arose mainly from the economic squeeze caused by continuing **austerity measures**. In December 1996, protesting farmers closed off the country's main road and rail arteries for several weeks, before dismantling the blockades in time for people to travel for the Christmas holidays. Teachers or students (or both) spent much of 1997 on strike over proposed educational reforms – essentially about imposing some discipline on the notoriously lax school regimens. September 1997 also saw a timely boost to national morale and economic prospects with the awarding of the **2004 Olympic Games** to Athens. Simitis sensibly warned against people treating it as an excuse merely for unbridled money-making projects, and hopefully more substantial and long-lasting benefits will accrue. The new airport at Spáta and (after a fashion) the Athens metro have been completed but, worryingly, much of the infrastructure for the Games has yet to materialize.

Simitis, by nature far more pro-European than his maverick predecessor, devoted himself to the unenviable task of getting the Greek economy in sufficiently good shape to meet the criteria for **monetary union**. The *Eforía* or Greek Inland Revenue has made some highly publicized headway in curbing the largest **black economy** in the EU, by requiring meticulous documentation of transactions and by publicly "outing" the more flagrant tax dodgers.

After some initial success with his "hard drachma" policy (often propping it up by dumping foreign currency reserves), Simitis was obliged to devalue it upon Greece's **entry to the ERM** in March 1998; however, with other internationally traded currencies badly exposed in the Far East economic crises, the drachma regained prior levels by October 1998. The fact that inflation has since 1997 stayed consistently down into single figures for the first time in decades is testament to Simitis' ability as an accountant; indeed his nickname, amongst both foes and supporters, is *o loyistís* or "the book-keeper". Simitis has also had the sense to delegate to the capable, and refrain from meddling, such that his Finance Minister Yannos Papantoniou had an unprecedented six years on the job before being shifted to Defence in October 2001.

Increasingly amicable relations with its Balkan neighbours – Greece is the principal foreign investor in Bulgaria and the FYROM, for example – promise to generate jobs and trim unemployment, currently just over nine percent officially (though among recent graduates it is more like twenty percent). But the most dramatic **improvement in international relations** has occurred with old nemesis Turkey, since the severe **earthquake** which struck northern Athens on September 7, 1999, killing scores, rendering almost one hundred thousand homeless (and immobilizing two of the three national mobile phone networks). It came less than a month after the devastating tremor in northwest Turkey, and ironically proved to be the spur for a thaw between the two historical rivals. Greeks donated massive amounts of blood and foodstuffs to the

Turkish victims, as well as being the earliest foreign rescue teams on hand in Turkey, and in turn saw Turkish disaster-relief squads among the first on the scene in Athens. Soon afterwards, **Foreign Minister George Papandreou** (son of Andreas) announced that Greece had dropped its long-time opposition to EU financial aid to Turkey in the absence of a solution to the outstanding Cyprus and Aegean disputes, and further indicated that Greece would not at present oppose Turkish candidacy for accession to the EU.

With his handling of the Turkish détente and progress towards EMU the main campaign issues, Simitis called **elections** five months earlier than required, on **April 9, 2000**. In the event, PASOK squeaked into office for an unprecedented third consecutive term by a single percentage point, 43.7 to ND's 42.7, with 158 seats against 125. The crucial factor that swung the cliff-hanger – not decided until 1am the day after – was voters' mistrust of Karamanlis the Younger's manifest inexperience. The KKE held steady at just over 5% and 11 seats, but Synaspismós barely cleared the three-percent hurdle for its six seats, while DIKKI didn't.

Simitis capped his narrow victory by announcing Greece's official **entry into the euro-currency zone** on June 20, at an EU summit in Portugal. He needed this bit of good news, as the country's international reputation had again taken a battering on June 8, when the terror group November 17 emerged from a couple of years' quiescence by assassinating **Brigadier Stephen Saunders**, the UK military attaché, while his car was stalled in Athens traffic. There were various mutterings abroad (again, especially in the US) that adequate security could not be guaranteed for the forthcoming, Greece-hosted Olympics. By the end of 2001, British detectives who had arrived in Athens to prod Greek law-enforcement personnel into some progress in the Saunders case, if not the others, reported gratifying progress in identifying the November 17 hierarchy, promising arrests as soon as air-tight evidence was secured.

Tourism, the most important foreign-exchange earner for the country, had a pretty good year in 1999 (after a rocky spring occasioned by the Kosovo war, roundly condemned by most, traditionally pro-Serbian Greeks), but a well-publicised spate of forest fires during an unusually hot summer, plus the *Express Samina* shipwreck (see box p.38), conspired to make 2000 an *annus horribilis* for tourist arrival numbers. 2001, with neighbouring Turkey enjoying an only partly justified reputation as a cheapo destination following a sharp March currency devaluation, was another bad season, ending on the sour notes of the September 11 US terror incidents (which could mean no significant American arrivals for the forseeable future) and Virgin Atlantic's announcement that it was abandoning its London–Athens routes as of October 28.

All this has made something of a mockery of government efforts to improve infrastructure, which in many cases have been stalled for some years. A few yacht marinas and roads have finally been completed with EU assistance, while spas, casinos and golf courses (Rhodes has all three of these) have been or are being renovated. On the aesthetic front, in late May 2001 Minister of the Aegean Nikos Sifounakis announced a strict new building code for the smaller islands of the Cyclades, Dodecanese and east Aegean, to check the spread of concrete monstrosities completely at odds with their surroundings. Measures to protect the larger islands are still on the drawing board, and it must be said that the last government minister to propose building controls for coastal Greece – the late Andonis Tritsis – lasted less than six months in the job.

Fluctuating visitor numbers have been particularly evident in the Dodecanese and east Aegean, where any consistent resurgence depends greatly on continued improvement in **Greek relations with Turkey**. Basic geographical realities dictate that the islands, the last territories incorporated into the Greek state, are those least securely clasped to the mother country. If push comes to shove, all of these islands are fundamentally indefensible; a Turkish bomb lobbed onto island airport runways every few hours will suffice to keep them from being resupplied and guarantee their capture by Turkey within a matter of days. Common sense would also suggest that Greece has much more to gain by encouraging weekend (or longer) tourism from Turkey to these islands, by abolishing or easing visa requirements, than in promoting international tension.

Greek society today

The foregoing summary of recent, salient events doesn't, however, give a full flavour of the massive changes which have occurred in Greece since the late 1980s. First and foremost, it's a conspicuously wealthier, more **consumerist society** than before, with vast disparities in income, imbued with the prevailing neoliberal mania for privatization. Athens, Thessaloníki and most large island capitals have their legions of **yuppies**, addicted to gourmet wines, properly made cappuccinos, designer trinkets, fast cars and **travel**; even small-town agencies promote junkets to Thailand and Cuba (the current trendy favourites). Greek domestic tourism is also heavily marketed, in particular weekend breaks to "name" islands like Corfu, Santoríni, Kós and Rhodes, or outdoor expeditions to the mountains; there are numerous Greek-language travel magazines, Sunday supplements and bound guides, advising people where to spend their surplus cash.

Mobile phones are ubiquitous – along with Italy and Cyprus, Greece has the highest per-capita use in Europe – and the success of the two private networks has forced OTE to offer its own mobile network at reasonable prices, and in general sharpen up. You can walk into an OTE phone shop and get any high-tech device or network service more or less instantly, unlike the bad old days – as recently as 1994 – when OTE was a national disgrace and provision of a simple analogue line could take years.

In tandem with this increased materialism, the **Orthodox Church** has declined from "guardian of the nation" to something of a **national embarrassment**. Rather than address the pressing social problems and hidden poverty occasioned by Greece's immigrant crisis (see p.456), its version of moral leadership has been to organize, in July 2000, a last-ditch attack, complete with street demos, on the **new-style national identity cards**, which omitted to state the bearer's religion. Government spokesman proclaimed that the old-style cards were illegal under EU regulations, and an ND-sponsored bill to allow for optional citation of religious faith was defeated in parliament. More understandably, the good bishops demanded (and got) from Pope John Paul II a grovelling apology for the 1204 sacking of Constantinople during his May 2001 visit to Athens.

But the Church's medieval mindset has really come to the fore in its continuing **ban on cremation**, and near-hysteria on the subject of bar codes. Greece is the only EU country where cremation is forbidden; every summer there's a malodorous backlog of corpses to be interred at the overcrowded cemeteries, whilst relatives surreptitiously cart their loved ones' remains to be burnt in more accommodating Bulgaria or Romania, under threat of excommunication – Orthodox doctrine is adamant that immolation would compromise the Resurrection, and that the bones of a saint (still revered as relics) might inadvertently be destroyed. But it's with **bar codes** on ID cards, and hand- or forehead-stamping for casino patrons or bank employees, that the Athonite monks in particular have really become exercised (and something of a laughing stock). They (and a considerable number of the lay faithful) see this as a Jewish-Masonic conspiracy in fulfilment of Revelations 13:16–17 and 14:9, which relates to the mark of the Beast, and vast stacks of printed leaflets – even an entire book – are distributed on the subject.

The clergy's rantings notwithstanding, bar-coded Greece is now firmly locked into the **global economy**, and not just in the matter of cross-border shipment of the dead. International franchises such as McDonald's, Next, Häagen Dazs, The Body Shop and the last continental outlets of Marks and Spencer proliferate in most larger towns; consumer interest rates have plunged, the Athens stock exchange burgeoned (before crashing spectacularly, prompting a wave of suicides by those who lost their savings), and foreign or multinational companies have flocked to invest. It is they who are funding and carrying out massive infrastructure improvements designed to long outlast the 2004 Olympics: the airport at Spáta, metros in Athens and Thessaloníki, the Río–Andírrio bridge over the Gulf of Corinth, the Via Egnatia expressway across Epirus, Macedonia and Thrace. **Overseas companies** are also quietly **acquiring** more (or less) productive elements of the Greek economy; Britain's Blue Circle, for example, in 1998 purchased Hercules Cement from Italian interests, while Cyprus Airways and an Australian group were among contenders to buy out troubled flag-carrier Olympic Airways. The 2003 end of cabotage – whereby only Greek companies have been allowed to provide ferry services within Greece – should weed out the flakier shipping companies and have the others pulling their socks up, under threat of possibly being challenged by the likes of P&O or Fred Olsen. Matters can only get better since the *Express Samina* sinking, which fully exposed the weaknesses in safety, pricing and personnel training of Greek Aegean transport – and most of all the oligopolies which have resulted from domestic companies following overseas examples and engaging in extensive **corporate takeovers**. Minoan (now Hellas) Flying Dolphins, the responsible party in the shipwreck, had acquired Ceres Hydrofoils, several smaller steamship outfits, and a majority interest in an airline, to become the largest domestic transport company (and, predictably, provide increasingly user-hostile schedules); Alpha Bank absorbed the troubled Ionian Bank in early 1999 and instantly became the second largest banking/insurance group in the country, before taking a majority interest in the National Bank of Greece in November 2001 to become the largest bank in the eastern Mediterranean.

It used to be that a lifetime sinecure with the civil service was the goal for most graduates, but no longer – now young people crave a **career** in the private sector, with unlimited salary prospects, and will initially work for low pay which older, less qualified professionals with families – who often must cobble together part-time jobs – simply can't live on. Yet most Greeks have now become too grand for menial jobs; the late Andreas once grumbled that Greece shouldn't remain "a nation of waiters", though it seems he needn't have worried.

Greece may continue to occupy the EU's economic cellar with Portugal, but it's still infinitely wealthier (and more stable) than any of its neighbours, and this has acted as a magnet for **a permanent underclass of immigrants**. Since 1990 they have arrived in numbers estimated variously as 800,000 to over a million, a huge burden for a not especially rich country of just over ten million (imagine Britain with six million refugees rather than a few hundred thousand). These days your waiter, hotel desk clerk or cleaning lady is most likely to be Albanian, Ukrainian, Bulgarian or Russian, to cite the four largest groups of arrivals. Mostly on the mainland, there are also significant communities of Poles, Filipinos, Romanians, Sudanis, Kurds, equatorial Africans and Georgians (not to mention ethnic Greeks from the Caucasus) – a striking change in what had hitherto been a homogeneous, parochial culture.

The **Greek response** to this has been decidedly mixed; the Albanians, making up roughly half the influx and found living on all the larger islands, are almost universally detested (except for the ethnic-Greek northern Epirots), and blamed for all manner of social ills. They have also prompted the first anti-immigration measures with teeth in a country whose population is more used to being on the other side of such laws – Greece is a member of the Schengen visa scheme and sees itself, as in past ages, as the first line of defence against the barbarian hordes from the Orient. All of the east Aegean islands regularly receive boatloads of people fleeing from every country in Asia, and the country's few refugee camps (near Athens) are grossly inadequate. In June 2001, as an attempt to cope, legal residence was offered to illegals who could demonstrate two years' presence in Greece, and pay a hefty amount for retroactive social security contributions; yet when this **amnesty period** ended in early September, only about 350,000 individuals had applied to be "regularised", leaving the remainder still subject to arrest and deportation.

On a positive note, these diverse groups, aforementioned travel by the Greeks themselves, touring bands or dance companies and programmes on the private television channels have created a taste for **exotic music and foods**. One doesn't always have to wait for the summer festivals to see name jazz, blues or soul acts in the biggest towns, and there are now decent foreign-cuisine restaurants there as well as in many of the major island resorts. All of these factors, however, have had the effect of making Greece less identifiably Greek and, it must be said, of making the native Greeks themselves rather less welcoming and more self-absorbed than before.

Wildlife

Dodecanese and east Aegean wildlife – in particular the flora – can prove an unexpected source of fascination. In spring, the colour, scent and variety of wild flowers, with the resulting wealth of insect and bird life, are astonishing. Islands cut off from continental landmasses have had many thousands of years to evolve their own individual species. Overall, there are some two thousand species of flowering plants on the islands (over half of which exist on Sámos alone), many of them unique to Greece.

Some background

In early antiquity Greece, including the islands, was thickly forested; Aleppo (*Pinus halepensis*) and Calabrian (*Pinus brutia*) pines grew in coastal regions, giving way to fir or black pine up in the hills and low mountains. But this **native woodland** contracted rapidly as human activities expanded. Already by Classical times, an artificial mosaic of habitats had been created through forest clearance, followed by agriculture (including the planting of olive groves), abandonment to scrub, and then a resumption of cultivation or grazing. Huge quantities of timber were consumed in the production of charcoal and pottery, metal-smelting, and in shipbuilding or construction work. Small patches of old-growth woodland have remained on the largest islands, but even these are under threat from loggers and arsonists (see box, pp.460–461).

Contemporary Greek **farming** often lacks the rigid efficiency of northern European agriculture. Many peasant farmers still cultivate little patches of land, without systematic use of pesticides and herbicides, while town-dwellers travel at weekends to collect food plants from the countryside. Wild greens under the generic term *hórta* are gathered to be cooked like spinach, while grape hyacinth bulbs are boiled as a vegetable. The buds and young shoots of capers are harvested, along with wild figs, carobs, plums, cherries, sweet chestnuts and the fruit of the strawberry tree. Emergent snails and mushrooms are collected after the first rains. The more resilient forms of wildlife can coexist with these uses, but for many Greeks only those species that have practical applications are regarded as having any value.

Now, however, increased access to heavier earth-moving machinery means farmers can sweep away an ancient meadow full of orchids in an easy morning's work – often to clear a field that is used for forage for a year or two and then abandoned to coarse thistles. Increasingly, the pale scars of dirt tracks criss-cross once-intact hill- and mountain-sides, allowing short-termist agricultural destruction of previously undisturbed upland habitats.

During the 1950s a policy of draining **wetlands** was instituted in order to increase agriculture, and many important areas were lost to wildlife completely. Those lakes, lagoons and deltas that remain on the larger islands are, in theory, now protected for their fragile biodiversity and their environmental and scientific value – but industrial and sewage pollution, disturbance, and misuse are unchecked. Local 4WD vehicles and noisy motorbikes race through dunes, destroying the surface stability and decimating nesting species; Greek military planes practice low-altitude flight over flocks of flamingoes; rows of illegally overnighting camper vans disfigure the beaches; and locals drive to the nearest ravine to dump unwanted televisions and fridges. On Lésvos, one of the island's main tourist attractions, the Kalloní saltpans, once beloved by rare birds, are being poisoned by sewage.

Since the 1970s, tourist development has ribboned out along coastlines, sweeping away both agricultural plots and wildlife havens as it does so. These expanding resorts increase local employment, often attracting inland workers to the coast; the generation that would have been shepherds and graziers on remote hillsides now work in tourist bars and tavernas. Consequently, the pressure of domestic animal grazing, particularly goat grazing on the larger islands, has been significantly reduced and allows the regeneration of tree seedlings.

Despite an often negative attitude to wildlife, Greece was probably the first place in the world where it was an object of study. Theophrastus of Lésvos (372–287 BC) was the first recorded **botanist** and a systematic collector of general information on plants, while his contemporary, Aristotle, studied the animal world. During the first century AD the distinguished physician Dioscorides compiled a herbal that remained a standard work for over a thousand years.

Flowers

Greek-island plants cease flowering (or even living, in the case of annuals) when it is too hot and dry – midsummer in Greece plays the same role for plants as winter does in northern Europe. Perennials survive in coastal Greece either by producing leathery or hairy leaves with a minimum surface area, or by dying back to giant tuberous rootstalks – both strategies for conserving moisture.

The arid Greek summers thus confine the main **flowering period** to **spring**, a climatic window when the days are bright, temperatures not too high and the ground water supply still adequate. Spring comes to the southern Dodecanese in late February or early March, with the east Aegean lagging behind until mid- or late April. The delicate flowers of early spring – orchids, fritillaries, anemones, cyclamen, tulips and small bulbs – are replaced as the season progresses by more robust shrubs, tall perennials and abundant annuals. May, marked by the yellow flowers of broom (*Spartium junceum*) or gorse (*Calycotome villosa*), signals the onset of **summer** at lower elevations; many plants close down completely now, though a few tough ones, like shrubby thyme and savory, continue to flower through the heat and act as magnets for butterflies. Once the worst heat is over, and the first autumn showers have arrived (usually by late September), there's another burst of activity on the part of **autumn** flowering species – on a much smaller scale than in springtime, but no less welcome after the brown drabness of summer. Mid- to late October will usually bring more rain, germinating seeds for the following year's crop of annuals, but **winter** flowers only get underway after Christmas, continuing into late February.

Seashore and watercourses

Plants on the **beach** tend to be hardy, salt-tolerant species growing in a difficult environment where fresh water is limited. Feathery tamarisk trees are adept at surviving in this habitat, and consequently are often planted to provide shade. On hot days or nights you may see or feel them "sweating" away surplus saltwater from their foliage.

Sand dunes on the southerly Dodecanese often support low gnarled trees of the prickly juniper. These provide shelter for a variety of colourful small plants like pink campions, yellow restharrow, white stocks, blue alkanet and violet sea lavender. The flat sandy areas or slacks behind the dunes serve as home to a variety of plants, where they have not been illegally ploughed for cultivation. Open stretches of beach sand usually have fewer plants, particularly nowadays in resort areas, where the bulldozed "spring cleaning" of the beach removes the local flora along with the winter's rubbish.

The spectacular yellow horned poppy (*Glaucium flavum*) can be found growing on shingled banks, and sea stocks or Virginia stocks amongst rocks behind beaches. The small pink campion (*Silene colorata*) is often colourfully present before June. Between August and October, look for the enormous, fragrant, white flowers of the sea daffodil (*Pancratium maritimum*) at the inland edge of sandy beaches, for example at Éristos on Tílos.

Forest fires – and other pests

Since 1928, **fires** have reduced Greece's proportion of forested land from just under one-third to just under one-fifth, with the most rapid loss since 1974. Huge infernos have raged almost annually on at least one of Rhodes, Kárpathos, Sámos, Ikaría and Híos from 1981 until 2000; of the larger islands of the east Aegean and Dodecanese, so far only Kós and Lésvos have escaped comprehensive damage.

A tiny fraction of these summer disasters occur naturally or accidentally, through a lightning strike during an electrical storm, sunlight refracted through a glass shard, or sparks from a badly insulated power pylon – any of these providing the necessary ignition to the highly volatile, resinous maquis shrubbery and pine which cover the middle altitudes of these islands. As for the other fires, conspiracy theories – ever popular in Greece – variously blame the CIA, KGB or its successors, the Freemasons, Mossad, the PLO, Turks, Albanians, etc, but the stark truth is that the vast majority are the result of arson perpetrated by the islanders themselves. Motives are simple and sordid: clearing land for grazing or building, touristic developers forcing stubborn farmers to sell up at depressed prices, or hampering tourism on a rival island or beach. There is always an upsurge prior to elections, the result of surreptitious promises by candidates to reclassify burnt forest land as suitable for development should they attain office. The Orthodox Church and the Forest Service own and administer vast tracts of land in a quasi-feudal system, implementing erratic methods and rates of taxation in addition to promulgating policies that enrage private owners and encourage firebugs. The arsonists themselves are usually locals with a grievance, but increasingly rent-a-thugs from elsewhere who are provided with sophisticated equipment (light planes and time-delay devices) by their employers.

The recurrence of blazes is often used as a justification by the Forest Service for the bulldozing of numerous dirt tracks through woods, presumably to allow fire engines easier access. Unfortunately this creates as many problems as it solves, since arsonists take advantage of the opportunity to drive their jerry cans full of petrol or time bombs to the scene of operations. Experience has shown that only Hercules transport planes, modified for dumping seawater on the flames, make a decisive difference in fire control, but these cannot fly at night, when only desperate crews digging trenches with hand tools can attempt to encircle the burn zone. Accordingly the arsonists generally do their dirty work just before dusk, on a windy day, setting blazes at several points simultaneously, so that by the time morning arrives the fire is far out of control. Once a conflagration is underway, pine trees are their own worst enemies, since pine cones explode grenade-like when set

Many **watercourses** dry up completely in the hot season, only being active after torrential rains during December to April. Consequently, there are few true aquatic plants compared with much of Europe. However, species that can survive the regular drying-out flourish – for example the giant reed or **calamus**, a bamboo-like grass reaching up to 6m in height and often cut for use as canes. It frequently grows in company with the shrubby, pink- or white-flowered and very poisonous oleander. Near the river mouths and in the damp ravines of Lésvos grows the yellow azalea (*Rhododendron luteum*), found nowhere else in Greece.

Cultivated land

Arable fields can be rich with colourful weeds in late spring: scarlet poppies, blue bugloss, yellow or white daisies, wild peas, gladioli, daisies, tulips and grape hyacinths. Small **meadows** can be equally colourful, with slower-growing plants such as orchids in extraordinary quantities. The rather dull violet flowers

alight, firing off blazing particles for up to 100m into unburnt tracts.

Since the mid-1990s the authorities have begun stationing **fire-extinguishing planes** at major east Aegean and Dodecanese airports (in theory two on each runway), but there are rarely enough to go around, with planes sometimes off combating fire on an adjacent island when disaster strikes. **Ground surveillance** can also be woefully inadequate; thus far only Lésvos has comprehensive, 24-hour summertime watches maintained on strategic ridges – though Sámos has also begun recruiting a corps of volunteers – and only Rhodes has installed anything resembling a network of rural standpipes (conspicuous in and around Petaloúdhes).

As if the fire threat wasn't bad enough, island forests have another, more insidious but nearly as destructive natural adversary: the **pine processionary caterpillar**. This is the larval form of a moth which lays its eggs near the apical bunches of pine needles; when they hatch, the caterpillars form densely webbed trapezoidal nests, inside of which they steadily munch away at the tender young shoots, denuding the growing ends of the tree and severely stunting it. Forest service employees are supposed to conduct springtime patrols in years of heavy infestation, collecting and destroying the nests, but they rarely if ever do – not too surprising in light of the caterpillars' highly irritant qualities (see Basics, p.27).

The underlying basis for both the blazes and the nonexistent pest control is social: there's simply no consensus in Greece that woodlands have any intrinsic value, now that few trees are tapped for resin or used in boatbuilding, so goats or villas will win hands down in any comparative assessment in rural minds. Only slowly is a connection being made between fire damage and subsequent winter flash floods or steadily dropping water tables; tentative anti-erosion terracing on Sámos hillsides following its July 2000 blaze was inadequate to prevent massive soil loss and flooding in December 2001, as unusually heavy rains simply failed to sink into the denuded, hard-baked soil. Only when tourist receipts begin to fall as a result of desolate scenery – as has happened on Sámos since 2000 – is there likely to be a belated conversion to "Green consciousness". The saddest element of the story is that most of the lost vegetation was a mature crop of Aleppo, Calabrian and (on Sámos) black pines, which will be replaced haphazardly if at all. Carob, the most fire-resistant species (often resprouting from scorched trunks within two months of a blaze), is seldom used in replanting schemes. In typical Mediterranean climatic conditions, native conifers grow so slowly – fifty to seventy years to attain any appreciable size – that few of the readers of this book will live to see a mature, regenerated forest on many islands.

of the mandrake belie its celebrated history as a narcotic and surgical anaesthetic. In the absence of herbicides, **olive groves** can host extensive underflora. Where herbicides are in use, there is instead usually a yellow carpet of the introduced, weedkiller-resistant *Oxalis pescaprae*, which now occurs in sufficient quantity to show up in satellite photographs.

Fallow farmland is good for bulbous perennials, in particular a gorgeous, multicoloured variety of anemone (*Anemone coronaria*) that blooms early in the year throughout most of the islands. The scarlet turban buttercup (*Ranunculus asiaticus*) on Rhodes, and Sámos' sweet-smelling blue hyacinths (*zoumboúlia* in Greek), ancestor of the cultivated variety, also emerge during late February and March.

Appearing between March and July is the wild snapdragon (*Antirrhinum majus*), which loves chinks in low **rock walls**. Here too, from May to August, blaze forth the white to pinkish flowers of the spiny caper; the unopened flower bud is not the only edible bit, since on many islands the thorny shoots are also pickled and eaten whole.

Among **exotics**, the century plant (*Agave americana*), naturalized around the Mediterranean since the eighteenth century, is a familiar sight on the islands; the plant flowers once in its ten- to fifteen-year (not 100-year!) lifetime during June, after which the formidably spiky leaf-rosette withers away. It's commonly used as a fence substitute, like another import, the yellow-flowered prickly pear (*Opuntia indica*), supposedly brought back by Columbus from the New World. Its scarlet fruit, ripening in September, tastes like watermelon but requires peeling and putting through a blender to get rid of spines and seeds respectively.

Lower hillsides

The rocky earth makes terracing for cultivation on some hillsides difficult and impractical. Agriculture is often abandoned here and such areas revert to a mixture of low shrubs and perennials – the **garigue** biome. With time, a decade of wet winters, and the absence of grazing, some shrubs such as juniper and kermes or holly oak develop into small trees – the much denser **maquis** vegetation. The colour yellow often predominates in early spring, with brooms, gorse, Jerusalem sage and the three-metre-tall giant fennel, followed by the magenta or white of bushy rockroses (*Cistus* ssp). An abundance of the last is often indicative of an earlier fire, since they flourish in the cleared areas. Strawberry trees (*Arbutus unedo*) are also fire-resistant; they flower in winter or early spring, producing an orange-red, edible (though disappointingly insipid) fruit in the autumn, fermented to make a more exciting if illicit liqueur. The Judas tree (*Cercis siliquastrum*) flowers on bare wood in spring, making a blaze of pink against the green hillsides. From late October until the New Year, heather (*Erica manipuliflora*) provides a blaze of pink on slopes with acidic soil.

A third habitat is **phrygana**, smaller, frequently aromatic or spiny shrubs, often with a narrow strip of bare ground between each hedgehog-like bush. Many **aromatic herbs** such as lavender, rosemary, savory, sage and thyme are native to these areas, intermixed with other less tasty plants such as the toxic euphorbias and the spiny burnet or wire-netting bush.

Orchids in Greece are much smaller and altogether more dignified than the tropical varieties in florists' shops. On both Rhodes and Sámos there are nearly fifty species, mostly of the genera *Orchis* and *Ophrys*, blooming from March until May, according to altitude. Their complexity blurs species boundaries and keeps botanists in a state of taxonomic flux. In particular, the *Ophrys* bee and spider orchids have adapted, through their subtleties of lip colour and false scents, to seduce small male wasps. These insects mistake the flowers for a potential mate, and unintentionally assist the plant's pollination. Other orchids mimic the colours and scents of honey-producing plants, to lure bees. Though all species are officially protected, many are still picked for decoration – in particular the giant *Barlia* orchid – and fill vases in homes, cafés, tavernas and even on graves.

Irises have a particular elegance and charm, appearing between February and June according to species and island. The blue to violet winter iris, as its name suggests, is the first to appear, followed by the small blue *Iris gynandriris*. The flowers of the latter open after midday and into the night, only to wither by the following morning. The widow iris is sombre-coloured in funereal shades of black and green, while the taller, white *Iris albicans*, the holy flower of Islam, is a relic of the Ottoman occupation. In the limestone peaks of Sámos, *Iris suavolens* has short stems, but huge yellow and brown flowers.

You can often find deserted, shady terraces full of **cyclamen**, either *Cyclamen persicum* (ancestor of the domestic variety) or *Cyclamen repandum*, sprouting from small tubers or corms. Both exhibit white to pink blooms in early spring; the Rhodes form has white blossoms with a pinkish throat. By contrast, the pink autumn *Cyclamen graecum* flowers in September.

Once the heat of the summer is over, **autumn bulbs** come into their own. The sea squill (*Drimia maritima*) occurs inland as well as near the sea, with tall spikes of white flowers rising from huge bulbs. Smaller bulbs or corms, including various crocus species and their relatives, the pink to purple colchicums and the yellow sternbergias, bloom from September until November.

Mountains and gorges

The higher **mountains** of Rhodes and Kós, or the east Aegean islands of Sámos, Ikaría and Lésvos, have transient winter snow cover varying with altitude, and cooler weather for much of the year, so flowering is consequently later than at lower altitudes. Their limestone or schist peaks hold rich collections of attractive flowering rock plants whose nearest relatives may be from the Balkan Alps or from the Turkish Toros ranges. Gorges are another spectacular habitat, particularly rich on Sámos and Ikaría. Their inaccessible cliffs act as refuges for plants that cannot survive the grazing, competition, or the more extreme climates of open areas.

Much of the surviving Dodecanese and east Aegean **island forest** is found in the mountainous areas of Rhodes, Kós, Sými, Sámos and Lésvos, with tree cover on Sámos and Rhodes much reduced in the wake of the aforementioned fires. Depending on the island, the woodland can comprise cypress (widespread at low altitudes), oak (on Lésvos) and a few species of pine: Calabrian or Aleppo at lower altitudes, and a few surviving black pine on Sámos' Mount Ámbelos. The cypress is native to the south and east Aegean, but in its columnar form it has been planted everywhere that has a Mediterranean climate. Some claim that the slim trees are male and the broader, spreading form are female, but female cones on the thin trees prove this wrong. On Kárpathos and Sými there are extensive stands of juniper in two species (as well as a few Aleppo pines), while shady stream canyons of the larger islands shelter plane, Oriental sweetgum, sweet chestnut (Sámos and Lésvos) and poplar. The cooler shade of woodland provides a haven for plants which cannot survive full exposure to the Greek summer – for example spectacular peonies, blooming during May on shaded slopes above 400m on several islands. Those on Kárpathos are white subspecies of *Paeonia clusii*, while those of Sámos and Rhodes are the more common, usually pink *Paeonia mascula*.

With altitude, the forest thins out to scattered individual hardy conifers and oaks, before finally reaching a limit ranging from 1000m to 1200m, depending on the island's latitude and rainfall. Above this treeline are limited summer meadows, and then bare rock. If not severely grazed, these habitats are home to many low-growing, gnarled, but often splendidly floriferous plants.

Birds

The Dodecanese and east Aegean host a large range of resident Mediterranean birds, with an additional bonus in the seasonal presence of **migratory species** that winter in East Africa but breed in Greece or northern Europe. Between January and mid-May – sometimes later, depending on the weather – they migrate up the Nile valley before moving across the eastern Mediterranean. These islands can be the first landfall after a long sea crossing, and smaller birds recuperate and feed for a few days before continuing north. Larger birds such as storks and ibis often fly very high, and binoculars are needed to spot them as they pass over. In autumn the birds return heading the other way, but usually in more scattered flocks. Although some species such as quail and turtle dove are shot, there is nothing like the wholesale slaughter that takes place in some other Mediterranean countries.

Seasonal **salt marshes** and **coastal lagoons** on Kos, Sámos, Límnos and Lésvos are excellent territories for bird-watching, especially during the spring migrations. Herons, egrets, glossy ibis, spoonbills, ducks, white pelicans and storks mingle with smaller waders such as the avocet and the black-winged stilt with its ridiculously long, pink legs. Greater flamingoes arrive in January, lingering until April; upwards of two hundred of them can be counted at the salt marsh near the easterly Psilí Ámmos (Sámos) on a given winter's day.

In, and just outside of **towns**, swallows (which prefer to nest under bridges and culverts), and their relatives the martins (which build mud nests on building exteriors), are constantly swooping through the air to catch insects, as are the larger and noisier swifts. In **lowland fields and olive groves**, especially on Lésvos, Sámos and Rhodes, hoopoes are a startling combination of pink, black and white, particularly obvious when they fly; they're about the only natural predator of the processionary caterpillar (see box, p.461). The much shyer golden oriole has an attractive song but is rarely seen for more than a few moments before hiding its brilliant colours among its favourite poplar tree. Rollers, which like to roost on wires, are bright blue and golden-brown, while multicoloured flocks of slim and elegant bee-eaters fill the air with their soft calls as they hunt insects. Tílos in particular, after several hunting-free years, has seen an explosion in the population of these last three species, as well as rock-partridges. Other small insect-eaters include stonechats, flycatchers and woodchat shrikes.

Hillside maquis, with its junipers and other dense, prickly scrub, is also a good habitat for birds. Warblers are numerous, with the Sardinian warbler often conspicuous on rough scrubby slopes because of its black head, bright red eye, and bold habits; the Rüppell's warbler is considerably rarer, and confined to thicker woodland. Lésvos plays host to two species of nuthatch native to Asia Minor: Krüper's nuthatch in the pine forests around Ayiássos, and rock nuthatch on the barer slopes throughout the west of the island. Also to be seen in the **mountains** are smaller birds such as black and white wheatears, and the blue rock thrush.

Larger raptors are relatively rare in the islands, but can occur around remoter gorges, cliffs and islets, for example on Rhodes west of Monólithos, or on neighbouring Hálki; on Télendhos and Tílos; and on Lésvos in the east Aegean, all locales which are famous for Eleonora's falcons, especially during late spring and summer. Buzzards are perhaps the most abundant type of raptor, mistaken by optimistic bird-watchers for the much rarer, shyer eagles, which do however appear in winter, when they're driven over from the mountains of Anatolia. Lesser kestrels are brighter, noisier versions of the common kestrel, and often appear undisturbed by the presence of humans, nesting communally and noisily in many small towns and villages. Equally bold red-footed falcons can often be seen perched on telegraph wires.

Seashore birds are also notable; the southern Dodecanese are home to a small population of Audouin's gulls, endangered by both human activity and the more versatile yellow-legged gull. Cormorants roost on and dive from cliffs, particularly on Sámos but also on certain Dodecanese, from autumn through until spring. Brightest of all is the kingfisher, more commonly seen saltwater-fishing than in northern Europe.

At **night**, the tiny Scops owl (*Otus scops*, in Greek *giónis*) has a very distinctive, repeated, single-note call, very like the sonar beep of a submarine; the equally diminutive little owl (*Athena noctua*, in Greek *koukouváyia*) is by contrast also visible and active by day, particularly on ruined houses or on power cables, and has a strange repertoire of cries, chortles and a throaty hiss. Certainly the most evocative nocturnal bird is the nightingale, which requires wooded stream valleys and is most audible on Sámos around midnight in May, its mating season.

Mammals

The variety of **mammals** is fairly limited, owing to long isolation from both the Anatolian and Balkan mainlands, and ruthless hunting. Most of the Dodecanese and east Aegean islands have the usual range of rodents such as rats, mice (many field varieties), hares and rabbits; the local hedgehog has a distinctive white underbelly. On the larger, more forested islands, particularly Sámos, which is separated from Anatolia by the narrowest of straits, there are fast-moving, ferret-like stone martens, weasels and even the odd jackal, but no foxes, badgers or larger predators, such as bears or wolves. Recently, however, wild boar have been (re)introduced to Sámos, where they have multiplied rapidly in the remoter stream canyons and are now causing extensive damage to crops; they will probably have to be culled (much to the delight of local hunters). Lésvos, alone of the islands, has a small population of Persian squirrels.

Dolphins and **porpoises** are a fairly common sight in the Dodecanese, often shadowing ferries to feed on fish stirred up in their wake. The extremely rare **Mediterranean monk seal** is still occasionally seen near Sámos (see box, p.332) and increasingly around Tílos; on Kastellórizo members of the clan resident in the island's sea cave (see p.182) have been glimpsed playing in the harbour. Despite these encouraging recent developments, this species remains highly endangered since losing many individuals – and most of its main breeding ground – to a toxic algal bloom off Morocco; on present trends it's unlikely to survive much into the new millennium.

Reptiles and amphibians

Reptiles flourish in the hot dry summers and rocky terrain of the islands, and there are many species, the commonest being **lizards**. Most of these are small, slim, agile and wary, rarely staying around for closer inspection. They're usually brown to grey, with subtle patterns of spots, streaks and stripes, though in adult males the undersides are sometimes brilliant orange, yellow, green or blue.

Flora and fauna field guides

In case of difficulty obtaining titles listed below from conventional booksellers, there is a reliable mail-order outlet for wildlife field guides within the UK. **Summerfield Books**, Main Street, Brough, Kirkby Stephen, Cumbria CA17 4AX ⓣ017683/41577, ⓕ41687, ⓔatkins@summerfield-books.com, not only has new botanical titles, but also rare or out-of-print natural history books on all topics. Postage is extra, but they often have special offers on select products. The shop is open Mon–Sat 9.30am–4.30pm.

Wildlife, general

A C Campbell *The Hamlyn Guide to the Flora and Fauna of the Mediterranean* (Hamlyn/Country Life). Very useful, but out of print, so try to find a second-hand copy; also published as *The Larousse Guide to the Flora and Fauna of the Mediterranean* (Larousse).

Flowers

Hellmut Baumann *Greek Wild Flowers and Plant Lore in Ancient Greece* (Herbert Press, UK). Lots of interesting ethnobotanical snippets about the age-old Greek relationship with plants, plus good colour photographs.

Marjorie Blamey and Christopher Grey-Wilson *Mediterranean Wild Flowers* (HarperCollins, UK). Comprehensive field guide, with coloured drawings; recent and taxonomically up to date.

Lance Chilton *Plant check-lists.* Small pamphlets which also include birds, reptiles and butterflies, available for Kárpathos; Kós; Kokkári (Sámos); Sámos; Sými; Líndhos/Pefkos (Rhodes); and Rhodes. Contact the author directly at ⓣ01485/532710 or ⓦwww.marengo@supanet.com for an up-to-date catalogue of this expanding series.

Pierre Delforge *Orchids of Britain & Europe* (HarperCollins, UK). A comprehensive guide, with recent taxonomy, though beware small inaccuracies in this translation.

Anthony Huxley and William Taylor *Flowers of Greece and the Aegean* (Hogarth Press, UK, o/p). The only volume dedicated to the islands (and mainland), with colour photographs, but now slightly dated for taxonomy.

Oleg Polunin *Flowers of Greece and the Balkans* (Oxford University Press, UK). Classic, older field guide (reprinted 1997), also with colour photographs, useful if Huxley and Taylor proves unfindable.

Oleg Polunin and Anthony Huxley *Flowers of the Mediterranean* (Hogarth Press, UK). The larger scope means that many Greek endemics are missed out, but recent printings have a table of taxonomic changes.

On most of the Dodecanese and east Aegean islands, you may see the angular, iguana-like *agama* or Rhodes dragon (*Agama stelio*). Attaining up to 30cm in length, these do look like miniature, spiny-backed dragons, their rough, grey-to-brown skin being vaguely patterned. Unlike other lizards, they will often stop to study you, before finally disappearing into a wall or under a rock.

Amongst the bushes of the maquis and garigue habitats you may see the Balkan green lizard, a brightly hued creature up to half a metre long, much of which is tail. You can often spot it running on its hind legs, as if possessed, from one bush to another; again they are shy unless distracted by territorial disputes with each other.

Geckoes are large-eyed nocturnal lizards, up to 15cm long, with short tails and often rough skins. Their spreading toes have claws and ingenious adhesive pads, allowing them to walk up house walls and upside down onto ceilings in their search for insects. Groups of them lie in wait near bright lights that attract

Birds

Richard Brooks *Birding in Lesbos* (Brookside Publishing, UK). Second edition of this superb little guide with colour photos, a list of bird-watching sites, and detailed maps, plus an annotated species-by-species bird list with much useful information. Contact the author directly at ©email@richard-brooks.co.uk

George Handrinos and T. Akriotis, *Birds of Greece* (A&C Black, UK). A comprehensive guide that includes island birdlife.

Heinzel, Fitter and Parslow *Collins Guide to the Birds of Britain and Europe*; **Petersen, Mountfort and Hollom** *Field Guide to the Birds of Britain and Europe* (both Collins/Stephen Green Press). Though obviously not specific to Greece, these two field guides have the best coverage of Greek birds outside of Lésvos.

Mammals

Corbet and Ovenden *Collins Guide to the Mammals of Europe* (Collins/Stephen Green Press). The best field guide on the subject.

Reptiles and amphibians

Arnold, Burton and Ovenden *Collins Guide to the Reptiles and Amphibians of Britain and Europe* (Collins/Stephen Green Press). A useful guide, though excluding the Dodecanese and east Aegean islands.

Jiri Cihar *Amphibians and Reptiles* (Conran Octopus, UK o/p). Selective coverage, but includes most endemic species of the Dodecanese and east Aegean isles.

Insects

Michael Chinery *Collins Guide to the Insects of Britain and Western Europe* (Collins/Stephen Green Press). Although Greece is outside the geographical scope of the guide, it will provide general identifications for most insects seen.

Lionel Higgins and Norman Riley *A Field Guide to the Butterflies of Britain and Europe* (Collins/Stephen Green Press). A thorough and detailed field guide that illustrates nearly all species seen in Greece.

Marine life

B. Luther and K. Fiedler *A Field Guide to the Mediterranean* (HarperCollins, UK, o/p). Very thorough; includes most Greek shallow-water species.

their prey, and small ones living indoors can have very pale, almost transparent skins. Not always popular locally – the Kós dialect word for them, *miaró*, means "defiler" after their outsized faeces – they should be left alone to eat mosquitoes and other bugs. The **chameleon** is a rare, slow-moving and swivel-eyed inhabitant of some eastern Aegean islands, particularly Sámos. Although essentially green, it has the ability to adjust its coloration to match the surroundings. It prefers bushes and low trees, hunting by day.

Greek land **tortoises** (*Testudo graeca*) occur in the Dodecanese and east Aegean. They have suffered to varying extents from (now illegal) collecting for the pet trade, but they are still commonly found basking on sunny or wooded hillsides. Usually it is their noisy progress through vegetation that first signals their presence; they spend their often long lives grazing the vegetation and can reach diameters of 30cm. Closely related stripe-necked **terrapins** (*Mauremys caspica*) are more streamlined, freshwater tortoises which love to bask on waterside mud; they're virtually a guaranteed presence at river mouths on Límnos, Ikaría, Lésvos, Kós and Rhodes. Shy and nervous, they're often only seen as they disappear underwater, with just the tops of their heads protruding like submarine periscopes. They are scavengers and will eat anything, including your fingers if handled or offered food.

Snakes are abundant on many islands (though Astypálea has none); most, such as assorted racers and grass snakes, are shy and non-venomous. Several species, including the Ottoman and nose-horned vipers, do have a poisonous bite, though they are not usually aggressive. These are adder-like, often with a very distinct, dark zigzag stripe down the back. They are only likely to bite if a hand is put in the crevice of a wall or a rock face where one of them is resting, or if they are attacked. Unfortunately, most locals attempt to kill any snake they see, and thus greatly enhance their chances of being bitten. Leave them alone, and they will do the same for you (but if worst comes to worst, see the advice on p.27). Most snakes are not only completely harmless to humans, but beneficial in that they keep down populations of rodent pests. There are also three species of legless lizards – slowworm, glass lizard and legless skink – all equally harmless, which suffer because they are mistaken for snakes.

On those islands with permanent streams, you can't miss **frogs** and **toads**, especially during the spring breeding season. The green toad has green marbling over a pinkish or mud-coloured background, and a cricket-like trill; the common toad can often be found some distance from open water. Frogs prefer the wettest places, and the robust marsh frog particularly revels in artificial water storage ponds, where the concrete sides magnify their croaking impressively. Tiny, jewel-like tree frogs (*Rana arborea*) have a stripe down their flank and vary in colour from bright green to golden brown, depending on where they are sitting – they can change colour like a chameleon. Obvious by their huge and strident voices at night, they rest by day in trees and shrubs, and can sometimes be found in quantity plastered onto the leaves of waterside oleanders

Insects and invertebrates

Greece teems with **insects**. Flies, wasps (especially on Ikaría, Híos and Kálymnos) and mosquitoes can be nuisances, but most other species are harmless to humans. The huge, slow-flying, glossy-black carpenter bee may cause alarm by its size and noise, but is rarely a problem; by contrast almost invisible gnats emerge on late summer nights and pack a mighty bite. Also harmless are the enormous, tarantula-sized hairy spiders found basking in spring on Sými stairways and balconies.

Grasshoppers and **crickets** swarm through open areas of grass and vegetation in summer, with several larger species that are carnivorous on the smaller and which can bite strongly if handled. Larger still is the grey-brown **locust**, which flies noisily before crash-landing into trees and shrubs. Grasshoppers produce their chirping noise by rubbing a wing against a leg, while house crickets do it by rubbing both wings together.

Cicadas are not related to the locust or grasshopper, but giant relatives of the aphids that cluster on roses. Their continuous whirring call is one of the characteristic sounds of the Mediterranean summer, from mid-morning until sunset, and is produced by the rapid vibration of two membranes called tymbals on either side of the body. If you look closely at the tree trunk from which the racket is emanating, you may detect this well-camouflaged, salt-and-pepper-toned insect. The high-pitched and endlessly repeated chirp of house crickets can drive one to distraction on autumn nights when temperatures fall to a range of their liking – they are silent by day, and usually all through mid-summer.

From spring through to autumn the larger islands are full of **butterflies**, particularly in late spring and early summer. There are three swallowtail species, so named for the drawn-out corners of their hind wings, in shades of cream and yellow, with black and blue markings. Their smaller relatives in the Dodecanese, the festoons, lack these spurs, but add red spots to the palette, or red and black zigzags. The rarer, robust brown-and-orange pasha is unrelated but is Europe's largest butterfly. Cleopatras are brilliant yellow butterflies, related to the brimstone of northern Europe, but larger and more colourful. Look out for green hairstreaks – a small gem of a butterfly attracted to the springtime flowers of the asphodel, a widespread plant of overgrazed pastures and hillsides. In autumn the black-and-orange plain tiger or African monarch may appear, sometimes in large quantities. In areas of deciduous woodland, look high up and you may see fast-flying large tortoiseshells, while lower down, southern white admirals skim and glide through clearings between the trees. Some of the smallest but most beautiful butterflies are the blues. Their subtle, camouflaging grey and black undersides make them vanish from view when they land and fold their wings.

Many of the Greek **hawkmoths** are equally spectacular, particularly the green-and-pink oleander hawkmoth; their large caterpillars can be recognized by their tail horn. The hummingbird hawkmoth, like its namesake, hovers at flowers to feed, supported by a blur of fast-moving wings. Tiger moths, with their black-and-white forewings and startlingly bright orange hindwings, are the "butterflies" that occur in huge numbers at Rhodes' "Butterfly Valley". The giant peacock moth is Europe's largest, up to 15cm across. A mixture of grey, black and brown, with big eye-spots, it is usually only seen during the day while resting on tree trunks.

Other insects include the well-camouflaged **praying mantis**, holding their powerful forelegs in a position of supplication until another insect comes within reach. The females are voracious, and notorious for eating the males during mating. Adult **ant-lions** resemble a fluttery dragonfly, but their young are huge-jawed and build pits in the sand to trap ants, while rhinoceros-horned beetles also dig holes in sand dunes. Hemispherical carob beetles collect balls of animal dung and push them around with their back legs. Cockroaches of varying species live in buildings, particularly hotels, restaurants and bakeries, attracted by warmth and food scraps. Glow-worms are occasionally found on hedges of Sámos. Centipedes are not often seen, but the fast-moving, twenty-centimetre *skolópendra* should be treated with respect since they can inflict very painful bites. Black millipedes or *vromoússes* ("stink-pots") are often found curled up on walls at night, their vernacular name a tribute to their pungent odour if disturbed.

Other invertebrates of interest include scorpions, which the islanders are terrified of but which, like snakes, are exceedingly shy and only out and about by night. Distantly related land crabs are found on most islands with running streams; they need freshwater to breed, but can cause surprise when found walking on remote hillsides. There are plenty of genuine **marine creatures** to be seen, particularly in shallow seawater sheltered by rocks – sea cucumbers, sea butterflies, octopus, cuttlefish, starfish and sea urchins. Octopus are bottom-dwellers, often hiding under rock overhangs or in the the discarded tyres which litter many coves; squid swim in large shoals near the surface, generally far from land. More solitary cuttlefish live in deeper water, but are often found close to shore; they typically swim with an undulating motion of their mantle, but if startled jet off at tremendous speed, leaving behind a cloud of their trademark ink. An abundance of sea urchins is indicative of clean seawater; as filter-feeders, they are extraordinarily sensitive to pollution and are in fact disappearing from many locales.

Lance Chilton, with Marc Dubin

Music

Music is central to the culture of the Dodecanese and east Aegean, and it's difficult to exaggerate its significance for those who have grown up with it. Even the most tone-deaf visitor will become aware of music's ubiquitous presence in vehicles, tavernas, ferryboats and other public spaces. Music and dance form an integral part of weddings, betrothals, baptisms, saint's days observed at local churches or monasteries, name days observed at private homes or tavernas (for those who share the name of the saint), Easter, and pre-Lenten Carnival.

Many songs and melodies, which vary from island to island, are specifically associated with **weddings**. Some of them are processional songs or tunes (*patinádhes*), sung or played while going to fetch the bride from her home, or as the wedding couple leave the church, and there are specific dances associated with different stages of a wedding ritual. It was common in the past (and in some places even today) for the music and dancing that followed a wedding feast to last for up to three days.

There are songs sung only at pre-Lenten **Carnival** (*Apókries* in Greek), accompanied by such rituals as shaking of large goat-bells roped together, or (as on Lésvos) lascivious dances and mummery. Such rituals (once widespread in Europe) date back to pre-Christian times.

Music also accompanies informal, unpublicized **private gatherings** in homes, kafenía or tavernas where music occurs. Ask people where you can hear *tá paradhosiaká* (traditional music). A few words of Greek (including names of instruments) go a long way towards inclining locals to help foreign travellers. Once it's clear that you're a budding *meraklís* (roughly, aficionado) and past the Zorba-soundtrack stage, people will be flattered by the respect paid to "real" music, and doors will open for you.

Questionable innovations

Be forewarned that *paníyíria* (**saints'-day festivals**), though often well-advertised occasions for live music, may feature ear-splitting, over-amplified music, with the inclusion of instruments from other genres of Greek music – notably the **bouzoúki** (which belongs to urban *rebétika* music and its offshoots). Electric bass has also been added in places, and is present in all too many recordings of *nisiótika* (island music). Even where more traditional instrumentation such as **violí** (violin) and **laoúto** is used, their tone may be distorted by the use of excessive reverb and/or electric pick-ups linked to poor sound systems. Many island-born musicians live and work mostly in Athens and only tour the islands in the summer, and most have rejected the older sound for the modern one as described above. All of the above is less true for **Kárpathos** and **Lésvos,** two of the more musically traditional islands.

This vulgarization of *nisiótika* (and indeed most Greek folk music) began during the mid-1960s, a trend accelerated by the values of the 1967–74 junta.

During this period many musicians were deprived of (or actively scorned) the oral-aural transmission of technique from older master players, though fortunately such attitudes have now changed. Also, recent CD re-releases of archival studio material, and high-quality field **recordings** of the last of the old-time players, are proving equally valuable to a new generation attempting to recapture traditional musicianship.

The older tradition

The music of the Dodecanese and east Aegean is wonderfully diverse, so only a general overview will be attempted here. Both archipelagos have their dances, songs and customs which vary between islands and even between towns on the same island. Different dances (or variants of the same dance) go by the same name (eg *syrtós*) from place to place, while different lyrics are set to many of the same melodies (or vice versa). The same tune can be played so idiosyncratically between neighbouring island groups (or between islands in the same group) as to be barely recognizable to an outsider. Compared to western styles, Greek music in general is far less linear and more circuitous, as would be expected from its Byzantine origins and later Ottoman influences. As in all "folk music", pieces are learned primarily by ear, though transcriptions exist and there are some who teach with written notes.

Given the intimate contact between Asia Minor and present-day Greece during the thousand years of the Byzantine empire and the four subsequent centuries of Ottoman rule, culminating in the mass eviction of Greek Orthodox from Asia Minor in 1923, Byzantine, Anatolian (especially Turkish) and Balkan influences on Greek music were inevitable. Many older songs have direct precedents in **Byzantine religious chant**, and the **modal system** used in most Greek music (related to the Arabic-Turkish modal system) also has correlates in the Byzantine ecclesiastical modal system. From the seventeenth century onwards, European instruments like the clarinet, violin, and accordion appeared in Greece, played with techniques developed for use with (and mimicking techniques of) earlier indigenous instruments. **Lyrics**, especially on the smaller islands, commonly touch on the perils of the sea, exile and – in a society where long periods of separation and arranged marriage were the norm – thwarted or forbidden love. More playful love songs, songs for before, during or after weddings, and historical ballads also appear. Lyrics are sprinkled with references to local landmarks (straits, islets, rural monasteries and their saints) with which their audience will be well familiar.

Dances and rhythms

Most island pieces, whether sung or instrumental, are in **dance rhythms**, with a vital interaction between dancers and the musicians or singers. Dancers and listeners may also join in a song (solo or as a chorus), or even initiate verses of commonly known pieces. It is customary for a lead dancer to tip the musicians, often requesting a particular tune and/or rhythm for his party to dance to. A dance is defined not only by its rhythmic count, but often as well by a certain characteristic lilt (way of swinging the rhythm) or by certain kinds of melodic phrases (as in the **bállos**, which has a repeating line that descends at the end of each part).

A dance common to most of the Dodecanese is the **soústa**, which may vary in details, but is consistently "springy" (*soústa* means spring) with an up-and-down movement. Also danced widely in the archipelago is the **siganós**, called **íssio** or **íssos** on Kálymnos, **melakhrinó** on Kós, and other names as well. This is a slower form of the *soústa*, and in some islands (eg, Kós, Kálymnos) leads directly into it, with just a couple of bars of the faster dance rhythm played to signal the dancers that the *soústa* proper is beginning.

A version of the Cretan dance called **Haniótikos** (after the city of Haniá, Crete) is known variously in the Dodecanese as **Krítikos**, **Rodhítikos** ("of Rhodes"), or **Pidikhtós** ("the jumping dance"). The **east Aegean islands** also share common dances such as the **syrtós**, the quintessential Greek circle dance; **bállos**, an up-tempo couples' dance; and the **hasápiko**, especially on Lésvos. The *hasápiko*, like the *kalamatianós* and *hasaposérvikos* which are also popular in the Dodecanese as well, are not indigenous to the islands or specific to any one Greek region, but "borrowed" from the mainland and old Constantinople.

On both Kárpathos and Sými, there are **fixed dance sequences** in which one dance leads into another without a break in the music. Yvonne Hunt (see below) notes that in northern Kárpathos "it is still not uncommon for the *káto horós*, which is danced to the singing of *mandinádhes* . . . to last for as long as six or seven hours. The music then 'shifts gears' so to speak from that segment to the next without any break or interruption; likewise the dance." More information on dances particular to specific islands or regions is given below, under the appropriate geographical region.

Yvonne Hunt's **Traditional Dance in Greek Culture** (published in Athens by the Centre for Asia Minor Studies, 1996) is an excellent introduction to the subject which, though primarily about dance, also covers important festivals and customs and the social role of music and musicians. A fine bibliography lists works of significant Greek musicological researchers, anthropologists and travellers. This book can be found most easily, and most reasonably priced (c.€12), at the Centre for Asia Minor Studies (Kydhathinéon 11) as well at the Folk Art Museum (Kydhathinéon 17) Plaka neighbourhood of Athens. Otherwise, contact Yvonne Hunt, 4837 38th NE, Seattle, WA 98105, USA Ⓔbg901@scn.org (North American price $25).

The Dodecanese

Of all the island groups in Greece, the **Dodecanese** arguably have the most vital musical tradition, owing to their isolation from the mainland, mutual separation and (until 1943) the political and emotional charge associated with preserving age-old customs in the face of Italian persecution.

In particular, the southerly arc of islands comprising Kássos, Kárpathos and Hálki is still one of the most promising areas for hearing live music at any season of the year. The dominant instrument here is the **lýra**, a pear-shaped, three-stringed fiddle played upright balanced on the thigh, with strings facing out; these are stopped with lateral action of the fingernails, and the bow held with the hand palm up. The Dodecanisian *lýra* is one variant of four similarly shaped instruments played in Greece. In Kárpathos, small bells are attached to the bow, providing rhythmic accompaniment as the bow moves. Three metal strings are tuned in fifths (G, D, A); melody is played on the outer two, while the middle one serves as a drone. The G-string is tuned one whole step below the A (rather than a fifth below the D).

At **Ólymbos**, north **Kárpathos** (see box on p.161), this instrument commonly accompanies *mandinádhes*. Similar to the ones sung in Crete, in alternation with instrumental interludes, these **rhymed couplets** about local personalities and incidents are often improvised on the spot, and may satirize, eulogize, commemorate, tease, and wish well, fresh verses being thought up during the instrumental interludes. (In Kálymnos, such couplets are called *pismatiká*.) There are also set phrases, as well as entire couplets, which have entered the traditional canon. **Kássos** is a rich repository for melodies and lyrics, which find favour even on neighbouring Kárpathos; many are based on the events of the 1824 Kassian holocaust.

Usually the *lýra* is backed up by one or more *laoúta*, a member of the long-necked lutes family, its name derived from the Arabic *al'ud* (known as the oud in the West). The *laoúto* shares the large rounded back of the oud (traditionally made with many wood-staves curled and joined over a mould), but unlike the short-necked, fretless, gut-strung oud, more resembles the old Byzantine *tambourás* in having a long neck with moveable frets and metal courses (pairs of strings each tuned in octaves. Interestingly, older *laoúta* (pl.) had the peg-head bent back from the neck as does the oud. The *laoúto* fulfils a strongly rhythmic role in most music from the Dodecanese, with few chord changes.

At several places in the Dodecanese, particularly northern Kárpathos, Kálymnos and Pátmos, a primitive (yet difficult to play, like many folk instruments) goatskin **bagpipe** with a double chanter – the *tsamboúna* – is heard, on its own or with the *lýra* and *laoúto*. The *tsamboúna* has no drone and two parallel chanters made of calamus reed. The left chanter does not vary between island groups, having five holes which allow an incomplete diatonic scale from "do" to "fa". The right chanter is of three types, with anywhere from two to five holes depending on the island. Some form of this instrument probably reached Greece from Asia Minor during late Roman times, though bagpipes have evolved independently (and more or less simultaneously) in most pastoral societies across Eurasia. During the colonels' dictatorship the playing of bagpipes was banned on some of the more accessible islands, lest foreigners think the Greeks too "primitive". The *lýra*'s tonal range matches that of the *tsamboúna* played in the Dodecanese and can be played alone; with *laoúto*; with *tsamboúna*; or both of these together, often accompanying vocalists.

On most of the other Dodecanese, you'll find the *lýra* replaced by a more familiar-looking **violí**, essentially a western violin, which reached Greece during the seventeenth century. The violin bridge may be sanded in Greece to a less highly arched form than that used for Western classical music (something done as well in some Western folk traditions). An alternate **tuning** known as *álla Toúrka*, more widespread in the past, is still used by some musicians on certain islands (eg, Kós). From high to low, its string values are D, A, D and G, with a fourth between the two higher-pitched strings instead of the typical all-fifths arrangement. The lowered high string is slacker and "sweeter", and the violin's tonality altered by the modified tuning. Some violinists have reported being pressured to tune *álla Fránga*, ie the standard European tuning with "E" on top. It is claimed that violin techniques on these islands mimic *lýra* techniques (past and present).

In some locales, music for **unaccompanied voices** exists: Arhángelos on **Rhodes**, generally conceded to be the musical capital of the island, is known for *kanákia* or wedding songs, based on Byzantine hymns and (supposedly) imperial palace music. Peculiar to **Hálki** are *helidhonísmata* or "**swallow songs**", chanted since Roman times in early March to welcome these birds, heralds of spring.

Kálymnos preserves a vibrant musicality, heavily reliant on *tsamboúna* and *violí*; the distinctive Kalymniot violin style features a fairly aggressive bow "attack", dubbed *khtipitó* or "beaten" by some players on neighbouring **Kós**. This is just one of many examples of audibly different violin styles between contiguous islands (though the difference may not be apparent unless one hears consecutive recordings of the same pieces from the two islands). One of Kós' older violinists, **Gavrilis Yialitzis** (d. 2001), made three recordings during the 1990s (see discography) with **Manolis Poyias**, who plays accordion, *sandoúri* (see below) and sings. Poyias still performs on Kós with **Manolis Kefalianos**, a violinist in his fifties who may well be the island's finest living violinist. Look for a planned CD sometime in the near future with this violinist, joined by Poyias on accordion, and Yiorgos Skarpathiotakis on Cretan *laoúto* (or ask where you might hear them should you visit Kós).

Despite its modest size, even on Kálymnos music shows regional characteristics; for instance, melodies and rhythms from Árgos, Aryinónda and Skália supposedly differ from those of the rest of the island. A legend claims that these villagers are descendants of Argive stragglers from the Trojan war; the village name of Árgos, and the fact that their *syrtós* exists only in one other, Peloponnesian Argolid village, are cited in support of this hypothesis.

The Kalymnian *mihanikós*, danced only by men, consists of two alternating melodies, one fast and one slow. During the slow melody, the dancers mimic the movements of sponge divers crippled by the "bends" (see box p.257) – an occupational hazard which afflicted many men in the Dodecanese for generations – then break into a faster dance, only to return to miming their affliction.

The *thymariótikos*, another dance found on Kálymnos, originally comes from Epirus on the northwest Greek mainland, where it is known as the *himariótikos* (after its village of origin, Heimara, now in Albania). This begins as a men's dance with an unusual clockwise *syrtós* (instead of the usual counter-clockwise movement elsewhere in Greece). Then the melody changes, a counter-clockwise *kalamatianós* takes over and the dancers launch into a song with lyrics from Asia Minor about a dark haired girl (dark eyes, hair, and even eyebrows being commonly praised features in many Greek songs).

If you remember Nikos Kazantzakis's classic novel (or the movie) *Zorba the Greek*, his hero played a *sandoúri* (**hammer dulcimer**) – though according to one *sandoúri* player who saw the film, Zorba (Anthony Quinn) was playing his upside down(!). Today, accomplished players of this difficult instrument are few, and it's usually relegated to a supporting role in *nisiótika*; in actual fact it was hardly known in the Dodecanese until well into the twentieth century, when Anatolian refugee musicians introduced it. The *sandoúri* is scarcely used on Kálymnos, as the local melodic intervals are unsuited to its chromatic tuning; by contrast, on neighbouring Léros, Pátmos and Lipsí it's one of the favourite instruments at festival times.

East Aegean islands

There's more obvious Anatolian and Constantinopolitan influence in both the music and instrumentation of these islands. Largely because of the refugee background of its population, there has never been much of an indigenous musical tradition on **Sámos**. Matters are rather better on adjacent **Ikaría**, where skilled musicians still perform in the west of the island at spring and

A selective discography

Almost every island described in this book is represented in the following discography; that said, coverage is thin and much has been lost by the failure to record worthy vernacular musicians. All the titles below are pressed in Greece, and fairly easily obtainable at any of the stores listed in the box on p.479.

Uniform series

The "**Songs of** . . . " releases issued by the Society for the Dissemination of National Music (Greece) is an older, inexpensive series collected from the 1950s through the 1970s under the supervision of Simon Karas. There are presently more than thirty of these, each covering one geographical area or type of traditional music. All (except the cassettes) include notes in English, and are available as LPs, cassettes or CDs.

Songs of Kassos and Karpathos (SDNM 103). The Kárpathos side is unremittingly poignant (or monotonous, depending on your tastes), enlivened by interesting passages on the *tsamboúna*. You'll still hear material like this at Ólymbos festivals. The Kássos side is more sweetly melodic, closer to Crete both musically and geographically.

Songs of Rhodes, Chalki and Symi (SDNM 104). The pieces from Sými are the most accessible, while those from Rhodes and Hálki show considerable Cretan influence. All material was recorded in the early 1970s; you're fairly unlikely to hear similar pieces live today, though Sými retains the instrumentation (*violí*, *sandoúri*) heard here.

Songs of Mytilene and Chios (SDNM 110), **Songs of Mytilene and Asia Minor** (SDNM 125). The Mytilene (Lésvos) sides are the highlight of each of these discs. Sublime instrumental and vocal pieces, again from the mid-1970s. Most selections are from the south of the island, particularly Ayiássos, where a tradition of live festival music was – and still is – strong.

Songs of Ikaria & Samos (SDNM 128). Much older material, from the 1950s; even then it was obvious that indigenous styles here were dying out, as there is extensive reliance on "cover versions" of songs common to all the east Aegean and Anatolian refugee communities, and the music – mostly choral with string accompaniment – is executed by the SDNM "house band" of the time. The Ikarian side is the more distinctive, though marred by irritating voice-over narration.

Songs of the North and East Aegean (SDNM CD7). Features music of Límnos, Thássos, Samothráki, Lésvos and Híos including local dances (*pyrgoúsikos, kehayiádhikos)* using local musicians recorded during the early 1970s.

Island-wide/archipelago anthologies

Paradosiaki Skopi kai Tragoudia tis Dodekanisiou: Mousika Taxidhia (CD E2–205 by the Kinotita Asfendhiou Kos). The final, 1996 recording of violinist Gavrilis Yialitzis of Kós island, with Manolis Poyias on accordion, *sandoúri* and some vocals. Their instrumental version of the wedding song *Tou gambrou* (The Groom's) is a wonderful example of Kós violin style. Poyias also appears on other 1990s recordings not on CD: 1994 **Omorfa Dodekanisa** (LP produced by Dimitris Kasiotis Bonapartis) and **Ta Dika Mas** (1995 LP and cassette) with Anna Karabessini.

Seryiani sta Nisia Mas (MBI 10371.2). Excellent CD compilation of various *nisiótika* artists and hits from the 1950s and 1960s, with Emilia Hatzidhaki (from Léros) and sisters Ann Karabessini and Efi Sarri (from Kós) all well represented. The high point is arguably Emilia Hatzidhaki's rendition of *Bratsera*, a song particular to Léros and Kálymnos.

Anatolika tou Egeou/East of the Aegean (Verso CD101). Nikos Ikonomidhis, though born in the islet of Skhinoússa near Náxos, has become an adopted son of Híos. One of the more traditional violinists under fifty years of age, he leads this set of lively dance tunes, with a few songs thrown in (he is a fine singer as well) all from the east Aegean islands. There's more genuinely Samian material here than on the SDNM disc, but the recording is marred by a persistently heavy electric bass line.

Ellines Akrites/The Guardians of Hellenism (FM Records). Vol. 1 of this series, "Chios, Mytilene, Samos, Ikaria" (FM 801) is a solid, if rather studio-ish, acoustic session of standards from each of the islands cited; vocalist Stratis Rallis, who also appears on the *Lesvos Aiolis* disc, is featured here on most of the Mytilíni (Lésvos) tracks, which make up nearly half the disc. Vol. 2 (FM 802), "Lemnos, Samothrace, Imbros, Tenedos", features excellent local *violí/lýra* players, plus top violinist Kyriakos Gouvendas from Thessaloníki. Volumes 9–11 (unreviewed) cover the entire Dodecanese.

Individual artists

Anna Karabessini & Effi Sarri Two singing sisters born at Andimáhia on the island of Kós during the 1930s. Performing only for private gatherings added to their status. *To Yialo Yialo Piyeno* from 1975 was one of their first big recording hits, reissued on CD (Lyra 0102067.2). Two other available CDs are *Tis Thalassas* (Lyra 10777) and *Ena Glendi* (Lyra 10717).

Emilia Hatzidhaki *Thalassina Tragoudhia* (LP: Panvox 16311, reissued as CD by Lyra-MBI). The sole easily available collection dedicated to this artist, who otherwise appears only on *nisiótika* anthologies.

Individual islands

Kassos: Skopi tis Lyras/Lyra Melodies of Kassos (Lyra-Papingo CD0113). Recordings of three generations of musicians from the Perselis clan caught live at a 1993 festival.

Tragoudhia keh Skopi tis Kalymnou/Songs and Melodies of Kalymnos (Syrtos 564). Harsh but haunting songs reminiscent of Kálymnos itself. No longer part of the island's repertoire but revived in this 1993 production by native musicologist Manolis Karpathios, featuring *tsamboúna*, *laoúto* and *violí*.

Skopi tis Kalymnou/Kalymnian Folk Music (Lykio ton Ellinidhon E2-276-97). Double CD with excellent notes and song translations. Traditional Kalymnian repertoire and native musicians features septagenerian Mikes Tsounias on violin, his young grandson playing unison violin on some pieces, plus good *tsamboúna* accompaniment.

Tis Leros ta Tragoudhia/The Songs of Leros (Politistikos ke Morfotikos Syllogos Neon Lerou/Instructive & Cultural Lerian Youth Society). Double CD produced by Music Folklore Archive. Live field recordings from 1996 and 1998 of island musicians and singers; *violí*, *sandoúri*, *laoúto*, and *tsamboúna* in various combinations, plus unaccompanied singing. Each disc finishes with an archival track of bygone greats Emilia Hatzidhaki and Manolis Skoumbouridhis, both Lerian.

Kastellorizo (Syrtos 561). Another Manolis Karpathios production, but the material, while worthy, is somewhat marred by studio-introduced echo.

Tragoudhia keh Skopi tis Patmou/Songs and Melodies of Patmos (Politistikon Idhryma Dhodhekanisou, Athens, CD 201). Yet another Karpathios project, but certainly the best of the three: live 1995 field recordings of well-edited pieces as raw but compelling as you'd hear them at a good festival. Local working singers and instrumentalists on *violí*, *tsamboúna* and (unlike Kálymnos) *sandoúri*.

Lesvos Aiolis: Tragoudhia keh Khori tis Lesvou/Songs & Dances of Lesvos (University Press of Crete/Panepistimiakes Ekdhoseis Kritis 9–10, 2 CDs). A decades' worth (1986–96) of field recordings of the last traditional music extant on the island, a labour of love supervised by musicologist Nikos Dhionysopoulos. Fairly pricey, but the quality and uniqueness of the instrumental pieces especially, and the monstrous, well-written and well-illustrated booklet, merit the expense.

Lesvos: Mousika Stavrodhromia sto Egeo/Musical Crossroads of the Aegean (University of the Aegean/Panepistimiou tou Egeou). A 5-CD set with an enormous book accompanying it: wonderful photos of many ensembles, seated and in street processions. Everything from Asia Minor music played in Lésvos (including some wonderful unaccompanied solo *taxímia* – unmetered solos in a particular mode) to carols, bawdy songs for *Apókries* and wedding songs. Again very pricey but worth it.

Thalassa Thymisou/Sea of Memories: Tragoudhia ke Skopi apo tis Inousses (Navtiko Mousio Inousson-En Khordais CD 1801/1802). The result of a "field trip" by the En Khordais traditional music school of Thessaloníki to Inoússes, a small islet northeast of Híos, to rescue vanishing traditional material with the help of the islanders' long memories; the result's superb, a mix of live sessions in Inoussan tavernas and some studio recordings. Thorough and intelligent notes, but no lyrics translations.

summer monastery-festivals, when goat skins, in no short supply on Ikaría, appear in the form of *tamboúnes*. On his recording *Anatolika tou Egeou* (see discography) **Nikos Ikonomidhis** plays an outstanding *kariótikos*, the most popular dance from this island, a fiddler's delight made up of set melodic fragments joined in spontaneous sequence. This is the real article, not to be confused with the eponymous, much more commercial, song written by Yiorgos Konitopoulos of Náxos.

On **Híos**, the more typical Aegean **violí**, **laoúto**, **and sandoúri** are played, as well as **tsamboúna** accompanied by the smaller two-headed drum called **toumbáki**. The latter is suspended to one side of the player's torso by a strap, and only one of the two heads is struck with two wooden (or bone) drumsticks. Of Hiot dances Yvonne Hunt writes: "Here the *syrtós* and *bállos* are frequently danced to lovely, lilting tunes. A form of the *syrtós* here is commonly referred to as *hiótikos*. It is done by couples moving counter-clockwise, each man leading his partner through his own series of variations . . . Though based on the same step found on so many of the Aegean islands, it is performed by crossing in front of the opposite foot on the slow count, which creates a definitive style that is not found on other islands." She also writes of the *Pyrgoúsikos* (from the village of Pyrgí): "a dance for groups of three, two men and one woman. A handkerchief links the first man and the woman while she and the second man are in a *klistó* (closed) handhold with fingers intertwined. The lines are directed wherever the leader desires, moving forward and backwards. The leader is free to improvise, performing squats, turning, forming a 'bridge', etc. After a while the two men change positions and the new leader will then do his variations . . . traditionally performed to the music of the *tsamboúna* . . . and the *toumbáki,* although these instruments are being rapidly replaced by . . . electrified instruments."

The island of **Límnos** also has its own dances, such as the *kehayiádikos*, a shepherd's dance "performed in a circle without the dancers holding on to each other…"(Yvonne Hunt). This dance is in a 7/8 rhythm (3+2+2) and the dancers do squats and leg-slaps at certain moments. Says Hunt: "Límnos is one of the few [east Aegean] islands on which the *lýra* can still be found . . . Unfortunately it will disappear from here also as younger members of the society have not learned to play it. The only hope is that someone will learn before the last generation of *lýra*-playing musicians is lost."

Lésvos (**Mytilíni**) occupies a special place in terms of island music; even before the turbulent decade of 1912–22 (followed by the influx of thousands of Asia Minor refugees), its "mainland" was Asia Minor rather than Greece, its urban poles Smyrna and Constantinople instead of Athens. Accordingly its musical tradition is far more varied and sophisticated than the Aegean norm, having absorbed melodies and instrumentation from the various groups who lived in neighbouring Anatolia; for example, Lésvos is the only island with a vital tradition of both brass bands and clarinet-playing, and virtually every pan-Hellenic dance rhythm is represented in local music. Favourite local dances are the **karsilamás** and the **zeïbékiko**, dances from Asia Minor. The latter, though it became famous as a solo dance with the *rebétika* music of the 1920s through the 1950s, is often danced in Lésvos by men in a circular formation, each doing his own movements.

Violin, *sandoúri* and guitar tuned like a *laoúto* – which itself is uniquely absent from the extraordinarily rich Mytilinian instrumental panoply – accompany *zeïbékika*; the violin is oddly often included in the **brass bands** which traditionally accompanied wedding marches or marked the start of horse-racing or bull-sacrificing festivals, part of the still-vital *paniyíri* tradition here. The keyed, single-reed European **clarinet** or *klaríno* – as opposed to the simpler, double-reed *zournás* – was unknown in Greece before 1830, and (depending on whom you believe) was introduced either by gypsies or Bavarians attached to the first royal court. As on the Anatolian mainland opposite, the lap drum (*toumbeléki*) or shoulder drum (*daoúli*) are preferred rhythm accompaniments to the clarinet. Other imports include the *gáïda* or bagpipe-with-drone of the northern mainland, instead of the *tsamboúna* known elsewhere in the Aegean; the accordion (also played on Kós); and of course the *bouzoúki*, which has in recent decades swept across most of the islands.

Susan Raphael, with Marc Dubin

Greek recording sources

UK

Trehantiri 367 Green Lanes, London N4 1DY ⓣ020/8802 6530. Run by the helpful Akis Patellis, with caches of rare/out-of-print discs, and also a worldwide mail-order service.

USA

Down Home Music 10341 San Pablo Ave, El Cerrito, CA 94530 ⓣ510/525-2129, ⓦwww.downhomemusic. Respectable Greek section in this Aladdin's Cave for world music enthusiasts.

Greece: Athens

Except for the first listing, the following shops lie within a few hundred yards of each other in central Athens, making it feasible to pop into all of them if you have half a day in Athens between connecting flights. All except the musical instrument museum and Okh Aman (both metro Monastiráki) are a few steps from the Panepistimíou metro station.

Museum of Greek Popular Musical Instruments Dhioyénous 1–3, Pláka (Tues & Thurs–Sun 10am–2pm, Wed noon–8pm). The gift shop of this highly worthwhile museum is a reliable if somewhat pricey spot to snag a range of folk recordings, including a few SDNM titles.

Xylouris Panepistimíou 39, in arcade. Run by the gregarious widow of Cretan musician Nikos Xylouris, this is usually the best spot for Greek folk recordings; despite the tiny space, stocks items unavailable elsewhere, in various formats.

Metropolis Multibranch chain. The one at Panepistimíou 54 has all musics; the outlet at no. 64 is for Greek music only.

Tzina Panepistimíou 57. Reasonable if somewhat chaotically organized stock (strictly CD), including its own label (Venus-Tzina) of *nisiótika* recordings.

Music Corner Cnr of Panepistimíou and Emmanouíl Benáki. Small but well-selected stock includes some of the better island recordings.

Okh Aman! Market Iféstou 24, Monastiráki. The best outlet for second-hand Greek music, all genres. Mostly vinyl, in good condition and well organized; some CDs as well.

Greece: Thessaloníki

In case you find yourself here between planes en route to Límnos, Lésvos, Híos, Sámos, or Rhodes, there are two good possibilities:

En Khordais Margariti 1, Platía Ippodhromíou. Lower-ground-floor shop devoted to traditional musical instruments and a careful selection of folk recordings. An affiliate of the traditional music school across the road.

Studio 52 Dhimitríou Goúnari 46. Cavernous basement premises, the oldest store in town, with lots of rare vinyl and cassettes, plus well-sorted CDs.

In addition, the capital towns of Rhodes, Kós, Kálymnos, Sámos, Híos and Lésvos all have decently stocked record shops where you can be fairly sure of finding at least a couple of the titles listed above.

The islands in literature

Secrets of Sými

William Travis and his wife Caroline came to live on Sými during the mid-1960s when it was still well off the tourist route, much less home to an expatriate community. Having set aside a bit of money in the yacht charter business, Travis was able to stay for three years, putting his boating skills to use along an island coast tailor-made for small craft. *Bus Stop Symi*, originally published in 1970 by Rap & Whiting, and unfortunately long out of print, is the chronicle of their time there. This extract is reproduced with the kind permission of Watson, Little Ltd.

The German forces finally abandoned Sými in December of 1944. When orders for their withdrawal were received they contained the instruction that the considerable stocks of explosives and munitions held on the island were to be destroyed rather than shipped elsewhere. At that time the major portion of these stores were held in numerous warehouses scattered about the town and, lacking time perhaps to move the explosives up into the hills and wishing to destroy them in one operation, German working parties set about the task of consolidating the various caches into one central dump. The final site selected for the operation was an unfortunate one.

The physical and spiritual centre of Symi's township is the old acropolis, a rocky outcrop atop the hillock separating the Upper and Lower Towns. This natural eminence bears upon it a complete record of the islet's human history, for Neolithic, Pelasgian, Classical, Roman, Byzantine, Crusader, Frankish, Venetian, Turkish and Italian remains can be traced there, often tiered one upon another within its one-acre extent. In 1944 the acropolis was topped by one of the island's finest churches, the Church of the Ascension of the Virgin, whilst around the base of the low cliffs on which it was perched clustered a whole complex of houses, storerooms and buildings belonging to the wealthier merchants of the Upper Town. It was here that the retiring German troops decided to consolidate their munitions and destroy them. A regrettable necessity of war made infinitely more regrettable owing to two grim factors. Firstly, the chosen method of destruction was by blowing up the whole dump and, secondly, and far more serious, the civilians living in and about the area were not consulted nor warned of the operation. In fact, some unknown officer had given precise instructions to the soldiers taking part that the whole scheme was to be carried out with the strictest military secrecy. Luckily for Symi, these orders were not obeyed.

Rudi – big, blond and Bavarian – Symi has no record of your surname, only of your religion which was Catholic, and your rank which was corporal. You, toiling day-long with your men, carrying ammunition boxes up the cobbled streets to their final destination beneath the walls of Our Lady of the Ascension, continually asked those of the villagers you met with and knew by sight: "Hey, Symiot – when is the celebration of the Ascent of the Virgin?" and when they replied, saying "August 15th of course, but why do you ask?" – you gave the cryptic reply: "Wrong, quite wrong. Ask me tomorrow and I'll tell you . . ."

And the next day you said the same and the day following as well. But by then your conundrum was well known, with people openly discussing the riddle, seeking to see within it some present application and, consequently, when on the fourth day you gave your version of the date of the Virgin's Ascension as . . . "tonight at eight you will see Her rise. Tonight at eight, mark you!" – it did not take the townsfolk long to tumble to your meaning. All that day, as unseen as mice behind the wainscot, the people of the Upper Town moved bed and baggage and what valuables they could from door to door and balcony to balcony, down a long corridor of neighbourly hands, to relatives and friends in other areas. Old people were carried piggy-back and small children in baskets. Caged birds went too, and so did those few cats that had remained uneaten. By dusk all was quiet and all was deserted with no sign of life about the citadel other than those few German soldiers detailed to guard the hidden mine. At eight o'clock an observer on a distant campanile saw two blobs of yellow light moving down the hill away from the doomed area and at exactly ten past eight the Church of the Virgin *did* ascend in a sheet of flame and with a roar that shattered windows throughout the town, besides totally demolishing over 260 houses adjacent to the acropolis. Had not a Bavarian corporal muttered his riddle to those he passed, how many Symiots might have died in that explosion? Five hundred perhaps – maybe more. As it was, the only fatality was an octogenarian known as Maria who, when told of what was going on, said: "I was born in this house. I have knelt in this one church all my life. I shall die here in my house along with my church" – and did.

And Rudi, what of Rudi, I asked?

Did anyone in the town ever hear from him afterwards? Did he write to those he had saved or did anyone seek to contact him?

"Hah! Rudi – no, he never wrote," I was told. "And you know why not, Vassili? The Germans left here the following day on board a ship that had called to collect them. Within an hour of leaving it struck a mine or was torpedoed. Out of the four-hundred-odd people on board some seventeen were saved. But not Rudi . . ."

The Church of the Virgin of the Ascension went up and within hours Rudi – surname unrecorded, Bavarian, a Catholic, serving as a corporal in the German Army occupying Greece – went down.

Thus war's see-saw.

****

One morning, shopping in Yalou, I came across a unique scene. There, clustered around a long table in the little square known as Pallas Athene – on account of the plaster statue of that Britannia-like deity which surmounts the gable of a house overlooking it – was a strange mixture of Symiots. At one end sat the mayor, Dr Nikitiades, flanked by his secretary and the Town Clerk. At the other sprawled the curly-bearded, piratical figure of Papas Anastasius with, in turn, two of his acolytes. Plumb in the middle of the table stood an ornate silver candlestick and in it a standard yellow offertory candle. Between the two groups and standing, not sitting, were a line of Symiot shepherds – lanky, sun-blackened creatures, characterized by their beautiful and uniform soft boots and divergent crooks.

"What goes on?" I asked.

"It's the auction of the grazing on Nimos [the islet just north of Symi], Vassili. It happens every four years."

"But what happens?" I insisted.

"Wait and see," I was told.

After a mumbled prayer Papas Anastasius lit the taper and silence fell. For five minutes nothing happened till the mayor, out of the blue said "Twenty thousand . . ." – thus setting, so I was told in a whisper, the arbitrary minimum price acceptable by the community as rent for that particular auction. Again silence, till a puff of wind caused the candle-flame to gutter. "Twenty-two", "Twenty-four", "Twenty-eight . . ." – the shouts came tumbling one upon the other for, as I now learnt the winner of the auction was he whose bid was uttered last before the candle went out – whether blown out by wind or burnt out by time. The sudden breeze dropped, the flame steadied and the bidding lapsed. Another five minutes passed, with random bids made partly in jest and partly by way of testing out the opposition, and the grazing rights stood at an even thirty thousand. The bidders grew silent, with eyes on the candle, for the day was calm and further wind-eddies seemed unlikely. There remained but a quarter-inch of wax before the offers started up once more, and then the cries flew thick and fast across the table: "Thirty-five, thirty-seven, thirty-seven fifty, thirty-eight two . . ." – the stump dissolved into a pool of dark wax overflowing the holder and still the little flame lived on. "Forty-one, forty-one and a half, forty-two, forty-two and two, forty-two and four . . ." – but it was too late, the flame had gone out in a little puff of oily smoke and the bidder of forty-two thousand and two hundred drachma had won the right to graze five hundred sheep on Nimos islet for the next four years. Making a quick calculation in my head I said to my companion: "But surely nearly eighty-five drachma per head is expensive grazing, when sheep and goats can free-range here on Symi? And which poor shepherd can afford to put down six hundred pounds in hard cash for the privilege, anyway?"

"Ssh, Vassili – it's not just the grazing, you ignorant foreigner! He who has the right to graze his sheep on Nimos has the right to go there anytime, right? Without causing comment or arousing suspicion. And the far side of Nimos faces Anatolia and can't be seen from Yalou or Horio, right? What better place to use as a starting point for a little trip to Turkey, eh – or at which to unload ships coming back . . . Nimos is uninhabited, remember? Now do you understand why some people give the shepherds money with which to bid? And what does it matter? The community chest gains ten thousand drachma a year it would not otherwise see and, if it were not Nimos, there would be some other place used for this night-traffic across to Turkey . . ."

Crooked captains

A diaspora Greek two generations removed from Kássos, bleakest of the Dodecanese, Elias Kulukundis visited his ancestral island for the first time in 1964. The result of a lengthy stay was *Journey to a Greek Island*, published by Cassell, London, in 1968, and now out of print. Often reading like non-fiction García Márquez, it is unsurpassed as an introductory exploration to local history, anthropology and genealogy, not just Kassian but Dodecanesian.

Like a number of other relatively barren Greek isles, Kássos has long made its living from the sea. At the time of the 1821 uprising, it possessed the fourth largest island fleet after Ídhra, Spétses and Psará. Of these, only Kássos remained a maritime power after independence, and Kassiots are still disproportionately represented in the contemporary Greek shipping industry. In his discussion of the history of Kasiot seafaring, Kulukundis does not shy away from the subject of piracy – occasionally indulged in by the islanders during the first half of the last century. What follows, however, details the other, less well-known practice of barratry.

It was customary at that time, as it is today, for the cargo owner to charter a captain's ship at a given rate. After the agreement had been reached, the captain would simply load the cargo on his ship and sail away with it, and unless the charterer posted a representative or supercargo to accompany the ship and protect his interests, he would have to trust the captain for the duration of the voyage. The voyages of sailing ships lasted several weeks, and during that time, anything might happen. The captain might encounter heavy weather and find himself in danger of foundering unless he lightened his ship by jettisoning all his extra masts and rigging and even a portion of the cargo if necessary. In that event, under the laws of general average, the captain would not be responsible for the loss of cargo, and it would have to be sustained solely by the charterer. This was where certain captains were cunning enough to see a special opportunity. A captain might not encounter heavy weather at all, only *claim* to have encountered it.

The coasts of the Aegean Islands and mainland Greece are full of tiny coves, secret places where a ship might put in unnoticed, under the cover of a moonless night. There, by prearrangement, a caique might come out to meet the ship, and as it drew alongside, the captain might strike a stealthy bargain with the caique's owner to *sell* him a portion of the cargo. After the agreement had been concluded, a portion of the cargo would be lowered into the caique. The captain would sail out onto the high seas again, then to the island of Zante where there were certain legal experts. They could doctor the log of the voyage to show that on such and such a day, under the stress of heavy weather, the captain had found it necessary to jettison his extra masts and spars and sails (items which might never have existed) as well as that portion of the cargo he had actually sold. At the conclusion of the voyage, the captain would enjoy a double profit: the rate of hire agreed upon with the charterer, plus the proceeds of the sale. Then, his winter's work done in a single voyage, he could return to his native island and roister in the café.

The practice was widespread in the Aegean after the [Greek] Revolution, taking the place of piracy of old. The island of Zante, which had probably begun as a natural haven for mariners after a storm, became a nest of log-doctorers. Gradually, it became so common for captains to put into Zante after the sale of cargo, that underwriters refused to pay a claim if the ship had stopped there for any reason. Meanwhile, the Greek Government, anxious to protect the reputation of its growing merchant marine, ran down offenders and imposed heavy penalties on them. And wherever Greek captains were suspected of barratry, the Greek Government posted a consul to report any illegal sales.

Barratry became very popular among certain Kasiots. It appealed to their naturally wily nature, as much for its own sake as for any profit it would yield. They would sail home to Kasos, anchor outside the Bucca [the port] and sell a portion of the cargo to the island merchants. Then, sending the ship on to Zante to its doctors, they would ascend victorious to the café.

But no Kassiot ever got rich on barratry, and the names of the barrators have dropped long ago from the shipping history of the island. After the captain had sold the cargo, he would be open to blackmail at the hands of his very accomplices; and often in the years ahead, he would have to pay out much more than he had made by the original transaction.

Sometime in the latter half of the nineteenth century, a Kasiot captain whom we can call Captain Nikos put into Salonika to find a cargo. It was a very slack season, and cargoes were difficult to find, so for lack of anything better he contracted with two Jewish rabbis to carry a cargo of flagstones at a very unprofitable rate. But the rabbis rubbed salt into his wounds.

"You're a Kasiot, aren't you?" they said.

Captain Nikos said he was.

"Well, in that case we shall have to post supercargoes to keep watch over our flagstones."

"Very well," said Captain Nikos, taking no offense at this discrimination. "Who will be your supercargoes?"

"We will," said the rabbis. "Both of us."

"You will?" said Captain Nikos, smiling. "Very well."

So the rabbis packed their belongings and prepared to sail with Captain Nikos to keep watch over their flagstones. And in the meantime, Captain Nikos was thinking: "Two supercargoes to watch over flagstones? What must they think of me? If I sold all their stones at twice their value, I still would not make enough to pay for my expenses. But very well. Let them come if they wish. I will see they have an exciting voyage."

In the meantime, an idea had grown on him. The rabbis had heard so much about the mischief of certain Kasiots, Captain Nikos thought he could not very well disappoint them. Since they distrusted him so openly, even with a cargo of flagstones, he would not be one to let them down. He would sell their cargo anyway, worthless as it was, under their very noses.

So Captain Nikos set sail from Salonika, already smirking over what he planned; and the two rabbis sailed with him. Standing stiffly on either side of the tiller in their black robes and beards and broad brimmed black hats, they watched Captain Nikos with eagle eyes. When the ship sailed out beyond the harbour, a strong wind came up. And although the rabbis did not realize it, Captain Nikos did what any seaman knows not to do. He steered the ship broadside to the wind, so that immediately it began to roll.

"What's that?" said the rabbis, taken by surprise.

"The wind," said Captain Nikos.

"Ah, the wind," said the rabbis solemnly, composing themselves once again on either side of Captain Nikos. But now the ship was rolling so fiercely they had trouble keeping their balance. Though neither of them said a word and did not even look at each other, very soon they were both pale as ghosts.

"Is this normal?" said one rabbi at last, in a voice weak with nausea and with fear.

"As normal as the wind," said Captain Nikos.

"But what will hapen?"

"I don't know. If you wish, you may go below where you can lie down and be more comfortable."

The rabbis looked at each other. For one longing moment they looked in the direction of their cabin. But at last, bravely, they decided against it.

"No, we must stay here to keep watch over our flagstones," they said.

"Very well," said Captain Nikos, raising his voice above the wind and water. "But if you must stand here, at least take hold of something. I'm afraid you may be thrown into the sea."

At that moment, appearing to be steering carefully in the face of danger, Captain Nikos turned the wheel violently one way and then the other, so that the ship plunged down towards the menacing white water, reprieving itself from catastrophe at the last moment, only to plunge down toward it again on the other side.

"But what is happening?" cried the rabbis. "Is this a storm?"

"Yes," said Captain Nikos, "a storm."

"Is it a bad one? Is it dangerous?"

"Any storm is a bad one, but this is the most dangerous storm I have ever seen."

"God of Moses. But what will happen? Will we drown?"

"We may," said Captain Nikos. "We are so heavy and the wind is so strong that at any moment we may go over."

"Go over? You mean into the sea?"

"Into the sea."

"God of Aaron, and is there nothing we can do?"

"Do? What should we do?"

"Is there nothing we can do to save ourselves?"

"Of course."

"What?"

"Pray. Pray to your God."

"Pray to our God? Is there nothing else?"

"Is that not enough?"

"God of Moses, is there nothing we can do to save ourselves? If we are so heavy, can't we lighten?"

"Lighten? How lighten?"

"If a ship is too heavy, they say the captain can throw some of the cargo overboard."

"Throw some of the cargo overboard?" said Captain Nikos. "You are asking me to throw some of the cargo overboard?"

"Why not?" cried the rabbis. "That would save us, wouldn't it? We would be lighter then, and we would be able to make it through this storm."

"Of course we would. We would be lighter in an instant, and the ship would right itself and be out of danger, and then there would be an end to this terrible sickness and dizziness and rolling first one way and then the other."

"Oh, dear God of Isaac, then let us lighten! God of Jacob, let us throw some of the cargo overboard."

"No," said Captain Nikos. "Upon my honour, as a captain and as a Kasiot, no."

"But why? Why in the name of God?"

"Because later, when we reached our destination, you would say we did not meet bad weather at all, that I didn't really throw the cargo overboard but sold it for my own profit. And as a Kasiot captain, I would rather drown than hear such accusations."

"Say you sold the cargo? Captain Nikos, put it out of your mind! We trust you completely!"

"Then why did you sail with me to watch over your cargo? That is the reason you find yourselves in this needless danger when you could be safe in your homes this very moment."

By now, the rabbis were close to tears.

"Oh why, Captain Nikos? We do not know why! We wish we had never sailed with you. But that is all forgotten. We promise you, on the bones of all the prophets, we shall never sail with you again. Only please, Captain Nikos, throw some of our flagstones overboard. You can trust us, Captain Nikos. We will sign a paper. We will do anything you say. Only please, Captain Nikos, before it is too late."

Captain Nikos deliberated for one unendurable moment.

"Very well," he said, "if you insist, I agree. But one of you must begin. That one." He pointed to one rabbi. "Let it be him. Let him cast the first stone."

"I will, I will," said the rabbi. "Only hurry, for the love of God, hurry before all is lost."

Captain Nikos directed his crew to open the cargo hatch and lift out one of the stones for the rabbi to throw overboard. As agreed, the rabbi awkwardly cast the first stone. Afterwards, at a signal from Captain Nikos, the seamen began to lift out a few of the stones, one by one, and throw them overboard. At that moment, Captain Nikos manipulated the wheel in such a way that a huge wave curled over the side and almost broke upon the rabbis.

"For the love of God," cried captain Nikos, "go below now, or the next wave will carry you away."

Without a word, the rabbis scurried below out of the menacing sea and wind. As soon as they disappeared, Captain Nikos ordered his men to stop what they were doing.

"What are you doing there, my lads?" he said. "Throwing stones into the sea? Have you lost your minds?"

Laughing, the crew stopped throwing stones into the sea, closed the hatch, and went about their business. After a discreet interval, Captain Nikos steered out of the wind, as even any landlubber knows he should. The ship righted itself, and the storm subsided into a placid Aegean afternoon.

The rabbis, by that time, were sound asleep. Delivered from the jaws of death and the terrible nausea which had menaced them far worse, they slept through the dinner hour and far into the night. And they were still asleep, near midnight, when Captain Nikos sailed into a deserted cove, and beckoning the owner of a caique to draw alongside, sold him the remaining flagstones. The next day, sailing toward their destination on an empty ship, the rabbis signed a paper Captain Nikos had prepared, attesting to the fact that the ship had met heavy weather a few miles out of Salonika, and at their insistence, the captain agreed to jettison the cargo. One of the rabbis, they admitted, had cast the first stone.

Captain Nikos' story became proverbial on Kasos. He was such a notorious barrator, he would sell flagstones for the sport of it, and he became the first Kasiot in history to get his supercargoes to doctor the log.

Lured from Léros

The British took over the administration of most of the Dodecanese, including Léros, in mid-September 1943, after the Italian capitulation. They had, as it turned out, barely two months in which to reinforce facilities inherited from the Italians against the massive German attack of November 12. Extra supplies could be landed by ship or submarine, but only under increasingly regular German air raids and via comprehensively laid minefields. The following self-contained interlude, narrated by a Maltese serviceman, is from a longer section devoted to Léros in *War in the Islands*, compiled by Adrian Seligman and reproduced by kind permission of Alan Sutton Publishing Ltd.

October [1943] was a disastrous month for the [British] Navy. Four cruisers, five more destroyers, an MTB, three MLs and numerous other smaller craft were lost or put out of action. The sowing of mines in the Kós and Kálymnos channels, and the arrival in the Aegean of the glider bomb, had completely altered the balance of power in the war at sea. The glider bomb in particular, launched and radio-controlled from an aircraft, and power-driven to its target with a warhead carrying well over 500lb of explosives, was a weapon against which there was no immediate defence . . .

From Navy House [a villa at Álynda used as British HQ] we had a clear view down the bay and out to sea. One night, early in November, we saw a glider bomb, easily recognizable by its red tail-light, pounce on a Brooklyn Yard Mine Sweeper (BYMS) passing the entrance to the bay. "Pounce" is an exact description of the way the bomb came cruising along, then suddenly tipped up and fell upon its wretched victim. The funnel and deck clutter aft took the full force of the explosion, thus saving the lives of the people in the great palace of a wheelhouse further forward. They now called us up to report the damage and request instructions. We signalled back telling the captain to make for Port Laki (Lakkí) round the northern end of the island. He would be met at the harbour entrance and piloted in.

I drove at top speed in my jeep down to the seaplane base [at Teménia on Lakkí Bay] to find our motor boat and, if possible, her crew. It was a moonlit night with a clear sky and [German] bombers overhead, which seemed to be concentrating on gun positions in the mountains and round the coast. I found our two boatmen turned fishermen, landing their evening's catch on the quay. We motored out to the harbour mouth and a mile or so beyond. In the bright moonlight, I remember, the sea looked black and bottomless. Then slowly round the northern cliffs and down past the Skrophes shoals came the BYMS which, we could see as she approached, had been badly damaged. And she was low in the water aft, where bomb splinters must have holed her. There was an air of silence about her above the slow, laboured beat of her screw turning at half speed.

I called her up with the recognition signal of the day, and when the correct reply came back I signalled "Follow me" and turned back towards the harbour mouth. Slowly she swung round after me, and we had almost reached the entrance, when all at once a loud voice speaking urgently in English rang out. I thought at first it must be the skipper of the BYMS calling us on his loud-hailer, but couldn't quite catch what he was saying. It sounded like a warning – certain the word "trap" came into it. Then to my horror, the BYMS began to alter course away down the coast toward German-held Kálymnos. I flashed and flashed, but there was no reply, and I realized that the voice on the loud-hailer was coming from somewhere to seaward.

There was nothing we could do but watch, appalled. The BYMS had increased to full speed, and it wasn't long before she rounded the southern headland of the bay and disappeared.

★★★★

By a remarkable coincidence, I heard the rest of the story in 1953, several years after the end of the war, from the captain of a "Hansa" cargo vessel on her maiden voyage out east. She was celebrating her first call at Chittagong with a party on board, and I, as manager of a firm of jute exporters, and therefore a major shipper, was received by the master personally. It wasn't long before we discovered that we had both been involved in the battle for Léros. And after we'd well-I-nevered and slapped each other on the back for a bit, Captain Loetzmann said, "I remember one night in particular, because it gave me my first chance of a decoration… I was just twenty, in command of an E-boat patrolling to the east of the island – and pretty pleased with myself, I've no doubt – when we saw what must have been one of the first glider-bomb attacks on a ship in the Mediterranean area. Poor creature, I felt sorry for her. She was a small and most unwarlike-looking craft with a tall and strangely palatial design of wheelhouse."

"Sure, she was a BYMS," I couldn't help butting in. "We were watching her from Navy House at the head of the bay."

The captain looked astonished. "Then it was you we saw signalling?"

"Not me personally, but never mind."

"Anyhow, that was when my four years at an English public school came in handy. I was able to read your signal."

"So you knew that she was bound for Port Laki north-about?"

"Indeed… and that gave me a better idea than wasting a torpedo on such an unimportant target. Instead I turned away to round the southern end of the island and be ready to meet and board her at my convenience." Loetzmann chuckled. "One gets a bit carried away when one's young. On the way round I called up Kálymnos, where we had two batteries of eighty-eights covered Léros strait, asking them . . . no, I expect I *told* them . . . on no account to fire on a small vessel which I proposed to board and capture. After that it was easy. When she was about to enter harbour I called her up from seaward by loud-hailer. I was down moon, so she couldn't see me properly. There was a small boat in the harbour entrance signalling her."

"That was me," I had to tell him, "and we could hear you shouting, but with your loud-hailer aimed at him, we could only make out odd words."

"I'm glad of that."

"Why?"

"Well, I hope you will forgive me, but what I said was: 'Take no notice of that fool flashing . . . it's an Italian trap . . . follow me'."

"And he did, poor fellow… kind of wolf and Red Riding Hood stuff."

We had a drink on that. Then he said, "I suppose it was, but if you'd seen the relief on the poor chap's face when we boarded him and he knew it was all over, you'd have felt, as I did, that it had all been worth while."

I met Captain Loetzmann again on several occasions, when we happened to be in Chittagong at the same time. But I never did remember to ask him which public school he'd been to.

Ikarian idiosyncrasies

Joseph Georgirenes was Archbishop of the diocese of Samos from 1666 until 1671, when – weary of Turkish interference – he voluntarily retired to the monastery of the Apocalypse on nearby Pátmos. Originally from Mílos, he had an involved outsider's view of his pastoral flock, if an occasionally jaundiced one. Following his residence on Pátmos, Georgirenes emigrated for unspecified reasons to London, where in 1677 he wrote *A Description of the Present State of Samos, Nicaria, Patmos, and Mount Athos*, which was translated into English by an unidentified acquaintance; its hundred-plus pages are packed with a wealth of detail, some of it doubtless exaggerated for effect, concerning Ottoman rule, religious observance, agriculture and ethnography. The good bishop was wrong in at least one particular, however; until the 1950s sleeping on the floor rather than in a bed was a widespread practice throughout village Greece.

The most commendable thing of this Island [Ikaría] is their Air and Water, both so healthful, that the People are very long liv'd, it being an ordinary thing to see persons in it of an hundred years of Age, which is a great wonder, considering how hardily they live. There is not a Bed in the Island, the Ground is their Tick, and the cold Stone their Pillow, and the Cloaths they wear is all the Coverlet they use. They provide no more Apparel than what they wear all at once, when that is past wearing any longer, then think of a new Suit. Betwixt their ordinary times of Eating, there is not a piece of Bread to be found in the Isle. A little before Dinner, they take as much Corn as will serve that Meal, grind it with a Hand-Mill, bake it upon a flat Stone; when 'tis Bak'd, the Master of the Family divides it equally among the Family; but a Woman with child has two shares. If any Stranger comes in, every one parts with a Piece of his own share to accommodate the Stranger. Their Wine is always made with a third part Water, and so very weak and small. When they drink it, so much as is thought sufficient is put into one large Bowl, and so passes round. The Nicarians [Nicaria was the medieval name for Ikaría] are the only Islanders of all the Archipelago, that neither keep Wine to sell, nor lay it up in Wooden Vessels, but in long Jars, cover'd all over in the Ground. When they have a mind to Tap it, they make a Bung-hole in the top, and draw it out with Canes. Their Houses are so plain, that all the Furniture you can see is an Hand-Mill, besides this, there is nothing but bare Walls: That little they have besides is all hid under Ground; not so much for fear of the Corsairs (from whom their Poverty is a sure guard) as out of Custome. Nor are they all so poor, as not to be able to buy Beds, but custome has brought them into a contempt of Beds, as meerly superfluous; insomuch, that when they Travel into other Islands, they refuse the offer of a Bed. A Priest of Nicaria coming into Samos, was courteously entertain'd by those of his Order, and at Night was offer'd a Bed to lye in; he thank'd them, but refus'd, nor could by any importunity be prevail'd upon, but told them the Earth was his Mother, from whence he would not keep a distance; besides he was afraid of being Sick, if he should lye in a Bed; and therefore if they had a kindness for him, they must give him the liberty of sleeping after his own Country way.

When I went to visit them as Arch-Bishop, and ignorant of the custom of the Country, carry'd no Bed. At Night, where I first lodg'd, asking for a Chamber, they told me they had not other than that where I first came; then asking for a Bed, they told me it was not the Custom of the Country; then desiring to borrow some Bed Cloaths for Love or Money, all they brought me was one Smock made of course Dimity.

They have no great communication one with another, any farther than the publick times of Sacred Solemnities, or Civil Business doth cause them to come together. At other times they keep strictly within the narrow Sphere of their own affairs. Formal Visits, Treats, and Entertainments are things unknown. If any business do put them upon a Visit to their Neighbour, they come not close to his Door, but stand off at a great distance, and call aloud to him; If he make them answer, they discourse the Business they came about, standing off at the same distance; except they be earnestly invited to come in. And this way of discoursing at a distance they practise more in the Fields and Mountains; their Voices being so strong, that 'tis ordinary to talk at a Miles distance; sometimes at four or five, where the Valleys interpos'd between two hills, give advantage to the Voice. Sometimes they can discourse at that distance, that the carriage of the Sound through the Winding of the Valleys, shall require half a Quarter of an Hours time; and yet they make distinct, and proper Answers, both audible and intelligible, without the help of a Stentorophonical Trumpet.

Their Habit for the Men, is a Shirt, and over it a short cassock, down to the Knees, to which, in Winter they add only a short Vest, that reaches a little below the middle. Stockings they never wear. Their Shoes are only a piece of thin Copper, bow'd to the shape of their Feet, and every one is his own Shoemaker. The Women have nothing but one Smock, but so large, that they wrap it double, or treble down to the Girdle, but below the Girdle single. The Priests, for greater reverence in the Church, tye two Towels about their Legs, the one is their usual Bonnet, and the other their Girdle: so that they perfom sacred Offices ungirt, as well as uncover'd.

Of all the Isles of the Archipelago, this only admits of no mixture with Strangers in Marriage, nor admits any Stranger to settle with them: They being, as they pretend, all descended of the Imperial Blood of the Porphyrogenneti, must not stain their noble Blood with inferiour Matches, or mixtures with *Choriats*, or Peasants, for so they term all the other islanders.

Porphyrogenneti, were those of the Blood Royal, in the Days of the Greek Emperours, so call'd, from their wearing of Purple, which was a Badge of Royalty, and allow'd only to Princes of the Blood; and not from an house call'd Porphyra, where the Empresses were wont to lie in. But Purple was throughout the East, the known Badge of Royalty. Hence came that unsanctify'd Wit, and learned'st Writer that ever oppos'd the Christian Religion with his Pen, to be call'd Porphyrius: For his true name in the Language of Syria, his native Country, was Malchus, or King; but the Greeks did paraphrase it Porphyrius, or Purple-robed; that being a Colour peculiar to Kings.

They have a great Happiness, by reason of their poverty, in not being molested by the Turks, who think it not worth their while to come among them, nor if they should, were they likely to enjoy any quiet, without keeping a stronger Guard than the Revenues of the Isle would maintain. Once they slew a Caddee [judge] sent by the Grand Signior [ie the Sultan], and being summon'd to Answer for their Crime, they by common consent own'd the Fact, but would name no particular Man. So that the Turkish Officers looking upon their beggarly Cloaths, thought there was neither gain nor glory in punishing such Miscreants, and that in Justice, they must punish all, or none, dismiss'd them untouch'd. From that time no Turk ever troubled them: For they take all courses imaginable to seem poor; and wheresoe'er they come abroad, they count it no shame to beg Alms: Yet they make a shift every year to levy three hundred Crowns for the Arch-Bishop. They are govern'd by a Proesti [council of village elders] of their own chusing, who also levys their Haratch or Tribute to the Grand Signior, and takes care to carry it to the Aga [local Turkish chieftain] of Scio [Híos]. As for their Religion, it is the same with that of Samos; but their Priests are more ignorant.

Thus you have an account of a small Island, the Poorest, and yet the Happiest of the whole Aegean Sea. The Soil is Barren, but the Air is Healthful; their Wealth is but small, but their Liberty and Security is great. They are not molested withe the Tyrannous Insolence of a Turkish Officer, nor with the frightful Incursions of barbarous and merciless Pirates. Their Diet and Apparel is below the Rate of Beggars in other Countrys, and their Lodging is a thying of no more care, or cost, than that of the Beasts of the Field, yet their Bodies are strong and hardy, and the People generally long liv'd. They live with as little forecast, as if they expected not to survive a day, being contented to satisfy the present necessities of Nature. They do properly *in diem vivere*, or as we say, From Hand to Mouth. They have but little, yet they never Want. Their Ignorance is equal to their Poverty, and contributes much to their content. And how well they esteem of their own condition, their contempt of their Neighbouring Islands, and scorning to mix with them in Alliance by Marriage, is a manifest sign. Whence we may learn, that they approach the nearest to Contentedness in this Life; whose desires are contracted into the narrowest compass.

Books

Where separate editions exist in the UK and USA, publishers are detailed below in the form UK publisher; US publisher, unless the publisher is the same in both countries. Where books are published in one country – or Athens – only, this follows the publisher's name.

An out-of-print but still highly recommended book is indicated by "o/p"; the recommended Greek-specialist book dealers often have large back-stocks of these. University Press is abbreviated as UP.

Books marked with ★ are particularly recommended by us. Titles marked with a ‡ are part of a highly recommended "**Modern Greek Writers**" series, currently numbering over thirty titles, issued by Kedros Publishers (Athens) and distributed by Central Books (London E9) in the UK, Paul & Co in the US.

Travel and general accounts

Howard Baker *Persephone's Cave* (University of Georgia Press, US, long o/p). Intimations of ancient worship on a reverential tour of Sámos, with good period detail (1960s) from before the advent of tourism.

★ **Gillian Bouras** *A Foreign Wife* (Penguin Australia). In which a woman who married a Greek-Australian during the 1960s consents to return permanently to the mother country in 1980. An excellent chronicle of cross-cultural/continental angst and the migrant experience in both directions, with penetrating insights into child-rearing, comparative views of leisure, local medicine and general expectations tempered of the grinding Messinian-mainland poverty of only a few decades ago – as well as the final, non-negotiable barriers of language and faith. It inaugurates a series of several works: *A Fair Exchange*, the sequel; *Aphrodite and the Others*, in which Bouras explores her always-difficult relations with her formidable mother-in-law, steeped in an oral culture which finds Bouras' obsession with reading and writing incomprehensible; the autobiographical novel *A Stranger Here*, in which the widespread ambivalence of being in Greece – never content there, can't keep away – is teased out still more exquisitely; and *Starting Again* (all Penguin Australia).

Joseph Braddock *Sappho's Island: A Paean for Lesbos* (Constable, UK, long o/p). Precious little on the modern island, but good background on ancient Mytilene and on the "primitive" painter Theophilos.

Lawrence Durrell *Reflections on a Marine Venus* (Faber & Faber; Marlowe & Co). Durrell spent 1945 to 1947 as a press officer on British-administered Rhodes; this was the result, rich in period detail but purple in the prose, alcohol-fogged as always, and faintly patronizing towards the "natives".

John Ebdon *Ebdon's Iliad* (Unwin, UK, o/p). Rhodes, Kós and Kárpathos as they (and their package trade) were in the early 1980s. No claims to profundity, but fun for light beach reading.

★ **Joseph Georgirenes** *A Description of the Present State of Samos, Nicaria, Patmos and Mount Athos*

(Noti Karavia, Athens; limited facsimile edition). An occasionally hilarious account of these spots as they were in the mid-seventeenth century, showing if nothing else that regional character was already well developed in medieval times. A choice morsel is excerpted on pp.488–490.

★ **William Johnson** *The Monk Seal Conspiracy* (Heretic Books, UK, long o/p). Johnson spent almost three years on Sámos (1979–82), employed by various conservation organizations, lobbying to establish marine reserves for the endangered monk seal. The alleged "conspiracy" he uncovered was that the seals were to become victims of Greco-Turkish tensions, the complacency of his employers and the ultimate supremacy of the Greek military and secret services. Johnson was clearly a prickly fanatic but even if half of what he says is true, you'll never donate to the WWF or Greenpeace again. Excellent on Sámos in pre-tourism days, and the mythology and life cycle of the seals in question.

Katherine Kizilos *The Olive Grove: Travels in Greece* (Lonely Planet Journeys). Returned, ambivalent Greek-Australian's musings on the country and Constantinople, which include vignettes of Pátmos, Ikaría and Lésvos.

★ **Elias Kulukundis** *Journey to a Greek Island* (Cassell, UK, o/p). More accurately, a journey back through time and genealogy by a diaspora Greek two generations removed from Kássos, poorest of the Dodecanese. Worth the effort of tracking down; a passage is excerpted on pp.482–486.

★ **Willard Manus** *This Way to Paradise: Dancing on the Tables* (Lycabettus Press, Athens). An American expatriate's memoir of four decades in Líndhos, Rhodes, beginning long before its sad descent into mass-tourist tattiness – he and wife Mavis were among the first foreigners to settle here in 1961. Wonderful period detail, including hippie excesses and hilarious appearances by the likes of S.J. Perelman, Germaine Greer and Martha Gellhorn.

Nicholas G Pappas *Castellorizo: An Illustrated History of the Island and its Conquerors* (Halstead Press, Australia). Recent (1994) account from a Sydney "Kassie" who has raised some eyebrows by asserting, among other things, that the islet never supported more than 10,000 permanent inhabitants.

James Pettifer *The Greeks: The Land and People since the War* (Penguin; Viking). A useful, if spottily written and now slightly dated introduction to contemporary Greece – and its recent past. Pettifer charts the state of the nation's politics, food, family life, religion, tourism, and other topics.

★ **Patricia Storace** *Dinner with Persephone* (Granta; Pantheon). A New York poet, resident a year in Greece, puts the country's psyche on the couch, while avoiding the same position with various predatory males. Storace has a sly sense of humour, and in showing how permeated – and imprisoned – Greece is by its imagined past, gets it right ninety percent of the time.

★ **William Travis** *Bus Stop Symi* (Rapp & Whiting, UK, o/p). Chronicles three years' residence there in the mid-Sixties; fairly insightful (if rather resented on the island itself), though Travis erroneously prophesied that the place would never see tourism. Two passages are reproduced on pp.480–482.

Faith Warn *Bitter Sea: The Real Story of Greek Sponge Diving* (Guardian Angel Press, UK). Fairly good potted history of the Kalymnian sponge industry, from the nineteenth century to the present day, by a British journalist now resident on the island; widely available locally.

The classics

Many of the classics make excellent companion reading for a trip around Greece – especially the historians Thucydides and Herodotus. Reading Homer's *Odyssey* when you're battling with or resigning yourself to the vagaries of island ferries puts your own plight into perspective.

Most of the standard undergraduate staples are part of the Penguin Classics paperback series. Routledge and Duckworth both also have a huge, steadily expanding backlist of Classical Studies, though many titles are expensive and quite specialized; paperback editions are indicated.

Herodotus *The Histories* (Penguin or A.D. Godley trans, Cambridge UP, o/p). Revered as the father of systematic history and anthropology, this fifth-century-BC Anatolian writer chronicled both the causes and campaigns of the Persian Wars, as well as the contemporary, assorted tribes and nations inhabiting Asia Minor.

Homer *The Iliad*; *The Odyssey*. The first concerns itself, semi-factually, with the late Bronze Age war of the Achaeans against Troy in Asia Minor; the second recounts the delayed return home of the hero Odysseus, via seemingly every corner of the Mediterranean. For a verse rendition, ★ Richmond Lattimore's translation (University of Chicago, *Iliad*; HarperCollins, *Odyssey*) has yet to be bettered. For a prose rendition, ★ Martin Hammond's *Iliad* (Penguin) and *Odyssey* (Duckworth, UK) currently edges out second-best choices by the father-and-son team of E.V. Rieu (*Iliad*, Penguin) and D.C.H. Rieu (*Odyssey*, Penguin). All the above are in paperback and modestly priced.

Ovid *Metamorphoses*, A.D. Melville, trans (Oxford UP). Though collected by a first-century-AD Roman writer, this remains one of the most accessible renditions of the more piquant Greek myths, involving transformations as divine blessing or curse. Ted Hughes' more recent rendition (Faber & Faber) has also been widely praised.

★ **Thucydides** *History of the Peloponnesian War* (Penguin). Bleak month-by-month account of the conflict, which involved most of the larger islands, by a cashiered Athenian officer who remains remarkably objective despite his affiliation and dim view of human nature; see George Cawkwell's book (review below) for a revisionist interpretation.

Xenophon *The History of My Times* (Penguin). Thucydides ended his coverage of the Peloponnesian War in 411 BC; this work continues events until 362 BC and the dawn of the Macedonian dynasty.

Ancient history and interpretation of the classics

★ **Mary Beard and John Henderson** *The Classics: A Very Short Introduction* (Oxford UP). As it says; an excellent overview.

★ **A.R. Burn** *History of Greece* (Penguin). Probably the best general introduction to ancient Greece, though for fuller and more interesting analysis you'd do better with one or other of the following, more specialized titles.

★ **Paul Cartlege** *Cambridge Illustrated History of Ancient Greece* (Cambridge UP). Large-format, pricey volume packed with information useful for both novices and experts.

George Cawkwell *Thucydides and the Peloponnesian War* (Routledge). Recent, revisionist overview of Thucydides' work and relations with prominent personalities of the war, challenging previous assumptions of his infallibility.

★ **M.I. Finley** *The World of Odysseus* (Pimlico, UK). Latest reprint of a 1954 warhorse, pioneering in its investigation of the historicity (or otherwise) of the events and society related by Homer. Breezily readable and stimulating, with prejudices apparent rather than subtle.

Michael Grant and John Hazel *Who's Who in Classical Mythology* (Routledge). Gazetteer of over 1200 mythological personalities, together with historical and geographical background.

★ **Pierre Grimal (ed)** *Dictionary of Classical Mythology* (Penguin). Though translated from the French, considered to still have the edge on the more recent Grant/Hazel title.

Simon Hornblower *The Greek World 479–323 BC* (Routledge). An erudite survey of ancient Greece at its zenith, from the end of the Persian Wars to the death of Alexander, which has become a standard university paperback text.

John Kenyon Davies *Democracy and Classical Greece* (Fontana; Harvard UP). Established and accessible account of the Classical period and its political developments.

Robin Lane Fox *Alexander the Great* (Penguin). An absorbing study, which combines historical scholarship with imaginative psychological detail.

Robin Osborne *Greece in the Making 1200–479 BC* (Routledge). Well-illustrated paperback on the rise of the city-state.

Graham Shipley *A History of Samos, 800–188 BC* (Clarendon Press or Sandpiper reprint). Somewhat dry treatment of Archaic-to-Hellenistic Sámos, though not without its moments of wit; most interesting for its catalogue of sites from all eras, and other unique appendices.

F.W. Walbank *The Hellenistic World* (Fontana; Harvard UP). Greece under the sway of the Macedonian and Roman empires.

Ancient religion and culture

★ **Walter Burkert** *Greek Religion* (Blackwell). Superb overview of ancient deities and their attributes and antecedents, rites, the protocol of sacrifice and the symbolism of major festivals; especially good on relating Greek worship to its antecedents in the Middle East.

Matthew Dillon *Pilgrims and Pilgrimage in Ancient Greece* (Routledge). Pricey hardback exploring not only the main sanctuaries such as Delphi, but also minor oracles, the role of women and children, and secular festivities attending the rites.

Nano Marinatos & Robin Hagg *Greek Sanctuaries: New Approaches* (Routledge). Form and function of the temples, in the light of recent scholarship.

Archeology and art

John Beckwith *Early Christian and Byzantine Art* (Yale UP). Illustrated study placing Byzantine art within a wider context.

William R. Biers *Archeology of Greece: An Introduction* (Cornell UP). A 1990s-revised and excellent standard text.

★ **John Boardman** *Greek Art* (Thames & Hudson, UK). A very good concise introduction: part of the "World of Art" series.

Reynold Higgins *Minoan and Mycenaean Art* (Thames & Hudson, UK). A clear, well-illustrated summary.

Sinclair Hood *The Arts in Prehistoric Greece* (Penguin; Yale UP). Sound introduction to the subject.

Roger Ling *Classical Greece* (Phaidon, UK). Another useful illustrated introduction.

Gisela Richter *A Handbook of Greek Art* (Phaidon; Da Capo). Exhaustive survey of the visual arts of ancient Greece.

R.R.R. Smith *Hellenistic Sculpture* (Thames & Hudson, UK). Modern reappraisal of the art of Greece under Alexander and his successors.

★ **David Talbot Rice** *Art of the Byzantine Era* (Thames & Hudson). Talbot Rice was, with Robert Byron, one of the pioneering scholars in the "rediscovery" of Byzantine art; this is an accessible illustrated study.

Peter Warren *The Aegean Civilizations* (Phaidon, o/p; P. Bedrick Books, o/p). Illustrated account of the Minoan and Mycenean cultures.

Byzantine, medieval and Ottoman Greece

Averil Cameron *The Mediterranean World in Late Antiquity, AD 395–600* (Routledge). Essentially the early Byzantine years.

Nicholas Cheetham *Medieval Greece* (Yale UP; o/p in US). General survey of the period and its infinite convolutions in Greece, with Frankish, Catalan, Venetian, Byzantine and Ottoman struggles for power. Very little specifically on the islands of this guide, but useful for keeping tabs on the main players.

★ **John Julius Norwich** *Byzantium: The Early Centuries*; *Byzantium: the Apogee* and *Byzantium: the Decline* (all Penguin; Viking-Knopf). Perhaps the main surprise for first-time travellers to Greece is the fascination of its Byzantine monuments. This is an astonishingly detailed yet readable trilogy, also available in one fat volume as *A Short History of Byzantium* (Penguin)

★ **Vangelis Pavlidis** *Rhodes 1306–1522: A Story* (Rodos Image, Rhodes). Caricature-illustrated history of the Knights of St John's occupation of Rhodes, by one of Greece's leading political cartoonists, but this isn't tourist pap – rigorous research and witty text illuminate a little-known era of the Dodecanese.

Michael Psellus *Fourteen Byzantine Rulers* (Penguin). A fascinating contemporary source, detailing the stormy but brilliant period from 976 to 1078.

Jonathan Riley-Smith *Hospitallers: The History of the Order of St John* (The Hambledon Press). Lavishly illustrated history of the Knights, from its beginnings in the Holy Land to its ultimate incarnation as an ambulance corps. Text is literate, but goes at a gallop to compress ten centuries into less than 150 pages.

★ **Steven Runciman** *The Fall of Constantinople, 1453* (Cambridge UP) is the standard account of the event; *The Great Church in Captivity* (Cambridge UP) follows the vicissitudes of the Orthodox Patriarchate in Constantinople up to the War of Independence. *Byzantine Style and Civilization* (Penguin, o/p in US) is more slanted towards art, culture and monuments.

★ **Kallistos (Timothy) Ware** *The Orthodox Church* (Penguin). Good introduction to what is effectively the established religion of Greece, by the Orthodox bishop resident in Oxford.

Modern Greece

Timothy Boatswain and Colin Nicolson *A Traveller's History of Greece* (Windrush Press; Interlink; Greek printing by Efstathiadis). Dated (coverage ceases in the early 1990s) but well-written overview of the important Greek periods and personalities.

★ **Richard Clogg** *A Concise History of Greece* (Cambridge UP). A remarkably clear and well-illustrated account of Greece, from the decline of Byzantium to 1992, with the emphasis on recent decades; there are numerous maps and lengthy feature captions to the artwork.

Douglas Dakin *The Unification of Greece, 1770–1923* (Ernest Benn; St Martin's Press, both o/p). Benchmark account of the foundation of the Greek state and the struggle to extend its boundaries.

★ **H.A. Lidderdale (trans and ed)** *The Memoirs of General Makiryannis, 1797–1864* (Oxford UP, o/p). The "Peasant General", one of the few honest and self-sacrificing protagonists of the Greek uprising, taught himself to write at the age of 32 to set down this apologia of his conduct, in vivid demotic Greek. Heartbreaking in its portrayal of the incipient schisms, linguistic and otherwise, that tore the country apart until recently.

★ **Michael Llewellyn Smith** *Ionian Vision: Greece in Asia Minor, 1919–1922* (C. Hurst; University of Michigan). Standard work, by the 1999-retired UK ambassador to Greece, on the disastrous Anatolian campaign which led to the exchange of populations, with many of the refugees ending up on the larger east Aegean islands. Diplomatic and military history cast as a Greek tragedy: Greece under Venizelos, egged on by Lloyd George, overplays its hand by leaving the relatively defensible confines of the Smyrna mandate. Evinces considerable sympathy for the post-1920 Royalists pursuing an unwanted, inherited war which they know is unwinnable.

Peter Varoulakis *The Greek War of Independence* (Hellenic International Press). Paperback furnishing a nice counterweight to the Brewer work, with lots of colour reproductions of famous scenes, with far less text.

C.M. Woodhouse *Modern Greece, A Short History* (Faber & Faber). Woodhouse was active in the Greek Resistance during World War II. Writing from a more right-wing perspective than Clogg, this history (from the foundation of Constantinople in 324 to 1990), is briefer and a bit drier, but scrupulous with facts. *The Rise and Fall of the Greek Colonels* (Granada, o/p; Watts), recounts the (horror) story of the dictatorship.

World War II and its aftermath

Winston Churchill *The Second World War, Vol. 5: Closing the Ring* (Penguin). Allied Aegean campaigns, with detailed coverage of battles on and around Rhodes, Léros, Sámos and Kós.

★ **David H. Close** *The Origins of the Greek Civil War* (Longman, o/p). Excellent, readable study that focuses on the social conditions in 1920s and 1930s Greece that made the country so ripe for conflict. Draws on primary sources, slays a few sacred cows along the way, and is relatively objective (though he's no great fan of the Left).

★ **Iakovos Kambanellis** *Mauthausen* (Kedros, Athens‡; Central Books, UK). Náxos native Kambanellis was active in the

Resistance, caught by the Germans, and sent to Mauthausen, the concentration camp to where many of the politicians and partisans who had opposed the Nazis' rise to power were deported. Harrowing atrocities in flashback there are a-plenty, but the main thrust of the book is post-liberation, describing the author's awkward romance with a Lithuanian Jew, and how the idealist inmates are slowly disillusioned as they see that the "New World Order" will be scarcely different from the old. The basis of a play, and the Theodhorakis oratorio of the same name.

★ **Mark Mazower** *Inside Hitler's Greece: The Experience of Occupation 1941–44* (Yale UP). Somewhat choppily organized, and just cursory coverage of the islands, but the standard of scholarship is high and the photos alone justify the price. Demonstrates how the complete demoralization of the country and incompetence of conventional politicians led to the rise of ELAS and the onset of civil war. The sequel to this, edited by Mazower, is *After the War was Over: Reconstructing the Family and State in Greece, 1943–1960* (Princeton UP), 14 scholarly articles on various aspects of Greece in the period specified.

Ministry of the Aegean *The Dodecanese: The Long Road to Union with Greece* (Kastaniotis Editions, Athens). Assembled diplomatic documents, recently released from the Greek Ministry of Foreign Affairs, from Italian, Greek, British and Turkish sources. Admittedly many are of specialist interest, but equally many are fascinating about inter-war intrigues, the abject state of the islands in the 1940s and the civic lustration campaigns of 1946–48 against Fascist collaborators. In case of difficulty, usually obtainable through The Hellenic Centre, 16-18 Paddington Street, London W1U 5AS ⓣ020/7487 5060.

Adrian Seligman *War in the Islands* (Allan Sutton, UK). Collected oral histories of a little-known Allied unit: a flotilla of caiques equipped to raid the Axis-held Dodecanese, Cyclades and east Aegean islands. Real-life *Boy's Own* stuff, a bit heavy on the service jargon and acronyms, but some pretty gripping tales, with lots of fine period photos and detail. One of the best episodes is reproduced on pp.486–488.

C.M. Woodhouse *The Struggle for Greece, 1941–49* (Hart-Davis, o/p; Beekman). A masterly and by no means uncritical account of this crucial decade, explaining how Greece emerged without a Communist government.

Ethnography

★ **Loring Danforth and Alexander Tsiaras** *The Death Rituals of Rural Greece* (Princeton UP). Many visitors find Greek funeral customs – the wailing, the open-casket vigils, the disinterment after three years – the most disturbing aspect of the culture; this book helps make sense of them.

Juliet Du Boulay *Portrait of a Greek Mountain Village* (Oxford-Clarendon, o/p in UK; Denise Harvey, Límni, Évvia). Specifically Ambéli on Évvia during the 1960s, and while falling outside the territory of this book, this classic observation of customs and mores is still applicable to most of Greece.

★ **John Cuthbert Lawson** *Modern Greek Folklore and Ancient Greek Religion: A Study in Survivals* (University Books, New York, o/p). Exactly as the title states, and still highly applicable a century after its writing. Well worth scouring libraries and antiquarian dealers for.

William McNeill *The Metamorphosis of Greece since World War II* (University of Chicago, o/p). In particular the progress of urbanization, engagingly covered; worth the effort to find in second-hand shops.

"Coffee-table" illustrateds

William Abramowicz *The Greek File: Images of a Mythic Land* (Rizzoli). Obstinately nostalgic black-and-white look at the country up through the 1980s, by this veteran Condé Nast photographer; main complaint is it fails to take on board the vast changes that had already swept through Greece since Manos' pioneering work (see below).

Liza Evert *Aeolian Lesbos* (Constellation Books, Athens). Archival material, plus evocative colour photos of Lésvos up to the early 1990s; such is the pace of change that many of the locales and activities no longer exist as shown. Useful introductory history text as well.

Jelly Hadjidimitriou *39 Coffee Houses and a Barber's Shop* (Crete University Press, Iráklio). Loving elegy to the traditional kafenía of Lésvos, many of which – as with Evert's subjects – have disappeared since documentation. Accompanied by excellent short essays which, among other things, explain their social role and why/how they arose in the nineteenth century.

★ **Constantine Manos** *A Greek Portfolio* (W. W. Norton). Long-awaited, reasonably priced reissue of a 1972 classic: the fruits of a gifted Greek-American photographer's three-year odyssey in the early Sixties through a country on the edge of modernization, still essentially unchanged from the 1930s. The quality and insight you'd expect from a member of the Magnum co-operative, in elegiac black-and-white photos strong on Kárpathos.

Clay Perry *Vanishing Greece* (Conran Octopus; Abbeville Press, both o/p). Well-captioned photos depict the threatened landscapes and relict ways of life in rural Greece; includes good coverage of Ólymbos on Kárpathos and Volissós on Híos. Look for either hardback or paperback second-hand copies, especially in Greece.

Suzanne Slesin et al *Greek Style* (Thames & Hudson; Crown). Stunning (if sometimes contrived) designer-tweaked interiors from various island interiors, including Líndhos on Rhodes.

Modern Greek literature

Roderick Beaton *An Introduction to Modern Greek Literature* (Oxford UP). Chronological survey of fiction and poetry from independence to 1821, with a useful discussion on the "Language Question" (see p.508 for this).

Fiction

Athena Dallas-Damis *Island of the Winds* (Efstathiadis, Athens; Karatzas, US, o/p). Rather breathy, overwrought historical fiction set around the 1821–23 events on Híos, by a Greek-American woman with roots on the island.

★ **Maro Douka** *Fool's Gold* (Kedros, Greece‡). Describes an upper-class young woman's involvement, and subsequent disillusionment, with the clandestine resistance to the junta.

Eugenia Fakinou *The Seventh Garment* (Serpent's Tail, UK). Greek history, from the War of Independence to the colonels' junta, as told through the life stories (interspersed in counterpoint) of three generations of women. It's a rather more successful experiment than Fakinou's *Astradeni* (Kedros, Athens‡), in which a young girl – whose slightly irritating narrative voice is adopted throughout – leaves the island of Sými, with all its traditional values, for Athens.

Nikos Kazantzakis Nobel laureate, woolly Marxist theorist, excommunicated Orthodox Christian and eventual self-imposed exile Kazantzakis seems to bear out the old axioms about prophets without honour in their own country, and classics being books praised but rarely read. Whether in intricate, translation-defying Greek or the resultant wooden English, he can be a hard slog. *Zorba the Greek* is a surprisingly dark and nihilistic work, light years away from the two-dimensional characters of the film. On the other hand, the movie version of *The Last Temptation of Christ*, despite its shortcomings, provoked riots amongst Orthodox fanatics in Athens during 1989. *Christ Recrucified* (published in the US as *The Greek Passion*) resets the Easter drama in the milieu of Christian–Muslim relations on Crete, while *Freedom or Death* (published in the US as *Captain Michalis*) chronicles the rebellions of late nineteenth-century Crete. *Report to Greco* – perhaps the most accessible of his works – is an autobiographical exploration of his Cretanness/Greekness (all titles Faber & Faber; Touchstone).

★ **Artemis Leontis (ed)** *Greece: A Traveller's Literary Companion* (Whereabouts Press, San Francisco, US). An overdue idea, brilliantly executed: various regions of the country as portrayed in (very) short fiction or essays by modern Greek writers. Both Lésvos and Kálymnos make cameo appearances.

Stratis Myrivilis *Life in the Tomb* (Quartet; New England UP). A harrowing and unorthodox war memoir based on the author's experience on the Macedonian front during 1917–18, well translated by Peter Bien. Completing a kind of trilogy are two later novels, set on the north coast of Lésvos, Myrivilis's homeland: *The Mermaid Madonna* and *The Schoolmistress with the Golden Eyes* (Efstathiadis, Athens). Heavily abridged translations of these are unfortunately not so good.

★ **Nick Papandreou** *Father Dancing* (Penguin). Thinly veiled *roman à clef* by the late Andreas' younger son. Papandreou Senior, not too surprisingly, comes across as a gasbag and petty domestic tyrant.

★ **Dido Sotiriou** *Farewell Anatolia* (Kedros, Athens‡). A perennial favourite since its initial appearance in 1962 (it is now approaching its sixtieth Greek printing), this chronicles the traumatic end of Greek life in Asia Minor, from the 1912 Balkan War to the catastrophe of 1922, as narrated by a fictionalized version of the author's father. In the finale, he escapes across the narrow strait of Mykale to Sámos, as so many did during those turbulent years.

★ **Tsirkas Stratis** *Drifting Cities* (Kedros, Greece ‡). Welcome reissue of this classic epic of leftist World War II intrigue in the Greek Army abroad in Jerusalem, Cairo and Alexandria. Tsirkas' scathing portrait of his hero's humanism clashing with Stalinist cadres got him expelled from the Greek Communist Party.

★ **Alki Zei** *Achilles' Fiancée* (Kedros, Athens ‡). Often moving portrait of the friendships and intrigues amongst a collection of Communist exiles floating between Athens, Rome, Moscow, Paris and Tashkent in the years between the Civil War and the colonels' junta. Largely autobiographical (the author is Samian on her mother's side), it captures the flavour of the illusions, nostalgia and party-line schisms endemic in this community.

Foreign fiction set in Greece

★ **Louis de Bernières** *Captain Corelli's Mandolin* (Minerva; Random House). Set on Kefalloniá during the World War II occupation, this accomplished 1994 tragicomedy by an author previously known for his South American extravaganzas quickly acquired cult, then word-of-mouth bestseller status, but has lately become a *succès de scandale*. When the islanders, Greek Left intellectuals and surviving Italian partisans woke up to its virulent anti-communism and disparaging portrayal of ELAS, there was a furore, with de Bernières eventually obliged to eat large quantities of humble pie in the UK press. It also seems the novel is closely based on the experiences of still-alive-and-kicking Amos Pampaloni, an artillery captain on 1942–44 Kefalloniá who later joined ELAS, who accuses de Bernières of distorting the roles of both Italians and ELAS on the island. The Greek translation has been suitably abridged to avoid causing offence, and the long-awaited movie (starring Nicholas Cage and Penelope Cruz), watered down to a pallid love story as a condition for filming on the island, sank without trace after a few weeks in 2001.

★ **John Fowles** *The Magus* (Vintage/Dell). Fowles' biggest and best blockbuster, inspired by his stay on Spétses as a teacher, in the 1950s. Post-adolescent mystification and sexual manipulation, ie the usual Fowles obsessions.

Peter Green *The Laughter of Aphrodite* (University of California Press). Reissue of a 1965 historical novel by a distinguished classicist, in the same vein as Marguerite Yourcenar's *The Memoirs of Hadrian*; this re-creates Sappho of Mytilene and her milieu, and largely succeeds.

Mary Renault *The King Must Die*; *The Last of the Wine*; *The Mask of Apollo* (Sceptre; Random House) and others (all Penguin except *Masks*). Mary Renault's imaginative reconstructions are more than the adolescent's reading they're often taken for, with impeccable research and tight writing. The trio above retell, respectively, the myth of Theseus, the life of a pupil of Socrates, and that of a fourth-century-BC actor. The life of Alexander the Great is recounted in *Fire from Heaven*, *The Persian Boy*, and *Funeral Games*, available separately or in one economical volume (all Penguin).

Modern Greek poetry

With two Nobel laureates in recent decades – George Seferis and Odysseus Elytis – modern Greece has an extraordinarily intense and dynamic poetic tradition. Translations of all of the following are excellent.

C.P. Cavafy *Collected Poems* (Chatto & Windus; Princeton UP). The complete works, translated by Edmund Keeley and Philip Sherrard, of perhaps the most accessible modern Greek poet, resident for most of his life in Alexandria. For some, *The Complete Poems of Cavafy* (Harcourt Brace Jovanovich), translated by Rae Dalven, or the volume done by John Mavrogordato (Chatto & Windus, UK), are superior versions.

Odysseus Elytis *The Axion Esti* (Anvil Press; Pittsburgh UP); *Selected Poems* (Anvil Press; Viking Penguin, o/p); *The Sovereign Sun* (Bloodaxe Books; Temple UP, Philadelphia, o/p). The major works, in good English versions, of a poet with roots on Lésvos. Easier to find is *Collected Poems* (Johns Hopkins UP), which includes virtually everything except *The Axion Esti*.

Yannis Ritsos *Exile and Return, Selected Poems 1967–1974* (Anvil Press; Ecco Press). A fine volume of verse by Greece's foremost leftist poet, from the junta era when he was internally exiled on Sámos. Look out also for *Romiosyne* (Louizou Publications, UK) with Greek–English parallel text.

George Seferis *Collected Poems, 1924–1955* (Anvil Press, o/p; Princeton UP, o/p). Virtually the complete works of the Nobel laureate, with Greek and English verses on facing pages. More recent, but lacking the parallel Greek text, is *Complete Poems* (Anvil Press; Princeton UP).

Archeological and site guides

A.R. and Mary Burn *The Living Past of Greece: A Time Traveller's Tour of Historic and Prehistoric Places* (Herbert Press; HarperCollins). Unusual in extent, this covers sites from Minoan through to Byzantine and Frankish, with good, clear plans and lively text – though only about a third of the book is devoted to the islands.

Paul Hetherington *The Greek Islands: Guide to the Byzantine and Medieval Buildings and their Art* (Quiller Press, UK). Usually reliable coverage of the monuments which are included, but some astonishing omissions (the painted churches of Rhodes, new basilica on Télendhos, etc).

Ellias Kollias *The Knights of Rhodes: The Palace & the City* (Ekdotiki Athinon, Greece). The last word on the Order's history and monuments, by the archeologist long in charge of Rhodes province.

Roy Lawrance *Where the Road Ends: Sigri* (Pinpoint Graphics, Milton Keynes). Everything you could possibly want to know about the western tip of Lésvos: wildlife, walks to local beaches (and their relative merits), plus the Ottoman monuments of Sígri village.

★ **Lycabettus Press Guides** (Athens, Greece). Although this series has not been updated in some years, the volumes on Pátmos and Kós in particular are still available, and well worth consulting.

Evi Melas (ed) *Temples and Sanctuaries of Ancient Greece: A Companion Guide* (Thames & Hudson, o/p). Excellent collection of essays on the main sites, written by archeologists who have worked at them.

Alexander Paradissis *Fortresses and Castles of Greece* (Efstathiadis Group, Athens). As it says, in three extremely prolix volumes; widely available in good Greek bookshops. Volume III covers the islands of this book.

Nikos Stavroulakis *Jewish Sites and Synagogues of Greece* (Talos Press, Athens). Lavishly illustrated alphabetical gazetteer of all Jewish monuments in Greece, including the islands, with town plans and full histories of the communities that created them. A few have been demolished since publication, however, and only the chapters on Rhodes and Kós apply to Dodecanesian travellers.

Hiking guides

Lance Chilton *Various Walking Pamphlets* (Marengo Publications, UK). Small but thorough, up-to-date guides to the best walks around various island resorts, accompanied by three-colour maps. Areas covered thus far within the Dodecanese and east Aegean include: Líndhos and Péfkos, Rhodes; Kokkári, Sámos; Pétra/Ayiássos, Lésvos; Sými; and western Kós. Available in specialist UK shops or by mail order catalogue from

Wildlife field guides

For a complete listing of recommended field guides to Greek flora and fauna, see pp.466–467.

17 Bernard Crescent, Hunstanton PE36 6ER, Ⓣ & Ⓕ01485/532710; Ⓔmarengo@supanet.com.

Marc Dubin *Trekking in Greece* (Lonely Planet, o/p). Includes many of the best day-hikes on Rhodes, Sými, Tílos, Níssyros, Sámos and northern Lésvos, in more detail than presented in this book, though some routes (Sámos and Lésvos especially) have been bulldozed beyond recognition since early 1990s research. Topographic maps, plus extensive preparatory and background information.

Yachting guides

H.M. Denham *The Aegean* (John Murray, UK, o/p). For many years, the standard cabin reference if you were out yachting; still found in second-hand bookshops, but a bit obsolete.

Rod Heikell *Greek Waters Pilot*. (Imray, Laurie, Norrie & Wilson, UK). Rather more current and thorough than the preceding, which it has superseded.

Food and wine

Rosemary Barron *Flavours of Greece* (Grub Street, UK). Probably the leading cookbook among many contenders, by an internationally recognized authority on Greek cuisine. Contains over 250 recipes.

Andrew Dalby *Siren Feasts* (Routledge). Subtitled "A history of food and gastronomy in Greece", this analysis of Classical and Byzantine texts demonstrates just how little Greek cuisine has changed in three millennia; also excellent on the introduction and etymology of common vegetables and herbs.

★ **Alan Davidson** *Mediterranean Seafood* (Penguin, o/p). A 1972 classic, periodically reprinted, this amazingly erudite and witty book

The islands covered in this guide are, with the exceptions of Rhodes, Kós and Híos, bereft of decent bookshops with any foreign-language stock. If you're stopping over in Athens, however, the capital has a number of excellent ones, at which many of the recommendations above should be available (albeit at a fifty-percent mark-up for foreign-published titles); all are centrally located. Try: Eleftheroudhakis, Níkis 20; Compendium, Níkis 28; Iy Folia tou Vivliou, Panepistimíou 25; and Pantelidhes, Amerikís 11. In London, the Hellenic Bookservice, 91 Fortess Rd, Kentish Town, London NW5 1AG Ⓣ020/7267 9499, Ⓕ7267 9498, Ⓦwww.hellenicbookservice.com, is the UK's premier walk-in Greek bookshop: knowledgeable and well-stocked specialist dealers in new and out-of-print books on all aspects of Greece, especially classics and educational texts. Rivals Zeno's, formerly in Soho, have reopened at 57A Nether Street, North Finchley, London N12 7NP Ⓣ020/8446 1985, Ⓣ8446 1986, Ⓦwww.thegreek-bookstore.com and have more of an antiquarian stress, with their own line of reprints.

catalogues (almost) all known edible species, complete with legends, anecdotes, habits, local names and a suggested recipe or two for each; no photos, but useful pen-and-ink sketches.

★ **James Davidson** *Courtesans and Fishcakes* (Fontana, UK). The politics, class characteristics and etiquette of consumption and consummation – with wine, women, boys and seafood – in ancient Athens, with their bearing on both historical events and modern attitudes. Highly recommended.

★ **Nico Manessis** *The Illustrated Greek Wine Book* (Olive Press Publications, Corfu; available at select retailers in Greece or through Ⓦwww.greekwineguide.gr). Covers almost all the wineries, including the islands, from mass-market to micro, with very reliable ratings; also fascinating features on grape varieties, traditional retsina-making, and even how Greeks were instrumental in introducing vines to the New World. Pricey but worth it.

language

language

Greek

So many Greeks have lived or worked abroad in North America, Australia and, to a much lesser extent, Britain, that you will find someone who speaks English even in the tiniest island village. Add to that the thousands attending language schools or working in the tourist industry – English is the lingua franca of most resorts, with German second – and it is easy to see how so many visitors come back having learnt only half a dozen restaurant words.

You can certainly get by this way, but it isn't very satisfying, and the willingness and ability to say even a few extra words will upgrade your status from that of dumb *tourístas/tourístria* to the more honourable one of *xénos/xéni*, a word which can mean foreigner, traveller and guest all rolled into one.

Learning basic Greek

Greek is not an easy language for English-speakers – translators' unions in the UK rate it as harder than German, slightly less complex than Russian – but it is a very beautiful one, and even a brief acquaintance will give you some idea of the debt owed to it by western European languages.

On top of the usual difficulties of learning a new language, Greek presents the additional problem of an entirely separate **alphabet**. Despite initial appearances, this is in practice fairly easily mastered within a few days – a skill that will help enormously if you are going to get around independently (see the alphabet box on p.511). In addition, certain combinations of letters have unexpected results. This book's transliteration system should help you make intelligible noises, but you have to remember that the correct **stress** (marked throughout the book with an acute accent or sometimes a dieresis) is crucial. With the right sounds but the wrong stress people will either fail to understand you, or else understand something quite different from what you intended. There are numerous pairs of words with the same spelling and phonemes, distinguished only by their stress (the classic, naughty example is *gámo*, a wedding, versus *gamó*, I fuck).

Greek **grammar** is more complicated still: nouns are divided into three genders, all with different case endings in the singular and in the plural, and all adjectives and articles have to agree with these in gender, number and case. (All adjectives are arbitrarily cited in the neuter form in the boxed lists.) Verbs are even more complex; they come in two conjugations, in both active and passive voices, with passively constructed verbs often having transitive sense (and you thought learning the alphabet was bad). To begin with at least, the best thing is simply to say what you know the way you know it, and never mind the niceties. "Eat meat hungry" should get a result, however grammatically incorrect. If you worry about your mistakes, you'll never say anything.

Katharévoussa versus dhimotikí

Greek may seem complicated enough in itself, but problems are multiplied when you consider that since the early 1800s there has been an ongoing dispute between two versions of the language: **katharévoussa** and **dhimotikí**.

Language-learning materials

Teach-yourself Greek courses

Breakthrough Greek (Pan Macmillan; book and four cassettes). Excellent, basic teach-yourself course; no Greek lettering, but good for classicists who need to unlearn bad habits.

Greek Language and People (BBC Publications, UK; book and two cassettes available). More limited in scope but good for acquiring the essentials, and the confidence to try them.

Anne Farmakides *A Manual of Modern Greek* (Yale UP; McGill UP; 3 vols). If you have the discipline and motivation, this is one of the best for learning proper, grammatical Greek; indeed, mastery of just the first volume will get you a long way.

Hara Garoufalia *Teach Yourself Holiday Greek* (Hodder & Stoughton, UK; book and cassette available). Unlike many quickie courses, this provides a good grammatical foundation, but you'll need a dictionary (see below) to supplement the scanty vocabulary lists.

Niki Watts *Greek in Three Months* (Hugo, Dorling Kindersley; book and four cassettes). Delivers as promised; equals or exceeds *Breakthrough Greek*.

Phrasebooks

Greek, a Rough Guide Phrasebook (Penguin, UK & US). Up-to-date and accurate pocket phrasebook not full of "*plume de ma tante*"-type expressions. The English-to-Greek section is sensibly transliterated, though the Greek-to-English part requires basic mastery of the Greek alphabet. Feature boxes fill you in on dos and don'ts and cultural know-how.

Dictionaries

The Oxford Dictionary of Modern Greek (Oxford UP, UK & US). A bit bulky in its wide format, but generally considered the best Greek–English, English–Greek paperback dictionary.

Collins Pocket Greek Dictionary (HarperCollins, UK & US). Very nearly as complete as the Oxford and probably better value for the money. The inexpensive *Collins Gem Greek Dictionary* (UK only) is palm-sized but exactly the same in contents – the best purse or day-pack choice.

Oxford Greek-English, English-Greek Learner's Dictionary (Oxford UP, UK & US). If you're planning a prolonged stay, this pricey, hardbound, two-volume set is unbeatable for usage and vocabulary. There's also a more portable one-volume *Learner's Pocket Dictionary*.

About the Greek language

Peter Mackridge *The Modern Greek Language* (Oxford UP). Analysis, by one of the tongue's foremost scholars, of contemporary "standard" Greek; the best resource if you get really interested.

When Greece first achieved independence in the nineteenth century, its people were almost universally illiterate, and the language they spoke – *dhimotikí*, "demotic" or "popular" Greek – had undergone enormous change since the days of the Byzantine Empire and Classical times. The vocabulary had assimilated countless borrowings from the languages of the various invaders and conquerors, namely the Turks, Venetians, Albanians and Slavs.

The finance and inspiration for the new Greek state, as well as its early leaders, came largely from the Greek Orthodox **diaspora** – prominent families who had been living in the sophisticated cities of central and eastern Europe, in Constantinople, or in Russia. With their European-Enlightenment notions about the grandeur of Greece's past, and lofty conception of Hellenism, they set about obliterating the memory of subjugation to foreigners in every possible field. And what better way to start than by purging the language of its foreign accretions and reviving its Classical purity?

They accordingly set about creating what was in effect a new form of the language, *katharévoussa* (literally, "cleansing" Greek). The complexities of Classical grammar and syntax were reinstated, and Classical words, long out of use, were resuscitated. To the country's great detriment, *katharévoussa* became the language of the schools and the prestigious professions, government, business, the law, newspapers and academia. Everyone aspiring to membership of the elite strove to master it, and to speak it – even though there was no consensus on how many of the words should be pronounced.

The *katharévoussa/dhimotikí* debate remained a highly contentious issue until the early 1980s. Most writers – from Solomos and Makriyannis in the nineteenth century to Seferis, Kazantzakis and Ritsos in the twentieth – have championed the demotic, or some approximation of it, in their literature, with advocacy of demoticism becoming increasingly linked to left-wing sentiments in the twentieth century. Meanwhile, crackpot right-wing governments forcibly (re)instated *katharévoussa* at every opportunity. Most recently, the **colonels' junta** of 1967–74 reversed a decision of the previous government to teach using *dhimotikí* in the schools, bringing back *katharévoussa*, even on sweet wrappers, as part of their ragbag of notions about racial purity and heroic ages.

Dhimotikí returned once more after the fall of the colonels and now seems here to stay. Perhaps the final blow to the classicizers was the official decision, in 1981, to do away with breath marks (which in fact no longer signified anything) and abolish the three different stress-accents in favour of a **single accute accent** (though there are still plenty of leftover road signs displaying the older system). *Dhimotikí* is used in schools, on radio and TV, and after a fashion in newspapers (with the exception of the extreme right-wing *Estia*). The only institutions which refuse to bring themselves up to date are the church and the legal professions – so beware rental contracts and official documents.

This is not to suggest that there is now any less confusion. The Metaxas dictatorship of the 1930s changed scores of village names from Slavic or Turkish to Classical forms, and these official place names still hold sway on most road signs and maps – even though the local people, three generations on, may continue to use the Turkish or *dhimotikí* form. Thus you may see "Plomárion" or "Innoússai" written on officially authorized maps or road signs, while everyone actually says Plomári or Inoússes. Posidhónio on Sámos is still referred to locally as Mulay-Brahim (ie Mullah Ibrahim) and Mólyvos on Lésvos is rarely if ever called Míthymna by the man in the street.

Dialects and minority languages

If the lack of any standard Greek were not enough, Greece still offers a rich field of linguistic diversity, both in its regional dialects and minority languages. Island **dialects** are alive and well in many a remote area, and some of them are quite incomprehensible to outsiders (which can mean inhabitants of the next island). The dialect of Lésvos is a particularly strong Aegean dialect, which owes much to migration from more southerly islands and influences from Asia Minor respectively. The dialect of Sámos and that of adjacent Híos are completely different from one another, Híos being considered a more pure "Ionian" (and this thousands of years after the Ionians arrived from the mainland), while the rough "Samian" variant owes much to the diverse origins of its settlers. On Rhodes and Kós there is a dwindling Turkish-speaking population, probably not in excess of four thousand persons as of writing.

Greek words and phrases

Essentials

Yes - Né
Certainly - Málista
No - Óhi
Please - Parakaló
Okay, agreed - Endáxi
Thank you (very much) - Efharistó (polý)
I (don't) understand - (Dhén) Katalavéno
Excuse me - Parakaló, mípos
Do you speak English? - Miláte angliká?
Sorry/excuse me - Signómi
Today - Símera
Tomorrow - Ávrio
Yesterday - Khthés
Now - Tóra
Later - Argótera
Open - Anikhtó
Closed - Klistó
Day - Méra
Night - Níkhta
In the morning - Tó proï
In the afternoon - Tó apóyevma
In the evening - Tó vrádhi
Here - Edhó
There - Ekí
This one - Aftó
That one - Ekíno
Good - Kaló
Bad - Kakó
Big - Megálo
Small - Mikró
More - Perisótero
Less - Ligótero
A little - Lígo
A lot - Polý
Cheap - Ftinó
Expensive - Akrivó
Hot - Zestó
Cold - Krýo
With (together) - Mazí (mé)
Without - Horís
Quickly - Grígora
Slowly - Sigá
Mr/Mrs - Kýrios/Kyría
Miss - Dhespinís

Other needs

To eat/drink - Trógo/píno
Bakery - Foúrnos, psomádhiko
Pharmacy - Farmakío
Post office - Tahydhromío
Stamps - Gramatóssima
Petrol station - Venzinádhiko
Bank - Trápeza
Money - Leftá/Khrímata

The Greek alphabet: transliteration

Set out below is the Greek alphabet, the system of transliteration used in this book, and a brief aid to pronunciation.

Greek	Transliteration	Pronounced
Α, α	a	a as in *fa*ther
Β, β	v	v as in *v*et
Γ, γ	y/g	y as in *y*es, except before consonants, α, ο or ου, when it's a breathy g, approximately as in gap
Δ, δ	dh	th as in *th*en
Ε, ε	e	e as in get
Ζ, ζ	z	z sound
Η, η	i	i as in sk*i*
Θ, θ	th	th as in *th*eme
Ι, ι	i	i as in sk*i*
Κ, κ	k	k sound
Λ, λ	l	l sound
Μ, μ	m	m sound
Ν, ν	n	n sound
Ξ, ξ	x	x as in bo*x*, medial *or* initial (*never* z as in *x*ylophone)
Ο, ο	o	o as in t*o*ad
Π, π	p	p sound
Ρ, ρ	r	r sound
Σ, σ, ς	s	s sound, except z sound before μ or γ; note that single sigma has the same phonetic value as double sigma
Τ, τ	t	t sound
Υ, υ	y	y as in barel*y*
Φ, φ	f	f sound
Χ, χ	h before vowels, kh before consonants	harsh h sound, like ch in lo*ch*
Ψ, ψ	ps	ps as in li*ps*
Ω, ω	o	o as in t*o*ad, indistinguishable from ο

Combinations and dipthongs

ΑΙ, αι	e	e as in h*ey*
ΑΥ, αυ	av/af	av or af depending on following consonant
ΕΙ, ει	i	long i, exactly like ι or η
ΕΥ, ευ	ev/ef	ev or ef, depending on following consonant
ΟΙ, οι	i	long i, identical again
ΟΥ, ου	ou	ou as in t*ou*rist
ΓΓ, γγ	ng	ng as in a*ng*le; always medial
ΓΚ, γκ	g/ng	g as in *g*oat at the beginning of a word; ng in the middle
ΜΠ, μπ	b/mb	b at the beginning of a word; mb in the middle
ΝΤ, ντ	d/nd	d at the beginning of a word; nd in the middle
ΤΣ, τσ	ts	ts as in hi*ts*
ΤΖ, τζ	tz	dg as in ju*dg*e; j as in *j*am in some dialects

Note on diereses

The dieresis is used in Greek over the second of two adjacent vowels to change the pronunciation that you would expect from the preceding table; often in this book it can function as the primary stress. In the word *kaïki* (caique), the presence of the dieresis changes the pronunciation from "cake-key" to "ka-ee-key" and additionally the middle "i" carries the primary stress. In the word *païdhákia* (lamb chops), the dieresis again changes the sound of the first syllable from "pay" to "pah-ee", but in this case the primary stress is on the third syllable. It is also, uniquely among Greek accents, used on capital letters in signs and personal-name spellings in Greece, and we have followed this practice on our maps, which are otherwise unaccented.

Toilet - Toualéta
Police - Astynomía
Doctor - Yiatrós
Hospital - Nosokomío

Requests and questions

To ask a question, it's simplest to start with *parakaló*, then name the thing you want in an interrogative tone.

Where is the bakery? - Parakaló, o foúrnos?
Can you show me the road to . . . ? - Parakaló, ó dhrómos yiá . . . ?
We'd like a room for two people - Parakaló, éna dhomátio yiá dhýo átoma
May I have a kilo of oranges? - Parakaló, éna kiló portokália?
Where? - Poú?
How? - Pós?
How many? - Póssi, pósses or póssa?
How much? - Póso?
When? - Póte?
Why? - Yiatí?
At what time . . . ? - Tí óra . . . ?
What is/Which is . . . ? - Tí íne/pió íne . . . ?
How much (does it cost)? - Póso káni?
What time does it open? - Tí óra aníyi?
What time does it close? - Tí óra klíni?

Talking to people

Greek makes the distinction between the informal (*esý*) and formal (*esís*) second person, as French does with *tu* and *vous*. Young people, older people and country people often use *esý* even with total strangers, though if you greet someone familiarly and they respond formally, it's best to adopt their usage as the conversation continues, to avoid offence. By far the most common greeting, on meeting and parting, is *yiá sou*/*yiá sas* – literally "health to you". Incidentally, as across most of the Mediterranean, the approaching party utters the first greeting, not those seated at sidewalk kafenío tables or doorsteps – thus the silent staring as you enter a village.

Hello - Hérete
Good morning - Kalí méra
Good evening - Kalí spéra
Good night - Kalí níkhta
Goodbye - Adío
How are you? - Tí kánis/Tí kánete?
I'm fine - Kalá íme
And you? - Ké essís?
What's your name? - Pós se léne?
My name is . . . - Mé léne . . .
Speak slower, please - Parakaló, miláte pió sigá
How do you say it in Greek? - Pós léyete stá Elliniká?
I don't know - Dhén xéro
See you tomorrow - Thá sé dhó ávrio
See you soon - Kalí andhámosi
Let's go - Páme
Please help me - Parakaló, ná mé voithíste

Greek's Greek

There are numerous words and phrases which you will hear constantly, even if you rarely have the chance to use them. These are a few of the most common.

Éla! - Come (literally) but also Speak to me! You don't say! etc.
Oríste! - Literally, "Indicate!"; in effect, "What can I do for you?"
Embrós! or Léyete! - Standard phone responses
Tí néa? - What's new?
Tí yínete? - What's going on (here)?
Étsi k'étsi - So-so
Ópa! - Whoops! Watch it!
Po-po-po! - Expression of dismay or concern, like French "O là là!"
Pedhí moú - My boy/girl, sonny, friend, etc.
Maláka(s) - Literally "wanker", but often used (don't try it!) as an informal term of address.
Sigá sigá - Take your time, slow down
Kaló taxídhi - Bon voyage

Accommodation

Hotel - Xenodhohío
Inn - Xenón(as)
A room . . . - Éna dhomátio . . .
for one/two/three people - yiá éna/dhýo/tría átoma
for one/two/three nights - yiá mía/dhýo/trís vradhiés
with a double bed - mé megálo kreváti
with a shower - mé doús
Hot water - Zestó neró
Cold water - Krýo neró
Air conditioning - Klimatismós
Fan - Anamistíra
Can I see it? - Boró ná tó dhó?
Can we camp here? - Boroúme na válume ti skiní edhó?
Campsite - Kámping/Kataskínosi
Tent - Skiní

On the move

Aeroplane - Aeropláno
Bus, coach - Leoforío, púlman
Car - Aftokínito, amáxi
Motorbike, scooter - Mihanáki, papáki
Taxi - Taxí
Ship - Plío/vapóri/karávi
High-speed catamaran - Tahýplio
Hydrofoil - Dhelfíni
Bicycle - Podhílato
Hitching - Otostóp
On foot - Mé tá pódhia
Trail - Monopáti
Bus station - Praktorío leoforíon, KTEL
Bus stop - Stássi
Harbour - Limáni
What time does it leave? - Ti óra févyi?
What time does it arrive? - Ti óra fthháni?
How many kilometres? - Póssa hiliómetra?
How many hours? - Pósses óres?
Where are you going? - Poú pás?
I'm going to . . . - Páo stó . . .
I want to get off at . . . - Thélo ná katévo stó . . .
The road to . . . - O dhrómos yiá . . .
Near - Kondá
Far - Makriá
Left - Aristerá
Right - Dhexiá
Straight ahead - Katefthía, ísia
A ticket to . . . - Éna isitírio yiá . . .
A return ticket - Éna isitírio mé epistrofí
Beach - Paralía
Cave - Spiliá
Centre (of town) - Kéndro
Church - Ekklissía
Sea - Thálassa

Numbers

1 - énas/éna/mía
2 - dhýo
3 - trís/tría
4 - tésseres/téssera
5 - pénde
6 - éxi
7 - eftá
8 - okhtó
9 - ennéa (or more slangy, enyá)
10 - dhéka
11 - éndheka
12 - dhódheka
13 - dhekatrís
14 - dhekatésseres
20 - íkossi
21 - íkossi éna (all compounds written separately thus)
30 - triánda
40 - saránda
50 - penínda
60 - exínda
70 - evdhomínda
80 - ogdhónda
90 - enenínda
100 - ekató
150 - ekatón penínda
200 - dhiakóssies/dhiakóssia
500 - pendakóssies/pendakóssia
1000 - hílies/hília
2000 - dhýo hiliádhes
1,000,000 - éna ekatomírio
first - próto
second - dhéftero
third - tríto

The time and days of the week

Sunday - Kyriakí
Monday - Dheftéra
Tuesday - Tríti
Wednesday - Tetárti
Thursday - Pémpti
Friday - Paraskeví
Saturday - Sávato
What time is it? - Tí óra íne?
One/two/three o'clock - Mía óra/dhýo/trís (óres)
Twenty minutes to four - Tésseres pará íkosi
Five minutes past seven - Eftá ké pénde
Half past eleven - Éndheka ké misí
In half an hour - Sé misí óra
In a quarter-hour - S'éna tétarto

Months and seasonal terms

NB You may see *katharévoussa*, or hybrid, forms of the months written on schedules or street signs; these are the spoken demotic forms.

January - Yennáris
February - Fleváris
March - Mártis
April - Aprílis
May - Maïos
June - Ioúnios
July - Ioúlios
August - Ávgoustos
September - Septémvris
October - Októvrios
November - Noémvris
December - Dhekémvris
Summer schedule - Therinó dhromolóyio
Winter schedule - Himerinó dhromolóyio

A food and drink glossary

Basics

Aláti - Salt
Avgá - Eggs
(Horís) ládhi - (Without) oil
Hortofágos - Vegetarian
Katálogo/lísta - Menu
Kréas - Meat
Lahaniká - Vegetables
O logariasmós - The bill
Méli - Honey
Neró - Water
Psári(a) - Fish
Psomí - Bread
Olikís - Wholemeal bread
Sikalísio - Rye bread
Thalassiná - Seafood (non-fish)
Tyrí - Cheese
Yiaoúrti - Yoghurt
Záhari - Sugar

Cooking terms

Akhnistó - Steamed
Frikasé - A stew, either lamb or pork, made with celery
Kourkoúti - Egg-and-flour batter
Pastó - Dry-marinated in salt
Psitó - Roasted
Saganáki - Cheese-based red sauce; also any fried cheese
Skáras - Grilled
Sti soúvla - Spit-roasted
Stó foúrno - Baked
Tiganitó - Pan-fried
Tís óras - Grilled/fried to order
Yakhní - Stewed in oil and tomato sauce
Yemistá - Stuffed (squid, vegetables, etc)

Soups and starters

Avgolémono - Egg and lemon soup
Dolmádhes - Vine leaves stuffed with rice, sometimes mince
Fasoládha - Bean soup
Florínes - Canned red sweet Macedonian peppers
Giouzlemés - Fried, cheese-stuffed crêpe; Lésvos only
Hortópita - Turnover or pie stuffed with wild greens
Kafterí - Cheese dip with chili added
Kápari - Pickled caper leaves
Kopanistí, khtypití - Pungent, fermented cheese purée
Krítamo - Rock samphire
Lahanodolmádhes - Rice-and-meat-stuffed cabbage leaves
Mavromátika - Black-eyed peas
Melitzanosaláta - Aubergine/eggplant dip
Pittaroúdhia - Egg, flour, courgette and herb frittata
Psarósoupa - Fish soup
Revythokeftédhes - Chickpea (garbanzo) patties
Skordhaliá - Garlic dip, for certain fish/fried vegetables
Taramosaláta - Cod roe paté
Tzatzíki - Yogurt, garlic and cucumber dip
Tzirosaláta - Cured and flaked mackerel dip

Vegetables and vegetable-based dishes

Ambelofásola - Crimp-pod runner beans; autumn only
Angináres - Artichokes
Angináres ala políta - Artichokes cooked with carrots and potatoes in a vinegar-based sauce
Angoúri - Cucumber
Ánitho - Dill
Bámies - Okra, ladies' fingers
Bouréki, bourekákia - Courgette/zucchini, potato and cheese pie
Briám - Ratatouille
Domátes - Tomatoes
Fakés - Lentils
Fasolákia - French (green) beans, flat-podded; summer
Fasóles - Small white beans, usually in sauce
Frésko kremýdhi - Spring onions
Horiátiki (saláta) - Greek salad (with olives, feta etc)
Hórta - Greens (usually wild), steamed
Kolokythákia - Courgette/zucchini
Koukiá - Broad fava beans; fresh in spring, dried otherwise
Maroúli - Lettuce
Melitzána - Aubergine/eggplant
Melitzánes imám - Very rich aubergine recipe, with oil, onions, garlic, tomatoes; vegetarian
Papoutsákia - Stuffed aubergine/eggplant "shoes"; has meat
Patátes - Potatoes
Piperiés - Peppers
Pligoúri, pinigoúri - Bulgur wheat
Radhíkia - Wild chicory – a common *hórta*
Rókka - Rocket greens
Rýzi/Piláfi - Rice (usually with *sáltsa* – sauce)
Saláta - Salad
Spanáki - Spinach
Vlíta notchweed - Another common *hórta ital* or colour
Yígandes - White haricot beans, large

Fish and seafood

Varieties recommended for taste, value, or dependable freshness are marked with an ★ on the table overleaf. This cites the most commonly offered fish species, in Greek alphabetical order, with English translation, their preferred method of preparation (this depends greatly on typical fish size and fat content), seasonal/local particularities, and other warnings. For more on individual species and what can be done with them, look no further than Alan Davidson's *Mediterranean Seafood* (see p.502).

Scaly fish

***Atherína** (Sand smelt) Fried whole in flour during autumn as an ouzerí snack; east Aegean speciality
Bakaliáros (Hake) Fried in slices, served with skordhaliá; fresh specimens rare, usually dried Icelandic
***Balládhes** (Large-eyed dentex) Reddish, medium-sized; grilled
Barboúni (Red mullet) Fried, sometimes grilled; famous smoky flavour, but fiddly to clean
Galéos (Hound shark, dogfish) Fried in slices, served with *skordhaliá*; fatty
Yermanós (Leatherback) Bony and tough-skinned, bland but pleasant white flesh; fried only. Found on Rhodes and surrounding islands, spring
***Gávros** (Anchovy) Fried whole, late summer, suprisingly mild-flavoured; east Aegean speciality
Glóssa (Sole) Lightly sautéed; mild flavour, springtime
Gópa (Bogue) Fried whole; very common
***Zargána** (Garfish) Small ones fried, big ones baked in sauce; east Aegean, autumn
***Kefalás** (Axillary bream) Grilled, late summer to autumn, often on Ikaría
Kéfalos (Grey mullet) Grilled; rich, but a scavenger, thus rarely offered
Koliós (Chub mackerel) Baked in tomato sauce, also grilled; rich
Koutsomoúra (Goatfish) Fried; same taste as *barboúni* but far cheaper
***Lakérdha** (White-fleshed bonito) Marinated; expensive treat, meant as an ouzerí starter, not a mains
***Lavráki** (Sea bass) Baked or grilled; gourmet fare, but usually farmed
Lithríni (Red bream, pandora) Large bones, but tasty grilled
Loútsos (Barracuda) Baked or grilled; usually caught May; heavy, mackerel-like flesh
***Marídha** (Picarel) Fried whole; common snack fish
Mayátiko (Amberjack) Bony, so best in soup, or baked; southern Dodecanese; spring to early summer
***Melanoúri** (Saddled bream) Grilled; springtime; good value
Menoúla (Sprat) Larger than *marídha*; often fried, but also marinated on Kárpathos
***Mourmoúra** (Striped bream) Grilled; not really a true bream, but quite tasty
Xifías (Swordfish) Baked, grilled; main season Feb–June; beware *galéos* as inferior substitute
Palamídha (Bonito) Grilled; autumn fish
***Pandelís, sykiós** (Corvina) Grilled; east Aegean native; flavour similar to *lavráki*
Pérka (Painted comber) Fried in batter; often frozen and rubbery, not esteemed
***Pescandrítsa, spehandrítsa** in some dialects (Monkfish) Usually fried, to its detriment; grilled by those who know; autumn
Rofós (Grouper) Unmistakably huge; cut into slices for grilling; texture like shark, but much tastier – like monkfish.
Sálpa (Salema) Explicitly not recommended; insipid, only for cat food
***Sardhélles** (Sardines) Grilled, wonderful east Aegean speciality
Sargós (White bream) Grilled; good value
***Skáros** (Parrotfish) Fried or grilled; rather bony but exquisitely flavoured white flesh, caught in drift nets and thus available much of the year
***Skathári** (Black bream) Grilled; the succulent king of the breams, most frequent in spring and on Foúrni
Skoumbrí (Atlantic mackerel) Baked in sauce; *estiatório* standby
Spáros (Annular or two-banded bream) Grilled or in soup
Savrídhi (Horse mackerel) Fried whole; ouzerí food
***Synagrídha** (Dentex) Baked in sauce; delicious
Tónnos (Tuna) Grilled or baked; light-fleshed variety much more satisfactory; autumn season
***Tsipoúra** (Gilt-head bream) Grilled; gourmet fare when wild, but usually farmed
***Fangrí** (Common bream, red porgy) Grilled; white, firm flesh
Hánnos (Comber) Fried or in soup; bony but flavourful
***Hióna** (Kind of bream) Excellent grilled, smoky flavour; may be the same as *psilomýtis*
***Khristópsaro** (John Dory) Baked, or in soup; rich white flesh, small bones

Other seafood

Ahiní (Sea urchin) Raw; only the very briny orange roe eaten as *ahinosaláta*; increasingly scarce and expensive
***Astakós** (Aegean lobster) Steamed, baked or flaked into pasta as *astakomakaraonádha*; gourmet fare; closed season Aug 15–Jan 1
Vátos, platý, seláhi (Ray, skate) Wings fried in slices, or as soup
Garidhákia (Miniature shrimps) Steamed whole, served in oil/lemon dressing; found on Rhodes, Hálki, Sými, Kastellórizo. Unmistakably sweet when fresh.
***Garídhes** (Shrimp, prawns) Preparation as for *garidhákia*, or stewed in sauce if big enough
***Hokhlí** (Sea snails) On Kastellórizo, served steamed in the shell; discard membrane and extract flesh with a pin (provided)
***Hokhlióalo** (Sea snails) Extracted from shells, blanched, salted, served in oil and vinegar on Sými
Kalamária, kalamarákia (Small squid) Lightly fried; overcooking toughens
Kalógnomes (Mussel-ish) Larger than *mýdhia*; steamed, served on Kálymnos
Karavídhes (Crayfish) Steamed or grilled; mostly carapace
Kydhónia (Warty Venus) Raw (alive) or lightly steamed; a delicacy despite the bizarre name
Mýdhia (Mussels) Steamed, or in saganáki sauce
***(O)khtapódhi** (Octopus) Grilled, stewed in wine; only tentacles used
Petalídhia (Limpets) Served live; ouzerí snack in spring or autumn
Pínna, spinóalo (Pinna-mollusc flesh) Served raw; another ouzerí snack, especially on Sými. Called *spiníalo* on Rhodes/Kálymnos
***Soupiés** (Cuttlefish) Grilled, or stuffed and baked; also cut up and cooked with their ink in rice and greens
Strídhia (Oysters) Raised in beds near Kálymnos; served raw; round, not lady's-slipper shape as elsewhere
***Foúskes** (Mock oysters, "blisters") Scooped fresh out of unprepossessing husk, or (less preferably) marinated in own liquor; most common on Rhodes and Kálymnos

Meat and meat-based dishes

Arní - Lamb
Bekrí mezé - Pork chunks in spicy red sauce, like Cypriot *afélia*
Biftéki - Hamburger, mince patty
Brizóla - Pork or veal chop
Hirinó - Pork (meat)
Keftédhes - Meatballs, with egg and bread-crumbs as binder
Kokorétsi - Liver/offal roulade, spit-roasted
Kondosoúvli, soúvla - Any spit-roasted beast, whole or in chunks
Kopsídha - (Lamb) shoulder chops
Kotópoulo - Chicken
Kounélli - Rabbit
Loukánika - Spicy home-made sausages
Moskhári - Veal
Moussakás - Aubergine, potato and lamb-mince casserole with bechamel topping
Ortíkia - Quail
Païdhákia - Rib chops, lamb or goat
Pansétta - Much thicker than Italian kind – more like spare rib
Pastítsio - Macaroni "pie" baked with minced meat
Patsás - Tripe soup
Psaronéfri - Medallion of pork fillet
Salingária - Garden snails
Soutzoukákia - Minced meat rissoles/beef patties
Stifádho - Meat stew with tomato and boiling onions
Sykóti - Liver
Tiganiá - Pork chunks fried with onions in oil or butter
Youvétsi - Baked clay casserole of meat and kritharáki (granular pasta)

Sweets and desserts

Baklavás - Honey and nut pastry
Bougátsa - Salt or sweet cream pie served warm with sugar and cinammon
Galaktobóureko - Custard pie
Halvás - Sweetmeat of sesame or semolina
Karydhópita - Walnut cake

Kréma - Custard

Loukoumádhes - Dough fritters in honey syrup, cinnamon and sesame seeds

Moustalevriá - Grape-must pudding

Pagotó - Ice cream

Pastélli - Sesame and honey bar

Ravaní - Spongecake, lightly syruped

Ryzógalo - Rice pudding

Fruit and nuts

Akhládhia - Big pears

Aktinídha - Kiwis

Fistíkia - Pistachio nuts

Fráoules - Strawberries

Himoniátiko - Autumn (casava) melon

Karpoúzi - Watermelon

Kerásia - Cherries

Krystália - Miniature green pears

Kydhóni - Quince

Lemónia - Lemons

Míla - Apples

Pepóni - Melon (honeydew/Persian)

Portokália - Oranges

Rodhákina - Summer peaches

Stafýlia - Grapes

Sýka - Figs

Vanílies - Plums

Yiarmádhes - Autumn peaches

Cheese

Ayeladhinó - Cow's-milk cheese

Féta - Salty, white cheese

Graviéra - Gruyère-type hard cheese

Kasséri - Medium-sharp cheese

Katsikísio - Goat cheese

Mastéllo - Grilling cheese of Híos, similar to Cypriot *halloúmi*; cow/goat

Myzíthra - Sweet cream cheese

Próvio - Sheep cheese

Drinks

Alisfakiá - Island sage tea

Boukáli - Bottle

Býra - Beer

Gála - Milk

Galakakáo - Chocolate milk

Gazóza - Generic fizzy drink

Kafés - Coffee

Krasí - Wine

áspro - white

kókkino/mávro - red

rozé/kokkinélli - rosé

Limonádha - Lemonade

Metalikó neró - Mineral water

Portokaládha - Orangeade

Potíri - Glass

Stinyássas! - Cheers!

Tsáï - Tea

A glossary of words and terms

Ancient architecture and history

Acropolis – Ancient, fortified hilltop.

Agora – Market and meeting place of an ancient Greek city.

Amphora – Tall, narrow-necked jar for oil or wine.

Apse – Polygonal or curved recess at the altar end of a church.

Archaic period – Late Iron Age period, from around 750 BC to the start of the Classical period in the fifth century BC.

Architrave – Horizontal masonry atop temple columns; same as Entablature (cf).

Atrium – Open, inner courtyard of a Roman house, as on Kós.

Basilica – Originally colonnaded, early Christian "hall"-type church adapted from Roman models, found at several sites in the Dodecanese and east Aegean.

Bouleuterion – Auditorium for meetings of an ancient town's deliberative council.

Byzantine Empire – The empire created by the division of the Roman Empire in 395 AD; this, the eastern half, was ruled from Constantinople (modern Istanbul). Sámos, Rhodes, Híos, Kós and Lésvos were all important members of the Aegean theme or province.

Capital – The flared top, often ornamented, of a column.

Cella – Sacred room of a temple, housing the cult image.

Classical Period – Essentially from the end of the Persian Wars in the fifth century BC until the unification of Greece under Phillip II of Macedon (338 BC).

Corinthian – Decorative columns, festooned with acanthus florettes; a temple built in this order.

Dorian – Northern (Balkan?) civilization that displaced and succeeded the Myceneans and Minoans through most of Greece around 1100 BC.

Doric – Minimalist columns with little ornament, dating from the Dorian period; a temple built in this order.

Drum – Cylindrical or faceted vertical section, usually pierced by an even number of narrow windows, upholding a cupola.

Entablature – The horizontal linking structure atop the columns of an ancient temple.

Exedra – Display niche for statuary.

Exonarthex – The outer west vestibule of a church, when a true Narthex (cf) is present.

Forum – Market and meeting place of a Roman-era city.

Geomatric Period – Post-Mycenean Iron Age era named for the style of its pottery; begins in the early eleventh century BC with the arrival of Dorian peoples. By the eighth century BC, with the development of representational styles, it becomes known as the Archaic Period (cf).

Hellenistic Period – The last and most unified "Greek empire", created in the wake of Alexander the Great's Macedonian empire and finally collapsing with the fall of Corinth to the Romans in 146 BC; thus, "Hellenistic" refers to the art and architecture of this era.

Heroön – Shrine or sanctuary, usually of a demigod or mortal; war memorials in modern Greece.

Ionic – Elaboration of the older Doric decorative order; Ionic temple columns are slimmer with deeper "fluted" edges, spiral-shaped capitals, and ornamental bases. Again, a temple built in this order.

Kouros – Nude Archaic statue of an idealized young man, usually portrayed with one foot slightly forward of the other.

Macedonian Empire – Empire created by Philip II in the mid-fourth century BC.

Megaron – Principal hall or throne room of a Mycenean palace.

Minoan – Crete's great Bronze Age Civilization, which dominated the Aegean from about 2500 to 1400 BC.

Naos – The inner sanctum of an ancient temple; also, any Orthodox Christian shrine.

Narthex – Western vestibule of a church, traditionally for catachumens and the unbaptized; typically frescoed with scenes of the Last Judgment.

Neolithic – Earliest era of settlement in Greece, characterized by the use of stone tools and weapons together with basic agriculture. Divided arbitrarily into Early (c.6000 BC), Middle (c.5000 BC), and Late (c.3000 BC).

Odeion – Small theatre, used for musical performances, minor dramatic productions, or councils.

Pal(a)estra – Gymnasium for athletics and wrestling practice.

Pediment – Triangular, sculpted gable below the roof of a temple; *aetoma* in Greek.

Pendentive – Any of four triangular sections of vaulting with concave sides, positioned at a corner of a rectangular space in a church to support a circular or polygonal dome; often adorned with frescoes of the four Evangelists.

Peristyle – Gallery of columns around a temple or other building.

Polygonal masonry – Wall-building technique of the Classical and Hellenistic period, which used unmortared, closely joined stones; often called "Lesbian polygonal" after the island where the method supposedly originated. The much-(ab)used term "**Cyclopean**" refers only to Mycenean and Bronze Age mainland sites such as Tiryns, Glas and Mycenae itself.

Propylaion – Monumental, columned gateway of an ancient building; often used in the plural, *propylaia*.

Pyliónas – (plural Pyliónes) Ornate decorated doorways found in Rhodion villages.

Squinch – Small concavity across a corner of a columnless interior space, supporting a superstructure such as a dome.

Stele – Upright stone slab or column, usually inscribed with an edict; also an ancient tombstone, with a relief scene.

Stoa – Colonnaded walkway in Classical-era marketplace.

Temenos – Sacred precinct, often used to refer to the sanctuary itself.

Tholos – Conical or beehive-shaped building, especially a Bronze Age tomb.

Medieval and modern Greek terms

Agorá – The commercial "high street" of any village or town.

Áno – Upper; common prefix element of village names.

Arhondikó – Elaborate mansions of the medieval upper classes, found for example at Hóra, Pátmos and Líndhos, Rhodes.

Astykó – (Intra) city, municipal, local; adjective applied to phone calls and bus services.

Áyios/Ayía/Áyii – (m/f/plural) Saint or holy. Common place name prefix; abbreviated Ag. or Ay., often spelt Agios or Aghios.

Dhimarhío – Town hall.

Dhomátia – Rooms for rent in purpose-built blocks or (rarely these days) private houses.

Eparhía – Greek Orthodox diocese, also a subdivision of a modern province analagous to a county.

Froúrio – Medieval castle; nowadays, usually means a modern military headquarters.

Garsoniéra/es – Studio villa/s, self-catering apartment/s.

Hamam – Turkish-style steam bath, dating from the Ottoman era; there are functioning ones in Ródhos Old Town and in Mytilíni on Lésvos.

Hokhláki – Mosaic of coloured pebbles, found in church or house courtyards in Rhodes and the southern Dodecanese.

Hóra – Main town of an island or region; literally it means "the place". An island *hóra* is often known by the same name as the island.

Icon – Representation of a saint or sacred event painted on a board, an object of veneration and pilgrimage in the Orthodox Church.

Ierón – Literally, "sacred" – the sanctuary between the altar screen and the apse of a church, reserved for priestly activities.

Ikonostási – Screen between the nave of a church and the *ierón*, supporting at least three icons. Also, a roadside shrine (see feature on p.xi).

Iperastykó – Inter-city, long-distance – as in phone calls and bus services.

Kafenío – Coffee house or café; in a small village the centre of communal life and possibly serving as the bus stop, too.

Kaïki – (plural **Kaïkia**) Caique, or medium-sized boat, traditionally wooden and used for transporting cargo rather than passengers; now refers mainly to island excursion boats.

Kalderími – Cobbled mule-tracks and footpaths.

Kámbos – Fertile agricultural plateau, usually near a river mouth.

Kantína – Shack, caravan or even a disused bus on the beach, usually serving just drinks and perhaps sandwiches or quick snacks.

Kástro – Any fortified hill (or a castle), but most usually the oldest, highest, walled-in part of an island *hóra*.

Katholikón – Central church of a monastery.

Káto – Lower; common prefix element of village names.

Kendrikí platía – Central square.

Kioupí, Koumári – Large Ali-Baba-style clay urns used for storing olive oil.

Meltémi – North wind that blows across the Aegean in summer, starting softly from near the mainland and hitting the Dodecanese and certain of the east Aegean islands full on.

Moní – Formal term for a monastery or convent.

Néos, Néa, Néo – "New" – a common prefix to a town or village name.

Nomós – Modern Greek province – there are more than fifty of them.

Paleós, Paleá, Paleó – "Old" – again a common prefix in town and village names.

Panayía – Virgin Mary.

Pandokrátor – Literally "The Ruler of All"; generally refers to the stern portrayal of Christ in Majesty frescoed or in mosaic in the dome of many Byzantine churches.

Paniyíri – Festival or feast – the local celebration of a holy day.

Paralía - Beach or seafront promenade.

Períptero - Street-corner kiosk.

Platía - Square, plaza.

Pýrgos - Tower-mansion found on Lésvos or Híos.

Skála - The port of an inland island settlement, nowadays often larger and more important than its namesake, but always younger since built after the disappearance of piracy.

Taverna - Restaurant; see "Eating and Drinking" in Basics, p.56, for details of the different types of specialist eating places.

Témblon - Wooden altar screen of an Orthodox church, usually ornately carved and painted and studded with icons; more or less interchangeable with the *Ikonostási*.

Vólta - Ritualised evening promenade on the seafront of a larger island town; akin to the Italian *corso*.

Acronyms and initials

DANE - *Dhodhekanisiakí Anónymi Navtiliakí Etería* (Dodecanesian Shipping Company Ltd), which runs many ferries between Rhodes and Pireás via intervening islands.

DIKKI - Democrat Social Movement, a more left-leaning spin-off from PASOK.

EAM - National Liberation Front, the political force behind ELAS.

ELAS - Popular Liberation Army, the main resistance group during World War II and the basis of the Communist army (DSE or "Democratic Army of Greece") during the civil war.

ELTA - The postal service.

EOT - Ellinikós Organismós Tourismoú, the National Tourist Organization.

KKE - Communist Party, unreconstructed.

KTEL - National syndicate of bus companies. The term is also used to refer to individual bus stations.

ND - Conservative (Néa Dhimokratía) party.

NEL - *Navtiliakí Etería Lésvou* (Lesvian Shipping Company), which runs many of the east Aegean ferries.

OTE - Telephone company.

PASOK - Socialist party (Pan-Hellenic Socialist Movement).

index

and small print

Index

Map entries are in colour

B

C

D

E

J

K

L

M

INDEX

Twenty Years of Rough Guides

In the summer of 1981, Mark Ellingham, Rough Guides' founder, knocked out the first guide on a typewriter, with a group of friends. Mark had been travelling in Greece after university, and couldn't find a guidebook that really answered his needs. There were heavyweight cultural guides on the one hand – good on museums and classical sites but not on beaches and tavernas – and on the other hand student manuals that were so caught up with how to save money that they lost sight of the country's significance beyond its role as a place for a cool vacation. None of the guides began to address Greece as a country, with its natural and human environment, its politics and its contemporary life.

Having no urgent reason to return home, Mark decided to write his own guide. It was a guide to Greece that tried to combine some erudition and insight with a thoroughly practical approach to travellers' needs. Scrupulously researched listings of places to stay, eat and drink were matched by careful attention to detail on everything from Homer to Greek music, from classical sites to national parks and from nude beaches to monasteries. Back in London, Mark and his friends got their Rough Guide accepted by a far-sighted commissioning editor at the publisher Routledge and it came out in 1982.

The Rough Guide to Greece was a student scheme that became a publishing phenomenon. The immediate success of the book – shortlisted for the Thomas Cook award – spawned a series that rapidly covered dozens of countries. The Rough Guides found a ready market among backpackers and budget travellers, but soon acquired a much broader readership that included older and less impecunious visitors. Readers relished the guides' wit and inquisitiveness as much as the enthusiastic, critical approach that acknowledges everyone wants value for money – but not at any price.

Rough Guides soon began supplementing the "rougher" information – the hostel and low-budget listings – with the kind of detail that independent-minded travellers on any budget might expect. These days, the guides – distributed worldwide by the Penguin group – include recommendations spanning the range from shoestring to luxury, and cover more than 200 destinations around the globe. Our growing team of authors, many of whom come to Rough Guides initially as outstandingly good letter-writers telling us about their travels, are spread all over the world, particularly in Europe, the USA and Australia. As well as the travel guides, Rough Guides publishes a series of dictionary phrasebooks covering two dozen major languages, an acclaimed series of music guides running the gamut from Classical to World Music, a series of music CDs in association with World Music Network, and a range of reference books on topics as diverse as the internet, pregnancy and unexplained phenomena. Visit **www.roughguides.com** to see what's cooking.

Rough Guide credits

Text editor: Alison Murchie
Series editor: Mark Ellingham
Editorial: Martin Dunford, Jonathan Buckley, Jo Mead, Kate Berens, Ann-Marie Shaw, Helena Smith, Judith Bamber, Orla Duane, Olivia Eccleshall, Ruth Blackmore, Geoff Howard, Claire Saunders, Gavin Thomas, Alexander Mark Rogers, Polly Thomas, Joe Staines, Richard Lim, Duncan Clark, Peter Buckley, Lucy Ratcliffe, Clifton Wilkinson, Matthew Teller, Fran Sandham (UK); Andrew Rosenberg, Stephen Timblin, Yuki Takagaki, Richard Koss (US)
Production: Susanne Hillen, Andy Hilliard, Link Hall, Helen Prior, Julia Bovis, Michelle Draycott, Katie Pringle, Mike Hancock, Zoë Nobes, Rachel Holmes, Andy Turner
Cartography: Melissa Baker, Maxine Repath, Ed Wright, Katie Lloyd-Jones
Picture research: Sharon Martins, Mark Thomas
Cover art direction: Louise Boulton
Online: Kelly Cross, Anja Mutic-Blessing, Jennifer Gold, Audra Epstein, Suzanne Welles, Cree Lawson (US)
Finance: John Fisher, Gary Singh, Edward Downey, Mark Hall, Tim Bill
Marketing and Publicity: Richard Trillo, Niki Smith, David Wearn, Chloë Roberts, Claire Southern, Demelza Dallow (UK); Simon Carloss, David Wechsler, Kathleen Rushforth (US)
Administration: Tania Hummel, Julie Sanderson (UK); Hunter Slaton (US)

Publishing information

This third edition published April 2002 by **Rough Guides Ltd**,
62–70 Shorts Gardens, London WC2H 9AH
4th Floor, 345 Hudson St, New York, NY 10014

Distributed by the Penguin Group

Penguin Books Ltd,
80 Strand, London WC2R ORL
Penguin Putnam, Inc.
345 Hudson Street, NY 10014, USA
Penguin Books Australia Ltd,
487 Maroondah Highway, PO Box 257,
Ringwood, Victoria 3134, Australia
Penguin Books Canada Ltd,
10 Alcorn Avenue, Toronto, Ontario,
Canada M4V 1E4
Penguin Books (NZ) Ltd,
182–190 Wairau Road, Auckland 10,
New Zealand
Typeset in Bembo and Helvetica to an original design by Henry Iles.
Printed in Italy by LegoPrint S.p.A

544pp – Includes index
A catalogue record for this book is available from the British Library

ISBN 1-85828-883-5

Help us update

We've gone to a lot of effort to ensure that the fifth edition of **The Rough Guide to the Dodecanese and the east Aegean islands** is accurate and up to date. However, things change – places get "discovered", opening hours can change, restaurants and rooms increase prices or lower standards. If you feel we've got it wrong or left something out, we'd like to know, and if you can remember the address, the price, the time, the phone number, so much the better.

We'll credit all contributions, and send a copy of the next edition (or any other Rough Guide if you prefer) for the best letters. Everyone who writes to us and isn't already a subscriber will receive a copy of our full-colour thrice-yearly newsletter. Please mark letters: "**Rough Guide Dodecanese Update**" and send to: Rough Guides, 62–70 Shorts Gardens, London WC2H 9AH, or Rough Guides, 4th Floor, 345 Hudson St, New York, NY 10014. Or send an email to:
mail@roughguides.co.uk or
mail@roughguides.com

Acknowledgements

The author would like to thank George & Barbara, and George & Effi on Lésvos; Markos Theodhore and Güher on Híos; Alexis and Dhionysia on Kós; David, Iain, Lynn, Joanna and Andrea on Tílos, plus Nigel for the loan of his lovely house; Paul and Stella, plus Efi, Spyros, Sotiris and Marianne (again) on Rhodes; Nikos, Wendy and Jean on Symi; Christine and Alex on Hálki; Nikos and Anna on Lipsí; Panayiotis and Aphrodite on Límnos; fellow guidebook-writers Daniel Koster, for the general errata, and Lance Chilton for masses of extra material on Kárpathos and Kálymnos (plus Greek proof-reading); editor Alison Murchie for indulging occasional prolixity, and last but not least to Pamela for over-eating once again for science, minding the farm in London and cheerfully island-hopping from Ikaría to Kós when we were supposed to be on Lésvos.

Thank also to Kingston Presentation graphics and Maxine Repath for cartography, Link Hall for layout, Sharon Martins for picture research and Susannah Wight for proofreading

Readers' letters

Our thanks to readers of the previous edition who sent in comments and suggestions. The roll of honour:
Nita Bennett, J. J. Blundell, Chloe Britton, Sue & Luke Carr, Matthew Chapman, Andrew Clarke, Joyce Cripps, Sam Davies, Ellen van Gogh, John Hancock, Duncan Illingworth, Andrew Land, Karen Mann & Kevin Marren, Gale Mead, Liz Mullen, Jan Nelder, Tony Nichols & Yves Jatteau, C. Power, Oded Shimshon, Hans Smit, Sven Sommer, Danièle Stewart, David Voas, Oyvind Westvik, John Woodhouse and mwalimu727@hotmail.com(!).

Photo credits

Cover

Main front cover, Kós © Robert Harding
Front (small top image) Sámos © Robert Harding
Front (small bottom image) Tsambíka Bay, Rhodes © Peter Wilson
Back (top) Kárpathos © Robert Harding
Back (lower) Vathý © Marc Dubin

Colour introduction

White cat in front of brightly painted house, Koskinoú, Rhodes © Peter Wilson
Goats on hillside, Rhodes © Peter Wilson
Lion-head fountain, Pylí Village, Kós © Marc Dubin
Ouzeri Ermis, Mytilíni Town, Lésvos © Marc Dubin
Easter procession, Kárpathos © Viesti Collection/TRIP
The watermill, Ayía Marina, Léros © Marc Dubin
Roadside shrine © Neil Setchfield
Kaïki-building, Patmos © Marc Dubin
Field of wild flowers, Lésvos © Roy Rainford/Robert Harding
Blue amulet © H. Rogers/TRIP

Things not to miss

1. Ayíou Ioánnou Theológou monastery, Pátmos © Marc Dubin
2. Kondias, Límnos © Marc Dubin
3. Aidhonokastro, Valeondádhes, Sámos © Marc Dubin
4. Rhodes nightlife © Alan Lewis/Travel Ink
5. Skála Eressoú, Lésvos © Marc Dubin
6. Mesakhtí beach, Ikaría, Armenistís © Marc Dubin
7. Time, Astypálea mosaic, Tallarás bath © Marc Dubin
8. Tomatoes drying, Híos © Marc Dubin
9. *Hokhláki* mosaics, Áyios Nikólaos church, Hálki © Marc Dubin
10. Terraced vineyards below Manolátes village, Sámos © Marc Dubin
11. The harbour with fishing fleet, Foúrni © Marc Dubin
12. Níssyros volcano © Neil Setchfield
13. Kastellórizo harbour © Marc Dubin
14. Lindos Acropolis, Rhodes © Marc Dubin
15. Yachters anchorage, Vathý © Marc Dubin
16. Rhodes, Byzantine frescoes © Marc Dubin
17. Ólymbos, Kárpathos © Marc Dubin/ Travel Ink
18. Ródhos Old Town © Stephen Psallidas/Travel Ink
19. Mandhráki, Níssyros © Marc Dubin
20. Khristós peak, Kós © Marc Dubin
21. Knights' castle above Plátanos © Marc Dubin
22. Italian Art Deco cinema, Léros © Marc Dubin
23. Kyrá Panayiá beach, Kárpathos © Marc Dubin
24. Harbour, Lipsi © Ian Booth/Travel Ink
25. Áyios Vassílios overlooking Lápathos bay, Symi © Marc Dubin
26. Housefront, Astypálea, Hóra © Marc Dubin
27. Brós Thermá thermal springs, Kós © Marc Dubin
28. Ayíou Pandelímona monastery, Tilos © Marc Dubin/Travel Ink
29. Télendhos straits, Kálymnos © Marc Dubin

Black and white photos

Lindos Acropolis, Rhodes © Marc Dubin (p.90)
Palace of the Grand Masters, Rhodes © B. Turner/TRIP (p.101)
Platía Ippokrátous, Ródhos Old Town © Stephen Psallidas/Travel Ink (p.106)
Fishing port of Boúka, Kássos © Marc Dubin (p.168)
Unusual round platía at Nikiá, Níssyros © Marc Dubin (p.212)
Trimming sponges for sale, Póthia, Kálymnos © Ian Booth/Travel Ink (p.256)
East fortification, Ayíou Ioánnou Theológou monastery, Pátmos © Marc Dubin/Travel Ink (p.289)
Archaic kouros, Archeological Museum, Vathý, Sámos © Marc Dubin (p.315)
Xistá technique on walls, Pyrgí, Híos © Marc Dubin (p.361)

around the world

Alaska ★ Algarve ★ Amsterdam ★ Andalucía ★ Antigua & Barbuda ★ Argentina ★ Auckland Restaurants ★ Australia ★ Austria ★ Bahamas ★ Bali & Lombok ★ Bangkok ★ Barbados ★ Barcelona ★ Beijing ★ Belgium & Luxembourg ★ Belize ★ Berlin ★ Big Island of Hawaii ★ Bolivia ★ Boston ★ Brazil ★ Britain ★ Brittany & Normandy ★ Bruges & Ghent ★ Brussels ★ Budapest ★ Bulgaria ★ California ★ Cambodia ★ Canada ★ Cape Town ★ The Caribbean ★ Central America ★ Chile ★ China ★ Copenhagen ★ Corsica ★ Costa Brava ★ Costa Rica ★ Crete ★ Croatia ★ Cuba ★ Cyprus ★ Czech & Slovak Republics ★ Devon & Cornwall ★ Dodecanese & East Aegean ★ Dominican Republic ★ The Dordogne & the Lot ★ Dublin ★ Ecuador ★ Edinburgh ★ Egypt ★ England ★ Europe ★ First-time Asia ★ First-time Europe ★ Florence ★ Florida ★ France ★ French Hotels & Restaurants ★ Gay & Lesbian Australia ★ Germany ★ Goa ★ Greece ★ Greek Islands ★ Guatemala ★ Hawaii ★ Holland ★ Hong Kong & Macau ★ Honolulu ★ Hungary ★ Ibiza & Formentera ★ Iceland ★ India ★ Indonesia ★ Ionian Islands ★ Ireland ★ Israel & the Palestinian Territories ★ Italy ★ Jamaica ★ Japan ★ Jerusalem ★ Jordan ★ Kenya ★ The Lake District ★ Languedoc & Roussillon ★ Laos ★ Las Vegas ★ Lisbon ★ London ★

ROUGH GUIDES
TWENTY YEARS

The ideas expressed in this code were developed by and for independent travellers.

Learn About The Country You're Visiting

Start enjoying your travels before you leave by tapping into as many sources of information as you can.

The Cost Of Your Holiday

Think about where your money goes - be fair and realistic about how cheaply you travel. Try and put money into local peoples' hands; drink local beer or fruit juice rather than imported brands and stay in locally owned accommodation. Haggle with humour and not aggressively. Pay what something is worth to you and remember how wealthy you are compared to local people.

Embrace The Local Culture

Open your mind to new cultures and traditions - it will transform your experience. Think carefully about what's appropriate in terms of your clothes and the way you behave. You'll earn respect and be more readily welcomed by local people. Respect local laws and attitudes towards drugs and alcohol that vary in different countries and communities. Think about the impact you could have on them.

Exploring The World – The Travellers' Code

Being sensitive to these ideas means getting more out of your travels - and giving more back to the people you meet and the places you visit.

Minimise Your Environmental Impact

Think about what happens to your rubbish - take biodegradable products and a water filter bottle. Be sensitive to limited resources like water, fuel and electricity. Help preserve local wildlife and habitats by respecting local rules and regulations, such as sticking to footpaths and not standing on coral.

Don't Rely On Guidebooks

Use your guidebook as a starting point, not the only source of information. Talk to local people, then discover your own adventure!

Be Discreet With Photography

Don't treat people as part of the landscape, they may not want their picture taken. Ask first and respect their wishes.